THE COLOR OF MODERNITY

A book in the series

Radical Perspectives: A Radical History Review book series

SERIES EDITORS: DANIEL J. WALKOWITZ, NEW YORK UNIVERSITY
BARBARA WEINSTEIN, NEW YORK UNIVERSITY

BARBARA WEINSTEIN

THE COLOR OF
MODERNITY

São Paulo and the

Making of Race and

Nation in Brazil

DUKE UNIVERSITY PRESS DURHAM AND LONDON 2015

© 2015 Duke University Press
All rights reserved
Printed in the United States of America on acid-free paper ∞
Designed by Heather Hensley
Typeset in Whitman and Univers by Graphic Composition, Inc.,
Bogart, Georgia

Library of Congress Cataloging-in-Publication Data
Weinstein, Barbara.
The color of modernity : São Paulo and the making of race and nation in
Brazil / Barbara Weinstein.
pages cm — (Radical pespectives: a radical history review book series)
Includes bibliographical references and index.
ISBN 978-0-8223-5762-9 (hardcover : alk. paper)
ISBN 978-0-8223-5777-3 (pbk. : alk. paper)
ISBN 978-0-8223-7615-6 (e-book)
1. São Paulo (Brazil : State)—History—20th century. 2. São Paulo (Brazil :
State)—History—Revolution, 1932. 3. São Paulo (Brazil : State)—Race
relations—History. 4. Racism—Brazil—São Paulo (State) 5. Brazil—
History—20th century. I. Title. II. Series: Radical perspectives.
F2361.w456 2015
305.800981′61—dc23
2014040373

Cover art: MMDC poster (detail), 1932.

For Sarah and Danny

CONTENTS

ACKNOWLEDGMENTS

Outside of academia, anyone embarking on a new enterprise—a software startup, a housing development, a widget factory—is likely to incur a certain degree of financial indebtedness. But we academics deal in a different currency; in the course of doing research, we usually accumulate intellectual, not financial, debts, and our moral economy dictates that we repay what we owe with our own peculiar bitcoin: profuse expressions of gratitude in the book's acknowledgments. Having run up an enormous bill over the many years during which I have researched and written this book, in the next few pages I will try to acquit myself honorably and metaphorically reimburse the many friends and colleagues to whom I am, in truth, forever indebted. But I worry that there will be some people who, early on, suggested sources or offered ideas whose origin I've long since forgotten; it's even possible that, against my better scholarly judgment, I've tricked myself into thinking that I came up with a particular idea all by myself. The eminent sociologist Robert K. Merton, apparently disgruntled that his colleagues were not citing him quite enough, termed a larger-scale version of this process "obliteration by incorporation"—by which he meant the way certain ideas get so embedded in the disciplinary "common sense" that they become untraceable to their original "inventor." Unlike Merton, I'm inclined to regard ideas as emerging from a collective process, not one individual person's "genius," so I'm hoping I can count on the generosity of the academic community and assume that my colleagues will not feel too "obliterated" should I inadvertently neglect to thank them for some excellent idea or suggestion that richly deserves to be acknowledged but whose origins have been rendered obscure by time.

There are three people who have been exceptionally supportive at various points in my ongoing struggle to finish this book, and to whom I owe an especially large debt. Maria Lígia Prado, the most wonderful friend and colleague one could ask for, suggested many sources, read the entire manuscript, and made many interventions that have helped me conceptualize what the book should be. Mary Kay Vaughan, my colleague for six years at the University of Maryland, has been an inspiration and a source of encouragement at every point along the way. And I can't begin to say how much I appreciate James Woodard's help and solidarity, made all the more meaningful by the fact that he would probably interpret much of the material I use in a substantially different way. Nonetheless, he has directed my attention to many sources, suggested any number of documents, and subjected the manuscript to the most incisive reading imaginable. Even an attentive reader will lose count of the number of notes in which I thank James for suggesting a particular source or bringing a specific problem to my attention.

Several colleagues in São Paulo have been extremely helpful, again including some who I know are skeptical about my interpretation. I want especially to thank my dear friend Maria Helena Capelato, whose own work on the 1932 uprising, the *paulista* press, and paulista identity has been essential for this study. Tania Regina de Luca, Vavy Pacheco Borges, and Michael Hall have all offered insights from their own work, and thoughtful comments about mine. Among the many other scholars who have shared their work and suggestions, I would like to thank Silvio Luiz Lofego, Cássia Chrispiniano Adduci, and Antonio Celso Ferreira. I hope it is apparent to readers how much I have relied on and remain beholden to their scholarly research.

At the Arquivo Público do Estado de São Paulo, I owe a particular debt to Lauro Ávila Pereira, who was a wonderful guide to the archive and its excellent collections. I thank the entire staff at APESP for the many ways they made my visits to the archive as productive and pleasant as possible, but especially for their dedication to keeping the archive open and functioning even as the new headquarters were being constructed right next door.

Also in São Paulo I owe many thanks to the staffs at the Arquivo Histórico Municipal, the Instituto de Estudos Brasileiros, and the Museu Paulista. At the Museu I am particularly grateful to the historians and archivists who provided me with research support, excellent company at lunch, and occasional car rides, including Cecilia Helena de Salles Oliveira, Solange Ferraz de Lima, and Miyoko Makino. In Campinas I had the pleasure of doing research once again at the Arquivo Edgard Leuenroth, a mecca for the student of social history.

In Rio de Janeiro the staff at the Centro de Pesquisa e Documentação at the Fundação Getúlio Vargas made doing research there a pleasure. For their friendship and excellent company in Rio, I thank Keila Grinberg, Cecilia Azevedo, Flávio Limoncic, and Olívia Gomes da Cunha. My thanks to Marcos Chor Maio for sharing his work and suggesting sources that I would never have found otherwise.

I began this book while still at my longtime academic home, Stony Brook University, did the last round of research and started the writing while at the University of Maryland, and finally finished while at my current academic home, the history department at New York University. In each place I had the great privilege of working with colleagues and graduate students who kept me on my toes and pushed me to think more critically and carefully. At Stony Brook I was especially fortunate to work with Brooke Larson, and to be surrounded by an exceptionally stimulating cohort of friends and colleagues (among them Paul Gootenberg, Gene Lebovics, Nancy Tomes, and Helen Cooper) and graduate students, including Stanley (Chip) Blake, whose outstanding study on *nordestino* identity has been a key reference for my own work. At Maryland, besides Mary Kay Vaughan, I had the pleasure of working with my fellow Brazilianist, Daryle Williams, and could draw on the comparative (and incomparable) insights of my colleagues Gary Gerstle and Ira Berlin. I also thank my former students, now colleagues, Ricardo López, Sarah Sarzynski, Patricia Acerbi, Paula Halperin, and Leandro Benmergui, whose own research has enriched my work in any number of ways.

I have had the rare pleasure of working with outstanding historians of Latin America in each of the departments where I have taught, and I am now privileged to count Ada Ferrer, Greg Grandin, and Sinclair Thomson as my colleagues whose own innovative scholarship inspires me to think more boldly about the implications of my work while trying to adhere to their standards of analytical rigor.

So many people have sent me messages alerting me to a particular document or relaying an idea that has proved crucial for my arguments in this book that there is no way I can remember them all, but aside from James Woodard, I would like to thank Márcio Siwi, Jeffrey Lesser, Cristina Peixoto-Mehrtens, Chip Blake, Sarah Sarzynski, Jared Rodríguez, Sinclair Thomson, Nancy Appelbaum, Marc Hertzman, Paulo Iumatti, Geraldo M. Coelho, Deborah Silverman, Jose Moya, Seth Garfield, and Paulina Alberto. I'm sure there are others that I am forgetting, but if they remind me, I'll be happy to buy them a drink at the next AHA or LASA meeting.

I have been fortunate to receive support for this research from several sources, including a fellowship from the John Simon Guggenheim Memorial Foundation, a semester fellowship from the University of Maryland, and a semester leave from NYU. But by far the most important institutional support for this project came in the form of a ten-month residence as a Joy Foundation fellow at the Radcliffe Institute for Advanced Study in Cambridge, Massachusetts. My time there was everything a historian could ask for, from the wonderful facilities in Radcliffe Yard to the outstanding cohort of 2011 fellows, to the research assistance and the fabulous treasures of Widener Library. I especially want to thank Kristen Ghodsee, Anna Maria Hong, and Caroline Bruzelius for helping to make my time at the Radcliffe Institute such a pleasure, and I am particularly grateful to my resourceful undergraduate research partner, Ivana Stosic.

Over the years I have presented portions of this book to more seminars, workshops, lecture series, and conferences than I can count; they are literally too numerous to list. But I do want those who invited me and took the time to hear me speak to know that in each and every location I received comments and questions that forced me to think harder and better about the results of my research. I would like to make special mention of my visit to the University of Wisconsin to deliver the Merle Curti lectures in 2011, and by the same token acknowledge my constant companions in academic life, Florencia Mallon and Steve Stern, whose intellectual creativity, enormous warmth, and unflagging encouragement have meant so much to me.

My pleasure at completing this book is mixed with some sadness at the loss of friends and colleagues who have lent me support and enriched my life over the course of my research and writing. Two outstanding historians of colonial São Paulo—Ilana Blaj and John Monteiro—shared their unpublished work with me and suggested crucial references. Their deaths are tremendous losses for the Brazilian academic community, but their work remains with us as a testament to their extraordinary contributions to historical scholarship. Closer to home, I had always imagined celebrating the completion of this book with my dear friend Rebecca Lord, perhaps with a wonderful dinner in her always charmingly disheveled home in Silver Spring, where the conversation could range from historical debates and pressing political questions to the latest celebrity scandal in *People* magazine. Rebecca, how I wish you were here.

It is a pleasure to acknowledge several friends and colleagues who have been steadfast sources of solidarity and inspiration. Many times when I felt overwhelmed or stumped, I was fortunate to have one of the finest historians I know, my dear friend Temma Kaplan, to cheer me on and suggest a way out of the rut in which I was stuck. Rachel Klein has been similarly supportive as we shared our anxieties about getting a book done and out. I have been lucky to count as my close friend and superb colleague Aisha Khan, first at Stony

Brook, and now at NYU. And Jim Green has been a staunch friend and ally, and someone whose intellectual energy I can only envy, not emulate.

A mere thank-you seems entirely inadequate to express my gratitude to Duke University Press, and especially to my editor and dear friend Valerie Millholland, who has been a model of patience and good humor. In the latter phase of this process I have had the good fortune to work with Gisela Fosado, who has been a welcome source of encouragement. Also at the press, Lorien Olive has provided indispensable assistance with the many images that appear in the book. And I offer my profound thanks to the two anonymous readers who did such a careful reading of the manuscript and gave me such constructive criticisms.

Some debts are simply incalculable, and that's certainly true of what I owe my husband, Erich Goode. If it were not for him, I would have given up on this long ago. Without him, I could not have made the many trips to Brazil that made this study possible, nor could I have managed to steal the time I needed to complete the manuscript. I owe every single page of this book to him, and much more than that.

Considering all the intellectual debts that I have accumulated over the years that I have been working on this book, it is a little ironic that I have dedicated it to two people who frankly were not the least bit helpful to me in its completion—*muito pelo contrário*. But my daughter Sarah and my son Danny fill my life with love and with meaning, and that is worth more than I can possibly say.

INTRODUCTION

I am off to São Paulo . . . a State . . . that is the exemplar of our progress, of our culture, of our civilization, and one that produces, not only for its own consumption, but also to furnish the wealth that all of Brazil requires for the satisfaction of its needs.

—Júlio Prestes, 1927, upon leaving Congress to assume the presidency of São Paulo

In *The Strategy of Economic Development* (1958), economist Albert O. Hirschman remarked at length on a phenomenon characteristic of many "underdeveloped countries," a process he dubbed "dualistic development." According to Hirschman, innovation and progress in underdeveloped economies cluster around "growth poles" that create significant, and escalating, interregional inequalities, a trend he considered both inevitable and, in the short run, desirable. "This transitional phase" would allow a nation to make the most of its existing resources and, if the conditions were right, the fruits of progress could be expected, eventually, to "trickle down" or diffuse out to the less developed region(s). He did readily admit that dualism "brings with it many social and psychological stresses" and expressed some concern about "the tendency to magnify the distance that separates one group or region from another," including the circulation of derogatory and racialized stereotypes.[1] But while Hirschman lamented the readiness of the average Italian "to declare that Africa begins just south of his own province," he betrayed no concern that he himself deployed adjectives that could serve to entrench the differences between regions in ways that went well beyond standard economic indicators or contingent economic advantages. Explaining the circumstances in which "polarization effects" would set the stage "for a prolonged split of [a] country into a progressive and a depressed area," he noted that these effects "were fairly typical of such *backward* regions as Brazil's Nordeste, Colombia's Oriente, and Italy's Mezzogiorno."[2] Even Hirschman, an astute and empathetic observer of the human condition, appears to have been untroubled by the polarizing effect of his own developmentalist language, routinely using terms such as "backward" and "progressive" to describe and naturalize regional inequalities.[3]

A central premise of this book is that these "social and psychological stresses" and racialized stereotypes are not just regrettable and ephemeral by-products of uneven economic development. Rather, I will argue that they are important constitutive elements of historically structured spatial inequalities.[4] For Hirschman, and for most other social scientists and historians, dualistic development, or economic divergence, is the result of the intrinsic logic of economic systems—a matter of labor supply, available inputs, adequate infrastructure, the needs of capital, and so forth.[5] Without dismissing these factors, I would argue that each and every one is mediated by historical circumstances that are shaped by discourses of difference and the grids of political and cultural power that they produce. The first wave of prosperity—always unequally distributed on both horizontal and vertical axes—in a particular locale is typically the result of a fortuitous coincidence of timing and topography. How that initial surge gets transformed into a sustained process of economic development, and how that locale becomes defined as a region, bounded and separate from other geopolitical spaces, is a consequence of a range of historical factors, including the capacity of well-positioned collectivities to construct an identity for themselves and their "region" that naturalizes its progress.[6] In other words, far from being just a by-product or reflection of already-existing uneven development, I would argue that discourses of difference are generative of policies and decisions that consolidate and exacerbate regional inequalities. Indeed, they are crucial to defining what we mean by a region in the first place, and to what David Harvey aptly calls the "the grossest of fetishisms"—the idea that a "place" has causal powers.[7]

It is not surprising that Brazil figures prominently among Hirschman's examples of dualistic development. Except perhaps for Italy, no nation has been more consistently associated with regional contrasts than Brazil.[8] The image of "the Two Brazils" has loomed large in the national imagination since the early twentieth century, and while the Norte or Nordeste has regularly been designated as the "backward" or "traditional" Brazil, the largely uncontested center of Brazilian progress and modernity has been the city and state of São Paulo.[9] By the 1880s São Paulo's booming coffee economy had already established it as Brazil's leading agricultural producer, and by the 1920s, it had emerged as the leading locus of manufacturing as well. Although it occupies less than 3 percent of Brazilian territory, São Paulo today accounts for well over a fifth of the national population and nearly a third of Brazil's gross domestic product. If it were a sovereign nation, São Paulo would rank fourth in terms of population (after Brazil, Mexico, and Colombia) and third in terms of wealth (after Brazil and Mexico) among the countries of Latin America.

Although paulista propagandists routinely insisted that the origins of São Paulo's surge could be found in the distant colonial past, the region's economic hegemony dates back only to the late nineteenth century. The coastal plain that formed the most fertile and accessible plantation zones in northeastern Brazil during colonial rule narrows to nearly nothing once it gets to São Paulo, so that the province played a marginal role in the early export economies. Lacking the sorts of irresistible inducements—such as precious metals—that drew waves of settlers to the inland province of Minas Gerais in the eighteenth century, São Paulo remained thinly populated, with large stretches of its interior inhabited by indigenous groups or *caboclo* farmers whose main goal was subsistence. Even during the mining boom, which stimulated internal commerce with paulista farms and estates, the scale of production remained modest compared to the strongholds of the plantation economies.[10] The provincial capital, near the littoral but perched atop a steep escarpment, remained little more than a large village well into the last quarter of the nineteenth century, and was briefly overtaken, population-wise, by the nearby city of Campinas, some sixty miles to its north. At first even provincial coffee production, located mainly on the slopes of the paulista portion of the Paraíba Valley, could be seen as a mere extension of the well-established plantation zones across the border in Rio de Janeiro province.

It was only in the final decades (1870s–1880s) of the Brazilian Empire, with coffee planting taking root on a significant scale in the paulista North and West, and with the railway system enlarging accordingly, that São Paulo, city and province, began to evince some of the characteristics later associated with its exceptional economic performance. Population growth—first mainly due to the forced relocation of African slaves, and then the more voluntary influx of European immigrants—expanded the labor force and the market. The maintenance demands of the railroad network fueled the growth of a half dozen major interior cities such as Jundiaí, Sorocaba, and Piracicaba, that became not only commercial entrepôts but centers of considerable industrial production as well. Santos, the main port city, drew both former slaves and immigrants searching for regular employment on the waterfront. But the most dramatic manifestations of the economic surge could be found in the state capital, where a previously compact, walkable city swelled into a sprawling metropolis with multiple working-class districts in the eastern quadrant and a growing zone of middle-class residences to the west and south. Wedged in between, and emblematic of the concentrated wealth derived from rapid economic growth, was the *bairro nobre* (noble neighborhood) of the Avenida Paulista, inaugurated in 1891, where the coffee barons and industrial magnates built their posh *palacetes*.[11]

The construction of regional ("paulista") identity has been inseparable from São Paulo's ever more spectacular economic success story. But it has also been inseparable from another "spectacular" narrative of a very different sort—the representations of poverty and backwardness in the Nordeste, a region routinely homogenized and rendered as a spectacle of "mayhem and misery."[12] The geographic area gradually being classified and homogenized as the Nordeste actually encompassed a very diverse set of topographical, social, and economic formations. The coastal zone was carpeted by fields of cane and dotted with sugar mills and industrial-scale refineries; the near interior was a semi-arid zone of cotton cultivation and subsistence farming; and the backlands or *sertão* was a region of cattle ranching and hardscrabble farming, relieved by fertile areas of natural and artificial irrigation. The region also included several large urban centers and some significant industrial enclaves, and had a population whose color and ethnicity were as varied as its landscape and social structure. From this strikingly diverse stretch of Brazilian territory emerged São Paulo's "Other," a uniformly backward region plagued by droughts, a stagnating economy, and, above all, a wretched population whose very bodies bore the stigmata of their poverty and misery. Without this regional "Other," the discourses of paulista exceptionalism would be far less compelling. The patently different life chances for a Brazilian from São Paulo and a resident of the Northeast has served to "naturalize" paulista claims about their region's exceptional capacity for progress and modernity.[13] Again, Hirschman was not unaware of this "tendency to magnify the distance that separates one group or region from another." However, what I think did escape him, at least in his study published in 1958, was the centrality of this tendency to the construction of regional and national identities, and therefore to the very politics of economic development.[14]

These qualifications aside, Hirschman's comments offer important insight into the use of racial stereotypes and innuendo to widen the distance between groups or regions. This was not an entirely startling revelation on his part; some forty years earlier, the Italian Communist Antonio Gramsci, describing the relationship between northern Italy and the Mezzogiorno (which he dubbed "colonialism of a special type"), said the following about northern Italian attitudes toward the southerners: "It is well known what kind of ideology has been disseminated in myriad ways among the masses in the North, by the propagandists of the bourgeoisie: the South is the ball and chain which prevents the social development of Italy from progressing more rapidly; the Southerners are biologically inferior beings, semi-barbarians or total barbarians, by natural destiny; if the South is backward, the fault does not lie with the capitalist system or with any other historical cause, but with Nature, which has made the Southerners lazy, incapable, criminal, and barbaric."[15] Hirschman was less confident than Gramsci that he could identify the precise origins of pejorative regional stereotypes, and less pessimistic about their sociopolitical implications, but he observed similar attitudes. Aside from the (northern) Italian claims about where "Africa starts," Hirschman noted "the derogatory use of the term 'indio' in some Latin American countries to designate whoever is economically or socially one's inferior."[16]

In Brazil, where the indigenous population had a relatively marginal presence by the late nineteenth century, the term "indio" was unlikely to serve this purpose (except perhaps in the Amazon), but there were other racial images readily available to those eager to construct a discourse of difference.[17] São Paulo—or more precisely, the paulista elites—emerged as major economic and political players during the final decades of legal, state-condoned slavery in Brazil, and during the heyday of what has been called "scientific racism."[18] It would have been literally unthinkable for those crafting narratives of paulista exceptionalism at the turn of the century to contest the link between whiteness and progress, or between blackness and backwardness. And this tendency was hardly confined to elites in São Paulo; throughout Brazil, members of the *classes conservadoras*—men of wealth and erudition—regarded European immigration as the key to modernizing the post-emancipation economy and considered the large population of color to be a "problem" for the future of the Brazilian nation.[19]

In some respects, the narratives of paulista exceptionalism that emerged in these decades could be categorized as a variant of the discourses of white supremacy that were widely disseminated during the height of European imperialism prior to World War I, and that endured well into the next global conflict.[20] But in São Paulo, as elsewhere in Brazil, there were discursive currents that questioned the "racial science" of the Northern Hemisphere, with its extreme pessimism about the effects of "miscegenation." Brazilian intellectuals and policy makers did embrace a certain version of eugenics; even a vocal critic of scientific racism, Antonio Baptista Pereira, defended Brazil's capacity for progress by insisting that Joseph Arthur de Gobineau and other racial theorists "didn't take into account the broad eugenic power of the Portuguese."[21] But historian Nancy Stepan has demonstrated that Brazilian enthusiasm for the "wellborn science" was tempered by a persistent Lamarckian version of evolutionary theory that made environment as important as heredity. And there was already, in the decades immediately following abolition, a sense that overly blunt public avowals of race prejudice were somehow "un-Brazilian."[22] Indeed, in São Paulo, as elsewhere in Brazil, there were individuals of (not too much) color, with talent and connections, who circulated within the ranks of the regional elite.[23] Thus, even as paulistas promoted the whitening of the regional population, whether through representational strategies or subsidized immigration policies, most did not adopt a full-blown discourse of white supremacy, or advocate sharply drawn boundaries between black and white.

At the same time, the relative sensitivity of the racial question and the instability of color lines in the Brazilian context help to explain the appeal of region as a marker of difference. Regional identity, I will argue, was a racialized category given its recourse to innate or natural characteristics to explain the contrasting trajectories of Brazilian regions. In privileging whiteness as a source of regional exceptionalism, paulista identity also implicitly drew on and reproduced negative constructions of blackness and African culture that were staples of Brazilian slave society.[24] But constructions of regional identity, both positive and pejorative, did not depend upon explicit references to racial difference, whether grounded in biological or cultural idioms, and thus maintained the standards of "cordiality" in Brazilian public discourse.[25] And as regional economies diverged, the tangible material differences between locales such as São Paulo and the Nordeste could be mobilized to legitimate narratives of modernity and backwardness. That the spaces respectively defined as São Paulo and the Nordeste were dramatically different, and that their populations bore the signs of this difference on their bodies and in their minds, became something that could go without saying—the ultimate sign of a successful, or hegemonic, construction.

Region and Nation

Regionalism is a long-standing theme in historical studies of Brazil and other Latin American nations. Colombia, for example, has been dubbed "a nation of regions," and until recently historians tended to treat such regional divisions—in Colombia and elsewhere—as resulting from self-evident and natural geographic features that separated and defined different climatic and geological zones of the nation, and generated specific types of economic activities and cultural proclivities.[26] Moreover, central to scholarly studies of regionalism has been the assumption that it was an impediment to the formation of homogeneous and cohesive national identities. In effect, regional loyalties were stubborn remnants of a colonial past, or the unfortunate consequence of natural geographic barriers.[27] As hindrances to national cohesion, they should or would fade away with the (inevitable) triumph of the nation.

Although regionally defined studies, as opposed to studies of regionalism, became a staple of the Latin American historiography when the new social history was in vogue,[28] most scholars doing research at the regional level failed to problematize or even contemplate the relationship between region and nation; typically historians simply treated the two as "the part and the whole" and assumed that regional identities were a priori categories, rather than the result of political struggle.[29] But some of the historians engaged in regional studies did try to think in more innovative ways about the articulation of region and nation. Starting in the 1970s a group of North American historians published a series of volumes that focused on the politics of Brazilian regionalism, with particular emphasis on the decentralized features of Brazil's First Republic (1889–1930). "Regions" in these works coincided entirely with the geopolitical boundaries of the various states being studied (Rio Grande do Sul, São Paulo, Minas Gerais, Bahia, Paraíba, Pernambuco), rather than being determined by geography.[30] Furthermore, these studies demonstrated that a reconfiguration of political arrangements that privileged political networks at the level of the individual states could produce or resuscitate regional identities. But the direct linkage between politics and regional identities drawn in these studies meant that they left undisturbed the standard historical narrative in which, ultimately, the centralizing power of the state suppresses regionalism and creates a more viable nation.[31]

Unlike the political-history bent of these monographs authored by North American scholars, studies of regionalism and regional identity published by Brazilian historians in the 1980s and 1990s tended to reflect the twin influences of neo-Marxist political economy and the new social history. Building on the concept of "internal colonialism" first broached in the Latin American context by Mexican sociologist Pablo González Casanova in the 1960s, this Brazilian historiography criticized the earlier tendency to naturalize regional divisions and identities, and argued that regions had to be historicized with reference to the process of capitalist development.[32] Moreover, this scholarship rejected the diffusionist reasoning that treated poorer regions as mere "residuals" of an earlier economic order. From this structuralist perspective regionalism, in the last instance, had to be understood in terms of the articulation of different modes of production or the uneven nature of capitalist development, and the role of the nation-state in mediating the interests of hegemonic and subordinate elites.[33]

This neo-Marxist approach had several salutary effects on the discussion of regionalism and regional identity. First of all, it emphasized the idea of a region as the product of historical processes, and not simply of geographic features or even geopolitical conventions, and it treated the definition of a region as inherently unstable, and apt to fluctuate from one era to another. And perhaps more important, it insisted that regional history could not be understood outside the context of national, and even global, history. Regional history was not merely a way to understand the particularities and peculiarities of a specific region, but a manifestation of broader national currents and tendencies. Thus, in her introductory essay to the important collection *República em migalhas* (roughly, Republic in fragments) Janaína Amado observed that several contributors to that volume defined "region" as a "spatial category that expresses a specificity, a singularity, within a totality; thus, the region configures a particular space that is articulated to a more broadly delineated social organization."[34]

Among the scholars adopting a "materialist" approach to Brazilian regionalism, those who hewed too closely to a literal conception of internal colonialism—which, as we have seen, was already present in Gramsci's writings on Italian regionalism—often found themselves engaged in a futile search for evidence of the actual transfer of wealth from the impoverished Nordeste to the economically robust Center-South.[35] The more sophisticated essays in *República em migalhas* favored, instead, the aspects of Gramsci's writings about regionalism that analyzed the region as the space where dominant classes form alliances and construct hegemony.[36] These insights were crucial to shifting the discussion away from regionalism as a source of fragmentation or distortion, and toward understanding how hierarchies of power and influence can be formed from regional identities. At the same time, this approach problematically assumes the existence of self-conscious social classes prior to the construction of the region, similar to Gramsci's consummately manipulative northern bourgeoisie, which, fully formed and conscious of its interests, cleverly promotes disparaging images of the southern populations among the susceptible northern working class. Moreover, even though the contributors to *República em migalhas* historicized the concept of region, rejecting the positivist notion of a region "as a *given*, already accepted and fully formed," and inserted regional history into a larger totality or historical narrative, they still accepted a certain fixity of categories, a certain stability of boundaries, between the region and the nation.[37]

It is at this juncture that the post-structuralist historiography of nations (and, by extension, regions) as imagined communities allows us to rethink regionalism now as a discursive effect and praxis inseparable from the construction of national historical narratives, and enables us to destabilize the very boundaries between region and nation.[38] One of the principal premises of this study is that there is no necessary opposition between region and nation; following Prasenjit Duara, I would argue that nation formation may actually produce or reinforce regional or provincial loyalties as competing political groups/projects imagine the nation through their assumed regional identities.[39] In other words, not only is region *not* the antithesis of nation, but it is an indispensable site from which to imagine the nation. Thus, regionalism in São Paulo should not be understood as a sign of the failure of the paulistas to construct a national project; rather, I would contend that regional discourse formed the basis for a national project that implied a hierarchy of regions and situated São Paulo at the center of the Brazilian nation. It was, to be sure, an inequitable vision of the nation, but it was a national project nonetheless. As historian Tania de Luca observes in her study of the pioneering paulista monthly the *Revista do Brasil*, "More and more the nation was being identified with the State of São Paulo."[40] This could be (mis)read as an allusion to growing separatist sentiment, but the meaning is actually the opposite. Once we eschew a strictly spatial notion of the region and the nation, it becomes easier to understand how the paulistas imagined their part *as* the whole. And once we take seriously the differences implied in the concept of internal colonialism, it becomes problematic to understand São Paulo as an instance of "incomplete hegemony."[41]

Orientalism in One Country

Given the regional disparities associated with "uneven development" in Latin America, it is not surprising that a Latin American social scientist coined the term "internal colonialism."[42] During the 1960s and 1970s this concept not only served as the standard analytical framework for understanding spatial inequalities in Latin America, but also proved to be an idea that "traveled" to contexts as diverse as Britain's "Celtic Fringe," Italy's Mezzogiorno, the Peruvian highlands, French-speaking Canada, Inuit peoples of Arctic North America, African-American and Chicano communities in the United States, and Brazil's Nordeste. Whether discussing the subordinate position of a specific region or minority community, academics applied the concept of internal colonialism to explain relations of domination and exploitation that seemed comparable to formal colonialism but that operated *within* a particular national space.[43]

Although the internal colonialism concept stimulated a great deal of interesting research, its structuralist/materialist roots meant that scholars employing this framework treated racial/ethnic difference as a preexisting condition that dominant elites could opportunistically exploit for economic advantage. Thus one researcher, writing in 1976, dismissed "racial-cultural heterogeneity" as an aspect of internal colonialism in Brazil since he perceived no significant distinctions in racial composition between the Northeast and the Center-South.[44] Such a conclusion rested upon an essentialized, objective definition of race, whereas both Hirschman and Gramsci understood that the racialization of regional difference operated mainly in the realm of representation. Historian Nancy Appelbaum traces the way nineteenth-century Colombians "elaborated a racialized discourse of regional differentiation that assigned greater morality and progress to certain regions . . . marked as 'white.' Meanwhile, those places defined as 'black' and 'Indian' were associated with disorder, backwardness, and danger."[45] Given that these "racial" categories were themselves unstable, the labeling of a region as "black" or "white" has to be understood as a process that is not reducible to local inhabitants' skin color or origins. Central to my own work is the contention that paulistas have routinely represented themselves as "white" and nordestinos as "nonwhite" regardless of genetics or physical appearance.

In the wake of the cultural and linguistic turn of the 1980s, the scholarly discourse shifted away from internal colonialism—a concept that emerged from the social sciences—to what we might call internal orientalism (or more fancifully, "orientalism in one country"), a concept that emerged from literary and cultural studies. Based on the critical theory first elaborated by Edward Said with regard to British imperial representations of Asia and the Middle East, it offers a more fluid and flexible framework for understanding spatially organized hierarchies of knowledge, wealth, and power than internal colonialism.[46] Rather than a set of specific socioeconomic processes and interests, orientalism emphasizes the emergence of discourses that permit a certain sociocultural group to create a sense of its superiority and its entitlement to wield authority over other groups. Said saw orientalism—that is, the construction of the "Orient" as Europe's Other—as an enabling rhetoric that underpinned the entire European imperial enterprise, and operated to produce hierarchies of power and authority whether or not an economic surplus was being extracted from the colony by the metropolis.[47] This same approach can be employed to explore the ways in which individuals and groups equate themselves with a particular region—assumed to be more modern, urban, and "progressive," while constructing other regions/populations as backward, stagnant, and semicivilized, thereby seeking to consolidate a dominant position for themselves within the boundaries of a single nation.[48] This rendering of the nation not only relies on a binary construction that "magnif[ies] the distance" between the dominant region and its "Other," but also requires the elision of portions of the nation that might attenuate regional difference.[49]

The concept of orientalism has yet another feature that makes it useful as an analytical tool for this study: unlike internal colonialism, it is specifically focused on the colonizing power. One of Said's principal points is that orientalism tells us much more about the desires, aspirations, and identities of its occidental architects than it does about the reputed "Orient." Although in certain venues regionalism might be associated with oppressed minorities, some of the most enduring regionalist movements of the last century emerged precisely from populations that, far from considering themselves as subaltern, oppressed, or exploited (in the usual sense), enjoyed or demanded a dominant position, to which they claimed to be entitled as a result of their superior qualities.[50] The aggressive assertion of regional supremacy usually comes accompanied by the insistence that the region in question is exclusively or disproportionately responsible for the greatness and sustenance of the nation; thus those who identify with that region chafe at having to share national political power or fiscal resources with other, "inferior" regions. This translates into a demand for a position of *superiority or privilege*, not equality, a mandate that would be difficult to assert without recourse to racist idioms and imagery, tropes supposedly frowned upon in Brazil's "racial democracy."

The Place of Racial Democracy in Brazilian Society

Even before the abolition of slavery in 1888, Brazil had earned something of a reputation abroad as a racially open, fluid, and tolerant society, particularly in comparison to the United States, with its rigid and frequently violent forms of racial exclusion.[51] Yet much of the historical literature dates the birth of the idea of Brazil as a "racial democracy," a phrase not widely adopted until the 1950s, to the publication in 1933 of Gilberto Freyre's *Casa-Grande e senzala* (translated into English as *The Masters and the Slaves*).[52] As Micol Seigel aptly puts it, Freyre's work is "too often credited (or blamed) with the stunning paradigm shift from whitening to 'racial democracy.'"[53] But precisely because of the inflation of Freyre's role in the crafting of this central element in Brazilian national identity, scholars have been inordinately interested in identifying the sources of inspiration for *Casa-Grande e senzala*. Freyre himself cites an episode in 1921, during his time as a graduate student at Columbia University, when he gazed upon a group of mixed-race Brazilian sailors disembarking from a ship "in the soft snow of Brooklyn."[54]

Freyre's remark that the sailors struck him as "caricatures of men" is striking evidence that the paulistas were hardly alone in associating shades of whiteness with degrees of fitness for citizenship. What distinguished paulista intellectual circles was not necessarily a greater inclination to treat racial difference as the central explanation for the contrasting fates of Brazilian regions, but a greater capacity to claim whiteness, and even to define what it meant to be white within the Brazilian context. Whether through policies of subsidized immigration or strategies of representation, the paulistas could claim an "essentially" white regional identity, and consign those "mulatto and *cafuzo*" sailors to the rapidly receding past.[55] But Freyre, from the declining northeastern state of Pernambuco, had no choice but to see in the sailors' faces his region's (and by extension, his nation's) future. Historians located in the United States, and many based in Brazil, tend to assume that Freyre constructed his vision of a racially harmonious Brazilian society vis-à-vis the racist United States, and his experiences in Texas and New York surely furnished part of the inspiration for his research. But his writings both prior to and after the publication of *Casa-Grande e senzala* suggest that he was, at least in some instances, imagining a Brazilian nation from the regional space of the "Nordeste" as against the whitening pretentions of the paulistas, which would have assigned his region and its "populations" to an ever more marginal position within Brazilian society.[56]

In contrast to the saga of progress and modernity emerging from São Paulo, whose central figure was the colonial pathfinder and enslaver known as the *bandeirante*, Freyre constructed a historical narrative that centered on the intimacies of the patriarchal plantation household in the colonial northeastern sugar-growing zones.[57] Unlike paulista writers, who zealously minimized the African influence on the society of the "plateau" (a reference to São Paulo's upland location away from the coast), Freyre celebrated the intermingling, both sexual and cultural, of Portuguese and African cultures in the coastal complex of plantation slavery. And he exalted this mixture, plus a lesser indigenous influence, as both the defining/distinctive feature of Brazilian national identity and the source of Brazil's unique racial harmony.

Despite the striking differences in these historical narratives, it would be inaccurate to describe Freyre's magnum opus as offering a vision of Brazil that was diametrically opposed to the paulista perspective.[58] Indeed, I would argue that *Casa-Grande e senzala* was so successful in part because it did not directly challenge existing assumptions about whiteness and progress, while foregrounding features of Brazilian culture (tolerance, benevolence) whose implications were highly gratifying to all but the most stiff-necked racists within Brazil's lettered classes.[59] In Freyre's heavily romanticized portrait of the patriarchal plantation, Europeans are still the source of civilized culture and erudition, selectively absorbing African and indigenous influences. And his introduction to the volume echoes the common elite expectation that the "African" influence in Brazilian culture would inevitably fade (though in Freyre's case, this prediction seemed couched in some regret).[60] Thus, *Casa-Grande* could serve as the foundational text for the discourse of racial democracy and provide a basis for thinking of Brazil as a modern nation, even as it left undisturbed certain assumptions about the relationship between whiteness and a more modern and progressive Brazilian future.[61]

There is no shortage of scholarly critiques of Freyre's work. He has been rightfully skewered for reinforcing the fiction of Brazilian slavery as a benevolent institution (though he may have been somewhat ambivalent on this question, given the many episodes of violence and cruelty detailed in his study of plantation life).[62] His claims about the special Luso-Brazilian proclivity for harmonious blending with non-Europeans would subsequently be deployed, with Freyre's blessings, as a justification for continuing Portuguese colonialism in Africa.[63] Most important, his promotion of the image of Brazil as a land of racial harmony—his early work makes no reference to racial *democracy*—has been repeatedly denounced as a myth that has served to mask enduring racial prejudice and to delegitimize racial identity as a basis for political activism.[64] In effect, it has been derided as the "myth of racial democracy" (with myth here meaning something false and misleading) and disdained as a convenient rationale that allows elites to dismiss protests against racial inequality as unfounded or even unpatriotic.[65]

In the past decade, the less polemical scholarship on race relations in Brazil has shifted away from simply denouncing racial democracy as a "myth," to recognizing the broad-based embrace of this idea, including among the poor and people of color, for whom it represents not so much a depiction of Brazilian reality as an image of the society to which Brazilians should legitimately aspire.[66] But this only further begs the question of how we are to explain the coexistence, in the same national space, of a robust discourse of racial democracy and copious evidence of racism and racial inequality. One common explanation is the gap between discourse and practice: Brazilians of all racial backgrounds want to claim that they are without prejudice, but in daily life still make decisions or engage in behaviors that privilege those with whiter skin or more European appearance.[67] This formulation of the problem, while making apparent sense, ends up treating racism in one of two ways, neither of which seems tenable. One is to see racial prejudice as existing outside the realm of rational thought or cultural meaning, as a sort of unconscious reflex or primordial reaction. The other is to see it as the product of cleverly deliberate individual and institutional calculation meant to favor whiter Brazilians over darker ones. Again, both seem unpersuasive explanations for the alleged discourse/practice gap.

I would like to suggest a different approach, one that precludes the idea of a gap between (racially democratic) discourse and (racist) action, and assumes instead that racialized images of modernity and progress have deeply informed discriminatory policies and practices. More specifically, I would argue that, historically, the economic success of São Paulo has cemented the widely assumed association between whiteness and civilization, between whiteness and modernization, between whiteness and productivity.[68] And the fact that this association can be expressed in regional terms, rather than explicitly racial ones, has meant that racialized discourses of modernity and progress have been able to coexist, or even mingle, with discourses of racial democracy for much of Brazil's post-emancipation history. As we will see, there have been moments when these different strands of national identity have not been so smoothly interwoven and have produced certain tensions and frictions. But more commonly, I would argue, one has informed the other, and together they have framed a vision of Brazilian society that eschews explicit expressions of racial prejudice but continues to link whiteness with progress. Rather than seeing these discourses as operating in opposition to each other, I would characterize their relationship as one of imperfect, and sometimes strained, complementarity.[69] There are, to be sure, political moments when these stresses and strains produce genuine shifts in the way paulistas, and Brazilians in general, conceptualize the meanings of racial difference. But for the period this book examines—the 1920s to the 1960s—I believe the more noteworthy, if disheartening, trend is the persistence of an equivalence between whiteness and progress.

What about Rio?

Thus far I have counterposed São Paulo's narrative of modernity and progress to the Nordeste's reputation as a region of backwardness and misery. Yet most Brazilians, when talking about São Paulo (usually meaning the city) in a comparative vein, would draw a contrast not with the Nordeste, but with Rio de Janeiro. Unlike most "hypercephalic" Latin American nations, Brazil has the distinction of being the home to two "megacities," separated by a distance of only some 250 miles, and these circumstances virtually invite comparison, both systematic and casual. Indeed, Brazilian culture is replete with jokes, anecdotes, and tropes about the different character of the nation's two leading cities, and about the divergent dispositions of the *paulistanos* and *cariocas*. Everyone knows the old saw that says paulistanos "live to work" while the cariocas "work to live." Not surprisingly, whenever I've given talks in Brazil about my work on paulista identity, someone in the audience has chided me for not paying greater attention to the rivalry between Rio and São Paulo.

It would certainly be a mistake to ignore the Rio/São Paulo competition altogether, especially when discussing the early decades of São Paulo's emergence as a major center of political and economic power. After all, Rio had been the capital of Brazil, whether as colony, empire, or republic, since 1763, and was the nation's most populous city until the 1950s, when São Paulo overtook it. Moreover, even as Rio's economic position waned, and it was supplanted by Brasília as the nation's capital, the "marvelous city" continued to be Brazil's most internationally renowned metropolis, the center of tourism, culture, both high and low, and the nation's media capital. As Tania de Luca found in her study of the *Revista do Brasil*, paulista intellectuals in the early 1920s were anxious to establish cultural parity with the federal capital, as well as to assert São Paulo's status as the more authentic Brazilian city. Contributors to the journal even resorted to linguistic comparisons to demonstrate that Rio de Janeiro was too "Portuguese" and cosmopolitan in its idioms to be the true center of the Brazilian nation.[70] In a similar vein, a study of Brazilian modernism and national identity by Angela de Castro Gomes reveals the "hegemonic perceptions" of the paulista modernist cohort, and the systematic minimization of carioca influences in the movement.[71] In other words, the rivalry with Rio certainly was a significant element in the way urban paulistas crafted their own identity. And race intermittently figured in the way paulistanos explained the contrasting characters of the two metropolises, as when Júlio de Mesquita Filho claimed that Rio's cultural "decadence" was a result of its excessively large population of African descent.[72]

However, for a number of reasons, the legendary competition between Rio and São Paulo will not occupy a major place in what follows. One minor consideration, for a study of regional identity, is Rio's status as a city or federal district, rather than a region per se. True, the referent for "São Paulo" typically oscillates between the city and the state, with the latter often being collapsed into the former. And one of the points of this study is that space, as a marker of place and identity, should not be treated as concrete or stable. Residents of Rio regularly comment that an advantage of being from that city is the absence of identification with a region—a specious claim that persists as a constitutive element of carioca (regional) identity.[73] Nonetheless, the exclusively urban character of Rio de Janeiro complicates any comparative discussion of paulista/paulistano and carioca identities.

A far more significant consideration is the relative absence of serious political implications in the rivalry between Rio and São Paulo. Indeed, the very term "rivalry" is a clue to this, for it implies a somewhat level playing field, a competition between near equals, whereas the São Paulo/Nordeste binary is not conceptualized on either side as a "rivalry," but rather in terms of domination and subordination, or superiority and inferiority. Such is not the case even in the more disparaging paulista depictions of Rio de Janeiro as a city burdened by its colonial/imperial past, whose residents—accustomed to living off government sinecures—lack the industrious and enterprising spirit of the modern metropolis.[74] Throughout the first half of the twentieth century, Rio would continue to be an obligatory destination for any paulista intellectual or professional who wished to claim polish and sophistication. It provided a space where journalists, artists, and literati from all regions of Brazil could exchange ideas and form friendships that did not necessarily erase regional loyalties, but did reinforce the articulation of region and nation.[75] The anthropologist Hermano Vianna cites the arrival in Rio in 1924 of French intellectual Blaise Cendrars as a significant moment in the growing vogue for things "authentically" Brazilian and mentions the names of a group of young intellectuals who went to the port to greet the French visitor—among them several paulistas, including the modernist poet and unapologetic regional chauvinist Guilherme de Almeida.[76] Many of these individuals maintained a lively correspondence that reveals an intimate transregional realm of communication. Thus the Minas-born historian and journalist Rodrigo de Mello Franco de Andrade, based in Rio, exchanged correspondence regularly with the paulista "bohemian" writer Antonio de Alcântara Machado. In a letter dated December 1931, he mentioned seeing "Gilbertinho" Freyre almost daily and remarked that Freyre had just signed a contract to publish a book on the history of the Brazilian family to be titled *Casa-Grande e senzala*.[77] And both politicians and intellectuals from São Paulo were keen to cultivate a positive image of themselves and their region among their carioca colleagues, maintaining a "Centro Paulista" in Rio where eminent sons of São Paulo presented lectures on the glories and achievements of their home region to an audience whom they clearly sought to impress.[78]

As should be evident, the "Rio" that paulista elites and intellectuals valued for its sophistication and culture was the "white" city inhabited by wealthy and/or educated Brazilians, many of them from other regions. As Vianna shows, some paulistas were also drawn to the other Rio—a city composed largely of Afro-descendentes and Portuguese immigrants struggling to get by, and an alluring source of distinctively "Brazilian" music, martial arts, and cuisine. But this aspect of the marvelous city also provoked considerable ambivalence: in contexts where paulistas sought to heighten the difference between their home city and the nation's capital, and insist on São Paulo's greater aptitude for progress, the focus might shift to this other Rio, with its more popular and disorderly character. For instance, in 1965, when Rio celebrated its own IV Centenário, the paulista daily *O Estado de São Paulo* took great offense at a carioca politician's claim that the ex-political capital was still Brazil's "cultural capital." Not only did the newspaper assert São Paulo's cultural preeminence, but claimed that the African influences in Rio's samba schools and religious practices were signs of the city's "social regression."[79] More typically, though, when paulistas imagined their urban "rival," they envisioned a place where Brazilians who exhibited a certain taste and cultivation would always be welcome and always feel at home.[80]

Defining Indefinite Terms

An introduction is customarily the place where an author defines what he or she means by terms such as "race," "liberalism," and "modernity." When we use terms such as these, we are expecting them to do interpretive work, and it is therefore reasonable for the reader to demand some explanation of what we mean by them, and what kind of work we want them to do. Yet, most scholars who are attentive to language these days know that the meanings attached to words like "race" and "modernity" are contingent—they shift over time, or from one context to another, and to fix meaning in these cases may be to sacrifice historicity in the interests of clarity. The word "race" (or the Portuguese *raça*) is notoriously polysemic; it could be used in the very same text as a synonym for people (as in the *raça paulista*) and for groups defined by supposed biological/somatic traits. And to make it more complicated, I would argue that the use of the term "raça" for something like "raça paulista," though apparently a different usage, may well have traces of that other, more familiar meaning. Modernity, meanwhile, has been imbued with a dizzying array of meanings. Oswald de Andrade, a leading paulista modernist, identified African musical rhythms as "the contribution of ethnic forces to the creation of modernity" in a lecture at the Sorbonne in 1923.[81] A year later, in his famous

"Brazilwood Manifesto," he expressed analogous sentiments, but also called for more inventors and engineers, instead of "speculators and dilettantes," invoking a productivist meaning of modernity that paulista industrialists were eagerly fashioning to heighten the contrast between themselves and "traditional" elites in other regions, and which they would have regarded—on *their* modernity meter—as the exact opposite of African contributions to Brazilian culture.[82]

To be sure, it is not just a matter of how words such as race and modernity are used in the sources that I will cite and quote, but also how *I* will be using these terms, or versions of them (e.g., "racialized discourses"). How will I be judging whether a particular position is being articulated in a way that draws on or reinforces racist premises? Are claims to an aptitude for modernity always complicit with hierarchical distinctions between backwardness and progress? These are questions best addressed in the body of the text, in the discussion of historical events that serve to clarify the meanings attached to certain language and phrases, and where an observable density of usage can make meanings more apparent. That said, I can identify some assumptions about categories such as race and gender that underlie this study. Not only do I operate from the widely accepted premise that these categories are cultural constructions, but also that how they are constructed and deployed, and what they signify, can be highly unstable, especially in the case of race and racism.[83] Many works in this vein draw a distinction between "biological racism" and "cultural racism," and those are distinctions worth making in some contexts since they help us understand how racist discourses might be contested, and to what extent they can be articulated with other discourses.[84] At the same time, I think we have to be careful not to treat the former ("biological racism") as the "real" racism and the latter as somehow less so. Virtually all racialized discourses are pastiches—rarely does an argument about "race" have strictly biological or cultural referents.[85] In this volume, I will generally be regarding a discourse as racialized if the language implies traits or characteristics that are supposedly innate in a particular group, identified with a specific place of residence or origin, regardless of what the alleged means of transmission of those traits might be. Moreover, even the adjectival categories of "biological" and "cultural" cannot exhaust the possibilities, as illustrated by the following quote—with a telluric logic—from an issue of the magazine *Paulista*, published in 1930 by the American Chamber of Commerce: "PAULISTA is the name commonly used to designate natives of the State of São Paulo. It implies that one's roots have penetrated deep into the rich soil of this great State and have drawn up the pioneer characteristics inherent in its development."[86] As should be apparent, racial difference in what follows is not confined to referents such as skin color or somatic appearance. On the other hand, ideas about race are not fashioned in an entirely arbitrary manner; given Brazil's long history of enslavement of people of African descent, and the advantages that have concomitantly accrued to those with lighter skin or more European lineage, we can expect certain historical assumptions about whiteness and blackness to shape the way Brazilians construct regional identities.

Compared to "race" and "modernity," the meaning of liberalism would appear to be considerably more stable and fixed. Thus, the eminent Brazilian literary theorist Roberto Schwarz famously declared that, in the postcolonial slave society of nineteenth-century Brazil, liberal ideas were "out of place," a claim that is viable only if we assume that there is a correct version of what constitutes liberalism, and a proper context that activates its essential features.[87] Schwarz's influential argument has been widely contested by historians from a variety of perspectives, and its very premises have been eroded by the post-structuralist turn in historical studies, with its approach to language that assumes unstable relationships between words as signifiers and what is being signified. Furthermore, a plethora of adjectives have been employed by historians to distinguish among the many versions of liberalism that have circulated in Latin America and elsewhere, including some (popular liberalism, authoritarian liberalism) that would seem utterly oxymoronic to a scholar with a narrower definition of the term.[88]

Although I would hardly advocate a return to a fixed and narrow definition of liberalism, I would insist that the latter term is certainly not as polysemic as "race" or as fluid in its meaning as "modernity"—hence the need for modifiers. Because, historically, a variety of ideas have been closely associated with liberalism, it is a political discourse that could be "at home" among elites in a slave society, where its defense of property rights would be foregrounded, but that might also generate contradictions—for example, demands for individual rights and equality before the law—which could not be readily dismissed. Particular groups in particular historical moments may seize upon a specific aspect or version of liberalism, and define it in that vein, but once they adopt the "liberal" label, they leave themselves open to the charge of betraying liberal principles if they ignore other claims for which they may have little need or sympathy.

The mid-nineteenth-century coffee boom in Brazil reshaped the political and cultural world of the province of São Paulo. Among the many consequences of this period of intense economic and demographic change was a revitalized regional identity that had among its formative elements a critique of the "excessive" power of the central/monarchical government and a demand for greater provincial autonomy. Such ideas could be comfortably articulated within a liberal or liberal/republican framework of federalism, private property rights, and limited (central) state power.[89] In that sense, paulista regionalism was an identity that was "born liberal."[90] At the same time, the paulista elites' intense apprehension about social disorder following the abolition of slavery (1888), and their jockeying for hegemony in the new federalized political system following the overthrow of the monarchy (1889), meant that theirs would *not* be an expansive definition of liberalism. As in many liberal-republican societies prior to the 1930s, paulista liberals privileged property rights and public order over social welfare and created a variety of barriers to greater popular participation in the political process. Even those paulista liberals who decried oligarchic politics and entrenched patron-client networks typically envisioned the ideal citizen-voter as having certain class, gender, and racial traits that would exclude the great majority of São Paulo's residents from the political sphere.[91] Thus, while liberalism served as a sort of ideological glue for an emerging regional elite, and remained an enduring feature of regional political identity, it tended to reinforce, rather than challenge, a hierarchical vision of Brazilian society both within and beyond the borders of São Paulo.

Special Occasions

The central chapters of this book are structured around two specific "events." One is the regional uprising in 1932 known as the Constitutionalist Revolution. The other is the commemorations in 1954 marking the four hundredth anniversary of São Paulo's founding. By focusing on two moments in history when, for quite different reasons, large numbers of individuals who identified with the city and/or state of São Paulo were actively engaged in producing representations of *paulistinidade*, and promoting paulista identity, I am seeking to reduce the risk of the evidence I offer being dismissed as arbitrarily selected or de-historicized. The 1932 uprising produced a torrent of print, visual, and oral representations of paulista history, economic life, and social character, as did the IV Centenário in 1954.[92] This rich evidentiary base offers the historian a range of representations, but also sufficient documentation to discern the way in which certain images were imbricated and reiterated, and certain meanings crystallized—at least for a while. Of course, I could imagine the opposite objection: that by concentrating on these two exceptional historical moments, my study is presenting a distorted view of paulista identity, one that merely reflects the special circumstances of these two historical instances. But I do not intend to make an argument about continuity or persistence per se.

I would readily admit that the intensity of regional sentiment manifested during these moments was not routine or typical, and that one cannot abstract from these "special occasions" to a stable, persistent tenor of regional identification. In particular, the willingness of tens of thousands of paulistas (and potentially many more) to kill and die in the name of São Paulo during the 1932 uprising is precisely what I am interested in explaining, rather than seeing it as a consequence of a fully formed, preexisting regional identity.[93] In both instances (1932 and 1954) I would argue that those engaged in formulating representations of paulistinidade drew from a stream of ideas and images that was already coursing through paulista society, but that only became the basis for collective action in very specific circumstances. And in both instances I would point to organizations, monuments, and locales that resulted from these historical events (the veterans' associations from 1932, the Parque Ibirapuera from 1954) that then became important referents, as agents or symbols, in the reproduction of paulista identity.

The timing of these two events, and their separation by more than two decades, are also features that make them especially appropriate choices for this study. Aside from allowing me to explore the changing meanings of race, gender, liberalism, and modernity in the context of shifting representations of paulistinidade, this chronological arc permits me as well to destabilize the linear narrative of the triumph of nation over region. The 1932 uprising, not coincidentally, occurred at a moment when regional political loyalties were coming under fire, and when the Vargas regime was seeking to dismantle the state machines that had been a key feature of politics under the Old Republic (1889–1930). As we will see, for many authors, the paulistas' defeat marked the end of an era, a sort of "swan song" of the republican regional elites.[94] In its aftermath, regional identities would be swept aside (according to this narrative) in favor of a burgeoning nationalism promoted by a robust recentralized nation-state. That is precisely why São Paulo's IV Centenário is such an opportune event for this study. It was a celebration of regional greatness and exceptionalism at a moment of escalating nationalist rhetoric and near-universal declarations of Brazil as a model racial democracy. As indicated above, my point is not to insist that regional identity was more (or less) important than national identity, but rather that neither region nor nation could be imagined separately from the other.

Finally, the focus on these two distinct moments, two decades apart, serves to illuminate changes in the venues and vehicles for identity formation. To be sure, some of the changes reflect the very different nature of the two events being analyzed: the types of publicity permissible for an armed insurrection are substantially different from those available to commemorative activity organizers. Others, however, reflect new ways of thinking about publics and about the relationship between self and society, as well as the shifting resources for shaping public opinion. During the mobilization against the Vargas regime and for a constitution in 1932, the major vehicles for political expression were, predictably, the press, radio, and public gatherings. Perhaps more important, writers and speakers routinely conceptualized their audience as "all of São Paulo"—an apparently inclusive category that, as I will argue, entailed its own exclusions. Periodically there were appeals to specific groups, such as workers or immigrants, but the basic script remained unaltered regardless of the social segment being addressed. By the early 1950s, in contrast, organizers of the IV Centenário could enlist the aid of public relations and opinion research firms, and target particular segments of the population for different publications, events, expositions, and activities. In an urban landscape that featured massive general strikes, sporadic protests about miserable living conditions on the periphery, and dramatically expanded political competition, it had become difficult, even impossible, to imagine São Paulo as a single "community."

A Note about Identity

In an article published in February 2000, sociologist Rogers Brubaker and historian Frederick Cooper took their colleagues to task for (over)using the category of identity, which they regarded as having become so ubiquitous as to be rendered meaningless. In a take-no-prisoners critique, they targeted virtually every school of thought that used identity as a category of analysis, including those who worked with a "harder," more essentialized notion of identity, and those who took what they called a "soft constructivist" position that emphasized fluidity and fluctuation. Scholars of the first tendency, according to Brubaker and Cooper, err in accepting a category of practice at face value, thereby reifying identities—a criticism I find completely convincing. As for scholars of the second, "soft" school, their treatment of "identity" as something fluid, unstable, and multiple, "leaves us without a rationale for talking about 'identities' at all," according to Brubaker and Cooper.[95] Here I am less persuaded. Despite the authors' call for careful attention to language, their own critical use of terms such as "soft" and "fluid" seems to have led them to the questionable conclusion that identity, from this perspective, is not a useful category for the (tough?) analytical task of understanding how identities can "harden, congeal, and crystallize" into something powerful and often dangerous. Not only do I find their point here unpersuasive, but I find their critique of constructivism markedly inconsistent. While they initially disparage the constructivist approach as too wispy and ambiguous, they later on insist that "even in its constructivist guise, the language of 'identity' disposes us to think in terms of bounded groupness."[96] This, however, is not a problem of constructivism per se, but of a poor application of the interpretive framework it offers.

In making this bold theoretical intervention, Brubaker and Cooper may be tossing out the baby with the bathwater. Again, I entirely agree with the authors' criticisms of the "hard approach" to identity and what I would call sloppy constructivism; we should never treat identity as "always already 'there,' as something individuals and groups 'have.'"[97] Instead, I regard identity as a discourse or truth claim available to certain groups or individuals, and not others. Further, I would argue that identities operate in different registers. Under certain historical circumstances (which I suspect are too idiosyncratic to lend themselves to any kind of social science modeling), political and cultural entrepreneurs can mobilize populations to take action, even take up arms. Here identity operates, not as the cause of the movement, but as a marker of difference that makes it unthinkable not to join, in part because one then risks being identified with the despised other. Such experiences may or may not harden boundaries of difference, but even if this intense identification proves ephemeral, traces remain as a way of thinking about the world that can reinforce hierarchies and divisions in more "casual," day-to-day encounters, regardless of whether one makes friends or finds marriage partners across shifting boundaries.[98]

One alternative would be to dispose of the admittedly overused term "identity" and just refer to "paulistinidade," or paulista-ness, instead of paulista identity. But aside from the clumsiness of the English translation, I think we lose something in excising the word "identity" since paulistinidade refers to an unstable bundle of traits associated with an imagined region called São Paulo; it omits the process—what Brubaker and Cooper would call "identification" or "self-definition"—by which individuals or groups claim or assume these traits.[99] Moreover, these alternative terms, though perfectly appropriate in certain instances, are less satisfactory when we shift to a more intense political register in that they involve an active, conscious, deliberate choice, and individuate the process in a way that obscures the role of collective "structures of feeling," which serve to make the refusal of certain identities almost unimaginable.[100] Thus the repeated use of phrases implying not only unanimity, but even the merging of minds and sentiments, in descriptions of the 1932 Constitutionalist Movement. Typical is the following commentary, by journalist Paulo Nogueira Filho, regarding the urgency of forming a "United Front" (Frente Única) against the Vargas regime: "It was hardly necessary to undertake a profound study, but merely a dispassionate one, to observe that in São Paulo what was happening was a phenomenon of the general will, whose dictates were consolidating with irrepressible power. Hence, the paulista masses, from the moment they became conscious of themselves, would under no circumstances allow themselves to be ruled by men in whose spirit there survived the vestiges of the dominant mentality in the slaveholding pens."[101] The point is not that paulistas were actually "thinking with one mind," or responding to the beat of "a single heart," to quote the title of a recently televised *novela* set during this period of paulista history. Rather, it is to see the way Nogueira Filho, by posing the issue in this manner, seeks to make it unthinkable for someone who would claim to be paulista *not* to join the movement. Self-definition implies a range of options, as if the individual were shopping for a suitable persona, but movements organized around an identity, whether socioeconomic, regional, racial, ethnic, or sexual, typically seek to erase other possibilities, and to make the identity in question the only imaginable choice. In his reminiscences of his service as a volunteer in the Constitutionalist forces, the former law student Luiz Gonzaga Naclério Homem repeatedly admits, with evident regret, to harboring doubts about the Causa Paulista.[102] Indeed, at various points he wonders why, in light of his lack of enthusiasm, he felt compelled to volunteer: Was he afraid of being considered a coward? Or of disappointing his family and friends? The case of Naclério Homem, far from calling into question the potency of paulista identity, does just the opposite. No identity, no matter how powerful, can be expected to erase individual idiosyncracies of thought and feeling. It is precisely his decision, despite a lack of conviction, to fight for "the beautiful ideal" that speaks to the strength of regional *identity*.

In the decades that are the focus of this book, any political or cultural entrepreneur intent upon producing a study of paulista identity that presented it as something stable and real would almost certainly open with the history of colonial "Piratininga," just as a narrative of (North) American exceptionalism would likely begin with the pilgrims landing at Plymouth Rock. Needless to say, that's *not* where this book will begin. Chapter 1, "Paulista Modern," centers on the initial period of economic and demographic growth following the coffee boom, but particularly on the 1920s. The latter decade was a time when paulista intellectuals, politicians, and journalists of various stripes advanced the notion that their home region had a special proclivity for modernity. But it was also a time when Brazilians from other regions, though expressing pride in São Paulo's prosperity, began to vigorously contest paulista claims to political hegemony, thereby prompting more elaborate assertions or defenses of regional superiority. The decade (and the chapter) ends with the seizure of power by the *gaúcho* politician, Getúlio Vargas.[103]

The next four chapters explore different aspects of the Constitutionalist Movement that culminated in the uprising against the Vargas regime in 1932, an event also known as the "Guerra Paulista." Chapter 2, "Constituting Paulista Identity," examines the discourses, many of them rooted in racist arguments, that circulated in São Paulo during the early 1930s and that served to intensify a sense of crisis and harden lines of difference between paulistas and Brazilians from other regions, especially the Nordeste. Chapter 3, "The Middle Class in Arms? Fighting for São Paulo," looks at the process of mobilization for war and the experience of combat, with attention to both the actual composition of the battalions that fought for the Causa Paulista, including the all Afro-Brazilian Black Legion, and the ways in which the paulista volunteer was imagined in print and visual representations of the armed struggle. In a similar vein, chapter 4, "Marianne into Battle? The Mulher Paulista and the Revolution of 1932," focuses on the prominent role played by women in the Guerra Paulista, and the gendered representations of paulista history and identity. In particular, this chapter examines what we might call the discursive management of the potentially disruptive presence of women in the public sphere, and the way in which the figure of the "Mulher Paulista" served to depoliticize women's participation. Closing this section, chapter 5, "Provincializing São Paulo," explores the responses to assertions of paulista superiority from various opponents of the Constitutionalist Campaign, but especially from the press in the Nordeste. These counter-discourses illuminate the limitations of a national community imagined through the lens of regional superiority.

The next section takes the reader to the 1950s and to an urban São Paulo that is preparing for its four hundredth anniversary celebrations. Chapter 6, "São Paulo Triumphant," examines the various "uses" of the IV Centenário, and more specifically, the structuring of the yearlong commemorations as a massive response to the question "Why São Paulo?"—that is, why, of all Brazilian regions, did São Paulo emerge as Brazil's center of modernity and progress? At the same time, it considers the tensions between organizers who sought to highlight São Paulo as a center of taste, refinement, and the latest trends in "highbrow culture" and those paulistas, especially elected politicians, who sought to give the commemorations a more "popular" character. Chapter 7,

"Exhibiting Exceptionalism: History at the IV Centenário," carries on this discussion, but in the specific context of historical reenactments and exhibitions during the IV Centenário. A principal concern in this chapter is to explore the different ways in which paulista history continued to be "whitened" even during the mid-1950s, the heyday of "racial democracy." It also illuminates the central role of the past even during an occasion apparently oriented toward the future.[104] Although the forging of collective memory is a theme throughout the book, it takes center stage in chapter 8, "The White Album: Memory, Identity, and the 1932 Uprising." Here I look at the changing forms of commemoration, and the shifting meanings embodied by the events of 1932. Starting with the fifth anniversary solemnities, just months before Vargas's declaration of an Estado Novo, and then continuing into the IV Centenário in 1954 and the "Silver Jubilee" in 1957, I examine the different ways in which the memory of the uprising served as a marker of paulistinidade. Finally, the epilogue/conclusion suggests some connections, if not continuities, between the developments of 1932 and 1954 and the paulista liberals' embrace of a profoundly illiberal seizure of power by the Brazilian military in 1964. Even that event, typically interpreted on a national or even international scale, cannot be fully understood without reference to the spatial inequalities and racialized discourses that have informed so much of Brazil's postcolonial history.

CHAPTER 1

PAULISTA MODERN

Now, if in addition to its opulent agriculture, São Paulo begins to achieve
substantial industrial development, very soon there will be an enormous
economic imbalance between this province and those of the North. And
then separation will be inevitable, unless this province wants to become
a California-type colony, exploited by the intransigent North for its own
interests and through the strength of its representation in Parliament.
—*Diário Popular,* **1887**

"At the present time there is no one who would call into doubt the prosperity and the socio-economic expansion of the province of São Paulo,
where each day, great enterprises, inspired by the most noble initiatives,
appear as if by magic." Thus observed a columnist in the Rio daily, *O
Jornal do Commercio,* in March 1887.[1] This quotation, and the one that
serves as the epigraph for this chapter, might seem entirely unremarkable given São Paulo's well-established reputation as the "engine" of the
Brazilian economy, but the timing and location of these comments make
them especially noteworthy. The foregoing flattering description of São
Paulo's socioeconomic progress appeared, not in a newspaper from that
province, but in the leading business daily of the Court (as Rio would
be known until the fall of the monarchy in 1889). Judging from this
statement, the perception of São Paulo as Brazil's economic "miracle"
was not just a product of inflated self-regard, but an idea already circulating beyond the regional borders, and as with the quote that opens this
chapter, the article in the *Jornal do Commercio* implies that São Paulo's
prosperity and promise consisted of more than the mountains of coffee
beans produced by the *fazendas* that stretched throughout the western

region of the province (the latter geopolitical designation being replaced by "state" with the founding of the First Republic).

Second, and perhaps even more striking, is the dateline of the two articles from which these quotes originated. Both appeared in March 1887; by then São Paulo had emerged as the leading hub of Brazil's coffee-exporting economy, but it was hardly the preeminent and diversified economic center that it would later become. The year 1887 was also one of unusual turbulence in the province, as the remaining enslaved workers began fleeing the paulista coffee zones en masse, forcing the hands of those politicians who were still wavering on the question of abolition.[2] And the notion of São Paulo as a center of industry was, at that point, little more than wishful thinking. True, the rapid expansion of coffee plantations into the Paulista West, from the 1850s on, and the construction of new railroad lines, urban services, and port facilities offered tangible evidence of economic effervescence, but these trends hardly provided incontestable indicators of modernity or incontrovertible proof of something *new and different* occurring in São Paulo. The economic prosperity of this "second founding"—the dramatic transformation of São Paulo city and state that began in the 1870s—rested largely on the traditional pillars of Brazilian wealth and power: the big plantation and enslaved African labor.[3] Historians of slavery and abolition have toiled tirelessly to lay to rest the myth of the progressive planter, showing that most paulista *fazendeiros* clung tenaciously to their slave workforce and only embraced alternative sources and forms of labor once the massive desertions of the plantations made emancipation a fait accompli.[4] Moreover, the city of São Paulo, despite its strong signs of dynamism, had a population that barely totaled sixty-five thousand in the final years of the empire—roughly a tenth the size of Rio de Janeiro, the imperial capital.[5]

Why this apparent discrepancy or disproportion between São Paulo's still arguably modest material achievements and these claims of regional opulence? Why this seemingly premature projection of São Paulo as representing something novel, even exceptional, on the Brazilian socioeconomic landscape? Although no historian should expect to find a perfect coincidence between the discursive representations of economic conditions and the material "reality" to which the sources refer, it seems difficult to ignore a puzzling prematurity in these congratulatory depictions/predictions of São Paulo's ascendancy.[6] Later paeans to São Paulo's greatness would highlight the initiative and industrious character of the *povo paulista*; perhaps what these opening quotes indicate is "industry" and initiative of a different sort. I would suggest that such portrayals stem from the imaginative and productive ideological labors performed by members of the paulista elite—ranging from leading coffee planters to prominent liberal professionals and men of letters—who sought to distinguish themselves and their home province, early on, as not only more prosperous but also more "progressive" than other provinces/regions of Brazil.

One might argue that São Paulo's provincial capital had long enjoyed a degree of prestige incommensurate with its size and economic significance.[7] As the home of one of only two law schools in imperial Brazil (the other located in the northeastern city of Recife), at a time when these schools effectively functioned as Brazil's main centers of higher education, São Paulo had an intellectual and academic cachet that set it apart from other small and sleepy provincial capitals.[8] And there were elements of São Paulo's colonial history that could, with relative ease, be composed into regional myth. One of the most eminent and oft-quoted visitors to Brazil—Auguste de Saint-Hilaire—back in the 1820s had obligingly declared, in response to regional tales of colonial exploits, that the paulistas of centuries past were a "race of giants," a remark that provided priceless raw material for future generations of regional chauvinists.[9] Even so, this hardly seems a sufficient explanation for the precocious emergence of a discourse of regional difference and superiority.[10] Indeed, Saint-Hilaire expressed his flattering, if fanciful, estimation of colonial paulistas in sharp contrast to his portrait of the rustic and penurious independence-era provincial capital.[11] And at least one historian of regional identity notes that the cariocas (residents of Rio) who came to study law in São Paulo during the middle decades of the nineteenth century found the "city" to be unrefined, provincial, and lacking in culture or entertainment, and were in the habit of calling the paulistas "caboclos," a term that signified rustic farmers of mixed racial backgrounds.[12]

One way to puzzle out the apparently premature claims of regional greatness is the very timing of São Paulo's emergence as a leading zone of coffee production. In her classic study of slavery and the early coffee economy, Emília Viotti da Costa emphasized precisely this factor to explain the paulista fazendeiros' greater disposition to adopt new production techniques and experiment with other forms of labor. Having taken up the enterprise of coffee production at a moment when slavery was widely regarded as headed for extinction, the paulista planters simultaneously sought to prolong the institution's lifespan and to identify measures and strategies that would allow their fortunes to thrive even after abolition.[13] With coffee prices booming and the Paulista West (in contrast to the older, nearly depleted Paraíba Valley coffee zone) offering seemingly endless stretches of rich, purple soil (*terra roxa*) for its production, the paulista elites had a palpable incentive to think beyond their immediate material circumstances. No extraordinary entrepreneurial proclivities were necessary to ascertain that a rigid reliance on established routine—whether economic or political—might shortly prove injurious to their individual and collective interests.

Returning to my earlier insinuation of "precocity," Edward Said offers us a way of understanding why the imaginative labor involved in crafting discourses of regional superiority or paulista exceptionalism began well before there were measurable markers of São Paulo's prosperity and modernity, or even before there was any consensus on what constituted modernity in this context. In his now classic study of "Orientalism" among nineteenth-century British scholars and opinion-makers, Said insisted that this discourse about the "Other," which helped to define Britain's (superior) place in the world, *predated* the heyday of the British Empire. In other words, it was not a post hoc reflection or justification of British imperialism, but rather an enabling rhetoric that helped constitute Britain as an imperial power.[14]

On a considerably less global scale, I would argue that the same applies to discourses of paulista regional identity. In this vein, we need to consider the political conjuncture in which the paulistas found themselves, and how the constraints and opportunities of that conjuncture shaped the regional identity that emerged in the final decades of the Brazilian Empire. It is important to take into account not only the rapid and robust growth of São Paulo's economy—the diffusion of plantation agriculture, the massive influx of labor via the internal slave trade, the multiplication of railroad lines—but also the evident and much-remarked signs of economic stagnation or decline in other regions of the nation that had dominated Brazilian politics for most of the imperial era. This lent an increasingly regional character to the two main imperial political factions, the Conservatives and the Liberals. Regarding the monarchy as ensuring both order and the enduring influence of their home bases, elites in the provinces of Bahia and Rio de Janeiro remained stalwarts of the centralist Conservative Party. In contrast, booming provinces such as São Paulo and Pará (a center of the Amazon rubber trade) became bastions of decentralizing sentiment, whether framed by liberal or republican precepts, during what proved to be the waning decades of the Brazilian Empire.[15]

In an earlier era, the provincial political elite might have simply pushed for more prominent positions in the emperor's court and heavier representation in the inner circles of the imperial bureaucracy. But by the late 1860s the impact of a protracted war against Paraguay, the growing pressure to initiate a process of slave emancipation, and the escalating dissension within the Liberal Party made the emperor and his court less attractive as a pole of political power.[16] Instead, paulista elites expressed their discontent with the perceived imbalances in the distribution of political power either by promoting a more federalist and decentralized national structure or by advocating the abolition of the (centralized) monarchy and the installation of a republican-federalist system of rule.[17] Both political visions encouraged a celebration of regional character and a conflation of regional and national greatness. Moreover, a political reform that federalized not only politics and administration, but also fiscal resources, had the additional advantage of allowing the provincial government to retain a larger share of revenue generated by the coffee boom, and to dispose of those funds in a way that would suit the interests of the planter oligarchy. By the mid-1880s, an intensified discourse of regional exceptionalism even produced a small but significant separatist movement that called for the creation of a "pátria paulista."[18]

In his brilliant study of the historical imagination within São Paulo's "lettered" circles during the decades from 1870 to 1940, Antonio Celso Ferreira informs his readers that he intends to "follow the textual meanderings of the invention of a regional tradition, not as some kind of false consciousness, destined to serve strictly functional purposes—in such a case, ideological ones—but as an expression of an imaginary, in this case a historical one."[19] This interpretive approach both acknowledges that all constructions of the past are, to some extent, an act of imagination, and allows the historian to move beyond merely debunking the self-congratulatory "myths" that paulista elites devised about themselves during this period. I agree with Ferreira that it is more productive to consider, first, what elements made a particular narrative or interpretation (or myth, if one prefers) viable and meaningful to those involved in its construction and dissemination, and why it resonated with a larger public. But unlike Ferreira, I would also insist on asking what ideological work that image or interpretation performed, even though a particular producer of images or narratives may have had no expressed or deliberate ideological purpose.[20]

It may seem natural that tensions emerged once regional elites "began to sense a contradiction between their degree of economic power and their degree of political power,"[21] but such tensions require a good deal of ideological labor to be "sensed" and translated into unifying and compelling discourses of regional identity—or in this case, paulista superiority—that can transcend, or at least paper over, political, spatial, and intellectual divisions within a particular regional society. Again, the discourses favoring regional autonomy that emerged in the 1870s and 1880s reflected the rapidly changing profile of São Paulo within the Brazilian nation, but they also *predated* that city/state's transformation into the engine of Brazilian economic growth and modernity. In other words, these regionalist discourses were not only reactive but productive; they not only indicated changing circumstances but enabled those transformations to occur. Tying together disparate political positions and social attitudes, regionalist writings fostered a discourse of paulista exceptionalism that bolstered demands for increased provincial autonomy, and thus for greater control over the region's revenues. This, in turn, facilitated such crucial initiatives as massive provincial subsidies for European immigration once the threat of abolition appeared imminent and unavoidable, and the valorization of coffee stocks when prices on the world market threatened to plummet. Regionalist discourses not only offered paulistas a language with which to understand and explain the rapid changes occurring in their region, but also helped to shape the form and direction those changes would take, and even to produce the political and fiscal reforms that enabled those changes to occur. And further heightening the efficacy of this discourse of paulista superiority was an increasingly pejorative representation of "Other" regions of Brazil, viewed as wracked by degeneration and decline, concepts that, in the late nineteenth century, inevitably evoked notions of racial difference.[22]

In the subsequent sections of this chapter I draw on developments in such diverse spheres as mainstream politics, public commemorations, history writing, labor recruitment, artistic expression, and travelers' accounts to explore the ongoing formulation and circulation of discourses that imagined São Paulo as whiter and more modern than the "Other" Brazil, and that increasingly conflated region and nation. These discourses of exceptionalism cannot be traced to a single social stratum, political organization, or economic interest group, but rather constituted an emerging paulista identity that could be claimed and invoked in a wide (but not unlimited) variety of contexts, and shared by segments of the regional population that might, at first glance, appear to have little else in common. To this end, the final section of the chapter focuses on some key political developments of the 1920s to highlight the considerable dissonance within São Paulo with regard to the existing republican order, and thereby call into question any interpretation of ensuing political conflicts as simply attempts to restore the "old regime."

Becoming the Povo Bandeirante

In a much-cited essay on the construction of regional identity, Pierre Bourdieu argued that regionalism is perforce "a *performative discourse*, which aims to impose as legitimate a new definition of the frontiers and to get people to know and recognize the *region*."[23] In many locales throughout Brazil one can observe the folkloric or theatrical elements that typically enable the recognition and enactment of regional difference. Centers of Gaúcho Tradition in Rio Grande do Sul encourage locals to dress and dance in a distinctive "gaúcho" manner; Amazonians celebrate their region's unique cuisine and indigenous myths; nordestinos—and other Brazilians seeking a timeless fragment of *brasilidade*—venerate their folkloric musical traditions, "naïve" artistic styles, and popular poetry.[24] The architects of paulista identity, in contrast, seem to have had few such performative elements at their disposal. But this is not because São Paulo, as a regional space, is literally deficient in the aspects of regionalism that Bourdieu cites as crucial to the cultivation of regional loyalties. It is not simply that there is no regional cuisine, or folktales, or customary dress, music, or dance—after all, these are always to some extent invented, and it is not unimaginable that zealous promoters of paulista regional culture could have "recuperated" any number of "authentic" cultural practices that would have enabled the performance of paulista identity.[25] For example, in São Paulo, as elsewhere in Brazil, there was a literary and artistic tradition of romanticizing the caboclo or *caipira*—a rustic man of mixed racial heritage whose homespun wisdom and virtues symbolized the "authentic" national character.[26] Even now, every year in the month of June, paulista children dress and dance as country folk and eat roasted corn around a bonfire during the Festival of São João, a celebration of the caboclo/caipira tradition.[27]

Yet, the *festas joaninas* aside, the cult of the caipira did not gain much traction. In 1918 the future media impresario Monteiro Lobato—already an influential figure in paulista literary circles—published *Urupês*, with its "acidic profile" of the caipira Jeca Tatu.[28] In contrast to the idealized figure of the humble but sagacious rustic of the romantic tradition, Jeca was a man of very few qualities, a caricatured antihero who quickly corroded the popular literary image of the venerable caboclo. In Monteiro Lobato's rendering, Jeca was more of an *antidote* to lingering nostalgia for a simpler, more pastoral existence than an emblem of regional identity.[29] In short, the "problem" was not an absence of raw (cultural) materials with which to construct a folkloric tradition. Rather, it was that emergent paulista regionalism already had certain meanings attached to it that were inhospitable to the incorporation of standard folkloric elements. *Paulistinidade* was an identity distinguished by São Paulo's supposedly exceptional disposition for the novel and the modern, and this emphasis on modernity rendered "traditional cultural practices" incompatible with or, at best, marginal to the ongoing construction of regional identity.

The *historic* (as opposed to folkloric) past, on the other hand, remained a vital source of building materials for the architects of paulista regionalism. Cultural theorist Anne McClintock, drawing on the insights of Walter Benjamin, contends that "the mapping of Progress depends on systematically inventing images of archaic time to identify what is historically new."[30] The enormous attention paid to São Paulo's past at the precise moment when so many paulistas were hailing their region's modernity is a perfect instance of what Benjamin observed. In a discourse on "São Paulo and the Modern Spirit," addressed to a carioca audience in 1926, modernist poet Guilherme de Almeida enunciated his (lyrical) perspective on past and present: "The modern spirit . . . The consciousness of the present. The moment, the fleeting instance, the geometric point without dimensions, that, having moved in space generated a line behind it: the past. Now, without a consciousness of the past there could not be this consciousness of the present: that [past] is the concrete reality of which this [present] is an abstract expression. Derived from its history—a history of tenacity, of energy, and of strength—is the magnificent present-day of São Paulo."[31] Thus "History" as a way of explaining the emergence of regional and national consciousness flourished during the second half of the nineteenth century, as did another intellectual enterprise intimately tied to the construction of national identities: scientific racism. Bourdieu closely associates representations of regionalism with the invention of ethnicity, a term he then dismisses as a "scientific euphemism" that has been "substituted for the notion of 'race.'"[32] Whether or not we agree that race always and everywhere informs the construction of regional identity, it seems evident that, in the nineteenth and early twentieth centuries, when scientific racism was at its height, in a nation where slavery was still a major institution in fact or (after 1888) in very recent memory, it would be extremely difficult to imagine regional identity apart from race. And even more so in the specific case of São Paulo, where a new and self-conscious elite, eager to demonstrate its modern and progressive character, formed the political leadership of a region where slaves and freedpersons of African descent were a demographic majority at the outset of the period under discussion—a feature of regional society widely regarded in elite and lettered circles as an impediment to modernity and progress, and requiring various measures to produce a whiter population.[33]

The whitening of paulista identity was a multifaceted and complex process. The most famous, or infamous, facet involved the literal transfer of white bodies from Europe, and especially from northern Italy, where labor-recruiters, armed with offers of jobs and subsidized transatlantic transportation, lured peasant families by the hundreds of thousands to the shores of southeastern Brazil.[34] From there, most of the newly arrived immigrants fanned out to coffee fazendas in the interior, where they took up the work previously performed by enslaved persons of African descent. Historians have sought to understand this dramatic transformation of the agrarian labor force either from an economic perspective (the need to find cheap, manageable labor for a booming coffee economy), or from a "civilizing" perspective (the anxiety to whiten and modernize the paulista population). Often these goals are counterposed, as if one motivation negated the other. And to be sure, if we consider prominent fazendeiro and politician Martinho Prado's observation that "immigrants with money are of no use to us," it would seem logical to conclude that his primary, and perhaps only, concern was to secure cheap able-bodied laborers for his estates.[35]

However, I think it is a mistake to pose this as an either/or proposition. As Matthew Frye Jacobson notes, any project to promote immigration is likely to generate tension between those who are primarily concerned with whether the immigrants will make suitable citizens, and those who are eager to expand the labor pool.[36] The latter position does not imply a complete lack of concern with the specific composition of the immigrant population—on the contrary, the very notion of "able-bodied" or "manageable" implies qualities that would be ascribed to some potential groups of immigrants and not others. When Martinho Prado famously expressed his preference for impoverished immigrants who would take any job they could get, he didn't need to specify that they should be "white" since the very word *imigrante* had embedded in it a racial genealogy, and elements of what Foucault termed "governmentality."[37] In the 1880s no member of the Brazilian elite would have thought of imigrantes as anything other than European.[38] The various efforts to bring in Chinese laborers to replace the soon-to-be-emancipated slaves had always positioned the Chinese as contract workers or "coolies" who were neither expected nor encouraged to remain in Brazil. Even so, these contract-labor initiatives provoked heated opposition in the Brazilian parliament, with some of the most vehement objections coming from coffee planters, whom one might assume would be eager to secure cheap, and reputedly docile, Chinese labor.[39]

Certainly Africans were not the people elites had in mind when discussing immigration; the Republican Constitution of 1891 included several provisions welcoming "persons healthy and able to work," but specifically forbidding entrance to Asians and Africans except with congressional authorization.[40] In fact, the only relevant distinction drawn by Brazilian elites with regard to immigrants' point of origin was between northern Europeans and southern Europeans, with the former seen as more suitable for smallholding agricultural colonies and the latter for labor on large estates.[41] Thus, when Martinho Prado referred to immigrants, with or without money, he was already using a term implicitly equated with "white" people of European descent.[42]

The massive, subsidized recruitment of European immigrants, however, was only one facet of the whitening enterprise. Indeed, the growing identification of European communities in São Paulo with labor militancy and subversive ideologies may have dimmed the gleam of their whiteness in the eyes of the paulista elites, and intensified other, more representational strategies for whitening regional identity. Historical interpretations of the preoccupation with whitening in post-emancipation Brazil have tended to interpret that process in narrow, biological terms and ignored what Matthew Frye Jacobson called "the alchemy of race,"[43] but there was an uncanny element to the construction of whiteness that went beyond any deliberate demographic engineering. In this context, the crucial character was not a recent European immigrant, but a figure from São Paulo's colonial past—the bandeirante—a figure who, oddly enough, was generally neither "white" nor entirely European by late nineteenth-century criteria. He was a historical character who, according to Ferreira, evoked among literary paulistas "the simultaneous sentiments of identification and distancing."[44]

As early as 1920, one can see this uncanny transformation in the remarks of Wickliffe Rose, a prominent public health educator employed by the Rockefeller Foundation. In his official report on his visit to Brazil to evaluate the conditions for sanitationist campaigns, he began by disparaging a population composed of "incompetent negroes, parasitic whites of Portuguese origin and a great percentage of their hybrid descendants." But he abruptly switched to a more optimistic register as he shifted his geographical compass:

> South Brazil, beginning with the State of São Paulo, was settled by adventurous, self-reliant Portugese [sic], who from the beginning crossed with the native Indians, developed a sturdy Brazilian stock, established themselves on the narrow coastal margin at Santos, and proceeded at an early date to explore and conquer the interior. This population has been re-inforced through a tide of immigration from Europe which continues to bring these southern states hardy types of colonists—Italians, Germans, Austrians, and Poles. Japanese also are now coming in considerable numbers. These immigrants take root in the soil, and tend in the second generation, to become a sturdy, *white*, Brazilian stock.[45]

Thus, in Rose's estimation, this "hearty Brazilian breed," though reinforced by the immigrant influx, could be traced back to the earliest colonial settlers and the emblematic colonial figure, the bandeirante.

The exploring, prospecting, and slave-hunting parties known as *bandeiras*—named for the banners that they carried aloft on their treks from colonial São Paulo into Brazil's vast, largely uncharted interior—had become the distinguishing feature of regional social and economic life by the early seventeenth century. Despite his legendary treks through Brazil's hinterland, at first glance the bandeirante does not seem a particularly promising candidate for the role of regional forefather, especially in an era when paulista elites were congratulating themselves on their progressive position on abolition and on their increasing whiteness. First of all, those who participated in the earliest bandeiras, including the leaders, were virtually all *mamelucos*—men of mixed Portuguese and Amerindian descent.[46] Second, the principal "moneymaking" purpose of those expeditions was the capture of indigenous peoples to be sold as slaves either in São Paulo or elsewhere in Brazil, an enterprise that earned the bandeirantes the eternal enmity of the Company of Jesus. And it was not only the Jesuits who registered their aversion to the colonial paulistas. The bishop of Pernambuco, who met with the venerable Domingos Jorge Velho in 1697 following the defeat of the massive maroon community at Palmares, spared no effort in expressing his distaste for the bandeirante captain:

> This man is one of the worst savages I have ever encountered. When he met with me he brought along an interpreter, for he cannot even speak correctly. He is no different from the most barbaric Tapuia, to say nothing of calling him a Christian. And although he was recently married, seven Indian concubines attend him; from this one can infer all his other habits. . . . He has roamed the forests hunting Indian men and women, the latter to satisfy his depraved appetites, and the former to work in the fields which he possesses.[47]

How, then, did these "half-breed" slave-catchers, portrayed in the standard Jesuit accounts of the colonial era as barbaric, brutal, and unsavory ruffians, morph into the revered progenitors of modern paulista identity?

The process of rehabilitation had actually begun two centuries earlier, with a three-volume genealogy produced by paulista Pedro Taques de Almeida Pais Leme (1714–1777), in which he "aristocratized" his bandeirante forebears and disputed the Jesuit portrayals of them as backwoods brutes.[48] Hence, there was already a "white legend versus black legend" tradition connected to the history of the bandeirantes for contemporary scholars to draw on. But the *bandeirologistas*, as this latter-day group of scholars came to be known, shifted the debate to a new level of erudition and to a new analytical plane. Associated with the recently founded Instituto Histórico e Geográfico de São Paulo, historians such as Afonso d'E. Taunay, José de Alcântara Machado, Washington Luís Pereira Sousa, Alfredo Ellis Júnior, Jaime Cortesão, and Sérgio Buarque de Holanda, with sharply varying degrees of scholarly subtlety, sensitivity, and sophistication, based their claims on systematic research in archival sources and primary texts, rather than simple polemics. In works whose publication dates stretched from the 1910s through the 1950s, the bandeirologistas painstakingly reconstructed the daily lives of the bandeirantes and the organizational details of their major expeditions. Despite the expectations sparked by its melodramatic title, Alcântara Machado's canonical text *Vida e morte do Bandeirante* (Life and death of the bandeirante) is in most respects a classic work of social history, based largely on inventories of estates left by men of (relative) substance and standing, who lived in and around the colonial village of São Paulo at the time of the bandeiras.[49]

This attention to the minutiae of the bandeirante phenomenon might seem an unpromising method for the production of an epic narrative of a glorious past, but from a rehabilitator's perspective such an approach had the virtue of presenting the bandeirantes and the men of their milieu as sober, serious, and respectable, as good citizens of the village of São Paulo and loyal (if unjustly neglected) subjects of the Portuguese Crown. In this rendering of the bandeirantes, they are men of austere habits and little culture, but hardly the brutes and barbarians depicted in the Jesuit accounts. Moreover, their lack of luxury and refinement is redefined as a positive trait that indicates their heartiness, their stamina, and their status as authentic Brazilian men.[50] As for their forebears' slave-catching activities, the bandeirologistas, as historians and historicists, accepted this as established fact, but insisted that it was a fact of life at the time throughout Portuguese America. In effect, the enslaving of Amerindians should be seen as a "normal" activity for men whose limited means meant they had no access to African slaves in an era when you could not be a civilized man of substance without "servants."[51]

Yet another strategy to neutralize the stigma of the slave-hunting expeditions was to argue that this was not necessarily the principal purpose of the bandeiras: Jaime Cortesão, for instance, focused on the legendary expedition (1648–1651) headed by Antônio Raposo Tavares and described it as having been primarily a geopolitical enterprise. Alfredo Ellis Jr., meanwhile, dismissed this vision of the bandeirante as a surveyor of continents and accentuated, instead, the search for precious metals and the need to defend São Paulo—perennially neglected and left to its own devices by the Crown—from Indian attack (an interpretation that established a *longue durée* argument for federalism).[52] In a similar vein, various historians noted the quasi-military character of the late seventeenth-century bandeiras, including the expedition led by Domingos Jorge Velho, which participated in the definitive destruction of the *quilombo* of Palmares, colonial Brazil's legendary runaway slave community. Yet other writers admitted that the bandeirantes did indeed enslave Indians and set them to work on their estates, but declared them to have been benevolent patriarchs who treated their charges well. As recently as 1965, Richard Morse asserted that "colonial paulista history was one of the most notable New World episodes of accommodation between European and Indian, and could ruminate about the relative merits, for an Amerindian, of life in a Jesuit mission, with its alien Christian discipline, and life in a bandeira, with its comparatively familiar nomadic *mestiço* culture and rough egalitarianism—a mental exercise clearly intended to add some shades of gray to the black legend versus white legend debate.[53]

As for the prototypical bandeirante being a mameluco, a man of mixed race, this "fact" yielded a range of interpretations and ramifications in both the scholarly literature and the popular appropriation of the bandeirante saga. Although there were many variations on this theme, the one common thread was the depiction of this particular mixed "type" as hardy and adaptable, rather than the sterile and decadent figure predicted by the most rigid "scientific" racial theories about miscegenation and degeneration circulating in the late nineteenth century. Again, Alfredo Ellis Jr., the bandeirologista most avidly engaged with racial theories, popularized the image of the colonial paulistas as a "race of giants."[54] Tania de Luca, in her analysis of racial discourses in the paulista periodical, *Revista do Brasil* (1916–1925), notes that by then the "negative view" of miscegenation "which never tired of calling attention to the pernicious effects of cross-breeding," was giving way to "an interpretation that identified mixture as a privileged conduit in the route to progress."[55] But not just any mixture (or any degree of mixture) would produce the desired results. Virtually every paulista writing about the bandeirantes and colonial São Paulo whose work appeared in the 1910s and 1920s insisted that there were few or no traces of "African" racial/cultural influence on the paulista plateau.[56] In his survey of articles published in the journal of the Instituto Histórico e Geográfico de São Paulo, Ferreira notes that "the dismissal of black culture" (*a desqualificação da cultura negra*) was evident even in "studies that took a favorable view of European/indigenous mixture."[57] One contributor to the *Revista do Brasil* went so far as to insist that the stereotypical claim that Brazilians' sensuality stemmed from African cultural influences was inaccurate: "Our savages [*sic*] were always infinitely more sensual than the blacks."[58] And not only did paulista writers construct hierarchies of racial desirability and miscibility that favored indigenous over African, but they also manifested clear preferences for some Indian ethnicities over others. That, according to

John Monteiro, is what explains the heated debates over the language-group affiliation of the Guaianá—recognized as the dominant ethnic group on the plateau at the time of Portuguese settlement—and the vehement rejection of claims that they might be Tapuia, "an indigenous 'race' disparaged by modern science and by the defenders of progress," rather than Tupi.[59]

While both the scholarly and the popular literature readily acknowledged the indigenous contribution to the bandeirantes' bloodlines and pathfinding capabilities, there was also a tendency to portray this contribution as transitory, as characteristic of a particular historical moment when local knowledge, and European women, were in short supply among the Portuguese settlers. Once white women became available as marriage partners, the leading paulista men naturally gravitated to them, thereby reducing the indigenous "element" in their lineage. Perhaps even more important, the bandeirologistas portrayed their forebears as "virile" men who were able to selectively absorb the positive traits of indigenous cultures while maintaining their superior European characteristics. In other words, these scholars wanted it both ways— they sought to depict the bandeirante as an authentically American/mestiço figure, while at the same time insisting that this temporary need to "mix" did not compromise his essential whiteness.[60]

This double representation of the bandeirante also made him a very useful figure for "old-line" paulistas, and those who identified with them, in establishing their preeminence vis-à-vis the new immigrant population.[61] The massive influx of immigrants—mainly from southern Europe—may have allowed the paulistas to assert a whitened regional identity and to claim the status of a "European Christian civilization," to quote Mário de Andrade.[62] And textile mills and ceramic factories bearing names like Matarazzo, Crespi, and Simonsen may have become key markers of paulista progress. But intellectuals and public figures from traditional paulista clans were hardly eager to cede credit for São Paulo's exceptional modernity to nouveau riche immigrant industrialists or to the restive immigrant working masses. Thus, an emphasis on the bandeirante spirit had the advantage of locating the source of São Paulo's superiority in a historical moment that long preceded the post-emancipation immigrant wave.[63] At the same time, the bandeirante's "virile" capacity to absorb the positive traits of other cultures provided a convenient foundation for assimilating these European newcomers, who were sometimes referred to as "novos mamelucos."[64]

If textual imaginings of the bandeirantes allowed for some ambiguities and complexities, visual representations exhibited little variation: painters and sculptors routinely produced a figure who was more European than indigenous in appearance, and who was unfailingly the embodiment of the tireless and intrepid pathfinder. When the Museu do Ipiranga (later renamed Museu Paulista) opened its doors to the public in 1890, the first sight to greet the visitors as they entered the museum was statues of the renowned bandeirantes Antônio Raposo Tavares (1598–1658) and Fernão Dias Pais Leme (1608–1681), both striking poses (see figs. 1.1. and 1.2) that indicated they were men of action, rather than the immobile figures typical of late nineteenth-century monuments. And when the distinguished paulista painter Benedito Calixto unveiled his 1903 portrait of Domingos Jorge Velho, this bandeirante, whom the bishop of Pernambuco had denounced as "one of the worst savages" he'd ever encountered, had become a slightly grizzled but well-turned-out patriarchal figure, bearing a suspicious resemblance to the former emperor, Dom Pedro II (see fig. 1.3). All of these figures appeared wearing ten-league boots, a tunic, and a leather hat with a turned-up brim—rustic apparel, to be sure, but European in its derivation. And it was nothing like the outfit worn by the colonial paulista depicted by Thomas Ender, the Viennese sketch artist who visited Brazil in the very early nineteenth century; in Ender's rendition, the bandeirante is imagined as barefoot and wearing a blanket-like garment that seems of indigenous origin.[65]

By the early decades of the twentieth century, the men engaged in historical research on the bandeiras, though strongly inclined toward certain favorable interpretations, endeavored to construct a more meticulous and detailed image of the bandeirante, and sought documentation to support their claims.[66] Thus the cartoonist Belmonte, whose text *No tempo dos Bandeirantes* (In the time of the bandeirantes), replete with his own illustrations, was clearly intended for a wide audience including paulista youth, used a minutely detailed account of the contents of a "typical" seventeenth-century home in colonial "Piratininga" to emphasize what had become one of the bandeirante's distinguishing features: his capacity for hard work and industry. After recounting the simplicity and rusticity of the furnishings, he goes on to assure his readers that "while the bandeirante dispensed with comfort in his furnishings, he did not skimp on work tools and instruments: hoes, axes, saws, adzes, wedges, sickles for reaping and harvesting, small sickles for gardening, shears . . . nor was there any lack of utensils for domestic use." He then lists at least a dozen other implements for use around the home, ending with the observation that "these are indications that, inside the home as well as outside the home, paulista life did not proceed in an idle manner."[67]

Popular poets and essayists, meanwhile, eagerly deployed a metaphorical bandeirante who, stripped of historical complexities, appeared even more ho-

FIGS. 1.1 AND 1.2. Statues of the bandeirantes Antônio Raposo Tavares and Fernão Dias Pais Leme at the entrance of the Museu Paulista, São Paulo. Marble sculptures by Luigi Brizzolara, 1922. Photograph for figure 1.1 by Aleks Politot. Used by permission. Photograph for figure 1.2 by Hélio Nobre, courtesy of the Museu Paulista da USP.

FIGURE 1.3. Benedito Calixto's highly idealized portrait of bandeirante patriarch Domingos Jorge Velho, painted in 1903. From *Benedito Calixto e a construção do imaginário republicano*, by Caleb Faria Alves (Bauru: Editora de Universidade do Sagrado Coração, 2003).

mogenized and essentialized than the statues in the Museu Paulista. The coat of arms designed for the city of São Paulo by poet Guilherme de Almeida and painter José Wasth Rodrigues, which won in an open competition sponsored by the prefecture in 1916, had at its center the arm of a bandeirante hoisting a flag, and bore the motto "Non Ducor, Duco" (I am not led, I lead) (see fig. 1.4). In his congratulatory remarks on the design, the editor of the *Revista do Brasil* (published in São Paulo) praised Almeida and Rodrigues for having "the felicitous inspiration of adopting the only emblem capable of condensing in an eloquent manner the entire history of our people: the symbol of the Bandeirante, title of Glory for the sons of this land."[68] In this case, a mere arm clutching a flag was regarded as sufficient to represent São Paulo's glorious past and promising future.[69] In his ode to the new coat of arms, Paraná-born poet Emilio de Menezes declared the São Paulo of the bandeirantes "wellspring of intrepidness, cradle of industry."[70] As paulistas active in overlapping literary, artistic, scholarly, and journalistic circles sought to make sense of the rapid changes

FIGURE 1.4. São Paulo city coat of arms with motto "Non Ducor Duco"—I am not led; I lead. Designed by José Wasth Rodrigues and Guilherme de Almeida, 1916.

in their home region, the bandeirante increasingly stood for the qualities of entrepreneurship and energy that supposedly set dynamic São Paulo apart from other regions of Brazil, with their stagnant seigneurial traditions, and that ultimately made São Paulo's history national, and not merely regional.[71]

In all these versions of the bandeirante, he is virile, he is tireless, and he is unimpeachably paulista. Attempts by various scholars, including Gilberto Freyre, to "nationalize" the bandeirantes, in the sense of connecting them to settlements in other regions of Brazil where they mixed with local populations, met with skeptical or irate responses from scholars in São Paulo.[72] But at the same time that the paulistas claimed the bandeirante as the exclusive symbolic property of the state of São Paulo, they also insisted that he was responsible for the construction of the Brazilian nation. As one article in the *Revista do Brasil* superciliously noted, "It should hardly be necessary for us to repeat the words of the Visconde de São Leopoldo to the effect that the history of São Paulo is the history of Brazil."[73] This became a regular theme in writings about the bandeirantes, whom the paulistas eagerly credited with the extension of Brazil's borders beyond the original contours defined by the Treaty of

Tordesillas, and thus being responsible for Brazil's most salient positive characteristic—its enormous territory. In the words of the irrepressible Alfredo Ellis Jr., speaking at the Centro Paulista in Rio, "it is beyond question that we owe our existence as a great continental nation to the paulistas of yesteryear."[74]

Increasingly, accounts of "Brazilian" history by paulistas foregrounded not only the role of the bandeirantes in the staking out of an amplified Brazilian territory, but also their contribution to the greater homogenization of Brazil by subduing refractory indigenous cultures and defeating the "quisto africano" (literally, African cyst) of Palmares.[75] But that was only the beginning of the enterprise of equating São Paulo's history with the history of Brazil. In both erudite and more popular circles, an entire narrative of Brazilian history emerged that was structured around the highlights of the paulista past—the independence-era Grito de Ipiranga, the regency of Padre Feijó, the abolitionist campaign, the Republican movement—as one writer in the *Revista do Brasil* put it, São Paulo was the historical "spinal cord" of Brazil.[76] Moreover, these paulista interventions in the historical narratives of the Brazilian nation were not confined to lecture rooms or scholarly journals, as exemplified by an outburst in a session of the Brazilian Chamber of Deputies in 1920 by paulista representative Eloy Chaves. Having addressed a specific charge in a Rio newspaper regarding the mysterious disappearance of a large quantity of paulista coffee that had been warehoused and subsidized by public monies, Deputy Chaves suddenly felt moved to denounce accusations (of unspecified origin) regarding separatist sentiment in São Paulo. This was a charge, he insisted, that was not just a lie but a crime:

> And it's a crime because it was S. Paulo, since the earliest days of Brazilian life, that looked toward the interior of our country, penetrating the backlands, clearing the forests, marking boundaries in distant lands with the bones of their children, the limits that later would be fixed by the great [minister of foreign relations] Rio Branco as the definitive contours of our national boundaries. São Paulo which thus lived Brazilian life so intensely could not possibly want to disconnect and estrange itself from the great family to which it belongs!!
>
> It was São Paulo, Mr. President and my fellow Deputies, where the idea of the nation first formed, where our independence had its birthplace, where all this country's noble and liberal ideas found their most intense echo; it was the place where abolition and the Republic had their most energetic and inspired proponents; in this [state] which, through its deeds and achievements, came to demonstrate what should be the definitive form

of government for Brazil, it would never be possible to consider the idea of separating itself from all this glory that belongs to it.[77]

It is a remarkable harangue, for in Deputy Chaves's zeal to affirm the patriotism of the *povo bandeirante*, he explicitly conflates Brazil with the state of São Paulo—or to quote Tania de Luca's insightful commentary on the regional chauvinism that filled the pages of the *Revista do Brasil*: "More and more the nation was being identified with the State of São Paulo. . . . The attributes of nationality—defined borders, the conquest of political sovereignty, glorious historic deeds, inhabitants endowed with specific ethnic traits . . . ended up being accredited exclusively to the paulistas."[78]

The 1920s: Triumphs and Challenges

The decade of the 1920s is widely regarded by historians of Brazil as a time of both cultural effervescence and political tension that culminated in the crisis that brought Getúlio Vargas to power in 1930 and marked the end of paulista hegemony. Yet from the perspective of those who sought to secure São Paulo's dominant position in the union, the decade began on a high note. Despite a state budget deficit, labor protests, and the persistent problem of overproduction in the coffee sector, the state capital was now incontestably Brazil's leading manufacturing center, and the Paulista West continued to be Brazil's most productive agricultural zone. Both the urban and rural populations of São Paulo were growing by leaps and bounds, and the population of São Paulo city, though still about half that of Rio de Janeiro, was rapidly gaining on the federal capital, which two decades earlier had literally dwarfed São Paulo in numbers of inhabitants. In the words of the *Revista do Brasil*:

> The city of São Paulo constitutes the sort of miracle of velocity in which the [North] Americans take so much pride, citing the metropolises that have emerged through improvisation in their nation. Look how, for example, the paulista capital a half century ago had no more than 23 thousand inhabitants. In 1920 its population reached 375,000 inhabitants. According to its most recent census, the city's population totaled 637,823 persons. Housing keeps pace with this demographic development. Just consider that, from January to the end of September 1923, there were 3,292 new buildings erected in São Paulo. This means 364 buildings per month, more than twelve houses per day, in short, a new house every two hours.[79]

Furthermore, the rapid diffusion of record keeping and statistical comparison created a representational genre with which one could succinctly but vividly express São Paulo's "superiority" over the other regions of Brazil, "enlisting the positivist halo that surrounds numbers," to quote Andrés Guerrero.[80] Typical was a pamphlet issued in 1917 by the state Department of Agriculture, Commerce and Public Works entitled *The State of São Paulo: Its Progress, Its Wealth*. After describing the state's astounding rate of growth over the past three decades, the text goes on to say that the purpose of this pamphlet is to illustrate this "admirable evolution . . . with the collection of synthesized statistics found in these pages. These data, appropriately expressed and organized, will present the truth without the adornment of unnecessary words."[81] In a similar vein, the authors of the many books published in the 1910s and 1920s cataloguing São Paulo's glories and accomplishments larded their texts with tables, graphs, and charts exhibiting how much more of *everything* São Paulo produced than the other Brazilian states, and especially how much more São Paulo contributed to the federal treasury. A particular favorite was to show that, during some years, all the other nineteen states of the Brazilian union (minus the federal district), combined, yielded less revenue for the federal coffers than did São Paulo on its own.[82] This might be supplemented with a quick reference to the stunning discrepancy between the value of São Paulo's export production and that of, say, an impoverished northeastern state such as Piauí, as we can see from table 1.1 adapted from T. de Souza Lobo's *O Brasil confederado*, a widely cited work advocating regional autonomy. The implicit argument—that it was absurd to regard these two geographic entities as in any way equivalent—hardly needed to be articulated. Indeed, the underlying theme of such publications was the now-familiar notion of São Paulo as the nation's locomotive, pulling a train of empty boxcars.[83]

One especially interesting source of contrasting images of São Paulo and the Nordeste can be found in the region's leading daily newspaper, *O Estado de São Paulo*, which from 1923 to 1925 published a series of articles entitled "Impressions of the Northeast" and "Impressions of São Paulo." The former portrayed the Nordeste as exotic and bizarre, dwelling on scenes of banditry and religious fanaticism that were explained largely through the peculiarity of the northeastern landscape and the racial/cultural regression of the nordestino population.[84] Maintaining the focus on the outsider's gaze, the editors then invited Brazilians from other regions to visit São Paulo and publish their impressions. This move allowed the newspaper to deny any trace of regional chauvinism; by having non-paulistas comment on São Paulo, they could emphasize the "objective" character of its superiority and its grandeur. But what is particularly notable in these "travelers' accounts" is not the repeated references to São Paulo's prosperity and modernity, or to the whiteness and

TABLE 1.1. Value of Exports by State (1930)

STATES	VALUE IN CONTOS	%
1. São Paulo	1,313,027	45.16
2. Minas Gerais	375,469	12.92
3. Rio Grande do Sul	259,773	8.94
4. Bahia	205,832	7.08
5. Paraná	146,941	5.06
6. Rio de Janeiro	112,567	3.80
7. Espírito Santo	87,081	3.00
8. Pernambuco	74,041	2.55
9. Ceará	59,678	2.06
10. Santa Catarina	51,336	1.77
11. Pará	43,550	1.50
12. Amazonas	42,794	1.48
13. Mato Grosso	27,617	0.95
14. Paraíba	26,252	0.91
15. Maranhão	25,348	0.87
16. Rio Grande do Norte	16,236	0.56
17. Distrito Federal	16,166	0.56
18. Piauí	11,145	0.39
19. Goiás	5,970	0.21
20. Alagoas	4,975	0.17
21. Sergipe	1,556	0.06
BRAZIL	2,907,354	100.00

Source: T. de Souza Lobo, *O Brasil confederado* (São Paulo: Lyceu Coração de Jesus, 1933), 216.

European character of its inhabitants (all thoroughly predictable), but rather the depiction of São Paulo as both exceptional and national, not so much a region as the epitome of the nation that all of Brazil should become.[85] From the perspective of a society whose flag was imprinted with the motto "Order and Progress," only exceptional São Paulo offered a national model that could be "generalized"—the rest of Brazil was the exotic, the archaic, and the particular.

São Paulo for the Whole World to See

The 1910s and 1920s would be a period of rising nationalism, but even so, it was still crucial to any assertion of paulista supremacy to reflect and record the admiring gaze of visitors from abroad. This was, of course, particularly true of the state capital—no city could claim to be modern and cosmopolitan without the global traveler's stamp of approval—but it could also extend to the region as a whole. To be sure, the city fathers of Latin America's growing urban areas all exhibited some concern with the face their hometown showed to "the world," but São Paulo's previous marginality as an urban center undoubtedly made its political, cultural, and commercial elites especially keen to place it on the metropolitan map. As the following remarks from a North American advertising journal indicate, "San Paulo" [sic] was hardly a household name in the United States in the 1920s:

> San Paulo! How many of us are familiar even with the name? It is true we ought to know, but no one will take it as a serious reflection of our national instructed-ness if it is said that probably not one in a hundred of us have ever had occasion to recall what teacher told us about San Paulo. Besides, sometimes it is spelled, Sao Paulo, which is confusing, to say the least. And then it is a long way off.
>
> It did not seem a very good prospect. So the bankers decided to advertise to tell about San Paulo, where it is, how large it is, what it does for a living and the kind of character it has for paying up without ugly looks from the sheriff. . . . These bank advertisements showed that the folk down at San Paulo are regular fellows, with automobiles, trolley cars and everything except prohibition.[86]

This desire to be seen in a certain light by the external gaze explains why, in its very first issue, the modernist journal *Revista Nova* (which began publishing in 1931) printed the text of a letter written by noted Portuguese writer Ramalho Ortigão way back in December 1887, following a visit to São Paulo. The majority of the letter, addressed to the prominent coffee fazendeiro and intellectual Eduardo Prado (whose nephew Paulo was an editor of the *Revista Nova*), consisted of observations about the insidious effects of slavery on the Brazilian home and family life. But the tone shifts as Ramalho Ortigão ventures a comparison between the cities of São Paulo and Rio de Janeiro: "São Paulo, which liberated itself long before Rio de Janeiro from the assistance of the slave, is from all points of view making greater progress. It is growing faster even though it doesn't have the Court to ignite the city's expansion. The level of difference is particularly perceptible in the character of the children, and it is immense. Your mother's home is a jewel, and without overstepping the boundaries, let me say that here [in São Paulo] you find a singularly clever sort of woman."[87] It was, in every sense, the sort of testimonial that paulista regionalists would prize, beginning with its authorship (a noted, erudite foreigner) and its early date (1887), which served to confirm the teleological character of São Paulo's success story, apparent even before a substantial number of immigrants had arrived on its shores. Furthermore, it reproduced the paulista elites' claim that they eagerly rid themselves of the institution of slavery even before abolition compelled them to do so. It underscored the modernity of the paulista woman while situating her within the home and family. And it constructed its praise of São Paulo in direct and disparaging contrast with its profile of Rio de Janeiro.

The letter recovered by the *Revista Nova* was an especially early instance of the outsider's endorsement that paulistas sought, but there would be many more over the years. Although there were no visits by foreign dignitaries that prompted the sort of pomp and spectacle that Sueann Caulfield analyzes in her account of the visit of the king and queen of Belgium to Rio de Janeiro in 1920, São Paulo hosted a steady stream of foreign officials, businessmen, technical personnel, and journalists who recorded their impressions of the city and state.[88] Several of these visits produced "coffee-table" type books that, despite being ostensibly about Brazil as a whole, typically focused on São Paulo, and on extolling its current achievements and future prospects. An early example of this is *Le Brésil*, a massive volume compiled by the foreign trade adviser of the French consulate and published in 1908. Despite its title, over two-thirds of the book was devoted to the city and state of São Paulo, with some 250 pages detailing industry and commerce in the state capital, and another 50 pages dedicated to the interior. Remarkably, in this volume the city of Rio— still substantially larger than São Paulo and a major center of commerce and incipient industry—merits a total of eighteen pages.[89]

Similarly effusive was the Portuguese visitor Arthur Dias, who published a state-by-state profile of Brazilian society following a visit in 1906. Although he was also quite enthusiastic about the federal district and predicted that Rio "will shortly be one of the best cities in this continent, no doubt, the first in South America," his prognosis for São Paulo as a region was even more optimistic. After detailing the fabulous amounts spent on public works, schools, hospitals, and so forth, he concludes, "The general progress of the state represented by its splendid Capital and by the principal cities of the interior, in the volume of factories, farms, banks, large buildings, railways, etc., not only places S. Paulo in front of all the other States of the Republic but its civilisation is over 20 years ahead."[90] A little further on Dias reinforces this point, claiming that "the progress of the scientific institutions, the culture of the cities and the public instruction in all the State is notably superior, and in an elevated degree, to the progress of other sections of Brazil." Having shown "conclusively" that no other Brazilian region can compare, he then places São Paulo's achievements in a transnational context, insisting that the state of São Paulo is not only the equal of Buenos Aires province but, in many ways, its superior.[91]

Nearly a decade later, business and travel writer L. Elwyn Elliott (whose first initial surprisingly stood not for Lawrence or Louis but for Lillian) published a survey of Brazilian social, cultural, and economic life entitled *Brazil Today and Tomorrow*. Elliott had already authored several articles on paulista history and economy for a special issue of the *Pan-American Magazine* (October 1915) on the state of São Paulo, and had predictably sanguine predictions about the region's "tomorrow." However, in the book she adopted a slightly more measured tone. She declared São Paulo Brazil's leading manufacturing center and claimed that "her industrial advance has been made possible in this direction, as in agriculture, by the influx of sturdy Italians, Portuguese and Spanish workers." But she made a point of acknowledging that several other Brazilian states had an incipient industrial economy.[92]

Two visitors from the Spanish-speaking world also wrote accounts that were ostensibly about Brazil in general, but reserved special praise and enthusiasm for São Paulo. One was José Vasconcelos, then Mexican minister of education and soon to be the renowned author of *La raza cósmica*, who visited Brazil and Argentina in 1922. Vasconcelos's chronicle is generally flattering and optimistic, as one might expect from an essayist whose trip was funded by the Brazilian government and who was himself eager to describe Latin America as in ascendance. Thus, even an unscheduled stop in Bahia, caused by a shipboard accident, prompted a description of "the modern buildings, the elevators that transport you up from one street to another, the trolleys and automobiles, the palaces and libraries, the constant movement of civilized peoples, tan, white, mixed; the tropical picturesque and the modernity of the pavements, of construction machinery: thus you have the landscape of Bahia. A land that is on the rise; nobody speaks with pride of Bahia, and yet even there, in the disdained city, there are signals of the potency of a people who are growing full of strength and hope."[93]

Given Vasconcelos's subtle whitening of the "disdained" Bahian population (thus whites and browns abound but blacks are erased) and his generous eye for the smallest trace of modernity, it hardly comes as a surprise that his visit to São Paulo evoked effusive praise, beginning with his pleasure at discovering the city's semi-temperate climate and relatively advanced industrial sector: "I confess that I imagined I would find a large town, but one that was a little rustic and ringed by the jungle, as are our villages in the tropics; I did not realize that [São Paulo] possesses such a temperate climate, nor did I presume that in this locale the most important industrial center in all of Latin America is being formed." Vasconcelos goes on to extol virtually every aspect of metropolitan São Paulo—its buildings, avenues, factories, commerce, its fashionable neighborhoods and clubs. He remarks on the "astonishing output" of the city's manufacturing sector and claims that "the humble" receive attention from the local government and business sector, "and have opportunities available to them to improve their conditions." As for the composition of the population: "Latin emigrations are coming there, and they are mixing to form an average type in which, one can say without stretching the truth, talent and beauty triumph."[94] The only discordant note comes in his description of the state penitentiary, but even then the objections have to do with the inhumanity of prolonged imprisonment in general, and not with the particular conditions in the paulista prisons: "We have seen all the bad sides of all prisons; but, on the other hand, in that of São Paulo there even exist magnificent workshops, with machinery for large-scale production. Also, one observes perfect cleanliness. . . . We cannot help but admire the perfect administration and the evidence not only of good management, as in a modern factory, but also penologists who observe and orient the conduct of the offenders, seeking to improve them by means of instructive lessons, diverse teachings, and some recreational activities."[95]

If Vasconcelos's philosophical objections to incarceration slightly dulled his enthusiasm for the São Paulo Penitentiary, the same cannot be said for the distinguished Spanish penologist Luis Jiménez de Asúa, who visited the prison in 1927 during a tour of Brazilian penal institutions. In his chronicle, *Un viaje al Brasil*, the Spanish visitor—who had recently spent some time as a prisoner himself due to his protests against the Primo de Rivera dictatorship in Spain—criticized all of the Brazilian prisons he toured for not adopting the latest reforms, with the "extraordinary" exception of São Paulo's penitentiary.[96] He then proceeds to recount his impressions of Rio de Janeiro's House of Corrections, which he finds unsanitary and lacking the proper rehabilitative atmosphere. In short, "the establishment that I have just finished describing is very far from perfect." His disapproval of the carioca penal institution only serves to heighten his praise for the paulista prison in the subsequent chapter, entitled (with an oxymoronic touch) "The Marvelous Penitentiary of São Paulo." Jiménez de Asúa lavishly praises virtually everything about the prison, which began operations in 1920. Like Vasconcelos, he notes the excellent sanitary conditions, the modern construction, as well as the many workshops: "The architectonic system they've adopted is of parallel pavilions, following the most modern criteria, and the magnificent factory seems nothing like a prison."[97] He goes on to detail the various types of work performed by the prisoners (carpentry, shoemaking, mechanics, tailoring, bookbinding, etc.), but also notes the attention to literacy and instruction, and the active use of the prison library, which boasts some six thousand volumes, all "carefully selected." He expresses pleasant surprise at the extremely thorough collection and recording of statistics and observations about the prisoners, and ends with a tribute to the prison warden, Franklin de Toledo Piza. By way of illustrating the character and dedication of this official, Jiménez de Asúa recounts an anecdote about a "revolution" in São Paulo that stirred fears of an attack on the prison by the rebels, which then prompted two-thirds of its employees to abandon their posts. Toledo Piza stoutly remained at the prison and was gratified to hear from the inmates that they not only had no intention of fleeing, but would help defend the penitentiary if it were attacked.[98]

A final comment by the Spanish penologist about the "marvelous penitentiary" is especially revealing for the purposes of this discussion. In closing, he mentions that this "house of reform" is "the object of constant pilgrimages by foreigners and nationals" and claims that in the first eight months of 1927 alone, some twenty thousand persons toured the facilities.[99] In other words, the penitentiary had become something of a showplace, and while at first glance it might seem odd for the state administration to make a prison an obligatory stop for visitors to São Paulo, the reactions of Vasconcelos and Jiménez de Asúa make it evident that it was not so odd at all. This new prison, with its up-to-date facilities, industrial discipline, attention to education, and scientific regulations, provided a highly condensed and visible confirmation of the civilized, modern, and progressive orientation of the state of São Paulo. In an ironic variation on Jeremy Bentham's "panopticon"—the model prison in which all inmates could be surveilled all the time—the paulista authorities used the penitentiary to allow themselves to be "seen" all the time, and always in the most favorable light.

Nationalism cum Regionalism

These years not only saw a rise in regional chauvinism, but also an intensification of nationalism, reminding us again that these two "isms" are not necessarily contradictory. In the late 1910s, the militaristic climate of a world at war had its repercussions in Brazil, and particularly in São Paulo. Furthermore, the devastation in Europe during those years fueled a discourse that presumed the decadence of the Old World and the youth and vibrancy of the New.[100] Following a visit to the São Paulo School of Law by poet and professional patriot Olavo Bilac, a group of paulista intellectuals and journalists, together with students from the law and engineering schools, founded, in 1916, the Liga Nacionalista.[101] The tenets adopted by this patriotic organization included support for compulsory military service, electoral reform (including the secret ballot), and the promotion of "national unity." The late 1910s and 1920s also saw increased interest among artists and intellectuals in brasilidade—that is, the incorporation of "authentic" elements of Brazilian culture/folklore in painting, music, architecture, and so forth, as opposed to an earlier tendency to value and imitate European cultural expressions.[102] Similarly, Brazilian artists and intellectuals began to question more loudly and insistently the claims by European race theorists that racial mixture inevitably led to social degeneration and decline, offering instead a more "optimistic" reading of the social and cultural consequences of mestiçagem. To be sure, there were often steep limits to that optimism—when Bilac spoke to the students of the São Paulo Law School, he referred to the men of the "rough backlands" (generally assumed to be "mestiço") as "not Brazilians, nor even true men; they are beings without free or creative spirits, like the beasts, like the insects, like the trees."[103] But unlike earlier reflections on the dismal state of Brazil's rural population, Bilac clearly saw a more active state and a stronger nationalist movement as a remedy for what ailed the Brazilian populace.[104]

As the founding of the Liga Nacionalista indicates, influential paulistas enthusiastically embraced nationalist trends. At the same time, the year 1922—a watershed in Brazilian history—offers two occasions that exemplify the continued conflation of regional and national identity in São Paulo. One is the centennial celebration of Brazilian independence, which took place in September of that year but whose commemorative activities, including multiple monument inaugurations, had been in preparation for several years prior to the event.[105] Of course, the most extensive centennial commemorations took place in Rio de Janeiro, but the São Paulo state government—now led by Washington Luís, himself a student of regional history—had no intention of being overshadowed or outdone by the festivities in the federal district. The state and municipal administrations had prepared an elaborate set of rituals, unveilings, speeches, processions, and firework displays in the state capital as well as in the port city of Santos and various towns throughout the interior.

The opening ceremonies, as one would expect, took place along the banks of the Ipiranga, the locale where Dom Pedro I declared Brazil's independence as well as the site of the Museu Paulista. Although probably exaggerated, contemporary accounts claim that the event attracted 100,000 spectators who listened to the various speeches and witnessed the unveiling of a monument to the Grito de Ipiranga (or at least what was available for public viewing—the monument, designed by an Italian sculptor, would take four more years to complete). Next there was a quick stop on the Avenida Paulista to inaugurate a statue honoring Olavo Bilac (to quote Mário de Andrade's observation, during these months "monuments germinated in a flowering of heroic gestures"). Then Washington Luís and several other leading dignitaries took the São Paulo Railway down to Santos. There they participated in another round of ceremonies, now in honor of the Andrada brothers (native Santistas), and particularly José Bonifácio, "patriarch" of Brazilian independence. This was followed by a procession to various historical landmarks that symbolized, according to historian Antonio Celso Ferreira, São Paulo's inexorable march toward civilization and progress.[106] The caravan of dignitaries subsequently returned to São Paulo, where the fireworks took place one day late because the fuses had been dampened by a steady drizzle.

It is hardly surprising that the organizers of the commemorations in São Paulo would choose to foreground figures and events related to Brazilian independence that were paulista in origin or location. Surely the other states of Brazil, to the extent that it was possible, did the same. But the content of the various speeches given during the ceremonies, and the coverage that the regional literati devoted to the events, indicate that this was more than just the routine recognition of local heroes. Tânia de Luca notes that the *Revista do Brasil*, despite numerous articles commenting on the commemorations in São Paulo both before and after the event, made no reference whatsoever to the parallel commemorations in Rio, a city that was, after all, the nation's capital.[107] But even more compelling evidence of the celebration as a narrative of São Paulo's evolution to greatness is the various discourses presented by leading political figures on the occasion. The speakers were not so much recounting paulistas' "contributions" to independence and the evolution of the nation, since that term implies that paulistas were one among many regional groups who forged Brazilian independence, the abolition of slavery, the rise of the republic, and so forth. Rather, the point was to insist that São Paulo was the region *primarily responsible* for all these liberationist trends.[108]

Up-and-coming Republican politician Roberto Moreira, who had the honor of delivering the closing address at the Ipiranga ceremonies, both incorporated many of the new nationalist themes, including an explicit rejection of the idea that racial mixture leads to social degeneration, and tied them to a celebration of São Paulo's creation of Brazil. According to one historian, "For the orator, it was in São Paulo that the Brazilian nation first germinated, as the fruit of the common effort to tame and expand its territory. An effort from which a racial and social cohesion resulted that would smash the pessimistic [racial] theses. Thus [Moreira's] conclusion, which left no room for doubt: 'Because, as is well-known, Brazil was made by the Brazilians, or to be more exact, by the paulistas.'" And Moreira closed his speech with a paean to the transformation of São Paulo city, now visible from Ipiranga "through the fantastic jungle of daring towers . . . of those chimneys bellowing smoke and through the enormous mass, compact, overflowing, unruly, of buildings . . . to attest, concretely, to the eloquence of these monumental lines, the progress of São Paulo, the civilization of Brazil, the greatness of the nation."[109]

Even more effusive was the address delivered by the state president's protégé, Júlio Prestes—the man who would later have the dubious distinction of being the (federal) president-elect prevented from taking office by Getúlio Vargas's seizure of power in 1930. Prestes, who spoke at the end of the quasi-religious procession down the coastal road, described the symbols erected along the route as "explaining the present" and then declared that "he who is only acquainted with our origins, but is not aware of our evolution from the melting pot of races, of our sufferings and triumphs, of the gloom of slavery and the radiance of liberty, even so will marvel before the splendors of São Paulo, which are as inexplicable as the legends of the magical cities that flourished in the Atlantis of our dreams and our imagination." Again, it is noteworthy that the leading speakers made a point of emphasizing race mixture as an aspect of brasilidade—or at least paulistinidade. But there were also limits to how that mixture might be conceived. Thus Prestes, in talking of São Paulo's colonial past, lauded "the first caboclo, blended from the two races that crossed, bringing, along with the superior qualities of the Portuguese, the resistance and the hot blood of the savage, forged for the adventures and for the diffusion of our nationality."[110] This formulation allowed Prestes both to rebuff the pessimistic forecasts of European race theorists regarding mestiçagem, and to locate that mixture in a receding past. It also eliminated any and all consideration of the genealogical contribution of Afro-paulistas, who only appear in these speeches as the fortunate beneficiaries of the (white) paulistas' distaste for the institution of slavery.

Although the centennial of Brazilian independence provoked a great deal of activity in São Paulo, the year 1922 is much more commonly associated with the occasion known as Modern Art Week, which took place in February of that year.[111] Organized by a core group of artists and writers (Mário de Andrade, Anita Malfatti, Paulo Menotti del Picchia, Oswald de Andrade, and Tarsila do Amaral), the event—which included art exhibits, poetry readings, and other activities—marked the advent of a new phase in Brazilian cultural life. To be sure, the work of the figures involved had already been circulating for some time, but the combined effect of their collaborative effort heightened the impact of their innovative and challenging artistic production. At the risk of oversimplifying a complex and minutely studied artistic movement, I would identify as the core principles of Modern Art Week a disdain for imitative, Europeanized artistic forms, but also a rejection of nativist and sentimentalized renditions of "authentic" Brazilian culture. The concept most readily associated with the Brazilian modernists is "anthropophagy," symbolically rendered as the indigenous Brazilian ingesting the European body. In other words, as artists they couldn't and wouldn't wall themselves off within the nation; they would consume new European cultural trends, but in digesting them, they would transform them into something novel and different, and something Brazilian, not European. This celebration of hybridity and mixture thus endorsed an eclectic melding of avant-garde techniques with "folkloric" elements, and critiqued the turn-of-the-century fixation on whitening and Europeanization.[112]

At first glance, the programmatic statements of the paulista modernists might seem utterly incompatible with the discursive trends feeding regional chauvinism. Yet, as we will see in chapter 3, all but one of the major modernist figures actively supported the paulista uprising in 1932, and several participants in Modern Art Week were among the most visible and prominent advocates of the regional insurgency. Far from this representing a break with their earlier convictions, I would argue that we can see a number of elements in Modern Art Week and the subsequent artistic ferment that indicates strong continuities in attitudes about São Paulo and the nation in the decade that stretched from 1922 to 1932. In the case of writer Menotti del Picchia and poet Guilherme de Almeida, fervent supporters of the Causa Paulista, one can readily discern the relationship between their particular nationalist orientation and their eventual political affiliations. When the paulista modernists splintered after 1924, Menotti and Guilherme, together with Cassiano Ricardo and Plínio Salgado, formed the group known as "Verde-Amarelo." In contrast to the other modernist factions (Pau Brasil and Terra Roxa), the verde-amarelistas aggressively insisted on the identification of São Paulo as the core of the Brazilian nation, simultaneously professing an anti-cosmopolitan perspective and endorsing the role of the immigrant in the construction of paulista/Brazilian modernity. As one student of this movement has argued, for Menotti and others, "São Paulo came to be the nation capable of Brazilianizing all immigrants."[113] Many of the crucial elements of paulista identity that would undergird the Constitutionalist Movement in the early 1930s were already present in the ideological and literary productions of the verde-amarelistas.

There was, however, a broader sense in which the modernists in general, for all their emphasis on artistic hybridity and their professed disdain for bourgeois culture, valorized São Paulo as Brazil's engine of social and cultural transformation. Prior to the decade of the 1920s, it would have been difficult for even the most dedicated disciple of paulistinidade to compare the city of São Paulo, as a cultural center, with the federal district. São Paulo (city and state) could claim economic supremacy and political primacy, but Rio de Janeiro remained the uncontested intellectual and cultural center of Brazil, and even paulista intellectuals regarded a sojourn in the national capital as indispensable for a serious man of letters. Modern Art Week certainly did not close this cultural "gap" between Brazil's two leading cities, nor did all the paulista artists and intellectuals necessarily seek to unseat Rio as Brazil's cultural capital. But their claim to having pioneered modernism in Brazil reinforced a sense of São Paulo as the center of modernity and as emblematic of the future Brazil.[114] In the pages of *Correio Paulistano*, Menotti del Picchia had this to say of a trip to Rio taken in 1921 by Mário de Andrade and Oswald de Andrade to read their work: "The paulistas, recuperating the exploits of their elders, reissued, in the century of gasoline, the epic of the 'bandeiras.' The day before yesterday the first 'futurist bandeira' departed for Rio. . . . The feat is a daring one! . . . the 'futurist bandeira' will have to confront . . . all the antediluvian fauna, that still survives, by a miraculous anachronism."[115] As historian Angela de Castro Gomes observes, this statement speaks volumes about the hegemonic pretensions with which the paulista artistic movement was imbued, and its insistence on São Paulo's salience as the future of the Brazilian nation.[116]

Menotti's assertion also exhibits the paulistas' appropriation of modernism—a literary and artistic tendency with concurrent expressions in both Rio and Minas Gerais—as a specifically, almost exclusively paulista phenomenon, sharply contrasted with the hidebound literary milieu of the federal capital. Moreover it was a highly successful campaign of regional branding. Two years after Modern Art Week, poet Manuel Bandeira (native of Pernambuco and resident of Rio), in a letter to Mário de Andrade about a furor involving Oswald, insisted that the latter could be denounced and trounced in any number of ways, but "never, however, shunted aside, because the modernist movement, the modernist wave *emerged from São Paulo* and he was a fighter [for it] from the outset."[117] As the long and lively correspondence between these two literary figures reveals, Mário de Andrade nursed a certain resentment toward the cariocas who he felt regarded paulista writers as competitors, as if "in literature one perpetuates rivalries as in soccer!"[118] However, it was

Mário who, despite his many criticisms of fellow paulista writers whom he considered excessively regionalist, made the most categorical claims about São Paulo's ascendant position within the Brazilian cultural universe. Writing in *A Gazeta* immediately following Modern Art Week, he declared São Paulo not just equal but superior to Rio in (nearly) all things cultural:

> The artistic hegemony of the Court [Rio] no longer exists. In commerce as in soccer, in wealth as in the arts, São Paulo has pulled out in front. Who was it that first manifested the idea of a modern and Brazilian architecture? São Paulo with the colonial style. Who was it that first manifested the desire to construct new bases for painting? São Paulo with Anita Malfatti. Who was it that presented to the world the greatest and most modern sculptor in South America? São Paulo with Brecheret. Where is it that poetry first turned into a vehicle for the modern sensibility free from the sing-songy rhyme and the bonds of metrics? In São Paulo. It is only in music that Rio with Villa Lobos is more advanced.[119]

And three years later, with the competition still on his mind, Mário famously complained to Manuel about "those people in Rio," whom he claimed "never forgave São Paulo for having first rung the bell."[120] Or to put it more plainly, he believed the cariocas could never forgive the paulistas for beating them to the modernist punch.

The Political Crises of the 1920s

Knowing how a story ends inevitably influences the way it is told. Because the standard narrative of the political crises of the 1920s is plotted as climaxing with the emergence of the Aliança Liberal in 1929, its defeat in the presidential elections of 1930, and then Vargas's military-backed seizure of power in October of that year, it is tempting to read the political twists and turns of the decade through the lens of the struggle against paulista hegemony in the First Republic, spearheaded by the ideologically motley crew of young military officers known as the "tenentes" (lieutenants). But that lens magnifies some issues and obscures others, including the considerable political contestation within São Paulo itself. As historian Vavy Pacheco Borges observes, the traditional historiography's tendency to summarize this period as "oligarquias versus tenentismo" can be highly misleading given that the discourses and practices of many paulistas associated with the so-called regional oligarchy coincided with those of the tenentes.[121] One of the more striking features of the discourses of paulista supremacy is that by no means did they track the political divisions of the time in any predictable or mechanistic way, especially if we are discussing what might be called "mainstream" politics. The one political milieu where there was a discernible skepticism, even scorn, for what was seen as the self-congratulatory postures of the paulista elites and their claims to regional supremacy was the left/labor movement and the working-class press.[122] But politically engaged paulistas who circulated in more "establishment" venues typically shared a common regional identification even as they vehemently disagreed about the course of regional and national politics, or even about the defining features of paulistinidade.[123]

Although in what follows I will be mainly discussing the more conventional forms of political activity, it is essential to note that the emergence of a popular sphere of political expression—and not just within the labor movement or the Communist Party—was one of the developments that provoked considerable debate and dissent within mainstream party politics.[124] Thus, it is inadvisable, even impossible, to entirely separate these realms of political participation, which also involved far more circulation and exchange, both of individuals and ideas, than usually assumed. Nor would I even argue that left-leaning political activists were immune to the conflation of regional and national identities that informed so much of the worldview of mainstream political actors and pundits. But because the subsequent chapters focus on an uprising that drew its strength from relatively privileged sectors of paulista society, the following discussion will mainly consider paulista political elites or near elites in the 1920s, and their multifarious interventions in the brewing conflicts of that decade.[125]

Divisions within the elite political community in São Paulo hardly began in the 1920s. There had been various dissidências—opposition factions—within the Paulista Republican Party (PRP) since the turn of the century, at least one of which led to a formal schism within the party.[126] But the level of contentiousness and criticism definitely intensified in what would prove to be the final decade of the First Republic. Moreover, there were rumblings and new pressures within and without, so that it was not simply a matter of an inert, unchanging PRP coming under "attack" from splinter factions or new interest groups; the composition, style, and leadership of the PRP itself were also undergoing significant changes, so that by the late 1920s one of the leading sources of support for the perrepistas was the industrialist association, the Centro Industrial do Estado de São Paulo (CIESP).[127] The robust and expansive paulista press also reflected the disquiet in this period; even the Correio Paulistano, the official mouthpiece of the PRP, started incorporating new voices into its roster of regular contributors (such as Menotti del Picchia, who signed his columns as "Helios"); O Estado de São Paulo, which positioned itself as a nonpartisan daily, became both increasingly critical of the established order and increasingly esteemed by the paulista readership.[128] This is not even to mention the labor press, the black press, and the numerous foreign-language papers that circulated during these years.

These indications of a vigorous and variegated public sphere—thoroughly documented in a recent study of paulista politics under the Old Republic—should move us to reflect upon the adequacy of existing labels, and particularly the standard reference to São Paulo's elites under the Old Republic as the "paulista oligarchy."[129] By using a term signifying "government by a small faction of persons or families," historians have sought to accentuate the concentration of wealth and power, the traditional (i.e., agrarian) sources of status and privilege, and the nondemocratic features of oligarchic liberalism—and understandably so, given the paulista elites' dominant position throughout most of Brazil's First Republic, the clubby character of that elite in terms of kinship and socialization patterns, and the apparent exclusion of the vast majority of the Brazilian population from the exercise of formal political power or participation during that era. In short, the designation of the paulista elites as an "oligarchy" makes a certain rough sense if broadly compared to ruling groups in more populist or democratic political systems.

At the same time, we need to consider what this designation may obscure or ignore. In discussing the use of the term "oligarchy," we need to do more than just interrogate its accuracy. Unless we proceed from the assumption that our categories are scientifically determined and that there is a complete coincidence between signifier and signified, we also need to ask what ideological work the term performs. Perhaps most important, we need to juxtapose our retrospective renderings of a particular political culture with the way it was presented and experienced by the historical actors in question. To take one example, an oft-used shorthand illustration for the oligarchic nature of politics under the Old Republic is the low percentage of the adult-male population that actually went to the polls and cast ballots.[130] Scholars have routinely identified the literacy requirement as the major explanation for the meager voter turnout even in *contested* national elections (as opposed to those where the outcome was a foregone conclusion). Yet the proportion of the paulista population that was sufficiently literate to qualify for the vote grew steadily throughout the 1910s and 1920s, and even so, the number of total voters remained low.

In his groundbreaking study of politics in São Paulo, historian James Woodard suggests that the common assumption that the polls were the exclusive preserve of the more privileged members of society may be wide of the mark.

Rather, it seems that "respectable" citizens regarded voting as a low-prestige activity appropriate for dependents and clients of political bosses. These cultured and refined critics of machine politics regarded such "professional politicians" as the true oligarchy (a term always pejorative in its implications) and bemoaned the fact that so many persons of quality—that is, members of the business, liberal-professional, and intellectual elites—refrained from actively participating in public life. Or as Monteiro Lobato alleged, in a letter sent to President Artur Bernardes in 1924, "We have automatically repelled from the polls precisely those men possessed of the natural capacity to vote."[131] In other words, the problem—in their eyes—was *not* a tight connection between the wealthy and the politically powerful, but rather the alleged estrangement between those who had achieved success through manly initiative, intelligence, and innovation, and those whose influence stemmed from the mere dispensing of political patronage or raw assertion of power. According to Woodard, when members of these dissident factions "complained of 'oligarchy' or 'professional politicians,' they were not bemoaning the marriage of public and private power, but rather their divorce: they found it galling that political power should be exercised . . . by men who lacked the customary trappings of sociocultural status . . . and socioeconomic success."[132] I would argue that their critiques reflected a germinating bourgeois sensibility that rejected politics for political power's sake, and disdained the attendant patrimonial machinations of "traditional" politicians. Instead, the critics sought to invest greater authority in those whose "legitimacy" stemmed from achievements outside the realm of politics, and for whom politics meant "public service," and not mere political power. In a similar vein, they sought to construct a competent electorate around the figure of the middle-class male head of household.[133]

Such expressions of dissatisfaction with paulista "politics as usual" can be traced to the period of World War I, with the formation of the Liga Nacionalista on the one hand, and the escalation of labor militancy—including general strikes in the state capital in 1917 and 1919—on the other. These deepening divisions were both manifested in and exacerbated by several unusually contentious presidential successions, one of which provoked the first tenente uprising, in 1922. Restricted to a few hundred dissident military personnel, most of them located at the Copacabana Fort in Rio, the revolt met with a quick but dramatic defeat when sixteen of the rebels chose to become martyrs rather than surrender to the government forces. Lacking any clear ideological position or fixed political agenda, "tenentismo" became a handy referent for the discontent and frustration of political factions throughout Brazil, *including* São Paulo.[134]

The second tenente uprising began exactly two years later, and this time the rebels' main strategic objective was to seize and hold the city of São Paulo (while a second tenente faction staged a revolt in Rio Grande do Sul). The 1924 rebellion, involving thousands of soldiers from army units stationed in São Paulo, constituted a far more serious challenge to the existing political order and briefly succeeded in bringing social and economic life in São Paulo's capital to a halt. Eager to ensure that the situation would not get completely out of hand or cause severe financial losses, Commercial Association president José Carlos de Macedo Soares negotiated an arrangement with the tenente leadership that allowed the resumption of some commercial activities and public services, but no such arrangement could be made with the federal forces, who began bombarding the metropolitan area with artillery in an attempt to dislodge the tenentes. Three weeks into the siege, the tenentes recognized that they had no hope of maintaining control of the city, never mind overthrowing the federal government, and decided to beat a stealthy retreat from the state capital and join up with the tenentes from Rio Grande do Sul to form what eventually became known as the Prestes Column.[135]

In light of subsequent events, it might be tempting to depict the tenente revolt of 1924 in São Paulo as a dress rehearsal for the overthrow of paulista republican rule, with most city residents keeping their distance or opposing the uprising altogether. But there are several chronicles and commentaries from contemporary witnesses and participants that offer a sharply different view of the situation, and a number of studies over the last two decades have provided us with a far more complex interpretation of the events of July 1924 in São Paulo. For example, Boris Fausto, in his introduction to Paulo Duarte's polemical account of the uprising (significantly entitled *Agora nós!*—"Now Us!" and subtitled *Chronicle of the paulista revolution*), contends that "the tenentes were not . . . unaware of the existence of political divisions in São Paulo, so much so that General Isidoro Dias Lopes tried to make contact with the editor of *O Estado de São Paulo* while organizing the revolution."[136] And James Woodard's chapter on the 1924 revolt describes in vivid detail the support that the tenentes received from prominent paulista figures in the Reação Republicana, who had spearheaded the most recent and serious *dissidência*.[137] There were, in addition, many politically influential paulistas who did not endorse the tenentes' recourse to violence, but nonetheless expressed considerable sympathy for the rebels' denunciations of the republican status quo. According to Paulo Duarte, although the tenente uprising was doomed to fail, "the sell-outs of the nation now no longer have the same tranquil slumber that the expectation of impunity gave them. And the oppressed learned to react, they felt the awakening of that old backlands energy from the seventeenth century; calculating accurately how many useless sacrifices an armed victory would entail, they today unite in a promissory enthusiasm, around an army that will save us through the ballot box."[138] As Boris Fausto concludes in his preface, this electoral army would be the Partido Democrático (PD), and while it would not score the victories that Duarte predicted, one can easily trace various links between the tenente uprisings and the creation of this new political party in São Paulo.[139]

Founded in 1926, the Partido Democrático was the first mainstream "opposition party" to challenge the Partido Republicano Paulista's monopoly on regional political power. Given the significance of this political development, for years historians struggled to find the socioeconomic key to the PD's founding, first asserting that its leadership reflected new industrial and commercial interests, then traditional and declining agrarian interests, then generational conflicts.[140] But each time closer inspection revealed the alleged social and economic bases for the schism to be statistically insignificant, or incompatible with the party's stated intentions. Finally, Maria Lígia Prado—starting with the premise that there were no substantial differences in the social profiles of the PRP and PD leaderships, and that explanations for political affiliations are not reducible to narrow definitions of economic or age-group interests— argued that the PD should be analyzed as an attempt to forge a more inclusive and reformist political project, though still within the confines of elitist paulista politics.[141]

Taking Prado's insights as my point of departure, and building on Woodard's recent research regarding the PD, I entirely agree that we need to think of the party in terms of a different political project that does not necessarily correspond to a narrowly defined set of interests. Pushing the critique a little further, I would argue that the use of a priori categories to understand the PD reduces its significance, for it assumes that the "interests" and identities of those involved in its founding were already fixed and stabilized; instead, I would propose seeing the PD as part of an ongoing project of identity formation whose central figure was the middle-class male citizen-voter. To be sure, PD proposals made many references to laboring men and workers' rights, but the PD's calls for moderate reforms and the secret ballot (the lodestone of its moralizing campaign) reflected not so much an incipient populism as an antidote to what the *democráticos* saw as the degradation of politics resulting from the patronage-fueled participation of uncultured and incompetent voters. And as one might expect, this campaign not only drew on class-based imagery, but on racial distinctions as well. Thus the "ignorant [and] truly beastlike multitude," who allegedly crowded out cultured and thinking Brazilians at the polls, were implicitly nonwhite in print, and explicitly so in posters and cartoons advocating the secret ballot.[142]

Not surprisingly, paulista pundits such as Monteiro Lobato couched their demands for the secret ballot in appeals to transnational modernity. In his letter to President Bernardes in 1924, he claimed that secret balloting "has already been adopted by *all cultured peoples with one single exception.*" Here the dividing line between those who favored the secret ballot and those who opposed it was culture. But he also goes on to equate support for the *voto secreto* with modern (middle-class) consumerism: "Can we play the part of a people that forbids the entry of a marvelous invention into its territory? Can one imagine a country that has resisted the adoption of the telephone, of the "Ford," of cinematography?"[143] Elsewhere, Monteiro Lobato and other paulistas called for the adoption of the secret ballot first in São Paulo—to them, the natural entry point for modern inventions and civilized practices—with the hope that it would then spread, like a benevolent contagion, to the rest of Brazil. Indeed, this was a familiar theme in writings by paulistas, including even those of the most "progressive" disposition. Thus Baptista Pereira, a paulista intellectual who avidly promoted antiracist ideas, nonetheless declared that São Paulo would always be in the "forefront" of Brazil's march to modernity, and that his home region was "the Apostle of the Peoples. . . . It is São Paulo that takes up the burden of the long crusades, to teach Brazil the meaning of Brazilianness [brasilidade], to show Brazil the path to a Greater Brazil [Brasil-Maior]."[144]

Although the PD could claim relatively few electoral successes, the formation of this political party, and its public statements through the PD daily *Diário Nacional*, and its unofficial and highly influential ally, *O Estado de São Paulo*, meant, somewhat ironically, that the most consistent and thoughtful mainstream critiques of the PRP and the "paulista oligarchy" emerged, in the late 1920s, from São Paulo itself.[145] Furthermore, in the presidential campaign of 1930, when Washington Luís, by then president of Brazil (1926–1930), violated the standard political practices of the era by designating paulista Júlio Prestes as his successor (rather than a politician from neighboring Minas Gerais), the overwhelming majority of the PD leadership decided to back the insurgent candidacy of Getúlio Vargas and his Aliança Liberal ticket. Vargas even made a brief campaign visit to São Paulo, where as many as 300,000 people turned out to greet him along his route, and where he delivered a speech packed with the usual tributes and accolades for the paulistas' extraordinary contributions to Brazilian civilization.[146] There were some dissenting voices, even within the PD; at least one young democrático militant declined to support Vargas because he suspected a "vendetta against São Paulo" in the gaúcho governor's campaign. And the independent-minded and irrepressible Monteiro Lobato sent a message of support to Júlio Prestes in which he declared that "it is not with cheese or cured beef [edible symbols of Minas/Rio Grande do Sul] that the grave problems facing Brazil will be resolved. It is with coffee, audacity, vision, initiative, and the other Yankee qualities that characterize the paulista."[147]

These deep divisions within the paulista political landscape would seem to give the lie to any attempt by the new political forces outside of São Paulo to present that state's regional political elites as uniformly opposed to significant transformations in the republican political system and unremittingly hostile to Vargas. But such efforts were made, even to the extent of altering visual evidence. As Jeziel de Paula reveals in his study of images and the Revolution of 1932, within weeks of seizing power, someone in Getúlio's inner circle deliberately altered a key photograph that would have indicated support for Vargas among paulista elites. The picture, which appeared on the cover of the November 8, 1930, issue of Rio's *Revista da Semana*, portrays the tenente leader Miguel Costa, Vargas himself (in military uniform), and General Góes Monteiro. The caption sets the scene of the photo as the "presidential [railway] car on the way to São Paulo." Documentation uncovered by de Paula indicates, first of all, that the photo was taken, *not* on the way to São Paulo, but in the Sorocabana train station *in* São Paulo. Even more important, the original photo shows Francisco Morato, a leader of the Partido Democrático, seated next to Vargas, but the version published on the magazine's cover had not only been cropped but retouched so that no vestige of the paulista politician remained (figs. 1.5 and 1.6).[148] The result of the altered photo and the misleading caption is a scene perfectly compatible with a representation of "São Paulo" as external and opposed to the Revolution of 1930; it composes a tableau that ignores the divisions within the paulista political class and literally erases any sign of enthusiasm within that class for Vargas's seizure of power.

While de Paula's discovery of this visual "purge" (to use his term) is surely significant, even fascinating, it does prompt me to ask whether the narrative imbedded in the *original* photograph could be seen as equally misleading in its expression of paulista solidarity with the newly triumphant regime. There was certainly a diversity of views and expectations regarding the soon-to-be-installed Vargas administration, but there was also considerable, maybe even overwhelming agreement about the position of São Paulo vis-à-vis the rest of Brazil. The collapse of coffee prices following the stock market crash in 1929

FIGURE 1.5. Photo of Miguel Costa, Pedro Góes Monteiro, Getúlio Vargas, and paulista Francisco Morato. Photographer unknown, October 29, 1930.

FIGURE 1.6. Retouched photo that erases Francisco Morato. From the cover of *Revista da Semana*, 47 (November 8, 1930).

had not dampened paulista elites' inclination to equate the nation's interests and progress with those of São Paulo; indeed, the precarious state of the coffee market may have made certain factions of that elite even more keen to insist that São Paulo's interests and those of Brazil were one and the same.[149] But Vargas, despite some conciliatory moves with respect to coffee prices, soon made it apparent that one of his principal objectives was to subordinate São Paulo's interests to those of the Brazilian nation that he and his inner circle envisioned. In short order, many members of the political leadership of both the PRP and the PD began to perceive a "vendetta" against the state of São Paulo in *getulista* policies. And it would take just a little over a year for the former rivals to decide that their shared concerns outweighed their political differences, leading them to form a "United Front" against the Vargas regime, and lodge an appeal to "Todo São Paulo" to rise up against those who would usurp Piratininga's primacy and autonomy.[150]

PART I　**THE WAR OF SÃO PAULO**

CHAPTER 2

CONSTITUTING PAULISTA IDENTITY

The paulistas constituted a blatant aberration within the race and the nation. São Paulo had become too great for Brazil. . . . Brazil had not yet become a civilization, [whereas] São Paulo was a European Christian civilization, with the mentality, the climate, the cosmopolitanism, the resources of a European Christian civilization.
—**Mário de Andrade, "A guerra de São Paulo"**

The War of 1932 was inevitable.
—**Benedito Montenegro, *Cruzes paulistas***

In the months before São Paulo declared itself at war with the federal government, those who supported an armed uprising began to frame an argument for the inevitability of the recourse to violence. São Paulo had been humiliated, insulted, and forced into submission by a dictator who drew his strongest support from the backward regions of the North. São Paulo had been stripped of its hegemony and then denied the autonomy necessary to continue to serve as Brazil's "locomotive." São Paulo, a society that thrived under the rule of law, could no longer abide a lawless political regime that operated without a constitution. Meanwhile, officials alien to São Paulo and lacking the necessary culture and competence had "invaded" the region and threatened its tranquility and prosperity by unleashing extremist forces. One *interventor* had even gone so far as to allow beggars free rein in the streets of the state capital.[1] Clearly, the povo bandeirante could no longer sit still for this endless stream of affronts and humiliations.[2]

The events of 1930 might be seen as setting the stage for these developments.[3] The nearly bloodless seizure of power by Getúlio Vargas and his civilian-military coalition of supporters in October of that year ejected one paulista politician from the presidential palace and voided the election of another. Also accompanying Vargas's ascension to power were some outbursts of popular unrest in São Paulo, which one observer described as "the drunken [common] people stomping on the ruins of a rotten oligarchy."[4] Nonetheless, the "Revolution of 1930" did not immediately or automatically generate an irreconcilable conflict between the federal government and São Paulo's political elites.[5] The fracturing of the PRP over the years, and the emergence of the PD in the latter half of the 1920s, meant that even mainstream politics in São Paulo were far from monolithic, making the response to Vargas's ascendancy very uneven. To be sure, those paulista politicians and journalists most closely associated with the PRP not only found their circumstances abruptly transformed for the worse, but a few (such as industrialist and coffee trader Roberto Simonsen) found themselves briefly incarcerated.[6] In contrast, the PD leadership manifested its support for Vargas, and its members greeted his arrival in São Paulo, on the way to assume power in Rio, with enthusiasm that ranged from measured to effusive. Indeed, the jubilant crowds that appeared at the São Paulo train station to cheer Vargas (who had yet to evince a particularly populist disposition) signaled how utterly discredited the PRP and the Old Republican order had become.[7] Under these circumstances, a vigorous protest against Vargas's seizure of power would have been both unlikely and politically unwise.

It was also not necessarily perceived as a problem for "São Paulo" (a term I'm using here as a shorthand for certain regional political factions) that a gaúcho politician had toppled a paulista president and taken control of the federal government. For a twenty-year stretch (1906–1926) during the First Republic not one paulista had occupied the presidential palace. And twice during that time segments of the PRP leadership had enthusiastically supported Bahia native Ruy Barbosa's campaigns for the presidency (1910 and 1919) only to see him go down in defeat.[8] In other words, the paulista political elite was hardly accustomed to *always* getting its way and always exercising direct political power. However, the configuration of politics and the fiscal system prior to the Revolution of 1930 meant that the state's elites could enjoy regional autonomy and wield national influence even with a somewhat hostile politician at the helm of the federal government.[9] It was not unreasonable, therefore, for large segments of even the PRP to assume, in October 1930, that they had little to fear from Vargas as provisional president.

But within a matter of weeks, it became apparent that Vargas had no intention of returning the federal government to business as usual. A month after taking power, Vargas appointed João Alberto Lins de Barros, a former tenente and a native of the Nordeste, as interventor of the state of São Paulo, and the radical tenente Miguel Costa (suspected by paulista elites of having Communist sympathies), as chief of the state's Força Pública, a move that outraged politicians in both the PRP and the PD.[10] The idea of an outsider being imposed upon the state of São Paulo as its chief executive was bad enough, but as we shall see, the appointment of João Alberto was especially difficult to swallow.

Soon petitions and manifestos began circulating that called upon friendly military officials to protect São Paulo from the possible predations of Miguel Costa's Legião Revolucionária, and most, though not all, of the members of the paulista political elite who had overtly or tacitly supported Vargas's rise to power shifted to a position of open and strident opposition. Over the next year and a half paulista politicians from both the PRP and the PD, allied in a "Frente Única" (Single Front), waged a near-constant struggle with the Vargas regime, ostensibly to secure the right to choose a paulista as interventor—the phrase was "um governo civil e paulista"—though the demands escalated over time. Thus by May 1932 the appointment of the eminent, if dottering, paulista statesman Pedro de Toledo as interventor would no longer appease the paulistas; the bandeirante leadership was stipulating that they would settle for nothing less than complete state autonomy. On May 23, 1932, the appointed government of São Paulo, in effect, staged a coup that created an autonomous executive and an "all paulista" cabinet in defiance of federal authorities. That day also marked the first clash that led to bloodshed, resulting in the deaths of four young paulistas whose initials, MMDC, became an almost mystical emblem of the resistance to Vargas. And on the ninth of July, São Paulo, with the support of a handful of high-ranking military officers and the state Força Pública, declared itself to be at war with the federal government.[11]

Unfortunately for São Paulo, the support it had expected from the neighboring state of Minas Gerais, and from Vargas's home state of Rio Grande do Sul did not materialize, and the paulistas found themselves in the difficult position of having to go it virtually alone.[12] In the first few weeks of the revolution, paulista troops (composed of the remnants of dissident federal battalions, the state Força Pública, and hastily trained volunteers) seemed to be having some significant successes, but they proved badly out-equipped and outnumbered, and it soon became apparent that they were fighting a losing battle, despite the state government's propaganda to the contrary.[13] In late September, after less than three months of armed warfare, the Força Pública cut a deal with the federal troops and on the third of October, the state of São Paulo formally surrendered. There is no exact body count, but we know that more than six hundred paulistas died during the fighting or of wounds sustained in combat, and it is likely that the death toll was higher on the federal side, so it is reasonable to estimate that between fifteen hundred and two thousand Brazilians lost their lives as a result of this brief civil war.

The story that I have sketched above is intended to acquaint the reader with what I judge to be the principal events of the period from 1931 to 1932 relating to the growing conflict and eventual war between the state of São Paulo and the federal government. It is a tightly condensed narrative, and in constructing it, I have tried to stick as closely as possible to the terrain of established fact. However, I am aware that there is no such thing as a historical narrative that precedes interpretation—even in this bare-bones account, I am choosing to mention some things and to omit others, and stating as "fact" some matters that are probably more accurately described as interpretation. Whether one identifies the federal authorities as "the Vargas regime," "the provisional government," or "the dictatorship" (a term Vargas himself used on occasion) already tells us a great deal about how the narrator sees the events that unfolded in 1931–1932.[14] But given how central the Constitutionalist Campaign and Revolution of 1932 will be to the next four chapters, it seems prudent to acquaint the reader at the outset with the basic outlines of this episode, though the reader should also be mindful that even in this "just the facts" narrative, many things are open to interpretation and contention.

Although this brief civil war is likely to be unfamiliar to the English-language audience, the Revolution of 1932 is hardly an obscure event in the Portuguese-reading world, at least if judged by the number of printed pages that have been devoted to it. Hundreds of books have been published about the uprising, ranging from firsthand accounts to personal memoirs to scholarly studies. The vast majority of the books in the first two categories, authored by men (and a few women) who participated in the rebellion on the paulista side, predictably paint a flattering picture of São Paulo's role in the events of 1932.[15] In contrast, the scholarly literature—that is, works written many years later by professionalized historians—offers a number of different approaches and ways of classifying the "Guerra Paulista."[16] One way to think about the Revolution of 1932 is as a military uprising—a reasonable choice when we consider that it was unlikely to have gotten off the ground if major military figures such as Isidoro Dias Lopes, Bertoldo Klinger, and Euclides Figueiredo hadn't sided with the paulistas. One of the leading historical texts on the "Brazilian civil war," a study published by Stanley Hilton in 1982, relies heavily (and in some sections, entirely) on documentation from the Arquivo do Exército (Army Archive). This is the case even in his excellent chapter "The People and the

War"; only in the section on the diplomatic aspects of the conflict does he shift away from military documents to the diplomatic archives of the Brazilian foreign ministry (Itamaraty). And for the story that he was seeking to tell, these were the appropriate sources. I'm sure Hilton did not regard his study as exclusively a work of military history, but he is a scholar from the "who done it" school of historical scholarship, and even though he may have been alert to the broader political and economic aspects of the era and the uprising, and even incorporated a smattering of social history, his primary protagonists were the military leaders of the *guerra civil*, and secondarily, their allies in the paulista bourgeoisie.[17]

The 1980s witnessed not only an "opening" in the Brazilian political arena, with the decline and fall of the military dictatorship (1964–1985), but also in the burgeoning academic sphere. Drawing on Gramscian theory and the new social history, critical historians produced a series of scholarly studies of the Constitutionalist Movement and the 1932 uprising that shifted the spotlight away from military maneuvers (both in the arena of armed and political struggle) to questions of class interests, hegemony construction, and social conflicts. Monographs by Holien Gonçalves Bezerra, Maria Helena Capelato, Antonio Pedro Tota, and Vavy Pacheco Borges emphasized both the alienation of the popular classes from a movement engineered by paulistas of the upper class, and the underlying socioeconomic interests that informed the actions of the civilian-bourgeois leadership. In this historiography, the paulista elite, accustomed (prior to 1930) to a free hand in suppressing labor militancy, acts out of fear of a burgeoning working-class movement supported by some factions of the new getulista regime, and of a small but active cohort of Communists with various ties to *tenentismo*. In other words, the uprising is seen as a counterrevolution, and the protagonists are civilians, whether segments of the paulista bourgeoisie who spearheaded the movement, or the popular classes that resisted the elites' calls to battle.[18]

As Emília Viotti da Costa observes, in a concise and insightful essay on the "contradictory images" produced by this episode, "as is true of every revolution, the one in 1932 generated its own mythology."[19] Indeed, given how brief the uprising was, one might argue for an inverse relationship between the duration of this conflict and the quantity of myths it produced. In light of this, another way to catalog the scholarly studies of the 1932 uprising is to consider how they engage with the dominant national-historical narrative of the Constitutionalist Movement. A firsthand formulation of this narrative would be the following remarks by General Pedro Góes Monteiro, the leader of the federal assault on São Paulo, in a report to Vargas:

> The dominant spirit in SAO PAULO is to emerge victorious, no matter what it takes, in an effort to satisfy the regionalist and particularist pride and to reacquire the political hegemony and monopoly of the national economy that it lost.
>
> It is evident that *constitutionalization* is nothing more than a farce to justify the paulistas resorting to arms, but in fact, everything indicates that should they meet with failure, they will mount an appeal for separatism, as the ultimate *logic*.[20]

One commentator, boiling this argument down to the basics, summed up its portrayal of the Causa Paulista as "the swan song of the coffee aristocracy."[21] A slightly more sophisticated statement of this perspective can be found in E. Bradford Burns's *A History of Brazil*, the text that was for decades the leading English-language synthesis of Brazilian history: "The significance of the revolt was readily discernible in its limited geographic and popular appeal. . . . More than anything else, the rebellion seemed to be a rearguard action by the Paulista oligarchy who looked to the past and desired a restoration of their former privileges and power, and the government treated it as such. Federal forces converged on the capital of São Paulo, and after three months of siege and desultory fighting, the revolt collapsed."[22] Though some of the more recent studies are too complex in their approach and their arguments to be easily catalogued in one camp or the other, much of the scholarly work on the 1932 uprising clusters around one of two poles. The critical social histories of the revolt tend to conform to the view that this was a restorationist movement of the paulista elites, who *cynically* sought a return to the status quo ante both to recover their national hegemony and to thwart the radical reforms proposed by a segment of Vargas's supporters.[23] In contrast, authors (such as Stanley Hilton, Hernani Donato, and Hélio Silva) who harbor some sympathies for the Causa Paulista, tend to insist that the regional elites were *sincere* in their liberal demands for a return to constitutional rule and concerns for the autonomy of their state, and sought neither a simple restoration of the Old Republic nor secession from the Brazilian nation.[24]

Cynicism and sincerity, however, are not especially useful categories of historical analysis, partly because historians rarely have the means to judge "interior" motives even for individual conduct, never mind collective actions, but also because the analytical payoff is very limited once we divorce intent from action and reception. Indeed, historical actors themselves should not be expected to have a particularly clear-cut notion of how "sincere" or "cynical" their statements and actions might be, and the very act of uttering certain ideas and asserting certain positions may constitute a subjectivity that becomes meaningful both to that individual and to his or her interlocutors regardless of how "deeply felt" these sentiments might originally be.[25] What I propose to do here, then, is to dispense with these categories and pursue an interpretive strategy that seriously addresses the discourses and practices of the Constitutionalist Movement (rather than seeing them as a cover for a different or truer set of interests and motives), but does so from a critical perspective that considers the meanings and identities constructed in the course of the movement, and what types of inclusions and exclusions these produced. I will also approach the Constitutionalist Movement and uprising as processes, rather than simply as events, which then allows me to highlight not a set of a priori interests and intentions that produced the Causa Paulista, but rather the ways in which the very process of forming, leading, and participating in the movement and revolt fashioned regional identities.

As a result, my narrative of the events of 1931–1932 departs from previous ones in a number of ways. For example, as I noted above, critical accounts of the anti-Vargas agitation typically emphasize the bourgeoisie's fear that the ex-tenentes João Alberto and Miguel Costa harbored sympathies for the Communist Party or would force employers to implement new labor laws.[26] Without discounting these factors, I would foreground instead the political affront that a nordestino interventor represented to paulistas from a wide range of social backgrounds, many of whom had no *direct* stake in "the social question"—the euphemistic term for class conflict in that era.[27] My preference for this approach reflects a number of assumptions, including my argument above that "interests" and identities are formed or reworked in the process of political conflicts rather than simply preceding and causing them. Discourses that historians previously tended to dismiss as mere facades are, in my interpretation, important constitutive elements of regional identity.

My approach also reflects one of my most fundamental departures from an earlier social-history literature. Whereas critical accounts of the uprising have assumed that there was little popular or mass support for the movement, and even questionable commitment within sectors of the elite, I am arguing here that the Causa Paulista in fact elicited strong support from large portions of the regional population.[28] Once we acknowledge the involvement of so many paulistas who could hardly be defined as members of the oligarchy or bourgeoisie (an issue that I will explore at greater length in chapter 3), we either need to subscribe to the highly problematic notion of ideological manipulation, or we have to seek to understand the meanings and tangible appeals of paulista identity and regional chauvinism, and why these could motivate so many people to participate in the anti-Vargas insurrection and risk their lives for the Causa Paulista.

As should be apparent, unlike many earlier studies, my primary purpose here is not to reconstruct the events or even explain the causes of the 1932 uprising. For this study, the important question is not exactly "what happened?" or even "why did it happen?" (although I am indebted to earlier studies that did take up these questions), but rather I am asking what political and cultural discourses and images "compelled" a sizable portion of the paulista population to join a movement that placed their region at violent odds with the federal government, and *how* leaders and participants in that movement crafted a regional identity that set São Paulo apart *and above* the rest of Brazil. And to do so, I would argue that we need to go beyond the earlier emphasis on class interests and partisan ambitions as a way to understand the intentions and limitations of the Constitutionalist Movement, and broaden our analysis to incorporate the categories of gender and, especially, race, which informed so much of the rhetoric and practices of the Constitutionalist Campaign.

As the previous chapter sought to demonstrate, a sense of São Paulo having a special role and destiny in the Brazilian nation long preceded the 1932 uprising. And by extension, the same can be said about the association of paulista regional identity with progress, modernity, and whiteness. As early as the turn of the century, Euclides da Cunha could declare in his masterwork, *Os sertões*, that "today, same as 200 years ago, the progress of São Paulo can still be seen as the progress of Brazil."[29] And a decade before São Paulo took up arms against the provisional government, a visitor from the Rockefeller Foundation could reflect in his report that "the northern boundary of the State of São Paulo divides Brazil into two sections presenting contrasts, with respect to populations, as sharp as those between Mexico and the United States"—a statement whose racial connotations hardly require elaboration.[30] Yet as long as São Paulo's hegemonic position, prior to 1930, could be treated as "established fact," it could also "go without saying."[31] Residents or natives of São Paulo could see themselves as "paulista" without giving much thought to what that might mean; and could engage in self-congratulatory rhetoric about their home region's singular success without going into much detail about why São Paulo had become so much more prosperous than other Brazilian states, or about what implications this might suggest for the future of the Brazilian nation. But once that hegemonic position came under fire, a number of different groups within paulista society found it increasingly urgent to explain, define, and fix the meaning of paulistinidade.[32]

There are many different ways to explore the meanings and workings of regional identity in São Paulo, but no episode seems more fortuitous for this purpose than the regional insurgency (civilian and military) from 1931 to 1932. The Constitutionalist Revolution of 1932 was a crucial moment for considering what it meant to be paulista, how this related to being Brazilian, and what this implied for other regional identities. Though São Paulo's act of defiance promptly ended in utter defeat, I would argue that the experience and memory of the uprising became an essential component of paulista identity. Moreover, the region's enduring position as the dominant economic center of the Brazilian nation allowed a particular racialized construction of paulista identity—and Brazilian modernity—to survive and thrive long after the Constitutionalist forces had laid down their arms.

A Note on Sources and Voices

One advantage enjoyed by the historian studying a movement that mobilized significant numbers of people from relatively educated and prosperous families is the extensive written material that participants have left in their wake. São Paulo at the time of the Constitutionalist Campaign had a robust periodical press, with over a dozen daily newspapers and assorted weekly and monthly journals, as well as a diverse and dynamic intellectual community that wrote and published ongoing commentaries on the political issues of the moment.[33] In addition, there were many literate paulistas who were not journalists, politicians, or intellectuals, but who were moved by the drama and emotion of the Guerra Cívica (Civic War) to pen letters, memoirs, manifestos, anthems, and poetry about their feelings and experiences.[34] Transcripts of notable radio broadcasts, which were a crucial means of rallying the population, were preserved in published form, and visual materials—photographs, films, posters, cartoons, sheet music and magazine covers, and so on—remain available in abundance.[35] And aside from the documentation produced during the Constitutionalist Campaign and uprising, there are the many retrospective accounts published by veterans of the movement, some of them written immediately after the events in question, and others authored or reedited years later.

The sheer quantity of materials produced by this relatively short-lived movement and uprising is a significant datum in and of itself. The paulistas' critics routinely claimed that the constant barrage of propaganda from the media, both press and radio, presumably orchestrated by the politicians and journalists who formed the Frente Única, was the principal mechanism for creating the overheated atmosphere that led to the uprising. Even a number of paulista memoirists who sympathized with the cause later recollected feeling initially hesitant or skeptical, but then finding the constant media appeals to paulista pride impossible to resist. One eventual volunteer recalled the desire to declare that they were all being "despicably deceived by a half-dozen unscrupulous journalists at the service of politicians without conscience."[36] This might seem to confirm the claim that the campaign was masterminded by a handful of resentful politicians who, using emerging forms of mass culture, manipulated a pliant public into a mass mobilization.[37] But that assumes that a small coterie monopolized the production of discourses and images, and that most paulistas passively received these messages, a very problematic assumption. At the same time, it is undeniable that certain individuals and groups "conspired" to heighten emotions, engender a movement, and incite protest against the federal government, and were far more likely than others to have access to the means of communication or to be in a position to script, shape, and censure public pronouncements.[38] The challenge for the historian is to figure out not only who is producing the language and images that constitute a particular political discourse, but how these are being circulated, and how they are being received, and perhaps then being reproduced or reshaped by those not involved in their initial production.

As the previous chapter should make evident, those crafting the rhetoric that made the mobilization possible were not inventing ideas and images out of thin air. Instead, they were drawing on several decades of scholarly, creative, and journalistic writing and images that helped form a regional identity and a sense of paulista exceptionalism. The increasing circulation and density of such discourses and imagery at a moment when old political arrangements had been disrupted and destabilized, and new ones were being hotly contested, undoubtedly served to create a widespread identification with the Causa Paulista throughout the state. And it is also undeniable that certain figures and factions had louder voices in the public sphere than others. Eminent poets and popular orators like Guilherme de Almeida and Ibrahim Nobre (dubbed the "Tribune of the Revolution") played an active role in stimulating the emotional atmosphere crucial to creating mass support for the movement. Journalists, politicians, and intellectuals who participated in the merging of the PRP and the PD into the Frente Única—Alfredo Ellis Júnior, Menotti del Picchia, Altino Arantes, Paulo Nogueira Filho, Paulo Duarte, Waldemar Ferreira, Júlio de Mesquita Filho, Aureliano Leite, and others—had ample means to disseminate their definition(s) of the Constitutionalist Campaign, as well as to shape the collective memory of the events of 1932.[39] Avid support from the Catholic hierarchy meant that even while worshipping in Church, paulistas would hear a sermon invoking the righteousness of the Constitutionalist cause,[40] but it was the omnipresence of the radio that turned pro-paulista propaganda into something approximating the "voice of God"—a speaker who could be heard almost anywhere at any time, and could create a sense of a statewide listening public all tuned into the same "revolutionary" wavelength.[41]

Thus, it is certainly true that there was a degree of orchestration of the popular fervor that made the uprising possible. At the same time, the massive turnouts for rallies and protests—both in the capital and in cities like Piracicaba, Campinas, Santos, and Franca—and the multitude of impromptu speeches, handwritten poems, and homemade posters indicates an audience that was already quite receptive to the messages being circulated, or that needed little prompting to engage with them. Indeed, one of the themes in various memoirs was the impossibility of restraining popular sentiment, or reversing the tide in favor of revolt, after the movement had gained a certain momentum. In his luridly titled *Martírio e glória de São Paulo*, Aureliano Leite issued the following caution: "Politicians, don't take it upon yourselves to guide the people in their eagerness to react. If some politicians previously possessed prestige among the masses to lead them, in this or that predicament, now they would be crushed by the population of Piratininga if they tried so much as a small maneuver; now don't even think of saying that you might intend to divert them from their path."[42] Although this depiction of an unstoppable popular will is surely exaggerated, it seems less farfetched than the notion of an otherwise indifferent populace being propelled into action by a barrage of media propaganda.

Furthermore, it's important to keep in mind that until May 1932, there were no significant restraints on media coverage or popular expression— mainstream newspapers such as *A Razão* and *Correio da Tarde*, which openly opposed the Frente Única, continued to publish, as did various periodicals from the working-class press such as *A Plebe*, which denounced both the Vargas government *and* the Constitutionalist crusade. While the escalating ardor of the paulista movement meant that more conciliatory voices, such as the democráticos J. A. Marrey Jr. and Vicente Ráo, or undecided figures such as José Maria Whitaker, were unlikely to get a full public hearing, it was still possible to argue for reconciliation with Vargas or against taking up arms without risking prison or worse.[43] After the twenty-third of May, when paulista protesters clashed with Miguel Costa's Revolutionary Legion, and an insurgent cabinet seized the state government, this was no longer the case: civil defense groups and Constitutionalist crowds attacked the offices of dissenting periodicals and threatened anyone who openly opposed the movement with violent retaliation.[44] And once the war began, predictably, the state authorities tightened control over the circulation of news, especially from the front. U.S. consular and embassy officials, including some quite sympathetic to the paulistas, commented on the highly distorted and absurdly optimistic reporting on the combat zones and the outcomes of various battles in the Constitutionalist-controlled press; coverage at this point seems to have crossed the line from highly partisan opinion to deliberate deception in the hopes of maintaining popular enthusiasm and a steady stream of volunteers.[45]

Even taking the wartime censorship of critical commentary into account, it seems inadequate, and perhaps misleading, to argue that the discourses and imagery of the Constitutionalist Movement merely represented the thinking and interests of a narrow group of politicians and politically affiliated intellectuals and journalists, and that the vast majority of the movement's participants were somehow co-opted or manipulated into following these leaders. Ibrahim Nobre's oratory, larded with melodramatic metaphors and heated polemics, would have seemed as ludicrous then as it sounds now except for the fact that he was usually speaking to immense and highly receptive crowds who created a context within which such florid rhetoric seemed entirely appropriate.[46] Menotti del Picchia, whose avid support for the Constitutionalist Movement did not cloud his wry powers of observation, vividly described the scene on the twelfth of July, when General Klinger arrived in the train station of the state capital. There he was greeted by ecstatic crowds, led by Ibrahim Nobre, whose "allegorical and refined speech [was] very much to the people's taste and in the flavor of the moment." He then recounts Klinger's remarks about unleashing his sword in favor of the law, followed by his very public and ceremonial mounting of a steed, and concludes his account by remarking that "the dawning of the revolution was entirely composed of the spontaneous theatricality that surrounds all the great events of history."[47] At first glance, the phrase "spontaneous theatricality" may seem like an oxymoron since we think of theatrics as being rehearsed and performed—the precise opposite of spontaneity. But I would argue that Menotti's phrase aptly captures the phenomenon of scripted rhetoric transformed into something more emotional, meaningful, even spectacular, when performed for an enthusiastic audience, itself willing and eager to join in the performance that was essential to Ibrahim Nobre's effectiveness as an orator or General Klinger's magnetism as a military leader.

What about the voices of the "rank and file" Constitutionalists? Can we only hear them in the cheers of the crowd? Since the heyday of the new social history, historians of social movements and political insurgencies have sought to uncover multiple and diverse voices, and have particularly warned against listening only to elites. I would certainly agree that we should strive to incorporate sources and hear voices articulated from a variety of standpoints, and I seek to do so below, but I would also caution against expecting a substantially different perspective on the Causa Paulista from a document produced by someone who was not of the elite. The poetry that "ordinary" paulistas sent into newspapers exalting São Paulo's place in the Brazilian union reveals even less nuance and more chauvinism than the writings of the eminent public figures in the campaign.[48] In part because the Causa Paulista was so thoroughly linked to a discourse of regional identity, and because its timing was so condensed, this was a tightly scripted, nearly univocal movement with little time or room for expressive variation among its leaders and/or followers. In the aftermath of defeat, we can hear some discordance: one veteran will claim the elites abandoned the people,[49] another will regret that he and his fellow paulistas let their zeal cloud their judgment,[50] while yet another will express even deeper abhorrence for the Vargas regime and declare newly found separatist sympathies.[51] But none of the above, no matter how bitter or disillusioned, questioned the fundamental premise of paulista superiority.

Constitutionalism—A Regional or Political Identity?

The titles of the many chronicles and memoirs produced by the 1932 uprising and the events surrounding it offer us a number of different ways to refer to the eighty-seven-day conflict between the paulistas and Vargas's provisional government. Alfredo Ellis Jr. adopts the intimate title "Our War"; Menotti del Picchia "The Paulista Revolution"; Nogueira Filho "The Civic War"; and Mário de Andrade "São Paulo's War." And then there are the more "fanciful" titles, such as Paulo Duarte's "Palmares in Reverse" or Leven Vampré's "São Paulo, Conquered Land." But the "official name" for the uprising, judging from the mode of reference in the mainstream press and documents issued by the leadership, is "A Revolução Constitucionalista"—The Constitutionalist Revolution.[52] Thus, we need to ask why the struggle for a constitution—whether the preexisting one or a new one crafted by an elected constituent assembly—became the formal motto or theme of the Causa Paulista. Once again, the question is not whether the "true" motivation of the paulista leadership and its followers was a return to constitutional rule—a claim that Góes Monteiro so scornfully dismissed—but rather what ideological work was performed by constructing the movement as a "Constitutionalist Campaign." What kinds of meanings for the movement did this label reinforce? What meanings did it marginalize? And how did constitutionalism—a political cause that was not necessarily of paulista origin—help the leadership navigate the tensions between the national and the regional aspects of the movement?

The Aliança Liberal justified the overthrow of sitting president Washington Luís in 1930 by contending that the victory of his elected successor, Júlio Prestes, over Getúlio Vargas was the result of massive voter fraud—a claim that was reasonable enough given that it was the rare election under the Old Republic in which the results corresponded to the actual votes cast. Thus, the Revolution of 1930 could be presented as a justifiable response to an illegitimate state of political affairs.[53] Yet once it became clear that Vargas would not even sustain the fiction of upholding the Constitution of 1891, and was also in no rush to call elections for a new constituent assembly, the illegality or, more precisely, the non-legality of the new regime became a matter of concern in political circles, both civilian and military. Elections, whether fair or fraudulent, were a crucial mechanism for creating political parties and alliances and for allocating public offices. The idea that Vargas and his closest supporters—especially the unpredictable tenentes—would have a nearly free hand in rearranging the Brazilian political sphere was disconcerting to those who had a stake in the previous political system and social order, and perhaps even to many who had little to lose with the dismantling of the Old Republic.[54]

The democráticos in Sao Paulo, who had backed Vargas as an alternative to their regional rivals, the perrepistas, were among the first political groups to withdraw their support. Although a faction of the PD—much reviled by their fellow paulistas—remained in the getulista camp, the majority of the liberal-reformist party chafed at the double disappointment of Vargas appointing an outsider as interventor and his refusal to adhere to the PD's agenda of a rapid return to (a reformed) representative democracy. In response they took up the mantra of constitutionalism, which also attracted adherents in liberal-reformist political circles in Rio, Pernambuco, Bahia, Minas, Pará, and Rio Grande do Sul.[55] Indeed, some contemporary sources indicate that the Constitutionalist Movement, for a time, was as vigorous in Vargas's home state as it was in São Paulo. But in the states to the north, constitutionalism remained confined to certain elite and near-elite sectors of the population. Meanwhile, in Minas and Rio Grande do Sul the compromise worked out between the dominant political factions and the provisional government meant that *constitucionalismo* faced substantial opposition. It also led to the odd spectacle of erstwhile loyal getulistas, such as former minister of labor Lindolfo Collor, siding with the paulistas after the tenentes orchestrated the shutdown of an opposition daily in Rio.[56] As gaúcho politicians like Collor and João Neves da Fontoura broke with the "dictatorship," Republican machine politicians in Rio

Grande such as Flores da Cunha became stalwart supporters of the getulista government. Only in Sao Paulo—where the absence of constitutional rule could be articulated to a sense of regional grievance and humiliation—did the movement secure a mass following. This also moved the perrepistas to adopt the Constitutionalist motto, thus allowing an alliance of convenience between the two paulista political factions, who announced the formation of a Frente Única—a single front—in January 1932.[57]

The formation of the Frente Única por um São Paulo Unido fortuitously coincided with the four hundredth anniversary of the captaincy of São Vicente (as the captaincy/province of São Paulo was originally named by the Portuguese). Cities and towns throughout the state marked this quadricentennial with celebrations that doubled as political protests, with the largest and most explosive occurring, of course, in the state capital. Among the many calls to paulistanos to attend the commemorative event was a mimeographed flyer addressed "To the People of São Paulo" that described the gathering as "a grand assembly for the exaltation and apotheosis of São Paulo." It bore the signature of twenty-three different political, recreational, student, professional, and commercial organizations, including the Textile Manufacturers Syndicate, the Paulista Academy of Letters, the Association of Commercial Employees, the Associations of Bakery and Butcher Shop Owners, the Frente Negra Brasileira, and the Associação Cristã de Moços de São Paulo.[58]

Estimates of the number of celebrants cum protesters who congregated in the Praça da Sé on January 25 ranged between 100,000 and 200,000 persons. Accounts of the gathering (all by sympathetic observers) are interesting for their insistence on three aspects of the rally. One was its massive character, typically described as unprecedented in the history of São Paulo; second was the fervor and intensity of feeling in the crowd that gathered that day; and third, in light of the tenor of the crowd, the remarkable discipline and orderliness of the gathering throughout the proceedings.[59] This last feature was clearly meant to strike a contrast with the disorderly protests, sackings, and vandalism (*quebra-quebras*) associated with popular groups, and especially those that supported the "dictatorship." In effect, the accounts were portraying a genuinely unprecedented event: a massive demonstration that was characterized by a middle-class notion of public comportment. This is not to accept the chroniclers' implied disparagement of popular protests; labor unions typically insisted on discipline among their members, and "disorderliness" often was the result of police assaults on working-class rallies.[60] It is not that *only* the middle class could be orderly, nor that all the demonstrators were white, male, and middle class—which they surely were not—but that the organizers

9 DE JULHO DE 1932

SÃO PAULO EM ARMAS PELO BRASIL!
(desenho alegórico de BELMONTE)

FIGURE 2.1. Drawing of volunteer with Bandeirante, Tiradentes, and the Law. Illustration by Belmonte, from *Álbum de Família, 1932* (São Paulo: Livraria Martins Editora, 1954).

and chroniclers made such a point of foregrounding the self-control of the protesters *despite* the generalized intensity of feeling in the crowd. The image conveyed is of a muscular middle class able to be simultaneously outraged and orderly, and thus eminently fit for public life.[61]

The dominant discursive tendencies within the Causa Paulista translated this emphasis on order into the motivation or rationale for the Constitutionalist Campaign. According to this argument, the paulistas were revolting not to subvert authority, even less to promote radical change, but to demand the rule of law. Once the civil war began, one of the many recruiting posters issued by the insurgent state government showed a modern volunteer shadowed by historical bandeirantes and clutching a volume entitled "LEX" to his manly breast (see fig. 2.1).

Indeed, the identification between military service and support for the law became so ubiquitous that when a family member volunteered to fight for the Causa Paulista, that home could proudly display a sign that announced "From

FIGURE 2.2. Poster—"From This House a Soldier of the Law Departed." Courtesy of the coleção iconográfico do Arquivo Público do Estado de São Paulo.

This House a Soldier of the Law Departed" (see fig. 2.2). Even when resorting to violence, a paulista could claim to be, first and foremost, a defender of law and order. Moreover, while this motivation might seem to be, at first glance, devoid of any particular regional connotations, the insistence that only paulistas (or those at the same stage of civilization as the paulistas) genuinely required or desired the rule of law turned what could have been a universal axiom into a regionalized slogan, and drew an equivalence between the campaign for the "rule of law" and a crusade for paulista hegemony.[62]

Regionalism as Racism

In his essay on "Racist Ideologies and the Media," Stuart Hall defines "inferential racism" as "those apparently naturalized representations . . . which have racist premises and propositions inscribed in them as a set of *unquestioned assumptions*. These enable racist statements to be formulated without ever bringing into awareness the racist predicates on which the statements are grounded."[63] Though Hall developed this concept with a very different "media" and historical moment in mind, it can still serve as an appropriate starting point for a discussion of racism and paulista regionalist discourses. In the early 1930s, even before the publication of Gilberto Freyre's *Casa-Grande e senzala*, and well before "racial democracy" became a defining feature of the imagined Brazilian nation, it had become impolitic to speak too overtly about racial difference in the public sphere.[64] Of course, this did not mean that no one in Brazil discussed race or openly uttered what we would consider racist language. On the contrary, the sources—both those aimed at scholarly readers and those targeted at wider audiences—are replete with overt references to race as an aspect of paulista identity and Brazilian society.[65] Nonetheless, the leadership of the Constitutionalist Movement rarely couched its goals and concerns in explicitly racial terms. Significantly, one of the few instances of this that I have encountered was a remark by the U.S. consul who claimed that São Paulo was "fighting for its white man's culture." In private, many "white" paulistas might have concurred with his assessment, but few would have expressed such motives in public.

Thus, I could imagine my concern with race and racism being dismissed by some as the typical fixation of a North American historian accustomed to a society where, historically, race has been a crucial axis of domination and division. Yet my point is not to produce startling revelations about the use of racist tropes and arguments, or to claim that the 1932 uprising was "really about race." Rather, it is to urge historians to look at the way in which that episode reinforced certain racialized understandings about the unevenness of Brazilian development, and promoted particular ways of defining whiteness together with modernity in Brazilian society. My objective is not to comb the writings, speeches, images, and so forth, of the Causa Paulista to expose the "real" racism beneath the "phony" racially tolerant rhetoric. Even less do I intend to argue that São Paulo was peculiarly racist compared to the rest of Brazil. What I am interested in is the particular way in which race becomes embedded in certain visions of modernity and progress so that they become and remain associated with whiteness—and not just from the paulista point of view.

We also need to be alert to the racist implications—or to use Hall's phrase, the inferential racism—of political discourse in this period precisely because open assertions of white supremacy were on the wane both in Brazil and beyond its borders. By the 1930s the era of biological or scientific racism was over, and despite some publications in Brazil by diehard advocates of racial science—such as Alfredo Ellis Jr.'s *Populações paulistas*, or Oliveira Vianna's *Raça e assimilação*—racial difference was increasingly being couched in historical/cultural terms. At the same time, certain "immutable" characteristics would continue to be attributed to Brazilians according to their region of origin, both in elite and popular culture.[66] Even as discourses of civilization, modernity, and progress replaced earlier preoccupations with race mixture and degeneration, notions of difference based on race (broadly construed), far from fading, flourished in new discursive contexts. Unless we regard more contemporary racisms as nothing more than lingering vestiges of older racial regimes, we need to consider how certain hierarchies and exclusions get reproduced, refurbished, and reinscribed even as their intellectual foundations seem to shift or dissolve.

Although expressions of paulistinidade that long preceded the Constitutionalist Movement fed the rhetoric and images that emerged in the early 1930s, I would mark the beginning of this intense period of regional identity formation with the appointment of João Alberto as interventor. Under the Old Republic the most crucial distinction between more and less powerful regions had been immunity from or vulnerability to federal intervention.[67] And whereas after 1930 ruling political factions in Minas Gerais and Rio Grande do Sul—states regarded as crucial and more reliable supporters of the October Revolution—retained the prerogative of choosing their own governors, São Paulo found itself ignominiously grouped with the poorer and less politically influential states of the Norte/Nordeste that were also subject to federal interventors appointed by Vargas.[68] And to make matters much worse, João Alberto was a native of Pernambuco, a feature of his biography that soon became a basis for vicious denunciations of his administration.

It is no surprise that the year 1932, which saw the emergence of a full-blown Constitutionalist Campaign, the seizure of the state government by an insurgent paulista cabinet, and the onset and defeat of the actual armed conflict between São Paulo and the federal forces, was a time when regional leaders forged particularly heated defenses of paulista superiority and unusually derogatory depictions of Brazilians from (certain) other regions, making explicit the assumptions that might remain implicit during normal times. Paulistas with access to the public sphere fulsomely celebrated the civic virtues of the regional population, which they routinely attributed to its more civilized and cultured character. In speeches, scholarly texts, polemical essays, and poetry, paulistas and their supporters extolled the civic and moral fiber of the povo bandeirante, and made a direct association between their region's economic progress, "stage of civilization," and concern for the rule of law.[69] Or as modernist poet Menotti del Picchia contended, "[the rule of] law is only interesting" to societies that are "cultured and policed."[70]

Though the paeans to São Paulo had a shared language and tone, they typically represented a mélange of different, and sometimes contradictory, discourses and tropes. Here, it might be useful to think of paulista discourse in this period as a palimpsest, with new themes and ideas being inscribed upon previous ones that had been effaced but not entirely erased. Consequently, a historian would look in vain for a consistent line of argument or logic in the way paulistas—including leading intellectual figures—crafted their claims about the superiority of their region in the early 1930s. For example, Alfredo Ellis Jr. seems at first glance to be the quintessential proponent of scientific racism, willing to make a case for paulista superiority in the most nakedly racially deterministic terms. In his *Confederação ou separação?*, published in early 1932, Ellis emphasized two themes: the ethnic "divergence" of the various regions of Brazil, and the extremely uneven development of these regions (with one obviously being, to him, a consequence of the other). Both features, he argued, had become much more pronounced since the abolition of slavery and the transition from monarchy to republic, as immigration further "whitened" São Paulo and the state emerged as by far the wealthiest in the nation.[71]

Ellis, unlike some of his more temperate colleagues in the movement, never shrank from deploying explicitly racial (and racist) "evidence" and arguments. For example, while acknowledging that *all* Brazilian regions had some mixture of races, he claimed that São Paulo was 85 percent "pure white," while Bahia was a mere 33 percent. He then argued—using a mash-up of color-based categories and biotypes—that such racial "divergences" automatically translated into weak national ties: "It would be pure sentimental lyricism if we were to regard as brothers of a *dolico-louro* from Rio Grande do Sul, of a *brachy-moreno* from S. Paulo, or of a *dolico-moreno* from Minas, a *platycephalo amongoilado* from Sergipe or Ceará, or a *negro* from Pernambuco."[72] Hence, in Ellis's view, one could detect a family resemblance among the blonds and brunettes of the more central and southern states, but that family could hardly include the "mongoloid flatheads" and "negros" of the Northeast.

None of the above is especially startling, given Ellis's intellectual background as a historian/ethnologist whose work on the bandeirantes helped construct the legend of a "race of giants" on the paulista plateau. What is less predictable is that most of Ellis's arguments in this text are not directly derived from racial categories, but instead rely on much more "mainstream" notions of São Paulo as culturally, civically, and economically superior. Indeed, the majority of the book consists of economic arguments in favor of paulista autonomy in the face of Vargas's centralizing thrust, with particular emphasis (amply illustrated by dozens of tables) on São Paulo's massive contribution to the federal treasury. Thus, as his argument unfolds, the *explicitly* racist elements fade, but then reemerge in the context of a language of stages of civilization, a concept that Ellis imbues with a range of cultural and political implications.[73]

Similarly, in *A nossa guerra*, Ellis contends that the *nortistas* support the Vargas dictatorship because their stage of civilization/economic development makes a "constitutional regime" unnecessary: "These small states, that have a much more backward level of civilization, much less economic development, etc., do not have the same needs [as São Paulo]."[74] We can find a similar multiplicity or heterogeneity in explanations for São Paulo's economic progress, with Ellis the racial determinist arguing at one point that the region's economic surge was due to a fortuitous coincidence of fertile soil and good timing, a position that a twenty-first-century economic historian might endorse. In contrast, Roberto Simonsen—generally regarded as a more "objective" historical scholar than Ellis, little influenced by racial thinking—evoked the classic regional chauvinist view that the paulista's capacity for hard work, dating back to the time of the bandeirantes, was the factor that best explained São Paulo's economic preeminence.[75] Surveying this mélange of ideological assumptions, we might be tempted to label only the explicit references to race as "racist" and assign racial rhetoric only a minor role in the formation of paulista identity during this era. But I would argue just the opposite since even those marshaling arguments having to do with stages of civilization, or the impact of climate or immiseration, were referring to circumstances that they regarded as producing innate characteristics that naturalized the hierarchical differences between São Paulo state and the other regions of Brazil. These are inferentially racialized arguments even when those articulating them aren't resorting to overtly racist language.[76]

Again, one of the reasons for the motley character of pro-paulista discourse in this era is its chronological coincidence with rejections of the more deterministic views of race, climate, and geography (a response, in part, to the looming threat in Europe of movements that seemed ready to take these ideas to their ultimate consequences). But there are other factors besides the shifting transnational intellectual climate that explain the highly variegated discourses that undergirded paulista chauvinism. Among them were the multiple ideological positions from which intellectuals and politicians exalted São Paulo's progress and modernity. Thus, Ellis (a PRP stalwart) and Paulo Duarte (an early member of the PD) could both construct their position, in part, on the basis of Sao Paulo's "racial supremacy," but even an outspoken antiracist like Antonio Baptista Pereira declared that São Paulo would always be in the "forefront" of Brazil's march to modernity.[77] In other words, this equation of paulista identity with modernity and progress allowed it to absorb a number of different ideological positions and sensibilities, and incorporate significant portions of the paulista population into the movement.

Identifying the Enemy

If efforts to exalt São Paulo's dynamism and progress preceded the Revolution of 1930, what had previously been a secondary but muted theme—an unflattering contrast with the rest of Brazil—now came to the fore.[78] And even more striking was the way in which pro-paulista discourse rapidly condensed the rest of Brazil into an entity referred to either as the Norte or Nordeste (both terms being used in the 1930s, though the former appeared more often than the latter), which came to represent São Paulo's opposite or "other." Whereas earlier commentators, whether historians, journalists, or politicians, who advanced the notion of paulista superiority constructed relatively subtle comparisons between São Paulo (city) and the "Court" (i.e., Rio de Janeiro), now discussions of regional identity were increasingly structured around a dramatic *contrast* between São Paulo (state) and the Norte, with far more disparaging implications for São Paulo's newly significant "Other."[79] The most immediate explanation for this increasing emphasis on the Nordeste's inferiority/barbarity is the appointment of *pernambucano* João Alberto as interventor, but it also reflected (and fueled) a growing association between the Norte and the Vargas dictatorship. Indeed, one of the most striking features of paulista discourse during this period is the routine identification of Vargas's regime with the impoverished and largely nonwhite regions of northern/northeastern Brazil—despite the fact that Vargas and many of his closest advisers were from the far *South* of Brazil.[80] And in the process, the paulista leadership converted what might have become a national movement demanding the convening of a constituent assembly into a regional movement that was primarily, or for some, exclusively paulista (though until July 1932, there was still considerable expectation that the *mineiros* and gaúchos would join the paulistas in their struggle against the provisional government).[81] And I would argue, further, that the regionalization of the movement reinforced its associations with certain racial, class, and gender identities.

The animus built up against the nordestinos drew on a range of disparaging tropes and stereotypes, but the foundational premise of all anti-nortista sentiment was the enormous economic, social, and cultural gap between São Paulo and the North. This "abyss," to quote writers as diverse as Menotti del Picchia, Mário de Andrade, Ellis Júnior, and Vivaldo Coaracy, made it patently outrageous for the paulistas to be subjected to the rule of a northeasterner and his regional acolytes, all of whom, because of their origins (and in marked contrast to the paulistas), would acquiesce or even enthusiastically adhere to a lawless and despotic regime.[82] Once João Alberto had taken up his post in São Paulo, the paulista press routinely ran stories whose point was to demonstrate how out of place nordestinos—derisively portrayed as rustic bumpkins and buffoons—were in São Paulo's modern, cosmopolitan milieu, and how comically inadequate they were to the task of governing a progressive society like São Paulo.

The paulista public had already been primed for such mockery; in 1926 a highly successful theatrical revue entitled "Brasil Pitoresco—Viagem de Cornélio Pires ao Norte do Brasil" had entertained audiences with "the picturesque, exotic, bizarre, ridiculous features of their Northern brothers."[83] Five years later, journalists and other writers regularly referred to nortistas as "cabeças chatas"—roughly, "flatheads"—which Ellis claimed, with a discernible lack of conviction, was meant as a term of endearment. In a similar vein, Leven Vampré insisted that "we [paulistas] have no prejudices based on race, color, or locale," but then goes on to refer to the nordestinos as "those formidable flat-headed Brazilians."[84] Mário de Andrade, drawing on material from his stint as editor of the *Diário Nacional*, put together a collection of anecdotes relating to this period, several of them organized around the comical "astonishment" of the nortistas at the modernity of the paulistas. And on a less jovial note, a pro-paulista manifesto directed at the cariocas referred to the Vargas regime as "um bando negregado de aventureiros," which roughly translates as "a negro'd band of adventurers."[85] Although such remarks tended to be directed at Brazilians outside of São Paulo, they inevitably had implications for people of color and humble origins closer to home. Thus perrepista Renato Jardim, in denouncing the "fascism and Bolshevism" of João Alberto and Miguel Costa's followers, claimed that "within a few days" of the arrival of the Revolutionary Legion, "there wasn't a single old black or newsboy in São Paulo who wasn't in the streets showing off his red armband."[86]

The most consistent and caustic mouthpiece for anti-nordestino sentiment was *O Separatista*, the short-lived weekly paper of the secessionist faction in São Paulo that filled its columns with degrading caricatures and racist commentaries about the nordestinos in their midst. In a bit of genocidal "humor," *O Separatista* playfully claimed that the paulistas were planning to erect a monument to the murderous northeastern bandit Lampião, in gratitude for his role in reducing the population of the Nordeste.[87] But the self-avowed separatists, widely regarded in São Paulo as a fringe group, were not the sole source of such extreme views. Paulo Duarte, in his polemic against the provisional government's treatment of São Paulo (and of Vargas's erstwhile supporters in the PD), described João Alberto governing São Paulo as performing "the same role as those negroes in Dakar, with top hat on their head and bare feet on the floor, who are convinced that they occupy the high position of 'French citizen.'"[88] The beleaguered pernambucano could even be turned into a verb: one of the most public faces of the Constitutionalist Movement, the poet and orator Ibrahim Nobre, would write in 1933 that like Germany, which was implementing "anti-Jewish prophylaxis," São Paulo should have sought to eliminate the "organisms" that "joão-albertized" (joanalbertisaram) its blood.[89] True, Duarte and Nobre tended toward the hysterical in their comments about 1932, but a more moderate and thoughtful commentator, such as Paulo Nogueira Filho (a self-styled "progressive bourgeois"), also larded his account of this period with claims that João Alberto, and the nortistas in general, were incompetent to rule São Paulo and had despicable intentions, including the desire to turn São Paulo into "a feudal estate."[90]

Especially elaborate expressions of anti-nordestino sentiment can be found in the polemics authored by Júlio de Mesquita Filho, publisher of the state's most prestigious daily, O Estado de São Paulo. Writing two decades later, in response to the publication of João Alberto's memoirs, Mesquita described the 1932 uprising as "a clash between the Brazil that was organically differentiated and the Brazil of the horde. In other words, it was civilization and barbarism that would meet to fight each other on the lands of the South Atlantic." He then goes on to say that it was beyond the mental capacity of João Alberto, "a mere artillery lieutenant," to understand what was going on in São Paulo, and then situates him within the stereotypical symbols of nordestino culture: "Thus it was only natural that he couldn't comprehend the true meaning of all that was unfolding around him, the drama resulting from the collision of two different mentalities, of two different conceptions of society, between the frontier and the Northeast, on one side, and order, social discipline and progress, on the other. Born under the sign of Padre Cícero and raised to admire [bandits] Antônio Silvino and Lampião, the social determinism of the milieu in which he spent his youth impelled him to side with Getúlio Vargas, man of the horde."[91]

The concept of "the Two Brazils"—one, a modern, progressive, cosmopolitan version concentrated on or near the coast, and the other, traditional, even backward, stranded in time in the backlands—long predated the 1932 uprising. Its most famous iteration is Euclides da Cunha's classic, Os sertões (1902), though that book's concluding pages made it evident that the boundaries between these two "nations" were not as fixed or stable as the author had imagined at the outset.[92] Constitutionalist discourse seized upon the crudest version of the Two Brazils, and condensed the poles of comparison even further, so that one pole was São Paulo, which embodied the modern, successful Brazil, and the other pole was the North, and really the Nordeste, figured as the failed Brazil—a land of unrelenting poverty and backwardness.[93]

This construction of the North as São Paulo's enemy did a great deal of ideological work for the Constitutionalist Movement. In practical political terms, it allowed the paulista leadership to continue to call upon elites and the middle classes in Minas, Rio Grande do Sul, even in the Federal District, to support their movement, and thus maintain the possibility that the other half of the Two Brazils could be extended beyond the geopolitical boundaries of São Paulo. While this "North versus South" configuration of the conflict never materialized, it strengthened the paulistas' hand to keep it alive as a possibility. Equally important, it allowed the paulistas to present their movement as a conflict between regions, as opposed to a conflict between one region and the federal government, or worse, between region and nation. Rather than being regional separatists or traitors, as their adversaries charged, from the perspective of São Paulo versus the Norte, the paulistas could position themselves as defenders of the "nation of laws."[94]

Perhaps most significant for my argument is the way in which this construction of the conflict allowed the paulistas to deploy a racialized explanation for the political rifts and economic gulfs in Brazilian society without necessarily having to use explicitly racial language. As we can see, there were many prominent paulistas who did not shrink from using racial arguments and racist language in certain venues. But most of the leadership would have disavowed any racially based motives for their actions. Rather, they generally claimed to share in the widely held belief that Brazil was a racially harmonious nation, devoid of harsh, North American–style racial prejudice, and that comments or actions that were explicitly racist were somehow "un-Brazilian."[95] Even Ellis contended that paulistas (by which he obviously meant *white* paulistas, an adjective that he would have regarded as superfluous) merely felt a certain "distaste" for blacks, in contrast to the "abhorrence" (*ódio*) evinced by (white) North Americans.[96]

The apparent contradiction between claims of racial harmony and evidence of racist thinking was hardly peculiar to São Paulo; elites everywhere in Brazil insisted on the absence of racial prejudice while maintaining and enjoying the privileges of whiteness.[97] However, it might be argued that São Paulo, with its massive European immigrant communities and its marginalized population of African descent, was a location where the flimsiness of claims about racial harmony would prove particularly palpable. Several recent studies have established that, within Brazil, the people of African descent who were the most likely to identify as "black" and to organize politically around their "blackness" were Afro-paulistas precisely because they routinely experienced exclusion or marginalization due to their skin color, and that even "mulattos" often found themselves relegated to the margins of paulista society.[98] But paulistas (white and not white) could still point to eminent scholarly and intellectual figures like Teodoro Sampaio, or Mário de Andrade himself, to prove that men of (some) color with sufficient talent could rise in paulista society. And like Brazilians elsewhere, they could insist on the absence of formal, de jure discrimination (though this was not entirely true—until 1932, the urban police force known as the Civil Guard was a "whites only" institution) as evidence of their shared Brazilian vocation for racial harmony.[99] Not only was a disavowal of explicit racism a way to undercut claims that the paulistas were un-Brazilian (or even anti-Brazilian), but such affirmations of racial inclusion became increasingly urgent as the movement shifted into the militarized phase of the struggle. Once the Constitutionalists' first priority became putting as many armed men as possible on the battlefield, a discourse that threatened to exclude substantial portions of the state's inhabitants from the Causa Paulista became inopportune, to say the least.

At the same time, avowals of racial tolerance did not mean foregoing racialized appeals to regional pride since these could be articulated to an anti-nordestino discourse that was racially inflected but not explicitly linked to a black/white axis of difference. Indeed, while the figure of the nordestino was clearly racialized—that is, defined by innate qualities/defects derived from place of birth—it was also a highly unstable, even fluid racial "type." At one moment a typical nortista might be a figure called *cabeça chata*, a pejorative stereotype to be sure, but one that cannot easily be accommodated by a conventional spectrum of skin color or origin. At another moment, he would be represented as a mulatto, and over time, as the term *bahiano* became synonymous with nordestino, the nortista was increasingly assumed to be of African descent.[100] Such inconsistency, far from being a problem, was expedient for a movement that based its political claims on a hierarchy of regional identities, but did not (and perhaps could not) openly avow an ideology of white supremacy.

Furthermore, whereas "simple" racism—that is, disdain for those with darker skin and more "negroid" features—might seem both un-Brazilian and arbitrary, even irrational, the paulista's contempt for the nordestino could be presented as a reflection of sociological reality. São Paulo, after all, *was* far wealthier, more urbanized and industrialized, than the states that constituted what became known as the Nordeste. Although the heyday of the ideology of national development was still two decades away, Brazilians of every region and social class already widely embraced the idea that commercial agriculture, urban growth, and industrial production were the foundations of national progress.[101] The very notion of development carried within it an image of those who forged ahead and those who lagged behind. The paulista Constitutionalists may have pushed this language of progress and development to its extremes, but they were echoing sentiments that were widely held throughout Brazil. Indeed, even in the Nordeste, elites increasingly appealed to the federal government for assistance by emphasizing the misery and backwardness of their home region.[102] In other words, the paulistas, in asserting their "right" to hegemony or autonomy, could draw upon a narrative of economic progress that was already widely familiar and credible in political and even popular circles throughout Brazil. And imbedded in this narrative were assumptions about what "peoples" were most fit to produce a society that was modern, progressive, and civilized.

All for São Paulo: Separatism and the 1932 Uprising

Since the most intensely studied civil war in the history of the Americas involved a region attempting to secede from a national union, it is hardly surprising to learn that a regional revolt against the federal government in Brazil both involved some secessionist sentiment and was widely reviled as separatist. It is also not surprising that São Paulo's adversaries sought to equate the Constitutionalist Movement with the separatist faction, thereby heightening the accusation that the paulistas were traitors to the nation, or were quite literally un-Brazilian and therefore unfit to lead the nation. To limit the potential damage from charges of separatism, the Constitutionalist leadership went so far as to ban publication of *O Separatista* in the months leading up to the outbreak of the civil war and strenuously disavowed any secessionist intent in the Causa Paulista.[103] Paulo Nogueira Filho mentions in his chronicle of the Guerra Cívica that at the massive rally on January 25, 1932, someone grabbed the microphone and yelled, "Long Live the Republic of São Paulo!" receiving approving cheers from the crowd. But Nogueira Filho dismisses this as a distraction from the main themes of the rally. In his chronicle of the campaign and uprising, he does acknowledge the "the exacerbation of regionalist sentiments in Piratininga." It was this intensified "collective state of mind, that had nothing, but absolutely nothing, of the separatist in it, that was identified . . . perversely, as a treacherous secessionism."[104]

FIGURE 2.3. Paulista separatist drawing depicting other Brazilian states as babies feeding off the "milch cow," São Paulo. Courtesy of the coleção iconográfico do Arquivo Público do Estado de São Paulo.

This is a perfect example of how the exigencies of political struggle and battles for power lead to the marginalization of some ideological positions and the foregrounding of others. Not that secession from the Brazilian union was ever a mainstream position within the Constitutionalist Movement—however much the paulistas might disparage the rest of Brazil as "twenty empty boxcars" or as babies feeding off the paulista milk cow (see fig. 2.3). This did not necessarily imply a rejection of the Brazilian nation per se. Aside from extensive affective, intellectual, and economic ties with other regions of Brazil, as long as there was some hope of an alliance with Minas and Rio Grande do Sul, even a hypothetical discussion of secession in the public sphere would have been extremely impolitic. The paulista Constitutionalists even went so far as to revise some revered emblems and symbols to rid them of the taint of separatism. Thus the state motto "Pro São Paulo Fiant Eximia" (For São Paulo Great Things Will be Done) became "Pro Brasilia Fiant Eximia" (For Brazil Great Things Will Be Done).[105]

In a literal sense, the denunciations of the Causa Paulista as a separatist plot were wildly exaggerated. Although there is no way to calculate their numbers, the segment of the anti-Vargas movement that supported an actual secession from Brazil was surely quite small. They were also somewhat shadowy, making it difficult to attach specific names to the faction.[106] One group whose spokesman was Bráulio dos Santos refused in mid-1931 to affiliate with the newly formed Liga de Defesa Paulista unless it came out in favor of a separatist program. The Liga responded by skirting the issue—neither embracing nor entirely denying separatist sympathies—a position that was more feasible in 1931, when the movement was first taking shape.[107] By the following year, there were few mainstream organizations that would countenance an affiliation with the overtly separatist factions.

As is often the case with a "fringe" group, however, their limited numbers and extremist views did not necessarily prevent the separatists from influencing more conventional participants, or from injecting their views of the regional conflict into the broader paulista campaign. At the height of the movement, some prominent paulistas privately expressed separatist sympathies. For example, Monteiro Lobato wrote to state minister of justice Waldemar Ferreira in August 1932 (prematurely) insisting that once they had achieved victory, they should adhere to the formula "Hegemony or Separation."[108] Moreover, the arguments for a related position—the demand for "full autonomy"—significantly overlapped with the separatist rationale. The most explicit version of this can be found in Ellis's polemic, *Confederação ou separação?* (1932), and a similar position can be found in works by T. de Souza Lobo and Vivaldo Coaracy.[109] In effect, these authors were calling for a degree of self-rule that differed only slightly from a demand for complete separation, and was predicated on a similar assumption that São Paulo had little or nothing to gain, and perhaps more to lose, from a continued relationship with the rest of Brazil. According to Ellis, the (getulista) revolutionaries of 1930 "cut the last cord that tied São Paulo to Brazil, the tie of sentimentalism." And Nogueira Filho readily admitted that, as the movement shifted into the armed phase of the struggle, "separatism dissolved into autonomist aspirations."[110] Many paulistas who would have been horrified at the thought of secession may well have sympathized with the call for complete autonomy, which was, in effect, what the leadership demanded when it seized control of the state government in May 1932.

The small but noisome group of paulistas who openly advocated separatism—what we might call nation building by other means—felt free to employ the most nakedly racist rhetoric. After all, they had no need to adhere to established codes of Brazilian public speech about race or to curry favor with the mineiros and gaúchos; and their political project depended upon invoking as negative a portrait of the rest of Brazil as possible, even on creating a sense of revulsion toward Brazilians of other regions. Predictably, the separatists expressed their strongest animus toward northerners or northeasterners—again, given the severe poverty and economic decadence (now dubbed "backwardness") of the region, as well as its largely nonwhite population, it provided the perfect foil for claims about São Paulo's enormous superiority.[111] As noted above, their short-lived newspaper, *O Separatista*, often resorted to degrading caricature and racist humor to lampoon Brazilians of northeastern origin. Articles in the separatist press oscillated between jovial anecdotes about "Cétinho," a bumbling, ignorant and pretentious cabeça chata, and comparisons between nordestinos and "semi-barbarians who lived in bands like animals."[112] But in their moments of greatest despair, the separatists dropped the tattered veil of cordiality altogether and resorted to the most vicious forms of racial demagoguery, as they did in a manifesto issued after the October defeat that urged paulistas to pursue secession and opt for being a "small nation" rather than continue as "mere associates of an unviable homeland, dominated by mestizos who have the souls of slaves, and who are but one step removed from their ancestors whose bodies were enslaved both here and in Africa." The flyer went on to describe these rapacious invaders as "Sons of the slave quarters and misery, victims of destructive climates, encrusted with the grossest ignorance, a people who are losing human form, such is the physical degeneration that ravages them." It ended by denouncing the "mestizos born of slaves, the foul offspring of the slave quarters, who now wish to enslave you."[113]

Again, leading paulista politicians were keen to suppress openly proseparatist agitation that could serve to legitimize the getulistas' most damaging representations of the paulista movement and justify military repression, especially during the tense months prior to the uprising. And the first manifesto issued by the insurgent government after the call to arms on July 9, addressed "To the Brazilian People," carefully avoided incendiary or disparaging language.[114] But to my knowledge, no paulista politician took the separatists to task for their racist portrayals of other Brazilians; moreover, a comic strip that ran in the aptly named *Jornal das Trincheiras*—a newspaper distributed to the paulista soldiers on the frontlines——depicted *sertanejos* from the Northeast in ways that were only slightly less demeaning than those found in *O Separatista*. The "Adventures of Jeremias and Zoroastro—Soldiers of the Dictatorship" followed two sertanejo recruits who were far more comical than menacing, but who were clearly being sharply contrasted with the more modern, dignified, and savvy paulista soldier.[115] And in the waning days of the war, a column entitled "Two Civilizations" opened with a portrayal of the conflict as a struggle between the forces of "civilization and barbarism." The article continued:

In all dynamic, evolving social milieux, there exists . . . a large, inferior mass . . . of unadaptables, of those ruled by the atavistic complexes of the primitive states, that rebel against civilization and seek to lower the general social environment to an inferior level, in a degenerative process of regression. . . . History registered examples in which these elements succeed in dominating society. If the superior elements, the enlightened forces of the elite and the middle sectors capable of moving upward, don't react; if that dominion [of the inferior ranks] manages to perpetuate itself, the society is doomed.[116]

In a sense, the separatists played the role of the court fool in the Constitutionalist Movement—that is, freed from the inhibitions imposed by the need to maintain political respectability and brasilidade, they could indulge in the sort of vituperative denunciations of "Other" Brazilians that resonated with more publicly circumspect insurgents. Indeed, much of the paulista rhetoric in this period could be described as a toned-down or cleaned-up version of separatist polemics. And as the above quote demonstrates, occasionally the "toning down" was very slight indeed.

Region versus Nation or Region cum Nation?

Those who believe that the attitude of São Paulo conceals separatist desires and is the work of political partisanship are completely mistaken. We can assure you that it is essentially nationalist and has not even the slightest partisan coloration.
—**Manifesto "Ao Povo Brasileiro" (To the Brazilian people), July 13, 1932—flyer dropped by planes over Minas Gerais and Rio de Janeiro and signed by several figures from the Commercial Association, including José Maria Whitaker and Alexandre Siciliano Jr.**

For São Paulo with Brazil, if possible; for São Paulo against Brazil, if necessary.
—**Vivaldo Coaracy, "São Paulo está só" (São Paulo stands alone), May 31, 1931—quoted in a flyer distributed by the Liga de Defesa Paulista, "Tudo por São Paulo!"**

The flip side of the effort to deny secessionist cravings was the challenge of reconciling an intensified paulista chauvinism with an insistence that the Constitutionalist Movement was essentially a nationalist cause. As noted in the previous chapter, during the decades prior to the 1932 uprising one could readily perceive a particular paulista nationalist vision that, rather than counterposing region and nation, imagined Brazil through São Paulo, and regarded São Paulo as the template for the nation's future. Maria Lígia Prado observes, in a discussion of the essayists who wrote for the daily newspaper *O Estado de São Paulo*, that their articles were replete with references to the present or future *grandeza* of Brazil, "but, in fact, the path leading to this culmination was always routed through paulista terrain; if the ultimate objective consisted of the enrichment and the increased economic power of Brazil, São Paulo would lead and command these initiatives; if São Paulo grew, consequently Brazil would grow."[117]

In other words, a strong regional identity did not automatically imply an absence of a "national" project; at the same time, there was still considerable potential for contradictions and tensions between regionalist loyalties and nationalist visions. Thus paulistas in the last decade of the Old Republic encountered increasingly fierce resistance from other regional representatives to their efforts to draw an equivalence between paulista interests and national welfare; indeed, the paulistas' critics argued that policies favoring São Paulo's economic growth might even be hampering the nation's progress—a contention that rested on the assumption that the rest of the nation could *not* be subsumed under São Paulo, and one that gained greater traction with the crash in coffee prices in 1929. And if there were already tensions in the 1920s generated by the paulistas' efforts to conflate the regional and the national, how much more would that be the case in 1932, with São Paulo first demanding "full autonomy" and then mounting a solo military challenge to the federal government? Thus spokespersons for the Constitutionalist Campaign frequently felt obliged to insist not only that the movement was free of even the slightest separatist tinge, but that it was actually nationalist and motivated primarily by a profound concern for the welfare of the Brazilian nation.[118]

The various ways in which writers and orators articulated these sentiments, however, often undermined their professed purpose. Thus Padre João Baptista de Carvalho, in one of his radio "sermons" in favor of the Causa Paulista, declared that "São Paulo is what Brazil is today because the civic soul of the nation has been transported here."[119] José Maria Whitaker, president of the Commercial Association, expressed similar sentiments when he announced that Pedro de Toledo had decided to give the name of each Brazilian state to a battalion fighting on the frontlines: "Brazilians! Pay no attention to the lies from Catete [the presidential palace], listen to the truth you're told by São Paulo, at this moment the most Brazilian of the Brazilian states animated by the most Nationalist of national movements!"[120] Then there was the speech broadcast by Professor Francisco Morato on Radio Educadora just two days after the outbreak of war insisting that "São Paulo's campaign is profoundly nationalist and civilizing; in it one cannot detect even the slightest hints or indirect thoughts of regionalism." And the Bandeiras Cívicas (Civic Brigades) distributed flyers throughout the war with patriotic declarations insisting that

"São Paulo doesn't make political revolutions to implant schisms, hate or rancor among Brazilians! Its revolution is a conscious revolution of the NATION against chaos, disorder and separatism."[121] Paulista ally, native mineiro, and former president Artur Bernardes, manifesting his support for the Constitutionalist uprising, declared that "São Paulo is a state that honors the Federation. It is the pioneer of our country's progress. . . . *She created the immense wealth in Brazil and for Brazil.* . . . Furthermore she deserves our appreciation for the high level of her intellectual culture which, in itself, enlightens the nation."[122]

These statements and many more like them indicate the eagerness of pro–São Paulo spokespersons—with a few pro-separatist exceptions—to assert the movement's nationalist tenor and to deny any lack of patriotism in the decision to revolt against the dictatorship. But even these utterances and slogans reveal an unavoidable tendency to proclaim São Paulo's superiority and paulistas' singular capacity to civilize Brazil, to promote a civic spirit, to create order out of chaos. This is not so much to deny the movement's nationalist claims, but to note again the regionalist position from which paulistas imagined the Brazilian nation. Their nationalism seems to have been especially deficient in the "deep horizontal comradeship" that Benedict Anderson sees as a central feature of the imagined national community.[123] But Anderson's construction is an ideal type, not a specific example; if we consider instead the historical formation of the nation and national identity not only as a series of inclusions and exclusions, but as producing hierarchies of national belonging, paulista "nationalism" and paulista claims to be the "apostles" of the nation seem substantially less peculiar.[124]

If the paulistas positioned themselves as the apostles of Grande Brasil, this raises the question of who could legitimately claim to be "paulista." Here I am asking not what it "meant" to be paulista—a closely related issue to be discussed in the next chapter—but a more immediate question of how the descriptor could be deployed. After all, unlike "Brazilian"—an identity that might be equated with the formal status of citizenship—there were no recognized guidelines to define who was and was not paulista. The narrowest definition of a "true" son, or daughter, of Piratininga was the *quatrocentão* (literally, a "big four hundred"), the paulista who could trace his or her genealogy back four centuries to the time of the first Portuguese settlers and the rise of the bandeirantes; this was São Paulo's version of the descendants of the passengers on the *Mayflower*. But at a moment of mass mobilization, such a narrow definition would be useful only for symbolic purposes—that is, to define elements of paulistinidade that could then be manifested by the movement's supporters, the vast majority of whom lacked even the faintest (or feigned) genealogical ties to São Paulo's bandeirante forbears.[125]

If we shift from the historical to the geographical, "paulista" could plausibly be defined as a matter of birthplace or residence. But such terms of inclusion or exclusion could be both too narrow and too encompassing. Place of birth would exclude the many immigrants resident in São Paulo but born abroad, while residence could include many im/migrants from the Nordeste whom some regarded as the opposite of paulista. Writing in the journal *Paulistânia* in 1939, eminent folklorist and jurist Dalmo Belfort de Mattos referred to the "immigrants" from the Nordeste *not* as *novos bandeirantes*, or even *novos mamelucos*—terms widely used to refer to immigrants from abroad—but as *sampauleiros*, a designation that explicitly situated them outside paulista identity.[126]

It was also the case that several of the most prominent and vocal participants in the Constitutionalist Movement—such as Vivaldo Coaracy and João Neves da Fontoura—did not hail from São Paulo and had not spent much of their lives in that state, whereas the oft-reviled Miguel Costa had been raised in São Paulo. Predictably, the insurgent leadership seized on the fact that men like Bernardes, João Neves, Coaracy, and Lindolfo Collor adhered to their cause to demonstrate that the movement was *not* a strictly regionalist one. And Brazilians outside São Paulo who sympathized with the Constitutionalist Campaign tended to emphasize the malleability of the designation "paulista." One northeastern state official, on the day after São Paulo's surrender, commented on the radio that paulistas always accepted residents from other states as "equals," citing as proof of this the absence of a clause in the state constitution requiring that the state president be a paulista native (a feature promptly amended in the new state constitution ratified in 1933 which, in what might be called the Miguel Costa clause, stipulated not only that the governor be paulista-born but resident in the state for at least twenty years).[127] A commentator from the state of Rio de Janeiro, writing just before the outbreak of war, contended that because of the influx of immigrants and migrants, São Paulo was the least "regionalist" of all Brazilian states, and that paulista "means all those who live and work in São Paulo."[128]

Not surprisingly, participants in pro-paulista protests and short-lived insurrections elsewhere in Brazil claimed kinship with their counterparts in heroic Piratininga. Some five hundred students in Bahia, most of them from the medical school, tried to ignite an uprising in favor of the Causa Paulista, and some two hundred students, workers, and state police in Belém do Pará staged a brief "armed" rebellion that lasted thirteen hours and cost six lives. Representatives of the latter group transmitted a manifesto addressed "To the Paraenses of São Paulo, from the Paulistas of Pará," a locution clearly intended to privilege political/cultural affinities over geographic location.[129] And the *Jornal das Trincheiras*—a publication that came as close as any to being the official mouthpiece of the Constitutionalist Revolution—insisted, seven weeks into the armed phase of the struggle, that paulista identity transcended regional boundaries; due to the uprising the meaning of the term *paulista* "had broadened, expanded, widened and extended to include in its purview more than just a simple designation of an accident of birth"; it had become a category that included all those who "think like São Paulo."[130] In other words, it defined São Paulo as a state of mind.

Both the nationalist sentiments and the expansive definition of "paulista" proved difficult to sustain in the aftermath of defeat. For some veterans, São Paulo as the antithesis of the Brazilian nation displaced the idea of São Paulo as the metonymic nation. Bitter about the limited support São Paulo received from other states, the paulista leadership and ex-combatants defined the movement more and more in strictly, and narrowly defined, paulista terms. It would have been difficult to do otherwise—a movement premised on the special character of the state of São Paulo and the povo bandeirante would be hard to redefine in a way that dispensed with specific historical and geographic coordinates. Following the military defeat, there was even something of a revival of explicitly biological explanations for São Paulo's extraordinary progress and the qualities of its population. Milton Carneiro, an eminent physician and zealous eugenicist from neighboring Paraná, had this to say about the victory of the federal forces: "We watched, unsurprised, the inevitable triumph of the most degenerate. It is Darwin in reverse. . . . The grotesque predominance of the Sub-human [Infer-homem]."[131] And just two years later, Ellis published his best-selling, and extremely racist, *Populações paulistas*, to great acclaim.[132] Meanwhile, memoirs about the uprising frequently claimed that only afterward did the author become sympathetic to separatism. In a volume of self-published poems, Lauro Teixeira Penteado included one called "Paulistas at the 'Front.'" It begins with Penteado saying that he went into combat with two flags, fighting for both São Paulo and Brazil:

But after the treachery
I felt such ingratitude
From the Brazilians of the North
That I became Paulista only,
And as a separatist,
I will fight to the death.

And his handwritten inscription in the volume reads "Don't forget, don't forgive. Abhor and avenge!"[133]

But perhaps the most eloquent statement of the collapse of the regionalist cum nationalist project in the aftermath of São Paulo's defeat can be found in the card filled out by Pedro de Toledo upon arriving, exiled, in Portugal. Under "nationality" he wrote simply "São Paulo."[134]

Paulistas never, never, never will be slaves!

One example of a theme that appears across the entire spectrum of pro-paulista discourse is that of a noble region "enslaved" by the Vargas dictatorship. The above riff on that old patriotic/imperial standard "Rule Britannia" serves to illustrate the specific way in which terms like "enslaved," "slaves," and "slavery" were deployed by the paulista movement. Written in 1740, "Rule Britannia"—despite its apparent objections to the enslaved condition—could hardly be interpreted as a call for the abolition of slavery or for universal emancipation. On the contrary, the point is not that slavery itself is wrong, but that the enslavement (whether literally or metaphorically) of the *British*—people who, *by their very nature*, must be free—would be abominable and impossible. Given that the circulation of this song coincided with an era in which the British were enslaving or subjugating a significant portion of the earth's inhabitants, clearly the majority judged to be unlike the British could, maybe even should, be slaves—whether meant in the chattel sense, or in the sense of politically unfree. Considered from this angle, the tune's lyrics serve, by implication, as a (circular) justification for the subjugation of those peoples who are, by their very nature, suitable for enslavement.

It is from *this* perspective that we can understand why the propaganda produced by the Constitutionalist Movement was littered with allusions to slavery.[135] Paulo Duarte bitterly declared a year before the civil war that Vargas's forces "instead of entering [São Paulo] as a liberating army, entered as enslaving hosts," and epitomized the 1932 uprising as "the man who wants to be free fighting against the man who wants to be a slave."[136] While this might seem, at first glance, to be evidence of identification with the subaltern or the oppressed, I would argue that, on the contrary, it was meant to invoke with particular force the absurdity of the existing political situation, in which cultured and civilized people were being subjected to treatment suitable only for Africans, nortistas, and other "barbarians." In many iterations of this theme, the humiliating nature of São Paulo's plight was heightened by the role reversal it involved, whereby the degenerate descendants of the slave quarters were imposing their will on the Europeanized and Christian people of São Paulo.[137]

Rather than drawing on a universalizing antislavery/human rights discourse, these writers were deploying the trope of "white slavery," with its outraged sense of the order of things being inverted by the scandalous enslavement of those whose "Christian and civilized nature" should make them fundamentally immune to or ineligible for the enslaved condition.[138]

Again, this theme appears almost constantly in the documentation produced to justify São Paulo's rebellion against the federal government. Inspiring the heading for this section, a priest whose radio broadcasts rallied popular support for the uprising declared in one address that, just as "Britons never shall be slaves, the paulista has never been and will never be a slave."[139] There were repeated references in speech and print to Vargas enslaving São Paulo and/or Brazil, typically with the qualification that only the paulistas actually objected to this enslavement, in contrast to the slavish "hordes" in other regions.[140] Thus the supposedly progressive *Diário Nacional* accused Vargas's dictatorship of seeking to "reduce Brazil to an African horde." Perhaps the most extreme expression of this sentiment can be found in the separatist manifesto cited earlier, which urged paulistas to defend their patrimony "against the barbarous horde that is swamping us from north and south, impelled by hunger and by envy."[141]

This document is clearly drawing upon the trope of white slavery, portraying São Paulo's subordinate position within the Brazilian federation as an abomination, an unnatural state in which the (degenerated) slaves have become masters, and the (enlightened) masters have become slaves. And while it might be tempting to dismiss this explicitly racist screed as reflecting a minority position, we can point to the very similar imagery in Paulo Duarte's combat memoirs. Duarte tellingly entitled his account of his experience as a volunteer soldier *Palmares pelo avesso* (Palmares in reverse), evoking the bandeirantes' widely celebrated role in defeating the seventeenth-century runaway slave community in Brazil's Northeast. In Duarte's memoirs, São Paulo's defeat by federal troops amounted to an invasion of the bandeirantes' homeland by the degenerate dark-skinned descendants of the *palmarinos*.[142]

Again, the repeated references to enslavement, far from reflecting a critical view of São Paulo's slave past or an acknowledgment of the sufferings and struggles of the slave labor force whose toil had made São Paulo's initial surge of prosperity possible, constructed the true paulista as the antithesis of the former slave. To say paulistas had never been, and never would be, slaves when there were still some people living in São Paulo who had once been literally enslaved, and many more who were their immediate descendants, implied that the nature of paulista character automatically excluded these ex-slaves and their offspring. Brazilians elsewhere or "exotic" residents of São Paulo might be characterized as spawn of the *senzala*, but not the true paulista. Similarly, the standard narrative of abolition—with the enlightened paulista planter bestowing freedom on his grateful chattel—reinforced the idea that those who had been enslaved had been natural objects of enslavement, incapable of gaining their own freedom, whereas paulista soil was "inhospitable" to slavery as a way of life. It was white paulistas' supposed distaste for slavery, not the efforts of the slaves themselves, that brought about abolition in this particular version of slave emancipation.[143]

It should also be noted that this *discursive* exclusion of the Afro-descendentes from the category of "paulista" was not usually replicated in the references to immigrants. Despite the rise of anti-immigrant sentiment among some conservative/nationalist sectors of the paulista elite, there seems to have been a near universal embrace of the immigrant as a full-fledged paulista during the Constitutionalist Campaign.[144] At least one separatist manifesto quite specifically assured the immigrants that they could consider themselves true paulistas.[145] In a sense, criticism of the immigrants tended to be focused on what they *did*—whether it was calling strikes, organizing unions, forming anarchist groups—but such criticism did not question whether immigrants, in their very "essence," could become part of the povo bandeirante. In contrast, the exclusion of Afro-descendentes stemmed not from any specified actions or behaviors on their part, but from their "essential nature." Thus, the pro-Constitutionalist literature repeatedly assured the paulista public that "there are no foreigners here" and claimed that the immigrant communities were avidly taking up the Causa Paulista.[146] Indeed, paulista writers regularly recognized immigration as a constitutive element of São Paulo's modernity, whereas "immigrants" from Africa and their descendants were represented as remnants of an anomalous and unpleasant phase of the region's distant past.[147]

Democracy: The Opposite of Dictatorship?

The portrayal of the Constitutionalist Campaign as a demand for the rule of law, and that demand as something emerging from São Paulo's special disposition for order and progress, helps explain a peculiar silence, or near silence, in the pro-paulista rhetoric. One might expect a movement that claimed liberalism as its defining ideology and that was rallying the masses against a lawless dictatorship to make extensive use of the term "democracy," a word that even in the early 1930s was widely regarded as embodying the antithesis of authoritarian rule. And yet there were remarkably few references to the need for democracy or democratization in the writings and speeches of the movement.[148] There were uncountable references to the pressing need for a constitution, for the restoration of order and the rule of law but, for the most part, the paulistas were silent on the matter of democracy. A Constitutionalist leaflet that circulated in Rio during the early days of the uprising claimed that paulista troops would soon be marching into the federal capital to "reestablish the regime of Law and of respect, the regime of Order and of hierarchy in Brazil." Significantly, there was no mention of the restoration of democracy.[149] On the rare occasions when the issue of democracy did appear, it was not so much to advocate it as to call it into question. Thus we have the particularly blunt assertion by Vivaldo Coaracy who, in *O caso de São Paulo*, wrote: "The difference in their evolutionary rhythms unavoidably establishes a hierarchy among the Brazilian States. . . . Democracy proclaims civil equality for all citizens and tends to concede them political equality. But it is incapable of creating natural equality."[150] Or this similarly pessimistic remark by PD militant Leven Vampré on Brazil's potential for "true" democratic rule: "We are an immense democracy of illiterates. Democracy, under these conditions, inevitably acquires features of a dictatorship."[151]

With such statements in mind, we can appreciate more fully the political vacuum that existed in Brazil during the early 1930s, as far as democracy is concerned, with Vargas edging toward an authoritarian/populist appeal to the popular classes, and the supposedly liberal paulista middle class identifying with a hierarchical and non-inclusive definition of political rights. Ironically, under these circumstances, it was the dictator Vargas and his allies, not the "liberal Constitutionalists" of São Paulo, who were more likely to benefit from an eventual transition to a broad-based democratic politics.[152] Paulista regionalism cum nationalism, so intensely identified with the white middle and upper classes in São Paulo, had little capacity for sustained popular mobilization, especially beyond the state's boundaries, making democratization an implicit challenge to paulista dominance or autonomy. Both before and during the Constitutionalist Campaign, paulista propaganda cited the benighted inhabitants of Brazil's less "advanced" regions as impediments to the formation of a modern, cohesive, and progressive national culture. But I would argue that the paulistas' insistence on a *hierarchy* (rather than a diversity) of regional identities posed the more serious and enduring impediment to the construction of a more progressive and democratic nation.

CHAPTER 3

THE MIDDLE CLASS IN ARMS
Fighting for São Paulo

Paulistas! The time has come to confront our oppressors. . . . We are united today as one man with one will. . . . Each paulista, whether by birth or sentiment, is duty-bound to become a soldier. There is no way you can free yourself from this obligation because what is at risk is not just this or that region, but our very nationality!
—Flyer distributed by the Liga Paulista Pró-Constituinte

In this case we saw a general explosion of the dominated classes under the leadership of the dominant classes, and the Revolution of '32, in my opinion, marked the last time that the dominant classes succeeded in incorporating the dominated classes into their political project, as if the people were a single bloc.
—Antonio Cândido de Mello e Souza

My first exposure to the "Guerra de São Paulo" was the brief discussion in E. Bradford Burns's *A History of Brazil*, which dismissed it as a resto-rationist movement with limited popular appeal that led to "desultory fighting," and then quickly collapsed.[1] Thus, it came as something of a surprise when I started reading contemporary accounts of the movement and uprising, both sympathetic and critical, and found one source after another describing near-unanimous support for the movement among the paulistas.[2] Of course, one has to start by asking what a par-ticular observer meant by "the paulistas"; typically, when someone said "all of São Paulo," he or she did not literally mean everyone who lived within the boundaries of São Paulo state, or even necessarily a majority of the state's residents. Nonetheless, it is striking that both supporters and opponents unfailingly described the Revolução Constitucionalista as having widespread and fervent support from the paulista population. To quote one particularly unsympathetic observer:

> In a unanimous gesture, worthy of a better cause, all the political clubs, all the propertied classes, all of the enterprises in agriculture, commerce, and industry, all of the academies and schools, all of the medical, legal, engineering associations, and those of scientific, literary, and artistic culture, including the Catholic schoolteachers, all of the Catholic, Protestant, spiritist, theosophic, Salvationist and masonic houses of worship, all of the associations of charity and assistance, all of the sports clubs invested their heart and soul, with all of their available resources, to the mobilization of the Constitutionalist armies and to the feverish preparations of all the elements of war and supply.[3]

Perhaps it is to be expected that a movement that cost lives and careers will spawn seemingly irreconcilable accounts of what happened and why it happened. But we also need to consider why a particular interpretation or narrative—exemplified by Burns's brief summary—becomes enshrined in scholarly texts as the accurate rendering of those events. One obvious explanation would be that the getulistas "won"—the paulistas, after all, did go down in defeat, the (armed) movement did collapse after less than three months of fighting, and Getúlio Vargas did subsequently secure a position that allowed him to remain Brazil's chief executive (whether as provisional president, elected president, or dictator) for seventeen of the next twenty-two years. As the dominant political force in Brazil for several decades, the getulistas were in a position to portray the paulista insurgency as the handiwork of conniving oligarchs who managed to inveigle a handful of disaffected military officials to turn against Vargas, and to stir up some short-lived and shallow civilian support with manipulative appeals to regional chauvinism.

This, alone, does not explain the tendency in scholarly circles (until recently) to dismiss the 1932 uprising as an oligarchic plot with little popular support since the same scholars who reproduce the getulista version of that event, practically word for word, have treated with skepticism Vargas's self-presentation as the "Pai dos Pobres" (Father of the Poor) whose labor legislation constituted a "gift" to the Brazilian working masses.[4] Thus I think we need to go beyond the tried and sometimes true assumption that the victors get to decide how history is told. After all, the pro-paulista version of events has hardly been "silenced." Even in the midst of getulista rule, the paulista press openly (if ambivalently) commemorated the fifth anniversary of the uprising. By the 1950s the single most recognizable landmark in the city of São Paulo was the obelisk marking the mausoleum for the remains of soldiers who died fighting for the Causa Paulista, and both a major avenue and the building that houses the state assembly bear the name "9 de Julho." The date even became a state holiday in 1997.[5]

I would argue, instead, that the widespread acceptance in academic circles of the getulista account of the paulista uprising reflects that version's compatibility with a certain set of scholarly assumptions—common until quite recently—about what social groups are "legitimate" historical participants in revolutions or insurrections.[6] The lack of enthusiasm for, and even rejection of, the Causa Paulista by most of São Paulo's labor unions, and the steadfast opposition of the Communist Party, inevitably marked the uprising—in historians' eyes—as having little "popular appeal." And the presence of paulistas from various segments of the regional elite in the leadership makes it, perforce, an oligarchic plot, at least from the social historian's perspective.[7]

In this chapter I will be starting with the premise that both the getulista claim that the Constitutionalist Campaign had little popular support and the anti-getulista claim that "Todo São Paulo" supported the movement have to be examined critically, and that neither can be taken at face value. At the same time, I think it necessary to concede that a cause able to rally hundreds of thousands of people across the state of São Paulo in simultaneous demonstrations and to speedily recruit over a hundred thousand volunteers for an armed insurgency should be regarded as a mass movement. But I am less interested in documenting the extent of paulista enthusiasm for the Constitutionalist Campaign (for which I think there is more than ample evidence) than I am in considering how the movement was defined in class, racial, and gender terms, and what this implied for paulistas from diverse backgrounds who participated in the movement. I would argue that throughout the 1932 rebellion there was tension between a discourse that insisted that the movement had the unanimous support of the povo bandeirante, including men and women of every class and color, and another discursive tendency that constructed the dominant image of the movement as white, male, and middle class.

To be clear, my argument is not that, if we could compose a profile of all of those fighting for the paulista side in terms of income, profession, and educational status, we would discover that a majority or plurality was middle class. For one thing, that would problematically assume that there already existed stable, empirical measurements of what it meant to be middle class in São

Paulo in the early 1930s. Rather, it is a question of the discursive construction of the Constitutionalist soldier and how that image shaped the regional experience/memory of the movement, as well as what it meant to be white, male, and middle class in São Paulo. It is the image of 1932 as an insurgency of the "respectable portion" of paulista society that made it so compelling for many journalists, memoirists, chroniclers, and devoted veterans of the movement, but this image also made the Revolution of 1932 virtually unintelligible to later generations of historians, accustomed to associating "genuine" rebellion with subaltern social sectors.[8]

All for São Paulo

Figuring out who fought for and what it meant to fight for São Paulo is complicated by the diverse segments and multiple stages that constituted the paulista insurgency. First of all, there were the eighteen-month-long preliminaries, which included various political alliances, negotiations, petitions, and denunciations, as well as massive marches and protests, one of which resulted in the first outburst of violence, on May 23, 1932.[9] These were all primarily civilian affairs that occasionally invoked the names of military figures, but were not necessarily linked to any military conspiracy. Furthermore, while São Paulo eventually emerged as the bastion of Constitutionalist sentiment, rallies and demonstrations calling for a return to a constitutional order were occurring throughout Brazil. Indeed, some contemporary commentators described the anti-getulista movement as even fiercer in Vargas's home state of Rio Grande do Sul than it was in São Paulo.[10]

Once we move into the period of actual civil war that began on the ninth of July, there are several different fighting forces to take into account. One would be the dissident elements of the federal armed forces, which turned out to be a relatively small contingent. General Bertoldo Klinger, perhaps the single most important military figure involved in the Guerra Paulista, had pledged to bring thousands of troops with him from Mato Grosso to São Paulo. But a rightly suspicious Vargas preemptively relieved him of his command, moving Klinger to pen a harshly worded letter of protest to the newly appointed minister of war, an action that forced a rupture with Vargas and prematurely forced the hand of the paulista leadership.[11] It also meant that Klinger arrived from Mato Grosso with only a fraction of the promised troops. In effect, the anti-getulista federal forces that sided with São Paulo were top-heavy with high-level officers such as Klinger, Isidoro Dias Lopes, and Euclides Figueiredo, and short on actual armed soldiers. Clearly the civilian leadership hoped that the backing of charismatic and influential officers, and especially the hero of the 1924 tenente revolt, Dias Lopes, would fracture the federal forces and undermine Vargas's military support, but General Góes Monteiro (whose brother Cícero would die fighting for the federal government) acted quickly to limit the damage from Klinger and other officers' move into the paulista camp.[12]

The second major contingent of paulista troops—and militarily, the most crucial—came from the state's Força Pública. As a result of the decentralization of finances and political authority in Brazil prior to 1930, the wealthier states could arm and train their own police forces that then effectively functioned as regional armies.[13] Indeed, several of the paulistas whom Vargas sought to appoint as interventor between 1931 and 1932 as a conciliatory gesture ultimately declined or resigned because the appointment did not include meaningful control over the state's Força Pública, which remained under the command of Miguel Costa until the seizure of the state government on May 23.[14] Judging from a number of accounts of the revolution and lists of paulista casualties, the Força Pública would appear to have been the most actively engaged segment of the paulista "armed forces." But it was also the contingent that provoked the greatest ambivalence among chroniclers of the revolt, and retrospective accounts almost uniformly question the dedication of the Força Pública battalions to the paulista cause, and attribute the "precipitous" surrender of the Constitutionalist forces to their lack of commitment to the struggle. In the hyperbolic words of Vivaldo Coaracy, "São Paulo wasn't defeated. Rather, it was sold and delivered."[15]

One reason for the ambivalent, even jaundiced, view of the Força Pública was the relatively "popular" composition of the state police force which, unlike the capital's Guarda Civil, had never been segregated by color, and thus aside from the commanding officers, consisted largely of poorer men of African or mixed descent.[16] At the same time, of the troops fighting for São Paulo, they were by far the best trained and most prepared for battlefield conditions a competence that, in certain situations, transcended the usual hierarchies of prestige and authority. Hence Alfredo Ellis Júnior, a volunteer wounded in battle during the revolution (and someone always alert to any slights to the privileges of whiteness), was horrified at the spectacle of "illiterate" members of the Força Pública, "true imbeciles," giving orders to "men of culture."[17]

Most of those "men of culture" served, of course, in the volunteer battalions. Ellis claims in his account of the Revolution of 1932, affectionately titled *A nossa guerra* (Our war), that some 200,000 men volunteered to fight for São Paulo, but shortages of arms and training facilities meant that only some 60,000 actually went into the trenches. Yet another source claims 100,000 enlisted "on paper," but only 50,000 took up arms, and of those a mere 30,000

FIGURE 3.1. Paulista volunteers in the capital going off to war. Photo from *O Mundo Ilustrado* (Rio), July 7, 1954.

actually saw combat (see fig. 3.1).[18] The volunteers were then further splintered into battalions and platoons, some of which were organized by place of origin (typical of troops from cities and towns on the coast and in the interior such as Santos, Sorocaba, Piracicaba, Buri, or Franca, or of units composed of São Paulo residents born elsewhere in Brazil), and others by profession or craft (as in the battalions of pharmacists, engineers, law students, shoemakers, and railway workers). I have only come across a single reference to a battalion organized around ethnicity (oddly, of "Germans" born in Brazil), but there was one defined by the racial identity of its members—the Legião Negra (Black Legion), which played a central role in several of the major battles between the paulista troops and the "forces of the dictatorship."[19]

In addition, there were the many thousands of paulistas who volunteered their time, money, and energy in auxiliary roles, or in carrying out war-related functions on the home front. As we will see in the next chapter, paulista women flocked to the Constitutionalist banner and filled the majority of non-combat posts, including serving as uniformed nurses who risked life and limb to treat the wounded at the front. Men of standing in commerce and industry arranged the revolution's finances, organized fund-raising drives, and retooled São Paulo's factories to place them on a war footing. Others joined the MMDC, a sort of civilian patrol responsible for keeping order and preventing sabotage in the urban areas. Named for four young men killed in a clash with the Legião Revolucionária, the MMDC attracted so many volunteers that some paulista officials began to express, in private, the suspicion that it was being used as a way to dodge more risky service on the frontlines.[20]

This roll call of participants in the 1932 uprising would seem to bear out the oft-repeated paulista claim that "Todo São Paulo" supported the revolution. Indeed, once the fighting got under way, nearly every public statement by insurgent officials emphasized the unanimity of the response, as one might expect. In the face of verbal attacks by the getulistas claiming the movement to be strictly an elite affair, or impugning the paulista leadership's attitudes toward workers or people of color, it became especially pressing for pro-paulista spokespersons to portray the movement as attracting adherents from every walk of life. Just as they had to repel accusations of separatism or paulista chauvinism by presenting the movement as an act of regional sacrifice for the nation as a whole, they had to rebut charges of elitism or restoration of oligarchic privilege by foregrounding the broad appeal of the liberal-Constitutionalist agenda, and presenting it as an expression of the "collective will" of the povo bandeirante.[21] Eyewitness accounts of a massive rally in the capital (as well as many smaller rallies throughout the interior) held the day after the paulista government declared war uniformly insisted on the presence of paulistas from "all social classes." A pro-Constitutionalist priest who made regular radio broadcasts to rally paulistas for the cause claimed that even children were participating in the movement. And the press published photographs to illustrate this diversity, with captions designed to make it even more apparent: "Young and Old, Students, Workers, Businessmen, All Linked by a Common Ideal!"[22]

Of course, not "all" of São Paulo supported the movement or joined the war effort. As we will see, there were certain segments of paulista society that actively opposed the uprising, and undoubtedly there were others who simply sat it out. But in many social circles and communities, it wasn't a matter of "deciding" for or against adherence to the movement. Rather, the power of paulista identity in certain milieux made a decision unnecessary—surely, as a paulista, one would support the uprising. To refuse to do so was probably for many unthinkable, and had they done so, they would have found themselves marginalized and despised by family and friends. Indeed, various Constitutionalist manifestos declared that it would be better to kill oneself than to refuse to volunteer and remain alive.[23] Afterward, many participants in the uprising described themselves as having been swept along by the intensity and fervor of the moment, or by the fear of being called a coward, but none indicated outright coercion (in the sense of threatened force) to join up.[24] It was a perfect example of how hegemony operates; for most paulistas, it went without saying that they would support the uprising. How could they be a paulista if they didn't?[25]

While there is considerable evidence that the movement attracted adherents from all social sectors and could claim a diverse following with regard to race, ethnicity, and social status, this does not contradict my earlier assertion that the imagined Constitutionalist soldier was white, male, and middle class. Again, I am not making a statistical or sociological claim: given the central role of the Força Pública, much of the fighting was probably done by men who did not consider themselves or were not considered middle class, and that's setting aside the racial question for now. And though reliable numbers are hard to come by, one source claims that within twenty-four hours of the outbreak of hostilities, the Liga de Defesa Paulista (the Paulista Defense League) had signed up 30 medical doctors, 30 engineers, 35 pharmacists, 29 typists, 10 telegraphers, 106 drivers and mechanics, 207 *operários* (workers), and 46 *diversos* (unspecified).[26] The total of liberal professionals on this list is impressive compared to any other revolt in Brazilian history, or to their proportion in the general population, but they still did not constitute a majority.[27] Moreover, once we move beyond certain well-established occupational categories, it is difficult to conclude in advance whether a particular volunteer regarded himself as middle class or not. Thus, even if we had employment data on every man who signed up to fight for the paulista cause, it would be problematic to make a priori assumptions about the social identities of the movement's participants.

In other words, I am not just contending that the Constitutionalist Movement had special appeal to the middle class, which I believe it did, but I would go further and argue that the movement played a major role in defining the contours and character of the paulista middle class. The critical historiography of the uprising has generally portrayed it as a "top-down" movement, instigated by the regional oligarchy, and it is certainly the case that the initial complaints about Vargas's insults to paulista pride emerged from groups that could be described as "elite" or "near elite."[28] For instance, Constitutionalist leader Aureliano Leite, addressing the commander of the Força Pública just a month prior to the start of the uprising, referred to the venue of his speech, the Clube Comercial, and declared the following: "If, perchance, there remains in your mind any shadow of a doubt that I am qualified to speak to you in the name of São Paulo, I would answer to you: I represent here the Commercial Club, and whoever says Commercial Club says São Paulo. . . . Cast your eyes around and you will see surrounding you politicians of every shade, merchants, lawyers, doctors, manufacturers, planters, engineers, functionaries—in a word, all the representatives of São Paulo."[29] But if we accept this characterization of how the Constitutionalist Campaign took shape, it immediately raises questions about whether we can clearly distinguish between "bottom-up" and "top-down" when it comes to movements that mobilize large numbers of people, and whether we can explain them without recourse to concepts such as manipulation or co-optation. And it becomes even more problematic once we identify the middle class as the stratum where these discourses are circulating most densely and effectively. If we look at the movement "from the middle," then using concepts such as "top-down" and "bottom-up" may prove more misleading than illuminating.

Critics of the Causa Paulista not only sought to question the legitimacy of the uprising by insisting on the top-down nature of the movement, but also by claiming that the better-off paulistas incited the war and then let the humble do their fighting (a charge that could be readily understood by later left-leaning social historians).[30] To be sure, there were numerous reports of volunteers performing badly on the battlefield, which is scarcely surprising given their inadequate training and faulty weaponry. But many volunteers who could hardly be called "humble" did put themselves in harm's way. A volume compiled in 1936 for the purpose of naming and honoring all of the paulista war dead arrived at a total of 632 men, a number that the publisher readily admitted was not the full list of those who perished, but was probably close to the total. Of the 632 identified, 371 were volunteers, 180 were members of the Força Pública, 57 were from army detachments, and 24 were from other units, such as firefighters. Contrary to the getulista claim, the war dead who were classified as volunteers included dozens of engineers, lawyers, pharmacists, and students from institutions of higher education.[31] There were also some twenty mechanics and many other manual workers, but the single most common "profession" among the volunteer war dead was "commercial employee." This last category indicates just how unstable and elusive an identity like "middle class" could be. After all, the typical commercial employee was likely to be no better off than a skilled manual worker, yet it is easy to imagine these young men joining the struggle in part to assert their membership in the civilized and cultured paulista middle class, and to distance themselves from "the humble."[32]

Even though the list of the war dead indicates that many better-off paulistas did take up arms, we have to be careful not to overstate their heroics. Again, much of the actual fighting for the paulista side seems to have been done by the state's Força Pública, whose troops were not likely to be middle class (or "white"), with significant reinforcements from the Legião Negra—by definition, not representative of the white middle class. This feature of the conflict was seized upon by the paulistas' opponents as a sign of the movement's hypocrisy, and the elite's cowardice. One memoir by a getulista combatant who was particularly vehement in his condemnation of the paulistas claimed that all eighty-five of the prisoners his unit captured in the region of Paranápitanga were from the Legião Negra. This prompted him to make the following sarcastic "suggestion": "To preserve the honor of the Constitutionalist Army, we would like to see included among the hundreds of combatants taken prisoner at least a few individuals of the white race. Thus, the now widespread commentary, in view of the current number of black prisoners, could be avoided. The talk among our soldiers is that the whites, the educated, the cultured, indeed, those responsible for this entire calamity, no longer want anything to do with what is now called the 'horror of the trenches.'"[33]

Though the particulars of this chronicle are almost certainly exaggerated, there is ample evidence that the Legião Negra saw more time on the front than most other units.[34] Even so, paulista press coverage, memoirs, and retrospective accounts of the fighting overwhelmingly highlight the contributions, sacrifices, and experiences of the middle class on the "battlefield" (whether political or literal). And they routinely and sharply contrasted these admirable middle-class *voluntários* with the wretched ruffians from the Nordeste recruited to fight for the federal government.[35] Even a quick survey of the various speeches, radio addresses, and newspaper articles presented by those rallying the "troops" confirms that the speaker or writer's interlocutor was a putative member of the paulista middle class (and typically male, though not always). Mário de Andrade, in his unpublished meditation on the war, declared that "São Paulo has just lived through one of the most impassioned pages of the history of the bourgeoisie."[36] Public addresses frequently called upon the paulistas to prove to the rest of Brazil that they had not become "soft" or "unmanly" as a result of their prosperity, surely not an anxiety associated with peasants or workers. Indeed, there is an underlying theme in many of the pronouncements that evokes the classic maxim, "War is a force that gives us meaning." Herbert Levy, a lieutenant in the civilian militia, dedicated a passage in his combat diary to the "intrepid youth": "Even boys [*rapazes*] who were known as society *dandys* . . . the fine flower of paulista youth planted their reserves of civic duty in the mulch of the trenches, revealing the fortitude [*fibra*] that they inherited from their ancestors and which endured in them, merely awaiting the right occasion to manifest itself in all its exuberance."[37] Similarly, the author of a column entitled "Cartas de Mulher" in the *Jornal das Trincheiras*, addressed to the "Voluntário Paulista Intelectual," assured her intended reader that he wasn't "pretending" to be a soldier—he really was one. The columnist goes on to say that she knew him when he was "rich and disdainful" but now he is "splendidly masculine, splendidly Brazilian."[38] In other words, the theme is war as a transformative experience, and particularly for those well-heeled paulistas who had voluntarily left the safety and comfort of their homes for the trials and tribulations of the trenches.

At times the central character in this imagined wartime setting is a solidly middle-class figure whose pleasant home life makes him initially reluctant to volunteer. Modernist writer Menotti del Picchia, in a fictional piece entitled "Vae" (Go), tells the story of Genny, described as a middle-class housewife who loves her husband Carlos so much that she begs him not to volunteer. But then her maid's son shows he "is a man" and enlists, as do Carlos's employees. Eventually, both Genny and Carlos realize that they will only experience true happiness once Carlos similarly proves that he's a [real] man and joins the others at the front.[39] At other times the figure being foregrounded is someone who might have regarded himself as part of the upper class but has learned to be less elitist, and more earnest, as a result of the combat experience.[40] Luiz Naclério Homem, in his wartime diary, noted how "catastrophes such as war and hunger blur the barriers that separate social classes. Here among us are rich and poor, students and workers, whites and blacks, but our common uniforms, needs, and risks bring us together as brothers in a most admirable way."[41]

This was also the theme of an item titled "The Benefits of War" that appeared in an issue of the daily paper *A Gazeta* on September 4. According to this article, the war had triggered a profound transformation in the region's elites. "Prosperity—their detractors said—had weakend [the elites'] combative spirit. . . . How untrue this [accusation] was is demonstrated by the sacred fury with which the paulistas are entering the battle." Here the elites (or a rehabilitated version of them) are elided with the paulistas. The article then goes on to discuss a piece that appeared in *A Folha da Noite* about a soldier from the elite whose confessions *A Gazeta* regards as both moving and revealing of the archaic attitudes that this "necessary" war had corrected. According to the paraphrased version, "before marching into battle, his image of the soldier was that which was common among the 'higher classes,' which was that he was a species apart, a different creature from the others. . . . The trenches revealed, however, to his astonished eyes, that they were 'men worthy of great attention,' that is, they were men and not animals, and that among the officers there were even some who were 'cultured.'" The (surprisingly human) "soldier" referred to here is either from the regular army or, more likely, from the Força Pública.[42]

As we have seen, even prior to the declaration of war, the journalistic descriptions of the major mass protests consistently emphasized the respectable middle-class comportment and discipline of the participants, and implicitly contrasted them with the more familiar (and presumably unruly) proletarian protests.[43] A letter sent to General Klinger regarding the massive rally on May 13 included the following description: "The balconies and terraces of the skyscrapers were loaded with people, including many ladies. I went down [to the street] to make contact with the crowd and feel its enthusiasm. I noted that within its diverse ranks, *there was no sign of the rabble*. There you encountered the people who think. The orators, all notable men of São Paulo, spoke one after the other, full of civic ardor."[44] And most of the published personal accounts of this three-month civil war contain the recollections of law students, journalists, or engineers who emphasized the unaccustomed daily hardships of life in the trenches, and who apparently had never expected to find themselves engaged in armed combat (and, not surprisingly, performed rather ineptly on the field of battle).[45] One particularly illuminating account of experiences on the frontlines can be found in the combat diary of José de Assis Pacheco, published twenty-two years after the fact (significantly to mark the quadricentennial of the city of São Paulo). Pacheco was a student at the Largo de São Francisco—the São Paulo Law School, a bastion of ardent Constitutionalist activism—when the uprising started. Sharing his classmates' intense enthusiasm, he quickly enlisted in the Batalhão Universitária Paulista, composed of students, doctors, lawyers, and engineers.[46]

Pacheco and his fellow volunteers were then sent directly to train with the Força Pública, at which point he writes in his diary: "I felt out of place in the midst of the crude individuals who made up the majority of those present. Where were the academic youth?" Still, his spirits remain high and he depicts the "festive" and cinematic scene ("like a movie") in which the members of the battalion said good-bye to their loved ones. But the tone quickly changes as he confronts the reality of his physical circumstances, including beds and bedding in their makeshift barracks so "repulsive" that he opts to sleep on the floor.[47] Once near the front in Itararé, according to Pacheco, he and his fellow volunteers kept receiving orders to make "strategic retreats," which he cites as a source of embarrassment. In other words, they were aware of the possibility that they might be considered cowards for not being more aggressive in the face of the enemy. It is also significant that he appended some footnotes to the published version of the diary, rebutting the claim by Clovis Gonçalves that the "academics" had tried to retreat in the face of fire, and only the threat of being shot by the Força Pública kept them from fleeing.[48]

Following a rainy night, awaking with chills, Pacheco recounts eagerly drinking three cups of hot maté, a beverage he had previously detested, provided by the kindly cook of the eighth battalion. "Never will I forget this kindness received from the calloused hands of an elderly black soldier." Continuing in this vein, he repeatedly mentions a "mulatto" in the Força Pública for whom he harbored some admiration and sadly notes a death among the soldiers of the Legião Negra. But the tone shifts dramatically in his next entry, when he describes being found and awakened, ill with fever, by two "ugly black" soldiers who at first he thinks are "troops of the dictatorship," but turn out to be from the Legião Negra. He refers to one as a "grotesque figure" and goes on to describe the ugliness of the other in detail. Pacheco portrays them both as *grosseiros* (coarse/vulgar) and is disgusted that he has no choice but to drink from a canteen soiled with their saliva. Rather than express gratitude for their aid and relief that they were not the enemy, he writes (with obvious unease): "I find myself amidst the soldiery [*soldadesca*] of the Legião Negra."

This is a remarkable passage in a number of ways, starting with its utter lack of self-awareness (after all, consider what *he* looked like—a pathetic, sweaty, fever-ridden white guy—to the two black soldiers in question). It is particularly striking that he expresses no relief when he discovers that the two black soldiers are not the enemy; indeed, it seems nearly impossible for him to imagine that these "repulsive" men are paulistas, fighting on the same side as Pacheco and his fellow academics. And the use of the pejorative term "soldadesca" indicates how removed the two *legionários* are from Pacheco's archetypical Constitutionalist soldier. To this young law student, being surrounded by the soldiers of the Legião Negra was little better than being surrounded by "the enemy."[49]

Herbert Levy, whose combat diary mainly focused on military maneuvers, made a point of dismissing the members of the Legião Negra as cowardly and disorderly. He describes one battalion of legionários as perpetually inebriated, and claimed that "when in combat, they abandoned their positions at the first shots, compromising the situation of nearby troops." He does, however, attribute this alleged lack of discipline to the absence of proper leadership (a theme that runs throughout the diary), and adds a remark that "softens" the harsh racial implications of his scorn for the Legião Negra. According to Levy, the legionários "didn't have adequate commanders, and thus constituted a real disappointment, particularly so when innumerable men of color, participating in other battalions, including our own, were genuine examples of discipline and valor."[50]

Vilifying the Enemy

Civil wars typically evoke disturbing visions of fratricidal conflict, and the Guerra Paulista was no exception. Both contemporary chronicles and retrospective accounts include references to soldiers' reservations about taking up arms against their fellow Brazilians.[51] One method to overcome this reluctance was, in effect, to define "the enemy" in such a way as to make his status as a fellow Brazilian questionable. As we will see below, the routinely racialized portrayals of federal soldiers as subhuman thugs from the northeastern backlands allowed paulista combatants to situate their antagonists outside the fraternity of Brazilian citizens. The flip side of this characterization of the enemy, however, was the more ambiguous attitudes expressed toward troops from Rio Grande do Sul or neighboring Minas Gerais. Both of these states had been quite powerful during the Old Republic and had been expected to ally with São Paulo against Vargas. And despite their "betrayal" of the paulistas, both states harbored sizable political factions with Constitutionalist sympathies. Furthermore, while stereotypes about the gaúchos of Rio Grande do Sul abounded, they were in a different register from the racialized or demeaning images associated with the nordestinos. Indeed, paulistas probably regarded most gaúchos as "white," given the limited role of slavery in the southern region's history, and its continuously growing population of European immigrants. When José de Assis Pacheco awoke amidst a group of black soldiers that he initially assumed to be the enemy, it is very unlikely that he thought they belonged to a battalion from the South of Brazil.

The different sentiments attached to soldiers from the North and the South can be seen in an account of an unusual encounter between paulista soldiers and federal forces on São Paulo's southern border. During an impromptu cease-fire, the paulista narrator and his companions engaged in a poignant conversation with their fellow Brazilians from Rio Grande do Sul in which both sides expressed regret at having to "fight against brothers" and agreed that "this war must stop!" But this idyll came to an abrupt halt when an "unhinged mulatto northerner" intruded himself into the conversation and began threatening the paulistas: "So, then, you paulistas want to fight with the rest of Brazil. . . . We're really going to thrash you!"[52] In other words, despite the war, there was a natural affinity between (presumably) white Brazilians from two different southern states, but the fly in the ointment was the nonwhite northerner whose backwardness and ignorance translated into irrational hostility and envy toward the paulistas.

In the standard portrayals of federal troops, those friendly (and implicitly white) gaúchos, however, were an exception.[53] Paulista media coverage of the uprising routinely highlighted the dramatic race/class differences between the rude, thuggish federal troops—virtually always portrayed as semi-savage conscripts from impoverished precincts of the Brazilian Nordeste—and the cultured, educated professionals who populated São Paulo's battalions.

It became a matter of course to refer to the "troops of the dictatorship" as the *jagunçada*, evoking the fanatical defenders of the backlands millenarian community, Canudos, profiled in Euclides da Cunha's *Os sertões*. An excellent example is the following description of the Vargas regime's efforts to crush the Constitutionalist Revolution, from the newspaper *O Estado de São Paulo*: "Against the youth of São Paulo, against the students, the doctors, the lawyers, the engineers, the merchants, the landowners, the men of industry and intelligence, [the government is] throwing a band of thugs [jagunçada] gathered and herded together in the backlands. . . . Against a civilized people, they hurl battalions of hoodlums."[54] Similarly, a headline in *A Gazeta* informed São Paulo's citizenry: "The Dictatorship Makes Use of Fanatical Jagunços against the Conscious Army of Liberty."[55] And *A Folha da Noite*, a few weeks before the surrender, described the federal forces as being like "hungry wolves" and a "mindless band of thugs" (*jagunçada bronca*), and accused Vargas of relying for support on "the coarsest barbarism, the pitiful and prolific spawn of backlands crime and banditry." The pro-Constitutionalist U.S. consul wrote to the State Department about reinforcements from the Northeast, whom he referred to as *jagunços* and described as fighting "principally with knives and under the inspiration of *pinga* [cane liquor]."[56] In short, the army of the dictatorship was a "torrent of primitives" sent to fight against the "fine flower" of paulista society.[57]

Immigrants, Foreigners, or Paulistas?

In sharp contrast to the disparaging depictions of their fellow Brazilians to the North, the paulista press and state government spokesmen uniformly praised the immigrant population of São Paulo and claimed its unanimous support for the Causa Paulista. But "immigrant" was an even more unstable category than nortista or middle class. In certain contexts it was equivalent to "worker" but typically was used in that vein when the speaker or writer's referent was an abstract one—not a specific group of workers but the muscle and sinew that were helping to make São Paulo more modern, more prosperous, and (implicitly or explicitly) whiter. As I will discuss below, immigrants *as workers* proved rather disappointing in their response to the clarion call of the Constitutionalists, but immigrants as an infusion of eugenically desirable labor power could be celebrated and appreciated regardless of their particular political inclinations. Hence the assertion in the first manifesto from the small but noisy separatist faction: "Foreigners' sons, born in Brazil, you are paulistas. Help us liberate our Homeland [Pátria]."[58]

Curiously, when a paulista journalist or government official cited a specific

ethnic group, the latter usually took the form of a "colony" or a "colony of foreigners"—as in the Italian colony (*colônia italiana*) or the Syrian colony or the
Jewish (Israelite) colony.[59] Thirty days into the uprising, Menotti del Picchia
described the contributions of various groups within paulista society to the
war effort, adding that "these gigantic activities have received the dedicated
collaboration of all of the colonies of foreigners in São Paulo, materialized in
the provision of ambulances, bandages, and bedclothes for the hospitals."[60] A
delivery of 942 knitted scarves and hoods to the Departament of Aid to the
Wounded by "Senhoras Mindlin and Klabin" was listed as being from the
"Colônia Israelita," and a contribution of 1,770 bone buttons from Theophilo
Haddad Baruky was attributed to the "Colônia Syriana."[61] It seems, at first
glance, an odd locution since it implies that these ethnic groups were not
immigrants in the usual sense and were somehow living apart from "native"
paulistas as temporary residents, though it is likely that most had settled per-
manently in Brazil (this was certainly true in the case of the Mindlins and
Klabins). And this at a time when one might expect vigorous efforts to portray
a united paulista people who all belonged to the same imagined community,
rather than a society with various separate colonies (or worse, "cysts") embedded in it. One possibility is that middle- and upper-class Italians and Syrians
preferred to be represented in this fashion, to distinguish themselves from the
proletarian immigrant community. Just as "all of São Paulo" could be taken to
mean the middle and upper class, the "entire foreign colony" could be meant
to refer to the more privileged segments of certain ethnic groups without
explicitly excluding immigrants of more modest status. Thus, in a photo cap-
tioned "The Italian Colony Contributes to the Victory," wealthy industrialist
Rodolfo Crespi appears as the central figure. But young Italian immigrant
women who volunteered in the surgical hospital were also identified as participating in the ceremony marking the donation.[62]

Again, we have to be careful not to assume that already-formed entities are
responding collectively to the appeals of the Constitutionalist Movement. For
example, women's clubs from several immigrant colonies contributed to the
war effort by sewing uniforms for the troops, which might indicate a robust
organizational tradition among women in the ethnic "colonies." But interestingly enough, a listing of these women's clubs indicates that most of them were
founded *during* the 1932 uprising, with the express purpose of participating in
activities to support the Constitutionalist Movement, and demonstrating the
loyalty of the particular ethnic colony to the paulista cause.[63] One consular
report claimed that many immigrants, and especially Italians, were enlisting in
the Constitutionalist forces, a contention that is difficult to confirm. Indeed,

judging from the family names of the soldiers listed on military rolls, or those of fallen combatants in *Cruzes Paulistas*, the immigrant presence among the Constitutionalist troops was rather modest.[64] Still, Alfredo Ellis Jr. claimed that his battalion was "saturated with the sons of exotics."[65] And there is occasional anecdotal evidence of immigrant support for the Causa Paulista: future jurist Miguel Reale, who would soon enlist in the ranks of Brazil's homegrown fascist movement, deflected charges of anti-Semitism in his memoirs by recounting his wartime friendship with a Hungarian Jew. According to Reale, José Preiz died fighting for São Paulo although he wasn't even a naturalized Brazilian.[66] The pro-Constitutionalist press also celebrated the paulista patriotism of two young voluntários of Japanese descent, both students at the law school. In an interview with *O Estado de São Paulo*, the father of José Yamashiro praised his son who "as a Brazilian and Paulista . . . obeyed the natural impulse to take up arms to defend [his] State."[67] Once again, we can see how the 1932 uprising provided an opportunity for immigrants to affirm their brasilidade/paulistinidade.

The precise participation of immigrants aside, the high-profile activities sponsored by the "foreign colonies" and the hefty monetary donations made by the Crespi and Matarazzo clans allowed these ethnic groups to assert their loyalty and devotion to their "adopted land"—by which they meant São Paulo, which was for them "Brazil."[68] Alfredo Ellis Jr., whose disdain for the "African element" in São Paulo was only matched by his enthusiasm for the European immigrant influx, ventured that "the hardships and the martyrdoms that have weighed upon São Paulo, especially during the dark days of the war of 32, were the best cement for the assimilationist process."[69]

Where Were the Workers?

One of the central assumptions of scholarly works about the Constitutionalist Campaign is that it elicited little or no sympathy from the working class. Writing nearly a decade after the uprising, and from a much more skeptical (if no less elitist) perspective, Mário de Andrade argued that the Causa Paulista was a movement to protect economic privileges, and therefore "consolidated itself within the propertied classes, while the proletarian classes refrained almost entirely from participation in it." He acknowledged that the Centro dos Operários Católicos in August 1932 published an appeal to workers in favor of the movement, but described this center as "chained to the bourgeois capitalist traditions of Christian civilization." He then went on to say that to the extent that the non-propertied participated in the movement, it was either "under orders" or due to "the pure mimicry of the uncultured classes."[70]

Documents produced during the three months of fighting—for example, notices circulated by the Federação das Indústrias do Estado de São Paulo (FIESP)—confirm these claims of proletarian apathy or hostility. Industrial employers who backed the Constitutionalist Campaign not only expressed concern about the seeming indifference of their workforce toward the Causa Paulista, but even funded a chain of free medical clinics to curry workers' favor.[71] It might then seem reasonable to assume that workers, by and large, did not share the enthusiasm of middle-class paulistas for the Constitutionalist Campaign and were not susceptible to the clarion call of regional chauvinism. But as with the discussion of middle-class identity above, such a conclusion rests on a priori reasoning: that is, that the working class already existed as a stable entity and fixed identity, and we need only know that someone was a worker to determine his (or maybe her) likely position vis-à-vis the Constitutionalist Movement.

If we approach the event, instead, as a moment that helped shape and solidify identities, we can better understand a certain degree of confusion about working-class participation in contemporary sources. Thus *A Plebe*, an anarchist periodical, described the workers as indifferent or even hostile to the Causa Paulista, while lamenting that "the people" were misled into volunteering by the appeals of the Catholic clergy.[72] This "confusion" appears even in some of the most credible chronicles. Florentino de Carvalho (the alias of Spanish-born anarchist Primitivo Soares), in his sharply unsympathetic account of the civil war of 1932, describes various centers of authority in São Paulo swiftly organizing "forces from all social classes" including "workers from all races, colors, and nationalities." Yet on the very same page, he claims that "the 'paulista surge' animated the bourgeois classes. Only the proletariat (*and not all of it*) responded with reserve, indifferent to that grandiose manifestation of civic sentiment."[73] What might seem like contradictory statements—workers of all colors and origins joined the movement; the proletariat alone remained indifferent to the movement—makes better sense when we look closely at his language and word choice. The first statement refers to "operários" which could be a general and descriptive term for manual workers (though it would be most commonly used for factory operatives). The second statement uses the term "proletariat," which carries with it certain assumptions about class identity and consciousness. Furthermore, Florentino is careful to insert the parenthetical "and not all of it" when he claims the proletariat remained indifferent. One can read his statements as indicating that significant numbers of manual laborers enlisted in the ranks of the paulista volunteers but that organized labor—workers who belonged to or identified with unions or parties of the left—for the most part refused to participate in the uprising. According to the openly pro-Constitutionalist U.S. consul in São Paulo in 1932, virtually the entire paulista population supported the war, "the only discordant element being the radical proletariat." Consul Cameron's report to the State Department went on to say that "such radicals" were the "only part of the population favorable to the Dictator but their influence is negligible and they are being kept down with an iron hand."[74]

There is plenty of evidence to indicate that significant numbers of workers supported the Causa Paulista, starting with the formation of battalions of railway workers, stonecutters, and shoemakers. Photos from towns on the coast and in the interior show battalions that probably encompassed members of the community from a variety of social classes and backgrounds. And the account of the war dead in *Cruzes Paulistas* includes a sizable number of volunteers whose "profession" is some sort of manual trade.[75] This should hardly be surprising: any serious study of workers in São Paulo during this period would readily acknowledge that not everyone who worked with his or her hands in an urban setting identified him or herself *primarily* as a "worker," much less as a proletarian. Especially in smaller cities and towns, it is likely that manual workers would be situated in a web of economic, political, and affective relationships that transcended a particular social class or occupational identity. But even in the big manufacturing centers, there certainly were workers for whom the regional identity of paulistinidade had considerable appeal, whether for its association with upward social mobility, or for the opportunity to demonstrate (in the case of immigrants) that they were genuinely "paulista" despite being born abroad, or being first-generation Brazilians.[76]

By the same token, the Constitutionalist Campaign had relatively little success in attracting workers *as workers* to its banner. The many petitions and proclamations calling for a "civil and paulista government," or denouncing the Vargas regime, carried the signatures of a remarkable range of societies, clubs, and associations, but typically the only "union" or "labor" entities that signed on were commercial employees' unions or Catholic workers' circles. Even the less incendiary call to the "People of São Paulo" to commemorate the four hundredth anniversary of the founding of São Vicente bore the name of the Textile Manufacturers' Syndicate, but not the name of the textile workers' union.[77] And the wartime notice of a memorial for young Benedicto Sergio of Taubaté, "a modest and retiring young man" who, "in a gesture of heightened nobility of sentiments, exchanged his worker's tunic for a uniform and, spontaneously headed to the battlefield in defense of the great cause, and there perished heroically," didn't include among the sponsoring associations a local labor union.[78] The flyer did list the Commercial Employees' Association, the Recreation Center of Taubaté, the Taubaté Sport Club, the Union of Young Catholic Men, the Benevolent Society of Taubaté, and the Workers' Mutual Aid Society, but no *sindicato*. Similarly, a program on Rádio Record dedicated to the "Laboring Classes," part of a series honoring all associations supporting the revolution, had guest speakers from the Paulista Institute of Accounting, the Center for Catholic Workers, the Association of Commercial Employees, and the Association of Bank Personnel, but no one from an industrial union.[79]

Most labor unions in São Paulo did not openly manifest their opposition to the movement, but to publicly criticize the Constitutionalist uprising was, of course, risky business during the actual conflict, and the arrests of dozens—and perhaps hundreds—of "Communists" in the state capital and in the port city of Santos indicate that the authorities were inclined to draw an equivalence among various types of "sedition" and label as Communist anyone who spoke against the Causa Paulista.[80] Whether the political police opportunistically used the wartime context to root out Communists, or simply defined all opponents as radicals and subversives, the period from July to October 1932 unquestionably saw an intensification of repression against leftist groups (the "iron hand" alluded to above by the U.S. consul). It is somewhat remarkable that the September 1932 issue of the paulista magazine *A Cigarra*—published in the midst of the civil war—devoted a full five pages to the subject "Repression against Communism" and printed photographs of dozens of arrested "Communists."[81] The same photographs also appeared in a September issue of the *Diário Nacional*, a newspaper that had earlier published an article congratulating the police on their arrest of "Communist" Eneida de Moraes, a government employee who had been mimeographing "subversive literature" to send to the front.[82]

Despite the repression, quite a few anti-Constitutionalist manifestos, mimeographed flyers, and short-lived gazettes aimed at workers circulated in São Paulo during the uprising. Typical of the getulista propaganda was a flyer addressed "To the Paulista Workers" reminding them that both former president Washington Luís and President-Elect Júlio Prestes regarded the social question as a matter for the police.[83] The text then contrasted the brutal treatment of workers under the Old Republic with the current regime's more enlightened policies—a claim made more credible by recent memories of Ibrahim Nobre's stint as state police chief when Júlio Prestes was governor. During his tenure as São Paulo's leading law-enforcement official, the "Tribune" of the Causa Paulista crushed a campaign by printers for implementation of the paid-vacation law and broke up families by deporting labor militants.[84]

Finally, the flyer described Vargas as having "unequivocal" sympathy for the workers' plight, but having been impeded in his progress toward labor reforms by Lindolfo Collor, now accused of "sabotaging the liberal [*sic*] intentions of the dictatorship." The reference to Collor, Vargas's first minister of labor, author of the initial round of labor legislation, and by 1932 a vocal supporter of the paulistas, marks this manifesto as very probably the product of political circles outside of organized labor. It also indicates the degree to which Vargas had yet to consolidate his position as a champion of the working class, given its emphasis on sympathies and intentions, and the contrast with his predecessors, rather than on actual benefits that had accrued to organized labor as a result of his regime.[85] A similar approach is adopted in a flyer issued by the federal "Army of the East" to the "Paulista Soldier and People" that declared the following: "All of Brazil, unified and cohesive, rejects the criminal assault on those in power, mounted by those politicos [*politiqueiros*] who have always, in the factory or in the coffee field, held the great working mass enslaved to their low and shabby interests and ambitions."[86]

A more extreme statement of opposition to the Constitutionalist insurgency could be found in the manifesto issued by the Regional Committees of São Paulo, of the Communist Party and Communist Youth and addressed to "Men and Women Workers, Peasants, Students and Poor Intellectuals, Youth, Soldiers and Sailors!" It begins by depicting the insurgent paulista government as the result of a "military coup spearheaded by Generals Isidoro and Klinger, in the pay of the big landowners and industrialists linked to the imperialists," and that had thus far "only meant more misery and hunger for the workers." In an even more incendiary vein, it next claimed that "workers and peasants are being dragged onto the battlefield," leaving wives and children hungry; priests then visit working-class homes with a bit of food to draft their daughters to work as seamstresses. It goes on to recount a series of alleged attacks on workers who dissented against the "revolution": according to the manifesto, the Constitutionalists "seize, beat and kill workers such as those in the Enlistment Post in [the neighborhood of] Braz . . . where three were killed who refused to join up, and two in the Alto da Môoca who were killed for the same reason." It then closes by condemning both Vargas's "bloody dictatorship" and the "bourgeois constituent assembly."[87]

It is difficult to know whether all the events described in the above manifesto actually occurred but there does seem to have been a widespread perception among workers that some of their *companheiros* were being coerced into military service on the paulista side.[88] Thus a notice issued by the municipality of Presidente Prudente during the uprising assured "the entire worker population" of that interior town that business was functioning normally and that nobody was being forced to volunteer.[89] Given the specific details provided in the Communist Party manifesto about the events in Brás and Moôca, it seems quite possible that there had been clashes, with lethal results, between pro-paulista authorities and opponents of the movement—the Constitutionalists were certainly keen to suppress any public manifestation of divisions within the paulista ranks. And there was probably some substance to the occasional anecdotes of proprietors, urban and rural, pressing their employees to join them in the fight for São Paulo. But given that the paulista authorities had more volunteers than they could adequately train and equip, and no shortage of women eager to sew uniforms for the troops, it seems most likely that these tales of coercion were, in part, a way to explain the presence of some of their fellow workers in the ranks of the Constitutionalist forces, rather than an accurate account of regular recruiting strategies.[90] In effect, labor leaders—whether of the more radical variety or those who were already seeking an accommodation with the getulistas—regarded the 1932 uprising as an event that helped define a proletarian identity and an appropriate degree of class consciousness. Those "workers" who did support the movement—and their numbers were not insubstantial—were deemed either victims of coercion or of false consciousness.[91]

As the health care clinics hurriedly founded by FIESP indicate, the leadership of the Constitutionalist Movement both recognized the limited enthusiasm that the movement excited among urban workers and attempted to do something about it. But the particular scripts that informed the discourses and images produced by the Causa Paulista were of little avail in enlisting working-class support, and for fairly obvious reasons. First of all, the association of the movement with the classes conservadoras and particularly with the perrepistas, notorious for their uncompromising, iron-fisted responses to labor militancy, made Constitutionalism a difficult sell among workers in the larger urban centers. True, the PD had maintained a somewhat more enlightened position regarding workers' rights and labor legislation, but once the democráticos had formed a Frente Única with the republicanos, the two parties probably became indistinguishable in the eyes of most working-class paulistas.[92]

Furthermore, the particular representation of São Paulo and paulistinidade that animated the Constitutionalist Movement would have been difficult to articulate to any of the central concerns and themes of organized labor. A perfect example is a communiqué issued during the first week of the uprising by the "Worker and Peasant Pro-Constitution Assembly" to the "Struggling

Classes" insisting that the paulista movement was the "true class struggle" and that the Vargas regime would only condemn workers to hunger and misery. It described the uprising as the combined effort of the "liberal classes and popular classes," and claimed that the true proletarian would fight for paulista autonomy and a constitutional assembly to initiate "a new period of plenty in favor of the producing masses, in which prosperity will turn this privileged land into a paradise open to all conquests of happiness and well-being." This was followed up, a week later, with another communiqué addressed to "Proletarians!" arguing that workers should oppose the Vargas regime because it had not provided the promised legal reforms, and should support São Paulo, the standard-bearer of "order," without which there could be no prosperity.[93]

The discursive efforts made specifically to enlist greater support from the "urban working masses" illustrate how difficult it was to couch the appeals developed for an essentially middle-class/regionalist movement in terms that would be meaningful to paulistas in the struggling working class. It seems unlikely that a call to arms based on the glory and prosperity of São Paulo would have had much resonance with the many workers whose straitened circumstances, worsened by the global depression, made the promise of a paradise of abundance seem ironic, if not downright insulting. Similarly, the slap at Vargas for not coming through with the promised labor legislation was a transparently flimsy argument given the far poorer track record of paulista politicians with regard to social reforms. As for injunctions to support the forces of "order," anyone with experience in the labor movement knew that elites typically expressed their opposition to strikes and May Day demonstrations by invoking the need for order.[94] Once again, this did not mean that the movement had no allure for those who made their living performing manual labor; one can easily imagine a person of modest means being eager to identify with São Paulo's progress and modernity, and the relative promise of prestige and social mobility that the rapidly expanding regional economy offered. In Gramscian terms, exemplified by the remarks by Antonio Cândido that open this chapter, one could argue that the "dominant classes" had articulated their interests, with (some) success, to nonclass aspects of popular culture, thereby attracting (some) support from the dominated classes.[95] But this ultimately rests on a conceptualization of society that seems overly static and dichotomous, and on a notion of class as real and other identities as constructed. Instead, I would contend that regional/paulista identity, with its particular class, gender, and racial referents, appealed to a broad swath of the paulista population that aspired to elements of a middle-class identity, and who were thus inspired to take up the regional cause.

Puzzle No. 1: The Legião Negra

If it was unlikely that someone whose primary identity was proletarian would vibrate to the call for paulista hegemony, it would seem doubly the case for someone who self-identified as black. The Constitutionalist Campaign may have been discursively tone deaf when it came to appealing to the working class, but it was still rare to encounter overtly disparaging remarks about the proletariat (as opposed to the *ralé*, or rabble, distinguished from the respectable working man or woman). Imagined as a white/European immigrant, the paulista worker could easily be absorbed into a hegemonic conception of a whitened, modern, progressive São Paulo.[96] But the same would not seem to apply to the Afro-paulista population, which had experienced considerable discrimination and bigotry in the post-abolition era as the (often-subsidized) European immigrants flooded the rural and urban labor markets. Several recent studies show that, as a result of this specific experience of marginalization, it was only in São Paulo that blackness became a primary identity among people of visible African descent for political organizing and social networking, with the black press becoming the central organ of the Afro-paulista community.[97] This is in contrast to the emphasis on *African* culture and religion in communities of African descent in Rio or Bahia. Politically active Afro-paulistas typically framed their activism in terms of blackness and distanced themselves from Africanness as an ethnic identity, as might be expected in a milieu where modernity was the coin of the realm, and where Africa was irredeemably associated with backwardness or, at best, primitive vitality.[98] And as historian Paulina Alberto notes, too close an association with Africanness could also undercut a major theme within the black press at the time, which was to insist on blacks' Brazilianness, in contrast to the foreignness of European immigrants.[99]

Given the vicissitudes of life in early twentieth-century São Paulo for men and women of color, the prominent role played by the battalions of the Legião Negra in the 1932 uprising presents something of a puzzle.[100] Precisely how many Afro-paulistas participated in the black legions is difficult to pin down. One source claims as many as 10,000 men enlisted in these battalions, but this number seems somewhat inflated; another source cites between 2,000 and 3,500 volunteers joining the Legião Negra, which seems a more reasonable estimate (see figs. 3.2 and 3.3).[101] Either way, there is no doubt that thousands of black paulistas—mainly men, but also women in auxiliary roles—joined the Legião Negra and fought fiercely against the federal forces even after many of their white, middle-class counterparts had fled the dangers and hardships of

FIGURES 3.2 AND 3.3. Battalions of the Legião Negra departing for the front. Photographer unknown, 1932. Courtesy of Ricardo della Rosa.

FIGURE 3.4. Typically diverse small-town battalion, this one from Iguape, on the southern coast of São Paulo. Photographer unknown, 1932. Courtesy of Ricardo della Rosa.

the battlefield.[102] It is, moreover, a double quandary since it raises the question of why black paulistas would fight for a movement grounded in idioms of (white) racial superiority, and how a movement that consistently portrayed itself as white and middle class represented the black troops in its midst.

Again, the very existence of a separate Legião Negra was peculiar to São Paulo; it is unlikely that blacks would have formed separate battalions in any other Brazilian state.[103] Note that the verb in the previous sentence implies agency on the part of the black legionnaires; all sources indicate that the legion represented a particular project of the black community rather than a deliberate attempt by the Constitutionalist leadership to segregate the fighting forces.[104] Indeed, in an article authored fifteen years later, Paulo Duarte would use the example of Afro-paulistas forming their own battalions in 1932 as evidence of their "pathological" hostility toward whites.[105] To be sure, there were many battalions—such as those composed of *universitários* or engineers—that were, by their nature, completely white, or nearly so (except for the company cook, who was typically an older man of color). But the photos of many other battalions, including those of manual workers, and units from cities such as Santos, Campinas, and Piracicaba reveal a highly diverse racial composition, including many volunteers who would be identified as black or men of color by the standards of paulista society at the time, not to mention Colonel Palimércio de Resende, chief of staff of the pro-paulista army forces in the Paraíba Valley, described as black in several sources (see fig. 3.4).[106]

What distinguishes the Legião Negra is that its troops self-identified as black and deliberately joined all-black battalions. Sources indicate that many were members of the recently formed Frente Negra Brasileira; the FNB adopted a formally neutral position on the conflict between the getulista regime and

São Paulo, but many of its adherents ultimately opted to fight for the Causa Paulista.[107] As noted above, several combat chronicles cited the rapid deployment of Legião Negra battalions to the front as well as their presence in the zones of most intense fighting, often with the intent of revealing that the Constitutionalist leadership valued white lives over black ones, or alternatively, of demonstrating the vigor and bravery of the black troops. But there is another possible and perhaps more plausible explanation: many of the original volunteers of the Legião Negra were reservists from the Força Pública and therefore already had some military training and experience.[108] Thus, among the Legião's war dead was one Anacleto Fernandes, from Santos, a reserve sergeant of the Força Pública, and veteran of the Revolution of 1924, "during which he suffered serious wounds in the combat that occurred in Cambucy." Following 9 de Julho, he joined the Legião Negra, eventually "attaining the commission of Captain."[109] Stanley Hilton cites instructions issued by the Constitutionalist authorities regarding railway passes for "all men of color, *especially reservists*, who wish to enlist in the Black Legion of São Paulo."[110]

However, it is likely that inexperienced soldiers who affiliated with the legion also were rapidly deployed to the front. The entry in *Cruzes paulistas* for Geraldo Benedicto da Silva, a legionário from the small town of São Joaquim who died in the fighting, bears the following description of his military service: "On the 14th of July, in that civic enthusiasm that electrified the spirit and the heart of the bandeirante people, he enlisted in the Constitutionalist Army. Four days later, as a soldier in the 'Henrique Dias' Battalion of the 'Black Legion' . . . he headed for the front." It is possible that Silva also had a military background since he was soon promoted to sergeant, and that he deliberately sought to join the Legião Negra. But it is conceivable that, being from a town too small to form its own battalion, he was directed by the authorities coordinating the volunteer forces to the Legião Negra because of the color of his skin. And then there is the curious case of Francisco Vieira, also listed on the roster of war dead, who was originally incorporated into the Legião Negra but was later transferred to the Batalhão Marcílio Franco—a previously all-white platoon, judging from the photos, and one that saw heavy fighting in the region near Buri. We have too little information to do anything other than speculate as to why Vieira changed battalions (or was ordered to do so). Did he feel uncomfortable in the Legião Negra? Did he have military skills that were badly needed by the embattled soldiers of the Marcílio Franco battalion? We also have no way of knowing why Thomaz de Araújo, who appears of African descent in his photo in *Cruzes paulistas* and was probably a reservist, "presented himself to the Força Pública when the war broke out," rather than joining the legion.[111]

What we do know is that many men of color, who self-identified as black and had political affiliations with clubs and movements dedicated to advancing the cause of racial equality, joined the Legião Negra and fought for São Paulo despite the prominent presence in the Constitutionalist Movement of several figures—such as Alfredo Ellis and Paulo Duarte—who openly promoted racist ideas, and the influence of a separatist faction that aggressively expressed the most racist attitudes imaginable. This is not even to mention the more general presentation of paulista supremacy as a consequence of the region's relative whiteness, a position that could be presented in relatively subtle ways, but sometimes with no subtlety at all, as when the *Diário Nacional* asserted the necessity of a paulista victory, "in the face of the miseries wrought by the dictatorship, which have reduced [the people of] Brazil to an African horde."[112] A somewhat embittered Mário de Andrade, retrospectively addressing this apparent paradox, returned to the theme of *mimetismo* (mimicry), claiming that the "uncultured people," including "the people of the [black] race . . . follow the example of the bosses," and dismissing the soldier of the Legião Negra as "[an] imitative negro."[113] A racialized version of "false consciousness," such an explanation demonstrates what an analytical trap it is to make rigid, a priori judgments about which political behaviors and interests properly inhere to particular identities.

Regrettably, we have few sources to explore how the members of the Legião Negra—male and female—conceptualized or expressed their decision to join the Constitutionalist Campaign. Petrônio Domingues, who has written the most detailed study of the Legião Negra to date, cites the legionários' desire to prove the mettle and valor of the black race, and to demonstrate their worthiness for full inclusion in paulista society, but ultimately concludes that material necessity, as much as anything else, drove Afro-paulistas into the ranks of the Constitutionalist army. This motive cannot be entirely dismissed—propaganda for the legion appealed to potential recruits with the claim that "to enlist in the Black Legion is to protect your family" (see fig. 3.5).[114]

Indeed, almost immediately following the formation of the LN, its architects founded the Institute of the Benevolent Association of the Black Legion with the purpose of offering to the legionnaires and their families "moral and material assistance services with the goal of assuring that once the war in which we are currently engaged has ended, and thus demobilized, the black soldiers will not find themselves facing misery."[115] And an article cited by Domingues, published first in a mainstream newspaper and then reprinted in the black press, claimed that for paulista blacks, in "their humble anonymity, it mattered little if we had a Constitution or endured a dictatorship."[116] But this,

FIGURE 3.5. Black soldiers departing for the front, bidding farewell to their families at the train station. Photographer unknown, 1932. Courtesy of Ricardo della Rosa.

I would argue, may go too far in the direction of denying a capacity for politically informed action and veers a little too close to the way white paulistas imagined the legionários. Thanks to São Paulo's zealous political police, we do have a copy of correspondence between one of the legion's (black) officers and Joaquim Guaraná de Sant'Anna, whom several sources identify as the legion's main founder. In the letter, written on September 5, Guaraná refers to the legionários as "selfless defenders of this our São Paulo." After relating various bits of news, he briefly reflects on his own decision, as a native of Bahia, to support the Causa Paulista:

> Here all is going well and we are increasingly excited by the success of our cause and bursting with pride for our unsurpassable São Paulo, which has astonished everyone with this memorable surge, manifesting the civic duty and grandeur of its sons. I, as you know, did not have the good fortune of being born here but, due to the 40 years in which I have lived the paulista

life with all of you; with my children all born here; I thus feel that to abandon [São Paulo] at this moment would be to betray them and the land to which I came as a child and which I adopted as my own, and I feel patriotic and proud to be living with you paulistas during these felicitous moments in our National History.[117]

Nothing in this statement immediately distinguishes Guaraná de Sant'Anna's motives from those of the many white paulistas who left us their thoughts on why they joined the Constitutionalist Movement. And given his background as a journalist and activist, this should not be entirely unexpected. There is, however, one slightly discordant note in the statement above, and that is his shifting relationship to São Paulo and the paulistas. Twice in the letter he refers to "our [adjective] São Paulo," implying full identification with the estado bandeirante, but then he later qualifies this by saying how proud he is to be living "with you paulistas"—almost as if he does not want to overstate his claims as an adopted son of São Paulo.

Flávio Gomes, in a thoughtful discussion of the politics of the Legião Negra, notes that the few articles and manifestos issued by members of the Afro-paulista community portrayed participation in the legion as part of the struggle against inequality; in his words, "the sense of belonging and integration evoked as much the desire to be recognized as the explicit recognition of inequality. To fulfill the law, the Constitution was the first step toward securing guarantees against that which the law should not permit: inequalities between whites and blacks."[118] To fully appreciate the legionários' position, it is crucial to keep in mind that the Causa Paulista, despite its racialized subtext, never explicitly presented itself as a movement in favor of white supremacy; rather, the leadership repeatedly claimed that, like all Brazilians, they valued racial harmony.[119] This ambiguity opened the possibility that a significant Afro-paulista presence in the war effort, and a demonstration of the black community's patriotism and civic spirit, could influence the direction of paulista politics with regard to the condition of the black race and its demand to be classified as part of civilized Brazil. Thus, a letter written from the front by legionário Antonio Rafael to his commander recounting a heroic and successful military maneuver by his battalion opened with the following phrases: "I salute you in the name of our compatriots and of the cause that we defend. This is to inform you of the bravery of the second battalion in its outstanding performance on the battlefront, where it received its baptism by fire. *This is a tribute that I want to make to my comrades in the Black Legion of São Paulo.*"[120]

We also have the lyrics of several marches written specifically for the Legião

Negra by members of the black community. The "Marcha aos Soldados da Legião Negra," by Lieutenant Laurindo Tavares, is indistinguishable in most respects from the many marches written by white supporters of the movement; the one difference is the degree to which it specifically exalts the exploits of the legionários, rather than the paulistas in general, ending with the lines "All we have left to say from all of our hearts / Is that we have no rival in this Revolution."[121] Then there are the intriguing lyrics penned by the eminent black poet Lino Guedes (1897–1951) for the "Marcha dos Henriques," dedicated to the Legião Negra. The final two stanzas are especially worth reproducing:

We do not fear the fight
We fight for an ideal
For the untainted grandeur
Of our native land!
Slaves all our lives
We dare to challenge death!
Paulistas from the same land
As the brave fighters for abolition
Side by side with Borba Gato
We conquered the backlands!
Paulistas, into battle
For law, and for reason![122]

Though the phrase "Slaves all our lives" can be read several ways—as an acknowledgment of past enslavement (indeed, both of Guedes's parents were slaves prior to abolition), and/or a metaphorical reference to the Afro-paulistas' continuing struggles for survival and full freedom—it is certainly an explicit rebuttal to the portrayal of São Paulo as historically inhospitable to anything but liberty. At the same time, the rest of the lyrics clearly assert the paulistinidade of the black community, including blacks' historical participation in the bandeiras, and their resulting determination to fight for the law and for reason.[123]

Extolling São Paulo as the land of the bandeirantes and the bastion of abolitionism was nothing new—the very same themes could be found in the most mainstream Constitutionalist writings. But the meanings and implications are altered when the lyrics insist that within the bandeiras were men of African descent, and when it is the sons of slaves saluting São Paulo's history of abolitionist activism—a process that occurred because of the bravos who fought against slavery, not because the paulistas were "by nature" opposed to enslavement. In more general terms, we can see the various statements that emerged from the Legião Negra as reflecting the aspiration to stake a claim to a regional identity that was modern and progressive, and to assert their blackness as fully compatible with the modernity of São Paulo. Domingues, in his study of the Legião Negra, identifies Vicente Ferreira as the leading pro-paulista orator within the black community and describes him as urging blacks to enlist by arguing that "participation in the Constitutionalist army formed part of their project of emancipation and of constructing a country free from all forms of oppression."[124] While it might seem implausible that support for the Causa Paulista would produce such results, it is notable that Ferreira did not merely repeat the objectives as outlined by the Constitutionalist leadership—that is, the restoration of the rule of law, and greater autonomy for São Paulo.

Moreover, recent research by Jared Rodriguez indicates that linking participation in the Constitutionalist Movement with demands for greater equality might not have been a pure pipe dream. The FNB and various black community organs, including the Centro Cívico Palmares, had for some time protested the persistent "whites only" policy of the Guarda Civil, the state capital's urban police force, and a rare instance of a public entity in Brazil that *overtly* refused black applicants.[125] In May 1932, when civil war began to seem inevitable, Pedro de Toledo reportedly counseled the various militias being formed to avoid recruiting "blacks and beggars."[126] But by mid-July Toledo was personally reviewing the black troops headed for the front, and then in September he ordered the chief of the Guarda Civil to integrate his units (possibly in time for a major parade by the Guarda Civil on the seventh of September—Brazilian Independence Day).[127] Apparently, the need to get men with prior military training into the field trumped whatever reluctance the paulista governor may have felt about incorporating blacks into the Constitutionalist army. And black political leaders understood that they could take advantage of this special historical moment, and the opening it provided, to advance their constituents' claims for greater formal equality.

In exchange for this fleeting sense of inclusion and short-lived political leverage, however, the members of the Legião Negra had to endure treatment that set them apart from the other voluntários in ways they almost surely did not welcome. Despite the fact that many of the legionários had more military training and experience than their white counterparts, the Constitutionalist leadership assigned a white officer, Gastão Goulart, to command the Legião Negra (see fig. 3.6).[128] Perhaps to soften the blow, the legion did have the post of civilian chief, a position that was filled consecutively by two men of color. The first was the aforementioned Joaquim Guaraná de Sant'Anna, a former member of the FNB and a radical nationalist. His tenure abruptly ended in

FIGURE 3.6. Battalion of the Legião Negra with white officer. Photographer unknown, 1932. Courtesy of Ricardo della Rosa.

mid-September for reasons that remain murky, but that involved accusations of financial impropriety and "defeatism." He was then promptly replaced by the lawyer and normal school professor José Bento de Assis.[129]

In addition, all military posts below commander (including battalion chiefs) were filled from the ranks of the Legião Negra itself, a practice that may have diminished the affront of having to accept a white commanding officer. Though Goulart must have been a difficult insult to swallow, no matter what the mitigating circumstances. In his memoirs, *Verdades da revolução* (Truths of the revolution), he had remarkably little to say about the Legião Negra per se, and instead peppered his recollections with flattering references to the work of Gustave Le Bon, a leading "theorist" of racial hierarchies, and endorsed Le Bon's concept of "residuals of ancestral personalities." Goulart did, at one point, wax euphoric about the performance of the Legião Negra, showering what he surely regarded as his highest praise on his subordinates: "Black in color, but white in their courage! How admirable are our black men."[130] These sentences, and especially the phrase "our black men," express a sentiment that often appeared in newspaper articles and chronicles about the Constitutionalist Revolution—the idea that blacks from São Paulo, though in need of moral supervision and improvement, were nonetheless (as quasi paulistas) more civilized than people of African descent elsewhere in Brazil.[131]

The imposition of the white commander was not the only "special treat-

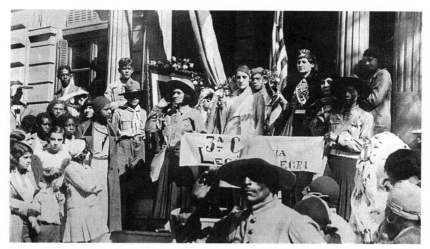

FIGURE 3.7. Battalion of the Legião Negra with a few members of the women's auxiliary. Courtesy of Ricardo della Rosa.

ment" that the Legião Negra received. It is revealing that when eleven "direct descendants" of the Botocudo Indians volunteered to fight for the paulista cause, they were lodged in the barracks of the Legião Negra.[132] Whether or not the leadership of the legion welcomed their presence is impossible to determine, but it seems unlikely that the black leadership was the source of this decision. And yet another feature specific to the Legião Negra was the formation of a women's auxiliary battalion, whose members wore wide-brimmed hats and long flaired skirts—outfits that were quite different from the modern, form-fitting uniforms of the white nurses, who were not linked to any particular combat unit.[133] What explains this idiosyncrasy is difficult to say in the absence of further information, but the available photographs definitely give the impression of a much more modest, rustic, and traditional appearance for the legionárias compared to other women in uniform (see fig. 3.7).

If the sources are nearly silent on the motivation—even the *stated* motivation—of the Afro-paulistas who joined the Legião Negra, they are much more eloquent on the other side of the question: how did white paulistas, participating in a movement that rested on racialized discourses of regional superiority, incorporate the Legião Negra into the Causa Paulista? A preliminary reading of the ample newspaper coverage devoted to the Black Legion reveals three main themes. First, the legion provided evidence that "all of São Paulo" was supporting the Constitutionalist Campaign, a rebuttal to the claims of their opponents that only a handful of privileged paulistas were responsible for the uprising, and that it had limited appeal beyond elite circles. Instead, the participation of black troops indicated that paulistas from all possible walks of life supported the movement. Second, the existence of a Legião Negra allowed the paulista leadership to dismiss insinuations of racism. Here it is important to stress again that the discourse of regional superiority did not rest upon a rejection of the idea of Brazil as a racially harmonious society; rather, these two different discourses of identity coexisted, if somewhat awkwardly, within paulista political culture.[134] For most of the paulista leadership it remained important to be able to deny accusations of racism, given the widely accepted notion that racial discrimination was somehow un-Brazilian. Third, and I suspect most important, was the claim that, because they lived in a modern, orderly society, the black legionnaires were superior to their dark-skinned counterparts elsewhere in Brazil. Moreover, in São Paulo, their military experience reflected the paulistas' concern with order and discipline, in contrast to the federal battalions whose troops—composed of "marginals and degenerates"—were not subject to the same benevolent tutelage. In other words, by this logic paulista blacks were *less* inferior due to their association with a superior culture.[135]

Depending upon the particular audience being addressed, paulista sources either highlighted the role of Afro-paulistas in the Constitutionalist struggle or effaced it. Photographs published in the regional press of the many battalions of volunteers heading to the front routinely included pictures of the Black Legion soldiers. But more representational or allegorical poster art consistently depicted the paulista soldier as white only. One widely distributed poster implying the massing of troops simply repeated the exact same "Roman" profile rather than portraying a diverse gathering of paulista males. Another recruiting poster, set in the paulista highlands, depicts a virtual Alpine scene, including an apple-cheeked lad wearing the volunteers' trademark "steel helmet" (see fig. 2.2). In all the many nonphotographic representations of the movement, I have come across only two that depict men of color. One is from the very first days of the war and portrays a black soldier from the Força Pública bidding farewell to his son.[136] The other is an etching done by the eminent artist and caricaturist Belmonte to commemorate the "Campanha de Ouro"—the campaign to collect funds for the war effort by asking paulistas to donate jewelry and any other items of gold they might be willing to part with (see figs. 3.8 and 3.9).[137]

To be sure, such an appeal would be directed primarily at better-off paulistas, but the theme of the Belmonte etching is the sacrifice made by paulistas

ELLES ESTÃO A
SUA ESPERA

PARA COMPLETAR
O BATALHÃO

ALISTE-SE

M.M.D.C.

FIGURE 3.8. Recruiting poster with identical images—"They are waiting for you to complete the battalion: enlist." MMDC poster, 1932. From *Álbum de família, 1932* (São Paulo: Livraria Martins Editora, 1954).

FIGURE 3.9. Belmonte commemorative poster for the Gold Campaign. From *Álbum de família, 1932* (São Paulo: Livraria Martins Editora, 1954).

from *all* walks of life, as indicated by the modest dress of several figures in the group depicted. Perhaps most striking is the framing of the picture by two male figures—on the viewer's right, a young white lad in clothes that indicate he is probably from an immigrant, working-class family; on the viewer's left, an elderly and frail black man, very much in the "Pai João" (Old Father John) vein. The only Afro-paulista out of fourteen figures, this elderly man not only serves as a sentimental, unthreatening presence, but also situates the black paulista as a remnant of the past, fast fading from the scene, to be replaced by the vigorous young white boy who represents the future. It is a kinder, gentler depiction of a process more brutally described by the noted folklorist Dalmo Belfort de Mattos, writing in the late 1930s, who claimed that whites outnumbered nonwhites three to one in colonial São Paulo, but that the coffee boom temporarily produced an African majority. However, "this soon passed. Mortality and mixture gradually eliminated the African *excess*."[138] Similarly, in his widely read *Populações paulistas*, Alfredo Ellis declared that in São Paulo, "blacks and mulattos . . . are rapidly marching to their graves."[139]

Puzzle No. 2: The Modernists

The soldiers of the Legião Negra are not the only group whose support for the 1932 uprising potentially complicates my contention that it was a movement discursively constructed as white, male, and middle class. The enthusiastic support for the Constitutionalist Campaign of almost every major figure in the modernist movement also raises questions about the way in which the Causa Paulista was conceptualized. Though the poet Guilherme de Almeida may have been the only leading modernist who actually took up arms, writers Tácito de Almeida, Sérgio Milliet, Antônio de Alcântara Machado, and Menotti del Picchia were zealous supporters of the uprising, using their pens as their weapons, and artists Tarsila do Amaral and Anita Malfatti signed petitions and helped raise money for the cause, while renowned pianist Guiomar Novaes gave public lectures and performances to help finance the war effort.[140] Mário de Andrade, despite his subsequent remorse, evidently shared his modernist colleagues' commitment at the time of the uprising.[141] Of the most visible modernist figures, only Oswald de Andrade, then a member of the Communist Party, denounced the uprising and refused to support it.[142] The challenge, then, is to explain the active role of the São Paulo modernists in the Constitutionalist Movement, given this artistic and literary group's association with constructions of cultural hybridity. Here I would emphasize the centrality of the trope of paulista exceptionalism, and how it enabled the modernists to imagine "Brazil" in a way that was neither Europeanized nor exoticized, but also reinforced notions of regional superiority.[143]

The modernists are most often cited and praised for their audacious attempts to create an aesthetic that was not merely imitative of European artistic ideas, but was genuinely Brazilian without being retrograde or traditional. They argued not for a rejection of European culture; in fact, several of them were initially devotees of Italian futurism. Rather, they called for a cannibalistic "ingestion" of European artistic and literary trends that could then be "digested" and transformed into something that embodied Brazil's mestiço culture—to use more current language, they aspired to appropriate rather than imitate, and thereby create an alternative modernity.[144] It might seem improbable that such a group of artists and literary figures would take up the Causa Paulista, but not only did some of them support the movement, but a few—Menotti del Picchia and Guilherme de Almeida—figured among its most prominent spokespersons. And even Mário de Andrade, the modernist most often credited with a critical eye for Brazilian racist stereotypes, supported the Causa Paulista—though he did later come to regret his role and see the movement as misconceived.

As noted in chapter 1, there had been a significant schism within the modernist movement just a few years after its spectacular debut in 1922 during Modern Art Week. Oswald de Andrade and Menotti del Picchia, who in the early 1920s had coedited a short-lived journal, veered off in opposite directions, with Oswald hewing closely to the anthropophagy theme in his "Manifesto Pau Brasil" and Menotti, together with Guilherme de Almeida, spearheading the nativist movement known as "verde-amarelismo" (literally, green-yellowism, a reference to the colors of the Brazilian flag). Mário de Andrade, meanwhile, adopted a more ambiguous position that incorporated intellectual and aesthetic elements of both factions. The enthusiasm of the verde-amarelismo group for the 1932 uprising is hardly mysterious; indeed, they could be cited as crucial producers of the images and ideas that made such an uprising thinkable in the first place. Monica Velloso, who has written extensively on this tendency within the modernist movement, aptly notes that "in defending the pragmatic spirit, the poet-educator and the soldier, the cult of hard work and of progress, the group, in reality, was designating São Paulo as the model for the nation." For the verde-amarelistas, "São Paulo figured as the core of the nationality."[145] Having adopted a vision of the nation that situated its center in São Paulo, and arrayed the rest of Brazil in a hierarchical relationship with that center, the verde-amarelistas suffered no sense of contradiction between their regional chauvinism and their nationalism; rather, they saw the former as constitutive of the latter.

Yet there were other modernists who were less inclined toward regional chauvinism, or were even critical of it, but who ultimately supported the Causa Paulista. In the mid-1920s Mário de Andrade engaged in a polemic with modernist polymath Sérgio Milliet because the latter, in Mário's view, had fallen into the error of regional chauvinism by exalting São Paulo: in a review of Guilherme de Almeida's *Raça*, Milliet had declared the author "profoundly Brazilian. That is to say, paulista," which moved Mário to reproach him for his "hysterical provincialism."[146] Tarsila do Amaral, though not sharing her ex-husband Oswald de Andrade's formal adherence to the Communist Party, had traveled in the Soviet Union in the year just prior to the 1932 uprising and as a result, her painting in this period reflected a new interest in proletarian themes.[147] At first glance, both Mário and Tarsila would seem poor candidates for recruitment into São Paulo's "Civic War."

In any particular individual's case, one might point to family pressures or sentimental motives, but I think, viewed as a whole, we can see the way the appeal of the Causa Paulista resonated with certain common elements of the modernist movement, and the way modernism, in turn, invigorated the association of São Paulo with modernity. Even the writings of that prince of ambivalence, Mário de Andrade, reveal many of the same assumptions as those articulated by such openly racist figures as Alfredo Ellis Jr. or Paulo Duarte (who were connected to the modernists in a variety of ways—Ellis published an initial chapter of his *Populações paulistas* in the modernist magazine *Revista Nova*, which Mário coedited with Paulo Prado and Antônio de Alcântara Machado). In his notes for a study of the "Guerra de São Paulo," Mário de Andrade recalls that he and other Constitutionalists would jokingly refer to the dictadura (dictatorship) as a *dictanegra* (replacing dura/hard with negra/black), to highlight Vargas's support from Brazilians of African descent. And despite his retrospective disenchantment with the Causa Paulista, Mário regarded the conflict between São Paulo, a "European Christian civilization," and the rest of (semicivilized) Brazil as virtually inevitable.[148]

Furthermore, he likened the "invading" federal forces to primitive Indian hordes.[149] In his own way, Mário de Andrade actively adhered to the discourse of paulista superiority; to the extent that he differed from the verde-amarelistas, it was not in denying that superiority but in insisting that the traditions and cultures of other Brazilian regions had a great deal to offer to São Paulo and to the nation. This would be particularly evident in his later initiatives to collect traditional musical forms from the North and Northeast of Brazil.[150] But even as he transitioned to a more skeptical, even critical, view of the 1932 uprising, Mário maintained a remarkable personal collection of the abundant paraphernalia associated with the Guerra Paulista. These ranged from coins and stamps to pins and stickers and belt buckles and tie clips and military badges. Produced during the revolt as a means to make money for the cause, or manufactured afterward to meet the demand for mementos of the struggle, these souvenirs of the Constitutionalist Revolution were carefully preserved in special scrapbooks, albums, and notion boxes, and seem to have been among Mário's most treasured possessions.[151]

Perhaps the modernists can be seen as particularly vivid examples of a tendency I would characterize as widely diffused throughout Brazilian society, and especially (though not exclusively) in those sectors that saw themselves as educated and cultured. On the one hand, there was the search for a national identity that was distinctively Brazilian and an effective rejoinder to those outside Brazil who viewed its racially mixed population as a fatal flaw. On the other hand, there was the fascination with the promise of modernity and productivity, and the strong association that they themselves drew between the modern world and white/North Atlantic culture. Even Oswald de Andrade, the one key modernist figure who later disdained the Causa Paulista, could not completely resist this vision of modernity. His call for more inventors and engineers, instead of "speculators and dilettantes," in his famous "Brazilwood Manifesto" (1924) invoked an image that paulista industrialists and techno-crats were eagerly fashioning to heighten the contrast between themselves and "traditional" elites in other regions.[152] At least in this respect, there was considerable convergence between the supposedly subversive modernism of Oswald de Andrade and the white, male, middle-class identity being crafted by the paulista leadership.[153]

Humble but Heroic: The Stories of Paulo Virgínio and Maria Soldado

As I will discuss in chapter 8, the collective and affective memory of the 1932 uprising became, over time, more and more the "property" of the paulista middle class. Indeed, participation in the Causa Paulista—whether by taking up arms or donating one's wedding ring—became emblematic of a certain paulista class identity.[154] As should be no surprise, most of the retrospective memoirs, chronicles, and commemorations of the uprising foregrounded the role of the cultured and educated voluntário, the scion of a comfortable pau-lista home who suddenly and unexpectedly found himself on the field of battle, heroically fighting for his "country" (or to use the appropriately ambiguous phrase, sua terra—his land). There were occasional references to the role of the black troops, or of Afro-paulistas in the firefighters' brigades, and many accolades for the "Paulista Woman," but if anything, the subsequent representations of the movement tended to be even whiter and more middle class than was the case during the war itself.[155] It is curious, then, that two of the most celebrated individuals in the chronicles of the Constitutionalist Revolution could definitely not be classified as members of the white middle class. Paulo Virgínio and Maria José Bezerra (a.k.a., Maria Soldado) were both recognized at the time of the revolution for their exceptional heroism and over the years became almost totemic figures in the epic narratives of the 1932 uprising. Paulo (a humble peasant from the interior) and Maria (an Afro-paulista who worked as a cook for an elite family) became fixtures in the iconography of the revolution, along with the dashing aviators and intrepid volunteers who most often incarnated the drama and sacrifice of that historic episode.

Paulo Virgínio gained his posthumous fame for his unexpected role in the Battle of Cunha, in the Paraíba Valley. This conflict was one of the few chapters of this brief civil war that could be described, in military terms, as a moment of glory for São Paulo since the Constitutionalist troops managed to halt the advance of federal forces from the neighboring state of Rio de Janeiro. Heightening the drama of this battle was the fleeting presence of the widely despised João Alberto, who briefly commanded a federal detachment in the area. In short, the stage was set for a tale of heroism and sacrifice, and the martyred Paulo Virgínio neatly fit the bill. According to multiple accounts, Paulo, a simple farmer, was suspected by the federal forces of knowing the whereabouts of the Constitutionalist battalions near Cunha. When he refused to divulge the desired information, the federal soldiers (so the story goes) mercilessly beat and tortured him, shot him eighteen times, and finally buried him alive, but to the end Paulo stubbornly refused to betray the location of the paulista troops. According to one (improbable) embellishment, Paulo's final utterance was "Morro, mas São Paulo vence!" (I will die, but São Paulo will win). Despite his modest circumstances, "Paulo Virgínio knew how to be paulista."[156]

Whatever the truth of this story, which was repeated in dozens of different contexts, usually without sparing any of the gruesome details, "Paulo the rustic and modest caboclo" became the official martyr of the Constitutionalist Movement. *Cruzes paulistas*, the volume compiled as an honor roll of the paulista war dead, devoted a full five pages to the story of Paulo Virgínio, more than any other hero of the revolution.[157] In October 1935 *A Folha da Manhã* published a long poem in his honor, and in 1937 the Commemorative Commission for the Ninth of July issued an elaborate flyer with a photograph of Juventina Maria da

Conceição, widow of Paulo Virgínio, and their children, surrounded by a black striped border evoking both mourning and the São Paulo state flag.[158] Interestingly enough, the photo shows Juventina and her children dressed in very simple clothing and visibly barefoot even though the Clube Piratininga had taken up a collection to ensure that the family of the martyred Paulo Virgínio would never suffer privations. It seems reasonable to assume, then, that the photo was deliberately staged to emphasize the authenticity and humility of the family, and to heighten the sentimental quality of the saga of Paulo Virgínio. The humble caboclo was a figure who embodied a certain romanticized conception of the paulista past, and thus could be deployed both to exemplify the broad appeal of the Causa Paulista, and to illustrate how a certain sense of honor and sacrifice was deeply rooted in the paulista soil.

Another individual from modest circumstances who became an object of sentimental adulation was "Maria Soldado," a black woman who, by most accounts, abandoned her job as a cook in the household of a wealthy family to join the nursing corps of the Legião Negra. Moreover, during the heated battles at Buri and Itararé, Maria actually engaged in combat and was wounded for her trouble. Unlike Paulo Virgínio, "Maria Soldado" survived the uprising, but her heroism was reported in *A Gazeta*, and she soon became part of the "folklore" of the Constitutionalist Revolution.[159] During the "silver anniversary" commemorations of the uprising in 1957, São Paulo's Commercial Association elected Maria Soldado the "woman-symbol of 1932."[160] And when she died a few months later, in February 1958, the Sociedade Veteranos de 32 MMDC issued a death notice with her photo and an accompanying "Farewell Song for Maria Soldado."[161] Curiously, despite all this attention, it's possible that both the Commercial Association and the Society of Veterans were not able to get their heroine's name right: they both referred to her as Maria José Barroso, but almost all the documentation from the black community indicates that her name was Maria José Bezerra.[162]

In a sense, it hardly mattered (to them) if they got her name wrong—what mattered was that they could point to a poor, plebeian black woman who was willing to risk her life for the Causa Paulista. As we will see in the next chapter, there were many women who played prominent roles in the civic campaign and the uprising, and thus the choice of Maria Soldado as the *mulher-símbolo* of 1932 was hardly selection by default. But as with Paulo Virgínio, it was precisely her humble origins that seem to have made her such an appealing candidate. Especially with the passage of time, and the increasing identification of the Constitutionalist Movement with a relatively privileged slice of paulista society, figures like Paulo Virgínio and Maria Soldado served to remind the public, and reassure the aging veterans, that "Todo São Paulo" supported the uprising. And in Maria's case there was the added advantage of allowing her admirers to repel lingering insinuations of racism within the Constitutionalist ranks.

São Paulo Defeated: To the Losers Go the Spoils

Having told themselves or been told repeatedly that São Paulo was the light and glory of Brazil, the resplendent, dynamic locomotive pulling twenty empty boxcars, the source of two-thirds of the federal government's revenue, the leading agricultural sector *and* the leading industrial center, many paulistas undoubtedly believed that the Constitutionalist troops could easily lick the federal forces in no time at all. Even with General Klinger's premature decision to initiate the armed struggle, and the unexpected resolve of the leadership in Minas Gerais and Rio Grande do Sul to stay in the getulista camp, a euphoric paulista population—or a substantial segment of it—expected a relatively easy victory.[163] Instead, what they got was a swift and humiliating defeat. Despite all the publicity about the well-funded and well-oiled paulista war machine— with FIESP speedily retooling factories to produce bullets, grenades, and steel helmets, the insurgent government purchasing airplanes and armoring trains, and the civic campaign coordinating everything from the sewing of uniforms to support services for the volunteers' families—São Paulo proved no match for a federal army that had a substantial stockpile of arms and munitions, and could purchase additional weapons and airplanes from foreign suppliers.[164] Similarly, despite the ardor with which paulista men, and some women, enlisted in the Constitutionalist forces, their numbers were no match for a federal force that included regular army soldiers, state police contingents, and rapidly conscripted troops from all over Brazil.[165] After the first few weeks of fighting the paulista forces suffered one reversal after another, and by the end of September surrender had become a foregone conclusion. On October 3, less than three months after the state of São Paulo had taken up arms against the federal government, Governor Pedro de Toledo announced that the war had ended.[166] São Paulo the invincible had been defeated.

Given this ignominious failure, one might expect large numbers of the paulistas who supported the Constitutionalist Movement to express regret at the decision to take up arms or to subsequently minimize the significance of the uprising. Instead, a sector of the population made the 1932 uprising into a defining moment for paulista identity. Guilherme de Almeida spoke for an entire generation of middle- and upper-class paulistas when he declared that his greatest source of satisfaction was having served as a *soldado raso* (foot soldier) in the Constitutionalist army.[167] But that sentiment raises the question of how those who so unconditionally supported the Causa Paulista understood and interpreted the movement's rapid defeat.[168]

To be sure, there is a long history of cultures that have glorified a "Lost Cause"—the most notorious being the cult of the Confederacy in the U.S. South.[169] And there was certainly an element of this "Lost Cause" romanticism in the way that veterans of the 1932 uprising talked about the movement and their experiences in it. But in the case of São Paulo, the loss to the federal forces had implications that could not be easily erased with assertions of honor and sacrifice. After all, the uprising had *not* been framed as an effort to maintain a "traditional" regional way of life, but rather to forcibly assert São Paulo's position as the center of Brazilian modernity. From that perspective, the defeat would seem to be a rebuke to São Paulo's pretensions to being vastly superior to the rest of Brazil, whether in matters of material wealth, technological organization, or self-discipline.

A common discursive strategy for expunging this stain from the region's name was to separate the event into two parts, one a civic uprising and the other a military operation. The civic movement included volunteers of every sort, both for combat and civilian-support duty, who would typically be portrayed as devoted to the Causa Paulista and willing to make whatever sacrifices were necessary for São Paulo to triumph. Paulo Nogueira Filho called his multivolume work on the Constitutionalist Movement *A guerra cívica* precisely to highlight this aspect of the movement. He referred to the civilian mobilization as the "Paulista Miracle" and quoted João Neves's remark that "the world will be astonished" when it learns of the rapid response of São Paulo's industrial sector.[170] The civilian authorities issued a final manifesto "To the People of São Paulo" which claimed that all able-bodied men, "in a single impulse," had volunteered without the slightest coaxing.[171] Even historian Stanley Hilton, writing years later with considerably more subtlety and restraint, referred to "a grand festival of civic sentiment."[172] In contrast, the (regular) military portion of the movement, including the army detachments that followed General Klinger and Major Figueiredo into battle as well as the Força Pública, tended to be portrayed, in the aftermath of the defeat, as having been insufficiently devoted to the cause, and maybe even betraying it.[173] Elite and middle-class paulistas had always regarded the Força Pública with some suspicion, given the notoriously plebeian and nonwhite composition of its troops.[174] Thus, it was easy for certain fervent factions of the movement to blame the defeat on a premature surrender by the Força Pública, a claim reinforced by the accord reached by its commander, Herculano de Carvalho e Silva, to occupy the state capital and ensure an orderly demobilization. Herculano himself later defended his conduct, saying that he avoided needless bloodshed by putting an end to an unwinnable insurgency, and also by keeping federal troops out of the city of São Paulo until the situation had been stabilized and tempers had cooled.[175] As for the dissident army units, although Klinger was originally hailed as a hero of the movement, in retrospect various memoirists and chroniclers contended that he virtually ensured defeat when he prematurely provoked a call to arms.[176] This then set the stage for claims that Klinger had negotiated a premature end to the conflict to secure personal political advantage.[177] The result was a narrative of the revolt that neatly split it into the heroic struggle of the civilian combatants (armed and not) on the one hand, and the self-serving maneuvers of the professional soldiers on the other.

Yet another line of explanation for São Paulo's failure was the (allegedly) last-minute betrayal of Minas Gerais and Rio Grande do Sul. Originally envisioned as São Paulo's junior partners in the struggle, both states remained loyal to Vargas. The case of Rio Grande do Sul was more ambiguous—there were popular manifestations of support for the Constitutionalists throughout the state, and four of the leading gaúcho politicians openly broke with Vargas and threw their support to São Paulo.[178] João Neves da Fontoura—an erstwhile stalwart of the Aliança Liberal—was present in São Paulo throughout most of the uprising and became one of the most celebrated orators of the movement. But Minas Gerais—guided by Olegário Maciel and Gustavo Capanema—remained solidly in the getulista camp, and troops stationed in Minas (including a young medical officer named Juscelino Kubitschek) stayed loyal to the federal authorities.[179] Detachments of the mineiro Força Pública stationed near the state's border with São Paulo arranged a "nonaggression" pact with paulista forces, only to violate it a month into the conflict.[180] Among eminent mineiro politicians, only former presidents Artur Bernardes and Wenceslau Brás backed the paulistas. And given Bernardes's unsavory role in suppressing the 1924 tenente revolt in São Paulo, his support came with a great deal of undesirable baggage.[181]

If, in the immediate aftermath of the surrender, the paulistas most devoted to the cause tended to point fingers at former allies they saw as insufficiently infused with zeal for and dedication to the movement, after some time had passed, yet another way to rethink the defeat emerged. In this narrative—which gained some currency on both sides of the conflict—São Paulo had lost the war but won the peace. That is, the indomitable povo bandeirante had succeeded in pressuring Vargas into calling elections for a constituent assembly in 1933 and had made sure that Brazil would soon return to constitutional rule. If the widely circulated poster declaring "Down with the Dictatorship"

FIGURE 3.10. Poster—Bandeirante clutching Getúlio Vargas—"Down with the Dictatorship." MMDC poster, 1932. Courtesy of the coleção iconográfica do Arquivo Público do Estado de São Paulo.

and showing a massive bandeirante clutching a pint-size Getúlio in his meaty fist had overstated paulista power, the heirs of the bandeirantes had nonetheless forced Vargas to yield on the crucial questions. Furthermore, the Causa Paulista had united the perrepistas and the democráticos into a Frente Única (Single Front) that, in the aftermath of the uprising, made possible a "Chapa Única" (Single Slate) for the elections of 1933, and a strongly unified paulista "bench" in the constituent assembly. Thus the paulistas, in the three years following the defeat, could claim to have forced the dictator to regularize and legalize his rule, and could present themselves as more unified than ever before (see fig. 3.10).[182]

The Generation of '32

However rough Getúlio Vargas may have gotten with São Paulo during the first years of his regime, he treated the rebellious state with kid gloves following the Constitutionalist surrender. There were no punitive attacks on the major cities, no prolonged occupation of the capital, no mass arrests—only a few dozen of the principal spokesmen and leaders of the movement suffered a brief imprisonment and then an abbreviated exile. The federal government absorbed some of the debts incurred by the insurgency, and Vargas appointed as interventor his brother-in-law, General Valdomiro Castilho de Lima, who during his nearly nine months in that office proved adept at managing the wounded sensibilities of the paulista political elite.[183]

Conciliatory gestures did not necessarily ease tensions on the streets of São Paulo, where the occupying troops—many of them nortistas—offered an obvious target for popular resentment. For the most part, paulistas restricted their "aggression" to insults and various forms of shunning. In her memoirs Paraná-born Deocélia Vianna, then eighteen years old and living in São Paulo, recalled being pressured by other passengers to get off a trolley when a nordestino soldier boarded. Not wanting to waste the precious trolley fare, she was reluctant to go, but found herself with no alternative. To quote her account: "The trolley wasn't full and I started to read my book, completely relaxed. Some stops later, a northerner in uniform from the 'Legalist' [federal] forces came on board. Immediately all of the other passengers, all of them except me, stood up and walked to the exit. I stayed seated, thinking of my 'pass' that was worth 200 reis, since it wasn't going to be returned to the passengers. Then a gentleman yelled at me: 'So now, young lady? Are you going to stay here with that flat-head?' And then the provocation: 'Aren't you paulista?'"[184] Occasionally, tempers flared and the encounters had graver consequences. The U.S. consul in São Paulo reported some serious outbreaks of violence between occupying troops of northeastern origin and paulista civilians during the Carnaval season of 1933, and the paulista authorities repeatedly called upon the population to avoid behavior that could escalate tensions. But the few episodes of violence seem to have been isolated incidents.[185]

Then, in August 1933, Vargas acceded to pressure from São Paulo's Chapa Única for an interventor who was "paulista e civil" and appointed the CU's preferred candidate—engineer, entrepreneur, and editor Armando de Salles Oliveira—to head the state government. The following year Armando oversaw the inauguration of the University of São Paulo, an institution that would reign as the uncontested center of Brazilian higher education for the next half century.[186] Ultimately, it made no sense for Vargas to be too harsh with the paulistas given his own interest in creating a more modern, industrialized, and powerful Brazil. Or as one U.S. official in Rio observed, "the intrinsic importance of São Paulo will insure its position regardless of the outcome of the present struggle."[187]

Not surprisingly, the paulistas most invested in the uprising did not show the slightest appreciation for Vargas's gentle treatment of his erstwhile enemies. On the contrary, the flood of memoirs and commentaries that emerged from local publishing houses in late 1932 and 1933 tended to highlight the trials and tribulations of a defeated people. Descriptions of the occupation of São Paulo treated the federal troops as if they were a foreign invasion force. In the words of journalist Vivaldo Coaracy: "They were soldiers of a strange sort, who seemed to belong to another race, short, yellow-skinned, with prominent cheekbones and slanted eyes. Many of them had teeth filed to a point. All carried in their dark eyes, mixed together with astonishment at the sight of the superb city, a glint of menace and provocation."[188] The images Coaracy evokes here are an interesting pastiche: teeth sharpening was a practice associated with sertanejos of African descent, but the other features (short, yellow, oblique eyes) seem more reminiscent of the derogatory "oriental" stereotypes associated with the Japanese troops that had recently occupied Manchuria.

Leading figures in the movement also recounted in great detail the unaccustomed hardships of life in confinement and exile. Aureliano Leite, Paulo Nogueira Filho, Sertório de Castro, and Austregésilo de Athayde all wrote of their escapades in the sala da capela, the chapel in the Rio House of Corrections that the Vargas government used as a ward for approximately seventy political prisoners—journalists, politicos, military officers, businessmen, lawyers, engineers—from the Constitutionalist Movement. Athayde, a pernambucano by birth and a young man at the time, recalls in his memoirs rising each morning eager for breakfast and shouting, "Wake up, paulista! Come fulfill your duty to give food to the northerners!"[189] But most recollections were not so comic or cheerful. Vivaldo Coaracy's bestselling A sala da capela offers a rather bitter portrait of men accustomed to a privileged existence suddenly reduced to being treated like common criminals (though it is quite apparent that federal officials went out of their way to treat them differently from other residents of the House of Corrections). Speaking of the occupants of the room, Coaracy notes that "all were highly educated men, drawn from the higher social classes." Being men of greater "civilization and education," he insisted they needed a higher degree of privacy than the other prisoners, who only needed privacy for "animal functions," according to Coaracy. He then goes on to remark on the habits of the "common" prisoners, including their same-sex liaisons, and their skin color(s). This leads to a diatribe about how "superior" men must sacrifice themselves in the interests of civilization. In short, as with much of the writing about the war itself, the author shows a constant preoccupation with the need for hierarchy, and a profound distaste for Brazilians of other social sectors.[190]

From there, federal agents transferred the paulistas and their confederates to a ship that transported them to exile in Portugal (or at least that was their initial destination). For those exiles who were not independently wealthy, support groups back in São Paulo organized frequent events to raise money to sustain them during their banishment from Brazil. Wealthy, sympathetic paulistas routinely offered money to those forced to go abroad.[191] In other words, though any exile is potentially unpleasant, for these men it did not involve great material hardship. Some stayed only briefly in Portugal. Paulo Duarte moved first to France and then spent the final leg of his exile in the United States. Still other militants from the Constitutionalist uprising—for example, Alfredo Ellis—went into hiding to avoid being forced into exile.[192]

Though compared to defeated political insurgents in other historical contexts, the paulista leadership suffered little in the way of abuse or privation; the peculiar experience of being subjected to various forms of state discipline/punishment strengthened the bonds among these men and reinforced a commitment to the commemoration and glorification of the 1932 uprising. Moreover, such a commitment extended well beyond the occupants of the sala da capela to include thousands of men and women who had fought for the Causa Paulista, or lost loved ones, or nursed the wounded, or raised funds, or donated their wedding rings—wearing with pride, for the rest of their lives, the simple metal ring with the inscription "Dei ouro para o bem de São Paulo" (I gave gold for the good of São Paulo) in place of the sacrificed gold band.[193] True, some veterans evinced a degree of ambivalence, remorse, or even bitterness about their role in the 1932 uprising. Mário de Andrade's unfinished and unpublished "A guerra de São Paulo" indicated its author's regret at having participated in the movement, though his paulista chauvinism continued unabated. A self-published combat chronicle by the physician Luiz Vieira de Mello similarly praised the unequalled bravery and spirit of the paulista people, but then unleashed a torrent of criticism against the instigators of the uprising: "São Paulo was defeated because the men who provoked the war knew beforehand that they wouldn't go [to war], nor would their sons." Instead they sent "the good and worthy [common] people" to the front like "cattle to slaughter."[194] And perhaps the most embittered commentator of all was Guaraná de Sant'Anna, the original civilian head of the Legião Negra, who in an opinion piece published in his journal Brasil Novo in 1933 claimed that after the combat ended, the black soldiers "were left huddled in the streets like human garbage" abandoned by their "good and affluent buddies from the hour of combat."[195]

The flood of postmortem celebrations of the uprising, however, likely drowned out these dissenting voices. Moreover, given the enduring influence, even dominance, in the region's social, cultural, and economic spheres of paulistas who favored the uprising, being able to claim a role in the Constitutionalist Movement, whether as an actual veteran or civilian auxiliary, had its advantages. As one might predict in a society where patron-client networks continued to have a robust presence in certain realms, paulistas who had enlisted in the Constitutionalist forces, or their families, cited such contributions and sacrifices to elicit favors—particularly in the form of employment—from well-connected political figures.[196] Aside from these scattered, individual efforts to wring some material advantage from service in the Guerra Paulista, there appears to have been a broader pattern of middle-class male employment that ostensibly relied on "merit," but in which participation in the 1932 uprising played a central role. According to Cristina Mehrtens, who has studied hiring patterns and practices in the municipality of São Paulo during the 1930s and 1940s, the "spirit of 1932" created a common bond among local government officials and aspirants to municipal employment; for the latter, military service in the Guerra Paulista could serve as a major source of social capital. Constitutionalist leaders such as Paulo Duarte openly acknowledged bringing to the prefecture "all [his] soldiers from the *blindado* [armored train] who needed employment." And this pattern was particularly pronounced among young men with engineering degrees who had used their technical expertise in the war effort. Mehrtens not only argues that the veterans of 1932 clustered around the "social middle," but also claims that those of more modest backgrounds could aspire to a certain degree of upward mobility as a result of the connections forged by the Constitutionalist experience. In effect, their service to the Causa Paulista helped to solidify their middle-class status.[197]

It is impossible to quantify how many "soldiers of the law" derived tangible benefits from their connection to the Constitutionalist Movement; we do know that some wounded veterans from modest backgrounds registered disappointment that they did not receive promised assistance. In any case, it seems unlikely that the average supporter of the uprising expected his or her contributions to translate into material rewards.[198] Instead, for many the "reward" was the less tangible, but no less valuable, social identity that it allowed them to claim. In the history of Brazil, the Guerra de São Paulo had been that rare revolt in which the common foot soldier could be a law student or engineer or even the fallen fazendeiro Fernão Salles. Never mind that many of the soldiers were paulistas of color and men (and a few women) of modest means—the allegorical figure of the "soldier of the law" was white, male, and middle class, a figure whose level of culture and education meant that his motives could only be liberal and pure—that is, neither the mindless obedience of the dependent nor the self-interested schemes of the professional politician. As Ernesto de Moraes Leme declared, before the São Paulo state assembly in 1935, "I count as perhaps the happiest day of my life . . . that moment when I removed my lawyer's robes to dress in the uniform of the soldier of São Paulo's Constitutionalist army."[199] And many decades after the paulista defeat, Francisco Ribeiro Sampaio, a philologist who was a founding member of the Academia Campinense de Letras, echoed the declaration by Guilherme de Almeida, cited above, and exemplified this vision of the 1932 uprising when he addressed the local Rotary Club:

> God be praised, I have a title that gratifies me to no end, it is my pride and my glory and I hope that my children and grandchildren will remember and esteem it always . . .
> It is worth more to me than all of the diplomas, all of the riches and honors of this world:
> —I was a volunteer in the paulista revolution of 1932, and, as a foot soldier, served in the Marcilio Franco Battalion.

As did so many of his compatriots, Sampaio then went on to insist on the all-embracing nature of the movement: "Everyone, all the paulistas and Brazilians residing in the Bandeirante State, all social classes, and women and children, with a unanimity never seen before, joined together to give Brazil . . . the dignity of life within a proper juridical order, the only soil in which the tree of liberty can grow, bloom and flourish." And what were they fighting against? "The audacity of our combatants super-exceeded itself in this holy war in which the banner of the law was hoisted to redeem Brazil from a social regime that oppressed and humiliated us, reducing us to the level of certain African states or African tribes governed by the whim or brutal tyranny of a despot."[200] Even many decades later, this veteran of the battles of Buri and Itararé, who spent several months behind "electrified wire" in the Ilha das Flores prisoner of war camp, denounced the Vargas regime not as an offense against the universal right to freedom, but as an insult to the paulista people, whom the dictator attempted to rule as if they were part of an "African tribe."

CHAPTER 4

MARIANNE INTO BATTLE?

The Mulher Paulista and the Revolution of 1932

Those nations that make a slave of the woman stagnate or regress.
—Antonio Baptista Pereira, *O Brasil e a raça*

All it takes is a dozen women from São Paulo to shake up Brazil.
—Valdomiro Lima, Interventor (1932–1933)

Brave young men who are departing for the front, LISTEN!
It is the Mulher Paulista who speaks to you.
—Maria Antonieta de Castro

Historians seeking to rescue women from the neglect or condescension of past scholarly generations usually have to painstakingly sift through piles of documents, reading between the lines, and even constructing imaginative scenarios to insert women into key historical episodes. This has been especially the case in the Brazilian context, where several so-called revolutions (such as the one that brought Getúlio Vargas to power in 1930, or the overthrow of the monarchy in 1889) were expeditious military affairs with little direct popular participation, and even less of an ostensible female presence. But thanks to the tireless efforts of such historians, we now know, for example, that women *did* mobilize in a variety of ways during key historical conflicts such as the Paraguayan War;[1] therefore, evidence that women played an important role in the 1932 uprising hardly counts as a startling revelation. What is remarkable, however, is the ease with which one can make this "discovery." Far from having to delve deeply into the documentation, a researcher merely has to scratch the surface to come upon dozens of references to the sacrifices and contributions that paulista women—typically referred to as A Mulher Paulista/The Paulista Woman—made to the Constitutionalist Movement. Nearly every chronicle, report, or memoir on the Guerra Paulista makes a point of underscoring the active role of the Mulher Paulista both prior to the uprising and during the conflict itself.

Those accustomed to the omission of women from such narratives and chronicles will be impressed, even astonished, by the frequency with which women's roles in the revolution are celebrated and affirmed by these accounts (mostly penned by men). Indeed, the one point on which both pro- and anti-paulista commentators seemed to agree upon was the salience of women in the movement. Their language and tone might differ, with those critical of the paulistas describing the women as "the most fanatical,"[2] while those sympathetic to São Paulo celebrate the moral fiber of the Mulher Paulista. But I did not encounter a single major source that ignored or dismissed the role of women in the Constitutionalist Campaign. Hence, in this chapter I will seek to answer two related questions: First, why exactly are these men talking about the role of women so much? And secondly, how are they talking about women, which "women" did they have in mind, and what did this imply both for the gendering of paulista regional identity and for women's ongoing presence in the public sphere?[3]

Again, it is hardly a challenge to demonstrate that women were nearly ubiquitous in the Constitutionalist Movement. According to the many sources at our disposal, women wrote and signed petitions, joined demonstrations, volunteered for nursing duty (including on the front lines), engaged in combat (occasionally), incited men to enlist, sewed uniforms, knitted scarves, cooked meals, rolled bandages, organized assistance to needy families of military volunteers, buried their husbands and sons, cared for the wounded, wrote patriotic poetry, delivered radio addresses, donated their gold jewelry, and later raised funds for men forced into exile. It might seem, then, that there is an obvious explanation for all the attention lavished on women's participation: they actually were more visible in this movement than in others. But I would caution against this easy conclusion for two reasons: One, I would argue that representations of political movements do not correspond to "real" events in any direct or predictable way. But perhaps even more important, I would argue that there was a clear interrelationship among the ways in which the movement was represented, its gendered construction of regional identity and modernity, and the many spaces that were created for women's participation (especially women of a certain social class) in the revolution. In other words, women's participation was as much an effect as a cause of the gendered representations of the movement.[4]

From the very outset of the Constitutionalist Campaign in early 1931, male politicians deliberately highlighted the role of the "paulista ladies [*damas*]" and treated their participation as emblematic of the movement, and indicative of São Paulo's extraordinary civic spirit. In his early diatribe against the Vargas regime, PD leader Paulo Duarte located the genesis of the campaign in petitions dispatched by "high society" paulista women to Getúlio Vargas, in which the signatories protested the imposition of non-paulista administrators and appealed to the president to allow the popular military official General Isidoro Dias Lopes to remain in command of troops stationed in São Paulo, and thereby "guarantee the integrity of the paulista home."[5] Thus from the very start women played and, equally important, were *portrayed* as playing, a vital role in defining the nature of the Causa Paulista. Speaking in the midst of the uprising, one leading orator referred to these petitions as the opening shot in the struggle against Vargas and declared that "for the first time in the history of Brazil, respectable women conspired in the light of day."[6] Accurate or not, this is a remarkable assertion on a number of levels, and particularly in its implicit acknowledgment that the participation of women in the movement, in and of itself, was not unusual. Rather, it is the specific (i.e., respectable) character of women who participated, and their willingness, even eagerness, to act in public rather than remain behind the scenes that distinguishes women's role in the Constitutionalist Revolution.

Two somewhat contradictory themes appear in this plethora of commentary on the role of the Mulher Paulista. One celebrates her participation as an example of São Paulo's modernity: whereas women elsewhere in Brazil led either frivolous or semi-cloistered lives, the modern Mulher Paulista has a sense of civic pride and a capacity for self-sacrifice, providing yet another example of the greater modernity and moral superiority of the bandeirante people. She is, in this sense, a modern woman and therefore willing to endure the glare of public life when civic duty requires it.[7] This theme at times comes close to portraying the Mulher Paulista as a political actor and an emancipated woman, but the second, and I would argue dominant, theme neutralizes whatever emancipatory implications might be lurking in the first. This second theme underscores the apolitical character of the Mulher Paulista, and the moral, not political, basis for her participation in the Constitutionalist Campaign. This reflects the desire, even the need, to represent the movement as primarily a moral, and not a political, campaign—a "human explosion" and a "reaction of sentiments," to quote José Maria Whitaker.[8]

The most damaging charge that could be leveled against the Constitutionalist Movement (aside from insinuations of separatism) was that it was a mere restorationist political maneuver aimed at resurrecting the thoroughly discredited pre-1930 republican regime. Within this context, both the cast-out members of the PRP (Partido Republicano Paulista), the former ruling party, and the jilted members of São Paulo's PD (Partido Democrático), who had previously supported Vargas and now cried betrayal, had to avoid any hint of their staging a campaign motivated by "mere" political interest. They also sought to invoke "moral" grievances that would conceal prior antagonisms between the two main political factions.[9] This led to the frequent use of family metaphors to express the widespread popular support for the movement, and more particularly, to the claim that even the Mulher Paulista was willing to leave her home and enter into the harsh glare of the public arena to manifest her moral opposition to São Paulo's relegation to the lowly status of conquered territory.[10] Clearly, this discursive strategy depended upon the classic gendering of politics and the public sphere as male, so that the very presence of women in the movement certified its moral and, hence, nonpolitical character.[11] This can be discerned in a range of speeches and articles from this era, but a predictably explicit version of the depoliticization of the Mulher Paulista can be found in the radio broadcast of Padre João Baptista de Carvalho, who simultaneously celebrated her self-sacrifice in the struggle and characterized the paulista woman as "modest, sensitive, affectionate, family-oriented," and as devoid of "any traces of exaggerated feminism, and never tainting herself with politics."[12]

Historicizing an Ahistorical Figure: The Mulher Bandeirante

Not only was regionalism gendered in this context, but gender was also regionalized (and, I would argue, racialized—surely no listener, when hearing João Neves da Fontoura exalt the "respectable women" who conspired against Vargas, imagined those women as nonwhite). The Mulher Paulista, like her older sister Marianne—symbol of liberty in the French Revolution—was an archetypical figure who could both represent "all" paulista women and indicate what qualities were necessary to claim the title of Paulista Woman. In this regard, it is significant that it became customary to refer to "A Mulher Paulista" (The Paulista Woman) with the first letters capitalized, a form that is unusual for a romance language and thus had the effect of enhancing her archetypical identity. Representations of "A Mulher Paulista" not only drew on images of her as innately moral and as alien to the hurly-burly of public life, but also figured her as a woman of exceptional fortitude as a consequence of long-standing regional traditions and social conditions. More specifically, paulista journalists, educators, and chroniclers fashioned an image of the Paulista Woman that drew upon the saga of the bandeirantes, São Paulo's widely recognized "master narrative of *discent*," to use Prasenjit Duara's apt phrase (that combines dissent and descent).[13] While (white) women did not participate in the bandeiras per se, the organization of economic life in colonial São Paulo inevitably meant that women would be overseeing the home and surviving alone without the masculine head of household for long periods of time.[14] Therefore, regionalist writers argued, the "bandeirante woman" had to become stronger and more self-reliant than women (particularly elite women) in other regions of Brazil.[15] The figure who emerges from these accounts is a woman of unusual moral strength and independence. Her beauty is of an austere (and by implication, white/European) character, in contrast to the more obviously decorative and sensual (and perhaps less white) women in the more tropical precincts of Brazil.[16] And though she is strong and independent, she is also profoundly tied to home and family, with little impulse to show herself off in public the way more frivolous and leisured women might tend to do.[17]

The historical construction of the colonial Mulher Paulista also highlights episodes in which individual women, to protect the sanctity of their homes, took up arms and engaged in warfare. Indeed, she is routinely compared to the "Spartan Woman," the paragon of female strength, loyalty, and stoicism.[18] Regional writers particularly enjoyed recounting the tale of the paulista women's role in the early eighteenth-century episode known as the "War of the Emboabas," a conflict that pitted the bandeirantes who settled in the recently opened gold-mining districts against the Portuguese newcomers trying to claim the riches of the "Minas Gerais" for themselves. The basic story line has the paulista women barring their husbands and sons, returning to São Paulo in defeat, from entering their homes, and thereby shaming the men into going back to the fray.[19] It is almost certainly an apocryphal story, and a slightly curious one given that the bandeirantes, numerically overwhelmed, ultimately surrendered to the Portuguese *emboabas*. But it did have the appeal of celebrating valor and sacrifice even when victory proved elusive.

This long-standing image of the Paulista Woman who will not countenance male weakness became especially popular and useful during the phase of the Constitutionalist Movement that involved military recruitment.[20] Four days after the declaration of war, one Eulália Marcondes dos Santos wrote to the *Diário Nacional* saying that it was time for the women of São Paulo, "we who actually have the virile courage of the race of Fernão Dias," to send their sons into battle.[21] A widely circulated poster showed a young, attractive, but stern-looking woman dressed in a nurse's uniform, with her finger raised and the caption "Paulista! I have fulfilled my duty. WHAT ABOUT YOU?" (see fig. 4.1).

And in one of the most famous public discourses of the era, the renowned

FIGURE 4.1. Recruiting poster with nurse: "I have fulfilled my duty. What about you?" MMDC poster, 1932. Courtesy of the coleção iconográfica do Arquivo Público do Estado de São Paulo.

orator Ibrahim Nobre extolled the strength, courage, and self-sacrificing nature of the Mulher Paulista, ending his peroration with the phrase "E então, homens?" (which translates, more or less, as "And what about you, men?").[22] In other words, the strength of the Mulher Paulista was a useful means to shame those paulista men who were reluctant to take up arms. Given the exceptional, almost masculine qualities of the Mulher Paulista—sometimes referred to even as a *mulher varonil*, or virile/manly woman—it was only in combat that men could genuinely distinguish themselves as the stronger sex.[23]

A Moral, not a Political, Struggle

This construction of the historical Mulher Paulista, for most male chroniclers, had the immensely satisfying effect of reinforcing their representation of the Constitutionalist Movement as a moral and civic campaign, rather than a "political" or partisan one, while not challenging the traditional associations

FIGURE 4.2. Recruiting poster with soldier: "You have a duty to fulfill. Consult your conscience." Poster by the MMDC, 1932. From *Álbum de família, 1932* (São Paulo: Livraria Martins Editora, 1954).

of the paulista woman with the home, the family, and the private sphere. Even the formidable nurse in the recruiting poster is pointing heavenward as she urges men to enlist; it is left to the male soldier in another widely circulated recruiting poster to adopt the now-familiar Lord Kitchener/Uncle Sam pose, pointing outward.[24]

Furthermore, the process of identifying women participants as A Mulher Paulista lent their presence in the campaign a comforting anonymity. Whereas the identities of individual men—whether due to their crucial roles in the regional administration, or their presence at key rallies, or their courage in the trenches—are frequently spotlighted in accounts of this period, women's contributions are most often subsumed under the rubric of the Mulher Paulista. It is the rare woman who is mentioned in the chronicles by name.

Anonymity apparently had multiple advantages, and the figure of the Mulher Paulista was by no means attractive only to men. Even the few women who did gain recognition as prominent figures in the movement often sought to portray their participation within the parameters of idealized paulista womanhood. An article in *A Gazeta* on July 22, 1932, reporting on the funeral cortege for fazendeiro Fernão Salles, killed in battle, highlighted "the expression of gratitude from the Mulher Paulista." According to this reporter (who used the typical locution that condensed many women into a single figure), "the paulista woman accompanied the hero's funeral procession and on each street, from the sidewalks and windows, she showered the coffin with flowers." Given the coordinated character of this elaborate homage, he was not surprised to discover that it had been supervised by "a lady from high society," but the woman in question declined to give her name because she "spoke through the heart of all the ladies of our land."[25]

The starkest example of this self-effacing stance comes from Olívia Guedes Penteado, a member of one of São Paulo's most prominent families, who delivered a memorable radio address appealing to the "women of Brazil" to support the regional revolt. Guedes Penteado began her address with the following explanation/apology for her foray into the public sphere:

> Never have I ventured a word in public, ladies.
> Never have I thought to make myself heard by
> anyone at all, beyond the intimate circle in which
> I live, as the simple mother of a family.[26]

There is no trace in this speech of a woman speaking out as a Brazilian citizen or seeking to advance her political rights or interests as a woman, individually or collectively, and this despite the recent issuing of a federal decree establishing female suffrage, and the increasing presence of middle-class women in the paulista workforce.[27] Furthermore, it is even more striking in the case of Guedes Penteado since she was patently not a "simple mother of a family" prior to the Revolution of 1932; rather, she had amassed a considerable reputation for her salon, which attracted leading intellectual and cultural figures from all over São Paulo, and for her patronage of avant-garde modern artists. She was, for example, a founding member of the Sociedade Paulista de Arte Moderna and was among the first Brazilian art collectors to purchase and exhibit the works of Fernand Léger and Pablo Picasso.[28] She also supported the campaign for women's suffrage.[29] Clearly, in Guedes Penteado's case, she was deliberately using the identity of the Mulher Paulista to efface the potential political implications of her radio address, and to make the "public" (i.e., political) character of her activities more palatable, both to male and female observers and, possibly, to herself.

However, as the campaign intensified, the category of the Mulher Paulista began to operate in ways that might not have been entirely foreseen by those who first exalted her as the embodiment of feminine virtue. At the same time that the Mulher Paulista functioned to obscure the crucial roles played by particular women, it also served to enable, perhaps even empower, women with less of a "natural" claim to participation in the public sphere than a privileged figure like Guedes Penteado.[30] Women speaking at rallies or on radio programs would identify themselves as the "Mulher Paulista," or in more local settings, a woman addressing a crowd in an interior town (say, Franca) would speak on behalf of the "Mulher Francana."[31] In what became increasingly standard practice, a woman bidding farewell to her husband departing for the front claimed that she was writing, not as a wife to her husband, but as the "Mulher Paulista" to her "Bandeirante Bravo."[32] Another woman ended a radio address with the declaration "Eu sou a Mulher Paulista!" (I am the Paulista Woman!), consciously using the archetypical nature of this image to legitimate her pronouncements, but also asserting herself as part of a collectivity that transcended her individual inclinations. Even a well-known educator such as Maria Antonieta de Castro, urging on the troops over the radio, began her broadcast with the words: "Brave young men who are departing, LISTEN!! It is the Mulher Paulista who speaks to you."[33] In effect, the Mulher Paulista became an identity that allowed women to claim a voice, exercise moral authority, and celebrate their own heroism within the movement without risking criticisms for transgressing traditional gender roles or abandoning familial obligations. They could enter the public sphere without becoming "public women"—a term that had long been a euphemism for prostitute in Brazil.[34]

It is instructive to contrast the considerable popularity of the Mulher Paulista with the limited circulation in Brazil of that famous feminine allegory of the republic, Marianne. José Murilo de Carvalho observes that Brazil's republicans had little success in using Marianne, a central image of the French Revolution, to disseminate a Republican visual culture in Brazil. In effect, he contends that Marianne, as a symbol, had little resonance among Brazilians because of the extremely limited participation of women in the overthrow of the monarchy, in contrast to their active participation in the battles of the French Revolution—in Brazil, he alleges, the signifier was too divorced from the signified.[35] On the surface, then, the successful deployment of the Mulher Paulista would seem to confirm his argument—we could conclude that this archetypical figure entered the popular imagination precisely because large numbers of women actively participated in the Constitutionalist Campaign. However, as I noted above, this sort of explanation seems inadequate, given its mechanistic assumptions about the relationship between the allegorical female figure and real, historical women. Indeed, as Murilo de Carvalho himself ultimately acknowledges, Marianne, rather than embodying women's role in the French Revolution, served to occlude it. In Eugène Delacroix's famous painting, and François Rude's iconographic sculpture, Marianne (a decidedly unreal woman) is leading only men into battle.[36]

In contrast to the failed introduction of Marianne in Republican Brazil, the Mulher Paulista proved to be a stunningly successful figure in the Constitutionalist Campaign precisely because she embodied, not an abstract, foreign icon, nor a realistic representation of actual women revolutionaries, but a collective image of idealized paulista womanhood that had a regional historical pedigree and a cultural resonance at a time when women's expanded presence in the workforce and the political sphere were matters of considerable debate and anxiety.[37] As for the relationship between real women's activities and the success of this archetype, I would also argue that Murilo de Carvalho's notion of cause and effect here is too reductive. At least in the case of São Paulo, the figure of the Mulher Paulista *enabled* women, especially "respectable" women, to participate in public life, even if in a circumscribed fashion, rather than their public presence inspiring the construction of the Mulher Paulista.

Perhaps nothing demonstrates better the ambiguities of the figure of the Mulher Paulista than the dedication and epigraph that open J. Rodrigues's account published in 1933 of women's participation in the Constitutionalist Campaign. He dedicates the book, predictably, to the Paulista Woman: "That angel, that companion, that marvel who, in her simplicity and beauty, can transform herself from one moment to the next into someone courageous and heroic, sublime and almost divine, making herself everything for everyone, she is the PAULISTA WOMAN." This clearly celebrates the Mulher Paulista's traditional virtues: while she may be capable of suddenly transforming herself into a courageous and heroic figure, she can also quickly morph back to her normative state as the simple and beautiful "angel of the home." But slightly less compatible with traditional gender roles is the epigraph—a comment made by the military interventor that Vargas imposed on São Paulo following the defeat of the Revolution of 1932: "All it takes is a dozen women from São Paulo to shake up Brazil."[38] In short, even though the figure of the Mulher Paulista was constructed in such a way as to reaffirm the conventional separation between public and private spheres, and to reinforce the image of women as alien to the world of politics, it did not always operate to that precise effect once it had become a major discursive strategy for women's mobilization.

Tradition and Modernity

As noted above, a significant source of ambiguity in the image of the Mulher Paulista was the tension between the notion of her as the feminine embodiment of the paulista/bandeirante "tradition" and the increasing emphasis on the Mulher Paulista as an emblem of São Paulo's "modernity." Similar to liberal movements elsewhere on the globe that used the expansion of women's rights and roles as a means to substantiate their society's greater fitness to rule than that of less civilized orders, paulista spokesmen invoked the civic spirit of the Mulher Paulista as further proof of São Paulo's superiority.[39] Though it might seem contradictory to deploy the same figure as representative of both tradition and modernity, gendered discourses often do precisely that since the teleological narrative of progress undergirding claims to modernity typically asserts continuities between traditional virtues and modern values. Indeed, there were significant overlaps in the image of the traditional Mulher Paulista and the modern paulista woman. Both were more self-reliant and civic-minded than the Brazilian woman of other regions; both eschewed frivolous and ostentatious behavior in favor of useful activities. Both were less likely to be cloistered from contact with the "real" world.[40]

At the same time, I would contend that the positioning of the Mulher Paulista as a badge of São Paulo's modernity stretched, and even frayed, the limits of a discourse meant to confine women's public participation within conventional gender boundaries. Just a few months before the outbreak of full-scale civil war, Sertório de Castro, a prominent member of the PRP, wrote an extended essay on party politics called *Política, és mulher!* (Politics, you are a woman!) The peculiar title, far from endorsing a larger role for women in political life or the public sphere, referred to a female stereotype—the woman as fickle, alluring, seductive—that instead reinforced the idea that (real) women had no place in the world he was describing: "I faithfully declare that I have never felt any enthusiasm whatsoever for any electoral reform that had as its purpose to draw the Brazilian woman into the turbulent world of our political activities."[41] However, once the most intense period of the Constitutionalist Campaign was under way, it became increasingly impolitic to insist that women did not belong in the public sphere at all, and it became increasingly difficult to contain the actual participation of women in the movement within "acceptable" limits, discursive or otherwise. Furthermore, as Constitutionalist discourse focused more and more on representations of São Paulo's superior modernity, and the orderly and civic-minded character of its population, especially when compared with the poorer and more "backward" areas of northern Brazil, representations of the Mulher Paulista also shifted to a more modernized register. Whereas in the late nineteenth century, the dominant discourses of civilization and cultural superiority underscored the extreme differentiation of gender roles in "advanced" societies, by the 1920s, modernity had become associated with a (sometimes disturbing) convergence of gender roles, whether in the realm of employment, child-rearing, or physical appearance.[42] In this context, the traditional image of the Mulher Paulista as having an almost masculine strength and virile courage could be reconfigured to demonstrate that she was very much the modern woman, but that same reconfiguration could threaten the carefully crafted boundaries of her political participation.

I would also argue that, as the campaign intensified and public discourse in São Paulo became increasingly and more overtly racialized, the idea of white women of good society participating in the formal political sphere became ever more appealing. As the allegedly degenerate, dark-skinned inhabitants of the Northeast and other "backward" regions of Brazil became the explicit enemy of the paulista cause, race in effect trumped gender as a source of anxiety. In this context, many paulista males (and females) undoubtedly regarded a literate, middle-class woman from São Paulo to be far more suited for full Brazilian citizenship than the typical jagunço (ruffian) from the backlands of the Northeast. Not only did this valorization of women as citizens, then, depend upon a devaluing of Brazilians of other regional, racial, and class backgrounds, but it also meant that the Mulher Paulista had to be represented as their opposite—that is, an immaculately white woman of good social standing.

White, Female, and Middle Class?

The political values signified by the Mulher Paulista, and the various representational purposes she served, are revealed by a range of paulista sources that highlighted the heroism and self-sacrifice of the Mulher Paulista, and applauded her civic virtue as a mark of modernity, but simultaneously attempted to construe women's participation in the Constitutionalist Campaign in ways that limited its potential to subvert existing gender hierarchies. Starting at the most elemental level, various writers had to reimagine São Paulo politically as it became more and more likely that women would be present in public spaces. Needless to say, the physical presence of "women" in public was absolutely nothing new; plebeian women, working-class women, women of color, typically did not have the luxury of deciding whether or not to appear in the city's streets and plazas.[43] But in terms of formal political participation, these women could easily be rendered invisible or inconsequential. In contrast, the mobilization of middle-class and elite women, and their increasing willingness to appear in public, were both more desirable and more subversive for established notions of the public, especially since it was in the leadership's interest to spotlight the participation of women.[44] The goal of many of the contemporary accounts was precisely to foreground the exceptional and circumscribed character of women's presence in the public sphere, with the clear implication that, once the Constitutionalist Campaign ended, women would retreat to their accustomed place in the private, domestic sphere.

One of the most interesting and revealing attempts to "manage" discursively this female presence can be found in the multivolume chronicle of the Guerra Cívica written by Paulo Nogueira Filho, a self-styled "bourgeois progressive." Volume 2, subtitled *The Civil Insurrection*, includes accounts of two massive rallies that crucially demonstrated widespread support, especially among middle-class paulistas, for a seizure of the state government by the Constitutionalist leadership. First Nogueira Filho provides his "I am a camera" account of the historic rally that took place on May 13, 1932, during which the protesters marched through the center of the city: "The procession [in the street] was immense; the balconies were teeming with ladies who applauded the popular slogans." This image could be taken as the "ideal" representation of gender roles in the movement, since it reserves the physical space of the public sphere for men. Women's presence is accented, but they are positioned as simultaneously in public and not in public since the balconies allow for their physical presence and their emotional support, but place them within a sheltered, semiprivate space. It is especially significant, then, that in his description of the climactic rally on May 23, Nogueira Filho observed a "surprising number of ladies and young women of all ages and social categories" who were actually in the streets, a phenomenon that initially produced in him something like cognitive dissonance. But then he goes on to make sense of their unaccustomed presence: "One might claim that they descended into the battlefield, vacating the trenches from which, in the sheltering buildings, they had participated in the previous protests in favor of autonomy. But that wouldn't be quite accurate since the balconies continued to be filled to overflowing. The truth is that, on this date, families came en masse—fathers, mothers, daughters and sons—in order to demonstrate that [the federal government] could no longer wound the pride of the bandeirante people with impunity." On this occasion, women and girls physically entered public space, but their presence was acceptable since they came as members of presumably respectable families, accompanied by male relatives. But there is at least one

FIGURE 4.3. Nurses wearing Constitutionalist caps. Photographer unknown, 1932. From *Álbum de família, 1932* (São Paulo: Livraria Martins Editora, 1954).

detail in Nogueira Filho's account that undermines his otherwise coherent and conventional gendering of the public sphere: noting that the tenor of the crowd became increasingly emotional, he remarks that even some "young women opened their purses in order to brandish revolvers. An uncountable number discharged and reloaded their weapons in view of everyone!"[45] It is this startling image, which a seasoned chronicler such as Nogueira Filho could hardly resist recording, that cannot be effortlessly absorbed either by "the ladies in the balconies" or "the whole family joins the protest" motifs. Instead, it allows us an unusual glimpse into the ways in which a revolutionary moment enabled women presumed to be "respectable" to transcend in rather dramatic terms the normal gender codes for public conduct, and ultimately blur the lines between respectable and not so respectable womanhood.[46] Judging from the abundant photographic evidence from this period, women began to routinely participate in political rallies and public ceremonies, often in enthusiastic and even ecstatic ways that seem to indicate the desire to erase the gender-restrictive character of public spaces.[47] But the photographs also reveal various strategies employed by middle-class and elite women to mark these public appearances as exceptional or unusual behavior. This sometimes took the form of wearing "uniforms": when the Constitutionalist government distributed caps that enabled the wearer to identify him or herself as a supporter,

FIGURE 4.4. Well-dressed women sewing uniforms. Photographer unknown, 1932. From *Álbum de família, 1932* (São Paulo: Livraria Martins Editora, 1954).

a spokesman noted that women had avidly taken to wearing them in public (see fig. 4.3).[48] While one could simply say that this indicated widespread enthusiasm for the movement among women, I would also speculate that the wearing of this partial uniform lent a desired legitimacy (via "extraordinary circumstances") to women's appearances in the public arena.

Conversely, middle-class and elite women who entered sewing shops to produce uniforms for the troops tended to employ what seems at first to be the opposite strategy—judging from the photographs, they deliberately wore clothing that would mark them as foreign to the industrial environment. No one viewing a typical photo of these women at work would ever mistake them for proletarian women whose everyday lives involved sweated labor in the needle trades (see fig. 4.4).[49] Given that the relatively formal dresses and jewelry worn by these women volunteers must have been rather cumbersome once they actually got down to work, it seems reasonable to assume that the decision to dress this way had been taken somewhat deliberately. Again, while this might seem to be the opposite strategy from the avid wearing of the Constitutionalist cap, I would argue otherwise. Both cap-wearing and over-dressing, in different contexts, served to mark the wearer as a "respectable" woman who, in the first case, would not normally or frivolously appear in a public space, and who, in the second case, should be seen as "just visiting" the factory.[50] Both have elements of a "masquerade" that allowed Constitutionalist women to adopt unaccustomed roles without directly defying either class or gender norms.

The ambivalence evinced by both men and women with respect to women's presence in the public sphere also manifested itself in the frequent references to women's heroism, patriotism, and self-sacrifice. As I noted above, the moral strength and *civismo* (civic consciousness) of the Mulher Paulista was a major element in the construction of paulista identity during the Constitutionalist Campaign. Family metaphors were also ubiquitous in public polemics. One typical paulista bulletin, addressed to "Cariocas" (residents of Rio de Janeiro), insisted that the "soul of São Paulo is in every way elevated and noble, and this manifests itself in the [paulista] family as a whole, in its women, in its men, in its youth."[51] These frequent references to the paulista "family" writ large and small also highlighted the nobility of those heroic mothers and wives willing to make what was deemed *their* ultimate sacrifice—urging their beloved husbands and sons to risk their lives in battle, or stoically accepting their deaths. Innumerable newspaper articles and radio addresses cited the example of Malvina Sampaio Melo of Piracicaba, whose son Ennes died in combat. Just before his coffin closed, Malvina reportedly held her son's icy hands in hers and declared, "Go, my beloved son: and may all the mothers of Piracicaba have courage, as I do! When facing the fatherland, one does not weep! [Diante da pátria, não se chora!]"[52] Once again we see touches of the Spartan woman in the idealized portrait of the Mulher Paulista; rather than the grieving, prostrate mother bathed in tears, she is portrayed as proudly and stoically accepting her son's sacrifice. Furthermore, bulletin after bulletin declared that it was preferable to lose a son in battle than to have a family dishonored by cowardice.[53]

Does Khaki Become Her?

Again, the organizers of the movement regularly used women's courage and fortitude as a means to goad men into taking up arms, which was, presumably, the only way in which they could surpass the bravery and sacrifice of the Mulher Paulista.[54] Indeed, to up the ante, or to demonstrate the extraordinary valor of the povo bandeirante, there were even sporadic accounts of women demanding to be allowed to put on a uniform and fight alongside the men. Or a "male" soldier who, upon being wounded, was discovered to be a female in disguise. Or a civilian woman who, in a situation of dire emergency, took up arms and fought "like a man."[55] Though not the principal theme in the literature celebrating the Mulher Paulista, it was a significant undercurrent, and it raises questions about the extent to which the 1932 uprising enabled paulistas to radically revise their images of women's proper roles. Or to put it differently, could the paulista imagination extend its image of the Mulher Paulista and her role in the march from mobilization to militarization?

Women who participated in combat, or were physically present in combat situations, tended to fall into one of three categories. The first, and the one least disruptive to dominant notions of gender roles, consisted of the nurses who dressed in uniforms and served on the front lines, but did not wield weapons or engage directly in combat. Even so, their obvious exposure to danger meant that only women who were single or widowed, and had completed a basic training course, could serve in this capacity.[56] Several accounts claimed that women competed fiercely for posts that would put them at the front and proudly wore the military uniforms provided to the nursing corps.[57] Antonieta Rudge, an internationally renowned pianist (and romantic partner of Menotti del Picchia), declared in a radio address to "artists and to Brazilian women" that "if the men have marched off [to the front lines], it behooves us women to provide all necessary services, whatever they might be; whether at the side of their sickbeds in the field hospitals, or in the most perilous posts to which we might be assigned. I, for one, would request such a post. I wish to run the same risks that threaten our most daring defenders."[58]

In the second category were the women who became impromptu combatants. Not surprisingly in a conflict where the line between soldier and civilian sometimes blurred, there were situations in which the local population, including the women, found themselves in the cross fire between federal forces and paulista troops, and spontaneously took up arms to defend the paulista cause. Such actions were often celebrated as latter-day versions of women's exploits under duress during the time of the bandeirantes. In a radio broadcast in August 1932 on the subject of "Paulista Heroines," Eurico de Góes regaled his listeners with the saga of Maria Dias Ferraz do Amaral, who accompanied her husband on a commercial expedition to Goiás during the early eighteenth century and "notably joined the combat like a man" when Indians attacked their convoy. According to the narrator, even the arrows that wounded Maria in the back "didn't weaken her masculine valor."[59]

Accounts of such heroics often portrayed the women as having been engaged in cooking or washing laundry or some other routine female task when suddenly they dropped everything to enter the fray. In another installment of his radio broadcast on "Paulista Heroines," Eurico Góes shifted the scene from the colonial period to the contemporary conflict and recounted the story of a group of "black women food vendors" in the area around Buri, who at the peak of combat abandoned their cooking pots "to raise the rifles and take part in the combat." He then extolled these women as "worthy descendants of Henrique Dias!" (Dias having led black militias in the seventeenth-century war to expel the Dutch from Pernambuco.) Similarly, he informed his audience that women in Cunha, "using sickles, shovels, axes, etc.," repelled an enemy attack and seized a number of weapons. Declaring them "veritable Amazons," he concluded that "they were well worthy of the Spartans of Thermopylae."[60] It was also common for accounts of women participating in battles under these unexpected circumstances to include a scenario in which some federal officer found himself in the humiliating position of being held captive by these provisional women warriors.[61] In other words, their participation in combat was portrayed as extraordinary and extemporaneous, a matter of intense fervor and sudden necessity, rather than an assertion of women's right or duty to serve on the field of battle.

The third category, and potentially the most disturbing to conventional notions of male and female roles in wartime, consisted of the women who donned male attire and passed as men on the front lines. Several stories about women in combat followed a narrative scheme that softened the subversive implications of women in the trenches. In these cases, a devoted wife pleads with her husband to let her accompany him to the front disguised as a man. Here the woman's devotion to the paulista cause can be conflated with her devotion to her husband; she is simultaneously masquerading as a man and affirming her wifely duty and devotion.[62] Her behavior can be seen as unconventional but not as transgressive. There were other instances of women serving in combat roles, however, that did not conform to this romanticized image of the hyper-devoted wife. The case of Maria José Bezerra (or Barroso), the Maria Soldado discussed in chapter 3, seems to be an instance of a woman being celebrated for her "manly" performance on the front lines, and without any softening elements to make her participation in combat more "acceptable" in gendered terms. On the other hand, as a cook and a woman of color, Maria did not have much claim to conventional measures of respectability or femininity, so that her performance in a typically male combat role could be seen as less "disturbing."[63] And even so, there were some ambiguities in narratives of her battlefield heroics. Certain accounts indicated that Maria was a member of the Legião Negra's nursing corps, and that only when the battalion was under fire did she grab a weapon and join the fighting. Another account, in contrast, claimed that there were five women in the Legião Negra who were "passing" as men and fighting alongside their male compatriots, with the implication

FIGURE 4.5. Maria Stela Sguassabia, "Soldado Mário." Photographer unknown, 1932. Courtesy of the coleção iconográfica do Arquivo Público do Estado de São Paulo.

that Maria was one of these—quite a different story from the nurse who grabs a rifle under duress.[64]

If Maria Soldado could become a celebrated and sentimentalized figure and the mulher-símbolo of the 1932 uprising, the same does not seem to hold for a superficially similar figure, O Soldado Mário. The latter was the nom de guerre of Stela Rosa Sguassábia, a forty-three-year-old widow and elementary schoolteacher who, disguised as a man, enlisted in a volunteer battalion near the border with Minas Gerais. According to one account, after a month of combat, the men in her unit discovered the ruse—that Mário was "really" Stela Rosa—but she pleaded with them to let her remain in the battalion and they apparently consented.[65] Compared to other stories of women in combat, there are several features of Mário/Stela's story that make it more transgressive. First of all, there's no ambiguity in the way her story is presented: she quite deliberately adopted an identity that would allow her to engage in combat. As a widow, she not only had no male partner accompanying her, but had left behind a nine-year-old daughter. And as a (probably) white woman who exercised the reputable (if meagerly paid) profession of schoolteacher, she had a certain claim to respectability. Moreover, the surviving photos of Mário/Maria poised for combat reveal an individual who felt no awkwardness or hesitation when wielding a weapon (see fig. 4.5). According to Herbert Levy, who claims to have served in the same battalion, Stela Rosa proved to be "as valiant as the most valiant men" and was later promoted to sergeant in recognition of her "diverse acts of valor."[66] Predictably, there is at least one account that claims a federal officer, already embarrassed at being captured by a Constitutionalist soldier, was mortified to discover that his captor was a woman. But beyond that, there were no accolades for Soldado Mário equivalent to the celebration of the more endearing Maria Soldado.[67]

Manly Men for Manly Women

The flip side of this near "masculinization" of the Mulher Paulista was the manifest anxiety about the manliness of the paulista male. A frequent theme in chronicles and newspaper accounts was the awful possibility that prosperity and luxury had eroded the manly legacy of the bandeirantes—a "fear" expressed by the paulistas themselves, as well as a taunt hurled at them by those outside São Paulo.[68] The very territory of São Paulo became gendered in the process; an article in *A Folha da Noite*, published in the midst of the civil war, claimed that when Vargas traversed São Paulo unimpeded in 1930, some observers "condemned us as a collectivity that had been rendered sterile by wealth and prosperity."[69] In the run-up to the outbreak of war, São Paulo was routinely figured as conquered, humiliated, forced into submission; indeed, one of the most popular visual images that circulated throughout this period was the map of São Paulo in the form of a head of a very white, European-looking woman (see fig. 4.6).

Those who were calling for forceful action against the Vargas dictatorship, therefore, dramatized, in as lurid terms as possible, the terrible humiliations being inflicted upon São Paulo and seized the opportunity this offered to demonstrate that São Paulo's mettle had not been weakened by money and modernity. One account/explanation of the Partido Democrático's decision to openly oppose the Vargas regime (a reversal of its position during the Revolution of 1930) foregrounds the impact of a poem written by a native of the northeastern state of Ceará, but addressed to the paulistas, which detailed the current mortification of São Paulo by the dictatorship and questioned whether the state still harbored the brave and bold bandeirante spirit.[70] At a crucial prewar rally, Roberto Moreira, a leading figure in the Paulista Republican Party, used steel as a metaphor for regional character and declared that "those who suppose us to be numbed by a corrosive opulence are mistaken." And in a more blatant (and bizarre) use of gendered imagery at the same rally, Waldemar Ferreira of the PD described the central government as a band of eunuchs who had managed to seize the "harem" (Brazil) including the "favorite" (São Paulo), but then had discovered that they had no idea what to do with her.[71] By this logic, the only thing preventing the "rape" of São Paulo was the impotence and incompetence of the Vargas regime.

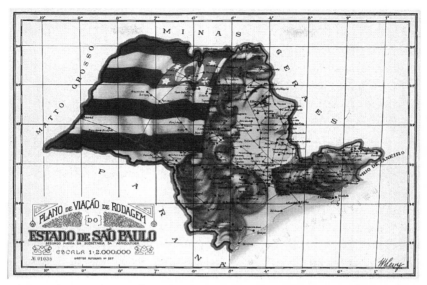

FIGURE 4.6. Iconographic map of São Paulo, with state flag/kerchief—sold to raise funds for the cause. Roadmap of the State of São Paulo by the Secretary of Agriculture, c. 1932. From *Álbum de família, 1932* (São Paulo: Livraria Martins Editora, 1954).

Predictably, the experience of war becomes the crucible to test and prove the true mettle of the paulista male. Various accounts from the front stressed the transformation of upper-class dandies, accustomed to late-night revelries and indulgence in wine and cocaine, into valiant, self-sacrificing soldiers— fitting heirs to the bandeirante legacy.[72] Photographs from the era portray "young men of good families"—particularly law students—posing eagerly, if somewhat awkwardly, with rifles in hand as they formed battalions or occupied the installations of the telephone company.[73] Indeed, the implication was that the Guerra Cívica was necessary, not only to "reinstate the rule of law" in Brazil, but to purify São Paulo and to restore the manly virtues of the povo bandeirante. The battlefield also provided the one venue in which men could surpass the quasi-virility of the Mulher Paulista.

The difficulties of simultaneously portraying the Mulher Paulista as almost "manly" while maintaining traditional notions about manliness and masculine identity become visible in a debate that transpired in the pages of the *Diário Nacional*. As a shaming ritual, various commentators (including Mário de Andrade) had suggested that, in good bandeirante tradition, men who refused to fight for São Paulo should not be allowed to dress in men's clothes in public.[74]

Indeed, one recruitment post went so far as to hang a brassiere outside its entrance with a banner that jeeringly declared "For those who stay behind." Clearly not pleased by the gender implications, several women wrote into the newspaper to protest the strategy of dressing cowardly men in women's clothes, calling it "a cruel irony" given the "innumerable paulista women who are competing for the glory of proceeding to the front lines in the first battalion of nurses." As one woman argued, "in order to stimulate indifferent weaklings or cowards, don't ridicule us women," suggesting that recruiters employ instead, as symbols of cowardice, a baby's pacifier and a bowl of porridge. In other words, the author of the letter had no qualms about shaming men into military service, but believed that the "cowardly" man should be infantilized, not feminized.[75]

Despite, or perhaps because of, these efforts by some women to gain parity with men in terms of their contributions and sacrifices (including appeals to be allowed to join the battalions headed for the front), the woman warrior hardly became the dominant motif in contemporary depictions of the Mulher Paulista. For one thing, the women who actively participated in combat, whatever the circumstances, were more likely to be of popular or modest origins than the women who were visible and active on the home front. References to the Mulher Paulista in the paulistano press made a point of describing her as hailing from "high society" or the "very best families," though often such distinctions could be made implicitly. Consul Cameron wrote admiringly of "wealthy women" doing the crudest sorts of manual labor to demonstrate their fervor for the cause.[76] In other words, with regard to social class, she was far more likely to be classified as someone from the elite or the paulista "blue bloods" than her male counterparts.

Again, given that a woman stepping into the public spotlight still risked damaging her reputation, it made sense to identify the Mulher Paulista with those actual women whose social status and family ties made their respectability unimpeachable. This included portraying her as a "simple mother of a family," a dedicated housewife, rather than a working woman. Significantly, in a handwritten draft of an "appreciation" of the "movement of 1932," probably authored by Carlota Pereira de Queiróz, who coordinated the movement's social services, there is a line that is crossed out referring to women who had to sew uniforms at night because they worked during the day.[77] The author seems to have been reluctant to acknowledge that some flesh and blood paulista women had to work for a living. Yet, early in the uprising a daily paper ran a brief article, "Mobilisação feminina," which reported that a group of women office workers (bookkeepers, typists, stenographers, and translators) had called upon their female colleagues to sign up with the Liga de Defesa Paulista to offer their temporary services to firms whose male employees had taken up arms.[78] These women almost certainly identified with the Mulher Paulista, but they did so by subsuming their own complicated lives under her more conventional representation since the Mulher Paulista continued to be portrayed as wife, mother, sister, or sweetheart, not as a working woman. And her contributions to the revolution, although lauded at every turn, were confined to the relatively feminine and mundane labors (compared to heroism and death on the battlefield) involved in sewing uniforms, nursing the wounded, sustaining the families of volunteers, and raising funds for the war effort.

During the final phase of the civil war this last activity gained particular attention as middle- and upper-class women became both the target and the visual embodiment of the "Campanha do Ouro" (Gold Campaign). Initiated in August 1932 by the Commercial Association of São Paulo, both to meet the costs of war and to mobilize the population in behalf of the revolution, the campaign appealed to paulistas to contribute their gold jewelry—earrings, cuff links, necklaces, even wedding bands—"for the good of São Paulo."[79] Since this campaign could "enlist" support from the many paulistas who were unable (or perhaps unwilling) to take up arms for the cause, it became one of the most memorable features of the Constitutionalist Movement, with some well-off paulistas, who could easily afford to purchase a new gold ring nevertheless proudly wearing the metal band inscribed with "Dei Ouro pelo Bem de São Paulo" for the rest of their lives. Although the Commercial Association ostensibly directed its appeal for gold at *all* paulistas, it was inevitable, given the nature of the campaign, that it would be identified with persons of specific class and gender positions. Obviously, women of middle- and upper-class backgrounds were much more likely to have significant amounts of gold jewelry than women of more modest means, or men in general. Thus the many celebrations of the highly successful campaign were testimony, first and foremost, to the generosity and self-abnegation of the Mulher Paulista, figured as a middle- or upper-class woman (see fig. 4.7).[80] At the same time, the chronicles of this campaign provide excellent examples of the way gender roles in the context of war tend to reinforce an inferior condition for women, even as they are being celebrated for their virtues and sacrifices.[81]

Particularly instructive is the widely read account of this campaign by Menotti del Picchia, one of Brazil's leading modernist writers, an ardent participant in the Revolution of 1932, and an active supporter of women's suffrage. Like other chroniclers of the Constitutionalist uprising, Menotti effusively acknowledged the efforts of the Mulher Paulista in many different venues,

FIGURE 4.7. Class, gender, and the Gold Campaign. Poster commissioned by the São Paulo Commercial Association, 1932. From *Álbum de família, 1932* (São Paulo: Livraria Martins Editora, 1954)

and attributed to her "miracles of zealousness."[82] Nevertheless, it is difficult to ignore the condescending tone in the phrase with which he introduces the subject of the Campanha do Ouro. "The women," he informed his readers, "overcame the most feminine and stubborn of their vanities: the love of jewelry."[83] The parallel being drawn here (consciously or not) between men giving up their lives on the battlefield and women giving up their gold baubles on the home front can only serve to heighten the very different character of the sacrifices being made by the Mulher Paulista, and the contrasting expectations that wartime placed upon men and women of the elite.

Similarly, while chronicle upon chronicle congratulates the Mulher Paulista for her civic fervor and devotion, there are no stories of women's transformation in the heat of the struggle comparable to those recounted for elite men who forsake a dissolute existence or acquire greater respect for Brazilians of less fortunate social positions as a result of their time in the trenches. The closest example would be Consul Cameron's somewhat condescending depiction of blue-blooded ladies breaking their nails and burning their fingers in their feverish efforts to contribute to the war effort.[84] Then there was Menotti del Picchia's account of a society lady who had initially decided to donate only half of her extensive jewelry collection to the Campanha de Ouro. However, upon learning that her maid had given up a gold chain that was her prized possession, the society dama resolved to donate *all* of her jewelry to the campaign.[85] A nice morality tale, perhaps, but one that pales besides the many dramatic accounts of privileged men's transformative experiences on the battlefield.

It should also be noted that, for all the attention lavished on the role of the Mulher Paulista in "shaking up Brazil," not a single woman suffered arrest or exile as a result of her role in the Constitutionalist Movement. There was no female equivalent of the sala da capela, where dozens of the most eminent (male) paulista politicians and military leaders were detained before being dispatched to Lisbon. Sertório de Castro, who spent the three months of the uprising stranded in Rio de Janeiro, does offer a description of a pro-Constitutionalist march in the federal capital, led by an especially zealous young woman, which indicates that women could not always support the movement with complete impunity. Brought to the police station with the other leaders of the protest, this young blonde (a feature of her appearance that's repeatedly noted) continues to harangue the police, at which point an officer smacks her in the face and tells her she should be "at home," an act that de Castro records with great shock and indignation.[86] But this is a rare, perhaps even exceptional, case of a woman who—judging from the description—was from a "respectable" family and suffered some form of abuse or punishment for her participation in the Constitutionalist Movement. Not that women in general were immune from police repression. We saw in chapter 3 that the paulista press noted with satisfaction the arrest of a female civil servant, labeled as a Communist, for producing subversive literature, and several women were among the alleged Communists rounded up by the Constitutionalist government during the time of the uprising. Similarly, there were four women among the eight *derrotistas* (defeatists) detained by the political police in the last few weeks of the uprising.[87] But these women, due to their affiliations (clearly figured as political, not moral) and social status, could not claim the halo of invulnerability that surrounded the Mulher Paulista. In a sense, both sides of the conflict "conspired" to define the Mulher Paulista as somehow outside of the political realm and therefore also exempt from the penalties that political subversives would normally incur.

Mulheres Negras and the Mulher Paulista

The Mulher Paulista is particularly illustrative of the way in which the Causa Paulista could be identified with whiteness even as the sources acknowledged the active participation of women who were not white, either in their own estimation or in the eyes of white paulistas. This raises the question of how the hundreds of women who joined the auxiliary ranks of the Legião Negra saw themselves and were represented by the paulista press and opinion-makers. Even a quick look at the visual sources (principally photographs) reveals a very different image for black women from the dominant portrayals of white women in the movement. Most of the time paulista women, when photographed in public, are wearing white dresses that create a virtual aura around them that serves to reinforce their angelic presence. When not dressed entirely in white, they are wearing jaunty little caps—indeed, in one photo the entire student body of the girls' normal school is adorned with the characteristic paulista headgear.[88] The nurses who served at the front did have full uniforms, but these were tailored in a way that was slightly mannish but modern and smart looking. And with the exception of the nursing corps, there were no women's units attached to the "regular" battalions.

In contrast, black women—that is, women who not only were of African descent but self-identified as black—were organized into a semi-militarized auxiliary battalion and wore distinctive uniforms. These consisted of broad-brimmed hats, khaki shirts, and very full skirts that were dramatically different from both the civilian clothes and the uniforms worn by white women.[89] Precisely who determined that black women would be enrolled in these quasi-military units and wear this particular uniform is unclear, but given the imposition of a white commander, it seems likely that the Constitutionalist authorities played a role in the matter. At the same time, it is entirely possible that the Afro-paulista associations involved in the formation of the Legião Negra also had some say about the way women were incorporated into the legion.[90] Either way, the black women's "battalions" indicate, by contrast, the limits and specificities of the white, middle-class Mulher Paulista's role in the Constitutionalist Movement. Despite all her zeal and devotion, the Mulher Paulista could not be imagined as a sort of support troop or *soldadera* (the term used for women who accompanied the Mexican revolutionary armies) who would fully share the harsh and hazardous living conditions and the menial labor required by life in the combat zones. Meanwhile, the particular dress and presentation of the *mulheres negras* indicated the very different exigencies of their articulation with the Causa Paulista. Compared to the jaunty cap and tailored uniform of the nursing corps, the black women's outfits were more traditional, even rustic, evoking rural/peasant dress. They looked decent and modest, not mannish and modern. And photos of the black women's units almost unfailingly appeared with captions such as "simple, modest, the black women work effectively at the soldiers' side."[91] Apparently, modesty and simplicity made them acceptable as participants in the movement, but still not eligible for inclusion under the mantle of the Mulher Paulista. Indeed, when Gastão Goulart, the white commander of the Legião Negra, did rhapsodize about the Black Woman, he resorted to a very different archetype: the Mãe-Preta, or Black Mother. Referring not to the women who served with the Legião Negra, but to a nameless black woman in Belém do Pará who many years earlier generously provided food and shelter for an impoverished João Pessoa (ejected from the army for participation in a tenente revolt), Goulart declared her "yet one more sublime example of the ardor and dedication of the Black-Mother: she who embraced in her soft bosom the youth of our nationality, singing songs of love, Christian faith, and civic virtue. . . . From the Black-Mother, ebony flower forever kind and maternal, daughter of Father John."[92] In this rendering, the black woman is extolled for her selfless nursing/nurturing of white men, and is situated as the daughter of "Father John," perhaps the most submissive figure from pro-slavery mythology. But she is still not even the stepsister of the Mulher Paulista.[93]

Marianne in Defeat and Retreat

Given the brevity of the Constitutionalist Campaign, and given its nearly exclusive focus on the struggle against Vargas, it is not surprising that neither women nor men used the occasion to aggressively advance women's claims to formal political participation or power. However, one might reasonably expect, as a consequence of such a massive mobilization and celebration of paulista women, to observe *some* tangible alterations in the position of women in regional political life, or *some* attempts to claim expanded political power on the basis of women's contribution to the 1932 uprising—at least during the five years of relatively open political activity prior to Vargas's seizure of full dictatorial powers under the regime known as the Estado Novo (1937–1945).[94] But I have come across only a handful of speeches and texts arguing that the admirable conduct of women in the Constitutionalist Campaign legitimated aspirations for greater gender equality (again, this despite the recent issuing of a decree granting women the right to vote throughout Brazil, which one would expect to create a propitious climate for such demands). One important exception is Menotti del Picchia, who gave a speech in early 1933 before São Paulo's Associação Cívica Feminina enthusiastically endorsing the vote for women, and women's more active participation in public life. In an interview prior to the speech, Menotti insisted that "it always seemed to me a complete political swindle to have prevented women from collaborating in public life." While describing the "Brazilian woman" as a novice in the political sphere, he assured his readers that she was prepared for this terrain as demonstrated by the "incomparable examples of civic culture that she provided in the recent movement in favor of the Rule of Law. The woman [A mulher] surpassed herself. She was beyond Spartan." And he ended by predicting that "the woman's soul, the woman's intelligence and, above all, the woman's intuition" would liberate Brazil from its errors and old ways.[95] In sum, even those who did call for wider electoral participation by women reproduced a discourse of feminine political virtue that entailed its own limitations and restrictions.

To be sure, there are indications that the war helped to open some new spaces for women in political and public life. At least one woman, Carlota Pereira de Queiróz, a medical doctor from a distinguished family who ran the main dispensary for the wounded in the capital, entered the formal political sphere after the war ended. Not only did she become a prominent figure within paulista political circles, but she managed to get elected, in the following year, as Brazil's first female federal deputy.[96] Similarly, Maria Tereza de Camargo, who participated in the directorate of the Partido Constitucionalista in 1934, was appointed mayor of the paulista city of Limeira, a highly unusual position for a woman to occupy. Later accounts, especially by women, would celebrate the election of Pereira de Queiróz as a particularly significant victory for the cause of gender equity, but not everyone at the time saw it exactly that way. Thus when Pedro de Toledo, the deposed head of the Constitutionalist government, visited the federal constituent assembly in 1934, he graciously requested permission to "greet the Mulher Paulista, who forms part of this august chamber."[97] Though I cannot say for sure, I would presume that he acknowledged the other members of the paulista contingent by their individual names, not by an allegorical figure.

With regard to changing gender roles, of more enduring and less purely symbolic significance is the substantial involvement of women in the social services created or expanded during the war. In the course of the three months of civil war at least a dozen organizations or institutions led and staffed by women provided a variety of support services for the movement (and in some cases such involvement extended beyond the end of the war, as women tended to the needs of families deprived of their primary wage earners by death or injury, and raised funds to support revolutionary leaders forced into exile). This "incomparable miracle" of speedily organized auxiliary services provided yet another basis on which to exalt the (mostly anonymous) women who were responsible for these initiatives. The tendency among male observers was to portray these efforts as a natural extension of women's Christian, charitable, and nurturing impulses, and to associate them with the philanthropic traditions of upper-class damas, such as the members of the Liga das Senhoras Católicas (League of Catholic Ladies). But this conventional rendering of women's contributions to the war seems inadequate in light of subsequent developments. First of all, as brief as the war was, it still meant that these services became, in effect, part of the official, public realm—an unusually elaborate, if short-lived, version of the welfare state in which women's efforts were not just philanthropic and episodic, but part of a systematic civic crusade. Furthermore, it was at this time that the very conception of Christian charity was starting to change among women themselves, with the emphasis shifting from the noblesse oblige of the upper-class lady to the professionalized assistance of the middle-class social worker. Thus, the woman who headed the revolution's Service for Assistance to the Family of Combatants, Carolina Ribeiro, was a trained educator and public lecturer who would later run for federal deputy. And one of the projects developed by Carlota Pereira de Queiróz in the aftermath of the revolution was the founding of São Paulo's first school of social work. Male observers may have relegated these activities to the realm of female compassion and charity, but at least some of the women involved in these efforts viewed them in a rather different light.[98]

Yet even if we foreground every one of the women who emerged as an important public figure following the Revolution of 1932, the results seem rather paltry and transitory given the hubbub that surrounded the contributions of the Mulher Paulista. Traveling forward in time to 1954 and the commemorations of the four hundredth anniversary of São Paulo's founding, we find that recollections of the Constitutionalist Revolution still acknowledged the active and vital role played by the Mulher Paulista in that formative episode, but this momentary political visibility does not seem to have been sustained. A rapid survey of hundreds of municipal and state officials, both in the capital and the interior, or of the various cultural and educational commissions in 1954, reveals a near-complete absence of women from public life in São Paulo more than two decades after the end of the uprising.[99] In other words, the celebration of the Mulher Paulista and her dramatic foray into politics and public life does not seem to have yielded or promoted any corresponding gains in terms of women's public and political roles in the region. Clearly the explanations for this cannot be reduced to the discursive strategies employed during and after the Revolution of 1932, but I would argue that these certainly helped to neutralize the potentially subversive implications of women's active participation in the Constitutionalist Campaign.

Particularly noteworthy is the convergence of men's and women's discourses on female participation in the public sphere (conceptualized as both a public space and a political terrain). Participants of both genders described women's presence in the public sphere as extraordinary, in the literal sense of the term (i.e., out of the ordinary). Furthermore, in virtually all accounts, irrespective of author's or speaker's gender, this participation is depicted as motivated by moral and civic fervor, not partisan or ideological motives. Under these circumstances, someone like Sertório de Castro, a major spokesperson and chronicler of the Revolution of 1932, could exalt the role of the Mulher Paulista in the movement without revising his opinion, stated just before the war began, that women had absolutely no place in the hurly-burly of political life.[100]

Indeed, I would argue that the archetypical nature of the Mulher Paulista rendered the female participants in the struggle visible but anonymous, and implied that her/their virtues were transcendental rather than the product of rational thought and political calculation (both in the positive and the negative sense). One of the central themes of feminist discussions of women, difference, and political rights has been the argument that liberal concepts of equality do not require uniformity of identity; women can be both "different" (from men) and "equal." Yet, just as important as difference across genders is the issue of heterogeneity and homogeneity within genders. Indeed, one could argue for the particular case under discussion here that the construction of a uniform or homogenized identity was highly incompatible with fundamental liberal notions of the autonomous subject.[101] In effect, a woman could *not* speak simultaneously as the Mulher Paulista and as a Brazilian citizen in full enjoyment of her rights.

However, we also need to recognize the limits of the Mulher Paulista's homogenizing power and capacity to silence challenging voices and subject positions. Certain "differences" could not be easily absorbed into her image. As should be apparent by now, she was not only a gendered construction, but one with specific racial and class characteristics as well. To be sure, women of color or women of little means could also claim to be A Mulher Paulista, and speak with her voice, but this access came with a specific script that did not allow even tangential references to racial discrimination or economic hardship. Thus Menotti de Picchia is careful to claim that the maid in his story can donate her gold chain because she has a good employer and wants for nothing.[102]

This silencing of other *mulheres paulistas* was the subject of a rare postmortem critique of women's roles in the 1932 uprising, published by the pacifist Isabel Ferreira Bertolucci in the pages of the anarchist newspaper *A Plebe*. According to Ferreira Bertolucci, despite being a native-born paulista whose grandfather fought in the Paraguayan War (1864–1870), she was never given the opportunity to speak with the voice of the Mulher Paulista. Continuing, she claims that "the woman worker and the mothers of anonymous soldiers could not speak in the name of the Mulher Paulista." Instead, the author contends that "she" was monopolized by "frivolous, bourgeois ladies."[103] Clearly, the portrayal of the Mulher Paulista as a sober, civic-minded housewife had not been entirely persuasive to all paulistas.

Finally, I would echo several of the conclusions drawn by Victoria de Grazia with respect to women and Italian fascism. On the one hand, the large-scale mobilization of women often has consequences unintended and unimagined by those initiating the mobilization, and creates exceptional opportunities to advance struggles for women's rights. At the same time, women's entrance into the public sphere should not be automatically viewed as "a progressive measure" regardless of the ends of the particular political movement, as de Grazia cautions. Just as fascism mobilized women and reveled in its fusion of tradition and modernity, it "sought as systematically as possible to prevent Italian women from experiencing these occasions as moments of individual, much less collective, emancipation."[104] This is not to say that paulista constitutionalism was analogous to Italian fascism, but the former certainly was not an emancipatory movement, given its emphasis on the rule of law without reference to a concept of justice or equality, its valorization of order and hierarchy, and its dependence upon a racialized construction of "other" Brazilians. Similar to Italian fascism, it glorified the Paulista Woman, and praised her as uniquely modern within Brazilian society, while retaining, even reinforcing, traditional ideas about women's role in the political sphere. In other words, it was a movement that sought to narrow, not widen, the notion of who could exercise full political rights in Brazilian society.[105] Under those circumstances, perhaps a thin wedge of privileged white and educated women could penetrate certain previously all-male bastions. But it was unlikely that the average paulista woman, despite the exhilarating experience of political mobilization, could or would use it as a path to emancipation.

CHAPTER 5

PROVINCIALIZING SÃO PAULO
The "Other" Regions Strike Back

The entire North is our instinctive enemy.
—Letter from Monteiro Lobato to Waldemar Ferreira, August 10, 1932

São Paulo . . . instead of giving the nation an example of spiritual growth, sank into an attempt at economic imperialism that lent to it, given the relative poverty in which we still live, a semblance of a nouveau riche in arms.
—Manoel Osório, *A guerra de São Paulo, 1932*

In his pathbreaking work on the "invention" of the Nordeste, Durval Muniz de Albuquerque Jr. observes that "the Nordeste is not only a northern invention but, in large part, an invention of the South, of its intellectuals who compete with the northern intellectuals for hegemony within the context of historical and sociological discourse."[1] I entirely agree with Albuquerque's insight about the role played by intellectuals in the South, and especially from São Paulo, in the creation of a region known as the Nordeste. My only reservation would be with regard to his claim about a "dispute" between North and South— at least for the period on which this study focuses. Perhaps on the slender terrain of literary production, one could discern an ongoing contest between northern and southern men (and women) of letters. But from the point of view of most paulistas, their region's superiority to the North/Northeast of Brazil was quite literally "beyond dispute." Given the high priority that a wide swath of politicians and intellectuals granted to the modernization of Brazilian society, and São Paulo's uncontested position as the center of Brazilian modernity, the ground on which spokesmen for "northern interests" could challenge São Paulo's claims to hegemony proved exceedingly narrow.

One indication of how successful the paulistas had been at defining the terms of regional success can be found in the ritualistic declarations of pride and admiration for São Paulo's growth and prosperity that accompanied even the most critical statements about the paulistas' political conduct. Some of these comments may have been a matter of political expediency, to salve the paulistas' wounded pride following Vargas's ascension to power, but the frequent iteration of phrases such as "the pride and glory of all Brazil" to describe São Paulo by its opponents indicates a broad, if sometimes grudging, acceptance of that state's preeminence within the Brazilian union. Thus, when Major Magalhães Barata, the strongly pro-Vargas military intervenor of the northern state of Pará, visited São Paulo in late May 1932 to encourage local industries to use raw materials from the Amazon, he felt obliged to declare paulista industry "the greatest expression of Brazil's vitality" and to describe the paulistas as "a people whose energy and activity honor the nation."[2] Similarly, Vargas's minister of war ended a flyer addressed to the paulistas with a declaration that "the grandeur of São Paulo [is] an object of pride for Brazil of which we are all in awe." Even Pedro Góes Monteiro, one of São Paulo's fiercest foes, insisted—at the moment of surrender—that no one in the federal government wanted to humiliate or dishonor São Paulo, "the leader state, the model state for Brazil."[3]

If by the 1920s São Paulo had a lock on the forefront of modernity, the Nordeste had consolidated its position as the site of mayhem and misery; one could even say that the region's calamities constituted nordestino identity.[4] With large sectors of the regional economy subject to stagnation or decline, and repeated droughts producing the spectacle of *flagelados* (drought victims—literally, flogged ones) fleeing to the coast or to other parts of Brazil in search of the means of survival, northern intellectuals, novelists, physicians, and politicians mobilized a discourse of immiseration to secure federal support and government subsidies to address regional tribulations.[5] Indeed, at the very moment that São Paulo was mobilizing against the "outrages" of the Vargas regime, yet another drought was afflicting the Nordeste, leading to frequent comments by the paulistas about their generous efforts to raise funds for the suffering nordestinos—a "kindness" that the latter "ungratefully" repaid by enlisting en masse in the ranks of the federal army.[6] The nordestinos, in turn, denounced the paulistas for their insensitivity in provoking a national political crisis at a moment when Brazilians throughout the Northeast were suffering the calamitous effects of the drought.[7] And at the same time that the paulista leadership constructed the Constitutionalist Movement as the epitome of order and discipline, it depicted the Nordeste as a place rife with banditry, messianic mobs, and impoverished hordes willing to sell their murderous services to anyone who promised them the means to survive.[8]

The disdain that "modern" Brazil exhibited toward the Nordeste—figured as traditional, even backward—had been evident well before the 1932 uprising. In 1926, at the Primeiro Congresso Brasileiro de Regionalismo, held in the northeastern city of Recife, the youthful Gilberto Freyre issued what he later dubbed his "Regionalist Manifesto" defending Nordestino culture and tradition from the derision of the Rio/São Paulo modernists, whom he accused of abandoning what was authentically Brazilian in their rush to adopt what they deemed modern and progressive.[9] Despite firm denials that he was assuming an antimodern position—Freyre insisted, instead, that nordestino culture offered a way to adopt/adapt certain aspects of modernity without obliterating what was pleasurable and useful in long-standing regional customs—much of the manifesto reads like a nostalgic rumination on nordestino culinary traditions. Freyre, for example, devotes close to half of his text to the sweets and other delights of the nordestino kitchen. This is not an entirely trivial matter, given how crucial food can be to a sense of place and how reflective it can be of ethnic influence, but there is something almost depressing about the spectacle of trying to halt the erosion of the northern states' position within the Brazilian nation with an assortment of sugary confections.[10] Only in the final pages does Freyre offer what will become his most formidable challenge to the "modernists" of the south. Returning to the subject of snacks, sweets, and cakes, Freyre affirms that in the Nordeste these morsels represent "a balance of the African and the indigenous with European traditions" and therefore the regional culture is "totally Brazilian. For this is what Brazil is: combination, fusion, mixture." The Nordeste, being the bowl in which these influences were most thoroughly mixed, could claim to be the most Brazilian region of all.[11]

Thus, a certain (largely one-sided) pattern of North/South "dispute" had already emerged when paulistas began framing their objections to the Vargas regime and the appointment of João Alberto as interventor in terms sharply hostile to nordestino society and culture.[12] At the same time, a new coalition of northern leaders sought to revive their region's political fortunes through a strong alliance with Vargas and his closest supporters.[13] The resulting political tension of the early 1930s created an atmosphere in which the nature of the "conflict" intensified and moved from the realms of relatively polite literary and cultural debate to a highly politicized and, from the paulista perspective, increasingly racialized exchange of charges and countercharges. In previous chapters I discussed the way in which the paulistas who supported the uprising condensed and transformed the "enemy" into the Nordeste, and what types of images they deployed to heighten the contrasts between these two regions and to question the legitimacy of the nordestinos' role in national politics. In this chapter I will be focusing on the way in which various individuals or entities situated in the Nordeste—and especially through the periodical press—responded to the paulistas' revolt against the Vargas regime, and to their disparaging representations of nortistas.

Before delving into the material from newspapers and other sources, I want to strike a note of caution. Paulista discourse in the early 1930s generally served to sharpen the differences and to exaggerate the antipathies between São Paulo and the North, and to treat these two locations as fixed, neatly bounded, and entirely separate.[14] Therefore, by constructing this chapter around the theme of the "nordestino response to São Paulo," I may seem to be giving a "voice" to the "subaltern" region, but this approach also runs the risk of reifying the paulista discourse of uneven development and regional difference, and treating the Nordeste as a fixed, coherent region rather than as an imagined locale produced by the political, economic, and cultural struggles of early twentieth-century Brazil. It also implies that "the paulista" and "the nordestino" speak from distinct and opposed subject positions, when it seems more accurate to say that there was extensive overlap in the way that paulista and nordestino politicians and writers represented each other and imagined the nation.[15] As Albuquerque notes in the study cited above, the image of the Nordeste as a decaying society and a land of poverty and misery can be found, first and foremost, in the novels and essays of nordestino writers themselves.[16] Even Freyre, in the *Manifesto regionalista*, pauses in his recitation of the regional culinary delights to assure his audience that "in seeking to rehabilitate northeastern values and traditions, we are not judging these lands, which are for the most part arid, heroically poor, devastated by banditry, malaria, and even hunger, to be the Holy Land or the Paradise of Brazil."[17]

At least one of the newspapers on which I will be relying in this chapter, the *Diário de Pernambuco*, is a perfect example of how misleading it would be to identify a singular or authentic "voice" of the Nordeste, or to treat regional difference as always operating against national networks and affiliations. The oldest continuously published newspaper in Latin America, located in the city Freyre explicitly identifies as the unofficial regional capital,[18] the *Diário* would seem to be the quintessential source for the "nordestino point of view." But it was also a major link in the periodical chain known as Diários Associados, owned by *national* publishing mogul Francisco de Assis Chateaubriand (often referred to as the William Randolph Hearst of Brazil). Though "Chatô" was a native of the northeastern state of Paraíba, he spent much of his early years as a newspaperman in Rio and São Paulo, and his business, political, and personal interests by the 1930s ranged across a broad portion of the Brazilian nation. He also had a rocky relationship with Getúlio Vargas, as demonstrated by the federal government's decision, at the height of the Constitutionalist uprising, to briefly shut down the *Diário de Pernambuco* and to arrest its publisher.[19] Thus, for several weeks in 1932, Chatô found himself in the company of various paulista opponents of the Vargas regime in the sala da capela, and the *Diário de Pernambuco* was compelled to refer to the paulista uprising as the "Subversive Movement in the South of the Country" to resume publication.[20]

At the same time, its location in Recife meant that the *Diário* could not reproduce without comment the highly disparaging images of the Nordeste being generated by the most fervent paulista supporters of the Constitutionalist Movement; its location was not made entirely irrelevant by Chatô's transregional interests. So, for example, an issue in late April 1932 vehemently criticized the federal government's plan to transport drought victims to the South of Brazil. Entitled "Depopulating the Nordeste," the article charged that "within a short while, the slave-trading ships [*navios negreiros*] will anchor on the beaches of Ceará in order to fill their hulls with human merchandise, which the Brazilian government intends to relocate to the labor markets of the south."[21] A few weeks earlier, a similar article about flagelados fleeing to the South had complained that the government of São Paulo offered a warmer welcome to foreign immigrants than to nordestino migrants.[22] As these articles demonstrate, the newspaper's location in Recife was not beside the point, but it also cannot be assumed that this location determined its position on the prevailing political issues.

The other newspaper that will be a major source for this chapter is *O Povo*, published in Fortaleza, capital city of Ceará. An independent paper founded in 1928 by Demócrito Rocha, its first editorial described the new daily as dedicated to "defending the interests of society against the dominant oligarchies" and "advancing the development of Ceará."[23] In other words, *O Povo* sought both to have the standard features of a mainstream newspaper and to cultivate a more popular image. In this regard, it could more appropriately be designated as the "voice of the nordestino," or at least that was how the editor projected it. This daily also served what was widely considered one of the most immiserated areas of the Northeast, and one of the states most severely affected by the drought of 1932. Indeed, until May 1932 the major theme in *O Povo* was *not* the increasing political turbulence in the state of São Paulo, but the suffering and dislocations caused by the catastrophic lack of rainfall in the interior of the Nordeste.

From National Movement to Causa Paulista

The history and memory of the Constitutionalist Revolution has been so thoroughly equated with the narrative of the Causa Paulista, that is, the resentment of the povo bandeirante at Vargas's impudence in imposing a tenente and nordestino on the government of São Paulo, that it seems impossible to imagine the movement as not strictly regionalist or paulista in origins. But the campaign in favor of the re-constitutionalization of Brazil was a much broader movement than paulista sources would indicate or acknowledge, and this transregional character is evident in the coverage of political developments by the two northeastern newspapers.[24] Even in the months leading up to the revolt, both dailies treated it as a national movement and emphasized the "triple alliance" of Minas, Rio Grande do Sul, and São Paulo, and not the "case of São Paulo." *O Povo*'s coverage of the specific situation in São Paulo paid more attention to labor agitation than it did to an impending political crisis. The DP, meanwhile, reflecting the political sympathies of its publisher, closely chronicled the "Campanha Pro-Constituinte" in the Nordeste, and in a late April article on the national political situation declared: "All political activity at the moment is revolving around the alliance among Rio Grande do Sul, São Paulo and Minas for a campaign in favor of the immediate constitutionalization of the nation."[25]

Shortly after the publication of that article, DP's coverage of the "political crisis" did decisively shift to a focus on São Paulo, including an item on May 13 claiming that São Paulo was demanding "unrestricted autonomy"—the first explicit reference to a movement motivated by more than the desire for a constitution.[26] But even then there were frequent references to *pro-constituinte* rallies in the federal capital, as well as an essay by Austregésilo de Athayde— soon to be recognized as a leading northeastern intellectual—insisting that the movement was a national, not a regional, one.[27] It is only after May 23, the day of the massive rally followed by the clash between paulistas and Miguel Costa's Revolutionary Legion that led to the deaths of four young men represented by the initials MMDC, that the coverage identifies the crisis as localized in São Paulo. Tellingly, the article recounting these events bore the headline "The Civic Movement That Animates São Paulo in Defense of Its Moral Autonomy," with nary a mention of the call for a constitution.[28]

The rapid transformation of representations of the movement from a national campaign for re-constitutionalization to a struggle for regional autonomy by the state of São Paulo placed Assis Chateaubriand and others like him in a delicate position. Chatô's attempt to parse the situation in a way that deflected the paulistas' most exaggerated claims while still sympathizing with their demands is evident in an editorial he published at the end of May entitled, significantly, "O Brasil das Capitanias"—the latter term referring to the original regional divisions of Portuguese America in the early colonial period. He begins by deriding remarks made by paulista deputies in the federal Chamber of Deputies during the 1920s such as "São Paulo *is* Brazil," and dismissing the notorious image of São Paulo as the locomotive pulling twenty empty boxcars. But he follows this with an acknowledgment that over half of Brazil's gross national product originates in São Paulo and then proceeds to make the rather tortuous argument that since federal policies continue to be favorable to the paulistas' economic interests, the current movement for autonomy must be motivated by (loftier) political goals, not economic concerns: "If São Paulo were the self-interested land that various people erroneously suppose it to be, she would have ample motive to be delighted with the Provisional [Vargas] Government."[29] Ventriloquizing the aggrieved paulista, he then goes on to say, "We not only lost federal hegemony with the victory of the Revolution [of 1930], but we are no longer even lords in our own abode." Switching to his own voice (by this point, barely distinguishable from the paulista's), he closes by declaring that "centralization is a political heresy that is at odds both with our traditions and with our present conditions."[30]

Throughout the month of June DP's coverage of the crisis continued to veer more and more toward the "Case of São Paulo." In mid-June the first article appeared citing the specter of separatism among the paulistas, and an article two days later commenting on the emotional tenor of events in the *estado bandeirante* observed that "these are truly heroic days for São Paulo."[31] Yet even in June there were repeated references to the robust alliance between São Paulo, Minas, and Rio Grande do Sul, and as late as the end of that month, a headline declared the alliance between São Paulo and Rio Grande "indissoluble."[32] At the same time, the aim of the movement was increasingly identified as federalism, rather than constitutional rule. With remarkably little foresight, one item in late June claimed that recent events demonstrated definitively that Brazil could not be centralized; referring to "this duel between paulista autonomy and the leveling will of the dictatorship," the article ended by prematurely declaring São Paulo the victor.[33] There were also ongoing editorial efforts to portray the struggle as *national* and to deny a "North versus South" characterization of the conflict. Hence a quote from the Rio-based Catholic publication *A Ordem* called upon Brazilians to "avoid allowing a North-South schism to affect our unity of action."[34] And a mere two days before the outbreak of war, DP insisted that "the movement in favor of re-constitutionalization is gaining space within the conservative classes." After all, as the Northeast's leading daily, it would have been awkward for the DP to throw its support to São Paulo if the conflict were strictly defined along a north/south axis.[35]

North versus South

Like its counterpart in Recife, O Povo treated the movement against the Vargas regime as not reducible to the "Case of São Paulo." Even in the first days of July, its coverage of the crisis seemed more focused on political tensions in Rio Grande do Sul than on São Paulo. Reporting on the latter tended to emphasize labor agitation and the intensifying roundups of alleged Communists by the insurgent state government.[36] However, in contrast to the DP, O Povo quite readily embraced the idea of the conflict as one that pitted North against South. Thus in June it reported that the "interventors of the North" were forming their own "Frente Única" to prevent the return to power of decadent political elements (i.e., the paulista oligarchy) and later referred approvingly to this "League of the North against the South."[37] Once the actual war (which the newspaper labeled "seditious and openly reactionary") had begun, O Povo escalated its polemic against the paulistas and intensified its appeals to nortistas to rally around Vargas's provisional government. On July 13 it reprinted the entire speech of Bahia interventor Juraci Magalhães in which the latter unreservedly identified Bahia as part of "O Norte," and even as the "most potent expression of the greatness of the North," and accused the paulistas of trying to take bread out of the mouths of the suffering drought victims. In the final lines of the speech, Magalhães declared: "The North is awakening. The North is speaking. The North is declaring itself a land that doesn't belong to anyone else!" And he closed by denouncing "this attempt at an invasion by the slavocrats!"[38] If the paulistas sought to disparage the nortistas as the descendants of slaves, the response was to associate the paulistas with an archaic and autocratic slaveholding mentality.

What is even more noteworthy is the language that O Povo used to rouse cearenses and coax them to volunteer for military service. In "Let's Save the Revolution!" it called upon cearenses to fight for Brazil and for the Nordeste, insisting that "the blood of the nordestino will always be prepared to sacrifice itself for Brazil" (see figs. 5.1 and 5.2).[39] With the aim of stimulating further volunteers, in mid-August it published a poem entitled "Rouse yourself, cearense peasant!" (Ergue-te, caboclo cearense!), which included the following lines, deliberately written in a regional colloquial style:

FIGURE 5.1. "Nortista" federal troops. Photographer unknown, 1932. From the collection of the Museu Histórico of Itapira. Courtesy of Marcio Carlos.

Chegô a hora im qui o Norte
Ou luta ou se dispedaça!
Vai mostrá qui a nossa gente
É mais maió quando sente
Qui é grande a sua desgraça.

The hour is arrived for the North
Either to fight or fall apart!
It's gonna show that our folk
Are more greater when they sense
How great is their disgrace.[40]

Similarly, *O Imparcial*, published in the northern state of Maranhão, argued that too much attention had been paid to whether Minas Gerais and Rio Grande do Sul would support Vargas. According to this daily, "the North is the indispensable element for the solution to this case." Furthermore, it claimed that the Revolution of 1930 would never have succeeded in bringing Vargas to power in the first place without the assistance of the nortistas.[41] And the *Diário de Pernambuco* quoted Major Magalhães Barata, who had so recently been extolling the virtues of São Paulo, as urging every able-bodied Brazilian man to offer his services, and citing "principally the North, which has been

FIGURE 5.2. Federal troops in the trenches. Photographer unknown, 1932. From the collection of the Museu Histórico of Itapira. Courtesy of Marcio Carlos.

the most direct and profound beneficiary of the arrival of the revolution."[42] In other words, at the very moment when the paulistas sought to identify the enemy as "the North," there was a concomitant tendency in the North to present itself as the principal foe of the paulistas, and therefore the principal champion of the Brazilian nation.

In Defense of the Nordestino

As part of its campaign to encourage nortistas/nordestinos to take up arms in defense of the Vargas regime (typically equated with "Brazil"), *O Povo* periodically recounted examples of the deep prejudices that paulistas harbored toward their northern compatriots. One of the most interesting articles that the cearense daily published in this vein was entitled "How One of the Paulista Leaders Judges the Man and the Land of the Nordeste."[43] The "leader" in question was Paulo de Morais Barros, then minister of finance in the insurgent paulista cabinet, and an eminent *sanitarista*—that is, a physician who specialized in the field of public health. Soon after Epitácio Pessoa (1922–1926) took office as president, Morais Barros participated in a three-man mission to the Northeast (the other mission members being Cândido Rondon and Ildefonso Simões Lopes) to investigate conditions for drought relief in the region. According to the article, the expedition was rushed and haphazard, and resulted in "a defeatist account," but particularly egregious in this regard were the writings and lectures produced by Morais Barros, which *O Povo* described as expressing "the most distressing pessimism" with regard to the Nordeste. Among other samples of his anti-nordestino disposition, Morais Barros claimed that the inhabitants of the Nordeste were "pygmies with bad complexions and little intelligence who lacked energy and initiative."[44]

What makes this article especially interesting is not just the dredging up of an unsavory series of writings by a member of the paulista insurgent government, but the strategy employed for refuting Morais Barros's disparaging assessment of the nordestino. According to *O Povo*, a North American engineer then residing in the Nordeste, Charles Comstock, was so incensed by Morais Barros's remarks that he took it upon himself to refute them, writing personally to the inspector general of works to combat the drought. Comstock claimed Morais Barros's viewpoint was that "the people of the Nordeste are not worth the money and the effort that these works would cost," and went on to defend the nordestino as hardworking, family-oriented, and cooperative. True, "he [had] deficiencies," but these were due—according to the engineer—to the widespread poverty and malnutrition in the region; indeed, Comstock insisted that the average nordestino's energy level was remarkable given the poor quality of his diet. As for his stature, Comstock admitted that the nordestino was short, but not a pygmy, and that "intellectually, they were immature"—that is, not very cultured—but this he attributed to the amount of effort they had to dedicate to sheer survival.[45] To be sure, these rebuttals were rather routine and relied on their own set of condescending, if more sympathetic, stereotypes. But what was significant in this case was the identity of the speaker—a foreign engineer (that is, an outsider with technical expertise), and even more important, a U.S. citizen. Since Comstock's countrymen were notorious in Brazil for their racism and ethnocentrism, the fact that someone from the United States defended the nordestino and held him in higher esteem than the paulista "expert" placed Morais Barros in an extremely unflattering, and un-Brazilian, light.[46]

Just as the paulista press was rife with articles that seemed nearly hysterical in their descriptions of nordestinos coming south to "drink the paulistas' blood," the northeastern press provided space for the most heated and alarmist polemics about the paulistas' intentions vis-à-vis the Nordeste. In late August *O Povo* published a story garrulously headlined "São Paulo and the Nordestinos—Now It's Not Just Disdain: It's Hatred for the States of the North." It started out by citing reports from nordestinos in São Paulo about their humiliating treatment at the hands of the paulistas, and the "terrible animosity" that the latter expressed toward them. But it quickly moved from this entirely credible claim to an apocalyptic register: "The current mood of the bandeirantes leads us to assume that if, in the past, the South has always disparaged the Nordeste, today, speaking hypothetically, if São Paulo were to reconquer its political hegemony, there would not be merely disdain, but rather a war of extermination against the Nordeste." And the article closed with the declaration that, to the paulistas, "the rest of Brazil represents nothing and deserves nothing."[47] Here there is no elaborate critique of the paulistas—they are simply presented as unpatriotically and irrationally hostile to the nordestinos. Indeed, the only brief explanation proffered in the article for these biased attitudes is the "exaggerated parochialism of that people." This charge also appears, in a somewhat modulated form, in O Imparcial, which claimed that "the provincialism peculiar to all the Brazilian States is exacerbated in the case of São Paulo."[48] An accusation of excessive parochialism, on the one hand, might seem perfectly justified and on target at a moment of flagrant paulista chauvinism; but on the other hand, it could be easily contradicted by pointing to the large, and largely welcome, presence of foreign-born residents of São Paulo. In other words, provincialism alone was an inadequate explanation since it evaded entirely the question of *why* paulistas displayed such special hostility toward the nordestinos in their midst.

The closing sentence of the article in O Povo, which cites São Paulo's disdain for "the rest of Brazil" (that is, not just the Nordeste), is highly intriguing in this regard. It implies that the paulistas' anti-nordestino prejudice is simply an element of their generalized disdain for the Brazil outside São Paulo's borders. But even a cursory examination of the paulista sources would call this claim into question. Despite their bitter disappointment at being "deserted" by Minas and Rio Grande do Sul, there were very few items in the paulista press or ephemeral publications from the period that manifested a similarly disdainful attitude toward mineiros and gaúchos. The exceptions were the overtly separatist manifestos, such as the one which described the "hordes from the South and the North and Minas," who "today, based on a common ideal . . . have allied to attack São Paulo, to loot São Paulo, to pillage São Paulo."[49] But more common was the claim that troops from Minas, Rio Grande do Sul, and Paraná displayed reluctance, even insubordination, when ordered to fight the paulistas, and that the federal government therefore had to rely on reinforcements from Pernambuco and other northeastern locations to maintain its offensive.[50] Clearly, there was a racial subtext to the paulistas' antagonism toward the nordestinos, and O Povo's alarmist comments about a future "war of extermination" indicate an awareness of this, but even at this moment of intense verbal and armed clashes, the author of the article preferred to skirt the issue.

Indeed, one of the interesting features of *O Povo*'s coverage of the political climate in São Paulo is the oscillation between identifying a particular animus toward the North and a claim that São Paulo's disdain extended to every corner of Brazil. An article on a speech by Pedro de Toledo to foreign consuls resident in São Paulo bore the headline "How Mr. Toledo Describes the Volunteers from the North" even though his remarks were not directed exclusively at the Nordeste. According to *O Povo*, the head of the insurgent paulista government made the following statement to his consular audience: "It is impossible that the most enterprising and progressive people of this beautiful nation and the leaders who have guided them to the most elevated degree of the present civilization would be crushed precisely by a caste of fanatics . . . who have yet to be exposed to the benefits of civilization, herded together in a violent cause by the delegates of that caste, just as yesterday in the Contestado, in the interior of Minas, or in the Brazilian Nordeste they were by the Silvinos and Lampeões."[51] Although this statement certainly disparaged the Northeast by implying that two notorious bandits and their ilk called the political shots in that region, it also classified parts of Paraná and Minas as uncivilized terrain. Perhaps it was evident that the areas being described were, in effect, being treated by Toledo as virtual extensions of the Nordeste, the embodiment of Brazilian backwardness.

Again, the options for refuting these negative portrayals of the Nordeste were limited; the one most often deployed was to simultaneously depict the Nordeste as the "real Brazil" while impugning São Paulo's "brasilidade." The *Diário de Pernambuco*, for example, quoted an apparently conciliatory speech by nordestino politician and novelist José Américo de Almeida in which he urged nortistas in São Paulo to try to convince the paulistas to put down their weapons: "Say to them that if the outcome of this drama were to be the mutilation of our Country, the North which is totally Brazil, which is the bedrock of our nationality *free of diluting cosmopolitanisms*, will always be Brazil."[52] In this short statement we can see both strategies: the assertion of the Northeast as the bedrock of Brazil, and the implication that São Paulo has been somehow polluted by the presence of foreign influences. In this vein, *O Povo* also congratulated Bahian interventor Juraci Magalhães for refusing an offer of aid from a retired British army officer, "even as the paulistas contract Hungarians and other [foreign] elements to engage in combat against Brazilians."[53]

Anti-paulista literature frequently aired the charge that paulistas received aid and comfort from foreigners, and that the region's vaunted cosmopolitanism was, in fact, evidence of its un-Brazilian character. Occasionally, this "nativist" attack on São Paulo took particularly unsavory turns. Thus a poem, "Ser Nortista—Não Paulista" (To be a Northerner—Not Paulista) authored by Dr. Magdaleno Girão Barroso, first published in *A Hora* in Ceará and then reprinted in Rio's *Diario da Noite* a few years after the Constitutionalist defeat, had this to say about the respective regional identities:

> To be a northerner is to be yet a cavalier
> Intrepid, serene and manly,
> It is to be free of mixture with the foreigner
> It is to be the number one Brazilian of Brazil
>
> To be paulista is to be a miserable hypocrite,
> It is to be nothing more than a pathetic Zebedee,
> It is to be Armando Salles—a Brazilian
> Disguised in the cloak of a Jew.[54]

An up-and-coming lawyer in Ceará, Barroso apparently was well aware that imputations of Jewishness, or associations with Jews—in this case directed at the editor of *O Estado de São Paulo* who became interventor and then governor in 1933–1934 and then presidential candidate in 1937—would be enough to depict the paulista as a "rootless cosmopolitan," and to imply a lack of patriotism or loyalty.[55] Most other accusations of fraternizing with foreigners did not resort to anti-Semitic imagery; indeed, more common was the claim that the paulista leadership, through the "good offices" of Count Francisco Matarazzo and other wealthy Italians resident in Brazil, was forming an alliance with Mussolini's fascist state.[56]

Needless to say, the paulistas sought to rebuff such accusations, presenting their movement as patriotic and as authentically Brazilian; hence the constant references to the bandeirantes and the use of the indigenous name Piratininga to refer to São Paulo. At the same time, their tendency to celebrate São Paulo as a modern and progressive city, and the region as more of a "European Christian civilization" than other parts of Brazil, left them open to charges of excessive cosmopolitanism, incompatible with a genuinely nationalist spirit. Indeed, this equating of the cosmopolitan with a lack of patriotism can be perceived in some of the paulistas' own statements. Thus Ana Maria Haddock Lobo, daughter of an elite paulista family, writing two days after the declaration of war, recalled her father saying that she and her siblings owed whatever love they had for Brazil to São Paulo. Inspired by the Causa Paulista, she went on to confess that "I had never dreamed that São Paulo would succeed in shaking my cynical cosmopolitanism, and in making me profoundly Brazilian."[57]

The Opposite of Progress

Given the paulistas' constant assertion of their unique and crucial role in the forward progress of the Brazilian nation, one potentially stinging rebuke was to characterize the paulista movement as reactionary or regressive. As discussed in previous chapters, the paulistas consciously sought to repudiate claims that the movement was merely a restorationist one, but the Constitutionalists' opponents kept up a steady barrage of denunciations in this regard. *O Povo* routinely referred to the movement as reactionary and regressive, as did virtually every anti-paulista chronicler of the uprising.[58] Much of the time, these terms were used with little specific content attached to them, or simply in the literal sense of "turning back the clock," a claim that the paulistas typically rebutted by describing the getulista "regime without law" as a throwback to a less civilized stage of human development. But in the case of *O Povo*, one can perceive a line of argument that goes beyond simply labeling the paulista movement as reactionary or regressive.

Throughout its coverage of the 1932 uprising, the cearense daily emphasized the orderly and patriotic conduct of the working class, both in São Paulo and in Fortaleza. When news of the paulistas' surrender reached Fortaleza, bells rang and sirens sounded, and *O Povo* reported spontaneous rallies and parades to celebrate the victory of the federal forces. It also mentioned some "disorders" among students, there and elsewhere in Brazil, who supported the paulista cause, but insisted that "the workers, who from the outset remained aloof to the struggle, continued to avoid becoming involved in the agitations."[59] Much of *O Povo*'s coverage of the situation in São Paulo during the three months of the insurrection came directly from the pro-tenente carioca daily *O Radical* and highlighted such issues as the repression against alleged Communists, and depicted paulista workers as victims of the oligarchy's insurgency. [60]

While *O Povo* heralded the working class as the voice of sanity, it portrayed the rest of the paulista population (minus the manipulative political bosses) as deluded fanatics. Here we can see quite deliberate efforts tu turn the tables and portray the paulistas in the terms the latter usually reserved for the nordestinos. In an article published on July 23 entitled "The Dream of Icarus," journalist Joaquim Gondim declared the movement in São Paulo "a fit of madness" and further claimed that the paulistas' "shameful egoism had moved them to cross the line drawn by the nation's dignity, with no other purpose but to restore the imperial regime of the misconceived political hegemony that for such a long time . . . subjected the north of the nation to a Babylonian captivity . . . exploited, flayed, and almost always prevented from choosing its legitimate representatives."[61] And even as the conflict was coming to an end, an article in O Povo cited the remarks of ship passengers arriving from São Paulo who were profoundly (if unfavorably) impressed by "the collective delusion that dominates the spirits of that city's population, with the ladies being the biggest zealots of all."[62] Two anti-paulista chronicles published soon after São Paulo's defeat went so far as to draw parallels between the paulista mentality at the time of the Revolution of 1932 and certain messianic movements in the Nordeste. Jurist and litterateur Almachio Diniz described the paulistas' delirium as reminiscent of Raimundo Nina Rodrigues's analysis of the insanity at Canudos—the millenarian community at the center of Euclides da Cunha's Os sertões.[63] And Manoel Osório declared that "the rebellious movement that is being promoted here is a vile exploitation through which the always insatiable press makes the paulista into a fanatic who is little different from those who, in Joazeiro, defended Padre Cícero."[64]

With varying degrees of subtlety, the anti-paulista polemics and the pro-Vargas press portrayed the decision by São Paulo to rise up alone against federal forces as an act that bordered on insanity. Whereas paulista sources depicted the extreme fervor of the povo bandeirante as being tempered by the civilized and disciplined character of the paulista people, their critics emphasized the "delirious" and irrational quality of the popular response, produced by the maneuvers of political bosses and the torrent of regionalist propaganda issuing from the radio and the press. One opponent of the Constitutionalist uprising claimed that the media propaganda had rendered the paulista population incapable of "deliberating and discerning."[65] It is interesting to note, however, that the images used to reinforce this representation were largely northeastern in origin: the "fanatic" backlands settlement of Canudos and the messianic community formed around Padre Cícero in Ceará.[66] There were no tropes of paulista "origin" or association that would be easily intelligible to a wider public as symbols of collective irrationality or regression, though terms like "oligarchy" or insinuations of "slavocratic" attitudes might serve a similar purpose.

Regionalism and Racism

Even in the midst of the civil war, some spokesmen for the Constitutionalist Campaign felt compelled to deflect charges of racial prejudice within the povo bandeirante. Thus high court judge Manoel Carlos Ferraz de Figueiredo, in a lengthy radio address, appended to the usual catalogue of São Paulo's virtues the following denial: "It is not a question of race, no one is insisting on pretentious and absurd superiorities." Then what explained São Paulo's supremacy? According to Figueiredo, "it is the power of the land, a telluric influence, exerting itself in a mysterious and inexplicable manner."[67]

The flagrantly preposterous "it's in the soil" explanation proffered by this distinguished jurist (as well as representatives of the U.S. Chamber of Commerce) to account for the singular character of the state of São Paulo indicates just how difficult it could be to sustain a discourse of regional superiority without implicit or explicit recourse to race.[68] Not that racial explanations weren't equally preposterous, but they nonetheless still commanded an audience and a following in large swaths of Brazilian society—including in regions well beyond the borders of São Paulo. The 1932 uprising occurred at a moment when the idea that racial distinctions had no place in Brazilian public discourse was already circulating widely—despite the fact that it would be another year until the publication of Gilberto Freyre's *Casa-Grande e senzala*, usually regarded as the foundational text of the concept of Brazil as a racial democracy. Yet there were many Brazilian intellectuals, physicians, sanitarists, and criminologists (among others) who persisted in relying on race-based epistemologies to explain the world around them, and to address questions such as why São Paulo had surged ahead of the rest of Brazil.[69]

The ongoing influence of eugenics and hereditarian thought is apparent in the remarks of Milton Carneiro, an eminent physician from the neighboring southern state of Paraná. In his preface for the combat memoirs of Elias Karam, a Constitutionalist volunteer of Syrian descent from his home state, Carneiro announces that his main purpose will be to present evidence "to demonstrate the splendors of [São Paulo's] civilization." He then follows the familiar route of praising the bandeirantes and applauding São Paulo's role in the abolition of slavery. But finally he must address the central question: Why has São Paulo progressed so much? His "preferred" answer? Heredity: "One can think, and I like to think this way, that heredity has led even the bandeirante of the present time to all the 'positives' of a brilliant historical tradition . . . that everything bears the mark of a good inheritance."[70] He then methodically eliminates all other "possible" forms of explanation—geography, Marxism/materialism, Comtean determinism—to conclude that "the traditions transmitted by heredity are what best explain" São Paulo's supremacy. But then how does Carneiro reconcile this claim with the supreme region's defeat at the hands of the federal forces? Here, again, the issue is heredity— but now in a negative vein: "We witnessed, with little surprise, the inevitable triumph of the most degenerate. It is Darwin in reverse . . . the grotesque ascendancy of the Sub-human."[71] In other words, São Paulo's defeat was the foreseeable outcome of a situation in which the government failed to favor the more eugenically fit region, giving preference instead to the rest of Brazil, which Carneiro characterizes as "this wasteland of men and ideas."[72]

Carneiro was not a paulista, but he did hail from Paraná, a southern state with a substantial immigrant population, and this might be seen as inclining him toward a favorable view of both São Paulo and eugenics. But race as a foundation for explanation appears in northeastern venues as well, and particularly in the *Diário de Pernambuco*. Throughout the months of July and August 1932, the DP published long articles authored by carioca journalist and conservative intellectual Azevedo Amaral, all of which explicitly linked the political crises of the moment to Brazil's regionalized racial heterogeneity. In "Raça e política," published on the eighth of July, Azevedo Amaral reviewed the recently launched book *Raça e assimilação*, by fellow conservative intellectual Oliveira Vianna.[73] In his review, he congratulates the book's distinguished author for arguing in terms of both material and biological factors: "The great merit of Mr. Oliveira Vianna lies in his daring reaction against the anti-racial [sic] prejudice." In other words, for Azevedo Amaral, the growing "prejudice" against using racial categories and terms was hampering intellectual debate in Brazil. For political reasons, he argued, talk of racial factors "has come to be considered an index of reactionary tendencies incompatible with the democratic spirit that we want to impress upon the nation's political organization." But Oliveira Vianna is bravely bucking this tide by emphasizing the contradictions created by the formation of "ethnic-regional groups," especially in southern Brazil. As for the current political problems, Azevedo Amaral applauds *Raça e assimilação* as a book that "shines a bright light on those facts, and that reveals profound causes of a crisis whose severity lies in the determinism of biological factors that are not perceived by the spectator who contents himself with an appreciation of the theatrics of the political comedy."[74]

In subsequent articles Azevedo Amaral returned to these themes, now directly expressing his own interpretation of Brazil's regional divisions, which he argued could not be resolved "by the methods that are applicable to racially homogeneous peoples."[75] In "The Problem of Unity" (published on August 27) he focused specifically on the growing divergence between North and South, and insisted that the paulistas' most serious error when in power was their failure to address this issue. As for the cause of this divergence, he contended that "it stems in part from the divergences in racial formation that were intensified during the last hundred years with the incoming currents of European immigrants." The result was a southern region with the "physiognomy of an Aryan society," while the North has "remained stationary."[76] As with most other writers of his time, Azevedo Amaral did not see race as the sole explanatory factor; he gestured, for example, to the coincidence of sugar's decline and coffee's expansion to explain the very different economic trajectories of North and South starting in the nineteenth century. But it is evident in all his articles that he feels that the racial factor is at the heart of the matter.

My point here is partly to demonstrate that "racial thinking" was by no means the exclusive preserve of the paulistas. It is also to show that discourses about regional difference and national (dis)unity, whether pro- or anti-paulista, relied on racial hierarchies to make sense of Brazilian "heterogeneity." Among other implications, this means that the paulista defeat at the hands of federal troops hardly resolved the racialized controversies provoked by a pattern of extremely unequal development. Though subsequent decades would witness surging nationalism and the celebration of Brazil as a "racial democracy," regional hierarchies, and the attendant images of dualism and difference, would remain staples of commentary about Brazilian society.[77]

Defending the Honor of the Nordeste and Brazil

In contrast to the *Diario de Pernambuco*, the cearense daily typically did not open its pages to racial theorists, and when *O Povo*'s contributors did turn their attention to regional divergence, this tended to be explained as a result of paulista rapaciousness and northerners' ill fortune. Interestingly, the only two articles I came upon that explicitly critiqued racialized images or interpretations of the Nordeste involved the gaze of non-Brazilians, whether that gaze be disparaging or flattering. In the article about Paulo de Morais Barros cited above, *O Povo* challenged his pejorative assessment of the nordestino population not by offering its own rebuttal to his claims, but by citing the outraged response of an engineer from the United States who spent two years working in the Nordeste. The editor almost certainly understood that the voice of an authoritative outsider would be more effective in this context than any argument, no matter how detailed or well informed, that a cearense journalist could muster. But the external gaze could look both ways, as was the case of an item in the French crime fiction magazine *Détective*. So infuriated were the editors of *O Povo* by this article, denounced as "mendacious and insulting to Brazil," that they reprinted a full version of it both in the original French and in Portuguese translation just three days after the armistice in São Paulo.[78] Set in the northeastern state of Rio Grande do Norte, the piece from *Détective* not only declared the Nordeste "the least civilized part of Brazil," but described it as populated by "blacks who still remember slavery, and dull-witted mestizos."[79] It then goes on to inform the magazine's extensive reading public that the big landowners have most of the power in the region, but that they ultimately take their orders from none other than the bandit Lampião, who, the article claims, makes the final decision on every election in the region. As if all of this were not insulting enough, it then goes on to say that "it is useful to note that, in the Parliament in Rio de Janeiro, those elected by Lampião are no worse as deputies than the others. On the contrary."[80]

Not only did *O Povo* express its outrage at this affront to regional dignity, but it called upon the entire "French colony" in Brazil to repudiate the article, which it described as an offense most of all to *Brazilian* honor. Although the majority of the denigrating remarks in the article were aimed at the Nordeste, the reference to the parliament in Rio made it clear that the article's author did not necessarily have a higher opinion of the "more civilized" regions of Brazil. Au contraire. It is this aspect of the article (meaning both the original publication in *Détective* and *O Povo*'s response to it) that makes the matter especially intriguing. The Constitutionalist Campaign—with its assertions of São Paulo's entitlement to special treatment and singular disposition for order and progress—rested on a notion of paulista exceptionalism, and a particular distancing of São Paulo from the "backward" precincts of the Nordeste. Foreign observers, however, were not always inclined to draw such fine distinctions, and negative perceptions of one region of Brazil could easily be extended to encompass all of Brazil, São Paulo included.[81]

The View from Minas Gerais

Although paulistas may not have regarded the populous neighboring state of Minas Gerais as São Paulo's full equal, throughout the Old Republic the two states had maintained (with some brief interruptions) an alliance known as "Café com Leite," and the politicians who formed São Paulo's "United Front" against Vargas hoped that their mineiro colleagues would join them in challenging the new national regime.[82] The paulistas did enlist support from a handful of eminent mineiro politicians, including two former presidents of the republic, and even claimed to have received a deathbed endorsement from the famed aviator and native mineiro Alberto Santos Dumont—possibly the most famous Brazilian on earth at the time of the uprising.[83] Rumor had it that units of the mineiro state police force posted near the shared border also reached an informal nonaggression pact with the pro-paulista forces.[84] But both established mineiro politicians, such as Governor Olegário Maciel, as well as the increasingly influential "young Turks"—principally Francisco

Campos and Gustavo Capanema—steadfastly supported the Vargas regime against the paulistas' pretensions.

Given that Minas Gerais had occupied a relatively privileged position under the Old Republic, the political leadership's decision to remain in the Vargas camp, and its stated reasons for doing so, had a special degree of significance for the paulistas beyond that of other states.[85] This applied as well to Rio Grande do Sul, where a very significant portion of the political leadership openly sided with São Paulo, and where there were numerous popular manifestations of pro-Constitutionalist sympathies—so much so that some paulistas chalked up Rio Grande's failure to break with Vargas to the treachery of political boss Flores da Cunha.[86] But there was no "consoling" narrative in the case of Minas Gerais: São Paulo's former partner had unambiguously declined to ally with the povo bandeirante in this latest bid for political power and state autonomy. It is also worth noting that in the paulistas' mental map of the racialized divisions of Brazilian territory, Minas represented transitional terrain.[87] Whereas Paraná, Santa Catarina, and Rio Grande do Sul, with their temperate climates and large immigrant populations, could be informally grouped with São Paulo in a multistate region called the South, and the Brazil from Bahia upward could be lumped together as the Norte and/or the Nordeste, Minas Gerais—with its vast territory and large, diverse population—defied easy categorization. It had a coffee-growing sector similar to São Paulo's, and a recently conceived and designed capital city, Belo Horizonte, that was as "up-to-date" as any urban center in Brazil.[88] But it had vast stretches of *sertão* (backlands) that were, in effect, extensions of the northeastern interior, and, in absolute numbers, it was home to Brazil's largest African-descended population. Consequently, Minas could be imagined in any number of ways, making the mineiros' discourse on the political crisis especially meaningful.

Mineiro politicians and intellectuals were themselves quite conscious of the political significance of their decision to side with Vargas, and the tenuous position it placed them in. A few days after the armed conflict began, *O Estado de São Paulo* published a lengthy "Manifesto to the Mineiros!," signed by nearly four hundred men described as "mineiros resident in São Paulo," that appealed to the state of their birth to ally with the paulistas.[89] What is significant about this manifesto, aside from the considerable number of signatures, is the reasoning employed to persuade mineiros to turn against the Vargas regime. There is a notable absence of the usual exaltation of São Paulo and the povo bandeirante; indeed, there is barely any direct mention of São Paulo after the opening paragraph. Instead, the manifesto emphasizes that Minas supported Vargas's seizure of power with the understanding that the provisional government/dictatorship would be short-lived and elections would be promptly called. Similar to paulista propaganda, it emphasizes the need for the rule of law, but not in the cosmic sense of the metaphysical relationship between law and civilized peoples, but in the practical sense of Brazil's economic and fiscal life being stalled by the political and juridical uncertainties of the moment. Implicit throughout the text is the positioning of Minas as a decisive actor, and a full partner, in the political struggles of the day—and not as a region whose inhabitants would be motivated by the glories and achievements of São Paulo.

In response to the considerable pressures to withdraw its support from the Vargas regime, the mineiro state government issued a series of manifestos and flyers to clarify its position on the matter, and to appeal to the paulistas to lay down their weapons. And like the paulistas, the mineiro leadership made ample use of the radio, especially in the region where their broadcasts could easily reach beyond the border with São Paulo. Within a week of the outbreak of war, noted mineiro educator Mário Casasanta began a series of radio addresses that lasted until mid-August in which he both refuted São Paulo's arguments for going to war against the Vargas regime and presented Minas's justifications for refusing to join its neighbor in revolt. Almost immediately after Casasanta completed the series of broadcasts, the texts of his speeches were collected in a volume and published by the official state press, with a long preface by Capanema, under the title *As razões de Minas* (which can be literally translated as *Minas's Reasons*).[90]

Nothing in this volume is, on its own, especially novel, but the source of the commentary makes it more curious and compelling. And unlike the pro-Constitutionalist manifesto described above, both the preface and the texts of the radio broadcasts insist on presenting the uprising as an expression of paulista chauvinism, and the selfish privileging of regional prerogatives over national interests. Thus Capanema asserts in his introductory comments that Minas has always sought its "perfect integration into the body and soul of Brazil. . . . Minas could never contemplate its own aggrandizement except as an element in the aggrandizement of the Nation."[91] This is an obvious rebuke to the paulistas for their tendency to present their state's prosperity as unlinked to any national process, as entirely due to paulista effort, and for conceptualizing the space of that prosperity as bounded by state borders. He then goes on to describe the promise of the Revolution of 1930 as "renovation and progress," which he contrasts to the paulista movement and its spirit of reaction and regression. And he closes the preface by insisting that "Brazil . . . will no longer tolerate the reestablishment of the old regime."[92] Again, such a remark might have little weight or impact if articulated by a politician in Alagoas or Piauí, or even in Pernambuco, but when uttered by an up-and-coming mineiro politician, it took on a different meaning.

Much of the subsequent text, by Casasanta, reads like the standard anti-paulista boilerplate. He acknowledges how much Brazil owes to the bandeirantes and to the state of São Paulo, but goes on to claim that the paulistas are fighting for a "return to the past." Then, in a section on "authority," he asks (rhetorically): "Is the nation São Paulo or is it composed of 20 States? São Paulo alone represents our Brazil, to the extent that, to fight for her [São Paulo], we are fighting for Brazil, or is it only one twentieth of that moral, political, and juridical unity that is our country?"[93] Ultimately, São Paulo may be prosperous and industrious, but it is still only one state, and he insists that all states should be treated equally—yet again, an assertion that is considerably more compelling when made by a spokesman for Minas Gerais. He then closes with a familiar strategy for contesting the superiority of a richer region or nation. As did the Uruguayan *pensador* José Enrique Rodó, in his essay *Ariel*, which famously compared the United States unfavorably with Latin America by contrasting its crass materialism with the spiritual tenor of Latin American society, Casasanta claims that São Paulo may be materially rich but lacks the "spiritual order" that defines mineiro society.[94] Paulistas had marshaled reams of statistics to demonstrate their greater wealth and productivity; the only feasible rejoinder was to foreground a sublime quality—in this case, spiritual values—that defied quantification.

Can the Subaltern (Region) Speak?

Minas Gerais, a state that enjoyed a central position in the politics and economics of the Old Republic, could repudiate São Paulo's claim to special status from a position of moral authority and rough equality within the Brazilian nation. Whatever its economic and social problems, Minas could not easily be reduced to the image of an "empty boxcar" being pulled along by a locomotive called São Paulo. But for the states of the Northeast, it was far more challenging to refute São Paulo's claims to superiority and (by implication) hegemony. How could a daily paper like *O Povo*, situated in the capital of Ceará, an impoverished state whose population was nearly 80 percent illiterate, claim political parity with the paulista leviathan? And how could elites in the Nordeste, themselves obsessed with the genetic, climatic, and physiological "causes" of their region's stagnation and decline, reject the paulistas' racialized claims to (white) supremacy? One strategy, as Durval Muniz de Albuquerque, Stanley Blake, and others have shown, was the invention of a region known as the Nordeste that could wield far more influence nationally than any individual northeastern states. To be sure, the primary connective tissue of this invented region was the shared poverty and hardships of its populations—its subalternity was the foundational feature of its regional identity. This identity allowed northeastern politicians, intellectuals, and labor leaders a voice, but with a very limited script.[95]

Another strategy, one that dated back to Euclides da Cunha's ambivalent celebration of the northeastern sertanejo as the authentic Brazilian type, was the representation of the Nordeste as the true Brazil, in contrast to cosmopolitan São Paulo, contaminated by excessive foreign influences.[96] This counterdiscourse, however, entailed its own exclusions and hierarchies. Thus one of the first northeastern regionalist novels, *A bagaceira* (1928) by politician and lawyer (and future presidential candidate) José Américo de Almeida, a native of Paraíba, echoed several of the most disparaging assumptions that could be found in paulista writings about the Nordeste. In seeking a way out of the Nordeste's degeneration and inferiority, he cites the "man of the backlands" as the true "nordestino" and as representing a "race" that identifies with the land and thus could be redeemed. This is in contrast to the men of the coast, whom he refers to as "the black hordes of the slave quarters, the result of arbitrary crossings, the dregs of race mixture, with their riotous hodgepodge of pigments."[97] These descendants of slaves were incapable, according to José Américo, of recuperating the region and restoring its former glory. Yet even the de-Africanized "Man of the Backlands" would provide a precarious foundation for visions of national strength. At a moment when the quest for greater modernity was an unquestioned objective for many Brazilians, the Nordeste at best could serve as a mine or wellspring of "authentic" folklore and traditions to be extracted and consumed by modernizing regions eager to maintain a sense of the past while plunging into the future.[98]

A famous example of the simultaneous celebration and distancing of "progressive Brazil" from the alleged authenticity of the "timeless backlands" is the music-hunting expedition mounted by Mário de Andrade in 1938. Mário, then secretary of culture for the Municipality of São Paulo, sent a four-man team to the North/Northeast to collect and record traditional musical forms so that the roots of Brazilian music could be preserved before the tentacles of modernity (e.g., electricity, radio, film) penetrated the northern hinterland.[99] In other words, the latter region could still function as a land outside of history, a "fossil culture" untouched by progress, thus allowing Brazilians from a rapidly changing locale like São Paulo to visit a piece of the nation's past as if the expedition's jeep were a four-wheel-drive time machine. Mário and his minions certainly treasured what they found in the Nordeste and did a service to music lovers everywhere by preserving the sounds of the sertão and other northern areas.[100] But this cultural rescue mission also reflected a kind of internal orientalism in which representatives from the realm of modernity collect, admire, and enjoy the products and practices of "traditional" societies that then serve as a foil for assessing the impact of progress and change in their "home" territory. One might assume that a shared national belonging would temper such orientalist tendencies, but the paulistas' habit of heightening the difference and exaggerating the distance between São Paulo and the rest of Brazil would operate to the contrary.[101]

Gilberto Freyre's *Casa-Grande e senzala*, published just a year after the defeat of the Constitutionalist Revolution, provided perhaps the most apposite strategy for revising the paulistas' vision of a regionalized, hierarchical nation. Though also argued from a regionalist position—one that identified the sugar plantation zones of the coastal Nordeste as the source of a distinctive Brazilian cultural identity—Freyre's "best seller" went beyond recuperating authentic/unchanged customs and traditions, highlighting instead the historical and dynamic blending of European, African, and Indian in the extended "family" of the plantation Big House.[102] In subsequent works he would consider the ways in which the competitive practices of urban, capitalist life threatened to erode the alleged racial harmony and cultural mixing characteristic of the rural estate under slavery. At the same time, he portrayed Brazilian racial tolerance—eventually fashioned into the concept of racial democracy—as robust enough to survive into the present and future, and to offer the possibility of a modernity that could escape the "cultural monotony" of homogenized, industrialized societies.[103] Whereas many paulista intellectuals, as well as non-paulistas such as Azevedo Amaral and Oliveira Vianna, regarded racial difference as an impediment to national unity and the chief explanation for increasingly severe regional inequalities, Freyre offered a route through which Brazil could be both a racially diverse society *and* a modern, unified nation.[104] Whatever the defects of a work that fed a "myth of racial democracy," Freyre's perspective on region and nation, I would argue, offered a far more appealing way for most of his compatriots to imagine a future Brazil than the paulistas' relentlessly hierarchical vision, with its implication that the only means to diminish regional inequalities was through a process of homogenization—that is, whitening—and exclusion.[105]

Putting São Paulo in Its Place

Surely the biggest boost to these multifarious strategies for valorizing the cultural, political, and economic contributions of the "Other" regions of Brazil was the swift and complete defeat of the pro-paulista forces. At the same time, it was the capacity of various groups invested in the new Vargas regime to portray the paulista movement as separatist, chauvinist, and profoundly incompatible with the interests of the Brazilian nation that helped make a swift victory possible. Given São Paulo's genuinely crucial role in Brazilian economic life and the many social and intellectual connections that paulistas had formed with elites in other states, it was by no means a foregone conclusion that Minas Gerais and Rio Grande do Sul would back the federal government and refrain from adding their substantial state police forces to the Constitutionalist ranks.[106] Indeed, some sources indicate that the energetic campaign to recruit volunteers from the northern states reflected concerns in getulista circles regarding the reliability of gaúcho and mineiro battalions.[107]

In this respect, a current of nortista discourse that accentuated the paulistas' apparent disdain for the rest of Brazil, and insisted that São Paulo's economic prosperity would not necessarily translate into a stronger Brazilian nation, defined northern "regional interests" in a way that served to enhance the federal government's capacity to repel the paulista challenge. Whether or not the North was "the indispensable element for the solution of this case," as the maranhense daily, O Imparcial, claimed, it certainly was significant that the central government could count on the support of factions of the elite and popular groups from that region. And even if their swift defeat did not diminish the paulistas' sense of their superiority to other regional populations, it offered them a rather compelling lesson in the limitations of a national project constructed on the assumption that "São Paulo is Brazil."[108]

PART II   **COMMEMORATING SÃO PAULO**

CHAPTER 6

SÃO PAULO TRIUMPHANT

The Quadricentennial awoke the pride of São Paulo, its capacity to build, a
consciousness that had been dormant since the crisis of 1929–30.
—Hernani Donato, "Histórias e memórias da cidade de São Paulo no IV Centenário"

Less than a month into the Guerra Paulista of 1932, the U.S. ambassador
to Brazil informed Washington that "the intrinsic importance of São
Paulo will insure its position regardless of the outcome of the present
struggle."[1] In the next two decades one could find ample evidence to
support that prediction in everything from statistical reports to the rapidly changing skyline of the state capital. And lest anyone still doubted
that São Paulo had leapt to the ranks of the world's leading cities, in the
early 1950s a circle of politicians, urban planners, cultural impresarios,
and businessmen forged plans for a massive program of commemorations, spectacles, and cultural events to mark the four hundredth anniversary (or IV Centenário) of São Paulo's founding. Unprecedented in
scale and scope for Brazil, this colossal, protracted birthday party was,
first and foremost, a celebration of São Paulo's remarkable triumph.
Despite repeated defeats for the paulista leadership on the battlefield
and in the political arena, the years between 1932 and 1954 would be
a time of explosive regional growth and rising prosperity—at least for
those paulistas with access to economic resources, educational institutions, and social connections. And the IV Centenário would be the
icing on the cake.

Developments over these two decades would give the lie to some
Constitutionalists' insistence that regional autonomy was the prerequi-
site for São Paulo's prosperity. During seventeen of those twenty years

Getúlio Vargas served as Brazil's chief executive, whether as provisional president, dictator, or democratically elected president, and his administrations took various initiatives to create a more "national" economy and to diminish regional inequalities. But the push for rapid industrialization, so central to the logic of developmental nationalism from the 1930s on, consistently favored those regions of Brazil that already had the factors regarded as necessary for a manufacturing economy. And in the course of these developments, no region was more highly favored than São Paulo. By the end of the 1950s São Paulo accounted for a full 56 percent of Brazil's industrial production, and over 60 percent of output from sectors classified as "dynamic industries."[2] If anything, São Paulo (city and state) had become even more indisputably the engine of Brazilian economic growth.

At the same time, increased popular political participation and intensifying nationalism across the political spectrum made social and spatial inequalities more evident and challenging. With these shifting circumstances in mind, the purpose of this chapter is to consider the ways in which the organizers of the IV Centenário—many of them veterans of the 1932 uprising—sought to represent São Paulo's triumph and to reshape paulista identity, with particular attention to the ongoing tension between the drive for unity and the growing sense of hierarchy and fragmentation. Despite my reservations about his overly dichotomous formulation of social relations, Antonio Cândido's suggestion that the Constitutionalist Revolution "marked the last time that the dominant classes succeeded in incorporating the dominated classes into their political project, as if the people were a single bloc," seems appropriate to reconsider here. If, indeed, "the people" could no longer be envisioned as a single bloc, then we need to ask how the promoters of the IV Centenário, two decades later, reconceptualized the paulista public(s) and to what extent they sought to tailor the festivities and solemnities to fit the more irregular outlines of postwar paulista society.[3]

Changing Places

For all their regional chauvinism, those paulistas who had supported the 1932 uprising and suffered the bitterness of its quick defeat would have been hard-pressed to share the optimism of the U.S. consul quoted above. Despite an initial spate of successes, the post-1932 Constitutionalists proved singularly ineffective at eroding Vargas's political power, even in their home state.[4] The sense of satisfaction that paulista political factions, united in a single slate, derived from the convening of a constituent assembly in 1933, the issuing of a new constitution in 1934, and the scheduling of presidential elections for

January 1938 turned out to be ephemeral. First, there was the splintering of the Chapa Única, as segments of the paulista political class threw their support behind different presidential candidates.[5] Then the internecine bickering proved to be for naught as Vargas, in November 1937, stunned Brazil's political class by canceling the presidential elections, assuming expanded dictatorial powers (with support from the armed forces), and issuing a constitution that wiped out the last shreds of regional political autonomy. If it was laws and a constitution the paulistas wanted, Vargas was happy to oblige—but of course, the corporatist Carta de 1937 was hardly the constitution that the paulistas had in mind.[6]

Vargas dubbed his new, enhanced dictatorship an Estado Novo (New State), a name redolent of fascist influences. For a while the regime did seem to be edging into an alliance with Nazi Germany and fascist Italy. He even used a trumped up "Cohen Plan"—an alleged Communist conspiracy that played to anti-Semitic sentiment—as a flimsy premise for the cancellation of the promised presidential elections.[7] But Vargas was always remarkably adept at keeping his options open and maintaining multiple sources of support, and as war erupted in Europe and Asia, he resolved to side with the "United Nations." This alliance, sealed with the dispatching of some twenty-five thousand Brazilian troops to the European theater, meant that Vargas was able to elicit various forms of economic and technical assistance from the Roosevelt administration, chief among them the building of Volta Redonda—Latin America's first fully modern steel mill.[8]

Though projects like Volta Redonda would be the marquee items for the Brazilian-American wartime alliance, it was the preexisting industrial sector in São Paulo that felt the most dramatic impact from the world going to war yet again. Since the conflict in Europe cut off most supplies of capital goods— machinery, chemicals—the war years were not a time when many new industrial enterprises could be launched or when manufacturing firms could easily upgrade their productive capacity. But it was a time when markets, at home and abroad, normally flooded with European and North American goods such as textiles and processed foodstuffs, were looking for new suppliers, with the result that factories in Brazil, long plagued by cramped and unstable markets for their output, suddenly found themselves working round the clock and to full capacity to meet internal and external demand and reap windfall profits.[9]

Government restrictions on workers' right to strike, imposed with the specious invocation of a wartime "emergency," meant that most factory operatives were unlikely to share in the bonanza of wartime production, even as they were grappling with the rising cost of living caused by wartime scarcity.[10]

Nonetheless, the increasing demand for industrial labor during and after World War II sharply accelerated a process that was already under way in the previous decade—the massive (internal) migration to Brazil's major urban centers, and especially to São Paulo, from the Nordeste.[11] Laws issued during the first years of the Vargas regime regulated and restricted the flow of immigrants into Brazil, and even that reduced stream of newcomers dried up with the outbreak of war. This created new spaces and opportunities for "national" workers; the first wave in this human tide of migration came primarily from Minas Gerais and the interior of São Paulo itself, but increasingly the new arrivals hailed from the economically struggling states of the Brazilian Northeast.[12] In the postwar decades, this growing stream of nordestinos, seeking employment and hoping for a better life, would produce profound changes in the city and state of São Paulo as industrialization expanded on a massive scale, and manufacturing replaced agriculture as Brazil's leading economic sector.[13]

These years also saw a dramatic transformation of the urban landscape as São Paulo's metropolitan area expanded to accommodate the car culture of the growing middle class and the steady stream of new arrivals from the interior and the Northeast (see fig. 6.1). Following the rechanneling of the Rio Pinheiros, which began in the late 1920s, previously flood-prone areas to the south and west of the central districts became available for residential construction, with the first wave of housing—in the "Jardins" (Gardens)—being designed for the upper middle class. This pattern of fanning out to the south and west continued in the next two decades as construction accelerated to meet the residential and recreational demands of better-off paulistanos, with new trolley lines and middle-class neighborhoods extending to subdistricts such as Vila Olímpia and Brooklin Paulista in the 1940s. And a decade later, the city inaugurated the Parque Ibirapuera, destined to become São Paulo's premier public space for leisure and recreation, and located in the midst of the new middle-class districts. Meanwhile, the city's eastern precincts continued to be home to a significant portion of the industrial economy and the working-class/immigrant population, but increasingly manual workers and the factories that employed them were locating in the metropolitan peripheries.[14] There the newcomers could find cheap if precarious housing, or occupy land and engage in "autoconstruction," but the services were scarce or nonexistent.[15]

Thanks to the recent study by historian Paulo Fontes, *Um Nordeste em São Paulo*, we now have a historical portrait of the postwar migration that goes well beyond demographic statistics, employment patterns, and standards of living.[16] In particular, Fontes's extensive use of oral histories enables him to

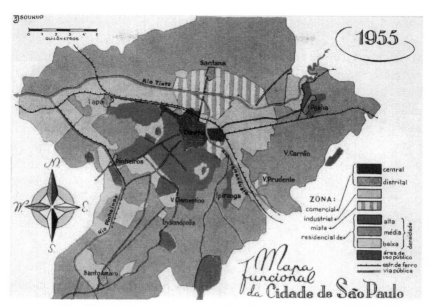

FIGURE 6.1. Map of São Paulo city showing growth, 1950–1962. Map by the Municipal Department of Urbanism, 1955. From Aroldo de Azevedo et al., eds., *A cidade de São Paulo: Estudos de geografia urbana*, vol. 3, *Aspectos da Metrópole Paulista* (São Paulo: Companhia Editora Nacional, 1958).

capture the impact of racism and anti-nordestino sentiment on the quality of the migrants' lives in realms ranging from employment opportunities to romantic possibilities. Both personal recollections and documentation from the 1940s and 1950s indicate that many paulista employers were reluctant to hire "nordestinos and negros."[17] In 1955, a series of articles in the getulista paper *Última Hora* documenting hiring discrimination in the metropolitan region caused such an uproar that there were demands for an official inquiry by the state assembly. Predictably, there were also the vehement responses from politicians and journalists for other dailies who indignantly denied that there could be any sort of prejudice, racial or regional, in the estado bandeirante.[18]

In the postwar period, however, not all major media outlets were so eager to express their adherence to the newly adopted vision of Brazil as a racial democracy. In April 1947 *O Estadão* ran a long two-part article by the irrepressible Paulo Duarte in which the noted journalist and Constitutionalist veteran took great exception to the claim, derived from "that minor sociology of the Northeast," that "the most characteristic type of Brazilian is the mulatto." He then went on to deride Brazil's black population—in what he insisted were entirely "objective" and "scientific" terms—as illiterate, alcoholic, syphilitic, and so forth. But the main thrust of this series was the claim that in Brazil, unlike in the United States, the chief problem was racial hatred against whites by blacks, and not the other way around. Adopting a particular version of the discourse of racial democracy, Duarte denounced all forms of political, social, and cultural organizing by color, which he regarded as both exacerbating animosities and diminishing opportunities for "miscegenation." The latter was an especially grave consideration for Duarte since, according to him, it was an objective fact that Brazilians wanted their country to be white. Or to cite his exact words, this was "a resolution marked by the unanimous consensus of lucid Brazilians: Brazil wants to be a white country, not a black country." As one would predict, he also noted regional differences: "[The Negro], which is the ethnic segment with greatest weight in some areas of the North, diminishes in intensity as we move toward the south, gradually becoming scarce as we move more and more in that direction, to the point of disappearing completely once we arrive in the temperate-zone Brazilian states." Moreover, in his zeal to rebut the "sociologia nigro-romântica do Nordeste" of Gilberto Freyre (whose name he misspelled) Duarte went so far as to argue that the typical nordestino was more of an Indian or caboclo type than an African.[19] In sum, in the pages of São Paulo's leading morning newspaper, even after the defeat of Nazi Germany and the widespread condemnation of certain explicitly racist doctrines, it was still acceptable to openly declare Brazil a nation that could and should be (overwhelmingly) white, as was (allegedly) already the case in the southern regions.[20]

Indeed, the very locutions that became the customary means of referring to the migrants from the North illustrate the racialization of regional origin, and the common use of apparently neutral referents as forms of stereotyping and disparagement. Thus it became a matter of routine among paulistas to refer to all nordestino migrants as "baianos" even though only a fraction of the migrants were actually from the state of Bahia, and even though Bahia, by some criteria, is not even a northeastern state. But it *is* widely identified as the most "African" state in Brazil, and thus the blanket use of the term *baiano* can be understood as a sort of "discursive darkening," to use Eileen Findlay's incisive phrase.[21] It is also a means of homogenizing a highly diverse population and drawing sharp lines of difference and widening distance between the new arrivals and the "legitimate" paulistas. And as with the "cabeça chata" of an earlier era, "baiano" became a regular refrain in disparaging jokes and anecdotes, which typically served to consolidate an image of "the" nordestino as backward, lazy, or unruly.[22]

Evidence of regional origin as a significant source of difference and distance can be found in an intriguing article published in 1950 by social psychologist

Carolina Martuscelli.[23] Based on a study of "acceptance" of "national groups, 'racial' groups, and regional groups in São Paulo" using the Bogardus scale to measure social distance, its author opens by assuring her readers that the 2,076 university students consulted for this survey were substantially more accepting of diverse populations than the North Americans canvassed for a similar study. Nonetheless, Martuscelli found the São Paulo students to be far more inclined to accept as a relative through marriage someone of European origin (74.7 percent would accept Italians, 72.7 percent Portuguese) than someone of Middle Eastern or Asian origin (40.3 percent Syrians, 23.4 percent Japanese). And the lowest percentages, by far, with regard to marital acceptability, were for "mulatos" (14 percent) and "negros" (9.9 percent).[24] The percentages for these last two categories rose dramatically when asked if they would accept someone in that group as a friend, neighbor, professional colleague, or citizen, but still remained well below that for Italian or Portuguese nationals.

As for the acceptability of different regional groups (paulistas, gaúchos, cariocas, baianos, nortistas), the results in this case both confirm and confound expectations. On the one hand, the respondents identified at least eight immigrant groups whose members they would be more inclined to accept as a relative through marriage than a baiano or a nortista. And over a third of the respondents indicated that an individual from the latter two categories would be unacceptable as a relative through marriage (whereas less than a quarter found a carioca or gaúcho unacceptable). But that is still a far smaller number than the 86 percent or 90 percent who rejected the possibility of kinship through marriage with a mulatto or black. And when the respondents were asked about acceptability as a friend, neighbor, or citizen, the statistical differences between nortistas, baianos, cariocas, and gaúchos virtually disappeared. In every category there is, of course, a clear preference for the paulista, but the gap between paulista and nortista or baiano is not nearly as dramatic as the one between Italian national and "negro." What this indicates is that, despite a degree of imbrication of race and region, there hadn't been a complete collapsing of the "racial" and "regional" categories. It is likely that these (probably middle-class) university students were aware that a nortista or baiano could be someone of mainly European descent, and that may have been the figure they had in mind when responding, whereas the categories "negro" and "mulato" left little room for ambiguity.[25] It should also be noted that this survey, by fixing categories and classifications that, in practice, could be quite fluid, "revealed" biases that might be negotiated differently in daily interactions.[26]

Martuscelli's study highlights the racial/ethnic preferences of middle-class university students, but Fontes's oral histories demonstrate that such prejudices could also be found among paulista workers, and especially those of European-immigrant descent. His interview subjects recall derisive remarks by workmates of "paulista" origin, and he also cites some of the first sociological factory studies, carried out in the 1950s, which observed tensions between workers of immigrant and nordestino descent. But perhaps the most telling commentary, from the reminiscences of worker Augusto Lima, has to do with life outside the factory: "I remember a baiano, a guy who was totally decent. He had an Italian girlfriend, daughter of an Italian woman and Senhor Manoel. That girl really liked that baiano, except he couldn't even pass by the front door of her house because of her father. The blue blood [sic] wouldn't accept the northern blood."[27] As Fontes aptly notes, the wording of this account, and especially the ironic use of the phrase "blue blood," skewers the paulista worker's pretensions. But it also illuminates the way in which paulistinidade could be cultivated as a source of superiority not just in the regional middle class, but in its working class as well, so that even a baiano who was totally decent ("decente para danar") was unacceptable as a romantic partner for Senhor Manoel's daughter. Despite the fact that many nordestinos who migrated to São Paulo shared with native paulistas a vision of the metropolis as the site of advancement and progress, and fled what they also perceived as the backwardness and stagnation of the Nordeste, once in São Paulo they often found themselves unable to shake the taint of their regional origins.[28]

In certain respects, the position of the nordestinos in São Paulo during the 1940s and 1950s seems analogous to that of the "guest workers" who left their homes in Turkey or Eastern Europe to seek employment in the Western European cities—their (cheaper) labor power may have been welcomed but they continued to be regarded as outsiders. Indeed, this analogy is made explicit by the "joke" in which a paulista asks a newly arrived migrant, "How are you liking Brazil?"[29] But there were important ways in which the nordestino in São Paulo was not like a "guest worker," for he (or she) was from the same "official" nation and, if literate, enjoyed the same formal rights in the political sphere as the most "authentic" paulista. As postwar Brazil entered its first era of mass politics, these new members of São Paulo's working class, together with more established urban workers throughout the state, became the potential constituents for a new generation of politicians who deliberately cultivated a popular image and a political appeal that was not intended for the "classes conservadoras."

Paulista Regionalism and the Populist Republic

The era of the "Populist Republic"—1946 to 1964—is typically regarded by historians as a time of surging political, economic, and cultural nationalism.[30] For many scholars, this inevitably means that it was also a time of waning regional identities.[31] Indeed, if our point of reference is the formal political sphere and if we adopt the First Republic as our base of comparison, then it could be argued that regionalism was a far weaker force in the aftermath of the Estado Novo than it had been prior to Vargas's seizure of power in 1930. Judging from the developments of the ensuing decades, the ceremonial burning of the state flags by the Vargas regime in December 1937 was not simply a symbolic event.[32] For example, whereas there had been virtually no transregional political affiliations of consequence during the First Republic, *national* political parties such as the União Democrática Nacional (UDN), the Partido Social Democrático (PSD), the Partido Trabalista Brasileiro (PTB), and Partido Comunista Brasileiro (PCB) structured much of the political patronage, competition, and mobilization during the Populist Republic. On the economic front, despite the growing presence of multinational firms and foreign investment, the Populist Republic was a time of economic strategies that envisioned a genuinely "national" economy that would integrate different productive sectors and serve internal markets. The expanded reach of radio programs, recording studios, the film industry, and eventually television meant that Brazilians in a large portion of the national territory could, with near simultaneity, enjoy similar or identical cultural products. Escalating patterns of internal migration meant that fewer and fewer Brazilians spent their entire lives in the location of their birth.[33]

Again, if we think of nationalism and regionalism as forming a zero-sum relationship, the surge in nationalist discourses, policies, cultural forms, and political movements would betoken a withering away of regionalist sentiment from the late 1940s on. But if we think of regional identity, instead, as a way of understanding and explaining spatial inequalities and hierarchically situated racial differences—which by no means were on the decline—then there is hardly any reason to expect regionalism to dissipate as a political and cultural force in this era.[34] Despite all the talk of national integration and internal markets, regional differences in standards of living became even more dramatic during these decades. And the migrants who poured into the southern regions of Brazil from struggling rural precincts of the central and northern sections of the nation often remained identified—whether in their own estimation or in the eyes of others—with their regions of origin. And now that Brazilians in the government and the media proudly proclaimed their nation a racial democracy, and more consistently censured overt expressions of racism, "regional" difference became an even more useful category to naturalize and explain the inequalities that defined so much of Brazilian society.[35]

Not that previous regionalist discourses survived unaltered and intact in this climate of near-compulsory nationalism. Compared to 1932, in the 1950s it was considerably more impolitic to revel in regional chauvinism—São Paulo might still be represented as Brazil's "locomotive," but no longer could anyone with a claim to public credibility describe the rest of Brazil as twenty empty boxcars. And local politicians with national ambitions had to be especially circumspect in their expressions of regionalist sentiments.[36] The expansion of the political and intellectual spheres also meant a proliferation of different regionalist discourses and historical narratives, making the consolidation of a singular, coherent, hegemonic regional identity increasingly challenging if not impossible. This is not to say that these new political and intellectual actors were less inclined to adopt a regionalist perspective than those in the early 1930s; in many ways, the regionalism of the 1950s could be even more encompassing than that of the 1930s. At the same time, the meanings attached to regional identity—or more specifically, paulistinidade—were multiplying and becoming increasingly unstable. Thus one could point to scholars as dramatically different as Alfredo Ellis Júnior, an unrepentant racist, and Florestan Fernandes, a pioneering academic critic of racism in Brazil, both of whom contributed to the regionalist discourses circulating in São Paulo during the 1950s—indicating both the extent to which São Paulo, as a region, was a privileged and unifying memory site, and how difficult it would be to define what paulista identity signified in that decade.[37] As Mona Ozouf has argued in her widely cited work on commemorations of the French Revolution, even festivities that seemed diametrically opposed in their representations of the revolutionary past ultimately converged to form a common identity.[38]

Such complications hardly led to the disavowal of regional identities, as is evident from the decision by various public and private groups in the region to sponsor the massive enterprise known as the IV Centenário da Fundação da Cidade de São Paulo.[39] According to regional lore (if not historical evidence), on January 25, 1554, the Jesuit Father José de Anchieta christened the future metropolis São Paulo de Piratininga, and thus in 1954 the state capital would celebrate four full centuries of existence. That such a major milestone would be marked in some way is hardly surprising. What is more remarkable is the extraordinarily elaborate plans developed by the quadricentennial organizing commission—with nearly nonstop activities set to run from the close of 1953 to January 1955—to commemorate this anniversary. This was, in some respects, an immense public relations boondoggle, with public and private funds being used to attract tourists (domestic as well as foreign) and investors (ditto) to "the fastest-growing city in the world." It was also an opportunity for financial profit—or at least the shareholders hoped so—through the advertising and admission fees for the events and spectacles sponsored by the commission.[40] But neither projected profits nor free publicity seems sufficient explanation for the extraordinary human and financial resources mobilized for the IV Centenário.

Instead, what the commission and its many boosters seemed to have been after was the more intangible cultural capital that they expected to accrue from the proposed commemorative programming.[41] Many of the key figures in the organization of the IV Centenário were also prominent participants in the ongoing commemorations of the 1932 uprising—a historical episode that, no matter how heroicized it might be, had still ended in defeat and in São Paulo's complete capitulation to federal forces that represented the "inferior" regions of the nation. The year 1954, in contrast, would be a time to celebrate São Paulo triumphant. In the words of Sílvio Luiz Lofego, a historian who has done pioneering research on the IV Centenário and regional culture, the commemorations constituted a massive effort to "produce the memory of a victory . . . a victory of São Paulo over its regional rivals and its affirmation as a model for the nation."[42] It was now the largest city in Brazil, having surpassed Rio in population a few years earlier, and by most indicators, it was the leading industrial center in all of Latin America. At a time when the words "nationalism," "industrialization," and "development" had become virtually synonymous, São Paulo could offer itself as evidence that nations like Brazil had the potential to become full-fledged members of the modern, industrialized world. To quote a special commemorative edition of A Folha de Manhã, "São Paulo is not just working for itself, but for the nation, which is increasingly integrated into the bonds of national communion."[43]

Despite this discourse of inclusion, many of the festivities of the IV Centenário were built around exclusions that reflected the organizing commission's notion of the true and proper paulista public. When the new crop of populist politicians spoke of the promise of industrial development, their imagined audience was, in the first instance, the industrial worker—or those who aspired to join the industrial labor force. But for those men (and a handful of women) most actively involved in the preparations for the IV Centenário, the principal promise of modernity, in terms of social formation, was the emergence of a cultured, sophisticated middle class, whether descendants of the original Luso-Brazilian settlers of the region, or the children of upwardly mobile immigrants of Italian, Spanish, Syrian, and Japanese descent.[44] One can discern the role of an imagined middle class as the lodestar for the commission in a variety of explicit and subtle ways, beginning with the intimate association of the festivities with the Parque Ibirapuera, the immense urban park whose many buildings and monuments would be inaugurated during the IV Centenário. Urban planners, rather than trying to revive declining districts of the city such as the area around the "Luz" Train Station, located São Paulo's version of Central Park at the far end of one of the city's most "noble" thoroughfares, the Avenida Brasil, and at the edge of an emerging middle-class neighborhood. And unlike other public spaces and recreational areas of the city, readily reached by train or trolley, easy access to Ibirapuera would require a car. This meant, among other things, that ensuring a large turnout for more "popular" events in the park routinely involved making special transportation arrangements.[45]

Even though the IV Centenário specifically referred to the founding of São Paulo city, and the urban middle class formed its target audience, this did not imply a split between the city and the region—the state capital frequently stood for the region, and essays explaining the city's formidable growth and development regularly cited the interaction of the capital, the state's many smaller urban centers, and its agrarian economy. Throughout the commemorations, historians, journalists, and literary figures regularly referred to the *civilização do planalto*—the civilization of the plateau that radiated from the colonial village/modern city of São Paulo to the region as a whole. Newspaper ads associated with the IV Centenário frequently portrayed piles of coffee beans side by side with panoramas of the São Paulo city skyline.[46] So the IV Centenário may have been urban-centered and primarily aimed at paulistanos and visitors to the capital from Brazil and abroad, but no one doubted that it was also a celebration of regional/paulista—not just paulistano—identity.

The Politics of Class and Commemoration

According to the subtitle of a commemorative article on "The Road to the Metropolitan Economy," São Paulo had undergone "three centuries of slow preparation and one of gigantic propulsion."[47] Indeed, as recently as 1854 São Paulo had been little more than a village, despite the budding coffee economy that was starting to transform the surrounding countryside. It is no surprise, then, that the three hundredth anniversary of São Paulo's founding passed virtually unremarked. What, after all, was there to celebrate?

A century later, the sleepy village had become a booming metropolis whose elites welcomed the approach of the four hundredth anniversary as an opportunity to display to the world their hometown's exceptional achievements. By 1948 plans were already afoot to mark the next centennial year with massive celebrations. A full six years before the august occasion, the municipal administration issued a decree forming the first incarnation of the Comissão do IV Centenário da Cidade de São Paulo (CIVCCSP). This exploratory committee included engineer and former prefect (1934–1938) Fábio da Silva Prado, FIESP stalwart and future prefect Armando de Arruda Pereira, and assorted other prominent individuals from the business, government, literary, and academic sectors of paulista society.[48] Their goals were to develop sources of funding, initiate a public relations campaign, and identify possible events and exhibits.

In early 1951, following the appointment of Arruda Pereira as prefect and the election of civil engineer Lucas Nogueira Garcez as governor, a new organizing commission was created whose mission would be to coordinate the funding, publicity, content, and timing of the quadricentennial activities.[49] Chosen to head the new commission was Francisco Matarazzo Sobrinho, nephew of Count Francisco Matarazzo, founder of the family's industrial empire. In a sense Matarazzo Sobrinho (familiarly known as Ciccillo) was the mirror image of Fábio da Silva Prado. The latter was from the powerful Prado family, which made its original fortune in coffee planting, and married Renata Crespi, the daughter of an Italian immigrant textile magnate, whereas Matarazzo was from an immigrant industrial clan but married Yolanda Penteado, from a traditional paulista landholding family. Both men and their wives were known for their active patronage and support for the arts and cultural initiatives. Indeed, as prefect Prado had founded the municipal Department of Culture, and appointed Mário de Andrade to head it.[50]

The selection of Matarazzo as president of the commission reflected a number of concerns, including the desire to lure the business community into contributing to the financing of the IV Centenário.[51] He also had extensive personal connections—regional, national, and transnational—to the plastic and performing arts.[52] Perhaps equally important, his presence at the head of the commission demonstrated that this was not just an initiative of the old paulista families—the blue bloods, or *quatrocentões* (literally, the "big four hundred yearers")—but an undertaking that encompassed the many paulistas of immigrant descent. Of course, Matarazzo's appointment did not speak at all to the question of whether the quadricentennial celebrations encompassed working-class paulistas, or paulistas of African descent (immigrants by other means), or mineiro and northeastern migrants. But the commission did repeatedly insist that the immigrant "colonies" should feel just as invested in these celebrations as paulistas who could trace their roots back to the bandeirantes.[53]

During the first two years of its existence, this new commission enjoyed a very friendly relationship with the municipal administration and could generally count on the state government for certain types of support, including the razing of a favela (squatter settlement) located on land destined for the Parque Ibirapuera.[54] But even during these years one can detect occasional tensions between the political concerns of the state administration and the orientation of the commission members. Governor Garcez, the embodiment of the conservative technocrat, made it clear from the outset that he expected the commemorations to be largely self-funding, either through private donations or the sale of shares in the quadricentennial enterprise. To be sure, some features of the more massive undertakings, such as works associated with the inauguration of the Parque Ibirapuera, would require public financing (and political muscle), but other commemorative activities, such as the cycle of ballets or the International Fair or the contracts for publicity, would not be financed primarily from the public coffers. As a result, nearly every commission meeting in the year leading up to the festivities opened with a discussion of their straitened fiscal circumstances; as of November 1953, the CIVCCSP estimated that, even with a budget of 600 million cruzeiros (approximately 30 million dollars), they were still short somewhere between 200 and 250 million cruzeiros to fund the completion of Ibirapuera.[55]

In addition to demanding fiscal discipline from the organizing commission, Governor Garcez and his representatives repeatedly insisted that at least a portion of the festivities have "a clearly popular stamp."[56] Though no populist himself, Garcez was an elected official (as opposed to Arruda Pereira, who was appointed prefect) and needed to give some consideration to the reception of the commemorations among the less privileged residents of São Paulo. Given the escalating protests over inadequate urban services, especially in the public transport sector, no elected official could avoid having misgivings about extravagant investments in an ephemeral program of celebrations oriented toward the more prosperous segments of paulistano society.[57] And such concerns became even more pronounced after elections were held for mayor and Jânio da Silva Quadros succeeded Arruda Pereira as municipal executive in May 1953. Quadros, a politician who would, in short order, run successfully for governor of São Paulo (1955) and president of Brazil (1960), met with the commission soon after taking office, and though he pledged his "moral support," made it clear that they could not count on him for another penny. Instead, he suggested that the commission make "drastic cuts" in its budget and shift to a more modest roster of events and activities. Soon after that meeting the commission arranged for a loan from the Banco do Brasil, facilitated by the outgoing federal minister of finance, paulista industrialist Horácio Lafer. Evidently, belt-tightening was not an endeavor that appealed to the commission's members.[58]

As for ramping up the popular appeal of its initiatives, despite intermittent references to spectacles and performances that would attract "the people," the documentation reveals the committee's preoccupation with foregrounding the modernity and sophistication of São Paulo as a cultural center, and the members' assumption that the modern and the popular were not compatible categories.[59] For example, one of the features of the IV Centenário on which the commission lavished funds and attention was the second Bienal Internacional de Arte—an international art exhibit of great prestige that began in December 1953 and continued through January 1954, with Matarazzo Sobrinho as its leading local patron and publicist.[60] Among its highlights was a room of paintings by Pablo Picasso, including the iconic *Guernica*. The importance of this art exhibit for the trajectory of modern art in Brazil is well established, but clearly this was an event entirely oriented toward the educated, cultured, and sophisticated visitor. Even if a working-class paulista had heard of Picasso and had interest in viewing his work, he or she was unlikely to feel welcome in the rarefied atmosphere of the Bienal.[61]

One can see in the very divisions of the services under the direction of the commission that its members had little notion of how to go about combining their concern to demonstrate São Paulo's cultural modernity with the political demands for activities of a more popular nature.[62] Thus there was a "Service for Cultural Commemorations" (whose "jurisdiction" would include a program item like the Bienal) and a "Service for Popular Amusements" (which would include an amusement park and certain folkloric performances). In other words, rather than trying to conceptualize festivities that would mingle these objectives and appeal to a wide-ranging audience, the commission simply decided to supplement its principal cultural activities with events that they assumed would attract the more humble paulistas. This sharp distinction between high and low culture was not always sustainable; for example, folkloric entertainments and even samba music were virtually always classified as "popular amusements," yet many of the "erudite" musicians and dancers who performed in civccsp-sponsored events drew heavily on "folklore" in their compositions and choreographies. Nonetheless, this division, or better, this hierarchy of festivities, continually informed the commission's deliberations, with popular activities generally being relegated to a lower priority.[63]

The treatment of such festivities as little more than an afterthought was particularly evident in the Carnaval celebrations in February 1954. As part of the effort to enhance its popular appeal, the Serviço de Divertimentos Populares had promised that this Carnaval would be the most spectacular in São Paulo's history. But from all reports, it was an unmitigated disaster, with certain samba performers and schools failing to show up as planned—possibly because the commission was reluctant to invest a significant portion of its limited funds in an event that it regarded as frivolous. Even worse, the occasion made a mockery of the commission's vaunted claims to organization and efficiency. Enormous throngs of spectators stood in the evening rain awaiting an unprecedented parade of decorated cars and floats, but the start time had to be repeatedly delayed due to malfunctioning equipment, and the event did not get off the ground until near daybreak, by which time most of the crowds had either dispersed or had become sullen and disorderly.[64]

This disastrous outcome exacerbated the already chilly relations between the commission and the municipal administration; as a result, in March 1954, Matarazzo Sobrinho—under pressure from the prefecture to resign—tendered his resignation as president of the commission, and soon after the other members followed suit. Quadros then appointed an entirely new commission, headed by poet and paulista patriot Guilherme de Almeida.[65] Given that Almeida could hardly claim to be a "man of the people," one can assume that Jânio had no intention of transforming the nature of the quadricentennial celebrations by dismissing Matarazzo (though, at a time of rising labor militancy, removing a member of a leading industrialist clan from the commission may have scored him some points with paulista workers).[66] And as Silvio Lofego points out, given that much of the programming was already in preparation or under way, the new commission had very little room to innovate or change direction, even if it had been so inclined. If anything Almeida's designation as the new president of the commission guaranteed greater continuity between the leadership of the 1932 uprising and the organizers of the commemorations of 1954.[67]

Aside from the members of the organizing commission proper, there were also paulistas from a variety of venues who populated the numerous consulting commissions, including Remo Forli, a leader of the São Paulo metalworkers' union. From the outset, municipal officials sought to include token representation from organized labor in the advisory committees, though their efforts were often politically clumsy. Thus, the first "labor leader" appointed, in 1952, to the technical consulting board for Popular Amusements was Luiz Menossi, a figure so thoroughly devoid of legitimacy in the labor movement that his appointment provoked a protest from five leaders of the National Confederation of Industrial Workers who were themselves widely regarded as *pelegos*—that is, labor leaders who collaborated with government and industry to maintain "social peace."[68] Their letter expressed enthusiastic support for the IV Centenário commemorations, and claimed that all unions remained entirely at the organizing commission's disposition, "because we understand that this crucial moment in our History should rally all of our efforts with the purpose of exalting and extolling our beloved paulistano terrain, which is the pride of all Brazilian lands and peoples." But they regarded Menossi as a completely unacceptable representative of their "classe."[69]

A year later, in 1953, São Paulo was the site of the largest labor protest to date in Brazil's history, the so-called Strike of the 300,000. One consequence of this surge in worker militancy was the diminution of the power of the pelegos in the labor movement. This, in turn, meant that there were fewer and fewer union officials of any ideological orientation willing to collaborate with the quadricentennial organizing committee and provide it with even a cursory claim to be incorporating the labor unions in its activities. The presence of Remo Forli on the consulting board following the resignation of Matarazzo in March 1954 is instructive. A member of the Socialist Party who tried to be an "authentic" labor leader while opposing the rising influence of the Communist Party within the principal industrial unions, Forli would probably have been regarded as too militant for the earlier incarnation of the organizing committee. Now, in 1954, he was a step behind much of the union leadership, who would have refused entirely to collaborate with the commemorative commission. Indeed, a list of all the organizations that participated in the parade marking the date of the four hundredth anniversary indicates that the only specifically working-class organization present was the Juventude Operária Católica (Catholic Worker Youth).[70] Similarly, the Ferroviários Católicos da Estrada de Ferro Central do Brasil was the only labor group to request commission funding for its May Day celebrations.[71] And the printers' union newspaper, *O Trabalhador Gráfico*, denounced in its issue of January 1954 the "false glitter" of the "bourgeois" commemorations of the IV Centenário in no uncertain terms. The paper claimed that the rich who run the factories and pay the workers so little "are the owners, the swindlers [*grileiros*], of the Quadricentennial." Moreover, it warned that the business sector would take advantage of the influx of tourists to raise prices on everything: "More than at any other time, in this year of the City's Quadricentennial it is necessary for us to remain vigilant and united."[72]

This is by no means to say that workers shunned events or amusements connected to the IV Centenário. Given the statistics on attendance, it is virtually certain that large numbers of working-class paulistas frequented the shows and spectacles designed for a mass audience, or the musical performances staged in specific "popular" neighborhoods. It is unlikely, for example, that a working-class family would refrain from enjoying an amusement park in Ibirapuera, created as part of the IV Centenário, or a nocturnal shower of silvery triangles, because the festivities had been denounced by a union newspaper as a bourgeois swindle. But when workers did attend, it was likely to be with their families, or as members of a particular community group, in a context in which their identities as workers would not be uppermost in their minds.[73]

If the type of union leader "eligible" to participate on the consulting boards was narrowly defined, the same could not be said of the academic and intellectual figures appointed to various advisory committees. The consultants for the historical exposition included everyone from the old-guard bandeirologistas Alfredo Ellis Júnior, Washington Luís, and Alfonso d'E. Taunay, to eminent university professors such as Sérgio Buarque de Holanda and Alice Canabrava. Commissions set up to judge submissions for the best historical and literary works included an even wider range of scholars, among them the Marxist historian Caio Prado Júnior and the sociologist-turned-literary-critic Antonio Cândido. These individuals did not necessarily pander to the preferences of the organizing commission—several panels of judges resolved not to award a prize because none of the submissions were considered worthy of recognition. But their presence on these prize committees gave the IV Centenário a degree of scholarly legitimacy it might otherwise have lacked.[74]

Programming Regional Identity

In October 1953 São Paulo's Institute for the Rational Organization of Work (IDORT) praised the quadricentennial organizing commission for its efficiency in planning the events of 1954.[75] Just a few months later, the entire commission would be pressured to resign amidst accusations of incompetence. To some extent, the very ambitiousness of the commission's vision for the IV Centenário made it inevitable that there would be delays, mix-ups, and misunderstandings, not to mention financial shortfalls. Among its other goals, the commission sought to offer a program of activities that would be impressive in its sheer size and variety. A pamphlet distributed at the beginning of 1954 listed the following features of the quadricentennial celebrations:

1. Exposition and First International Fair of São Paulo
2. Bienal de Arte
3. Exposition of the History of São Paulo vis-à-vis the History of Brazil
4. Theater
5. Ballet
6. Scientific and Cultural Conferences
7. Wax Museum
8. Folklore
9. Sports Competitions
10. Popular Festivities[76]

While this was an impressive list in and of itself, it by no means encompassed all the activities and programs produced under the commission's auspices. For one thing, there is no overt reference to the inauguration of the Parque Ibirapuera—a massive undertaking, often compared to New York's Central Park, that included multiple buildings designed by world-renowned architect Oscar Niemeyer, and extensive landscaping overseen by Roberto Burle Marx, as well as the long-delayed inauguration of Victor Brecheret's Monument to the Bandeiras just outside the park.[77] Similarly, events timed to coincide with the commemorations, such as the consecration of the new metropolitan cathedral, do not appear on this list. It also omits the many publications subsidized by the commission that formed a collection of "paulistiniana," which it distributed to libraries throughout and beyond Brazil.[78] And some items give little indication of how much was involved in their realization, such as the Exposition and First International Fair, which was itself an immense undertaking with many constituent parts, including pavilions from Denmark, the Dominican Republic, the Vatican, Syria, Japan, Holland, Czechoslovakia, Paraguay, Italy, Great Britain, Portugal, Malta, Canada, the United States, Venezuela, France, Spain, Belgium, Switzerland, Bolivia, Uruguay, Chile, Sweden, Lebanon, Yugoslavia, Finland, the Federal Republic of Germany, Trinidad, and Austria. In a sense, one goal of the organizing commission was to replicate the enormity and the complexity of São Paulo—the fastest-growing city in the world—with a dizzying, nonstop program of activities and spectacles.

Yet, as indicated above, this did not mean that the commission was indiscriminate in its selection of items for the program, or lacked preferences and priorities. Indeed, precisely because the program seems, at first glance, so inclusive, it is revealing to consider what initiatives were especially prized by the commission, and what proposals it refused or accepted with reluctance, and what issues were never even raised. Again, the commission's proceedings and correspondence indicate that it lavished funds and attention on items such as the São Paulo Ballet and the Bienal, whereas there is a slapdash quality to the plans for popular entertainments. There was also a great eagerness to invite distinguished foreign artists, writers, and intellectuals; among those who accepted invitations were sculptor Henry Moore, architect Walter Gropius, novelist William Faulkner, and choreographer Aurelio Milloss (who assumed direction of the ballet company).[79] Significantly, the commission offered a 50,000-cruzeiro subsidy for a scholarly history of the city of São Paulo, not to a local historian, but to a young North American scholar named Richard Morse.[80]

The cosmopolitan orientation of the commission, and its efforts to secure legitimacy for its activities by associating them with internationally prominent figures, inevitably raised hackles at a time of growing cultural nationalism. When choosing the novel to be awarded the IV Centenário prize, the panel of judges reported a "tie" between the two best submissions, but decided in favor of the one that "had the distinction, if that is what we can call it, of being a more essentially Brazilian novel."[81] And no less a cultural icon than Heitor Villa-Lobos, the most celebrated composer of erudite music in Brazil, wrote a letter vehemently protesting the commission's choice of compositions for the Ballet do IV Centenário, and other musical performances, noting its indifference "toward subjects that could be regarded as Brazilian, which is not the case of those that are foreign." Although the lineup did include Villa-Lobos's "Uirapurú," and pieces by Brazilian composers Francisco Mignone and Souza Lima, the other nine were all compositions by classical European composers. According to Lofego, "the cultural practices and representations promoted by the commission tended to valorize in Brazilian art only that which had some parallel in Europe."[82] In effect, despite the terms of the Brazilian composer's protest, it was not so much a question of Brazilian versus foreign, since the addition of a few more pieces by Villa-Lobos or Camargo Guarnieri could easily satisfy a demand for national parity. What it could not undo was the sharp distinction that the commission drew between erudite and popular culture, with the former typically having foreign/European referents and the latter being consistently equated with cultural forms from other, less modern regions of Brazil. Thus a proposal for a wax museum—hardly a high-cultural art form by most measures, but which promised to depict figures of international renown—received ready endorsement and funding from the organizing commission, whereas regional performance troupes would be carefully scrutinized and often rejected as "inauthentic."[83]

Despite the commission's condescending attitude toward what it regarded as popular culture, its members were aware of the need to show that the IV Centenário was having ample repercussions. And this was not just a matter of political pressure from elected officials. The goals embedded in the gigantic undertaking that was the IV Centenário could be roughly described as three-fold: to secure São Paulo's place among the progressive and modern cities of the world, to perform a pedagogical function, and to engage the attention and sympathies of the "masses."[84] Again, these goals were not necessarily regarded or treated as being of equal importance by the organizers. The commission, especially during Ciccillo Matarazzo's tenure as president, seemed most enthusiastic and invested in the first goal, and to the extent that it was attentive to the pedagogical opportunities of the IV Centenário, it seemed more in the vein of shaping the appropriate cultural tastes for the growing paulista middle class than reaching out to or forming new audiences and constituencies.

This disposition is especially apparent in the organization in 1953 of a survey of households to inquire about awareness and expectations regarding the upcoming IV Centenário. Both public-opinion firms that competed for the lucrative contract claimed in their proposal that they would take a systematic sample of homes from all social strata. Yet, in its report on the results from a survey of four hundred households, the Institute for Opinion and Market Research (IPOM) stated that it had restricted its interviews "to persons of the upper and middle classes, with schooling at the intermediate level (secondary, normal or commercial) or higher . . . *in accord with the instructions of the Committee on Public Relations of the IV Centenário.*" Further on it returned to this theme: "It is essential to remember that our sample is not representative of the entire population of the capital, but only of one segment. In fact, the interviewees were persons of the middle class, with those from the lower class being almost entirely excluded, and persons from the upper class, principally its middle tier."[85] Apparently, the organizing commission had little use for the opinions of paulistas who resided in neighborhoods that marked them as beneath the middle class. As for initiatives to cultivate the sympathy of the "masses," these the commission members seemed to regard as regrettable concessions to popular tastes that would do little to advance, and might even undercut, its other goals.[86] In a sense, the commission members still thought of paulistinidade as the property of a particular social sector, even as the rapidly changing political and socioeconomic conditions in São Paulo made it inadvisable, even impossible, to conceptualize the IV Centenário in such exclusionary or segmented terms.

The two full-time staff members who were directors of the Departments of

Public Relations and Cultural Commemorations from 1953 to 1954 were less inclined to define their mission as providing cultural stimulation for a select few and repeatedly made proposals that could expand the audience for various artistic, musical, and theatrical productions. José Roberto Whitaker Penteado, director of public relations, was particularly alert to opportunities to reach out to the "povo"—especially if it could be done at little cost. Thus, in March 1954, when the Brazilian team traveled to Asunción to play the Paraguayan national soccer team, he urged the commission to issue a certificate with a message of encouragement from the "people of São Paulo represented by the Commission of the IV Centenário." Penteado opened his recommendation by insisting that it was "very important for the commission . . . to be identified with the people [povo]. This match, in our opinion, offers us the immediate possibility of a profoundly sympathetic connection with the people, by means of soccer."[87]

Another, more significant example of Penteado's penchant for seizing opportunities for low-cost publicity in more "plebeian" venues was his proposal to stage a public event honoring Mário Zan. A popular musician of Italian birth, widely regarded as the leading accordionist in Brazil, Zan was the composer of the "Anthem of the IV Centenário," an extremely successful dobrado—a musical style that might be described as a syncopated march—in which he sang the standard praises of São Paulo. In a March 1954 memo Penteado claimed that the record had already sold over 600,000 copies, and that with its robust celebration of paulistinidade, the "Anthem" represented a goldmine of free publicity.[88] Indeed, he described the anthem as "one of the greatest contributions to popular joy [alegría popular] in the city's IV Centenário." Furthermore, Rádio Record—a leading broadcaster—had promised to invite a number of major recording stars for the event. The public relations director hoped to build on the song's success and solidify a connection between the official organizing entities and Zan's independent initiative. But apparently members of the newly appointed organizing commission, including Guilherme de Almeida, were reluctant to recognize or "officialize" Zan's contribution. This may have been partly due to the "popular" nature of the music, but the commission—lacking Penteado's pragmatic opportunism—may have also resented the fact that the most resoundingly successful feature of the IV Centenário up to that point was a "freelance" composition that had been produced without the imprimatur of the official organizing apparatus.[89]

Penteado coordinated the various advertising campaigns for the IV Centenário as well, and it becomes readily apparent from the correspondence that the publicity and marketing firms involved in the commemorations were keen to appeal to a broader public. At least one firm cited the coronation of Queen

Elizabeth II in 1953, which attracted an enormous radio and television audience, as a model for the IV Centenário.[90] Of course, strategies varied according to the event or experience being marketed—the J. Walter Thompson Company recommended television advertising in Rio de Janeiro at a time when TV ownership would have been confined to the well-heeled few precisely because only financially comfortable cariocas could contemplate coming to São Paulo as tourists. But Standard Propaganda—which won the major contracts for advertising the IV Centenário—sounded a more disturbing note. The firm insisted that "there are differences in the mental attitude of the [common] people of both our state and other states," and offered the following frank assessment of the commemorations midway through 1954: "The extraordinary activities that have been put into effect thus far, notably in the artistic sector (II Bienal of São Paulo) and the cultural sector through highly prestigious scientific meetings—have not produced a corresponding repercussion on the part of the broad paulista public." Standard attributed this, in part, to "elements" interested in creating "in the hearts of the people a certain skepticism and disbelief with regard to the official commemorations of the IV Centenário." And then it finished by assuring the commission that "we can and want to contribute toward refuting this false notion."[91] This is an especially interesting commentary since it not only points up the continuing tension between the commission's elitist standards of success and the intermittent concern to involve a broader public, but also demonstrates the impossibility of confronting this problem outside the context of a political climate in which an increasingly militant labor movement played a prominent role.

If Penteado's post as director of public relations and tourism "naturally" inclined him toward greater outreach, the position occupied by Roberto de Paiva Meira as director of cultural commemorations was much more fraught with ambivalence. Meira could have simply catered to the commission's preferences for (what they considered) erudite cultural activities; in most respects, he probably shared its members' views of what constituted high and low culture. But his proposals to the commission indicate that he sought not only to diversify the commemorative offerings, but to broaden the definition of "cultural commemorations" to include productions and performances with more popular appeal. His attempt to both widen the audience and remain within certain boundaries of respectability is evident in the following proposal presented to the commission: "In all of our programming here, we are directing our attention to the most tasteful theatrical elites of our nation, and to a certain extent, also to social elites. But we have tended to neglect somewhat the popular tastes with regard to the commemorations of the IV Centenário.

All of this is very beautiful, but I have been thinking that we should also organize a popular extravaganza, a type of revue, and naturally one that is purged of all the pornographic [sic] features that appear in spectacles of this type in São Paulo."[92] Meira's specific proposal was to sponsor a series of plays or shows, all of them Brazilian, to be presented in different neighborhood theaters each week, for a total of sixteen performances. Free tickets for these shows would be distributed in factories and shops in poorer neighborhoods. In a somewhat different vein, Meira's predecessor as director, Acyr Teixeira, endorsed a proposal by the Rio *sambista* Heitor dos Prazeres to bring his twenty-six-piece band to São Paulo to stage "popular music extravaganzas." Not surprisingly, there was some doubt as to whether such activities were the province of "Cultural Commemorations" or "Popular Amusements."[93]

The scale of the IV Centenário festivities, and the limited subsidies from public sources, meant that even the most stubbornly elitist commission members might come to see the value of appealing to a broader public. An excellent example is the one-man campaign mounted by Guilherme de Almeida to extend the life of the Ballet do IV Centenário beyond 1954. First the commission, in November 1954, approved a request for the ballet to perform in Rio de Janeiro, a trip that would cost 2 million cruzeiros (~75,000 dollars). Then in February 1955 Almeida approved another request for funds, this time for the ballet to perform in Buenos Aires. By the following September, the commission had closed up shop, and responsibility for the ballet company had been transferred to the municipal Department of Culture, which shortly thereafter received a letter from Almeida requesting funds to send the company to Montevideo and New York (where it would participate in the International Festival of Dance). His rationale for the request was predictable: "It is hardly necessary to emphasize to your excellencies the importance and the exceptional value of both of these invitations being that, in all certainty, they will grant the 'Ballet of the IV Centenário' the possibility to make a definitive impression abroad, and thus honor our culture and our organizational capacity."[94]

It appears that these funds were not forthcoming, and by the final months of 1955, the ballet company was struggling to survive. At that point, Almeida turned to his strategy of last resort. Writing again to the municipal Department of Culture, he suggested a series of ballet "spectaculars" at very modest prices, "to the extent that it will allow the popular classes the opportunity, which up till now they haven't been given, to attend one of the highest expressions of our elevated cultural status." (Apparently, the "our" in the phrase "our elevated cultural status" did not include the popular classes.) This was followed, in mid-December, by one last letter from Almeida, this time contending that weak publicity and lack of novelty had meant a poor turnout for the ballet's performances, and pleading with the Department of Culture to set ticket prices low enough so that they would be affordable to the "grande público paulista." Almeida's pleas evidently fell on deaf ears, and the ballet company soon folded. This cultural initiative, whatever its merits, had neither the public nor the public subsidies needed to sustain it. The story of its failure aptly illustrates the difficulties created by the commission's adherence to a conventional divide between "high" and "low" culture, and its privileging of cosmopolitan and European-influenced cultural forms as emblems of modernity and sophistication.[95]

Folklore from the Other Brazil

Nearly two years before the commemorative festivities were scheduled to begin, the newly appointed Ciccillo Matarazzo received a letter from one Amancio Moreira Gomes who sought to interest the commission in including his Bahian dance troupe in the programming of the IV Centenário. According to Gomes, the troupe specialized in "indigenous and Afro-Brazilian dances," among them "Dança de Omulu, Jogo de Capoeira, Cena de Senzala, Bumba Meu Boi, Babalouchá, Candomblé de Caboclo, e Toque de Santa Barbara." Since his troupe had no particular connection to paulista history or culture, this inquiry reflected a small-time cultural entrepreneur's wager that there was money to be made and publicity to be gained from the extravaganzas being planned by Brazil's largest and wealthiest urban center.[96]

Gomes's inquiry seems to have been tucked away in the folders of the Department of Popular Amusements until April 1954, when the new incarnation of the commission, now under Guilherme de Almeida's direction, began considering participants for a "folklore parade" that would accompany the official inauguration of Ibirapuera. Inquiries were made about the troupe, and the findings were not encouraging. According to a report from Oswald de Andrade Filho, "we are talking about a purely commercial extravaganza, which could not be considered (not by a longshot) to be authentic folklore."[97] The commission thus responded by informing Gomes (who had first contacted it two years previously) that the program for the festivities was full, the funding was entirely committed, and therefore his troupe would not be included. Similarly, an offer to participate by the Rio-based Academia de Samba Jaime Portela led to a consultation with the noted Bahian anthropologist Edison Carneiro, who opined that this school's performances were too sensual ("with their legs displayed and with provocative gestures") to be appropriate for the festivities.[98]

This is not to say that cultural forms from other regions of Brazil did not have a place in the IV Centenário celebrations; an advertisement for the First Brazilian Folklore Festival, to be held in August 1954, envisioned "all of Brazil within São Paulo at the same time" and promised that in the festival all the different regions "will be linked by their most intimate popular traditions."[99] But such traditions were only welcome if they conformed to certain requirements for "authenticity" and respectability. To be sure, there were predictable concerns that public performances not violate standards of decency for events deliberately designed for the whole family (as Meira had put it, they had to "purge the pornographic features" that he perceived in much of Brazilian popular culture). But the insistence on "authentic" folklore (as opposed to commercial entertainments) also reflects the role that these performers from other regions of Brazil would play in the construction of the symbolic edifice of São Paulo triumphant. They represented the primordial past, the traditional Brazil, a world and a time that paulistas might still enjoy having access to, but which mainly served as a sharp contrast to the awesome modernity and progress of São Paulo. At least one observer of the folkloric parade itself commented, somewhat sardonically, that the various rituals and traditions portrayed in the procession were as "foreign" to the average paulista as to visitors from abroad. While there was a slightly critical connotation to this comment—as if the paulistas were not fully Brazilian—in a sense that was precisely the point of including these folkloric acts. While it would have been impolitic for anyone in an official position to say it explicitly, it was a badge of pride, not a mark of shame, that paulistas had only a passing familiarity with these supposedly archaic customs, these vestiges of the past. Or if they were familiar with them, it was as objects of curiosity and preservation, similar to the many "experts" who flocked to São Paulo in 1954 for the International Congress of Folklore.[100]

Not all popular traditions had to be "imported" from other states. São Paulo—or to be more precise, remote corners of rural São Paulo—could also be a source of folkloric entertainment. Indeed, an article in a special commemorative issue of the paulista daily, *A Folha da Manhã*, complained that for some time paulista folklore had been virtually forgotten. Instead, "all eyes are turned toward the Nordeste, the El Dorado of Brazilian folklore. And what is being whispered . . . is that São Paulo no longer boasts of any folklore worthy of attention."[101] But an article in the commission's monthly bulletin in October 1953 promised that the "Folclore no IV Centenário" would include "a typically paulista festival, with exhibitions of such dances as the Cururú, Congadas, Caiapós, Moçambiques, Fandango and the traditional dances of Saint Gonçalo that still survive among the good and simple people of our peasantry."[102] Yet at the same time as the commemorations valorized these "remnants" of rustic country life that had somehow survived on the margins of the paulista modernizing juggernaut, they too were classified as relics of the past, rather than as meaningful elements of the regional present, and even less so of its future.[103]

Possibly because of mounting pressure to ensure large turnouts, especially in the vast indoor and outdoor spaces of Ibirapuera, the commission seems to have relaxed some of its standards about folkloric and popular entertainments, and invested greater effort in projects such as the construction of an amusement park to accompany the official opening of the Parque Ibirapuera. According to coverage in A Folha da Noite, thousands of people attended the inaugural festivities in August for the Exposition of the IV Centenário, and the article described the "Festival for the People" as a particular success. The account of the proceedings began by expressing sentiments that surely would have pleased the organizing commission: it claimed that "the capital city applauded the tasteful simplicity of the folklore that had come from afar." It then went on to report that the event was a huge success, and especially the performance by Portela. The latter had the distinction of being the oldest samba school in Rio de Janeiro but, despite its historic importance, represented something of a concession by the organizers since it certainly did not conform to the commission's notion of authentic folklore. Nonetheless, it was so well received that the festivities would have continued into the wee hours, according to the Folha, had the park authorities not insisted on closing the premises for the night.[104]

Yet another occasion during the IV Centenário that did not neatly and cleanly fit in either the cultural commemorations or popular diversions categories was the "old-timers' show" or Festival da Velha Guarda, which took place on April 25, 1954, in Ibirapuera. Organized by the composer and music impresario Almirante, the Festival da Velha Guarda included, among other performers, Pixinguinha, perhaps the most celebrated popular musician in Brazil, as well as such esteemed figures in the music world as Donga, João da Bahiana, and Benedicto Lacerda. Almost all were men of African descent who were natives of Rio de Janeiro. And not only were most of the performers now of an age where they could be legitimately referred to as "old-timers," but they performed mainly choro—a musical genre from an earlier era that had been supplanted by samba, but that was undergoing something of a revival. Whereas the folklore pageant held a few months later emphasized the archaic and the exotic, the Show da Velha Guarda was a festival of nostalgia, or as the Boletim Informativo of the commission noted, it was an "evocation of the Brazil of yesteryear," highlighting music that many older paulistas had listened to in their youth, and which undoubtedly seemed less commercial and less sensual than the samba that had taken its place at the top of the popular music pyramid.[105] Neither specifically paulista nor an emblem of modernity and progress, the show of the Velha Guarda was an enormous success—indeed, the president of the Union of Paulista Journalists sent a letter congratulating the performers, claiming that "among all the extraordinary festivities with which the quadricentennial has been commemorated, none has had a stronger repercussion in São Paulo, none has managed to touch more profoundly the hearts of the people."[106]

The Long Shadow of Getúlio Vargas

One not so subtle irony of the timing of the preparations for the IV Centenário was that they coincided with Getúlio Vargas's return to power, in 1951, this time as the elected president of Brazil. Moreover, paulista voters favored Vargas in the presidential elections by a nearly two-to-one margin.[107] Now committed to a more populist politics, and loaded with baggage from his fifteen-year-stint as dictator (or unelected executive), Vargas proved, once again, to be a highly polarizing figure.[108] In 1953–1954, the Brazilian opinion-research institute IBOPE (Instituto Brasileiro de Opinião Pública e Estatística) conducted polls in the cities of Rio and São Paulo that indicated widespread dissatisfaction with the federal government and pessimism about the future of the Brazilian nation. Specific sources of discontent included the strike movements in São Paulo, the rapidly rising cost of living, and ongoing electric-power shortages that caused frequent factory shutdowns and loss of wages. Because of the class configuration of residence in Brazil's urban centers, and the particular polling techniques employed, these surveys tended to be weighted toward middle-class opinion and cannot be regarded as a national referendum on the Vargas presidency. But these polls do illustrate the paradox of organizing a celebration of regional optimism at a moment of (middle-class) pessimism about the state of the nation.[109]

Trends in public opinion aside, protocol meant that President Vargas had to be invited to São Paulo to preside over the inaugural ceremonies. The nationalist tenor of the times made it unthinkable to snub the democratically elected chief executive on an occasion as august as São Paulo's four hundredth anniversary. But there were still many regional writers and politicians for whom it was an abomination to allow the "executioner of Piratininga" (in the words of one local journalist) to participate in the upcoming festivities.[110] Nonetheless, the organizers held their noses and invited Getúlio, who dutifully followed the standard script and offered the usual praise of the povo bandeirante as a hardworking and industrious people. He did go slightly off script when he acknowledged the workers' struggles, and the role of migrants from the Nordeste, but otherwise he behaved as the occasion demanded.[111] A few newspapers continued to complain about Vargas sullying the solemnities with his presence, but most took note of his anodyne speech and assumed that this cameo appearance would be the last that São Paulo would see of him in its quadricentennial year. It even seemed possible, as the months passed and the scandals multiplied, that Vargas would be forced to resign his office in disgrace, and that the commemorations might outlast his presidency.

In a sense, they did. On August 24, 1954, Getúlio Vargas committed suicide. A few weeks earlier, a botched assassination attempt against Vargas's arch-nemesis, journalist Carlos Lacerda, had made the president's already precarious position virtually unsustainable.[112] Rather than yield to pressure from his civilian and military adversaries to resign his office, Vargas—in his private quarters in the presidential palace, still dressed in his striped pajamas—placed a gun to his heart and shot himself, dying instantly. For the press in São Paulo, as elsewhere in Brazil, Vargas's decision to take his own life came as a shock—so much so that A Folha da Noite, in the same edition that announced the suicide, also printed an article about a contingent of law school students heading to Rio to demand Vargas's resignation.[113] For the organizers of the massive International Fair and the formal inauguration of the Parque Ibirapuera, the timing could hardly have been worse. The "tragedy of Catete" followed immediately on the heels of the gala opening of the fair, with a reported million people visiting the park during the first two days of the exposition. Vargas's suicide distracted public attention and interrupted the momentum that had been building around the various exhibits in Ibirapuera.

Perhaps even more discomforting for the organizers was the massive expression of popular sentiment in response to Getúlio's suicide. In Rio alone, hundreds of thousands of men and women took to the streets to pay their last respects as the motorcade carrying Vargas's body—being flown to his native Rio Grande do Sul for burial—wended its way through the federal capital. The throngs of mourners that seemed to appear spontaneously throughout Brazil provided a dramatic visualization of what it meant to mobilize the masses or to engage the popular imagination. It formed an uncomfortable contrast to the lukewarm popular response to some of the events organized to mark the IV Centenário. To be sure, many middle- and upper-class paulistas who disdained Vargas's escalating populist appeal dismissed these crowds—especially those that attacked individuals, institutions (such as the Paulista Law School), or newspapers known for their anti-Vargas position—as the "ralé" or rabble. But the frequent photographs of middle-aged women with white handkerchiefs pressed to their brows, or praying on their knees for Vargas's soul in front of the cathedral, made it difficult to attribute the popular outpouring of emotion to the mob or riffraff.[114]

At least one paulista magazine could not resist running a photo of the elderly Washington Luís—whom Vargas had overthrown in 1930—waving to reporters, with a caption noting that the paulista ex-president had outlived his adversary.[115] But the undeniable depth of popular sentiment in the aftermath of Vargas's suicide undoubtedly put something of a damper on any inclination to publicly take pleasure in his passing. Instead, the organizing commission attempted to pay as little attention to the dramatic events of the moment as possible, announcing that the historical exposition—a set of exhibits on which they had lavished funds and energy—would be opened the week following Vargas's suicide, as planned—though, in fact, the inauguration had to be postponed for an additional two weeks. Surveying the sources available to us, there is no indication that the organizers noted the irony of ignoring the drama of history in the making or of Vargas's enduring ability to appeal to a broader section of the Brazilian—and paulista—public.[116]

Civic Vibrations

The organizers of the festivities may have had difficulty sustaining popular interest in the various cultural expositions and educational exhibits that dominated the final months of 1954, but there were moments when the confluence of a widely recognized historical date, an enormous publicity campaign, crowd-pleasing amusements, and a crescendo of spectacular, almost cinematic events produced the sort of "civic vibration" that many of the commentators on the festivities regarded as a crucial measure of the IV Centenário's success. Three particular dates—the twenty-fifth of January, designated as the formal anniversary of São Paulo's founding; the ninth of July, the day that the 1932 uprising against the Vargas regime began; and the twenty-first of August, the official inauguration of Ibirapuera and the accompanying International Fair— became the occasions for highly orchestrated attempts to foster an intense and collective sense of excitement and belonging. Not surprisingly, these moments counted among those most vividly remembered in recollections of the IV Centenário.[117]

The very phrase "civic vibration" indicates what the organizing commission and its various auxiliary entities were after—an experience that would encompass all of São Paulo city, and whose manifestations would be so ubiquitous that its effect would not be a matter of conscious participation or attendance.

Like the tremors of an earthquake, anyone living in the city, within earshot and eyeshot of the festivities, could not help but "feel" these vibrations and consider themselves part of the celebrations. To accomplish this effect, the commission deliberately unlinked the festivities that would mark the anniversary on the twenty-fifth of January from the principal location of the commemorations—Ibirapuera—and endorsed a more decentralized program of parades and performances. The festivities began on the evening of January 23 with a flag-raising ceremony in the traditional center of the city, Anhangabaú, presided over by the president of Brazil, the governor of São Paulo, and the city's mayor. Also on the program that evening were musical performances by various civic bands in fourteen different neighborhoods throughout the city, followed by firework displays in the locales where the bands had played. The monthly bulletin of the commission judged this initiative a great success and reported that their employees who oversaw the festivities in situ were "unanimous in emphasizing the considerable turnout from the popular classes [as well as] the orderliness and the reigning sentiment of civic jubiliation."[118] Apparently, there had been some anxiety beforehand not only about attendance, but about whether the crowds in these more popular districts would comport themselves appropriately. The following day, the twenty-fourth, the same bands competed in the Pacaembú gymnasium; also on the next day's program were various athletic events and religious ceremonies, along with performances by a chorus composed of university students, who toured different neighborhoods throughout the evening.

The festivities entered their most intense phase as the clock struck midnight on the evening of the twenty-fourth. To mark the beginning of São Paulo's four hundredth "birthday," the commission had arranged for all factories to sound their sirens and all churches to toll their bells, so that all of São Paulo would know that the majestic moment had arrived. The ensuing program for the day of the twenty-fifth was a full one, with events as diverse as the inauguration of the new cathedral, multiple military and civic parades in Anhangabaú, the awarding of prizes at the Bienal, and a swimming competition at the reservoir formed by the Billings dam. Capping it all off was a massive outdoor show, in the center of the city, featuring circus, theater, and radio performers, and followed by an elaborate fireworks display and confetti shower.[119]

Many retrospective accounts identify the spectacle known as the "chuva de prata Wolff" (Wolff silver shower) as the most remarkable and memorable moment of the festivities. Indeed, an article about reminiscences of the IV Centenário published four decades later claimed that the vivid memory of the "silver shower" had obliterated or obscured the recollection of other major events. But as will come as no surprise to those who study memory, this very memorable event is not necessarily remembered with great accuracy. Whereas most personal recollections of it (which are often quite detailed) indicate that this "silver shower" formed part of the festivities on January 25 and describe it as a singular and unique event, documentation from the time establishes beyond a doubt that this spectacle took place as part of the commemorations of the ninth of July, the other major date punctuating the yearlong calendar of events.[120] Financed by industrial magnate and international playboy Francisco Matarazzo (Baby) Pignatari, owner of Wolff industries, the event involved several planes from the Brazilian Air Force that were rigged to release millions of cardboard triangles laminated with aluminum foil—reportedly, six tons of them in all—over the center of São Paulo.[121] For maximum effect, searchlights, both stationary and mobile, illuminated the night sky, enhancing the visual impact of these triangles as they fell to earth, where the astonished crowds scrambled to catch a falling fragment of "silver"; half a century later many paulistas still kept one of these triangles among their personal memorabilia.[122]

The appeal of the chuva de prata for the crowds in Anhangabaú—estimated to have numbered anywhere from 300,000 to a million people—needs little explanation. Like the sounding of the sirens and the church bells, it had the effect of enveloping the entire city in a shared emotional experience, made even more intense by the staging of a startlingly novel visual phenomenon. And precisely because it was all-encompassing, it was also accessible to all. Any resident of São Paulo could join the throngs on the Viaduto do Chá, or along the Avenida 9 de Julho, and have a privileged position from which to view the extravaganza and to snag a treasured triangle. And while the effect of the chuva de prata might be described as "magical," it was not in the literal sense of something inexplicable. Rather, it exemplified the kind of "magic" that São Paulo's technical and industrial prowess made possible. The coordination of the planes and the floodlights, and the manufacture of millions of laminated triangles, each stamped with the characteristic spiral that was the symbol of the IV Centenário, were what made the moment so sublime.

The spectacles that mark these two major celebratory occasions produced a sort of ecstatic collective experience whose impact transcended quantitative indicators such as numbers of people in attendance. After all, one did not have to be in any particular location to hear the sirens sound or to watch the planes unloading their silvery cargo, and to feel oneself a part of the celebration. Contemporary depictions of these "civic vibrations" all emphasize that these sights and sounds enveloped the city in a way that made conscious participation unnecessary, or beside the point. The description in the issue of O Estado *de São Paulo* published on January 25 is exemplary of this type of account and is worth quoting at length:

> Exactly at midnight all the [church] bells of the city began to toll festively, while one could hear everywhere the sirens of the factories, the firecrackers that exploded, the car horns that were noisily honked, the radios that played commemorative songs, and the people in the streets celebrating with great enthusiasm the dawn of the grand and historic day. From the top of the Banco do Estado building, in an unprecedented spectacle, awe-inspiring fireworks were launched. . . . [It was] a really beautiful and emotional moment, made so by the civic vibration, by the profound feeling of love and admiration for this great city of nearly three million inhabitants, that unites us all in the work of construction, in the communion of patriotic sentiments, in the virtues of the proper Brazilian family, and in this well-earned pride in a land that has so generously rewarded the efforts of its sons, and that is truly blessed by God.[123]

Even more dramatic and evocative was this description that appeared in the issue of the newspaper *Correio Paulistano* published on January 26:

> Streamers of confetti, inflated balloons, toys all combined to celebrate the august event and to translate the joy of the paulistano at reaching yet another stage in the life of the city. In sum, the shared enthusiasm, as all awaited the clock to strike midnight in order to experience, together with all of São Paulo, this precious moment of the great anniversary. When it sounded midnight, echoed in the streets by the buzz of radios and loudspeakers, the sirens of the factories and presses began to soar through the air of Piratininga, along with the ringing of all the church bells. . . . Everyone was then overcome with excitement [*delírio*] and began hugging each other and exchanging good wishes, as if it were New Year's Eve. . . . Never has the city been more jubilantly alive than in these few hours that preceded the dawn of the 25th of January and all who shared in this civic vibration certainly will never forget the joy and the satisfaction that they felt in being present and participating in this great occasion.[124]

Most of the deliberations of the organizing commission concerned projects and programs that the members valued for their promise of permanence and lasting importance, whether they be buildings in Ibirapuera, or commemorative books that would remain on library shelves, or a ballet company that they hoped would endure beyond the close of the festivities. They did not ignore the need for spectacles and extravaganzas, but they treated such events as more frivolous, and as less deserving of time, attention, and money. Indeed the funding for the chuva de prata came entirely from Baby Pignatari and his metallurgical firm, Wolff. And the three days of festivities held to commemorate the ninth of July (see chapter 8) were almost entirely arranged and financed by the leading broadcasting companies in São Paulo.[125] One could argue that making brick-and-mortar projects a high priority made sense since they would have a more enduring impact, but the irony here is that what seems to have made the most wide-ranging and lasting impression—the sirens, the fireworks, the chuva de prata—were precisely those events that were the most ephemeral, and were therefore the most "out of the ordinary."

Commemorative Supplements

Although accounts of the IV Centenário tend to focus either on major spectacles or monumental structures, the commemorations also produced a plethora of print material, much of it issued by São Paulo's many newspapers. Since the early twentieth century, São Paulo had been home to a robust daily press, with dozens of newspapers circulating within the city. By midcentury the number of small-circulation newspapers, catering to foreign-language readers or revolutionary sympathizers or the black community, had declined somewhat, but there continued to be an impressive number of major dailies, among them *A Folha da Manhã*, *Diário de São Paulo*, *O Tempo*, *Diário Popular*, *A Gazeta*, *Correio Paulistano*, *Última Hora*, and the venerable morning paper, *O Estado de São Paulo*. Each of these newspapers marked the four hundredth anniversary of São Paulo with special commemorative editions on the twenty-fifth of January, including supplements dealing with topics ranging from the colonial history of São Paulo and the history of regional agriculture to the role of women and immigrants in paulista society. They also were replete with ads for everything from clocks to cars that in some way paid homage to the IV Centenário. Therefore, no discussion of the IV Centenário and the production of regional identity would be complete without some attention to the role of the press as publicist for and commentator on the commemorative events.[126]

The mainstream media, like the organizing commission, regarded the IV Centenário as what would now be called a "teachable moment." It was a welcome opportunity to offer their readers pages and pages of enlightening discussions of São Paulo's past, present, and future. A few of the commemorative editions included over a dozen *cadernos*, or supplements, and some ran to nearly two hundred pages. Unlike the typical daily newspaper, a piece of ephemera expected to be tossed out in a day or two, the publishers apparently hoped that these commemorative editions would become a permanent addition to the paulista home—or at least to the homes of those paulistas educated and cultivated enough to appreciate the long, detailed, erudite articles that filled the pages of the supplementary sections.[127] Indeed, these supplements sometimes seem to have been deliberately designed to have limited popular appeal. In several cases the front page of the commemorative edition was devoted to an eye-catching sketch of a historical episode or an epic poem. The *Diário de São Paulo*, for example, introduced its commemorative edition by devoting two entire pages to verses by Guilherme de Almeida, "Acalanto de Bartira," which traced the high points of São Paulo's history starting with the birth of the first offspring of a European man and indigenous woman. Significantly, Almeida dedicated the poem to "Guilherme Egydio—grandson of Bartira, and my grandson."[128] *Última Hora* opted for a full-page color illustration of Father Anchieta converting the Indians. *A Folha de Manhã*, meanwhile, filled its front page with an aerial photo of the city and a long caption about São Paulo's meteoric rise, including a quote from famed architect Walter Gropius: "This city isn't just growing, it's exploding with vitality, dynamism, and fortitude."[129]

In contrast, the supplements themselves favored articles that were sober in tone, scholarly in format, and replete with details—thus, they seem more like a test of the reader's perseverance than a sincere attempt to edify the paulista public. A special section on industry included articles on the role of São Paulo in the formation of Brazilian labor legislation and a discussion of the changing character of the industrial employer. A supplement on agriculture offered, in addition to predictable articles on the economic importance of coffee, detailed pieces on cotton, sugarcane, and virtually every other agro-pastoral commodity produced in São Paulo. An extreme example was *O Estadão*'s special section on colonial São Paulo, with articles by historians Jaime Cortesão, Afonso Taunay, Jorge de Lima, and Serafim Leite, S.J., and anthropologist Egon Schaden.[130] Some of these articles seem almost perversely tedious, likely to interest only the most dedicated antiquarian. But they also served to imbue the commemorative editions with a certain degree of gravitas. Rather than superficial and extravagant celebrations of São Paulo's glories and achievements, they provided the reader with yet more evidence of the serious, sober, and rational paulista character, and postulated a literate, tasteful middle-class household able to appreciate the publication of such erudite, scholarly articles—whether or not middle-class paulistas ever actually read them.

From the perspective of the early twenty-first-century reader, one of the most curious features of these supplements is their palpable eclecticism. This was most likely a reflection of the mid-1950s as a transitional period in which one can see the persistence of certain ways of explaining the world that *explicitly* located causality in climate, geography, or race—or some combination of the three—which by the next decade would enjoy very little scholarly credibility. At the same time, one can detect the growing influence of Marxist and Annales school interpretative approaches that emphasized social conflicts, structural opportunities and constraints, long-term transformations, and fortuitous conjunctures.[131] To be sure, many of the articles written from the latter perspectives still had embedded in them certain assumptions about climate, geography, and race, but others directly challenged the deterministic interpretive frameworks of earlier scholarship. Thus *O Estadão*'s commemorative edition included an article by Sampaio Ferraz, "O homem do planalto paulista," (The man of the paulista plateau), that relied on the concept of "biotypes" to explain São Paulo's evolution. In contrast, Giles Lapouge's article "São Paulo's Industrial Vocation" stressed the timing of abolition and immigration, the consequent increase in local demand, and the emergence of a middle class.[132]

There was, however, one bright, unifying thread that ran through all these articles, no matter how apparently diverse in their approaches, and that was the question "Why São Paulo?" Whatever the answer, the question was always the same: why had São Paulo (city and state) surged ahead of the rest of Brazil and become its most modern, progressive, dynamic center of commerce, industry, and agriculture? Despite the striking heterogeneity in the ways the authors addressed this question, they all shared a linear/progressive vision of the world that placed São Paulo "ahead" of the rest of Brazil, and treated its status as the most modern and advanced region of the nation as a given. This illustrates with particular force how certain ideas can attain a hegemonic status even within a discursive field that seems ideologically heterodox.[133]

To be sure, in contrast to 1932 most contributors to these commemorative editions were less inclined to use their essays as an occasion to *openly* disparage the rest of Brazil. More typical of these paeans to São Paulo's progress was an emphasis on its leading the whole Brazilian nation into the future, as in the following declaration that closed *A Folha da Manhã*'s section on "Four Centuries of Paulista Life—Four Decades of Industrial Toil": "We are on the march; nothing will hold us back in our effort to transform Brazil into a great industrial power. . . . That note of confidence is justified when we glance back at the recent past and we see that in a mere 40 years we have built something of which all of Brazil is proud and from which all of Brazil benefits. Because, as in the era of the bandeiras, São Paulo is not just working for itself, but for the nation."[134] The European correspondent for *O Estadão*, meanwhile, drew an analogy between São Paulo's relationship with Brazil and that of the (postwar) United States with Latin America: "São Paulo is the hope of Brazil. Paulista capital fertilizes [fecunda] even the most distant regions [of Brazil]. There are those who construct petroleum refineries, who apply their funds in the mines of Central Brazil. One hears talk of a sort of Point IV program promoted by this city and implemented to benefit all of Brazil. In the space of 20 years, São Paulo has lifted the Nation out of the torpor in which it has been slumbering since the Conquest."[135] And even when an author did veer in the direction of a regional chauvinism that overtly positioned other regions of Brazil as starkly inferior to São Paulo, there would be some attempt to dress up the comments with a few diplomatic qualifications. For instance, an article in the *Diário da Noite* on 1932 argued that the impulse to revolt against the Vargas regime "was born from the consciousness that emerged from a superior stage of civilization, and the consequently more advanced economic and cultural conditions." The presumably less civilized regions "rose up against the dominion of São Paulo, and tried to impose the laws of a lower mentality on the more advanced." This may sound identical to the claims made in the 1930s, but the author then felt obliged to soften the potential insult to the rest of Brazil: "We do not mean to say, with this, that the other States languished in a stage of barbarism, which would be absurd." But he ended by insisting that it was "undeniable that the very economic conditions attested to that fatal difference on the cultural level. Agricultural and pastoral regions inevitably clashed with the superior stage of industrialization on the plateau."[136] This article, however, was somewhat exceptional in its use of "stages of civilization" rhetoric; more common was a discourse of modernization and development that often deployed a similar notion of historical stages, but in a way that seemed less disparaging and judgmental toward Brazil's "less advanced" regions.

Pitching Paulista Identity

In many ways, the IV Centenário was an ad man's dream. Not only did the organizing commission solicit bids from major advertising firms such as J. Walter Thompson and Standard Propaganda for campaigns to publicize the commemorations and to attract tourists as well as local visitors, but the commemorative newspapers also afforded opportunities to market every conceivable product with a IV Centenário "tie-in." And all this was occurring at the very moment when advertising was assuming a whole new level of innovation and sophistication with an emphasis on novel psychological and visual techniques, and use of the brand-new medium of television.[137] The prospectus submitted by

J. Walter Thompson for the contract to conduct publicity for the International Fair in Ibirapuera reflected a keen awareness of the class and regional issues involved in publicizing the IV Centenário. For example, since the commission wished to attract visitors from other states, the firm—which had been in Brazil since 1929—promised to "show not just the paulista side, but the national aspect of this undertaking." And the Thompson representatives assured the commission that "it was our concern to make it very clear that Ibirapuera is for everyone, including for children." Similarly, Standard noted that the programming in the artistic and cultural spheres, such as the Bienal and various scholarly conferences, though of excellent quality, had not resonated with the "wider paulista public." To ensure a broader audience, the firm promised to counteract any negative propaganda or popular skepticism that might exist with regard to the IV Centenário.[138]

As early as 1952, the staff office for the commemorations mapped out an advertising plan which would have as its principal objective "the affirmation of São Paulo as the center of civilization and engine of propulsion for national progress."[139] The very first concrete decision that had to be taken vis-à-vis publicity for the commemorations was the designation of a symbol that would appear in all of the advertising related to the IV Centenário. This concern with an apt trademark, what we might today call "branding," indicates just how thoroughly the whole commemorative enterprise resonated with the emerging public relations ethos. And even though existing symbols such as the city's coat of arms, with its literal "arm" of the bandeirante, or the state flag of São Paulo would appear in some of the flyers and announcements of the various festivities, the adoption of a symbol expressly designed for the IV Centenário indicates the desire to imbue the commemorations with a significance all their own.[140] As befits an occasion highlighting São Paulo's modernity and progress, the symbol adopted was the "aspiral" created by the firm of famed modernist architect Oscar Niemeyer. Since the Grupo Niemeyer was the primary firm in charge of the construction projects in Ibirapuera, the aspiral became particularly important as a symbol of that portion of the commemorative undertakings. Indeed, the original plan had been to include an enormous concrete and steel reproduction of the aspiral, over five stories high, among the other buildings and structures in the park.[141] But precisely what made the symbol appealing from a modernist perspective—its combination of curved and angular lines—made it too challenging from an engineering perspective to turn into a permanent monument. Ironically, it was the modernism of an earlier era—embodied by Brecheret's Monument to the Bandeiras, finally inaugurated in 1954—that most prominently graced the new park. Nevertheless, through its

FIGURE 6.2. The "aspiral" in an announcement of the IV Centenário Expositions. Courtesy of the coleção iconográfico do Arquivo Público do Estado de São Paulo.

use in advertising, the aspiral became a ubiquitous image, emblematic of São Paulo's dynamism and upward trajectory (see figs 6.2 and 6.3).[142]

If the aspiral pointed to the future, the IV Centenário–themed advertisements that appeared in the commemorative newspaper editions were more likely to conjure up São Paulo's past. The purpose in doing so seems not so much to stimulate a sense of nostalgia—which would be, in any case, an unsuitable strategy for firms hawking modern household appliances or the latest automobiles. Nor does it seem to have been to highlight the modernity of the present by juxtaposing it to the past. Rather, the goal of these ads seems to have been to provide a sense that despite all the dramatic changes in urban life over the last century, there was something enduringly familiar and famil-

FIGURE 6.3. Victor Brecheret's Monument to the Bandeiras. Color photograph by Fernando Quartarolo Marques, June 2011. Used by permission.

ial about São Paulo. Thus one could purchase the most up-to-date gizmos, or dress in the latest styles and fashions, yet still feel a reassuring sense of stability and continuity provided by an imagined bond to an earlier incarnation of São Paulo. To be sure, there were some ads that simply amplified the message of industry, progress, and national development that ran through so much of the commemorative activities. Thus the industrial firm Briganti described itself as "100% Paulista, contributing to the emancipation of National Industry." At the end of the ad it took this identification one step further, proclaiming "I Am São Paulo. I Am Brazil." And an ad for the timepiece maker Westclox declared São Paulo "the city of the men who wake up earliest in all the world." It also noted that in São Paulo "men walk in a hurry, because they know that time is money."[143] In effect, these ads went well beyond earlier depictions of the paulistas as hardworking when compared to the "indolent" cariocas or nordestinos, portraying them instead as on a par with the most industrious/industrial societies anywhere in the world.[144]

Other advertisements were more colorful and complex, weaving their marketing message into a condensed narrative of São Paulo's historical trajectory. Several ads put special emphasis on the diverse and expansive character of the paulista population (and hence of its consuming public). An ad for the Ford Motor Company "quoted" an elderly white male describing what he likes about São Paulo: "She has children with names from every race. . . . The name of one is Luigi, the other is called Manoel, there is Salim, Kamoto, Zankowski, and there are many others who were born in other lands and who, in their hearts and through their children, are sons of São Paulo."[145] In a slightly different vein, SEMP Radio and Television declared the founding of São Paulo "an act of faith. . . . Faith in the mixture of three races that would form the foundation for a tropical civilization."[146] Perhaps the most extravagant version of this "São Paulo as melting pot" narrative could be found in an ad for Mineração Geral do Brasil. It celebrated the bandeirantes who "imparted a sense of historical predestination to the indomitable spirit of the paulistas," and praised "those men who came from other lands to mix their sweat and their blood to forge a race of daring people. . . . Paulistas from every State of Brazil and from all the nations of the world who here have fused together in the heat of a shared ideal of hard work."[147]

Often the text in these advertisements portrayed São Paulo as a site of diversity, but the illustrations unfailingly depicted the paulista as white and middle class (hardly surprising given who the targeted consumer would be). Thus an ad for Escritório Levy, with a text that read "Homage to the Men Who Came from All Over the World to Forge the Greatness of São Paulo," featured an illustration of the conventional middle-class family, with a father seated in an armchair, wearing a tie, looking off into the future while his daughter sleeps peacefully on his lap, and his wife, wearing the inevitable pearls, looks lovingly upon her husband and child.[148] In a different vein, an ad for Negrita rum carried a caption informing the reader that this beverage was 100 percent Brazilian and contributed to the "industrial emancipation of São Paulo." The accompanying illustration depicted four typically middle-class men playing cards while being served drinks by a "mulata" dressed in iconic Bahian garb. If Aunt Jemima Pancake Mix promised North American households—in the words of one historian of consumerism—a "Slave in a Box," Rhum Negrita offered male paulistas a "Bahiana in a Bottle."[149]

Not that the ads were all directed at male consumers. Certainly the prominent role played by middle-class women in household shopping decisions and the substantial market sector devoted to women's apparel meant that at least some of the ads would be addressed to the "Mulher Paulista." Once again, this archetypical phrase seems the most appropriate since a number of the ads quite explicitly drew on the allegorical figure of the Paulista Woman, rather than addressing a diverse population of paulista women. Hence, an ad for the clothing stores Casas Mousseline featured the following text beneath a feminine silhouette:

São Paulo owes so much to the Paulista Woman—400 years of São Paulo history is a documentary of four centuries regarding the valor of the paulista woman.

Stem of the incredible fiber of the bandeirante in the War of the Emboabas, as in the daily struggle for life.

Her kiss is a prize. Her smile is an order. Her tear is a battle flag.[150]

An even more elaborate celebration of the Mulher Paulista could be found in an ad for the Brazilian version of *Vogue* magazine. Beneath a sketch of a well-dressed white woman, ran the following text:

Our homage to the MULHER PAULISTA.

It wasn't just HIM penetrating the backlands, creating with his bold steps the greatness of our land . . . It wasn't just HIM cultivating the virgin soil and transforming it into oceans of coffee fields . . . It wasn't just HIM alone hammering in the forge of industry and constructing the wealth of São Paulo with his strong arms . . . It was HER—the paulista woman as well—mother, sister or wife, raising us with her tenderness, educating us with her love, making us greater bandeirantes, greater farmers, greater workers, greater and more legitimate paulistas.

To the Mulher Paulista, our appreciation.[151]

What is especially striking about this advertisement is its implied proto-feminist critique of an excessively male-centered narrative of paulista history. Although the Mulher Paulista is equated here with the traditional roles of mother, wife, and daughter, she is also associated with all the great "feats" of the paulista past. To be sure, the elegantly dressed female figure in the ad signals that we are not to take the references to farmers or workers too literally (whether with regard to her or to her male counterpart). In both this and the Casas Mouselline ad, the Mulher Paulista is imagined in her archetypical guise as a white woman of the middle class.

Nationalizing Regional Development

If we compare the discussions, public and private, that shaped the IV Centenário to the discourses produced in the era of the Constitutionalist Revolution, we can easily discern thematic continuities linking 1932 and 1954. The tropes of the bandeirante saga, paulista exceptionalism, the locomotive, and the civilization of the plateau, among others, are all in evidence in the 1950s as they were in the 1930s. True, ways of explaining São Paulo's singular trajectory had become more eclectic, and by the mid-1950s explicitly racialized modes of interpreting regional success were falling into disfavor, but these trends did little to alter the major elements that constituted paulista identity since the 1920s.

There were, however, two appreciable shifts that altered the reception and resonance of the discourse of paulista exceptionalism. The first had its main ramifications within the borders of São Paulo. In 1954, as in 1932, the most audible and visible boosters of paulista identity presumed their typical inter-locutor to be a member of the white middle class. Yet in 1932, it was still possible to imagine a single paulista public that could be appealed to with the same posters, flyers, anthems, broadcasts, and addresses. To be sure, even then the leadership recognized that residents of São Paulo who defined themselves as "proletarian" proved somewhat immune to these appeals. But those dissent-ers could be shrugged off as a small minority who were not genuine paulistas. In part, the protean character of the middle class at that moment in time made it possible for the larger "public" to identify as paulista, and to resonate with elements of paulistinidade that they could claim even if their conditions of life placed them well beyond common notions of middle-classness. In 1954, by contrast, a focus on the middle class entailed more evident exclusions. In an era of multiplying publics, prioritizing the tastes and preferences of the middle class (whether catering to them or shaping them) inevitably meant that the IV Centenário would have limited emotional resonance for signifi-cant portions of São Paulo's population. Furthermore, while the members of the organizing commission might have had few qualms about indicating the better-off paulistas as their target audience, they had to answer to a range of "authorities"—whether government officials or market researchers—who associated the narrowness of their appeal with failure. Of course, even in 1932 the claim that "Todo São Paulo" supported the Constitutionalist Revolution was, at best, a useful fiction. But it was a fiction that could be maintained, and would even be reproduced by many who opposed the paulistas. In 1954, with the brief exception of the moments of "civic vibration," there wasn't even a serious effort to create a similar fiction.

The second aspect of regionalist discourse, or its reception, that changed perceptibly had implications that extended beyond the borders of São Paulo. This was the claim that all of Brazil benefited from São Paulo's successes. Starting with its initial "Plan de Propaganda," the organizing commission was keen to insist that the IV Centenário, "far from being of interest only to the paulistas, should profoundly interest all of Brazil."[152] In itself, this was not a novel argument—in the 1920s and 1930s paulista politicians (for example, Júlio Prestes) already contended that the nation as a whole derived benefits from São Paulo's modernity and prosperity, and even the paulistas' most severe critics ritually acknowledged that São Paulo was a "source of pride for all of Brazil." What had changed was the degree of receptivity to the idea that regional progress and national development were, in effect, one and the same.

Such an equivalence had been difficult to draw in an earlier era. The debates in the Chamber of Deputies during the 1920s are replete with evidence that politicians from other regions of Brazil regarded São Paulo's prosperity as coming at the cost of other, less politically powerful regions. The use of public monies, whether state or federal, to provide price supports for coffee was a source of ongoing resentment among elites in other regions of Brazil whose exports were entirely vulnerable to the vagaries of the international market. In the typically overheated rhetoric of the times, a deputy from Pernambuco had this to say in response to a proposal made in 1921 for a new round of coffee price supports: "Here's what will happen with this emission for the defense of coffee. Sugar, cotton, rubber and all the other national products will have to kneel before São Paulo and beg it for the crumbs that might drop from the banquet table of [coffee] valorization." He then denounced this as one of the injustices "that is continually and increasingly feeding the spirit of separation among the States of Brazil."[153] There were also frequent complaints about São Paulo draining labor from other areas of Brazil, with members of parliament arguing that price supports allowed paulista coffee planters to pay higher wages, and thereby lure laborers away from economic sectors that lacked public subsidies.[154]

In this earlier era, three intimately related factors seem to have been working against any effort to equate, in the public imagination, São Paulo's interests with those of the nation. One was the continued association of São Paulo's progress and prosperity with its coffee economy. Despite the paulistas' emphasis on the modernity of the coffee sector, it was difficult to argue that the latter was *qualitatively* different from, say, the *babassú* economy of Piauí.[155] Coffee might bring in revenues and pay for railroads, but it could not be persuasively presented as having a transformative effect on the national economy. And its success could easily be dismissed as the result of fortuitous timing and repeated subsidies, the latter a product of political muscle, not hard work and technological innovation. This leads directly to the second factor undermining claims that what was good for São Paulo was good for Brazil—the region's disproportionate political influence, widely perceived as allowing the paulistas to tilt the playing field in their favor, and accrue advantages to the detriment of other regions. Third, and most intangible, was the paulistas' own representation of São Paulo's success as the result of regional exceptionalism, a discourse constructed not only on the basis of certain qualities specific to São Paulo, but also on a disparaging contrast with those of other, lesser regions. Once again, in metaphorical terms, it was not just a matter of São Paulo being the locomotive; equally relevant was the claim that it was pulling empty boxcars.

As early as the 1920s, there were prominent figures in the paulista political sphere and the business community—Roberto Simonsen chief among them—who were arguing for the crucial role of industry in boosting productivity and raising *national* standards of living. Ironically, it was only with the consolidation of the Vargas regime in the 1930s, and the turn toward an elaborate program for national development, that industrialization and technological change became the touchstones of Brazilian nationalist discourse.[156] This shift also facilitated a transformation in the image of São Paulo from a largely agrarian, export-oriented economy to Latin America's leading manufacturing center. And it inclined the meaning of "São Paulo" away from the state as a whole, and toward the region's principal metropolis. By the 1950s, the idea that underdeveloped societies needed to rapidly industrialize in order to become truly independent nations had been enshrined in policy throughout the Third World, and São Paulo's progress—now linked mainly to manufacturing—could thus be more readily interpreted as a portent of the future for all Brazil. Its economy could be portrayed as qualitatively different from those in the past, or in other locations, and as having the potential to transform an entire nation.[157] Now the hundreds of thousands of internal migrants struggling to make their way to São Paulo were not simply workers being drained away to perform the same labor at slightly higher wages; rather, they were aspirants to modernity searching for steady jobs in industry, for new skills and educational opportunities, and perhaps a degree of security and social mobility.[158] Equally important, the more national configuration of Brazilian politics meant that São Paulo's triumphs could no longer be so easily attributed to political favors. Ironically, if anything, this reinforced a certain discourse of paulista superiority for if political advantage could no longer be cited as the principal explanation for São Paulo's success, then one had to look for traits intrinsic to the history, geography, climate, and demography of the region to explain its precocious transition to a modern, industrialized society.

A striking example of the effort to fold the story of São Paulo's triumph into a larger narrative of Brazilian history is an extended essay written by Catholic intellectual, industrialist, and Rio native Alceu Amoroso Lima on the occasion of the IV Centenário.[159] Entitled *A missão de São Paulo*, the argument of the text, according to the author himself, could be summarized as "I see the North as representing tradition, the Center as representing equilibrium, the

South as representing progress."[160] Lima—who published under the pen name Tristão de Athayde—repeats many of the same claims that could be found in the most chauvinistic paulista texts. Reflecting the increasingly eclectic interpretations of São Paulo's success, he cites four principal factors that explain its economic growth: fertile soil, strong men (i.e., miscegenation with European immigrants), technical resources, and the multiplication of smaller cities.[161]

After having indulged in the usual praise for São Paulo's remarkable trajectory, and having acknowledged the weight of whitening in the region's success, Lima then shifts gears and distances himself from certain reactionary attitudes of "paulista high society" and assures his readers that "in no way do I wish to ally myself with any sort of neo-bandeirante utopianism, which would consider São Paulo to be the only model for Brazil's future." He goes on to insist that Tradition, Progress, and Equilibrium are all equally essential elements for any nationality and warns that "excessive growth" in one region, and stagnation in others, "will not result in progress, but in digression or regression. That would be the march to separatism, to conflict, to wars of irredentism." Furthermore, if the North, "guardian of Tradition," risks succumbing to xenophobia, the "South" risks lapsing into a "sterile cosmopolitanism or a hedonism of wealth and pragmatism." Fortunately, according to Lima, internal migrations have brought these three regions closer, and the days when São Paulo was pulling twenty empty boxcars are at an end. Rather than seeing Brazil and São Paulo as two parallel realities, he pronounces them as being "as the part to the whole and the whole to the part."[162]

In *A missão de São Paulo*, this leading Catholic intellectual overtly rejected the most chauvinistic paulista claims and attempted to construct an organic vision of the Brazilian nation that implied a nonhierarchical relationship of interdependency among three regions, broadly construed. But at a time of national preoccupation with economic growth and industrial development, it was impossible to attribute equal significance to "Tradition," "Equilibrium," and "Progress." And the claim that internal migration had brought the regions closer together ignored the hierarchies of class and race that kept nordestinos on the periphery—literally and figuratively—of paulista society. Ultimately, even this mildly critical text could not avoid the language of predestination, and therefore, exceptionalism, in discussing the historical trajectory of the "povo bandeirante." Thus as São Paulo entered its fifth century of existence, it emerged as the standard of modernity and progress to which other regions, maybe even other nations, could aspire, while maintaining, even enhancing, its self-image as exceptional, as "o Brasil que deu certo"—the Brazil that turned out right.

CHAPTER 7

EXHIBITING EXCEPTIONALISM
History at the IV Centenário

Long Live the Cry of Ipiranga
That history has consecrated
It was here, my dear São Paulo
That Brazil became free.
—Mário Zan, Hino do IV Centenário

The coastal plateau was the sieve that strained the courage of the first
settlers. The weak ones remained on the shores of the coast. Those that had
the power of the eagle [and] conquering muscle ascended to the heroic ether
of the Plateau.
—Helena Silveira, "Carta a quem faz 4 séculos"

"São Paulo—The Fastest Growing City in the World." This slogan was
proudly proclaimed on buses, trolleys, and billboards as São Paulo's
state capital approached its putative four hundredth birthday in 1954.[1]
Together with the onward-and-upward pointing "aspiral," official symbol of the quadricentennial celebration, these words reflected the IV
Centenário's presentation of São Paulo as the metropolis of the future.
While, in theory, what was being celebrated was the birth of the village
that became the twentieth-century metropolis, in practice the most
ecstatic and elaborate celebrations looked to the future, to a São Paulo
that would soon take its place among the most modern and progressive cities of the world. In that sense São Paulo's IV Centenário more
closely resembled the New York World's Fair of 1940, whose theme was
"Tomorrow's World," than Lisbon's contemporaneous Exposition of the
"Portuguese World," which had vainly sought to burnish the empire's

greatly diminished present by reinforcing associations with its Golden Age past.[2]

In certain ways, however, the festivities in São Paulo reflected an almost obsessive attention to regional history, and to understand this, we need to consider both the national and the transnational contexts. Whereas New York City's professed modernity was only *relatively* greater than the nation surrounding it, and thus required little explanation, São Paulo's claim to be the city of tomorrow positioned it as exceptional within the Brazilian nation.[3] Not only was São Paulo's rise to the status of global metropolis unusually meteoric, even compared to New York, but it occurred within the context of a nation still struggling to claim its place in the modern world. By the mid-1950s, Rio de Janeiro—the only Brazilian city that could compete with São Paulo as a metropolitan center—was in a phase of economic and cultural stagnation. Not only had it recently been surpassed by São Paulo as Brazil's biggest urban area, but it faced the impending loss of its status as Brazil's capital district to the newly projected city of Brasília. Rio's own IV Centenário commemoration, held a decade later, proved to be a somewhat melancholic affair, owing in part to a lack of funding, but also to the cloud of political and economic uncertainty that hovered over Brazil's "marvelous city."[4]

In many respects, twentieth-century São Paulo exemplifies Marx and Engels's famous claim about the modern bourgeois world, in which "all that is solid melts into air."[5] As an urban landscape, it evinces little regard for the material remnants of the past. Thus, the following comment from one of the leading historians of paulistano identity:

> It would appear that a widespread process of forgetting has been characteristic of the creation of modern megalopolises. . . . But in São Paulo this process of metropolitanization seems to have been of such intensity that it brutally destroyed not only any and all material reference, but also any remnant of a stable symbolic reference. São Paulo in the guise of a metropolis was thus born in anonymity, eliminating its past or extracting from it only that which would be useful to reinforce the thesis of progress for progress' sake. Its only signs of identification were not stable elements, but processes taking off at dizzying speeds: fusion, speculation, expansion, acceleration.[6]

Yet, however heedless paulistanos were toward the *physical* remnants of the past, the persistent trope of regional exceptionalism, the ever-present question of "Why São Paulo?" made history an indispensable element of the city's IV Centenário. Even more than usual, the paulista past had to be scrutinized for clues to provide explanations for the region's contemporary triumph and future prospects, and to credit particular groups, traditions, or forces within paulista culture for this success. While this may fit within the rubric of "extracting . . . only that which would be useful to reinforce the thesis of progress for progress' sake," it was extraction on a fairly extravagant scale.

As noted in previous chapters, this excavation of the past for intimations of the future had been under way since the late nineteenth century, but by the 1950s an emerging national-populist sensibility made it more complicated and challenging to articulate the particular regional history of São Paulo to a narrative of the history of Brazil. In his study of national identity and popular culture, Hermano Vianna argues that, during the 1930s, Rio's popular-cultural traditions became identified as the authentic national cultural identity through the mutual constitution of mainstream samba music and Gilberto Freyre's concept of racial harmony.[7] But whereas cariocas had persistently sought to position their culture and identity as typifying a Brazilian ethos, São Paulo's regional identity had long rested on a notion of paulista *exceptionalism* that could not be so easily reconciled with Brazilian national identity in the mid-1950s, when nationalism and populism were reaching their height, and Freyrean interpretations of Brazilian character, now refashioned as "racial democracy," served as the bedrock of brasilidade.[8] Thus the challenge facing the organizers of São Paulo's quadricentennial celebrations was how to present their home region as both exceptional—that is, superior to or in the forefront of the other regions—and yet as authentically Brazilian.[9]

History Lessons

Those involved in organizing the 1954 festivities readily acknowledged the pedagogical goals of the IV Centenário and saw "history" as playing a crucial role in fulfilling those objectives. In this regard, the commemorative activities in São Paulo were hardly exceptional. The voluminous historiography on officially sponsored public commemorations and expositions has repeatedly demonstrated that these were typically designed to teach an imagined regional, national, or even transnational public about the nature of progress and modernity and, by extension, to offer lessons in good citizenship.[10] This insight needs no further elaboration here. What seems more interesting to explore is how new trends in both regional demographic composition and Brazilian historical interpretation produced alterations or challenges to the existing narratives of paulista exceptionalism. Further, as in the previous chapter, I will consider how those most actively involved in shaping the quadricentennial celebrations imagined their prospective public(s). The members of the official organizing commission, by taste and personal association, surely preferred to imagine their target audience as the middling sorts in Brazilian society, but as we have seen, they did not always have the luxury—politically or financially—of defining their audience in such narrow terms. During an era of intense populist political mobilization and agitation, with São Paulo just having witnessed its first major general strike since 1919 (not to mention the melodrama of Vargas's suicide in August 1954), it was unwise to ignore the "povo" altogether as an element of the public and as a target of commemorative pedagogy.[11]

In other words, the various meanings intended for or derived from the myriad activities and exhibits that constituted the commemorations in 1954 cannot be treated as simple, direct manifestations of discursive positions.[12] Even those expositions elsewhere that were largely vanity productions of particular dictators—such as Antonio Salazar's celebration of the "Portuguese World," or Rafael Trujillo's megomaniacal Fair for Free World Peace and Fraternity in the Dominican Republic—might create spaces for narratives and images that escaped the control of the original conceptualizers of the event.[13] If anything, this makes these occasions even more interesting to the historian, who can read them as part of the struggle over regional and national identities, and transnational image-making. In this case, what I am especially interested in is the extent to which paulista constructions of the region's triumphs reflected and reinforced racialized understandings of modernity and progress. As an extension of this, I will explore the implications of a racialized regional identity for São Paulo's relationship with the Brazilian nation, especially in light of the triumph of racial democracy as the dominant discourse of national identity, even as a "whitened" São Paulo consolidated its position as the nation's economic juggernaut.[14]

It should be noted that the architects of the IV Centenário did not regard pedagogical opportunities as being confined to the more erudite or scholarly features of the commemorations, such as the Historical Exposition. Recreational activities and spectacles could also be expected to perform a pedagogical function—more specifically, to give working-class residents of the metropolitan area (not all of them necessarily regarded as "paulistas") a sense of belonging, a sense of awe at São Paulo's modernity, and a sense of the city's future promise. Through the use of spectacle and technical virtuosity, it was relatively easy to present the "future" of São Paulo in a way that appealed to all social sectors, but especially to the laboring poor, many of whom had staked what little they had on that very future by migrating to Brazil's booming urban center.[15] More challenging was the representation of the past in a way that could be meaningful to this wider audience. Still, there was a broad consensus among the organizers that this challenge had to be met, and that the celebrations of the future had to be anchored in an appreciation of the past. João Batista de Arruda Sampaio, a member of the original organizing commission, in requesting additional funds for the Historical Exposition explained its significance in the following insistent terms:

> I regard the São Paulo Historical Exposition . . . as the fundamental and indispensable feature of the festivities of the IV Centenário. . . . If it becomes necessary, we could sacrifice any other aspect; this one, never. The Quadricentennial undoubtedly has substantial commercial, scientific and cultural goals of great scope in the economic and cultural development not only of São Paulo, but of Brazilian civilization. All of this, however, has to conform to a basic principle . . . which is that of the historical background, that marks the path, that gives it direction, that forms character. And our [historical background], whose origins lie in the tiny and immense Portugal, is among the most beautiful, whether in its territorial expression, which represents the conquest of a heroic people, or in the spiritual sense of its civilization, which is profoundly Christian. Therefore, the characteristic tone of the celebration . . . can only be that of moral and civic instruction. And this rests entirely on the Historical Exposition.[16]

Or as the director of Rádio Bandeirantes, in a prospectus for a radio show on paulista history, more succinctly put it: "History is the underpinning on which we base the Present in order to better guide ourselves to the Future."[17]

An underlying theme in the correspondence between the various paulista broadcasters and the Service for Public Relations and Tourism (SRPIPTUR) is not only the recognition of "History" as an essential element in public pedagogy, but also the claim that the official historical exhibits would prove to be too erudite and complicated for the "povo," who needed history lessons delivered in some other fashion geared to "popular tastes," such as novelization.[18] The Rádio Bandeirantes director recommended that these "lessons" be presented as semi-fictionalized episodes in a twelve-month radio series (accompanied by advertisements every half hour for quadricentennial activities). Judging from their responses, the commission members generally agreed that an exhibit designed to provide a coherent history lesson for the middle-class paulista, or familiarize a well-heeled tourist with São Paulo's past, might prove overly taxing and tedious for a member of the "popular classes." Thus, the main History Lesson "delivery system" for the middling sorts could be an elaborate, scholarly, and tastefully constructed exposition (supplemented with a historical library subsidized by the commission), whereas radio shows that "popularized" and even "novelized" paulista history were designated as the preferred means to deliver those same lessons to the masses.

It should be noted that not all of those involved with the historical programming of the IV Centenário harbored such a bifurcated view of the audience for these history lessons, or was so quick to dismiss the ability of poorer paulistas to appreciate a scholarly presentation of historical events. Jaime Cortesão, the eminent Portuguese historian who organized the historical exhibits, viewed the official exposition not as a strictly elite affair but as "essentially for the people."[19] In one communication with the consulting board, he insisted that "from the outset . . . my proposal was for the Exposition to have a didactic character, that is, for it to become a lesson in history and civics for the larger public."[20] And postmortem appraisals of the exposition, including attendance figures, indicate that it did have considerable popular appeal, contrary to the (low) expectations of the commission. But Cortesão also insisted that the "scientific side" of the exposition would not be forgotten—that is, it would be constructed according to professional standards and norms of academic argument and presentation. Apocryphal historical anecdotes, such as the "prophecy" of Padre Anchieta, would be excluded as having no place in "an exhibit that is logical and scientific in character."[21] In other words, his intent was to mount an exhibit that would be both edifying and entertaining, and would pass scholarly muster.

History on the Air

For regional radio stations, the major inducement to participate in the teaching of history to the paulista public was almost certainly the organizing commission's generous advertising budget, rather than a desire to produce a better-informed citizenry. But regardless of motive, the IV Centenário created an occasion for several broadcasters to offer radio programs devoted to historical themes with formats considered sufficiently simple and entertaining to attract the uneducated public. Although the full transcripts of these programs are not available in the commission's archives, summaries of their content allow us to consider what modifications were made in this effort to reach a wider audience. For example, did these presentations of paulista history on the airwaves make any concessions to the "povo" in terms of content, or was it mainly a matter of form? And how was the povo, as an audience, being defined? Did it include working-class descendants of European or Japanese immigrants? Did it include paulistas of African descent or recent migrants from Brazil's Northeast? Were any or all of these groups entitled to representation in the popular version of São Paulo's historical narrative? And how did the popularized, not to say "vulgarized," histories compare to the more "scholarly" historical interpretation offered in the official exposition?

For the most part, if we juxtapose the content of the radio presentations and the historical exposition, what is striking is not the differences between them but their extensive similarities, and particularly their common exclusion or trivialization of the African contribution to São Paulo's "progress." With one important exception, all opened with the premise pronounced by the Brazilian ambassador to Portugal: "Brazil is a conquest and a gift from São Paulo, from the strong and generous race that the blood of the Portuguese molded in this favored region, transmitting to [São Paulo] the enterprising impulse and the civilizing instinct."[22] And as they moved forward in time, they acknowledged the contributions of the various immigrant "colonies," and especially those from Italy, Spain, and Japan. In the case of the more elaborate and expensive historical exposition, there would be far greater attention to presenting a "full" account of São Paulo's evolution, thereby making it more likely that Afropaulistas would receive at least cursory recognition. But the basic story line, uncluttered by token acknowledgment of Indian or African influences, would be the one echoed in the popular radio programs. According to this narrative, São Paulo had always been the leading force of civilization and enterprise in Brazil, and its history had been a continuous process of forward progress led by white Europeans who strategically absorbed the specialized knowledge and backbreaking toil of non-European peoples toward the goal of constructing a predominantly white and progressive society.[23]

Correspondence from several of the leading radio stations indicates that there was general agreement that, given the "low cultural and educational level" of the audience, novelization was the best means to convey paulista history to the "povo." This was the proposal of Rádio Bandeirantes, as well as Rádio América, which planned to dramatize the historical novela *O romance dos quatro séculos*, by Otávio Augusto Vampré. Similarly, Rádio Gazeta contended that the history of São Paulo easily lent itself to novelization: "The sacrifices, the hardships of the treks, the animosity of the savages, the strong spirit of the bandeirantes and, at the same time, the brutality of those who tamed our backlands, are all themes that can be developed to produce *novelas* with a strong historical significance and, why not say it?, to enlighten the masses."[24]

Rádio de Piratininga proposed a series of programs entitled *Itinerary of the Bandeiras* that would trace the bandeirante spirit throughout the history of São Paulo. "We will relate through these impressive programs the greatest chapters in paulista history. The epic story of the bandeiras, the lessons in boldness, tenacity, and industry that is the history of the bandeirante capital.

The magnificent contribution of the immigrant. Coffee. Cotton. Our industry and commerce. A series of broadcasts exalting the civic spirit of the people of São Paulo." And Rádio Nacional described its intended program as "paying homage not only to the great City and its people, but also, and especially, to the vast immigrant colonies that helped to constitute the Bandeirante prosperity."[25] In short, these radio programs, due to their fictionalized format, melodramatic structure, and episodic character, were even less likely to include significant information on the lives of enslaved Africans and their descendants, slave and free, than the official historical exposition. And to the extent that they shaped their programming to have greater popular appeal, this seems to have entailed highlighting the contributions of European immigrants, not Afro-paulistas or northeastern migrants. If anything, the São Paulo whose history they recounted was even whiter and more Europeanized than the one represented at the Ibirapuera exhibit. Rádio de Piratininga designated law professor and folklorist Dalmo Belfort de Mattos as its principal scriptwriter; given that Belfort de Mattos was among a group of historical researchers who adamantly insisted on the whiteness of São Paulo's colonial population, one can presume that blacks and Indians would get little air time on *his* program. He was also a pioneering opponent of nordestino migration to São Paulo, calling them "sampauleiros" (to situate them outside the charmed circle of paulistinidade), and disparaging them as carriers of both disease and subversive ideas.[26] Clearly, they would not be candidates for inclusion in the heroic narrative of paulista history.

The programming proposed by Rádio Cultura—a public broadcasting company—constituted a partial exception to this trend. While very much adopting a "popular" format—four youngsters meet Father Time in a park and are transported back to great moments in São Paulo's past—the script summaries included some discordant notes when compared to the other radio programs. True, it starts with the usual account of Padre Anchieta and the defeat of the Tamoios, but at one point a character says that the Indians refuse to be taken prisoner because "in this land there will be no slaves." This statement is especially ironic (and surely unintentionally so) given the future slaving expeditions of the bandeirantes and the heavy presence of enslaved Africans during the coffee boom. But it does trace the claim about paulistas' natural antipathy to slavery back to a non-European source. Next there's a scene of Borba Gato and Fernão Dias Pais—two leading bandeirante figures—bidding farewell to their stoic, iron-willed wives and setting off on an expedition. And a chapter from more contemporary history applauds the Revolution of 1932 as a "just cause" and recounts a son going off to battle with his mother's blessing and a girl shouting "we want to donate our wedding rings for the good of São Paulo." Indeed, this segment seems so relentlessly cheerful and upbeat that one would never know from the script summary that São Paulo suffered a quick and sobering defeat at the hands of the federal forces.[27]

Like the other radio programs, this one also has dialogue of immigrants (Italians, Portuguese, Sirio-Lebanese, Japanese) arriving on Brazil's shores "to help with the progress of São Paulo." But not only is the immigrant population slightly more diverse in this rendering, but the following statement indicates a somewhat different notion of their role in São Paulo: "Immigrants. Blessed art thou who, arriving in this good and bountiful land, helped to make it greater. You worked, you mixed with the black, with the bandeirante, and thus emerged a new race of heroes." This might be read as the standard injunction for the immigrants to whiten the existing population of São Paulo but in the very last chapter, devoted to the marvels of modernity and industry, a narrator concludes by declaring the greatness of "São Paulo of the white man, the black man, and the yellow man."[28] This final remark is especially significant because it describes a genuinely diverse São Paulo; it can't be read as yet another reference to the fleeting contribution of nonwhite groups, just "waiting" to be overwhelmed by the vigor of European blood. In this respect, Rádio Cultura was adopting a perspective on race "mixture" that was closer to that associated with Gilberto Freyre and the concept of Brazil as a racial democracy than with the paulista discourse on "racial amalgamation" as a process of whitening.

History on Display

Among the many fans of the Historical Exposition of the IV Centenário was the literary critic Valdemar Cavalcanti, who was so impressed by the exhibit that he urged the authorities (unsuccessfully) to make it a permanent installation. Rhapsodizing about the experience of visiting the exposition, he remarked: "I immediately think of the pedagogical effect of such an exhibit with respect to the thousands upon thousands of individuals who pass through it each day: they 'see' history."[29] A great deal of time, money, and effort had been expended to make São Paulo's history "visible." It took the better part of two years to collect the documentation, artwork (including paintings and murals by Di Cavalcanti, Tarsila do Amaral, Estrela Faria, and Fernando Lemos), and artifacts showcased at the exhibition, and the organizing commission regularly expressed its anxiety about possible setbacks and inevitable cost overruns. As the date of the inauguration approached, there were increasing expressions of doubt—both within the commission and in the press—about whether the buildings and grounds in Ibirapuera would be ready in light of construction delays and a last-minute strike by workers involved in the decoration of the facilities. Newspapers even reported that the organizers were prohibiting the press from photographing the installations in Ibirapuera because it would reveal how poorly prepared the site was on the eve of the scheduled inauguration. But the strike was quickly settled, the unfinished structures made to look complete, and some of the exhibits were inaugurated on August 21, as planned. Except for the interruptions associated with the inconveniently timed suicide of President Vargas, the expositions of the IV Centenário stayed close to the original schedule, with the history exposition mildly delayed until the Seventh of September, Brazilian Independence Day.[30]

The history of São Paulo presented in the exposition (which was on display throughout the last five months of the commemorations) was chronologically organized in an intricate series of panels (some 150 in all), with each set devoted to a specific era and/or theme. The foundational period included panels devoted to (1) the conquest of the coast, (2) indigenous cultures, and (3) the place of Portuguese/Iberian society among the classical (Greek, Roman) cultures. In regard to the indigenous cultures, a caption on the display explained how "the Lusitanian, in order to survive, tupinized [sic], meaning, he adapted himself to the economic, social and ethnical regimes of the natives." The next set of panels, on the bandeirantes, was especially elaborate and presented the mainstream/White Legend paulista view of these figures. According to Cortesão's own notes on the exhibit, "There has been far too much emphasis with regard to the goals of the bandeiras on the merciless hunting of Indians for the purpose of using their slave labor." Instead of this Black Legend narrative, the exhibit emphasized the bandeiras' economic goals (search for minerals) and geopolitical goals (conflicts with Spain, expansion of borders). The central theme was the role of the bandeiras in creating a paulista identity, "ennobled by their epic actions," and expanding the frontiers of "Grande Brasil."[31] It also described the bandeirantes as "the fusion of two cultures—Portuguese and native"—and praised the Indian as "the living compass and map for the incursions into the interior."

Lest one surmise that colonial paulista society was being depicted as entirely composed of Portuguese, mestiços, and Indians, there is a brief reference to "other" paulistas in the panel on the church in São Paulo, which included watercolors "portraying ceremonies and conga dances in which male and female blacks blend Catholic rites and African rhythms." But it is interesting to note that the sole attempt to incorporate artistic objects of African origin—a collection of Benin sculptures belonging to the Geographical Society of Lisbon—foundered because the organizers decided that the insurance required to ship the valuable sculptures was too expensive.[32] In contrast, no expense was spared in acquiring a collection of Jesuit-authored documents that allegedly absolved the bandeirantes of the most serious Black Legend accusations.

After that homage to the Indian and the brief "cameo appearance" by paulistas of African birth or descent, the story shifts back to the predominantly European population, citing the contribution of paulista naturalists and intellectuals first to Portuguese Enlightenment thought, and then to the formation of Brazilian national identity. Two turn-of-the-century works (by Silva Pontes and Aires do Casal) are presented as particularly significant and introduced as "the remote but logical consequence of the bandeirante tradition, presag[ing] the movement for Independence." Furthermore, "the two [works] provided Brazilians with a physical portrait of Brazil, the knowledge of its frontiers and territorial unity, the primary and indispensable basis for State formation. But São Paulo remained the radiating center and focus, that inspired and gave life to these works."[33] Also eagerly noted is São Paulo–born Teresa Margarida da Silva e Orta (1711–1792), credited with being the first woman to write a novel in the Portuguese language. As one might expect, less attention was given to the fact that she spent only the first five years of her relatively long life in Brazil.

The next series of panels opens with São Paulo's role in the movement for independence—a panel which, interestingly enough, begins in 1765 with São Paulo's separation from Rio and the restoration of provincial autonomy. Particular attention is given to the long-standing "nativist" outlook in São Paulo, which allegedly made it a stronghold of anticolonial sentiment. This is followed by São Paulo in the First and Second Empires; in the latter (1840–1889), the emphasis shifts to the building of railroads and the "immigration of European workers," which "would consolidate the bases for the contemporary progress of São Paulo."[34] Given the massively important role of African slavery in this particular phase of the province's economic and demographic growth, the decision to highlight new technology and European immigration (which was little more than a trickle until the final years of the empire) is especially telling.

Other themes from the Second Empire that received attention included the intellectual influence of the growing periodical press and the law school, and the crucial role of paulistas in the republican and abolitionist movements. Cortesão's notes indicate that objects and documents relating to life and work under slavery would indeed be included in the imperial portion of the exhibit, but entirely within the context of the abolitionist movement in São Paulo—by then the standard means to simultaneously incorporate and marginalize the history of African slaves in the region.[35]

Once into the republican period—the ninth and last section—the exhibit proceeds to become an unrestrained celebration of São Paulo's emergence as, by far, the most important economic center of Brazil, "surpassing all other regions in agriculture, industry, transport, and education." The initial cause of this sudden prosperity is identified as "administrative autonomy" due to the new republican system, which allowed São Paulo, from 1889 to 1930, "to develop its economic resources in an extraordinary manner." And among the other factors explaining this explosive growth, the documents cite "the great waves of immigrants endowed with the industrial tradition."[36] This section also includes a panel on the Constitutionalist Revolution of 1932, placing it within the "longue durée" of paulista history, which is described as composed of three "conquests": "The conquest of the land, the conquest of gold, and the conquest of the law. . . . Hence, equal in valor/value to those who tamed a land, and those who discovered a treasure, were those who insisted on a Constitution."[37] The panels traced a direct and unbroken line from Padre Anchieta to the bandeirantes to the Revolution of 1932.

The final panel of the exposition was inscribed with the following declaration, which is worth quoting in full:

With the legacy of the European cultures, transplanted to the lands of America by the audacity of the Portuguese navigators; with the knowledge of the paths and the land taught by the Indians; with the spirit of Christianity transmitted by the apostles and missionaries; with the tenacity and bravery of the bandeirantes discovering and populating new territories; with the humble and formidable labor of the blacks and mestizos; with the nativist sentiments and patriotic impulses that led to Brazilian Independence; with the struggles of the soldiers on the battlefield; with the experience of the immigrants of São Paulo.[38]

This recitation of the historical elements that constituted São Paulo's glorious present seems, at first glance, quite inclusive—it mentions both the indigenous influence and the African contribution. But only rarely did the dominant representations of São Paulo and its history completely expunge those groups from the narrative; more typically, they placed them on the margins, or in discrete intervals of the rapidly receding past. Whereas the bandeirante spirit runs through the entire narrative, and gets credit for everything from paulista nativism to capitalist entrepreneurship, Indians and blacks are situated as groups that "lent a hand" at crucial moments, only to fade from the landscape, overwhelmed by the virile Portuguese blood of the original settlers, or by the recent immigrant tide with its reputed "industrial tradition" (no matter that the vast majority were peasants with little experience of either urban or industrial life).[39] Moreover, the above historical laundry list did not include even a token reference to the hundreds of thousands of migrants from Minas Gerais and the Northeast who had been steadily moving to São Paulo since the 1930s. This historical construction of the paulista, rather than emphasizing an open-ended, continually changing regional identity, in effect used the 1932 uprising as the outer chronological boundary of paulistinidade.

Although attendance at the exhibit was ample and press commentaries were enthusiastic, the exposition did come under fire from some members of the paulista historical establishment: Aureliano Leite, a leading figure in the Paulista Academy of Letters, openly criticized the choice of Cortesão as organizer of the exposition and deplored what he saw as an exaggerated emphasis on the "Portuguese" contribution in the central narrative.[40] But Leite was hardly calling for more attention to African or even European-immigrant populations; rather, his preference would have been to foreground the hardy New World hybrid that emerged in colonial São Paulo, and whose way of life "on the plateau" he regarded as a dramatic departure from Portuguese culture.[41]

It may be unsurprising that a historical exposition created within the context of a regional commemoration would highlight São Paulo's importance to the nation, sanitize the historical conduct of the bandeirantes, and downplay the role of human enslavement in the region's progress. Yet, this was in notable contrast to the widely celebrated work of Gilberto Freyre, who foregrounded slavery—or a sentimentalized version of it—in his construction of regional cum national identity.[42] Moreover, Freyre himself became involved, both directly and indirectly, in some of the debates over race and history in São Paulo. First, his name was invoked in connection with the mildly controversial work of historian and folklorist Ernani Silva Bruno, whose manuscript "Café e Negro" was submitted for the commemorative prize in economic history, and who also published his three-volume *História e tradições da cidade de São Paulo* as part of the bibliographical tributes to the IV Centenário.[43] In contrast to an earlier generation of students of paulista history such as Alfredo Ellis Júnior, Dalmo Belfort de Mattos, and Aureliano Leite, who claimed that colonial São Paulo had been predominantly white and "suffered" little African cultural influence, Silva Bruno insisted that even prior to the nineteenth century, African slaves and freedpersons had formed a major portion of the paulista population, and that many cultural and artistic traditions in the region could be traced back to African influence.[44] Commentators immediately dubbed Silva Bruno a disciple of Gilberto Freyre (who authored the preface for *História e tradições*), but Freyre himself coyly insisted that he had no "school." Freyre's denials aside, Silva Bruno undoubtedly had been influenced and emboldened by *Casa-Grande e senzala* and subsequent works by Freyre. In "Café e Negro" he is clearly seeking to make São Paulo's agrarian past compatible with the increasingly hegemonic historical narrative of Brazil as a racial democracy that emerged from the intimate bonds forged under the regime of plantation slavery.

It is a sign of the shifting tenor of historical research in São Paulo, and in Brazil generally, that Silva Bruno's work turned out to be only slightly controversial within the restricted circles where such scholarly studies would initially be read. Submitted for the prize in economic history, "Café e Negro" was one of only two historical works that were judged worthy of recognition by the official juries—though Silva Bruno received a special commendation rather than a prize because the jury (which included the eminent Marxist historian Caio Prado Júnior) did not regard his manuscript as a work of economic history per se. Silva Bruno also assisted Jaime Cortesão in collecting materials for the Historical Exposition and had the honor of organizing the panels related to slavery and abolition. In other words, he was hardly a marginalized or ostracized figure.[45]

Moreover, his influence quickly expanded beyond scholarly circles. In July 1954 the Diários Associados—Brazil's largest newspaper chain—issued a special commemorative edition dedicated to the theme of "Coffee." Much of the first section was devoted to a polemic by publisher Assis Chateaubriand, a vehement defender of agrarian interests, who fulminated against the "abuse" of coffee in preference to industry, and called coffee (anthropomorphically) "the only Brazilian that even today has not been emancipated. He is a king who is no more than a slave, given that Brazil lives and moves as a nation thanks to his sweat and blood." The second section, however, opened with a series of long and contentious excerpts from Silva Bruno's "Café e Negro." The article begins with Silva Bruno informing his readers that there's still no systematic study of coffee and slave labor, "as there is still no study that defines the cultural values with which the Negro contributed to what we could call 'paulista civilization.'" He then goes on to assert the decisive role played by black slaves in the implantation and expansion of the coffee economy in São Paulo, "to the dismay of those who defend at all costs paulista Aryanism and believe because of this that the coffee plantations only occasionally relied on the servile regime [slavery]." He does readily concede that São Paulo was in the best position to make a transition to free labor, but disparages as an "excessive simplification" the claim by some observers that the mere presence of immigrants in the coffee fields as early as the 1840s can be taken as evidence that African slavery, and Africans themselves, were of only minor and transitory importance.[46]

In a similar vein, the eminent French sociologist Roger Bastide, resident in São Paulo since 1938, contributed a chapter, "O Negro em São Paulo," to the massive two-volume commemorative publication of São Paulo's Instituto Histórico (*São Paulo em quatro séculos* [São Paulo in four centuries]); his essay challenged the tendency to dismiss the African contribution to paulista society. According to Bastide, Afro-paulistas played important roles in the abolition of slavery and the rise of popular republicanism. He also decried the negative impact of massive European immigration on blacks in São Paulo and attributed their numerical decline to social factors, not the racial and climatic factors foregrounded by Alfredo Ellis Jr. And he closed his contribution by lamenting the persistence of racial prejudice in São Paulo.[47]

On a less scholarly note, Isa Silveira Leal, in the article "Four Centuries of Feminine Values," inserted a pause in the standard narrative of indigenous women assisting the Portuguese male colonists until European women arrived and displaced them, to acknowledge the anonymous "first Black woman to set foot on paulista soil." According to Leal, this woman "had lost all her rights to happiness, to motherhood, to the very condition of human dignity." She then goes on, in a Freyrean vein, to praise the black woman's culinary skills, musical rhythms, and affection, and ends the pause by expressing "a sentiment of gratitude to the Black Mother from all paulistas."[48] Other writers explicitly cited Freyre's oeuvre. Almeida Magalhães, in a piece entitled "The Birth of São Paulo," claimed that the multiplication of the original four hundred settlers from 1530 to 1554 "exemplify the robust aptitude for mobility and mixture of the Lusitanian people as studied by Gilberto Freyre."[49]

To be sure, there were numerous scholars who resisted Freyre's influence, or who adopted a very particular interpretation of Freyre's concept of *lusotropicalismo*. Tito Lívio Ferreira, who contributed the chapter "The Portuguese in the Formation of the Bandeirante" to *São Paulo em quatro séculos*, constructed an argument based entirely on the Freyrean notion of the unique "miscibility" of the Portuguese. This, he claimed, explained the more humane nature of slavery in Brazil, especially compared to the treatment of Africans and Indians by the English and the Spaniards. In making such arguments, he readily acknowledged his intellectual debt to "Gilberto Freire" [*sic*], whom Ferreira described as the "master of Brazilian sociology," and quoted Freyre's declaration that "after Christ, no one has contributed more than the Portuguese to fraternity among all men." Yet Ferreira argued in another essay (discussed below) that slavery had only a brief and transitory significance in São Paulo's coffee economy. An even more dubious use of Freyre's concept of luso-tropicalismo can be found in one of the unpublished theses presented at the Historical Congress entitled "The Influence of São Paulo in the Solution of the Brazilian Indigenous Problem." This work equated the "Indian problem" in Brazil with the "native question" then facing the Portuguese in Africa—that is, the question of what to do about its "primitive colonial population." The author claimed that Portuguese policies on this question, always imbued with their more humane disposition, had excited considerable interest among authorities in South Africa, a country he described as deserving "kudos for the orientation it has adopted on this matter." And he ended by dismissing criticisms of South Africa's recently imposed racial-segregation policies as unfair and misguided.[50]

The work of Silva Bruno and others generated some ripples of criticism, but more noteworthy is how painlessly it was incorporated into the regional historical narrative. Although "Café e Negro" was an important corrective to the elision of African slavery from the history of São Paulo, it did not challenge the foundational narrative of paulista identity. Nor, for the most part, did Freyre, who extolled the "living tradition of the bandeirantes " as responsible for "the numerous cases of conversion, among Europeans of the most diverse origins, or among Brazilians from the most remote provinces, to the particularly dynamic and creative spirit of the paulistas."[51] This statement, however, does draw an equivalence between the European immigrant and the Brazilian migrant, both of whom have to undergo a "conversion" to become a dynamic, creative paulista—which implicitly rejects the claim that European immigrants deserved special credit for the modernity of São Paulo.

Like modernist poet Cassiano Ricardo's insistence on the African presence in the bandeiras, the African influence cited by Silva Bruno did not necessarily diminish the generative role ascribed to the bandeirantes in the construction of the Brazilian nation and the region's spirit of enterprise, nor did it deny the impact of European immigration on São Paulo's post-emancipation economic trajectory.[52] As long as "Africanisms" could be relegated to the realm of nostalgia or popular culture, they did not undermine São Paulo's claims to being in the vanguard of civilization and modernity in Brazil because of its peculiar colonial history. Indeed, I would argue in broader terms that the discourse of racial democracy, though insisting that racial heterogeneity was no impediment to modernity, left undiminished the generalized Brazilian tendency to associate modernity and progress with whiteness or Europeanness. And as long as this association remained unchallenged, paulista elites could continue to construct a compelling "history of the present." That is, with São Paulo's exceptional progress and future prospects as their starting point, they could selectively read back into the region's (whitened) past a narrative that would explain this eventual triumph—and much of the Brazilian "public" would find an interpretation that foregrounded the bandeirantes and European immigration far more compelling than any of the alternative explanations.[53]

This "easy" association between whiteness and progress did not go entirely unchallenged. Freyre himself directly intervened in the discussion. In an article entitled "An Interpretation of São Paulo," published in a special commemorative issue of the *Diário de São Paulo*, he sounded a rare, genuinely critical note regarding the paulistas' unbridled advocacy of industrialization and progress:

> Progress, perhaps, does not exist in any absolute sense, but only in a relative one. Industrial capitalism itself . . . in order to correspond to the best of the national spirit needs to be as egalitarian with regard to an individual's race—biologically evident—as to his "status"—sociologically or culturally obvious. A Brazilian, whether old or young, blond or dark in appearance, should become a member of the Brazilian industrialized community. And there can be no doubt that the tradition that Prof. Ascarelli calls "egalitarian" runs the risk, with regard to race, of becoming "Americanized" in São Paulo, in the worst sense of Americanization—esteeming the white newcomer, offspring of a European worker or peasant, who transforms himself through his own effort ("self-made man," "strenuous man," etc.) into an industrial magnate, but then creates obstacles to the social ascent of the Brazilian or the paulista who has been here, if not for 400 years, for 300 or 200, and who retains, on his face and body, overly visible marks of his African origins.[54]

Moreover, Freyre did not simply construct the issue as a question of European versus African, but implicitly recognized the racialization of regional identity in São Paulo, and insisted, when speaking of immigration, that paulistas should include "the immigration of Brazilians from the North, lured by a messianic São Paulo." In some ways, this insistence on the "immigrant" status of nordestino migrants was even more challenging to the ongoing reproduction of a whitened paulista identity than Silva Bruno's claims about African influences in colonial paulista culture. It is also worth noting the shrewd use of the term "messianic," an adjective normally used pejoratively to refer to the Nordeste; in this case Freyre is deploying it to metaphorically reposition São Paulo as an immense, industrialized Canudos.[55]

Whose History?

The above statement by Freyre argues that European immigrants to São Paulo had been preferentially welcomed into paulista society and had been fully, even excessively recognized for their role in the explosion of regional prosperity. Yet there are other sources from the era of the IV Centenário that indicate an ongoing tension between those who would locate the "origins" of São Paulo's exceptional historical trajectory in the colonial saga of the bandeirantes, and those who would attribute the region's success to the post-emancipation immigrant wave.[56] While there were various discursive and representational efforts to make these two perspectives compatible—including the notion of the immigrants as "novos mamelucos"—at least some public figures believed there was political hay to be made from this "dispute" and consequently played up the opposition between the two positions. One notorious example was a speech given by Emílio Carlos—manager of Jânio Quadros's campaign for governor—in the interior city of Assis, reprinted in *A Folha da Noite*, a newspaper that vigorously supported the candidacy of Quadros's chief opponent, Prestes Maia. According to the *Folha*, Emílio Carlos made the following declaration to his audience in Assis: "Gentlemen, there are certain candidates who boast of having the honor of being descended from the bandeirantes. But the greatness of São Paulo isn't due to the bandeirantes. Rather, it is the result of the toil of Italian, Portuguese, Spanish, Syrian, Japanese, German, etc., immigrants, who cleared the fields for coffee and built the great paulista industrial sector. I don't see any reason to take pride in being descended from Fernão Dias' harem."[57] *A Folha da Noite*, correctly interpreting these remarks as an attack on the "blue-blooded" Prestes Maia, accused Jânio of sowing divisions among paulistas. It also claimed that immigrant paulistas identify with "the same historical traditions that are a source of pride for the descendants of the heroic bandeirantes" and observed that no one would imagine a European arriving in the United States denigrating the memory of Washington or Lincoln. And to make it clear that the real bone of contention was the IV Centenário, the *Folha* noted that Governor Garcez had appointed Francisco Matarazzo Sobrinho—the descendant of immigrants—to head the organizing commission, and that Matarazzo resigned only because of pressure from Jânio himself. The article ended by claiming that Emílio Carlos—and by extension, Jânio—was somehow implying that immigrants and their offspring were not fully paulista, but the *Folha* insisted otherwise: "Yes, we are all paulistas—good, genuine, authentic paulistas—working in harmony to make São Paulo even greater, because what distinguishes 'the paulista' . . . is not simply the fact of having been born here, but the pioneer spirit, the capacity for achievement, the sense of collective well-being, the eagerness for progress."[58] As should be apparent, both sides in this "debate" were reproducing a whitened version of paulista history—ironically, the more populist Quadros campaign even more explicitly so, given the reported remark about immigrants "opening the coffee fields."[59] In general, Jânio kept his distance from the commemorative proceedings, which made him the target of repeated denunciations by certain publications for being "insufficiently paulista." But it also allowed him to portray the festivities as elitist, on the one hand, and himself as a man of the people, on the other.

Some of the authors of articles in commemorative supplements also entered this debate. Sampaio Ferraz, who wrote a long piece on "The Man of the Paulista Plateau" in *O Estadão* insisted that, despite the important contribution of both immigrants and migrants, the principal issue was to determine the cultural and geophysical elements that produced the "paulista character."[60] Other commentators placed more emphasis on the definitive role of the immigrants in making São Paulo different from the rest of Brazil. According to an article in *A Folha da Manhã*, "Many observers tend to attribute the development of São Paulo, which has been more intense than in the rest of Brazil, to the preponderance of immigrant waves that have had our state as their destination."[61] Several articles, especially those focused on paulistas of Italian descent, highlighted the disposition of these immigrants to make the leap from proletarian to petty proprietor. And the multiple articles that openly celebrated the statistics indicating that a large majority of paulistas and paulistanos were "white" attributed this "achievement" to the influx of European immigrants. One article in the *Diário de São Paulo*, detailing "essa alvura paulistana" (that paulistana whiteness), noted—in an unmistakably celebratory tone—that São Paulo city, principally due to immigration, was 87.8 percent white, 10.23 percent black and brown, and 1.89 percent yellow. And it also made an obviously invidious comparison with other parts of Brazil, mentioning how much higher the percentage of "black and brown" was in Rio (29.8 percent), Pernambuco (50.3 percent), and Bahia (66 percent). The *Diário Popular* trumpeted the same statistics as revealing the "hegemony of the white race over the rest" in São Paulo.[62]

Several articles in the commemorative supplements stressed the crucial role of São Paulo's climate and geographic location—a point made by historians as diverse as Caio Prado Jr., Oliveira Lima, and Pierre Monbeig, according to Frederico Heller's essay "The Road to the Metropolitan Economy."[63] In one of the more lurid versions of this interpretation Helena Silveira made the Darwinian claim, quoted at the start of this chapter, about the plateau straining out the weak.[64] More sober analyses simply argued that settlement on the plateau meant that the paulista colonists had to be more self-sufficient and more oriented toward the interior. The French geographer Monbeig cited the temperate conditions on the plateau, noting that "the climate of São Paulo was quickly recognized as particularly favorable to settlement by whites."[65]

The next key factor—implicitly determined by paulista "character"—was the early and enthusiastic transition to immigrant/wage labor. Typical of this would be a piece written by historian Tito Lívio Ferreira, titled "The Economic Path of Coffee," which insisted that long before abolition, the paulista fazendeiro "considered slavery to be extinct."[66] Indeed, it was probably Ferreira that Silva Bruno had in mind when he denounced the excessive simplification that led some historians to downplay the role of African slavery in the coffee boom. But Ferreira was hardly an isolated case: a writer for *A Folha da Manhã* claimed that "even before 1850 . . . there was a sense of the need to replace the slave laborer with the European."[67] *O Tempo* ran an article titled "Immigrants: Powerful Lever in the Development of São Paulo—1827 Signaled the First Step in the Replacement of Slave Labor with the Foreigner."[68] And a writer for *O Estadão* claimed that if it hadn't been for the disruptions attendant upon the war with Paraguay (1864–1870), São Paulo would have made a full transition to free labor even earlier.[69] Only the Communist Party paper, *Notícias de Hoje*, emphasized the "broad popular struggles" involved in the abolition of slavery, in an article authored by historian and black militant Clovis Moura.[70]

This, of course, sets the stage for the final crucial factor—the influx of hundreds of thousands of immigrants into the region from the 1890s through the 1920s. Portrayed as skilled, literate, and enterprising, these new arrivals are celebrated for their whiteness (in both a biological and cultural sense), their habits of consumption, and their social mobility. The ethnic group that received the most attention, unsurprisingly, was the Italians—some supplements included several pages about Italian immigration alone. A few made reference to the history of labor militancy within the Italian community, and one article even insisted that some mention should be made of those Italian immigrants who did not "succeed" and instead endured a life of poverty and hardship after relocating to Brazil.[71] But such remarks were exceptional. More typical were essays or exhibits that presented the immigrant wave as precisely the infusion of progressive, European virtues that São Paulo needed to make the leap into the modern/industrial world. As a letter from Rio's Rádio Nacional put it, its broadcasts for the IV Centenário would not only honor "the great City and its people, but also, *and especially*, the vast immigrant colonies that helped to construct the Bandeirante prosperity."[72]

Immigrants were visible not only in the newspaper supplements, but also in a number of events programmed for the IV Centenário. In part this reflects the financial contributions that the more prosperous segments of immigrant "colonies" could offer to make certain events or installations possible. But it is also apparent that the organizing commission readily accepted suggestions for programming that celebrated Spanish music or Italian art, especially of the more "erudite" variety, and presented these as recognition of the cultural heritage of immigrant/ethnic communities. Various cultural entrepreneurs discerned this receptivity as well as the continued pressure on the commission to appeal to a broader audience. Thus the famed theatrical impresario Ruggero Jacobbi—an Italian who resided in Brazil from 1945 to 1960—wrote to Guilherme de Almeida in mid-1954 proposing that a Portuguese-language production of the play *La figlia di Iorio*, by Gabriele D'Annunzio, be made part of the official IV Centenário program and requesting that the commission purchase all the seats for one performance to distribute to the larger public. Jacobbi's "pitch" for this proposal, which seems to have been approved, is worth quoting at length:

> Considering that the Italian colony, the largest in São Paulo, has done much to enrich and enhance the festivities of the IV Centenário, in the technical and industrial sector;
>
> Considering that these unifying ties, between the colony and the City, should also be extended to the sphere of culture and the arts, and in this case, the theater;
>
> It seems to us to be, more than merely interesting, but necessary and urgent, to take the initiative of staging, this year and in this city, an immortal work of Italian dramatic literature, in the Portuguese language, inviting the population to attend free of charge, in a genuine festival of confraternization.[73]

We cannot easily surmise from the above quote how Jacobbi imagined the "povo" that would attend this theatrical production for free, but he clearly conceived of it as somehow separate from an "Italian colony" with whom it would be able to "fraternize." Indeed, the very persistence of the term "colony," which routinely appeared in references to the immigrant populations of São Paulo, indicates an abiding sense of separateness, though one that may well have been cultivated by certain sectors of the immigrant communities as a way to distinguish themselves from Brazilians of more questionable whiteness and/ or status, even as they sought to assert their integration into paulista society.

Perhaps the most interesting case of an immigrant "colony" using the IV

Centenário to highlight its particular heritage and affirm its paulistinidade was that of the Japanese community. At first glance, one might conclude that the ample attention dedicated to Japanese culture and the colony's contributions to São Paulo refute the argument that whiteness and immigration tended to be associated and celebrated together. But one could also argue that the Japanese immigrant community enjoyed a certain status as "honorary whites"—perhaps not entirely white, but embodying the immigrant virtues of hard work, social mobility, and aptitude for modernity that were generally considered the attributes of European immigrants.[74] At the same time, the Japanese evinced more anxiety than other immigrant groups to demonstrate that they were genuinely paulista and eager to be a part of the IV Centenário. Rather than just engaging in occasional, piecemeal initiatives, there was an active and well-endowed Collaborative Commission of the Japanese Colony for the Quadricentennial of São Paulo that funded an elaborate Japanese Pavilion as part of the exhibits in Ibirapuera. Together with the public relations director of the IV Centenário, this collaborative commission also organized a "popular spectacle" in Ibirapuera to honor the Japanese community and staged traditional cultural performances for the crowd's amusement.

According to the description submitted by the public relations director, the ceremonies would include the awarding of medals to the "pioneers of immigration" as well as to their descendants who represented the fourth Nippo-Brazilian generation. The "spectacle" portion would consist of "typical dances" such as the "dance of the sabers" and demonstrations of judo and jiujitsu. Newspaper coverage of the event referred repeatedly to the Japanese as a "hardworking colony" and quoted acting mayor Porfírio da Paz, who congratulated the colônia japoneza for its "perfect integration into Brazilian life and collectivity, and its profound respect for our laws." This tribute, scheduled at the tail end of the IV Centenário festivities, was regarded as so successful that the director proposed that a similar event be staged for each of the other immigrant communities (Italian, Spanish, Portuguese, Sirio-Lebanese, and German). Unfortunately, with the official closing of the IV Centenário commemorations fast approaching, the commission decided that there was no time to accommodate such an ambitious proposal.

All the major immigrant communities, or segments of them, sought to take advantage of the IV Centenário to affirm their place in a dynamic, progressive São Paulo, but only the Japanese manifested such anxiety about their claim to be genuinely paulista. To be sure, they were still regarded by many Brazilians outside of their community as the most "exotic" immigrants—a feature that the collaborative commission actually foregrounded in organizing a "popular spectacle." But as an Asian community long associated with an exceptional aptitude for modernity—in contrast, say, to the Chinese—the paulistas of Japanese descent could take comfort in their routine inclusion among the immigrant groups that "undeniably contributed much to the greatness of São Paulo, and therefore of Brazil."[75]

The one group of "immigrants" that, despite their increasingly massive presence in the regional workforce, were routinely omitted from the universe of those who helped make São Paulo great, were the internal migrants from Minas and the Nordeste. No newspaper supplements celebrated their struggles and sacrifices. No panels in the Historical Exposition illustrated their role in the recent history of São Paulo. The Nordeste only appeared in the cultural programming of the IV Centenário in connection to the folklore pageant, a context that reinforced the image of that region as a "living museum" frozen in the past, one whose authentic cultural traditions provided a convenient contrast to the modernity of São Paulo. The Department of Popular Commemorations did receive a proposal from Rádio Record to organize, as part of the IV Centenário, an event in Ibirapuera on the occasion of the Festa de São João (June 26–29), a traditional celebration of rustic life. It would include a contest of *músicas sertanejas*—folk music from the interior and backlands of Brazil—as well as a traditional "country dance" and *casamento caipira* (peasant wedding) with *desfile de carros de boi* (parade of oxcarts) and other typical features. Finally, the radio station proposed the participation of ten *desafiadores do Norte*—practitioners of traditional oral poetry whose verses were composed in the process of the competition. To calm any concerns about the quality and authenticity of the event, Rádio Record promised that the entire production would be overseen by the composer and impresario Almirante, "a name that needs no further commentary as an expert on matters of our music and folklore," who would "then create . . . a special presentation, describing [the backlander's] peculiar mode of singing, dancing, declaiming, etc." The commission, seeing this as an event that would "attract the masses," responded positively. Though it was not stated explicitly, we can safely surmise that these masses included the otherwise invisible nordestino migrants.[76]

"With the Exception of the Blacks"

Lest I leave the impression that these issues of inclusion and exclusion from the historical narrative were of immediate concern to a mere handful of Brazilian intellectuals, cultural entrepreneurs, and radio programmers, I want to close this chapter with a particularly intriguing episode from the protracted negotiations over the content and character of the commemorations of 1954. Toward the end of the yearlong celebrations, Guilherme de Almeida received an appeal for support from the Commission of the Festivities for the Erection of the Bust of the Black Mother. This entity had been formed to raise funds and plan the program for the inaugural ceremonies attendant upon the unveiling of the monument to the Black Mother, the only African or Afro-Brazilian figure to be thus memorialized during a year when monuments once again sprouted up like mushrooms on paulista soil. This sculpture had been contemplated and proposed by the black communities (and some white allies) in both São Paulo and Rio de Janeiro since the mid-1920s.[77] The figure it was intended to honor was not simply a mother who was black, but rather a specific figure from Brazil's slave past—the enslaved black woman who suckled and cared for the master's white children. Thus, the "Mãe Preta" could serve as both a historical symbol of the toil and sacrifice of the black woman, and an allegory of racial intimacy and mixture in Brazil.[78] In the latter regard, the original campaign to erect a monument to the Black Mother can be seen as anticipating the Freyrean rejoinder to the concept of whitening, still so widely embraced in São Paulo during the 1920s. At the same time, as Micol Seigel observes, the commemoration of the Mãe Preta did not challenge assertions of paulista whiteness since it memorialized an "extinct" figure from the distant and rapidly receding past. It is, thus, not surprising that many white politicians and journalists enthusiastically endorsed the intermittent efforts by the Afro-paulista community to erect such a monument.

Undoubtedly spurred by the preparations for the quadricentennial celebrations, several groups within the paulistano black community, together with supporters on the city council, revived the movement in favor of a monument to the Mãe Preta in 1953. After securing a site on the Largo do Paissandú—an area in the center of the city long associated with the black community—the committee issued a call for proposals from sculptors, ultimately accepting the projected design submitted by Júlio Guerra. The result was a statue that was very much in the paulista modernist style of the 1920s. Unlike earlier proposals that had presented a sentimental image of an attractive black woman discreetly cuddling a white child, Guerra's black granite monument showed a woman with clearly African and slightly geometric facial features and exaggerated limbs, with ample bare breasts at which she is feeding a baby presumed to be "white" (see fig. 7.1).[79]

To make sure the sculpture would be ready in time, the unveiling of the monument had been scheduled for January 1955, the last month of the IV Centenário commemorations. The head of the committee in charge of the

FIGURE 7.1. Monument to the Black Mother, Praça Payssandu, São Paulo. Color photograph by Regina Kalman, September 2005.

inaugural festivities, Frederico Penteado Júnior, wrote to Almeida and his colleagues to request that the quadricentennial commission grant official recognition and sponsorship to the unveiling of the monument and the attendant festivities. He also, as one would expect, requested funding for the related events. Initially, he may have hoped to convince the commission to cover the entire bill, but the chilly reception from Almeida eventually led him to reduce his appeal to a modest 15,000 cruzeiros (less than 600 U.S. dollars). Penteado opened his letter by challenging the historical marginalization of Afro-paulistas, arguing that in all the most glorious moments of São Paulo's past, "blacks have participated in a decisive manner." He went on to couch his request in the following terms:

> The very fact that the Monument to the Black Mother is being erected under the auspices of paulistana officialdom, shows that now, *although belatedly*, recognition is being given to the important role of the black race in the development of the civilization of the plateau, recognizing what historians and sociologists have acknowledged—ever since Cassiano Ricardo's research confirmed the participation of blacks in the bandeiras and in the

heroic expeditions that expanded, to the point of immensity, the geographic frontiers of the nation.

Under these circumstances, it would only be fair to associate these commemorations with which today the city of Nobrega and Anchieta celebrates the triumph of its culture with the participation of the black race through the inspiration which it contributed to create original motifs in popular and erudite music, in the theater, in poetry, in Brazilian art, marking some of the high points of the national artistic sensibility, and influencing our ways of life.

All of this makes imperative the participation of the black race in the festivities with which all of Brazil is celebrating São Paulo's IV Centenário, and above all because *all the human elements that have contributed to the greatness of the city that is today a motive for national pride are being represented in the commemorations currently being held, with the exception of the blacks.*[80]

The letter proceeded to detail the ambitious program of performances and presentations that would take place during the weeks prior to the unveiling. These included a staging of the play *Aruanda*, by the Teatro Experimental do Negro, and lectures by scholars of Afro-Brazilian culture and history, including Florestan Fernandes and Oracy Nogueira. There would be readings of works by black poets or poets who dealt with "afro" related themes, such as Castro Alves, Jorge de Lima, Mário de Andrade, Raúl Bopp, Guilherme de Almeida (author of "Raça"), Langston Hughes, Claude McKay, Nicolás Guillen, and Jacques Romain. The municipal orchestra would be performing works by Villa-Lobos, Francisco Mignone, and Camargo Guarnieri that reflected motifs from "black folklore," and there would also be an evening of popular music collected by folklorists, including performances by Portela and Heitor dos Prazeres, and compositions by Hekel Tavares. Finally, on the day of the unveiling, there would be an open-air mass involving all entities representing people of color in São Paulo.

Given this carefully constructed roster of events, involving many distinguished groups and individuals, the quadricentennial commission readily agreed to "officialize" the program. But it refused to provide any funding. This prompted yet another appeal from Penteado, who this time emphasized the continuing poverty of the Afro-paulista community and claimed that many people of color would be unable to participate in these festivities and ceremonies unless there was some sort of subsidy to allow free admission. To evoke the sympathy or guilt of the commission members, Penteado noted that many people of color "continue to be poor in fortune just as was the case of their forebears when they arrived here, way back 400 years ago, to collaborate in building the civilization that today this commission celebrates with such well-deserved splendor." And he ended by insisting that "it is also to the blacks that is owed the jubilation with which today all of Brazil celebrates, with pride, the IV Centenário of São Paulo."[81]

Yet another letter addressed to the commission and written by Penteado arrived at the very end of December, but this one, aside from the usual pleas and appeals, included a petition from the "Clube 220" (whose stationery described it as "The Largest Association of People of Color in the Nation"), with approximately a hundred signatures asking for the sum of 15,000 cruzeiros to fund the inaugural festivities planned for the unveiling of the monument to the Black Mother, contending that with this small sum, the commission "would pay homage to this 'WOMAN SYMBOL' of the humble race that helped create the greatness of Brazil and the vigor of São Paulo."[82] Judging from the difficulty with which some of the petitioners signed their names, this was indeed a club whose members included many people of color who were "poor of fortune."[83]

This last appeal seems to have done the trick: the IV Centenário commission finally agreed to provide the subsidy, but it did so with much reluctance and little enthusiasm. While one might argue that the commission was virtually tapped out by this late date, thus explaining its willingness to "officialize" the inaugural ceremonies but not finance them, the small amount in contention seems to indicate that there were other considerations. To get some sense of how modest this sum actually was, it came to less than a third of the 50,000 cruzeiros awarded to the Brazilianist Richard Morse to write a history of São Paulo.[84] So what would explain the commission's reluctance? As in the case of the unwillingness to pay the insurance costs for the Benin sculptures that were to be included in the Historical Exposition, it seems to be a question of low priority. Even in the heyday of (the discourse of) racial democracy, the organizing commission had little interest in foregrounding the African influence in São Paulo, or making financial contributions to events organized by paulistas of African descent.

Who's History?

Despite a few significant incursions into paulista scholarly circles by Freyrean representations of Brazil as a tenaciously, even increasingly, multiracial society, the "official" paulista historical narrative continued to be one that emphasized whitening, and that associated whiteness with civilization, progress, and modernity. It did this *not* by denying the very existence of nonwhite groups, such as the indigenous peoples and the forced African immigrants, but by assigning them to a particular era when they fulfilled a specific function, only to recede to the margins of paulista society when that era had ended. Conversely, other ostensibly "nonwhite" groups, such as Japanese colonists, were whitened by their inclusion in the wave of immigration that consolidated São Paulo's claim to primacy in the Brazilian race to modernity.[85]

What we can see in the case of the representations of history in the IV Centenário is not so much a rejection of the concept of racial democracy, but rather the ways in which that representation of Brazilian society could be folded into the narrative of paulista whiteness and progress without disturbing its fundamental elements.[86] While in certain contexts the Freyrean construction of Brazilian history might permit genuine criticism of racism in São Paulo, for the most part the two discourses about race could easily coexist, and even combine, since racial democracy did not call for a fundamental reconsideration of Brazilian historical narratives or contemporary attitudes about the relationship between "racial traits" (biological or cultural) and progress. That said, the ways in which Frederico Penteado and the Clube 220 presented the concerns and demands of Afro-paulistas allow us to appreciate how members of the black community could maneuver in the spaces opened by even a reluctant embrace of racial democracy. Certainly their posture vis-à-vis the organizing commission indicated a refusal to retreat into marginality—Penteado did not mince words in denouncing the exclusion of blacks from the historical pageant that was the IV Centenário. At the same time, his arguments in favor of inclusion were couched in terms entirely compatible with the dominant view of São Paulo's history. In this regard he was following in the footsteps of many other black paulistano leaders who, since the early decades of the twentieth century, had sought to position themselves as modern political subjects and therefore legitimate paulistas.[87] And while Penteado and the Clube 220 might have been primarily motivated by the desire to secure a financial subsidy from the commission, they also seemed genuinely eager to enjoy the prestige and legitimacy of having their activities recognized as part of the official commemorative program.

The focal point of the inaugural festivities—the unveiling of a monument to the Black Mother—could be seen as a triumph for the Afro-paulista community, many of whose members had campaigned long and hard for this statue. Yet this symbolic figure was also of a piece with Freyre's sentimentalized vision of Brazilian race relations, and (for whites) one of the least "threatening" archetypes that could be summoned from Afro-paulista history. Rather than contesting the fundamental lineaments of official paulista history, Penteado (and the Woman-Symbol he championed) claimed a place in it for Afro-paulistas, reminding the commission that there had been blacks among the bandeirantes, and in the coffee fields of their paulista forebears, and therefore the black community should be recognized for its contribution to the grandeur of São Paulo and Brazil. [88] Instead of turning their backs on the IV Centenário, they did something potentially more audacious: they insisted on their right to be celebrated as paulistas and as those primarily responsible for São Paulo's prosperity. While this did not halt the commission's active dissemination of the "White Legend" (in every sense) of São Paulo's historical exceptionalism, it did make it apparent that the discourse of racial democracy, at the very least, entailed a more diverse roster of historical actors.

CHAPTER 8

THE WHITE ALBUM

Memory, Identity, and the 1932 Uprising

The second [motive], and without a doubt the stronger one, is the intention to remind today's paulista youth, disillusioned and indifferent to almost everything, that in their veins flows the ardent and audacious blood of the bandeirante, that merely dormant in their chest is the ancient strength of the race that manifested itself in their elders in 1932; to make [the youth] believe that wherever there is a great ideal that sets hearts to beat quicker, the paulistas of yesterday, today, and tomorrow will always know how to say: We are here!

—Souza Queiroz, *Batalhão 14 de Julho*

One of the high points of the yearlong celebrations of São Paulo's IV Centenário were the ceremonies to mark the ninth of July, the day in 1932 that the state government declared war against the Vargas regime.[1] On the evening of July 9, 1954, hundreds of thousands of paulistas took to the streets, not to protest, but to enjoy a jam-packed program of performances and spectacles, and especially the awesome "silver shower" described in chapter 6. Speaking over the airwaves on that enchanted evening, radio personality Randal Juliano announced that "the paulista sentiment has the entire city on the move to the Viaduto do Chá." Following this anthropomorphic rendering of the state capital, Juliano went on to describe the visual effect of the laminated triangles falling from the sky, "translating the joy of the paulista people on this 9th of July, [a date] that commemorates a defeat. . . . Perhaps [the paulistas] have been the only people to commemorate a defeat."[2]

This latter claim was, to be sure, wildly inaccurate.[3] But that detail aside, one can easily understand the radio announcer marveling at the sustained emotion and energy invested in remembering an event that lasted a mere three months and ended in what some considered a shameful surrender. How many of the celebrants that evening were drawn to the Viaduto do Chá by regional pride and an urge to mark the august occasion is literally impossible to determine; it seems reasonable to assume that the principal inducement for the vast majority was the free program of musical performances and visual spectacles organized by the Association of Radio and TV Broadcasters.[4] But the very choice of 9 de Julho as the date for this extravaganza served to reinforce its central place in regional identity even though more than two decades had passed since São Paulo had briefly risen up in arms.

The purpose of this chapter is to consider the enduring significance of the 1932 uprising, and the shifting meanings attached to the Causa Paulista, in three different moments: the years immediately following the uprising (roughly 1933–1937), the IV Centenário (1954), and the year of the revolt's twenty-fifth anniversary commemorations (1957).[5] In the first moment, various memoirs and commentaries dealt with the challenge of acknowledging defeat and justifying the loss of life and resources, while several different organizations initiated rituals to mark the occasion and honor the (paulista) war dead. Complicating this process were the diverse ways in which former combatants and supporters vilified or reconciled with the Vargas regime.[6] Moreover, Vargas's official shift to a more authoritarian register in late 1937, with the declaration of the Estado Novo, made it difficult to publish critical commentaries or publicly celebrate an uprising against his regime. The second moment, the IV Centenário, offered an occasion of intense regional triumphalism, with the celebrations choreographed by representatives of the intellectual and business elites, among them men and women with direct ties to the 1932 uprising. It was a moment rife with tension between the impulse by certain groups to use that connection to the Constitutionalist Revolution as a marker of paulistinidade that was as much exclusive as inclusive, while other groups, engaged with the formal political sphere and more alert to burgeoning nationalist sentiment, sought to broaden the meaning of the uprising. And all of this was further complicated by the fact that, on July 9, 1954, Vargas—though virtually under siege and on the verge of "leav[ing] life to enter history"—was once again Brazil's chief executive, this time as its elected president.[7] Finally, in the third moment, the twenty-fifth anniversary commemorations in 1957, the discourse shifts to a reimagining of the Causa Paulista as a struggle for democracy, but we also see the way in which a particular "liberal" paulista construction of democracy remained anchored in a notion of citizenship rights as something that should not be equally distributed across the different regions of Brazil.[8]

One of the most important contributions of the massive scholarly literature on historical memory has been to demonstrate how difficult, even futile, it is to separate the significance of a particular historical event from the multiple and contested ways in which it is remembered. Even efforts to make memories more "concrete" by constructing monuments and museums often fail to fix the character and significance of an event.[9] If that is *generally* true, it seems especially the case with the Constitutionalist Revolution. Given the brevity of the uprising, and the density of publications surrounding the event, it is almost as if there was no interval at all between the actual historical conflict and the contest over its memories and meanings.

From the Jaws of Defeat

Speaking in 1937, on the occasion of the fifth anniversary of the paulista call to arms, the folklorist Dalmo Belfort de Mattos derisively referred to a book published right after the uprising that had claimed that within three months of the armistice, no one would remember the Constitutionalist soldiers' struggles and sacrifices. Mattos noted the sizable crowd that had gathered in the São Paulo Cemetery, and the masses that would be celebrated in every church in the state for the souls of the departed soldiers, as abundant proof that the author had spoken too soon.[10] It was certainly true that the fallen volunteers and other war dead had not been forgotten, but at the same time, contemporary descriptions of the commemorations on what would normally be considered a symbolically important anniversary indicate that they were rather subdued. Even a year earlier, on July 9, 1936, there were more robust and rousing ceremonies, among them a parade composed of veterans from over fifty different volunteer battalions, including the Legião Negra, and a procession to the São Paulo Cemetery to transfer the mortal remains of forty-two paulista soldiers who originally had been buried in Rio de Janeiro State.[11] Other highlights of the program in 1932 included the unfurling of an immense flag of São Paulo, and a banquet at the Instituto de Contabilidade to celebrate the role of accountants (!) in the Constitutionalist Revolution. An organizing commission, amply funded by São Paulo's Commercial Association, oversaw the solemnities, and the newspaper *A Gazeta* declared that 9 de Julho was a day to "put aside political resentments," filling its entire front page with an ode to regional chauvinism by the schoolteacher and popular poet Isabel V. Serpa e Paiva.[12] To be sure, it is not that the occasion of the fifth anniversary, the following year, went entirely unremarked, but absent was the sort of pomp and circumstances that would later become a hallmark of the 9 de Julho celebrations. And this despite the fact that Vargas's declaration of an Estado Novo—with its attendant escalation of the mechanisms of censorship and repression—was still several months off in the future. Ultimately, the muted tone with which paulistas marked the fifth anniversary of the state's Guerra Cívica reflected the difficulty of setting aside political resentments during a major electoral campaign, even out of respect for the war dead.

As discussed in chapter 3, in the wake of São Paulo's surrender leaders and promoters of the Causa Paulista consoled themselves with the notion that their actions had pressured Getúlio into meeting several of the movement's chief demands. Thus he abided by his promise to hold elections for a constituent assembly, which in 1934 produced a new constitution. And following a ten-month period of demobilization and occupation under the administration of General Valdomiro Lima, Vargas acquiesced and appointed an interventor who was "paulista and civilian"—the engineer, entrepreneur, and publisher Armando de Salles Oliveira. Perhaps equally important, the paulista insurgents could salve their wounded pride by pointing to the greater unity among mainstream political factions that resulted from the regional rebellion, starting with the Frente Única Paulista formed in January 1932, and then leading to the Chapa Única por São Paulo Unido (Single Slate for a United São Paulo) campaign for the national constituent assembly.[13] At least on the surface, and at least for a while, the bitter discord between the PRP and the PD, or between the situationist and dissenting factions within the PRP, had subsided and paulistas on the national stage could speak with what sounded like one voice.[14]

Even during this festival of regional unity, there were paulistas—whether in the press or in personal memoirs—who grumbled about Armando being too eager to reconcile with the Vargas regime. There were charges about his refusing to reinstate government functionaries dismissed by João Alberto, and allegations that he agreed to ban public commemorations of 9 de Julho during his first year in office.[15] But these complaints seem to have been confined to a small minority; most of the representatives in the newly elected state constituent assembly were allied with the Partido Constitucionalista, formed in 1934 from the remnants of the defunct Partido Democrático and a dissident wing of the Partido Republicano Paulista. With their votes, Armando became the (indirectly) elected governor of São Paulo in April 1935.

The real cracks in the thin façade of regional unity began to form when the various political factions had to consider whom to back in the upcoming presidential elections, scheduled for January 1938. Most (though not all) of the cohort that had founded the PD plus the dissident perrepistas supported Armando as its presidential candidate under the banner of the newly inaugurated Partido Constitucionalista, eventually forming the União Democrática Brasileira in an attempt to make his candidacy more viable on the national level.[16] But the mainstream perrepistas—who included figures such as Alfredo Ellis Júnior and Paulo Menotti del Picchia—couldn't swallow the former democrático as their presidential candidate.[17] Not only was Armando an early member of the rival PD, but for several years he served as copublisher of *O Estado de São Paulo*, a major organ of criticism directed against the PRP, and he was married to Júlio de Mesquita Filho's sister Raquel. It is likely that members of the PRP feared that a victory in the presidential elections for Armando would consign them to political oblivion. They may also have suspected that a candidate so closely identified with paulista interests would have little chance of winning a national election. Thus, in a move that would have been unimaginable a few years earlier, the PRP gave its endorsement to José Américo de Almeida, a candidate who not only did not hail from São Paulo, but who was from the northeastern state of Paraíba. True, José Américo was a novelist and intellectual, quite different from the despised João Alberto, but he not only was a nordestino but appeared to be Vargas's anointed successor.[18] Meanwhile, Armando, eager to establish the credibility of his campaign beyond São Paulo, allied with Flores da Cunha, the gaúcho politician widely regarded as directly responsible for the failure of Rio Grande do Sul to join with São Paulo in the 1932 uprising. In other words, by 1937 the Constitutionalist Revolution was no longer an experience that predictably determined lines of alliance and political identification, even as it was invoked by both sides as a means of impugning the integrity and loyalty of their adversaries.[19]

The shift in political discourse about the 1932 uprising is particularly evident in *O Estado de São Paulo*, the main champion of Armando's candidacy, and in *A Gazeta*, which supported the presidential aspirations of José Américo.[20] By July 1937, the principal concern of *O Estadão* was to demonstrate that Armando was a viable *national* candidate, who could enlist support beyond the borders of São Paulo. Thus, most of the coverage of the presidential campaign in the pages of *O Estadão* recounted Armando's trips to the Northeast, to Minas, and to the Far South—almost anywhere but São Paulo. Typical of the tone was the banner headline on the front page of the issue published on July 4: "In All of the Social Sectors of the North of the Nation the Name of Mr. Armando de Salles Oliveira Is Enthusiastically Submitted."[21] But at the same time that *OESP* was downplaying Armando's connections to São Paulo, *A Gazeta* was accusing him and the *OESP* circle of claiming to be the "owners" of the 1932 uprising, and of abusing the campaign slogan "A Paulista doesn't vote against a Paulista."[22]

In this political context, coverage of the 9 de Julho commemorations posed a particular dilemma for *O Estadão*. The newspaper could hardly ignore the festivities altogether without alienating regional voters for whom Armando was the authentically paulista and anti-Vargas candidate. At the same time, too much attention to the event could have the effect of identifying Armando too heavily with regional, not national, interests. The front page of OESP on 9 de Julho indicated the ambivalence with which São Paulo's leading morning paper was marking the august occasion. The words "9 de Julho," a paulista flag, and the poem "Nossa bandeira" (Our flag) appeared in the upper left corner, and beneath this were the words "Homage from Commerce and Industry in São Paulo—1932–1937." Ads for various commercial enterprises filled the rest of the page. In other words, it was São Paulo's industrial and commercial sectors, not *O Estadão*, that were paying homage to the 1932 uprising. Meanwhile, to read the articles on the actual commemorations, one had to turn to pages 11 and 12. There the coverage was ample in space but subdued in tone, and there was only the briefest mention of Armando going to the São Paulo Cemetery to pay his respects to the fallen paulista soldiers.[23]

Although the fissures in paulista political circles can best be understood as reflecting short-term electoral ambitions and, to a lesser extent, conflicting sensibilities, rather than deep ideological differences or divergent "interests," they should not be dismissed as superficial. The splits produced by the presidential campaign generated more than just a war of words. In early July 1937, less than a week before the 9 de Julho commemorations, former police chief Sylvio de Campos—now a member of the dissident *armandista* wing of the PRP—stormed into the offices of the perrepista paper, *Correio Paulistano*, with a group of his cronies. After a heated exchange with Alberto Americano, the *Correio*'s editor, who had published a letter that had proved embarrassing to Campos, the latter opened fire, seriously wounding Americano. Soon after this incident, the PRP voted to expel the armandistas from the party.[24]

If the circle around Armando faced the challenge of squaring their appeal to paulistas with their claim that he was a viable national candidate, periodicals like *A Gazeta*, which supported José Américo, faced an even more daunting discursive task. One article in *A Gazeta*, for example, informed its readers that Armando, when interventor, forbade commemorations of 9 de Julho, whereas "Catete" (the name of the presidential palace) had always respected the right of paulistas to celebrate this date—the same way the Portuguese respect Brazilians' celebration of 7 de Setembro, Independence Day. In other words, through some fairly tortuous logic, *A Gazeta* was contending that Vargas was more indulgent of regional sensibilities than Armando. Another concern in *A Gazeta* was to contest the armandistas' claim to represent a certain technocratic and meritocratic ideal. One editorial ridiculed the OESP circle's self-definition as an "aristocracy of talent" and accused the armandistas of tolerating corrupt practices and collaborating with the *cangaceiros de gravata*—that is, white-collar bandits. And after the Sylvio de Campos episode, *A Gazeta* charged the pro-Armando faction with protecting the PRP renegade and declared that politicians like him threatened to transform "the civilized capital of São Paulo into a new Canudos." Both of these comments indicate that *A Gazeta*—though endorsing the candidacy of nordestino José Américo— still looked to the Nordeste for pejorative images (cangaceiro, Canudos) to attach to the armandistas.[25]

It was in this highly fraught political atmosphere that paulistas commemorated, in rather desultory fashion, the fifth anniversary of the 1932 uprising. The coverage in *A Gazeta* exemplifies how, in certain circles, the occasion had become completely conflated with partisan conflicts. The ninth of July edition of that newspaper carried not a single allusion to the commemorations on its front page, and according to the headline the next day, "The 9th of July, which took place yesterday, encountered an indifferent and disillusioned paulista population." The "commemorative" event that enjoyed the most attention from the daily was a bicycle race.[26] In short, *O Estadão* minimized its coverage of the commemorations to deflect insinuations of regional chauvinism while *A Gazeta* dismissed the solemnities as tarnished by the armandista circle's efforts to use them to political advantage.

The Racial Politics of Paulistinidade

The withdrawal from an active role in the commemoration provoked by these partisan rivalries also meant its increasing monopolization by representatives of groups that treated the uprising as "beyond politics," at least in the narrow sense of the term. These included the Federação dos Voluntários de São Paulo, the main veterans' association, and various clubs founded after the uprising for the veneration of paulista history and culture. This guaranteed that the anniversaries would be occasions for the most unbridled expressions of regional chauvinism—the sort of sentiments that could be found in a self-published volume of poetry (1935) by veteran Lauro Teixeira Penteado. A handwritten inscription on the frontispiece closes with the pronouncement "Never forget, never forgive. Hate and Avenge!"[27]

One indication of the trend toward hyper-regionalism in the commemorations was the prominent role played by folklorist Dalmo Belfort de Mattos, a guiding light of the Clube Piratininga, who was a featured speaker in both

1936 and 1937. The Clube Piratininga, according to a retrospective account in its bimonthly publication, *Paulistânia*, was founded in 1935 as an alternative to the excessively politicized Clube Bandeirante; the members of the new club reportedly wanted an organization where "love of our land" would transcend political competition.[28] Aside from the journal, whose publication began in 1939, the club sponsored weekly lectures and raised funds for various initiatives of regional significance, such as Victor Brecheret's Monument to the Bandeiras. While many of its leading members—the engineer Gaspar Ricardo Jr., the physician Wladimir de Toledo Piza—could be identified as liberal professionals, this hardly meant that they were "above politics." For example, Toledo Piza, who was the club's president in the late 1930s, would later serve as interim prefect of São Paulo and would make a run for governor. But the club did not have a particular partisan affiliation and did not endorse specific political candidates, and this gave its journal a certain latitude in the way it represented paulista identity, and the way it characterized other regions of Brazil.[29]

Virtually every early issue of *Paulistânia* carried an article authored by Belfort de Mattos, a leading member of the Society for Ethnography and Folklore of São Paulo. And almost all of his contributions either drew a connection between São Paulo's civilized, progressive character (especially compared to other regions of Brazil) and the absence of African influence, or expressed alarm at the growing concentration of nordestinos within São Paulo's borders. Typical of his openly racist observations was his argument, in the third issue of *Paulistânia*, that São Paulo's marginality during the colonial period actually worked to its advantage because, while "the North stuffed itself with blacks," few Africans came to São Paulo.[30] And even that slight influence had been largely expunged, he contended, by the "Aryanizing contact" with immigration—a remarkable comment to make at a moment when, in Europe, the Nazis were initiating a genocidal onslaught on various "non-Aryan" populations.[31] In a similar vein, he objected strenuously to any claim that the São Francisco River served as "the great homogenizer of the backlands," insisting instead on the stark separation of the "Afro-Lusa" culture of the Northeast and the bandeirante culture of the paulista plateau. As for the early eighteenth-century conflict known as the Guerra dos Emboabas between the paulistas and the newer arrivals (nortista and Portuguese) in the gold mining districts, Belfort de Mattos described the paulistas' rivals as "the profligate and bastard rabble, generated in the 'matriarchal/negroid civilization' of the sugarmills. Individuals who were totally lacking in scruples."[32] And in an article published in 1939 on the influx of Bahians and nordestinos to São Paulo, he dubbed the migrants "sampauleiros"—not new paulistas or "novo mamelucos," as had been the practice with European immigrants. He also called for strenuous measures to limit the number of these "colonos" entering São Paulo, and claimed they posed multiple threats to paulista society since they were carriers of both disease and subversive ideas.[33] Moreover, in the pages of *Paulistânia* Belfort de Mattos was hardly alone in his racist portrayals of the paulista past and present. Another regular contributor, Américo R. Netto, in a piece entitled "Southerners and Northerners in Brazil: A Case of Human Geography," reminded his readers that the phrase "cabeça chata" to describe nortistas was "both popular and accurate." He went on to describe the short stature, brown color, and "superficial" intelligence of the nortista "type." But when he turned his attention to the *sulistas*, he concluded that they, unlike the nortistas, were too diverse to describe as a "type." According to Netto, the modern, individuated southerner could not be subjected to the anthropological gaze.[34]

Apparently, no aspect of Brazilian culture could escape the "Aryanizing" effect of São Paulo. Thus, Belfort de Mattos went so far as to insist that samba, which in Rio was "100% negro," would "come to echo in the paulista firmament in new racial accents."[35] He then went on to reproduce the lyrics of a samba, "Paulistinha querida" (Dear little paulista girl), written in 1936 by the renowned composer Ary Barroso, whose greatest fame would derive from composing the nationalist standard, "Aquarela do Brasil," just three years later. Barroso, a native of Minas Gerais and a resident of Rio, was the rare "sambista" with a law degree, and he reportedly harbored sympathies for the Causa Paulista at the time of the uprising. While that may be the case, it is difficult to read the lyrics of "Paulistinha querida" without sensing, beneath the surface celebration, an undercurrent of irony that apparently went unnoticed by the staff of *Paulistânia*:

> Dear little Paulista girl
> What is your real color
> That you disguise so much
> With your rice powder?
> You are not blond or brunette
> You are not the least bit mulata
>
> Dear litte Paulista girl
> Your color is "thirty-two"![36]

To be sure, one could read the lyrics of this samba as insisting that "1932 has no color," since the dear little paulista girl is described as neither blond nor brunette, but the fact that she's also described as "not the least bit *mulata*," the identity so central to so much samba imagery, inclines the listener to associate the color of 1932 with whiteness and with a certain lack of brasilidade. It also alters the intonation of the line about disguising color with rice powder; rather than the usual connotation—hiding a too-dark complexion—here the powder seems to serve as a means to further whiten the already whitish paulista physiognomy.[37] Of course, what Barroso may have intended as gentle sarcasm, Belfort de Mattos eagerly embraced. The idea of "32" being the paulistinha's "color" sounded a note that would have been most welcome in the pages of *Paulistânia*, not only for its celebration of an essential moment in the regional past, but for its implication that paulista identity was culturally, perhaps even "genetically," inseparable from support for the 1932 uprising.

Flag Burnings and Other Conflagrations

The consoling conviction that São Paulo, despite its defeat, had emerged triumphant in its battle with the dictatorship proved short-lived. Even as the various paulista factions were at each other's throats in an effort to determine Vargas's successor in the ill-fated presidential election scheduled for January 1938, Vargas himself was busy planning a coup that would allow him to seize full dictatorial powers and issue unilaterally a new, more authoritarian constitution to replace the one produced by the constituent assembly in 1934. Following the declaration of the Estado Novo in November 1937, the central government banned all political parties (including those that had numbered among Vargas's most fervent supporters), suspended publication of newspapers regarded as hostile to the dictatorship, and sent the erstwhile presidential candidates into exile. In a more ritualized vein, on November 27, 1937, the regime staged an elaborate "burning of the (state) flags" on a beach in Rio de Janeiro, symbolically cremating the remains of the state political machines and the regional oligarchies, and signaling what it hoped would be the definitive centralization of political authority.[38]

Outraged by both the cancellation of the elections and Vargas's move toward even greater centralization of the Brazilian state, the paulista "liberals"—including *O Estadão* and the armandistas—resorted to an alliance with the most illiberal of Brazilian political parties, the Ação Integralista Brasileira. The Integralists, Brazil's homegrown fascist movement, expected to have a significant presence in Vargas's newly declared and fascist-inflected political regime, but soon discovered that no exception had been made for the AIB—it had been declared illegal along with all other Brazilian political parties. This led to an Integralist plot to attack the presidential palace and assassinate Vargas, and the formation of a peculiar partnership between the fascist conspirators and the paulista "Constitutionalists" (always referred to in the police files as "armandistas"). In the aftermath of the failed assault, the Vargas regime first imprisoned and then exiled the paulista conspirators, including Júlio de Mesquita Filho and Paulo Nogueira Filho. And even those Constitutionalists who suffered neither imprisonment nor exile found themselves closely monitored by the political police and banned from writing for publication.[39]

If the events of 1937 and 1938 solidified an enduring animosity toward Getúlio Vargas among certain paulista political factions, other segments of the regional political and economic elites sought a modus vivendi with the authoritarian regime. In particular, the industrialists and technocrats associated with the Federação das Indústrias do Estado de São Paulo (FIESP) increasingly perceived Vargas as an ally in their campaign to make industry the foundation of the Brazilian economy, and to do so with a minimum of social disruption. Roberto Simonsen, the principal spokesman for FIESP, regarded Vargas's statist turn and populist rhetoric with some unease, but accurately assumed that the dictatorship needed the paulista industrialists' cooperation as much as they needed the government's backing.[40] So while the Estado Novo may have deepened hostility toward Vargas among segments of the paulista intellectual and political *classe*, it by no means restored the fragile unity that had briefly characterized the regional elites in the early 1930s.

Whatever their specific posture vis-à-vis the Vargas regime, paulista politicians, journalists, and intellectuals adapted to the changing national and transnational political climate. Leafing through the pages of *Paulistânia*, a journal founded at the height of the Estado Novo, one can detect by the 1940s a more eclectic approach to questions of race and identity that contrasted with its consistently racist tone during the first two years of its existence. Following an involuntary pause in 1941 "to fulfill certain legal obligations that today regulate Brazilian publications," the monthly journal of the Clube Piratininga resumed publication, but now with a more restrained and tactful approach to issues of racial identity and the role of São Paulo in Brazilian history.[41] This shift reflected not only the central government's intensifying promotion of the idea of Brazil as a racial democracy, but also the impact of the nation's entrance into World War II on the side of the antifascist struggle. Under these circumstances, the journal seems to have been considerably less inclined to run articles on the "Aryanizing" effect of European immigration, and even the piece by Americo R. Netto on northerners and southerners, published in 1944, relied heavily on anthropological language about culture and climate rather than a strictly biological-racist formulation of difference. More striking, though, were articles on themes that would have been impossible to imagine appearing in the early issues of the journal. For example, the image on the cover of the issue published in October–December 1942 was Rafael Galvez's sculpture *The Death of Zumbí*, and the accompanying article portrayed the leader of Palmares—Brazil's most famous runaway-slave community—as a courageous figure and a national hero.[42]

Moreover, this new orientation cannot be attributed exclusively to the coercive effects of Estado Novo censorship. *Paulistânia* did cease publication again (due to financial difficulties and political disputes) from 1945 to 1946, but when it reappeared in 1947, after the fall of Vargas and the return to a semblance of democratic rule, it seemed even more thoroughly transformed in the way it dealt with certain themes.[43] The first issue to appear in 1947 included an article entitled "The False Sentimentalization of Slavery," which took to task those commentators who claimed slavery wasn't so bad, who talked of the "good master" and of "Pai João" (the loyal family retainer) who lived to be one hundred years old. The article ended by citing demographic statistics on slave mortality as evidence that Brazilian slavery was anything but mild. The next issue included a relatively innocuous article by Belfort de Mattos about the various sites where the bandeirantes sojourned and left their mark, but appended to his essay was a note from the editor that quoted Jesuit sources regarding the number of Indians killed and native villages destroyed by the bandeirantes. Moreover, the very same issue featured an article entitled "Palmares 1697–Canudos 1897" by Rego Canticaval, the author of the earlier article on slavery. This time around, Canticaval declared Palmares the greatest feat of African heroism in Brazil and an act of resistance against the "tyranny of the whites," as well as the first cry for independence. The latter claim is particularly striking since it inserted Palmares into the master narrative of Brazilian national history, rather than treating it as a curious episode from the colonial past. Moreover, Canticaval described bandeirante Domingos Jorge Velho, noted for his role in the destruction of Palmares, as fighting "on the side of authority and against liberty."[44]

The roster of contributors also became more diversified. Issues in the late 1940s included several articles on the legacies of colonial paulista life by Sérgio Buarque de Holanda, a piece entitled "Economic Factors of Colonization in São Paulo" by the young sociologist Florestan Fernandes, and an essay by poet Carlos Drummond de Andrade. Perhaps most striking of all, for a journal that a decade earlier had dismissed migrants from other regions as "sampauleiros," was an article entitled "The Contribution of the Immigrant to the Progress of São Paulo." Although it began with conventional praise for the role of European and Japanese immigrants in São Paulo's growth and development, it then went on to say the following: "And that is not all. We have to highlight, on the other hand, the activity, in every way magnificent, of the national worker, who migrated here during the last fifty years, and who played a very valuable part in the advance of the bandeirante civilization."[45] As the final words of the quote indicate, the new orientation of *Paulistânia* did not mean that its editors had renounced regional chauvinism. On the contrary, the journal continued to dedicate an issue each year to the memory of the 1932 uprising, and routinely described its sponsor, the Clube Piratininga, as having been born "in the trenches" of the Guerra Paulista. Its debut issue in 1947, following a two-year cessation of publication, included a facsimile reproduction of Ibrahim Nobre's "Minha Terra, Minha Pobre Terra," and an issue in 1948 featured the poem "Paulista thanks to God" (Paulista por mercê de Deus) by "Ceciliana," a work of unrestrained regional chauvinism. And there were at least half a dozen articles that touched on the theme of the abominable "enslavement" of civilized São Paulo by the Vargas dictatorship, including one that referred to 9 de Julho as "the day of the liberation of the slaves."[46] There was still plenty of space in the pages of *Paulistânia* for articles such as one published in 1948 that referred to São Paulo prior to the 1932 uprising as a land of "giants in chains": "But this hardworking people, who were never weakened nor corrupted by the fictitious luxury of the salons or by the comforts of palatial antechambers . . . this people who were so accustomed to freedom as the air they breathed to live, could not be lulled to sleep in servitude."[47]

However, even some of the representations of the Constitutionalist Revolution started taking on a slightly different cast, especially from 1947 on. The issue published in July–August 1947 declared it a singularly important year to celebrate 9 de Julho because of Brazil's return to "liberty and democracy."[48] An editorial published in 1948 in support of the monument and mausoleum for the Constitutionalist soldier described the revolution as a fight for democracy and compared it very explicitly, if somewhat absurdly, to World War II ("Instead of Klinger, Montgomery: In Place of Palimércio, Eisenhower"). And yet another article claimed that the 1932 uprising was emblematic of Brazilians' (not just paulistas') refusal to acquiesce to restrictions on their liberty.[49] This celebration of Brazilian democracy, however, encountered its limits in the reality of the electoral results of 1950. Several months before the election, *Paulistânia* published an especially elaborate tribute to the Constitutionalist Revolution and explained to its readers that it was doing so "because São Paulo is feeling the threat of Brazil returning to the hands of the one against whom it wrote the epic of the 9th of July."[50] Then, in the month after Brazilians went to the polls and, as feared, brought Getúlio Vargas back to power, *Paulistânia* published an article denouncing the elections as marred by fraud, bribes, and other irregularities. The article expressed particular outrage at the alleged inclusion of "illiterates" on the voter rolls and advocated the promulgation of "a law that would make it impossible for [the elections] to be subject to the will of barely literate men."[51] In other words, the only explanation for the undesirable outcome in the elections was the participation of voters (in São Paulo and elsewhere) who were not as fully competent to be electors as the civilized paulistas.

The significant shifts in the treatment of race-related questions in the pages of *Paulistânia* reflect both the transnational decline in the legitimacy of biological-racist ideologies and the nearly ubiquitous adoption of the discourse of racial democracy in Brazil. At a more local level, they also indicate growing diversity within São Paulo's intellectual sphere, which had expanded to include many historians and social scientists affiliated with parties of the left. By the early 1950s, intellectuals such as Dalmo Belfort de Mattos, Paulo Duarte, and Alfredo Ellis Jr., who still employed openly racist idioms, were in the minority. And new ways of thinking about race and national identity had even provoked some discernible revisions in the discourse of paulista exceptionalism. Yet we can also see the limits of revisionism in the continuing uncritical celebrations of 1932, and in a definition of democracy contingent upon outcomes judged as reasonable by those the journal anointed as the modern, cultured, and progressive segments of Brazilian society.

Commemorating 1932 in the IV Centenário

In the Historical Exposition that was a centerpiece of the elaborate commemorative displays for the IV Centenário, one of the panels described the history of São Paulo as consisting of three stages: the conquest of the land, the conquest of gold, and the conquest of the law.[52] The latter "conquest," of course, referred to the Constitutionalist Revolution of 1932. In classic fashion the inscription went on to say that, during the three months of this Guerra Cívica, "the paulistas fused into one single human figure who felt, thought and acted without reference to social, political, religious, racial or sexual differences." One can easily understand the appeal of this paean to regional unity, both for the organizers of the exhibit and for their intended audience. Given the many "stresses" generated by São Paulo's ballyhooed growth and industrialization—including a rapidly expanding "migrant" population from Minas and the Nordeste, and unprecedented episodes of working-class militancy—it is unsurprising that various groups involved in the IV Centenário would want to recall and exalt a moment that they associated with a transcendent regional solidarity.[53] At the same time, the dominant representations of the 1932 uprising and the emphasis on a shared past could situate large swaths of São Paulo's population outside, or even on the wrong side, of regional memory.

Those who conceptualized and organized the actual celebrations that took place over three days, July 9–11, during the IV Centenário clearly hoped to define the occasion in the broadest and most inclusive terms possible. Among the factors that influenced the nature of the commemorations was the central role played by the Associação de Emissores—an entity that represented radio and television broadcasters in São Paulo (with the emphasis on radio since there was only one paulista TV station, TV Tupi, in operation at the time). Unlike the anniversary celebrations on the twenty-fifth of January, and the inauguration of the Parque Ibirapuera and the International Exposition in August, the official organizing commission appears to have played a limited role in the 9 de Julho festivities. Perhaps the disastrous outcome of the Carnaval parade in 1954, which led to the dismissal of the original organizing commission, made its members eager to transfer responsibility for this elaborate set of popular events to the broadcasters' association. It may also be that the new commission president, Guilherme de Almeida, preferred to associate 9 de Julho with solemnities rather than spectacles, and therefore resolved to keep his distance. In any case, the events of July 9–11 bore the imprint of the broadcasters' association and its eagerness to reach as broad an audience as possible. An official wrap-up statement from the festivities' sponsors gleefully announced (perhaps with some hyperbole) that a million people, from all sectors of paulista society, had participated in the commemoration of São Paulo's *arrancada cívica*. The latter phrase, which roughly translates as "civic rising," portrays 1932, not as a war with guns and trenches, or even as a regional insurrection, but as a burst of civic enthusiasm that ignited all of São Paulo, little different in tenor from the excited throngs celebrating its anniversary.

A documentary film, *São Paulo em festa* (São Paulo in celebration) made by the Vera Cruz Studio in cooperation with the Association of Broadcasters, recorded the highlights of the three-day festivities.[54] Not only is the film a useful chronicle of the commemorative activities, but its narration and scene selection underline the way the organizers wished to present the events. To be sure, certain solemnities and rituals had to be observed regardless of who the organizers might be. Thus the official 9 de Julho program began with a flag-raising ceremony at the Pátio de Colégio, the re-created "colonial square" of the state capital. Among the individuals present at the flag raising was the Afro-Brazilian woman known as Maria Soldado, whose presence served as evidence that "all of São Paulo" had supported the uprising. The next major item on the agenda was the inaugural ceremonies for the new cathedral, in the Praça da Sé. As with so many of the events of the next few days, there was no ostensible connection between these ceremonies and the historical episode supposedly being commemorated. But the regional ecclesiastical authorities had been ardent supporters of the 1932 uprising, and the inauguration ceremony underlined the "Christian" character of paulista society as young girls dressed in white and waving state flags lined the walkway to the new cathedral.[55]

The camera then zooms in on a parade of musical bands that includes ensembles from the Brazilian Armed Forces and the Rio de Janeiro Fire Department, whose participation confirms that "the paulista festival is a Brazilian festival." The narrator also waxes enthusiastic about the presence of the Miami-Jackson High School marching band—the one foreign entrant in the parade. But it is the band of the Força Pública Paulista that receives the most animated reception from the narrator, who describes the state police force as an entity that has been present whenever the "povo" has taken to the streets of São Paulo to demand "democracy, law, and justice." Meant as an allusion to the force's role in the 1932 uprising, this comment could also be understood in a more ironic register as a reference to the many working-class protests where the Força Pública was present—to repress and disperse the protesters. But those memories, and that particular "povo," were not the ones being evoked by a "São Paulo em festa."[56]

The scene then shifts to the city's center, to the massive crowds gathered at the Viaduto do Chá for the nighttime celebrations, including the "chuva de prata," a spectacle that suffered a significant loss of visual impact when transferred to the silver screen (and thus oddly ends up getting less footage than the mundane, and predictably all-white, Miami-Jackson High School band). This is followed by a nocturnal parade that included São Paulo's leading sports teams—with the Corinthians soccer club enjoying an especially ecstatic reception. And capping off the evening was a procession of some fifteen thousand automobiles, many of them decorated for the occasion. Closing the scene, the narrator assures the viewers that, despite the chilly weather, paulistas came out to celebrate as if it were Carnaval.

The next major segment of the film takes place during the following day, in Pacaembú Stadium, filled to capacity, where four complete circuses performed for the delight of the lucky children and their families in attendance. This "Children's Festival," recorded in tedious detail, was devoid of any reference to the historical occasion supposedly being commemorated and thus reinforces the sense of the festivities being principally geared toward entertainment. The scene then changes from day to night and from Pacaembú to the Parque Dom Pedro II, where the festivities climaxed with a musical show featuring various popular singers and musicians whose performances would be broadcast on the sponsoring radio stations. Interestingly, after recording rather standard circus and marching-band performances in great detail, the camera only briefly dwells on the famous performers in this outdoor concert—perhaps because they demanded additional compensation to appear on film. It is therefore especially intriguing to note that the one performer who appears in close-up on the screen—the popular crooner João Dias—is captured by the camera singing the line: "São Paulo where there is no racial prejudice, no color prejudice." This was surely not a random selection but a deliberate effort to assert São Paulo's full membership in Brazil's "racial democracy."[57] The film's final segment is devoted to the massive fireworks display that closed the festivities (a spectacle that also lost much of its luster when transferred to black-and-white film footage). Described as the grandest such display in the history of the world, the fireworks included exploding lights on various iconic images such as the broadcasting tower on the Banespa building and São Paulo's coat of arms, with the motto "Non Ducor, Duco." And the scene closes with the narrator declaring that "after three days of festivities, the paulista people will return to the workshop, to the factory, to the office with the knowledge that São Paulo is the great locomotive of Brazilian progress."

At least as presented in this fifty-minute documentary, the 9 de Julho festivities for the IV Centenário seem like a cross between popular entertainment and an extended infomercial for the city of São Paulo. The opening scene, with the camera predictably panning the city skyline, has a voice-over declaring São Paulo "the fastest-growing city in the universe"—apparently, it was no longer sufficient to be the fastest-growing city on *Earth*. The message was that anyone who was willing to come to São Paulo and work hard and strive could be a paulista and share in the rewards, tangible and intangible, of modern life. Even the location of the festivities' finale, the Parque Dom Pedro II, highlighted the popular and inclusive character of these commemorations. Located between the downtown area around the Praça da Sé and the working-class neighborhood of Brás, this park was a site where paulistas of more modest means could comfortably congregate, in contrast to the soon-to-be inaugurated Parque Ibirapuera, located in a new and more middle-class zone of the city, and virtually unreachable by public transportation.[58] And despite Randal Juliano's claim that the throngs in the park were commemorating a defeat, it seems much more likely that they were celebrating São Paulo's triumph as the center of industry and modernity in Brazil, if not in all of Latin America.

The White Album

The 9 de Julho festivities in 1954 may have seemed only loosely related to the motifs of the 1932 uprising, but other commemorative artifacts and activities were much more direct and explicit in their efforts to construct and consolidate a particular collective memory of the Constitutionalist Revolution. Among these was a widely circulated volume entitled, significantly, *Album de família 1932*. Compiled by José de Barros Martins, publisher and veteran of 1932, this "family album," with its off-white cover embossed with a medallion bearing the profile of a paulista volunteer, stood out from the many other commemorative publications issued in 1954 for being lavishly and lovingly produced to an exceptional degree.[59] Aside from a very brief introduction and a series of explanatory captions, the book is almost entirely composed of visual materials; Martins himself explains that "in a work like this, more than words, it is symbols that speak—photos, posters, slogans." Moreover, he informs his readers that to ensure maximum "authenticity," great effort was taken to reproduce the visual materials in their original colors and, wherever possible, in their true dimensions. Considering the technology of photographic reproduction at the time, this surely meant that the "family album" was both time-consuming and costly to produce.

This former "soldier of 1932" turned publisher is very explicit about his objectives: the album is not intended to be a full chronicle or visual history of the uprising, but rather is offered as a memento, an instant scrapbook that can both evoke and preserve the memory of that majestic moment in the paulista past. His intention is for the album "to have a place in every paulista home . . . as a repository of memories, where the retrospective gaze of the sons of Piratininga can, from time to time, focus nostalgically." Martins regards his handiwork as a way of preserving in material form "the glorious moments that São Paulo lived through during the Constitutionalist campaign."[60] And the actual organization of the album reflects its purpose as a remembrance of the *epopéia paulista*—an epic tale of regional heroism. The epic form seems especially appropriate since the emphasis on heroism makes the "tragic" defeat of the movement beside the point.[61] What matters is the courage and spirit of the participants, the supposed unanimity of sentiment, the willingness of the populace to mobilize in the face of overwhelming odds. Both the failure of the movement, and its specific ideological implications, are treated as secondary or irrelevant in this context. Instead, it evokes a nostalgic yearning for the days of glory when "all São Paulo" united in a heroic campaign.

The album opens with reproductions of the front page of six different pau-

FIGURE 8.1. Demonstrations in the spirit of the *Album de família 1932*. From *Álbum de família, 1932* (São Paulo: Livraria Martins Editora, 1954).

lista newspapers announcing the outbreak of the revolution—a very effective, almost cinematic, device for quickly situating the reader in the proper historical context. The first major section of the album documents the months in which the movement gained momentum, and during which the first violent incidents occurred. Photographs depict the events of May 22–23, showing streets packed with immense but orderly crowds of well-dressed, and overwhelmingly male, paulistas. The sense one gets from the photographs and the captions is that, despite the emotional pitch of the occasion, the crowd manages to remain restrained, orderly, and disciplined (see fig. 8.1).

The theme then shifts to preparations for war, including recruitment posters and the mustering of volunteers. Reminiscent of Mário de Andrade's carefully preserved collection of "ephemera" from 1932, the album lovingly reproduces the minutiae of the insurgency, including the paulista currency, coins, bonds, postage stamps, pins, and picture postcards for the troops. These are interspersed with photos of women, often dressed in luminous white, seeing off their sons and sweethearts, or staffing the support services. Again, the impression the reader gets is of intense activity and emotion; one unusually zealous recruitment flyer advises "he who is not prepared to fight, commit suicide, since it is better to die in this way than to die an immoral death."[62] But all of this is occurring within a framework of order, discipline, and rational planning—a peculiarly paulista style of revolt.

The next major section, "At War" ("Em plena guerra"), opens with a dozen different pictures from "the Front," including obviously staged "battle scenes," as well as photos of cleverly improvised war machines and the insurgent "air force." Many of the shots invoke themes that had become standard tropes of combat imagery in the aftermaths of the two world wars, including the classic "men in the trenches." The scenes of a diverse band of soldiers standing around a grenade launcher or heavy artillery would be instantly recognizable to anyone acquainted with twentieth-century war photography.[63] But this is a genre in which Brazilians rarely figured as the main visual subjects, especially prior to World War II. The exceptional nature of this "war experience" for Brazilians is undoubtedly part of the appeal of these photos, and the Guerra Paulista in general: it shows paulistas engaged in *modern* warfare, complete with trenches and tanks, and with all the attendant danger, heroism, and camaraderie. The unstated message is that when paulistas took up arms, it was to fight a modern, European-style war, in contrast to the backlands skirmishes or caudillo-led charges that were the defining images of previous regional revolts.[64] At least one chronicler of the Causa Paulista, Alfredo Ellis Jr., claimed that the politicians had only expected a "revolution," but the people wanted a "war."[65] That was certainly how Martins wanted to remember 1932 in his *Album de família*.

The platoon composed of men from all walks of life is yet another trope that had become a staple of representations of World War II, a cliché of the many Hollywood films that feature a multiethnic (if all-white) combat unit whose members put aside their minor differences to fight for a greater good. In the *Album de família* there are a few pictures that hint at the genuine diversity of the paulista forces, and one caption identifies "young and old, students, workers, businessmen, all connected by a common ideal." But most of the photos portray volunteer troops whose appearance and body language indicate that they were from the "academic youth" wing of the paulista Constitutionalist army. Less evident are soldiers from the regular army or the Força Pública, and there isn't a single reference to the Legião Negra despite its considerable role in the actual combat phase of the campaign. In contrast, several photographs depict church dignitaries blessing the flags of battalions headed to the front, which a caption recalls as "moving spectacles of Christian faith."

The tragic side of the conflict appears in Martin's album, but certainly not in an antiwar register. Several pages are devoted to scenes of funeral corteges and mourning for soldiers fallen in battle. But these photographs of ornate and stately funeral processions, far from evoking the horrors of war, foreground the fortitude and grandeur of the paulistas in that moment of ultimate sacrifice. The theme is the honor and glory of these selfless acts, as São Paulo "cries for its heroes," whereas the antiwar literature and iconography typically emphasized the insanity of war, and the waste of human life that it entailed. As the album comes to a close there are a few bittersweet pages devoted to the theme "Off to Exile" but the very final images—including a model of the soon-to-be-completed monument and mausoleum for the soldier of 1932 and reproductions of the covers of various memoirs (some published by Livraria Martins Editora)—confirm that the "Guerra Paulista" lives on in the regional collective memory. These images position the album not as a lone voice recalling São Paulo's forgotten splendor but as part of a panoply of written and visual materials meant to preserve the memory of those "glorious days"—a memory still alive within households that could be defined as authentically paulista.[66]

The references to memoirs previously published about the Causa Paulista are also apt in underscoring the continuity between the representations of the 1932 uprising in the album and those that can be found in sources more contemporary to the events being chronicled. But there are some significant silences and omissions in this commemorative volume that reflect the circumstances of its publication. Perhaps most notably, the "conflict" portrayed in the pages of the *Album de família* appears to be a war without an enemy. A close reading of the tiny print in the reproduced newspaper articles might reveal a reference to the dictatorship or to Getúlio Vargas, and the feverish recruiting flyer does declare that it is time for paulistas to "confront their oppressors." It is only in the closing pages that the text attributes São Paulo's defeat to the "tremendously superior forces" (in numerical terms) of the "dictatorship," and claims that, nonetheless, São Paulo came out "the winner" because it compelled the "dictatorship" to return to the rule of law. The album is full of nouns such as "imperative" and "sacrifice" and "enthusiasm," but is notably vague about what the paulistas were enthusiastic about, and even vaguer as to whom they were fighting against. To be sure, earlier accounts also had to deal with the potentially awkward fact that the Constitutionalist forces were fighting against other Brazilians, but typically those chroniclers dealt with this awkwardness by denigrating the troops from other regions, reducing them to particular "types," and placing them outside the realm of civic consciousness and decency, often in racialized terms. In contrast, the *Album de família* simply elides the enemy, a discursive strategy that makes perfect sense following two decades of semi-reconciliation, a burgeoning myth of racial democracy, and the emergent nationalist mood in Brazil during the mid-1950s. Under the circumstances, it is unimaginable that Martins's pictorial account would, in words or image, dismiss the federal troops as a "jagunçada," or echo Alfredo Ellis Jr.'s denunciation of the "flatheads and mongoloids of the North." Similarly, there are no reproductions of articles or cartoons from *O Separatista*, with its frequent references to "cabeças chatas," nor are there any images such as the widely distributed drawing that portrayed São Paulo as a shiny new car on a road called "Progress" whose forward motion is being blocked by a rickety oxcart called Brazil.[67] By 1954 language that *explicitly* stressed the inferiority of other Brazilian regions had been expunged from the official story. Indeed, even the slogan "Tudo por São Paulo," so ubiquitous during the Constitutionalist Campaign, never appears in the *Album de família*.[68]

Again, it is easy to imagine the appeal, to Martins and many other veterans of the Guerra Paulista, of rekindling the memory of that historical moment, and particularly of remembering it as a moment of absolute unity and social solidarity. The mid-1950s were a time when the city of São Paulo was growing exponentially, with many of the new arrivals being nordestinos who seemed (to "native" paulistas) even more foreign and difficult to assimilate than the previous wave of European immigrants.[69] Just a year earlier São Paulo had been the site of the Strike of the 300,000 — the largest labor stoppage in the history of Brazil up to that point — and worker militancy showed no signs of abating.[70] Under these circumstances, it is hardly surprising that Martins and others would want to revive the memory of and encourage *saudades* (roughly, nostalgia) for a time when "all of São Paulo" united in an epic struggle, even if that unity was, in fact, illusory and ephemeral.

Yet neither the glossy representation of the Revolution of 1932 in the *Álbum de família*, nor the very idea of situating that experience as central to paulista identity, was likely to advance the cause of regional "unity," at least in the sense of transcending other divisions within the state population. The strongly coded class and racial meanings of the Constitutionalist Campaign made it a very unreliable vehicle for popular unity, and even in his brief introduction to the *Álbum*, Martins cannot avoid indicating the specific class-based appeal of the movement. When he states his objective as simply to provide a symbolic site, a sort of handy *lieu de memoire*, "in every paulista home," we can reasonably surmise that "every paulista home" does not include the residences of recent migrants from the interior of Minas or from Bahia, nor perhaps the homes of workers active in union politics and labor struggles.

The use of the term "family" in the volume's title might signal an attempt at inclusiveness, but the expectation of familiarity that underlies the book's emotional effects ultimately implies that the album is directed at those who have a personal recollection of or connection to the events being memorialized, and who can see themselves (literally or figuratively) in the photos and posters. A similar assumption can be found in another volume especially prepared for the IV Centenário, *A Mulher paulista na história*, by Adalzira Bittencourt.[71] When the author profiles the late Dona Nicota, known for her philanthropic efforts on behalf of the Constitutionalist exiles, she claims that "São Paulo still sheds tears of nostalgia [saudades]" for this departed upper-class "dama." Here again, the "imagined community" called "São Paulo" was not likely to include the majority of its poorer, darker, or more recently arrived inhabitants. In this context, "saudades" for 1932, or for Dona Nicota, rather than serving as a unifying sentiment, was instead a way to mark off the "genuine" (white, upper- or middle-class) paulistas from those who could be dismissed as interlopers or outsiders.

There were, to be sure, ways of "remembering" the 1932 uprising that might have appealed to a more extended paulista family. By highlighting the struggle for a constitution and for representative government, the veterans of 1932 could, in theory, connect their memories to the democratization of Brazilian politics in the postwar period. But the populist tendencies in the political arena of the 1950s, and the increasing demands for a more "social" democracy, gave the narrowly legalistic version of democracy advocated by the Constitutionalists little traction with a broader populace. Moreover, the specific political context at the outset of 1954 complicated any such strategy since the restoration of constitutional rule and the electoral process had placed none other than the former dictator Getúlio Vargas in the presidency, with strong support from working-class Brazilians (including many who called São Paulo their home). Under these circumstances, even an emphasis on the 1932 campaign's opposition to dictatorship tended to reinforce its anti-populist implications.[72]

All for Democracy?

On July 9, 1957, paulistas marked the *jubileu de prata*—the silver anniversary—of the Constitutionalist Revolution of 1932. Although only three years had passed since the massive IV Centenário festivities, "9 de Julho" had become so embedded in the construction of paulistinidade that it would have been impossible to let its twenty-fifth anniversary pass without elaborate solemnities. Moreover, the meanings attributed to the uprising had shifted tangibly over this brief interval. Most striking is the almost universal (re)definition of the Constitutionalist Revolution as a struggle for democracy—a motif that was present but more muted in the celebrations in 1954. In 1957, by contrast, the theme of democracy was front and center, evoked at every turn. To quote the coverage of the 9 de Julho festivities in the newspaper *O Dia*, "Yesterday São Paulo lived through moments of intense democratic emotions."[73]

The term "democracy" proved both ubiquitous and polysemic; some commentators (including President Juscelino Kubitschek) cast the Constitutionalist Movement as a precursor of the democratic ethos now embraced throughout Brazil, while others, such as Júlio de Mesquita Filho, drew a direct connection between the *defeat* of the 1932 uprising and the continuing fragility of Brazilian democratic politics.[74] These divergent views of the state of democracy in Brazilian society, and of the very meaning of democracy, are of a piece with the highly contradictory images associated with the Kubitschek period (1956–1960). Although the phrase "Brazilian economic miracle" (with or without qualifying quotes) is more commonly associated with the middle years of the subsequent military dictatorship, in some sense the JK presidency could be described as Brazil's first "economic miracle," characterized by massive rates of industrial growth, and genuine improvements in standards of living, at least for those workers fortunate enough to find steady employment. It was also a time of increased grassroots democracy within labor unions and other popular organizations, and ample press freedoms. And despite the charges of corruption and cost overruns, the construction of the new federal capital of Brasília in less than five years seemed nothing short of miraculous.[75] However, the rising rates of inflation, stagnation in the agricultural sector, and continued frequency of strikes and other forms of labor protest fueled anxieties in certain social milieus that Brazil was entering a period of crisis.[76] This latter interpretation of the era tended to be articulated by those for whom Kubitschek's election indicated the continuing "malfunction" of Brazilian democracy. Although JK was a more moderate politician than his predecessor in almost every sense, he was someone who had a long record as an ally of Vargas, and his electoral success represented, yet again, the failure of the opposition loosely grouped around the União Democrático Nacional (UDN) to break the getulista "stranglehold" on national politics.

Whether a commentator was expressing confidence in Brazil's political future or concern about the tenuousness of its existing democracy, the Silver Jubilee offered an apt occasion for the construction of a historical narrative to bolster either interpretation. In certain ways, the meaning of 1932 had been fixed and stabilized: it was something that was recognized, both within and beyond São Paulo, as having a sentimental and emotional significance. Thus even a slightly skeptical article published in the Rio daily *O Correio da Manhã* informed its readers that the 1932 uprising might be politically "debatable," but that no one could deny the sincerity of people who risked their lives for a cause. It then went on to present an account of the 9 de Julho solemnities that foregrounded a dead soldier, a crippled father, and a disfigured nurse—figures that could be honored and admired without reference to any controversy about the uprising's political motivations or implications.[77] Not only had the Constitutionalist Revolution become so fully incorporated into regional identity that almost no mainstream media outlet could dismiss its significance, but it had been incorporated in a way that, for the most part, transcended the sorts of partisan disputes that had interfered with its memorialization twenty years earlier.

One indication, however, that the 1932 uprising still evoked some class and regional connotations that were undesirable for a politician with national ambitions in Brazil's "populist republic" was the decision by São Paulo governor Jânio Quadros to absent himself during the festivities of 1957. Although Governor Quadros gave a speech on the sixth of July in which he acknowledged that the 1932 uprising was São Paulo's finest "civic moment," he then took off for a sixty-day visit to various European capitals, leaving the state government, and the ceremonial functions, in the hands of lieutenant governor Porfírio da Paz.[78] The latter was, in several ways, the perfect man for the occasion. Though a former military officer and a mineiro by birth, Paz had volunteered to fight on the paulista side of the Constitutionalist Revolution and remembered his service to the Causa Paulista with pride.[79] Thus, he could both represent a direct connection with the 1932 uprising and confirm the now dominant paulista contention that this had not been a strictly regional affair.

The roster of festivities for the Silver Jubilee repeated many of the same events that had marked the commemorations of 1954, including circus performers in Pacaembú, multiple parades, a fireworks display in Ibirapuera, and a "chuva de ouro e prata"—a rain of silver *and* gold, perhaps to give the spectacle a touch of novelty. However, the overall tone of the commemorations in 1957 was less celebratory and more somber. A major focal point for the solemnities was the recently inaugurated "obelisk," which functioned as both monument and mausoleum to the paulista war dead and veterans of the conflict. Ceremonies marking the transfer of mortal remains of departed Constitutionalist soldiers from their original burial sites to the mausoleum had already become a staple of the 9 de Julho solemnities, but in 1957 it was especially elaborate, with 144 different "entities" (battalions, support groups) participating in the procession. On the Sunday preceding 9 de Julho there was a Catholic ceremony and mass for the war dead held before a packed crowd in Pacaembú Stadium. And in a sign that direct, personal recollection could no

FIGURE 8.2. The Obelisk—Monument and mausoleum to the paulista war dead and veterans. Black-and-white photograph by Edgard Leão, April 2011

longer be counted on to keep the memory of 1932 alive, Guilherme de Almeida and Antônio d'Avila offered minicourses on the history of the Constitutionalist Revolution to auditoriums filled to capacity (see fig. 8.2).[80]

Whatever the intentions of the organizers, the media coverage of these events revolved around three principal themes regarding the 1932 uprising: first, that it was much more than just a defense of regional interests; second, that it had significant popular support, including among the less privileged sectors of paulista society, and third, that it was a struggle for democracy.[81] The first theme probably represented the sharpest departure from the commemorations of 1954; perhaps it was inevitable that festivities organized during the city's IV Centenário would portray the movement as made by and for the povo bandeirante. Certainly that was the message of Martins's *Album de família 1932*. In contrast, the coverage of the Silver Jubilee commemorations reiterated at every opportunity that the movement was one that transcended the borders of São Paulo, whether in terms of support for the revolution or the goals of the participants. Kubitschek, in his address to the state legislative assembly, declared that "the men of São Paulo rose up not to demand privileges but to recover the public rights and liberties of all Brazilians."[82] Adhemar de Barros, then mayor of São Paulo (and, like Jânio, someone with national electoral ambitions), went so far as to repeatedly refer to "Brazilians of São Paulo" in his "salute to the heroes of 1932."[83] Acting Governor Porfírio da Paz insisted that "as a consequence of its objectives the revolution of 1932 ceased to be exclusively paulista," and an article on the industrialists' role in the conflict observed that Roberto Simonsen always referred to the movement as the "causa *brasileira*," not "paulista."[84] Even a newspaper ad for Presidente Wines was addressed "to the paulistas and our brothers from all the other states who, in 1932, united to defend the Constitution."[85] And finally, the lead editorial in *O Estado de São Paulo* on 9 de Julho told its readers, in no uncertain terms, that "the fact is that [the movement] followed principles that were infinitely broader and deeper than the mere defense of regional interests. . . . The cause was not exclusively São Paulo's: it was for all of Brazil."[86]

Not that these invocations of "all of Brazil" erased every trace of the claim that São Paulo represented the "leader-state," the most civilized, progressive, and civic-minded state in the Brazilian union. The OESP editorial, for example, after denying that 1932 was merely regional in character, and insisting that the demand for constitutional rule was of national concern, then went on to explain that "São Paulo, due to its economic and social position, was the state most consciously inclined to understand [this principle] and defend it." As for the other regions, "the economically impoverished peoples have never been the first to clamor for liberty. . . . What São Paulo had, and the other States lacked, was an awareness of the treason that was victimizing the Nation, which was a foreshadowing of everything that we are now experiencing at this moment."[87] Thus, not only did *O Estadão* persist in its portrayal of São Paulo's civic superiority, but it drew a direct parallel between 1932 and the contemporary political "crisis." It is difficult to read the final phrase without perceiving it as auguring the decision by São Paulo's premier morning paper to support the military seizure of power seven years later.[88]

Writing in the *Correio Paulistano* with reference to the Constitutionalist defeat, Catholic intellectual João de Scatimburgo took a similar tack. He lamented São Paulo's continuing frustration "in this nation with a low level of political education, and little civic commitment." And another article in that daily insisted that it was "sentiment, not demagoguery" that brought out the huge crowds of paulistas this 9 de Julho, and that (federal) government officials should interpret this public manifestation as a clear warning that the paulistas will refuse to tolerate their shenanigans.[89] Since the "demagoguery" invoked here almost certainly referred to the rhetoric of populist (and getulista) politicians, it also doesn't require a difficult stretch of the imagination to detect a subtext in these commentaries that will become an overt political stance in the early 1960s, as paulistas of certain ideological orientations positioned themselves as arbiters of appropriate "democratic" behavior and mobilized for the overthrow of the Goulart presidency.

Portrayals of the Constitutionalist Campaign as extending beyond São Paulo's borders tended to be coupled with claims about broad-based and popular participation in the movement. This was hardly a new theme in commentaries on the 1932 uprising, but it seemed to be asserted with particular force in the commemorations of 1957. Thus, a separate solemnity organized to honor "MMDC" included a special homage to "the caboclo Paulo Virgínio," who had been elevated to the status of "hero of the Battle of Cunha." Similarly, a banquet sponsored by the Commercial Association of São Paulo to recognize the participation of women in the 1932 uprising had as its special honoree Maria Barroso, a.k.a., Maria Soldado, named by the association as the "Woman Symbol of 32." Thus, the dais at this event offered the unaccustomed sight of a working-class woman of African descent (Barroso) sitting side by side with the "blue blood" Olga Ferraz Pereira Pinto, president of São Paulo's Associação Cívica Feminina.[90] Indeed, accounts of the role of the Mulher Paulista seem to have been the preferred occasion for elaborating on this theme. Thus, in an article entitled "The Mulher Paulista Also Went to the Battlefield in 32," published in the *Correio Paulistano*, Carlota Pereira de Queiroz made a particular point of highlighting the role of women from humble backgrounds in the revolution. To be sure, the article included the usual praise for the "ladies of high society," who didn't hesitate to perform any services needed, "*including the most unsavory.*"[91] But Queiroz, more unusually, also noted that there were some women of modest means who volunteered for combat and took up arms, and then went into particular detail about the role of indigent women. Among the anecdotes she recounted from her experience as head of the Department of Social Services during the uprising was one in which a poor woman came to volunteer but since she didn't know how to sew, readily agreed to wash floors instead. To emphasize that this wasn't an isolated case, she then shared another, similar recollection: "On a certain occasion, a lady [senhora] of color, poorly attired, showed up at the Department and offered to collaborate. She had no money with which to help São Paulo, but she would buy a pack of cigarettes for the soldiers. She was poor, but with some sacrifice she would continue to help out."[92] These detailed memories of the time dovetailed perfectly with the words of Pedro de Toledo (who died in 1935), reprinted in the same issue of the *Correio Paulistano*. According to the article, the official leader of the insurgency had observed that "the unity of the paulistas, without distinction regarding origin, party, or class, constitutes the greatest astonishment for the masses, and the most moving spectacle ever observed in our land."[93]

With regard to the "origins" of the combatants and supporters of the Constitutionalist Revolution, aside from the attention to Maria Barroso, there were several items in the mainstream press that confirmed the presence of black paulistas in the movement. *A Gazeta*, in its ninety-six-page commemorative edition, ran an item on the São Paulo firefighters, a unit that, at the time, had been composed almost entirely of men of color, including its charismatic commander, Lieutenant Colonel Alvaro Martins. Described as both "defending the home front," and fighting "the dictatorial horde," the Corpo de Bombeiros lost several men during the uprising, and the article mentions at least one member who left to join the Legião Negra.[94] The *Tribuna de Santos*, the leading daily paper in São Paulo's principal port city, ran photographs of several volunteer battalions that included significant numbers of black paulistas, among them a rare shot of a detachment of the Legião Negra taking a break for lunch while stationed at the front.[95]

Yet, as with the repeated references to the trans-regional character of the movement, the media coverage was full of arguments and idioms that undercut these attempts to construct a more "popular" image of the 1932 uprising and to celebrate the diversity of its supporters. The article that reprinted Pedro de Toledo's paean to cross-class cooperation also included his reminiscences of the massive paulista response to the visit by Vargas's emissary, Oswaldo Aranha, in May 1932: "That visit, received with undisguised suspicion by the people, who saw in it a repetition of the events that led to Capt. João Alberto taking power, provoked an indescribable manifestation among the popular masses, in which one could find not only the people [povo], *who are so easily suggestible*, but also the entire academic class, the conservative and liberal classes, and even those elements most representative of paulista society, including the ladies [senhoras], who participated in the series of rallies held on the 23rd of May."[96] Thus even as he celebrated the expressions of outrage from all sectors of paulista society, Toledo both disparaged the response of the "povo," too easily provoked into action, and exalted the participation of elite and middle-class paulistas, whom, one assumes, would only come out to protest when the situation genuinely required it. Of course, these were comments that the departed paulista leader had made some twenty-four years earlier, but the decision to reprint such remarks in their entirety indicates that it was still acceptable to take special pride in the "cultured" character of the movement.

Finally, there was hardly an utterance during the Silver Jubilee that didn't characterize the Causa Paulista as a struggle for liberty and democracy. No matter the topic, there would inevitably be some reference to the paulistas' commitment to a free and democratic order. Thus an article honoring the Mulher Paulista by a former army officer ended with the exclamation "Glory to democratic Brazil!"[97] The lead article in the issue of A Gazeta published on 9 de Julho described the paulistas as mobilizing in 1932 "in order to write an unparalleled chapter of our democracy."[98] And when crowds enthusiastically applauded U.S. sailors who participated in the parade in Anhangabaú, OESP reported the episode as a manifestation of solidarity among peoples who shared a commitment to democracy.[99]

While the term *democracy* may have been ubiquitous in commentaries about the Causa Paulista during the Silver Jubilee, the meaning of this term was far from uniform or consistent. When President Kubitschek extolled the Constitutionalists as champions of democracy, he was reinterpreting the movement in a way that allowed him to ignore its more politically problematic or unsavory features while acceding to the paulistas' demand that the memory of the uprising be respected. And after all, the Guerra Paulista was a struggle against a dictatorship and in favor of constitutional rule—objectives that could be easily equated with the fight for democracy. Thus shorn of its regionalist, racist, and elitist implications, the 1932 uprising could be portrayed by Kubitschek and others as part of the inevitable unfolding of a democratic politics in Brazil.[100]

In contrast, references in O Estadão to the continued malfunctioning of democracy in Brazil, or Rubens do Amaral's claim, in the pages of A Gazeta, that the paulistas of 1932 wanted "democracy, which consists of a balance between liberty and discipline," indicate both a different historical narrative, and a different definition of democracy.[101] Not only did various articles in these and other newspapers explain São Paulo's "solo" uprising against the Vargas dictatorship through the classic tropes insisting on the region's higher economic stage, more modern and progressive disposition, greater civic consciousness, and so forth; but they also gave no indication that the other regions of Brazil had "caught up" with São Paulo. On the contrary, Scantimburgo, writing in O Correio Paulistano, lamented the "meager civic consciousness" still rampant in the Brazil beyond São Paulo's borders.[102] And as noted above, the lead editorial in *O Estadão* on 9 de Julho insisted that, then as now, only São Paulo understood the nature of the threat to the nation. In other words, they continued to regard democratic process as something that could only function properly if the nation consisted of citizens who thought and acted in particular ways. And they continued to see the "paulistas" (a category that did not necessarily include all who lived in São Paulo) as the segment of Brazilian society that could perform the rites of citizenship in a way they considered appropriate to a modern, liberal democracy.

The year 1957 was also a time of Cold War and rising anticommunism, in Brazil and elsewhere in Latin America, and it was not at all unusual for democracy (especially when paired with "freedom") to be invoked as the antithesis of Communist/totalitarian regimes. Certainly, the remark about crowds applauding U.S. sailors as defenders of democracy, or the denunciation of excessive nationalism by the president of the Institute of Engineering sounded a recognizable Cold War note.[103] Therefore, it is both curious and intriguing that specific references to the Communist threat were absent from the speeches delivered and the articles published to commemorate the 1932 uprising. This may be, in part, because it was so patently absurd to characterize the Kubitschek administration, with its robust support for rapid capitalist development and warm welcome for multinational corporations, as influenced by or "soft on" Communism. But I would also argue that the growing sense of "crisis" among sectors of the Brazilian political class, which even Kubitschek obliquely acknowledged in his speech on 9 de Julho, was not a response to anything as specific or tangible as a rising threat of radical change or socialist revolution. And despite the claims of OESP, it was surely not provoked by a sense that Brazil was insufficiently democratic, if we measure democracy by the degree of effective popular participation. Rather, it seems to have emerged from quite the opposite concern—a sense of outrage (among "cultured" Brazilians) that social sectors allegedly lacking the capacity to make decisions essential to a modern, orderly society were increasingly in a position to play a decisive role in the course of Brazilian life, including in that embodiment of the nation's progress, the state of São Paulo.[104] It was a version, writ large, of a retrospective remark made by Aureliano Leite in a lecture on the forerunners of the Revolution of 1932. Fulminating about Vargas's decision to appoint João Alberto as intervenor of São Paulo, Leite noted the absurdity of "an inexperienced youngster governing this State which is the equivalent of a nation!"[105] In a sense, the paulista political elites, and much of the region's middle class, viewed large swaths of the Brazilian electorate as a collective "inexperienced youngster" and still regarded their state as a virtual nation.

The Politics of Memory

Beyond the realm of scholarly research, pundits and commentators remarking on the past are wont to lament the shallowness of historical memory, and the consequent failure of the public to learn from the experiences of those who have gone before them. Despite the commonsense quality of this complaint, it relies on a number of debatable premises. First, it assumes that the "lessons" of history are transparent and obvious, rather than a matter of interpretation, and second, it posits a linear deterioration of collective memory that rests on a notion that, in the immediate aftermath of an event, people had a clear and accurate idea of what it was about. What the history of commemorations of the Constitutionalist Revolution teaches us is something substantially different with regard to historical memory. One could argue that "9 de Julho," in 1957, was more central to the representation of regional identity than it had been just a few years after the uprising, and that "memories" of the event were, in a sense, more "vivid" in 1957 than they had been in 1937.[106]

Not that there was *ever* any danger of the Causa Paulista being forgotten. Given its heavily middle-class social base, and the loss of life it entailed, there were segments of paulista society that would nurture the memory of this historical episode and would have the wherewithal to do so. Many paulistas today can still remember their parents and grandparents wearing with pride the metal "wedding ring" that they received in exchange for the gold band that they donated to the Constitutionalist cause. Even when material circumstances would have easily allowed the purchase of a new ring, their elders deliberately persisted in wearing this precious token of past sacrifice. Groups like the various veterans' associations and the Associação Cívica Feminina could be expected to perpetuate a "cult of 1932" with annual solemnities and continuous fund-raising drives to finance monuments and mausoleums. So the question was not whether the "memory" of this event would persevere, but whether the imagined collective to whom this memory held significance would be broadened, and in what ways this historical episode would be re-signified over time.[107]

In the years immediately following the uprising, it was virtually impossible to unlink the event from the specific political circumstances that gave birth to it. Thus, it briefly served as a source of regional unity during the period of the Chapa Única (1933–1934). But this political cohesion proved transitory at best, and by the fifth anniversary of the uprising, the two major regional political factions had retreated to a partisan position that made an extravagant celebration of the Constitutionalist Campaign impolitic. At that slender remove, the close association between the 1932 uprising and paulista demands for either hegemony or autonomy turned it into a liability for any partisan group that harbored national ambitions. The result was not only a subdued commemoration of the Constitutionalist struggle on its fifth anniversary, but also the reinforcement of the claim that the authentic memory keepers should be those who treated the "paulista epic" as a transcendent event that should not be tainted by political squabbles. To paraphrase Ary Barroso's musical quasi homage to the Constitutionalist Revolution, they believed the true paulista's color should be "32."[108]

This cult of regional memory sustained the rituals and networks that made the annual commemorations of 9 de Julho a centerpiece of paulistinidade. This is evident in a short film produced in 1950 by the Department of Culture in the state capital to promote tourism in the nearby "colonial" town of Santana de Parnaíba. Entitled *Viagem ao passado* (Voyage to the past), this travelogue— intended to educate visitors about São Paulo's colonial history—opens with a shot of the local headquarters of the "Veteranos de 1932," apparently to establish it as an authentically paulista location.[109] It is hardly surprising, then, that the yearlong celebrations of the IV Centenário would be punctuated with especially elaborate festivities and pageantry around the date of 9 de Julho. But by the mid-1950s there was a new set of tensions that influenced the way the occasion could be commemorated. The broadcast media that organized and funded most of the festivities for that date sought to emphasize entertainment and amusement that would ensure the presence of large, enthusiastic crowds. While there were the usual nods to honoring the war dead, 9 de Julho in 1954 was a decidedly festive occasion, with the highlights being spectacular events (the chuva de prata, the massive fireworks) meant to induce a sense of wonder and awe. It was a celebration not of São Paulo's past, but of its future—when all denizens of the great metropolis might enjoy the benefits of its modernity and progress, and when "sampauleiros" might become full-fledged "paulistas." Again, it can hardly be a coincidence that the film made by Studio Vera Cruz chronicling the festivities captured a lead performer singing about the alleged absence of racial and color prejudice in São Paulo. In contrast, Martins's *Album de família 1932*—which I have coined "the white album"—constructed a genealogy of paulistinidade that privileged a direct connection to the regional past and assumed an audience that remembered firsthand the episode it memorialized.

Finally, the commemorations of 9 de Julho in 1957—its Silver Jubilee—indicated how thoroughly the Constitutionalist Revolution had been re-signified as a struggle for democracy, with virtually every orator and commentator foregrounding the movement's democratizing objectives, rather than its demands for regional hegemony and/or autonomy, which had been far more in evidence at the time of the uprising. Yet despite the apparent rhetorical consensus in this regard, there were sharp disagreements over both the meaning and the state of democracy in Brazilian society that manifested themselves in the narratives constructed by different writers and speakers. Thus, Mayor Adhemar de Barros and President Kubitschek hailed the paulista insurgents as precursors of the ongoing process of democratization in Brazilian society, while the editors of O Estadão and the udenistas traced what they considered the failure of democratization back to the defeat of the 1932 uprising. By their logic, that defeat meant that the most progressive and civic-minded Brazilians had been placed on the same political footing as the least cultured, least educated, and most suggestible of their fellow "citizens." Under such circumstances, it was little wonder that they regarded Brazilian democracy, despite the best efforts of certain paulistas, as plunging the nation into a state of crisis.

EPILOGUE AND CONCLUSION

Making historical analysis the discourse of the continuous and making human consciousness the original subject of all historical development and all action are the two sides of the same system of thought.
—Michel Foucault, *The Archaeology of Knowledge*

Only ignorance explains why São Paulo, with all its advantages and defects, still isn't regarded as the best synthesis of Brazil.
—Gilberto Dimenstein, "Capital de São Paulo é o Brasil," *A Folha de São Paulo*

Historians, as Michel Foucault observed, have tended to privilege continuities, deep structures of unbroken thought or tradition, in their construction of historical narratives or modes of interpretation. Though the analysis of "change over time" often serves as a shorthand for the historian's craft, what use is the study of the past unless we can discern a thread, no matter how tenuous, between what has gone before and the present? Of course, Foucault was critiquing, not congratulating, historians for their focus on continuities, which he regarded as inseparable from their tendentious belief that documents could reveal "real" traces of the past. For the most part, I find this critique persuasive and am sympathetic to postmodern scholars who emphasize rupture over continuity, and instability (if not indeterminacy) of meaning over persistence. But every now and then the sources make it almost irresistible to argue for continuity, or to draw a direct line from historical point "A" to historical point "B."

This was my initial response to two editorials that appeared in *O Estado de São Paulo* just before and after the Brazilian military's seizure of power on March 31, 1964, an act that initiated twenty-one years of authoritarian rule. The first, published on March 21, 1964, described in nearly ecstatic language the "March of the Family, with God, for Liberty" that had taken place in São Paulo two days earlier. Entitled "The Paulista and the Nation under Threat," the editorial claimed that half a million "paulistanos and paulistas . . . the largest human throng ever gathered in any locale in our national territory to defend an idea" had turned out for this right-wing rally against the left-leaning populist government of João Goulart. (Elected vice president in 1960, Goulart had assumed the presidency following Jânio Quadros's sudden resignation in August 1961.) It then went on to claim that this fervent but orderly outpouring of paulista indignation demonstrated "their disposition to defend their liberty with the same heroic determination with which paulistas, 32 years ago, defended the sacred territory of São Paulo against Getúlio's soldiery [soldadesca]. Yes, it was São Paulo that marched [in protest]." Not only did the editorial draw analogies between the two moments of paulista outrage, it implied a virtual reenactment, with the crowds converging "on the same site where, in 1932, the paulista multitudes manifested the intention of challenging, with arms in hand, the Vargas regime.[1]

Ten days later, the commanding officers of the Brazilian Armed Forces overthrew Goulart and initiated the dictatorship that would rule Brazil for the next two decades. *O Estadão* celebrated the event with an editorial entitled "São Paulo Repeats 32." Without subtlety or qualifiers, São Paulo's leading daily paper declared that Goulart had sealed his own fate by ignoring the protests of "the former combatants of 32 and their descendants," and now "as if one man, today São Paulo finds itself in full mobilization, and with the same spirit from three decades ago, it rises up in defense of the existing constitution." Even the mathematics of the moment seemed to conspire to confirm this claim of repetition—after all, thirty-two repeated/doubled equaled sixty-four. True, not everything was exactly the same as before: "Minas, this time around, is on our side."[2] However, this was presented not so much as an inconsistency but as a corrective for a past error, a decision that would set "history" right.

Given Julio de Mesquita Filho's strong identification with the Constitutionalist Movement, one might attribute these references to the particular history of this one newspaper. But we can see the same tendency in the coverage of *A Folha de São Paulo*, which declared that the paulistas were defending democracy and the Constitution "within the same spirit that drove the Revolution of 32." Perhaps even more noteworthy are the references to 1932—in a very different register—in the columns of the decidedly pro-Goulart daily, *Última Hora*. Under the headline "Return to 32," it began its coverage of the right-wing march by remarking that "as was expected, the evocation of the movement of 32 constituted a constant theme during the rally."[3]

For a historian seeking continuities, there is no need here to search for subtle clues or to tease out hidden meanings. Obviously, the editorial writers for *O Estadão* and other dailies sought to draw a bright, straight line between these two "revolutions" and thereby legitimate their support for the unconstitutional overthrow of a legal, democratically elected government while foregrounding the civilian participation in an essentially military operation. But that is precisely why it would be unwise to succumb to the temptation of tracing "continuities" and to the teleological thinking that would claim some kind of underlying causal connection between the 1932 uprising and the coup of 1964; it would mean accepting the mainstream media's self-serving interpretation at face value. To be sure, I do think there is a causal connection, but not of the sort that a Hegelian or materialist interpretation might reveal. Rather, I would argue that the 1932 uprising was a moment when certain notions of paulista exceptionalism crystallized and when certain derogatory views of Brazilians from "Other" regions gained special currency within São Paulo. The personal experiences of the revolution, the epic narrative that emerged from it, and the continuing commemorations of that event meant that "1932" became a politically useful trope whenever "São Paulo"—meaning, in the first instance, its white, liberal, middle-class incarnation—could be portrayed as being buffaloed by lesser regions of Brazil or victimized by the inversion of natural hierarchies of civic virtue. The availability of this political language, with its antidemocratic implications, helps to explain how "liberal" media outlets such as *O Estadão* and *A Folha de São Paulo*—the two leading dailies in Brazil's largest metropolis—could so seamlessly connect a past mobilization against a dictatorship with subsequent support for a military seizure of power.

My point here is surely not to insist that a racialized regional identity was the literal cause of the coup of 1964, or of paulista support for the "Revolution of 1964," as the military liked to call it.[4] Rather, I am arguing that the discourse of regional superiority served to make particular political positions more "thinkable" or acceptable for a sizable segment of the paulista population.[5] By no means would I deny that anticommunist sentiment—the fear that Goulart was being manipulated by "subversive" forces on the left—played a central role in mobilizing middle-class (and some working-class) Brazilians in favor of a military seizure of power. But given the widely recognized influence of anticommunist "hysteria" in the overthrow of Goulart, it is curious to note that explicit references to the "Communist threat" were nearly absent from the editorials in *OESP* at the time of the coup.[6] One can detect it as an element in repeated claims that the Goulart government was subverting the Constitution and threatening Brazilian freedom, but only rarely do the editorials invoke the "Communist menace" in an explicit way. And significantly, one commentary that did address rising Communist influence—in this case, within the Brazilian labor movement—couched its claims in a regionalized discourse that displaced that "threat" to the disorderly Nordeste. The editorial, entitled "The Paulistas Refused to Be Intimidated," claimed that leftist nordestino union leaders had tried to take over the recent and "inappropriately named" *National* Convention of Railroad Workers, held in Recife, but the paulista delegation had boldly challenged this attempt by the left to seize control of the proceedings. Moreover, the editorial extended its praise well beyond this specific coterie of railroad workers, declaring that the paulistas' protest at this gathering "translated the general sentiments of the working classes in this State in response to the tricks with which the Marxists . . . have been seeking to confuse the working masses."[7] The paulista middle class might be the "vigorous core" of regional identity, but even the state's working classes were more resistant to Communist influence by virtue of their paulistinidade.[8]

Once again, we can see the way positive representations of paulista identity went hand in hand with disparaging representations of the Nordeste. Moreover, similar to "1932," these negative images of nordestinos should not be regarded as "remnants" of an earlier conflict, but rather as shifting visual and verbal tropes that circulated widely in Brazilian society, and were available for revival, reconfiguration, and deployment when hierarchies asserted as "natural" came under attack. Thus, as OESP intensified its criticisms of the Goulart administration, it repeatedly targeted the president's campaign to expand voting rights to illiterates, typically figured as *analfabetos nordestinos*, though the latter adjective was not always necessary given that most of its paulista readership would automatically associate illiteracy with persons of nordestino origin.[9] And the Northeast was designated as the locus of not only backwardness and ignorance, but also extremism and disorder, and therefore was represented as the region most susceptible to Marxist subversion.[10]

As with most racialized discourses, these disparaging characterizations of nordestinos—whether on their native terrain or in their adopted homes in São Paulo—tended to be inconsistent and even contradictory, so that at one moment the nordestinos would be derided as too prone to disorder, and at another moment would be scorned for their supposed submissiveness to an authoritarian regime.[11] During the 1970s, when São Paulo emerged as a major center of *opposition* to the dictatorship, paulista critics of the regime routinely derided northeastern voters for casting their ballots in favor of pro-military candidates in exchange for the meager rewards of patronage.[12] Pejorative comments of a different sort circulated in the decades of economic recession following the end of the dictatorship. Maureen O'Dougherty, studying regionalist sentiments among middle-class paulistas in the 1990s, found that her subjects simultaneously regarded "baianos" in São Paulo as lazy and unreliable, and as only interested in making money.[13] And even representations meant to reflect concern for the suffering of the nordestino often reinforced the negative images attached to that identity. In *O que é Nordeste brasileiro?* (What is the Brazilian Northeast?), a brief book published in 1984 as part of a series of inexpensive paperbacks intended for the general reading public, author Carlos Garcia included a drawing of a barefoot, stooped nordestino, bereft of any sign of modernity, with the following caption: "There is today, in the Northeast, more than 24 million Zecas-Tatu [*sic*], the symbol of malnutrition, of laziness, of obstruction, of physical and mental incapacity, created by Monteiro Lobato."[14] It is little wonder that, a year later, one of Brazil's leading human rights lawyers published a polemic entitled *Are the Nordestinos a Racial Minority?*[15]

These recurring racial/regional stereotypes, however, do not tell the full story of evolving attitudes toward nordestinos, whether among paulistas in particular, or Brazilians in general. Perhaps the most significant political development in Brazil during the final years of the dictatorship was the formation of the Workers' Party (Partido dos Trabalhadores—PT), which emerged in São Paulo from an alliance between a segment of the regional middle class and an increasingly militant working class, largely of nordestino origin and based in the industrial suburbs of Greater São Paulo.[16] And the man widely recognized as the most important political figure of his generation—Luiz Inácio Lula da Silva—hailed from the northeastern state of Pernambuco but made his career as a union leader and political activist in the state of São Paulo. A recent biopic of the former president bears the title *Lula, Filho do Brasil*, and while "son of Brazil" is a phrase that suggests multiple referents, surely one of them is Lula's notable ability to transcend any single regional identity.[17]

Despite Lula's remarkable popularity—he ended his two-term administration with an approval rating well over 80 percent—not all paulistas are reconciled to the PT's electoral successes or the heightened influence of the Nordeste in national politics. In the election for Lula's successor in 2010 the PT candidate, Dilma Rousseff, secured a strong majority in the second round of voting, defeating the former paulista governor José Serra, but the geographic distribution of support for Rousseff and Serra reflected a potentially troubling degree of political division based on location. Reminiscent of an earlier political configuration, Dilma, though a longtime resident of Rio Grande do

Sul, received her most robust support from the states of the Nordeste. An electoral map illustrated this regional divergence: almost all the states from Rio de Janeiro north gave a majority of their votes to the PT candidate, whereas all the states from São Paulo south gave majorities to Serra. Since Brazil has direct presidential elections, rather than an electoral college, this regional division isn't necessarily decisive in terms of electoral outcomes. It also should be kept in mind that a substantial minority of voters in the southern states did give their votes to Dilma, and she gained clear majorities in the center-south states of Minas and Rio; even in his home region of São Paulo, Serra's lead was relatively thin. Furthermore, the dramatic preference for Dilma in the North and Northeast, where incomes are lower, can be seen as largely a function of the PT's greater commitment to income redistribution and social welfare programs compared to Serra's Brazilian Social Democratic Party (PSDB). At the same time, the fact that Dilma's support came disproportionately from the North and Northeast of Brazil apparently rendered her victory less "legitimate" in the eyes of some southern Brazilians, as we know from the instant reactions posted in cyberspace. One young woman from São Paulo, a law student no less, infamously tweeted her outrage to her regional compatriots, declaring that "Nordestisto [sic] não é gente" (roughly, Northeastist isn't human), and ending with an odious suggestion: "Do SP a favor: strangle a nordestino to death!"[18]

As one might expect, this explicitly racist and vicious tweet elicited condemnation from all quarters and immediately inspired a website entitled proudtobenordestino. It also, less predictably, prompted legal action and an eighteen-month prison sentence (commuted to community service and a fine). Even in the bare-knuckled world of contemporary Brazilian politics, Mayara Petruso had crossed the line of acceptable discourse. But it is difficult not to speculate as to how many paulistas, and Brazilians from other southern states, though more restrained or discreet, nonetheless share some of her sentiments and regard nordestinos as less deserving of the rights of citizenship than "those who labor to support the bums who just have children so they can get the 171 subsidy."[19] It also seems possible to detect in her comments a faint echo of the "jocular" proposal made by the paulista separatists, some seventy years earlier, to erect a monument to the murderous bandit Lampião for reducing the nordestino population.[20] Or the quip that one of Maureen O'Dougherty's informants shared with her, which he claimed he had heard (to his dismay) from several people in response to the killing of 111 inmates—assumed to be mainly dark-skinned nordestinos—following a prison riot in São Paulo. According to his account, the joke was "Only 111?"[21] Whether or not those expressing such sentiments would actually condone systematic violence against people from the Nordeste, these comments represent a sort of "distancing strategy" that can serve to justify the durable inequalities that continue to characterize Brazilian society.[22]

Race, Region, Nation

This book began with some of Albert O. Hirschman's thoughts on the consequences of "uneven development." One of the principal purposes of this study has been to show that there is no way to neatly separate causes and consequences. Rather, I have maintained that racialized, classed, and gendered discourses of modernity have been constitutive elements in the production and reproduction of inequalities—material, political, cultural—naturalized through association with a particular geographic space denominated as a region. Only by questioning anything designated as "natural," whether it be regional boundaries or economic processes, and focusing instead on the historical (de)construction of bounded spaces or discrete populations, can we fully contest a way of viewing the world in which those who "naturally" have a certain propensity for modernity end up "logically" enjoying, or deserving, a much larger share of the material and political resources it entails.[23]

It is hardly surprising that dramatic shifts in the fortunes of the local economy from the mid-nineteenth century on moved men (and a few women) of property, prestige, and education in São Paulo to search for the roots and ponder the causes of these changes, and to seek a position within the Brazilian nation consonant with their newfound prosperity. Drawing on existing regional narratives, they refurbished and reworked the figure of the bandeirante, making him the state symbol and the central character in the myth of paulista exceptionalism. Both provoking and seizing upon a moment of political crisis, they adopted a liberal/federalist stance that allowed the paulista elite to assume a dominant position within the newly formed republic while maintaining a great deal of regional autonomy. Closing ranks at key moments, the regional elite used the resultant political power and fiscal resources to create first a massive program of subsidized European immigration, and then a publicly financed valorization scheme of coffee price supports, both of which helped to sustain regional prosperity (at least for the elites) and fuel the emergence of São Paulo's industrial economy.[24]

By the early decades of the twentieth century, São Paulo had not only become more urbanized and industrialized, but also whiter, both in demographic and representational terms. Even as various scholarly, literary, and artistic cohorts rejected the pessimism of scientific racism and celebrated Brazil's racially mixed population, the dominant regional narrative remained one that prized whitening, and associated whiteness with modernity and progress. Similarly, the archetypical paulista family was increasingly represented as bourgeois or middle-class, with a competent, industrious male head of household assisted by his domestically oriented but civic-minded wife/partner. And all of these constructions of race, class, and gender were brought into sharper relief by being contrasted to those "Other" regions of Brazil whose economic stagnation or decline could be explained by their "darker" racial composition and moral and civic defects.

It is crucial to bear in mind that the regional cum national identity that emerged, piecemeal, from these various political, cultural, and social venues was never uncontested or universally embraced. Large segments of the population composed of struggling immigrants or migrants performing poorly paid manual labor were unlikely to swallow whole hog the invocations of São Paulo's exceptional prosperity. The Afro-paulista community, though claiming a stake in São Paulo's modernity and progress (a leading publication of the black press was titled *O Bandeirante*), nonetheless challenged the equation of whiteness with paulista exceptionalism.[25] Brazilians from other regions, while ritualistically expressing pride in São Paulo's economic success, derided its political elite as a provincial "oligarchy" and intermittently attributed the prosperity of the "estado bandeirante" to federal favors secured through political muscle, rather than the virtues of hard work or innovation. Even within the paulista elite, where notions of regional exceptionalism gained particular traction, this shared investment in paulistinidade did not necessarily smooth over thorny political and cultural disputes. Nor did it resolve tensions over questions such as the relationship between region and nation or between the privileged classes and the lower orders, as exemplified by the founding of the Partido Democrático in 1926.[26]

Therefore, the Constitutionalist Campaign that would begin to take shape in 1931, within months of Getúlio Vargas's rise to power, cannot be understood as the product of a fully formed and firmly entrenched regional identity, even within groups that we could designate as elites. Instead, it was a moment when an unprecedented challenge to the paulista position within the Brazilian nation spurred overt expressions of regional chauvinism as well as disparaging representations of Brazilians from the "upstart" regions seeking to dislodge São Paulo from its perch at the center of national political power. The repeated denunciations of the humiliations being visited upon the "povo bandeirante" by Brazilians from less wealthy, less modern, and (implicitly) less white regions of the nation resonated deeply with large segments of the paulista population, including many who had no apparent stake in the material interests supposedly under threat from the tenente interlopers. Although the archetypical paulista that emerged from this regional discourse was white, male, and middle-class—an identity that excluded or marginalized the vast majority of the paulista population—the need to mobilize an impressive number of "citizens" meant that the discourses of the Constitutionalist Movement could not be too exclusionary. Women from middle- and upper-class families proved to be among the earliest and most fervent supporters of the movement; represented as the "Mulher Paulista," and as venturing into the public sphere only due to extraordinary circumstances, their participation did not directly challenge the manly character of the Constitutionalist Campaign, but could be cited as evidence of the civic spirit of the povo bandeirante. Industrial workers as a class, in contrast, proved much less responsive to the clarion call of the Causa Paulista, with its refusal to acknowledge any degree of exploitation of labor by capital, though many individual artisans and manual laborers enlisted in the volunteer battalions. And upwardly mobile immigrants, eager to demonstrate their loyalty to their regional cum national home, supported the movement in both combat and noncombat roles.[27] Finally, the black soldiers of the Legião Negra played a crucial part in military phase of the movement and presented the most significant challenge to the dominant/whitened representations of paulistinidade.[28]

Despite the brevity of the armed phase of the movement, and its quick defeat at the hands of Getúlio's "soldadesca," the experience of combat was a defining moment for many paulistas, one that reinforced their tendency to imagine Brazil through São Paulo. And for a few years following the uprising, the different factions of the regional political class were able to forge a degree of unity based on this shared experience. But once again, regionalist discourses, no matter how appealing to certain segments of the population, did not imply a monolithic approach to politics even within the paulista elites. Well before Vargas seized fuller dictatorial powers and declared his regime an Estado Novo (1937), paulista cultural, business, and political elites had fragmented, with some accommodating themselves to the dictatorship and others—many of whom would go on to found the União Democrática Nacional (UDN) in 1945—remaining steadfastly opposed to Vargas and his ruling clique.[29]

The conservative, anti-populist tenor of udenista politics ill suited the party to the world of electoral competition that emerged after 1945, in Brazil's so-called Populist Republic, and paulista politicians who sided with the stridently anti-getulista fraction found themselves unable to revive their political fortunes, especially at the national level. But São Paulo, city and state, fared considerably better than its "liberal" political elite in the aftermath of World War II, growing economically and demographically by leaps and bounds. In April 1948 *Life* magazine ran a ten-page feature article on the city of São Paulo, lauding it as "a roaring metropolis of 1,600,000 people who live in a dramatic skyscraper city that has about as much Latin languor as a New York subway at 5 P.M."[30] That same year the state and municipal governments of São Paulo, together with assorted representatives of the private sector, began planning the commemorations of the four hundredth anniversary of São Paulo city's founding.

It would be overreaching to draw too close a parallel between 1932 and 1954. Despite their shared instances of theatricality, mobilizing a population for war is a very different matter from enticing people to attend exhibitions and watch firework displays. The surging nationalism at the time of the IV Centenário also meant that the paulistas had to be more circumspect in their comments about other regions, and therefore sought to consistently portray São Paulo's regional success as a contribution to *national* development. Still, I think we can discern some analogous features in these two rather different moments. The IV Centenário, like the Constitutionalist Campaign, offered a context in which segments of the paulista elite (broadly defined) could not only celebrate the modernity and progress of their home city and region, but also shape the image of São Paulo at home and abroad. It created a multi-faceted space in which to assert São Paulo's primacy within Brazil. But as in 1932, the IV Centenário generated significant tensions between the ideal audience imagined by the organizers of the festivities—one composed of white, middle-class paulistas of good taste and refinement—and the need to appeal to a broader public.[31] The routine valorizing of whiteness in a variety of venues prompted the reputed architect of racial democracy, Gilberto Freyre, to publicly scold the paulistas for their un-Brazilian and quasi-American attitudes toward racial difference. And the petition from the Afro-paulista community seeking support for the unveiling of the monument to the Black Mother indicates how little recognition black paulistas had been allotted in the program for the IV Centenário, and their awareness of this erasure. Perhaps even more striking is the virtual absence of references to the hundreds of thousands of residents of Greater São Paulo who had recently migrated there from Minas or the Nordeste, even as the European and Japanese immigrant communities were being feted as genuinely paulista.

Then there was the quite literal imbrication of 1932 and 1954. The commemorations of "9 de Julho" were among the most memorable features of the IV Centenário, equaled only by the elaborate solemnities staged in 1957 for the revolution's silver anniversary. These repeated commemorative cere-monies might be interpreted as "keeping alive" the memory of 1932, but that too would connote a degree of continuity or persistence that I think would be profoundly misleading. Although the occasion had been marked with some sort of solemnity by veterans and relatives of the war dead every year since the uprising, the 1950s saw not so much a continuation of these practices as a substantial escalation of the commemorations and a reworking of their mean-ings. Thus the long-proposed obelisk and mausoleum for the heroes of 1932 was finally inaugurated (though not actually completed) in July 1955. And the *Album de família 1932*—what I have dubbed "the White Album"—was among the most widely circulated publications to emerge from the IV Centenário. It was also one of a handful of books that would be reissued in 1982, in time for the fiftieth anniversary of the Constitutionalist Revolution.[32]

Perhaps the most significant "rupture" with past commemorations was the insistent representation of the 1932 uprising—now routinely dubbed the "epic of 32"—as a crucial moment in the ongoing but inevitable transformation of Brazil into a democratic society.[33] Framed in this way, the commemorations of the Constitutionalist Revolution could be embraced by almost any political entity or media outlet in São Paulo, and even beyond the state's borders. At the same time, certain segments of the paulista population that regarded them-selves as the guardians of the memory of 1932 were defining the struggle for democracy, past and present, more narrowly, and arguably more in keeping with the original "spirit" of the 1932 uprising. Thus, Júlio de Mesquita Filho and his "liberal" circle at *O Estado de São Paulo* increasingly defined the "de-mocracy" championed in 1932 as the opposite of leftist political projects and warned that it was being undermined by populist appeals, political reforms, and campaigns to extend the vote to illiterates.[34] It was a small step from this argument to the exaltation of the rally in March 1964 against President Gou-lart as "São Paulo in protest," and the endorsement of the military seizure of power in 1964 as a victory for democratic forces.[35]

Region versus Nation: Some Final Thoughts

For all the current talk of globalization and international aid programs, and the high-profile role of nongovernmental organizations (NGOs) in initiatives for development, human welfare, or social justice, the nation continues to be the arena where disadvantaged groups or regions can most effectively seek redress for systematic inequalities. Despite the scurrilous remarks of the paulista law student, a large minority of voters even in São Paulo backed the presidential candidate for 2010 whose party is the most closely identified with redistributive programs such as Bolsa-Família, which has been especially crucial for lifting households out of extreme poverty in the Nordeste.[36] Although the population of São Paulo may be no more (directly) responsible for the privations of Brazilians in less advantaged regions than, say, the population of the United States, as citizens of the same imagined community paulistas are much more likely to be prevailed upon to channel a significant portion of their national patrimony to fund such programs than North Americans with no sense of a stake in Brazil's future.

Redistribution on a national level, whether based on tax receipts or income from "natural" resources, is never entirely painless, and it may also require the redistribution of political authority in a way that will chafe sensibilities and pique resentments that are not reducible to economic concerns. In settings where there are already available regional identities and discourses of regional difference, those threatened politically, economically, or even culturally by such initiatives—a sentiment rarely confined to the ranks of the elite—can challenge the national agenda by invoking regional rights, or, in extreme cases, by imagining the region as a separate nation. As in the case of São Paulo's small separatist faction in the 1930s, such secessionist movements, based on simultaneous claims of superiority and oppression, rarely gain enough traction to secede from the union and create a new national community. Thus Italy's longstanding Northern League might garner a troubling percentage of the votes in certain locales, but presently poses no real threat to the territorial integrity of the Italian nation. Nevertheless, the racist discourses that such movements typically deploy—to reinforce their own identities and delegitimize the claims of citizens in other regions—can have an impact on the tenor of debate and the breadth of support for social-justice initiatives that goes well beyond the number of active adherents. In other words, without literally splintering the nation, they can render the nation a less unified space and a far less effective arena for addressing material inequalities and social discrimination.[37]

A recent example of the role that "race" almost inevitably plays in such movements can be found in the Bolivian province of Santa Cruz. This lowland region of the Bolivian nation with a long history of federalist political sympathies also happens to be the locale with the largest reserves of natural gas and other exportable resources.[38] The income derived from these reserves has served as a crucial source of funding for redistributive programs promoted by the government of Evo Morales, Bolivia's first indigenous-identified president. This perceived "transfer" of wealth from the region to the nation, compounded by the expanded political power of indigenous groups in the Bolivian highlands, has (re)animated a movement for autonomy, and even secession, among the *cruceños*. Its followers, who hail from all social classes, cite their region's higher standards of living, its greater modernity, and the whiteness of its population as both the basis of a regional identity, and as a justification for refusing to submit to the authority of the "backward" and indigenous regions of the Bolivian nation.[39]

As always, these claims of "whiteness" have to be treated as contingent and placed in context—a glance at a photograph of any regionalist protest in Santa Cruz will reveal an assemblage of individuals who, from this outsider's perspective, seem to be themselves of indigenous descent. Clearly, a great deal of political and ideological work has gone into defining Santa Cruz as a distinct region and the cruceños as a separate, whiter people.[40] One is tempted to say that the whiteness they are claiming is of a cultural sort, defined by their way of dress and by their everyday practices, but the "innate" difference that they are seeking to invoke between themselves and Bolivians of the highlands regions seem as fully racist in its "logic" and implications as what has conventionally been termed biological racism.[41]

Not all regionalisms are so pervaded by racial thinking; some that emerge in response to forms of exclusion and oppression may even have an emancipatory quality.[42] And conversely, national identities, with their rosters of required traits and peculiarities, are hardly innocent of racial thinking. Indeed, Paul Gilroy has argued that the shift to "cultural racism" has been especially expedient in this regard: "The emphasis on culture allows nation and race to fuse. Nationalism and racism become so closely identified that to speak of the nation is to speak automatically in racially exclusive terms."[43] The problem resides not so much in our tendency to reinscribe difference, per se, but to construct hierarchies of difference that become measures of worthiness. National identities, in Brazil and elsewhere, will always be imagined through regional referents.[44] What we might hope is that an emphasis on diversity, not hierarchy, will mark regional identities, as will an awareness of the fluidity of their boundaries. Regions, like nations, are products of history, not nature, and are always subject to change.

NOTES

Introduction

Epigraph. Cited in Centro Paulista, *São Paulo e a sua evolução*, 7. Note that state "president" is equivalent to a governor.

1. Hirschman, *The Strategy of Economic Development*, 132, 185.

2. Hirschman, *The Strategy of Economic Development*, 185. Emphasis mine.

3. Hirschman is rightly recognized as an exceptionally humane economic thinker, which makes his unreflexive use of such language especially noteworthy. On his life and work, see Adelman, *Worldly Philosopher*.

4. Harvey, *Spaces of Global Capitalism*, 75.

5. See the discussion in Leff, "Economic Development and Regional Inequality," 243–262.

6. For an extended discussion of this see my "Developing Inequality," 1–18.

7. Harvey, *Justice, Nature and the Geography of Difference*, 320. My thanks to Seth Garfield for bringing this comment by Harvey to my attention.

8. On the Italian case, see Schneider, *Italy's "Southern Question."*

9. The foundational text for this vision of Brazil is Euclides da Cunha's *Os sertões*, first published in 1902, and translated into English (1957) by Samuel Putnam as *Rebellion in the Backlands*. It has been reiterated by many scholars and journalists since, including Jacques Lambert, *Os dois Brasis*. Throughout I will be using the more familiar term "Nordeste," but during the period under discussion the more common term was "Norte."

10. Among the many fine monographs on colonial São Paulo, see especially Monteiro, *Negros da terra*; Metcalf, *Family and Frontier in Colonial Brazil*; and Blaj, *Trama das tensões*.

11. For a fuller discussion of the changing layout and ongoing transformation of the city of São Paulo, see Saes, "São Paulo republicana," 226–234.

12. On representations of the Nordeste as a region of misery and mayhem, see Sarzynski, "Revolutionizing Identities"; see also Albuquerque, *A invenção do Nordeste e outras artes*; and Blake, *The Vigorous Core of Our Nationality*.

13. For example, a mass-market paperback (published in 1984 in São Paulo in the

popular "What is . . . ?" series), Garcia, *O que é o Nordeste brasileiro?*, included a drawing (p. 65) of a decrepit-looking northeastern rural figure.

14. Fan, "Uneven Development and Beyond." Fan argues that Chinese economic planners in the 1990s, inspired by Hirschman, adopted economic policies and incentives that deliberately heightened regional inequalities.

15. Gramsci, "Notes on the Southern Question," esp. 71; "The Southern Question," 28–51.

16. Hirschman, *The Strategy of Economic Development*, 185.

17. The indigenous "element" in Brazilian identity in the nineteenth century tended either to be erased or idealized. See Sommer, "*O Guaraní* and *Iracema*."

18. There is an immense literature on Brazilian reception and appropriation of scientific-racist ideas. Leading studies include Schwarcz, *The Spectacle of the Races*; and Skidmore, *Black into White*.

19. Pereira, in *O Brasil e a raça*, critiqued claims by Gobineau, Buckle, Bryan, and Lapouge that doomed Brazil to backwardness due to its racial composition. Yet even Pereira, who explicitly rejected biologically based racial difference, accepted the notion of European cultural superiority.

20. On the transnational politics of whiteness in this period, see Lake and Reynolds, *Drawing the Global Colour Line*.

21. Pereira, *O Brasil e a raça*, 31.

22. Stepan, "*The Hour of Eugenics*"; Alberto, *Terms of Inclusion*; Seigel, *Uneven Encounters*.

23. Woodard, "Of Slaves and Citizens"; Costa, "The Myth of Racial Democracy."

24. On the particular challenges faced by paulistas of African descent during the period of slave emancipation, see Xavier, *A conquista da liberdade*; Alberto, *Terms of Inclusion*; Domingues, *A Nova Abolição*; Butler, *Freedoms Given, Freedoms Won*; and Andrews, *Blacks and Whites in São Paulo, Brazil*.

25. On the "homem cordial" see Holanda, *Raízes do Brasil*, 106–107.

26. David Bushnell refers to Colombia as a "nation in spite of itself." *The Making of Modern Colombia*. Frank Safford's national history is tellingly entitled *Colombia: Fragmented Land, Divided Society*. Despite the strong tradition of seeing its "natural" physical diversity as the cause of its disunity, recent Colombian historiography has begun to critique this geographic-determinist approach. See Múnera, *El fracaso de la nación*; Serje, *El revés de la nación*; and Appelbaum, *Muddied Waters*.

27. Geographic determinism and its regionalizing implications can be found in classic Brazilian works as different as Euclides da Cunha's *Os sertões* (1902) and Caio Prado Jr.'s *Formação do Brasil contemporáneo* (1942).

28. As Steve J. Stern notes, "Narrowing the unit of analysis down to a specific region or locale enabled one to explore the problems of human agency and domination historically and specifically." "Between Tragedy and Promise," 36.

29. The many regional studies of the Mexican Revolution are, for the most part, symptomatic of this approach to regionalism. See, for example, Wasserman, *Persistent Oligarchs*; and LaFrance, *Revolution in Mexico's Heartland*. Even Alan Knight's magisterial study of the Mexican Revolution uses regional difference mainly to map broad variations in political culture. *The Mexican Revolution*. For a different approach to

Mexican regionalism that treats region as, in part, a cultural construct, see Lomnitz-Adler, *Exits from the Labyrinth*. For a critique of the "whole is the sum of its parts" approach to region and nation, see Oliven, *A parte e o todo*, especially chapter 2.

30. Studies of Brazilian regions as geopolitical entities include Love, *Rio Grande do Sul and Brazilian Regionalism*; Wirth, *Minas Gerais in the Brazilian Federation*; Levine, *Pernambuco in the Brazilian Federation*; Love, *São Paulo in the Brazilian Federation*; Pang, *Bahia in the First Brazilian Republic*; Lewin, *Politics and Parentela in Paraíba*; and Gomes, *Regionalismo e centralização política*. For a review essay on the Love-Levine-Wirth series on regionalism, see Weinstein, "Brazilian Regionalism."

31. See, for example, Love, "A república brasileira."

32. Silva, *República em migalhas*; Silveira, *O regionalismo nordestino*; Weinstein, "Brazilian Regionalism." Similar approaches for the Mexican context can be found in Van Young, *Mexico's Regions*. For a hyper-materialist interpretation of regional conflict, see Zeitlin, *The Civil Wars in Chile*.

33. Harvey, *Spaces of Global Capitalism*, 72–73.

34. Amado, "História e região," 8.

35. Oliveira, "A Questao Regional"; Chaloult, "Regional Differentials and Role of the State."

36. See, for example, Martins, "O Nordeste e a questão regional"; and Pesavento, "História regional e transformação social."

37. Amado, "História e região," 8; Weinstein, "Regional vs. National History." Judith Bieber's work on nineteenth-century Minas Gerais is an excellent example of how regional identity—and a regional elite—take shape within political struggles, rather than inevitably emerging from a particular fragment of territory. *Power, Patronage, and Political Violence*.

38. The foundational text for this shift is Anderson, *Imagined Communities*. For a brilliant discussion of the processes by which India emerged as a bounded national space, see Goswami, *Producing India*. For an intriguing discussion of Brazil along similar lines, see Oliven, *A parte e o todo*, chapter 2.

39. Duara, *Rescuing History from the Nation*, chapter 6. Other studies that underscore this relationship between region and nation include Lebovics, *True France*, esp. chapter 4; Confino, *The Nation as a Local Metaphor*; Waldstreicher, *In the Midst of Perpetual Fetes*, esp. chapter 5; and Radcliffe and Westwood, *Remaking the Nation*.

40. de Luca, *A Revista do Brasil*, 78.

41. Oliveira, "A questão regional." I would also echo Florencia Mallon's point that there is "no single 'real' version" of nationalism. *Peasant and Nation*, 4.

42. González Casanova, "Internal Colonialism and National Development."

43. The decade of the 1970s was the heyday of internal colonialism studies. See, among others, Hechter, *Internal Colonialism*; Havens and Flinn, *Internal Colonialism and Structural Change in Colombia*; Zureik, *The Palestinians in Israel*; and Blauner, "Internal Colonialism and Ghetto Revolt." In July 1979 an entire issue of the new journal *Ethnic and Racial Studies* (vol. 2, no. 3) was devoted to articles on internal colonialism, including studies of Alaska, Eastern Finland, Austria-Hungary, Brittany, Quebec, and southern Italy.

44. Chaloult, "Regional Differentials." Chaloult insists (p. 58) that "racial-cultural

heterogeneity is not substantially relevant in the Brazilian regional relationships, although there are racial groups in the society. In other words, the social groups in the two regions are not necessarily of different racial or cultural origin." Although I would agree that standardized racial categories might confirm his contention, I would also claim that racial categories defy standardization, and that identities are racialized in ways that do not register within fixed categories.

45. Appelbaum, *Muddied Waters*, 4; see also Wade, *Blackness and Race Mixture*. On the racialization of regional identity in Cochabamba versus the altiplano region of La Paz, see Gotkowitz, *A Revolution for Our Rights*, 11–12.

46. Said, *Orientalism*; in response to criticisms of his over-dichotomization of imperial power and colonial subjects, Said refined certain aspects of his central argument in *Culture and Imperialism*. See also Burke and Prochaska, *Genealogies of Orientalism*, especially the chapters by Nicholas B. Dirks and Ella Shohat; and Schneider, *Italy's "Southern Question."*

47. Even as we critique internal colonialism's tendency toward economic determinism, it would be problematic to dismiss the relationship between colonialism and expropriation of material resources. On this point see Sinha, *Colonial Masculinity*, 3.

48. See Appelbaum, "Whitening the Region," and the essays in Schneider, *Italy's "Southern Question."* It should also be noted that the phrase "internal colonialism" continues to be used in post-1980s theoretical and historical works, but typically in a way that approximates what I am here calling internal orientalism. See, for example, Rivera Cusicanqui, "La Raíz."

49. Thus when wishing to heighten claims to exceptionalism, paulistas draw a contrast with the Northeast, rather than Minas Gerais or Rio Grande do Sul. Within Europe, Eastern Europe blurred the lines between the West and the Orient, though its alleged backwardness could also serve to heighten the exceptionalism of "Western" Europe. See the pathbreaking work of Larry Wolff, *Inventing Eastern Europe*.

50. On regionalism as a subaltern identity, see Bourdieu, "Identity and Representation," 221–223. A classic example of self-racialized region-based subalternity is the polemical autobiography of a self-styled Quebecois terrorist, Vallières, *White Niggers of America*. Some regionalist movements can draw on historical experiences to combine a sense of subalternity and superiority—for example, the case of Catalonia in Spain. Michael Hechter (*Internal Colonialism*, xix) groups Catalonia with Scotland as examples of regional cum national identities that highlight prosperity and exceptional industry. Within Latin America, another example would be *antioqueño* identity in Colombia. Wade, *Blackness and Race Mixture*, 73–78.

51. For early representations of Brazil as a racially fluid or "mixed" society, see Seigel, "Beyond Compare"; and Lima, *Cores, marcas e falas*.

52. Freyre, *Casa-Grande e senzala*.

53. Seigel, *Uneven Encounters*, 221. See also Araújo, *Guerra e paz*.

54. For different arguments about Freyre's source of inspiration, see Vianna, *The Mystery of Samba*, chapter 6, and Needell, "Identity, Race, Gender, and Modernity in the Origins of Gilberto Freyre's *Oeuvre*."

55. Again it is important to emphasize that whiteness constituted a major resource

in the construction of hierarchies throughout Brazil. On whiteness in Rio de Janeiro, see Dávila, *Diploma of Whiteness*.

56. Freyre, *Manifesto regionalista de 1926*; on Freyre and modernity, see Oliven, *O parte e o todo*, chapter 2. Oliven notes that the manifesto, which Freyre read aloud in the Primeiro Congresso Brasileiro de Regionalismo (Recife, 1926), wasn't published until 1952, and thus the print version may present some elements that were not in the original oral presentation.

57. For a statistically based analysis of the real-world extent and limits of Freyre's vision of the plantation household, see Barickman, "Revisiting the Casa-Grande."

58. On "Gilberto Freyre and São Paulo," see the articles in part 2 (pp. 121–221) in Falcão and Araújo, *O imperador das idéias*.

59. For an interesting discussion of the compatibility between the Freyrean interpretation of Brazilian "reality" and the project of conservative modernization, see Mitchell, "Miguel Reale and the Impact of Conservative Modernization."

60. Freyre, "Prefácio à primeira edição," in *Casa-Grande e senzala*, lvi–lvii.

61. On racial democracy as a discourse of modernity, see Gomes and Domingues, "Raça, pós-emancipação, cidadania e modernidade no Brasil."

62. There's no sign of such ambivalence in his earliest work. In his master's thesis, published in 1922 in an issue of the *Hispanic American Historical Review*, he claimed that "slavery in Brazil was anything but cruel. The Brazilian slave lived the life of a cherub [sic] if we contrast his lot with that of the English and other European factory-workers." Quoted in Blake, *The Vigorous Core of Our Nationality*, 192.

63. The publication of Freyre's major study of "luso-tropicalismo," *O mundo que o português criou*, coincided with the Exposição do Mundo Português in Lisbon in 1940 and inaugurated Freyre's role as an official apologist for Portuguese colonialism in Africa. Williams, *Culture Wars in Brazil*, 247–249.

64. On the absence of the phrase "racial democracy" in *Casa-Grande e senzala*, see Vianna, "A meta mitológica da democracia racial," 215–221. Vianna uses this absence to argue that Freyre—and by extension, Brazilian intellectuals—never took literally the idea of Brazil as a racial democracy. If we pose the question in such narrow terms, Vianna's claim is beyond dispute but of limited utility.

65. For an early and oft-invoked denunciation of the "myth of racial democracy," see Nascimento, "Inaugurando o Congresso do Negro," 1, cited in Alberto, *Terms of Inclusion*, 11–12.

66. For more nuanced discussions of the idea of Brazil as a racial democracy, see Alberto, *Terms of Inclusion*, especially 14–17; Caulfield, "Interracial Courtship in the Rio de Janeiro Courts"; McCann, *Hello, Hello Brazil*; Sheriff, *Dreaming Equality*; Maio, "Tempo controverso"; Winant, "Racial Democracy and Racial Identity"; and Guimarães, *Classes, raças e democracia*.

67. For different approaches to the persistence of racism in everyday life, see Twine, *Racism in a Racial Democracy*; and Telles, *Race in Another America*.

68. This despite paulistas' celebration of modern elements in African aesthetics (Vianna, *Mystery of Samba*, 70). For the broader transnational context, see Gilroy, *Black Atlantic*, 2, and Stam and Shohat, *Race in Translation*, 175–238.

69. Mitchell, "Miguel Reale and the Impact of Conservative Modernization," 116–137.

70. De Luca, *A Revista do Brasil*, 280.

71. Gomes, *Essa gente do Rio*, 48. Mário de Andrade, in a retrospective account of the modernist movement, claimed that it started in São Paulo rather than Rio because the latter was an "imperial city," oriented toward Europe (and implicitly static), whereas the former was an "imperialist city" (and explicitly dynamic). Cited in Morse, "The Multiverse of Latin American Identity," 19.

72. "Os negrinhos do Rio desgostam S. Paulo," 53–57. This article was an appropriately indignant response to an editorial that Mesquita Filho published in *O Estado de São Paulo* (January 5, 1965) dismissing Governor Carlos Lacerda's claim that Rio was Brazil's cultural capital. My thanks to Paula Halperin for bringing this article to my attention.

73. Many important scholarly works on Rio de Janeiro treat it as a synecdoche for the nation—conclusions drawn about Rio are assumed to apply to Brazil as a whole. For a work that consciously constructs its argument around the equivalence of Rio and the Brazilian nation, see Vianna, *The Mystery of Samba*.

74. De Luca, *A Revista do Brasil*, chapter 5.

75. For an insightful discussion of the relationship between provincial intellectuals and the "corte," see Lazzari, "Entre a grande e a pequena pátria." The correspondence between Antonio de Alcântara Machado and Rodrigo Mello Franco de Andrade (a Minas-born journalist and cultural critic) provides an interesting window on Rio as an intellectual crossroads for Brazilian men of letters from various parts of the nation. Coleção Antonio de Alcântara Machado, Instituto de Estudos Brasileiros (São Paulo), December 15, 1931; February 1, 1933.

76. Vianna, *The Mystery of Samba*, 67–73.

77. Rodrigo Mello Franco to Alcântara Machado, Col. Arquivo Antonio de Alcântara Machado, Instituto de Estudos Brasileiros, December 15, 1931.

78. A sample of these lectures can be found in Centro Paulista, *São Paulo e a sua evolução* (1927).

79. "Os Negrinhos do Rio Desgostam S. Paulo," 53–57. My thanks to Paula Halperin for bringing this article to my attention.

80. Thus Paulo Duarte, in a pair of articles on what he regarded as the declining significance of blackness in Brazilian life, argued that most Brazilian cities, including Rio and Bahia, were (like São Paulo) becoming predominantly white. Duarte, "Negros do Brasil." In the second segment of the article, Duarte claimed (without evidence) that "there is perhaps no city in Brazil where the black or mulatto population is numerically superior to the white." "Negros do Brasil," 5.

81. Vianna, *The Mystery of Samba*, 70.

82. Sevcenko, *Orfeu extático na metrópole*, 295–296.

83. While I agree with Barbara J. Fields that talk of "race" typically serves to shift our attention away from racism, I think analytically collapsing the two categories has the (unintended) effect of making "racism" ahistorical. Fields, "Whiteness, Racism, and Identity," 48–56.

84. Gilroy, "One Nation under a Groove," 357.

85. A particularly compelling discussion of this problem can be found in Wade,

Race and Ethnicity in Latin America. On the limits of the culturalist "rupture," see Martínez-Echazábal, "O culturalismo dos anos 30 no Brasil e na América Latina," 107–124. On biology, culture, and national identities, see Appelbaum, Macpherson, and Rosemblatt, "Introduction," 1–31.

86. AmCham-São Paulo, *Paulista,* third quarter (1930): 3.

87. Schwarz, *Misplaced Ideas.*

88. The foundational text for the concept of popular liberalism is Mallon, *Peasant and Nation.*

89. Unsurprisingly, São Paulo and Pará, centers of the era's two leading export booms (coffee and rubber), were strongholds of liberal-federalist sentiment. Love, *São Paulo in the Brazilian Federation,* 240–266; and Weinstein, *The Amazon Rubber Boom,* 99–109.

90. Here I am borrowing Tulio Halperin Donghi's famous remark about Argentina. See Halperin Donghi, "Argentina," 99–116.

91. On the extent and limits of popular participation in the formal political sphere in São Paulo under the First Republic, see Prado, *A democracia ilustrada;* and Woodard, *A Place in Politics.*

92. For an excellent sample of the print and visual materials produced, see Camargo, org., *São Paulo, 1932.*

93. This well-known "gauge" of national feeling, here transposed to the regional context, is from Anderson, *Imagined Communities,* 7.

94. Blurb (cover flap) for Hilton, *A guerra civil brasileira.* The blurb acknowledges this view but questions it, as does Hilton.

95. Brubaker and Cooper, "Beyond 'Identity.'"

96. Brubaker and Cooper, "Beyond 'Identity,'" 27.

97. Brubaker and Cooper, "Beyond 'Identity,'" 27.

98. Daphne Patai, in *Brazilian Women Speak,* offers the most striking example of this when two sisters raised in the same household but of different "phenotype" discuss how they suffered racial stereotyping within their own family (10–15).

99. An illuminating example of this process can be found in an interview with a migrant from the North of Brazil that appeared in the film *Viramundo* (1965): "Inside my house I have a television, I have a refrigerator. . . . I like São Paulo very much, I really adore this people, a people who look to the future. I don't consider myself a northerner but rather a paulista and I intend to spend my life here. . . . I will not return to the North because if I went back there, I would be going backwards; therefore, I am in São Paulo and I want to march forward."
Quoted in Fontes, *Um Nordeste em São Paulo,* 77.

100. On the concept of "structures of feeling," see Williams, *Marxism and Literature,* 128–136.

101. Nogueira Filho, *Ideais e lutas de um burguês progressista: A guerra cívica 1932,* [hereafter *A guerra cívica 1932*], vol. 2, Insurreição Civil, 9–10. The final manifesto issued by the insurgent civilian authorities acknowledging the surrender by the state's military forces opened with a claim of unanimity: "In a single impulse, everyone volunteered and organized." Reprinted in Andrade, *Tudo por São Paulo,* 114.

102. Homem, *Lembranças de um belo ideal,* especially 2 and 80.

103. "Gaúcho" refers to Brazilians from Rio Grande do Sul, the southernmost state.

104. Florestan Fernandes declared, in a text written for the Congresso Internacional de Americanistas, which was on the official calendar of events of the IV Centenário, that "the past contains little meaning. What is important is the present and, above all, the future." Cited in Arruda, *Metrópole e cultura*, 30.

Chapter 1: Paulista Modern
Epigraph cited in Adduci, A "*Pátria Paulista*," 129.

1. *O Jornal do Commercio*, Rio, March 14, 1987, cited in Adduci, A "*Pátria Paulista*," 197.

2. One of the first major studies to highlight the role of the slaves' mass "desertions" from the coffee fazendas was Costa, *Da senzala à colônia*, 305–319. See also Toplin, *The Abolition of Slavery in Brazil*; Dean, *Rio Claro*; Machado, *O plano e o pânico*; and Azevedo, *Onda negra, medo branco*.

3. On coffee expansion into the Paulista West, see Costa, *Da senzala à colônia*; and Silva, *Expansão cafeeira*. Some recent work emphasizes the role of smaller estates in the early paulista coffee economy. See Frank, "Wealth Holding in Southeastern Brazil"; and Marcondes, "Small and Medium Slaveholdings in the Coffee Economy."

4. While virtually all studies over the last four decades agree that the paulista planters reluctantly shifted to non-slave labor, there is some disagreement over whether this reluctance was primarily an effect of economic considerations or whether there was a cultural attachment to the prerogatives of slave ownership. Darrell Levi argues for little non-economic commitment to slavery; Emília Viotti da Costa claims that until railways lowered transport costs and world prices rose, wage labor couldn't be employed profitably, whereas Warren Dean disagrees and argues that autocratic fazendeiros clung to slave ownership even though profits could have been sustained with wage labor. Levi, *The Prados of São Paulo*, 73; Dean, *Rio Claro*; Costa, *The Brazilian Empire*, chapter 5.

5. For a brief period around midcentury, Campinas boasted a larger population than the provincial capital. On the Campinas region during this period see Xavier, *A conquista da liberdade*.

6. Many scholars dismiss the very notion of a reality outside those discursive constructions, but here I think we need to consider discourses about the future (or what was the future in 1887), and why they project a certain trajectory. See, for example, Richard Morse's chapter "Coffee . . . and Premonitions," in *From Community to Metropolis*, 111–119. On the history of the future, see "*AHR* Forum." On the political ramifications of the formation of the "coffee complex," see Beiguelman, *A formação do povo no complex cafeeiro*.

7. For two different views of life in the capital prior to the boom of the 1870s, see Morse, *From Community to Metropolis*, 60–104; and Dias, *Power and Everyday Life*.

8. A. Almeida Jr., "A Faculdade de Direito e a cidade"; Morse, *From Community to Metropolis*, 139–165; and Kirkendall, *Class Mates*, 86–88.

9. Saint-Hilaire, *Viagem à provincia de São Paulo*, vii. This phrase had its most notorious iteration in the work of Alfredo Ellis Jr.; see, for example, *Raça de gigantes*.

10. This regional chauvinism seems in line with Homi Bhabha's observation that

challenges to homogeneous national identities emerge from marginal spaces, except that from the outset it was accompanied by assertions of regional superiority. Bhabha, *The Location of Culture*, 149.

11. Saint-Hilaire, *Viagem à província de São Paulo*, 32–33; Blaj, *A trama das tensões*, 47.

12. Ferreira, *A epopéia bandeirante*, 34.

13. Costa, *Da senzala à colônia*, 108–204.

14. Said, *Orientalism*, 2–5.

15. Love, *São Paulo in the Brazilian Federation*, 102–110; Weinstein, *The Amazon Rubber Boom*, 100–109.

16. Dissenting factions in the Liberal Party during the 1860s called for more direct elections, expanded individual rights, (gradual) abolition of slavery, and, increasingly, the abolition of the monarchy and the creation of a republic. See da Costa, *The Brazilian Empire*, 72–75.

17. Love, *São Paulo in the Brazilian Federation*, 106–110.

18. The most detailed discussion of this brief flirtation with separatism can be found in Adduci, *A "Pátria Paulista."* See also Queiroz, "Ufanismo paulista," 78–87.

19. Ferreira, *A epopéia bandeirante*, 24.

20. The concept of ideological work comes from Poovey, *Uneven Developments*.

21. Adduci, *A "Pátria Paulista,"* 65.

22. On the role of São Paulo in the construction of an image of the Nordeste as intractably backward, see Albuquerque, *A invenção do Nordeste*, 57–62. On the ways in which the policies of the late imperial period contributed to growing regional inequalities, see Melo, *O Norte agrário e o império*. For an excellent discussion of Brazilian intellectuals' use of ideas of degeneration, see Borges, "'Puffy, Ugly, Slothful and Inert.'"

23. Bourdieu, "Identity and Representation," 221–223. Emphasis in original.

24. On gaúcho folk culture, see Oliven, *A parte e o todo*, 69–98; on Amazonia, see Slater, *Entangled Edens*; on the Nordeste, see Lima, *Um sertão chamado Brasil*.

25. My thanks to anthropologist Gastón Gordillo, of the University of British Columbia, for making this point in response to an earlier draft of this argument.

26. On caipira culture celebrations, see Lima, *Um sertão chamado Brasil*, 133–154.

27. For a discussion by Gilberto Freyre of the "Clube Caboclo," formed by a circle of paulista intellectuals and politicians during the Old Republic, see *Order and Progress*, 199.

28. de Luca, *A Revista do Brasil*, 62.

29. On Monteiro Lobato's ambivalence regarding caipira culture, see Ferreira, *A epopéia bandeirante*, 217–218, and Lima, *Um sertao chamado Brasil*, 145–164.

30. McClintock, "'No Longer in a Future Heaven,'" 263.

31. Almeida, "São Paulo e o espírito moderno," 107. The lecture was delivered at the Centro Paulista in Rio in 1926 and published the following year.

32. Bourdieu, "Identity and Representation," 220.

33. Among the many studies that discuss this issue, see Skidmore, *Black into White*; and Azevedo *Onda negra, medo branco*.

34. For an excellent overview of the history of immigration (European and non-European) to Brazil, see Lesser, *Immigration, Ethnicity, and National Identity in Brazil*.

See also Andrews, *Blacks and Whites in São Paulo*, especially chapter 2; and Holloway, *Immigrants on the Land*.

35. For a pioneering study that stresses labor supply over whitening, see Hall, "Origins of Mass Immigration in Brazil." See also Beiguelman, "A grande imigração em São Paulo." The Martinho Prado quote appears in Andrews (p. 58).

36. Jacobson, *Whiteness of a Different Color*, 15–38.

37. On the concept of governmentality, see Burchell, Gordon, and Miller, *The Foucault Effect*.

38. On opposition to nonwhite immigrants see Lesser, *Negotiating National Identity*, especially 13–40; Meade and Pirio, "In Search of the Afro-American El Dorado"; T. Gomes, "Problemas no paraíso"; and Gomes, Domingues, and Fagundes, "*Idiossincrasias cromáticas.*"

39. Lesser, *Negotiating National Identity*, 13–40.

40. Meade and Pirio, "In Search of the Afro-American El Dorado," 85–110.

41. For an intriguing discussion of the political implications of German immigration to agricultural colonies in Rio Grande do Sul, see Kittleson, *The Practice of Politics in Postcolonial Brazil*, 46–73.

42. Although he may continue to disagree with me, I thank Michael Hall for his critical comments, which moved me to think through this question more carefully.

43. The subtitle of Jacobson's pathbreaking study *Whiteness of a Different Color* (1999) is *European Immigrants and the Alchemy of Race.*

44. Ferreira, *A epopéia bandeirante*, 69. See also Souza, "Vícios, virtudes e sentimento regional."

45. Rose, "Public Health Situation and Work of the International Health Board in Brazil" (October 25, 1920), Rockefeller Archive Center, Hyde Park, NY, Record Group 5, Series 2, Box 25, Folder 152, p. 8. Emphasis added. Also cited in Marinho, "A presença norte-americana na educação superior brasileira," 65.

46. Two excellent introductions to the immense literature on the bandeirantes are Morse, *The Bandeirantes*; and Monteiro, *Negros da terra*.

47. Quoted in Morse, *The Bandeirantes*, 125.

48. Morse, *The Bandeirantes*, 32; also Gaspar da Madre de Deus, "A Defense of the Paulistas," 92–99, in Morse, *The Bandeirantes*. By far the best discussion of this first wave of bandeirante rehabilitation can be found in Abud, "O sangue intimorato e as nobilíssimas tradições."

49. Dozens of studies on the bandeirantes were authored during the first four decades of the twentieth century. Perhaps the most representative of this historiography were Machado, *Vida e morte do bandeirante*; and Taunay, *História geral das bandeiras paulistas*. Laura de Mello e Souza ("Vícios, virtudes e sentimento regional") describes *Vida e morte* as diverging from the mainstream depiction of the bandeirantes as rich and powerful, but I would argue that by the 1920s the more modest/industrious bandeirante had become the prototypical figure.

50. Oliveira Vianna insisted on the aristocratic character of the leading bandeirantes whereas Alfredo Ellis Júnior highlighted their democratic/egalitarian inclinations. On this debate over the character of the bandeirantes, see Ferretti, "A construção da paulistinidade"; and Ferretti, "O uso político do passado bandeirante."

On the bandeirantes in the separatist-tinged work of Paulo Prado, see Gouveia, *The Triumph of Brazilian Modernism*, 151–161.

51. Ellis, *Evolução da economia paulista*, 35. The leading scholarly study of slavery in colonial São Paulo is Monteiro, *Negros da terra*.

52. Ellis, *Os primeiros troncos paulistas*, 343–350; M. Ellis, "The Bandeiras in the Geographical Expansion of Brazil," 48–63.

53. Morse, *The Bandeirantes*, 24, 36; for a deeply researched reconstruction of rural life in colonial São Paulo, see Metcalf, *Family and Frontier in Colonial Brazil*.

54. Blaj, *A trama das tensões*, 42–54.

55. de Luca, *A Revista do Brasil*, 170.

56. Ferreira, *A epopéia dos bandeirantes*, 68, 146–147.

57. Ferreira, *A epopéia dos bandeirantes*, 147.

58. de Luca, *A Revista do Brasil*, 172. The use of the term *selvagens* here is reminiscent of the "noble savage" trope used in the North American context.

59. Monteiro, "Tupis, Tapuias e história de São Paulo," 127.

60. An excellent discussion of this is Monteiro, "Caçando com gato," 79–88.

61. Queiroz, "Ufanismo Paulista"; Arruda, *Metrópole e cultura*, 74–75. See, especially, the section "Modernos mamelucos," in Ferreira, *A epopéia bandeirante*, 304–327.

62. Andrade, "A guerra de São Paulo."

63. Ellis, *A evolução da economia paulista*, 180.

64. Queiroz, "Ufanismo paulista," 83. In the dedication of his affectionate fictional chronicle of immigrant neighborhoods in São Paulo, António de Alcântara Machado cites "the triumph of the novos mamalucos," and names, among others, Paulo Menotti del Picchia, Víctor Brecheret, Anita Malfatti, Conde Francisco Matarazzo Jr., and Sud Menucci. *Brás, Bexiga e Barra Funda*.

65. For a particularly unflattering but more accurate image of the bandeirante, see Mioto et al., "Apesar da aura mítica, bandeirante era assassino do sertão" (2011).

66. Washington Luís, as prefect (1914–1919), used municipal funds to collect historical documentation. Ferreira, *A epopéia bandeirante*, 114–125.

67. Belmonte, *No tempo dos bandeirantes*, 34.

68. "As armas de S. Paulo," *Revista do Brasil* (April 1917): 505–508.

69. Sevcenko, *Orfeu extático*, 138.

70. Menezes, *Útimas rimas*. "Non Ducor Duco" appears on page 4 of the electronic version.

71. For a critique of the way this national/regional binary has seeped into the historiography of Brazil, see Janotti, "Historiografia," 81–101.

72. Freyre, *New World in the Tropics*, 106–108.

73. "As armas de São Paulo," *Revista do Brasil*, 2, no. 8 (August 1916): 386; the same quote opened the first issue of the *Revista do Instituto Histórico e Geográfico de São Paulo* 1 (1895) 1, cited in Ferreira, *A epopéia bandeirante*, 110. The *visconde* was born in Santos and died in 1847, long before São Paulo had been launched on its upward trajectory.

74. Ellis, "São Paulo e o Brasil-Colonia," 71.

75. Rubens do Amaral, "À Margem da História," in IHGSP, Arquivo da Rev. Consti-

tucionalista de 1932, Recortes de jornais, doc. 25. In defense of the bandeirantes, Amaral noted that they fought against Palmares, "which was a black cyst [quisto negro] capable of shattering national unity."

76. "Factos e Idéias: A terra paulista e as suas grandes legendas," *Revista do Brasil* 2 (July 1916): 272–277; Brazil, *Anais da Camara dos Deputados* 9 (October 11, 1920): 541–542.

77. Brazil, *Anais da Camara dos Deputados* 9 (October 11, 1920): 541–542.

78. de Luca, *A Revista do Brasil*, 78. One of the earliest versions of this argument can be discerned in an article by Maria Lígia Prado, though it still invoked an opposition between region and nation. See "O pensamento conservador paulista," 233–245.

79. de Luca, "O centenário da independência em São Paulo," 136–150.

80. Guerrero, "The Administration of Dominated Populations," 286. An early example (1875), replete with foldout tables, is Godoy, *A província de S. Paulo*. On this mode of representation of "facts," see Poovey, *A History of the Modern Fact*.

81. São Paulo (State), *O Estado de São Paulo: Seu progresso, suas riquezas*.

82. Lobo, *São Paulo na federação*, 7–14; Ellis, *Confederação ou separação*, 113.

83. This oft-repeated saying is usually attributed to the eminent hygienist Arthur Neiva, who was born in Bahia. Nunes, *O patriotismo difícil*, 20.

84. In a similar vein, a theatrical revue written in 1926 by Cornelio Pires (who would later volunteer to fight for the Causa Paulista) entitled "Brasil pitoresco—Viagem de Cornélio Pires ao Norte do Brasil," amused the paulista public with the "picturesque, exotic, strange, ridiculous aspects of their Northern brothers." Latter quote from *O Estado de São Paulo* (OESP), cited in Albuquerque, *A invenção do Nordeste*, 45.

85. See, for example, Paulo Morais Barros, "Impressões do Nordeste," OESP, August 15, 1923, 2; Dionísio Cerqueira, "Impressões de São Paulo," OESP, October 28, 1923, 4; Oliveira Vianna, "Impressões de São Paulo," OESP, February 7, 1924, 6; João Lima Verde, "Impressões de São Paulo," OESP, January 14, 1925, 3. This series is discussed in Albuquerque, *A invenção do Nordeste*, 40–44.

86. "Selling San Paulo Loan Here by Advertising," *Printer's Ink*, April 28, 1921, 42–44, cited in Seigel, *Uneven Encounters*, 56. Seigel incisively notes how this ad exemplifies the "pleasures of ignorance," and the portrayal of condescension as harmless fun.

87. *Revista Nova* 1, no. 1 (March 15, 1931): 5.

88. Caulfield, *In Defense of Honor*, 63–78.

89. Though published in French at the behest of the French consulate, the book was produced in Buenos Aires and overseen by an Argentinian journalist, Manuel Bernardez. *Le Bresil*.

90. Dias, *The Brazil of To-day*, 11, 455.

91. Dias, *The Brazil of To-day*, 458. For a similar set of flattering quotes about São Paulo's progress and promise from visitors ranging from Rudyard Kipling to Stefan Zweig, see Woodard, *A Place in Politics*, 1.

92. Elliott, *Brazil Today and Tomorrow*, 265.

93. Vasconcelos, *La raza cosmica*, 65.

94. Vasconcelos, *La raza cosmica*, 73–74.

95. Vasconcelos, *La raza cosmica*, 77.

96. Jiménez de Asúa, *Un viaje al Brasil*. My thanks to Marc Hertzman for bring this source to my attention.

97. Jiménez de Asúa, *Un viaje al Brasil*, 122–127.

98. Jiménez de Asúa, *Un viaje al Brasil*, 131–132. The "revolution" the author refers to is almost certainly the 1924 *tenente* uprising. The classic study of the revolt is Corrêa, *A rebelião de 1924 em São Paulo*. For an important reinterpretation of the revolt see Woodard, *A Place in Politics*, 108–142.

99. Jiménez de Asúa, *Un viaje al Brasil*, 132.

100. Pereira, *O Brasil e a raça*, 54–55, 62; Velloso, "A brasilidade verde-amarela," 89–112.

101. On the Liga Nacionalista, see Woodard, *A Place in Politics*, 74–76; and Silvia Levi-Moreira, "Ideologia e atuação da Liga Nacionalista," 67–74.

102. For an intriguing discussion of this trend, see Vianna, *The Mystery of Samba*, 10–31.

103. Woodard, *A Place in Politics*, 75.

104. On the tendency throughout Latin America to interpret eugenics/racial improvement through a Lamarckian/environmental lens, see Stepan, *"The Hour of Eugenics."*

105. Sevcenko, *Orfeu extático*, 138.

106. Ferreira, *A epopéia bandeirante*, 270–284; the Mário de Andrade quote is from de Luca, "O centenário," 8.

107. de Luca, "O centenário," 3.

108. Blaj, "O paulista enquanto construtor da nação," 16–19.

109. Ferreira, *A epopéia bandeirante*, 276–277. Most of the foregoing account of the bicentennial celebrations in São Paulo is derived from this source.

110. Ferreira, *A epopéia bandeirante*, 282.

111. De Luca rightly notes that the centennial commemorations have been obscured in the scholarly literature by all the attention to Modern Art Week that same year. "O centenário," 2–3.

112. A classic account of Modern Art Week is Morse, *From Community to Metropolis*, 260–270. See also the discussion of Brazilian modernism in Morse, "The Multiverse of Latin American Identity," 17–26. For a more recent study that nonetheless relies on historical sources that are several decades old, see Gouveia, *The Triumph of Brazilian Modernism*.

113. Velloso, "A brasilidade verde-amarela," 18.

114. Gomes, *Essa gente do Rio*, 48.

115. Gomes, *Essa gente do Rio*, 49.

116. Gomes, *Essa gente do Rio*, 49.

117. Moraes, *Correspondência Mário de Andrade e Manuel Bandeira*, 138 (emphasis in original).

118. Moraes, *Correspondência Mário de Andrade e Manuel Bandeira*, 62, 66; Velloso, "A brasilidade verde-amarelo," 5.

119. Mário de Andrade, "Notas de Arte," *A Gazeta*, February 13, 1922, cited in de Luca, "O centenário," 11–12 (paper). The use of the term "Court" (Corte) for Rio was

both anachronistic and deliberate—it reinforced a sense of Rio as more patrimonial and less modern than São Paulo.

120. Moraes, *Correspondência*, 201.

121. Borges, *Tenentismo e revolução brasileira*, 18.

122. The most virulent radical critic of paulista chauvinism was *A Plebe*, which referred to the 1932 uprising as an "abomination" and as "those cursed and horrendous three months of war, of counter-revolution and of unspeakable violence." It also dismissed the very notion of paulista identity in a region whose population was of such diverse origins. "O ano terrível de 1932," *A Plebe*, January 7, 1933, 2; "Um patriota," *A Plebe*, March 4, 1933, 3.

123. On disputed versions of paulista identity, see Woodard, "Regionalismo paulista e política partidária nos anos vinte," 41–56.

124. Prado, *A democracia ilustrada*, 158–172; Woodard, *A Place in Politics*, 32–70.

125. Here I am borrowing the very useful category of "near elites" from Roger Kittleson (*The Practice of Politics in Postcolonial Brazil*).

126. On the early dissidências in the PRP, see Levi-Moreira, "Liberalismo e democracia na dissidência república paulista."

127. On the shifting social base of the PRP, see Decca, *1930: O silêncio dos vencidos*, 135–182; and Weinstein, *For Social Peace in Brazil*, 13–50.

128. On the mainstream press in São Paulo during this period, see Capelato, *Os arautos do liberalismo*.

129. The study referred to here is Woodard, *A Place in Politics*. For an uncritical use of the term "oligarchy," see Cerri, "NON DUCOR, DUCO."

130. Love, *São Paulo in the Brazilian Federation*, 138–145.

131. Woodard, *A Place in Politics*, 126. Hilda Sábato makes a similar point about electoral participation in Argentina in the late nineteenth century. See *The Many and the Few*.

132. Woodard, *A Place in Politics*, 58. Vavy Pacheco Borges discusses the tenentes' use of the term "oligarchies" in a similar vein. *Tenentismo e revolução brasileira*, 140–144.

133. On the legitimating effect of public service, especially for the generation of the 1920s–1930s, see Mehrtens, *Urban Space and National Identity*, 98–109. A prominent figure in the Partido Democrático (PD) claimed that a law for the secret ballot would be the equivalent of a "13th of May [date of abolition of slavery] for whites." Mario Pinto Serva, "A Redempção dos Brancos," in *Problemas Brasileiros*, 235.

134. See Borges, *Tenentismo e revolução brasileira*, 27–32.

135. Corrêa, *A rebelião de 1924*; and Woodard, *A Place in Politics*, chapter 4. The "Prestes" invoked here is not the Republican politician but Luiz Carlos Prestes, the famed tenente leader and future general secretary of the Brazilian Communist Party.

136. Boris Fausto, "Apresentação," v–xxxi, in Paulo Duarte, *Agora nós!*

137. Woodard, *A Place in Politics*, 112–113.

138. Quotation in Fausto, "Apresentação," xxx–xxxi, in Paulo Duarte, *Agora nós!*

139. Fausto, "Apresentação," xxxi, in Paulo Duarte, *Agora nós!*

140. Fausto, *A revolução de 1930*, 32–38; Love, *São Paulo in the Brazilian Federation*, 164–168.

141. Prado, *A democracia ilustrada*, 172–174.

142. My discussion here comes almost entirely from Woodard, *A Place in Politics*, chapter 5.

143. Woodard, *A Place in Politics*, 126–127.

144. Pereira, *Pelo Brasil Maior*, 347.

145. Prado, *A democracia ilustrada*, 56–96; Woodard, *A Place in Politics*, chapter 5.

146. Woodard, *A Place in Politics*, 198.

147. Woodard, *A Place in Politics*, 190–191.

148. Paula, *1932*, 48–53. The photos in question, original and retouched, are on page 49.

149. Love, *São Paulo in the Brazilian Federation*, 50–52.

150. On the process by which the formerly fierce rivals, the PD and the PRP, gradually allied following the Revolution of 1930, see Prado, *A democracia ilustrada*, 123–133. Piratininga was reputedly the indigenous name for the locale that the Portuguese renamed "São Paulo dos Campos de Piratininga." As the regional movement intensified, the use of this indigenous name became more common.

Chapter 2: Constituting Paulista Identity

Epigraph. An annotated but still unpublished version of Mário de Andrade's "Guerra de São Paulo" has been edited by Angela Maria Gonçalves da Costa, Faculdade de Filosofia, Letras, e Ciências Humanas, Universidade de São Paulo. The quote appears on page 14 of that version.

1. Jardim, *A aventura de outubro*, 280–281.

2. For a narrative of the escalating momentum toward revolt, see Leite, *Martírio e glória de São Paulo*, 48.

3. Costa, *1932*, 1.

4. Osório, *A guerra de São Paulo, 1932*, 18.

5. Borges, *Getúlio Vargas e a oligarquia paulista*; Capelato and Prado, *O bravo matutino*, 34–40.

6. Weinstein, *For Social Peace in Brazil*, 58.

7. On the reception of Vargas in São Paulo as he made his way to the federal capital, see Paula, *1932*, 75–84.

8. By far the best discussion of the paulista Republicans' frustrated enthusiasm for Ruy Barbosa's presidential campaigns can be found in Woodard, *A Place in Politics*, 63–70, 93–104.

9. Even a paulista in the presidency did not ensure that federal policies would advance paulista elites' financial interests. Both Campos Sales and Washington Luís adopted economic policies that were somewhat controversial in their home state. See Topik, *The Political Economy of the Brazilian State*.

10. On Miguel Costa and the Revolutionary Legion of São Paulo, see Borges, *Tenentismo e revolução brasileira*, 63–108.

11. The two best accounts by witnesses of the events leading up to the armed conflict are Leite, *Martírio e glória*, vol. 1; and Nogueira Filho, *A guerra cívica—1932*, 4 vols.

12. General Klinger did bring some troops and arms from the western state of Mato Grosso, but support from this thinly populated state was inconsequential. Hilton, *A guerra civil brasileira*, 107–110.

13. National Archives and Records Administration (NARA), RG59, M1472, Reel 7 (Revolutions): Morgan, Rio de Janeiro, July 10, 1932, "Political Situation in Brazil."

14. It is interesting to note that Vargas himself occasionally referred to his regime as the *ditadura* during these years. Vargas, *Diário*, vol. 1.

15. In the 1950s, historian Aureliano Leite compiled a list of all publications on the 1932 uprising and printed it in *A Gazeta*, July 9, 1957, 27; more recently Jeziel de Paula appended an updated list of 272 publications on 1932 in his book *1932: Imagens construindo a história*.

16. For an excellent discussion of the way in which the relationship between Vargas and the paulistas has shaped the Brazilian historiography, see Woodard, "'All for São Paulo, All for Brazil,'" 83–108. For an insightful overview of the historiography of 1932, see Rodrigues, *1932 Pela força da tradição*, 24–44.

17. Hilton, *A guerra civil brasileira*. For more insight into the military aspects of the conflict, see McCann, *Soldiers of the Pátria*.

18. For a study that stresses elite manipulation of popular sentiment, see Bezerra, *O jogo do poder*. Other studies of 1932 that emphasize elite interests and concerns about the rise of labor militancy and Communist influence within the working class include Capelato, *O movimento de 1932*; and Borges, *Getúlio Vargas e a oligarquia paulista*; and *Tenentismo e revolução brasileira*.

19. da Costa, *1932*, 1.

20. FGV, CPDOC, GVc 1932.08.28, r2f0925–0932. Emphasis in the original. Góes, at the time the most influential military figure in Vargas's inner circle, called the paulistas "incomplete Brazilians, who have lost national sentiment." His opinions would become even harsher after September 1, when his brother Cícero, a major in the army, was killed in battle.

21. This phrase is from the cover flaps of Hilton, *A guerra civil brasileira*, but is used as an example of an oversimplified (and overly materialist) interpretation that Hilton contests.

22. Burns, *A History of Brazil*, 294.

23. Again, the best example of this view can be found in Bezerra, *O jogo do poder*. For a study that emphasizes the role of anticommunist sentiment within the paulista elite, see Borges, *Tenentismo e revolução brasileira*, 177–220.

24. Hilton, *A guerra civil brasileira*; Silva, *1932*.

25. For an excellent discussion of the role of "sincerity" in the construction of the modern self, see Martin, "Inventing Sincerity, Refashioning Prudence."

26. This was the motivation that I highlighted when I discussed the paulista industrialists' support for the 1932 uprising. See Weinstein, *For Social Peace in Brazil*, 62–63. But mainstream political figures, intellectuals, and journalists in São Paulo had long discussed and endorsed the idea of labor reforms that would reduce the incidence of class conflict, so that Vargas's proto-populist tendencies would not automatically cause a uniform rejection of the new regime. See Weinstein, "Impressões da elite sobre os movimentos da classe operária."

27. I am certainly not the first historian to make such a contention. In the documentary *1932: A guerra civil* (1992), historian Boris Fausto similarly insists that the mistreatment of "São Paulo" by the Vargas regime, and the appointment as interventor

of someone whom paulistas saw as "a little tenente of no importance" [um tenentinho qualquer] were "what explains this galvanization, that sensation of profound injustice and profound duty in the name of Brazil that traversed the population. Without this sentiment, without this type of attitude, the mobilization would be inexplicable."

28. Burns, *A History of Brazil*, 294. In a meeting with Vargas in 1937, Waldemar Ferreira, who was a member of the insurgent cabinet, claimed that it was the military that had unleashed the uprising, and that the civilian politicians supported it under threat of being deposed if they refused. Vargas, *Diário*, vol. 2, 27. Recent works have put more emphasis on mass support for the uprising. See, for example, Paula, *1932*, and Rodrigues, *1932 pela força da tradição*, chapter 2.

29. Sevcenko, *Literatura como missão*, 140.

30. Wickliffe Rose, "Public Health Situation and Work of International Health Board in Brazil," 8, Rockefeller Foundation Archive, cited in Blake, *The Vigorous Core of Our Nationality*, 105.

31. Sevcenko, *Literatura como missão*, 124.

32. On regional identity as an "arm of combat," see Rodrigues, *1932 pela força da tradição*, 141–165.

33. On the paulista press in this era, see Capelato, *Os arautos do liberalismo*; Capelato and Prado, *O bravo matutino*; and Woodard, *A Place in Politics*, especially chapter 3. On the influential paulista journal, *Revista do Brasil*, see de Luca, *A Revista do Brasil*.

34. Nearly every anniversary of the uprising brings a revelation of an unpublished memoir or diary. The July 9, 2013, issue of *O Estadão* (a commonly used nickname for *O Estado de São Paulo*) quoted various entries in the recently discovered combat diary of Aurélio Stievani, who fought in the second platoon of the Batalhão Universitário Paulista. "O diário de um combatente de 1932," OESP, July 9, 2013, A17.

35. On the "sonic" aspects of the Constitutionalist Campaign, see Tota, *A locomotiva no ar*.

36. Mário de Andrade, for example, retrospectively reflected on the way in which diverse media gradually created a false sense of "unanimity." "A guerra de São Paulo," 5. The quote in the text is from Luiz Gonzaga Naclério Homem, who recalled being hesitant to enlist but being influenced by the superheated atmosphere created by the constant propaganda in favor of mobilizing against the Vargas regime. *Lembranças de um belo ideal*, 2.

37. The narration in the documentary film *1932: A guerra civil* (1992) stresses the role of a relatively new "mass culture" in the mobilization, but does not equate this with manipulation.

38. There is some irony in the decision of Lindolfo Collor and several other leading gaúcho politicians to break with Vargas and support the paulistas purportedly because of the tenente attack on the *Diário Carioca*, an opposition newspaper in Rio, since any publication deemed too pro-Vargas suffered the same fate in São Paulo. NARA, RG59, 832.00, Reel 7, "Military Attaché Report: Disorder in São Paulo," May 26, 1932, refers (p. 2) to the sacking of the offices of the paulista newspapers *Razão* and *Correio da Tarde*, which were viewed as too sympathetic to Miguel Costa's Partido Popular Paulista.

39. On the "reconciliation of old enemies," see Prado, *A democracia ilustrada*, 123–133.

40. Carvalho, *O clero solidário com o povo em*, 32. The Instituto Histórico e Geográfico de São Paulo published this volume as part of a "Curso de Historia da revoluçao Constitucionalista de 32" offered on the occasion of the uprising's twenty-fifth anniversary.

41. Carvalho, *A guerra civil de 1932 em São Paulo*, 54; Tota, *A locomotiva no ar*, 97–105. Many of the key manifestos and decrees were broadcast by the twenty-two-year-old César Ladeira, who would eventually become one of the most recognizable radio voices in all of Brazil.

42. Leite, *Martirio e glória*, 48. This is a frequent theme in reminiscences. Linguist Francisco Ribeiro Sampaio, in a speech to the Rotary Club of Campinas in 1975, insisted repeatedly that 1932 "was not the work of politicians . . . as the dictatorship declared in its radio broadcasts. . . . It was not the politicians, but all the people." *Renembranças*, 213.

43. Leite (*Martírio e glória*, 48) claims that fear of popular retaliation forced Marrey and others to join the movement.

44. A left-wing anti-Constitutionalist manifesto issued by "Regional Committees of São Paulo, of the Communist Party and Communist Youth," and addressed to "Men and Women Workers, Peasants, Students and Poor Intellectuals, Youth, Soldiers and Sailors!" claimed that workers who refused to volunteer were being beaten up and abused. Museu Paulista, Coleção Revolução 1932, Doc. 2766.

45. NARA, RG59, M1472, Reel 7 (Revolutions): Morgan, Rio de Janeiro, July 10, 1932, "Political Situation in Brazil." This report claimed that both sides were broadcasting lies and exaggerations about the conflict, but São Paulo even more so than the federal government.

46. On Ibrahim Nobre see Donato, *A revolução de 32*, 62.

47. Picchia, *A revolução paulista*, 42; also cited in Silva, *1932*, 113.

48. For a wonderful collection of popular poetry (wonderful for its historical value, not its literary merits) submitted to the *Diário Nacional* in 1932, see Andrade, "A guerra de São Paulo," appendix. Here I would cite the now well-known objections expressed by Gayatri C. Spivak to the historian's effort to "give voice" to the subaltern. "Can the Subaltern Speak?"

49. Interview with veteran, *A respeito do Movimento Constitucionalista de 1932*, documentary film; Loureiro Junior, *São Paulo Vencido*, chapter "Desorganizacao Militar," 22–36. For a particularly bitter commentary see Mello, *Renda-se, paulista!*, 3. After extolling nearly every aspect of the war effort, he goes on to claim that "São Paulo lost because the men who promoted the war knew beforehand that neither they nor their sons would be going [to the front]."

50. This is more or less the perspective of Mário de Andrade in "A guerra de São Paulo," xxxix; see also *Cartas Mário de Andrade/Oneyda Alvarenga*, 30.

51. Penteado, "Paulistas no 'Front,'" *O Inevitável*.

52. For an excellent discussion of the role of constitutionalism in the construction of narratives and memories about the 1932 uprising, see Rodrigues, *1932 pela força da tradição*, especially 329–411. Rodrigues emphasizes the consolidation of the designation "Constitutionalist Revolution" in the subsequent "battle for the memory" of the uprising. Here I am accentuating it as a major theme even during the uprising

itself, though I would agree that it does not become the standard designation until the period after the uprising.

53. On the electoral system of the Old Republic, see Carone, *A república velha*.

54. Prado, *A democracia ilustrada*, 97–114. A political cartoon by popular caricaturist Belmonte, which appeared shortly before the uprising, shows Vargas dismissing the idea of a constitution because "its only purpose is to be violated by politicos." This elicits a response from "Juca" suggesting that then, perhaps, Brazil should abolish its criminal code, since "its only purpose is to be violated by criminals." The original appeared in *A Folha da Noite*, April 6, 1932; reproduced in Donato, *A revolução de 32*, 73.

55. Love, *São Paulo in the Brazilian Federation*; and *Rio Grande do Sul and Brazilian Regionalism*; Levine, *Pernambuco in the Brazilian Federation*; Wirth, *Minas Gerais in the Brazilian Federation*.

56. The opposition paper was the *Diário Carioca*. Vargas, *Diário*, vol. 1, 32, n.7.

57. Prado, *A democracia ilustrada*, 123–133.

58. Arquivo Público do Estado de São Paulo (APESP), Col. 32, Caixa 64, Pasta 360B, Doc. 900.

59. Acervo B. Klinger, Fundação Getúlio Vargas, CPDOC, 1932.05.22/433; Nogueira Filho, *A guerra cívica*, vol. 2, 26.

60. As Angela Castro Gomes has shown, May Day rallies became more orderly under Vargas in part because workers stopped being attacked and harassed by the police. *A invenção do trabalhismo*, 235.

61. Letter to Klinger, FGV, CPDOC, 1932.05.22/433; "Um grande espectáculo de civismo paulista," *A Folha da Noite*, February 24, 1932, 1.

62. Nogueira Filho, *A guerra cívica*, vol. 1, 84–90.

63. Hall, "The Whites of Their Eyes," 12–13. Emphasis in the original.

64. See, for example, Vampré, *São Paulo terra conquistada*, 266.

65. An apt example is the nakedly racist discussion (1924) of "The Land and the Racial Resources," in Lobo, *São Paulo na federação*, 130–145. The books and lectures of Antonio Baptista Pereira, a self-defined "antiracist," are full of assumptions about racial difference. See, for example, *O Brasil e a raça*. But it clearly had become controversial by the early 1930s to treat race as an explanatory variable on its own. Hence, in a review of three essays by Oliveira Vianna on race, Azevedo Amaral congratulated him for "courageously reacting against the anti-racial prejudice [*sic*]." "Raça e política," *Diário de Pernambuco*, July 8, 1932, 2.

66. For overviews of changing notions of race, see Graham, *The Idea of Race in Latin America*; also Maio and Santos, *Raça, ciência e sociedade*. For discussions of the way biological notions of race continue to inform "culturalist" approaches to difference, see Blake, *The Vigorous Core*, 136–142, 212–216; and Cunha, *Intenção e gesto*.

67. For a discussion of states that could and could not be "intervened," see Pang, *Bahia in the First Brazilian Republic*, 122–123.

68. The interventions that occurred after 1930 in the northern states, which had sharply declined in political influence during the Old Republic, could be interpreted not as a humiliation, but as an opportunity to replace ineffective regional oligarchies with a new political leadership invigorated by its close working relationship with the Vargas regime. See Pandolfi, "A trajetória do Norte," 339–425.

69. Coaracy, *O caso de São Paulo*, 135–136.

70. Picchia, *A revolução paulista*, 21.

71. Ellis, *Confederação ou separação?*, 12–20.

72. Ellis, *Confederação ou separação?*, 20.

73. On the impact of evolutionary notions of race, see de Luca, *A Revista do Brasil*, 90.

74. Ellis, *A nossa guerra*, 128–132.

75. Roberto Simonsen, "A evolução economica de São Paulo," *Paulistânia* 6 (March–April 1940): 17–18.

76. For a discussion of a similar process of regional racialization in Colombia, see Wade, *Blackness and Race Mixture*, 51–105.

77. Pereira, *Pelo Brasil maior*, 347.

78. On anti-nortista sentiment in São Paulo prior to the 1930s, see chapter 1 of this volume.

79. Albuquerque, *A invenção do Nordeste*, 57–62.

80. Among advocates of the Causa Paulista, it became common to refer to the "Viceroyalty of the North" and its reputedly unquestioning, quasi-colonial support of the Vargas regime. See Nogueira Filho, *A guerra cívica 1932*, vol. 2 (*Insurreição civil*), 86–88.

81. On the machinations between various figures in the armed forces and politicians in Minas and especially Rio Grande do Sul, see Hilton, *A guerra civil brasileira*, 41–62.

82. Picchia, *A revolução paulista*, 14; Ellis, *A nossa guerra*, 128–132; Andrade, "A guerra de São Paulo"; Coaracy, *O caso de São Paulo*, 18.

83. Cited in Albuquerque, *A invenção do Nordeste*, 45.

84. Ellis, *Confederação ou separação?*, 36; Vampré, *São Paulo terra conquistada*, 266.

85. Andrade, "A guerra de São Paulo," 92. This section of the unpublished manuscript includes many other examples of "Constitutionalist humor," much of it at the expense of the nordestinos. The manifesto can be found in APESP, Col. 32, Pasta 353, Doc. 556. And one ex-combatant recalled that he and his fellow soldiers, upon sighting federal airplanes (that to their relief, dropped no bombs), broke into a chorus of the hit song from Rio's Carnaval in 1932, "Teu cabelo não nega" with the lines "Teu cabelo não nega, mulata / Porque és mulata na cor" (Your hair doesn't lie, mulata / Because mulata is your color). Moura, *A fogueira constitucionalista*, 61.

86. Jardim, *A aventura de outubro*, 174. In this text, written before the uprising, Jardim even claimed that members of the state Força Pública sported red armbands.

87. "Monumento a Lampeão," *O Separatista* 3 (June 1932): 2.

88. Duarte, *Que é que há? . . . Pequena história de uma grande pirataria*. This comment recalls Homi Bhabha's discussion of the "mimic man"—the colonial subject who is ridiculed precisely for his futile effort to emulate the colonizer. *The Location of Culture*, 85–92.

89. APESP, Col. 32, Pasta 357, Doc. 658—Letter from Ibrahim Nobre, 1933.

90. Nogueira Filho, *A guerra cívica*, vol. 2 (*Insurreição civil*), 84–90. Juarez Távora, chief of Vargas's northern forces, became known as the Viceroy of the North. This "title" evoked the colonial/backward character of the Nordeste, and its alleged susceptibility to rule by a strongman.

91. Mesquita Filho, *Memórias de um revolucionário*, 35.

92. On Euclides's social concerns, see Sevcenko, *Literatura como missão*, 130–154.

93. On misery as a central element in representations of the Nordeste, see Albuquerque, *A invenção do Nordeste*, 242–251; and Sarzynski, "Revolutionizing Identities." São Paulo maintained an ambivalent relationship with the coast; many paulista authors claimed that the exceptional civilization of the *planalto* resulted from the capital's location on a plateau and consequent orientation toward the interior. See chapter 6, herein.

94. Picchia, *A revolução paulista*, 21, 26–27. See also Reale, *Memórias*, vol. 1, 67.

95. Vampré, *São Paulo terra conquistada*, 266; Ellis, *Populações paulistas*, 64.

96. Ellis, *Populações paulistas*, 97.

97. See, for example, Dávila, *Diploma of Whiteness*.

98. Butler, *Freedoms Given, Freedoms Won*, 88–128; Domingues, *Uma história não contada*. Recent research on other regions of Brazil, especially the Far South, indicates that São Paulo was not quite so exceptional in this regard. See the essays in Gomes and Domingues, *Da nitidez e invisibilidade*.

99. Rodríguez, "Black on Both Sides."

100. Although "cabeça chata" was the term most often deployed when referring to nordestinos, an individual nordestino might be described as mulato or mestiço. In his regional/racial classification of the Brazilian population, Alfredo Ellis Jr. referred to a native of Sergipe or Ceará as a "platycephalo amongoilado" but called a native of Pernambuco simply "negro." *Confederação ou separação?*, 20.

101. In *For Social Peace in Brazil*, chapters 1–2, I argue that the widespread embrace of the discourses of productivity and development can be traced back to the 1920s.

102. Albuquerque, *A invenção do Nordeste*, 68–106.

103. On the suppression of the separatist movement, and its absorption by the autonomists, see Nogueira Filho, *A guerra cívica*, vol. 2 (*Insurreição civil*), 146–147.

104. Nogueira Filho, *A guerra cívica*, vol. 1, xxv.

105. Museu Paulista, Col. 32, Doc. 2759.

106. For example, on the masthead of their short-lived newspaper, *O Separatista*, the names of three renowned seventeenth-century bandeirantes appeared as publisher, editor in chief, and general secretary. On the connection between the cult of the bandeirantes and the 1932 uprising, see Abud, "O bandeirante e a Revolução de 32."

107. Nogueira Filho, *A guerra cívica*, vol. 1, 139.

108. Quoted in Silva, *1932*, 282.

109. Pro-autonomy/confederacy works include Lobo, *O Brasil confederado*; Ellis, *Confederação ou separação?*, and Coaracy, *O caso de São Paulo*.

110. Ellis, *A nossa guerra*, 42; Nogueira Filho, *A guerra cívica*, vol. 2, 146.

111. Duarte, *Que é que há?*, 257–258.

112. *O Separatista*, April 1932, 2.

113. "Paulista, não te desanimes," APESP, Col. Rev. de 32, Pasta 357, Doc. 673.

114. As one might expect, the text of the manifesto issued "To the Nation" on July 12, 1932, by a joint committee of civilian and military leaders of the Constitutionalist uprising, had a very different tone. It made no explicit reference to São Paulo's special place in the nation, and even spoke of the necessity of "constitutional repre-

sentative democracy"—a rare instance in which "democracy" was invoked as a goal of the uprising. Manifesto reproduced in Donato, *A revolução de 32*, 197.

115. A film produced in 1978 about the Revolution of 1932 included "re-created" scenes of interactions between paulista volunteers and federal soldiers from the Nordeste. Though the film seeks to highlight fraternal feelings between the opposing sides, the paulistas mock the nordestinos, and especially their excessive consumption of cachaça. *A respeito do Movimento Constitucionalista de 1932.* For other pejorative images that appeared in the *Jornal das Trincheiras*, see Tota, *A locomotiva no ar*, 103.

116. *Jornal das Trincheiras*13 (September 25, 1932): 1.

117. Prado, "O pensamento conservador paulista," 236.

118. As is to be expected, the flyers and manifestos directed to Brazilians outside São Paulo, such as the ones cited in notes 98 and 99 above, were especially insistent about this. But even some explicitly directed at paulistas emphasized that what was at risk was the very nation itself.

119. Carvalho, *Irradiações*, 134.

120. "Ao Povo Brasileiro," Museu Paulista, Col. Rev. de 32, doc. 2.777. The target for this flyer was probably the neighboring state of Minas Gerais.

121. *A Gazeta*, July 11, 1932, 4; APESP, Caixa 337–43, Pasta 342, Doc. 273.

122. APESP, Pasta 342a, Doc. 314, emphasis in original. Bernardes's endorsement of the 1932 uprising was a somewhat mixed blessing given his association with the bombardments of São Paulo in 1924.

123. Anderson, *Imagined Communities*, 7. Of course, Anderson realizes that this comradeship would not imply literal equality. To quote him: "Regardless of the actual inequality and exploitation that may prevail in each, the nation is always conceived as a deep, horizontal comradeship."

124. Here again, the comparison with Italy is an apt one. See Schneider, *Italy's "Southern Question."*

125. Even those members of the paulista elite who were of Portuguese descent tended to be much more recent arrivals. The founder of the wealthy and powerful Prado clan, Antonio da Silva Prado, arrived in the captaincy of São Paulo in the 1710s, during the region's "decadent" post-bandeira period, though he did manage to marry two women from the more established paulista families. See Levi, *The Prados of São Paulo*, 17–20.

126. "O drama dos sampauleiros," *Paulistânia* 5 (December 1939).

127. Though he spent nearly his entire childhood and early adulthood in São Paulo, Miguel Costa was born in Buenos Aires. See entry for Miguel Costa, website "A Era Vargas: dos anos 20 a 1945," FGV, CPDOC, 2012, accessed September 2013. http://cpdoc .fgv.br/producao/dossies/AEraVargas1/biografias/miguel_costa.

128. Anon., "São Paulo, sua terra e sua gente," ms. in Museu Paulista, Col. Rev. de 32, Doc. 2.777; Discurso de dr. Júlio de Faria, Radio-Jornal (October 4, 1932), APESP, Col. Rev. de 32, Pasta 342b, Doc. 360.

129. "Mocidade Paulista!" Manifesto (October 29, 1932) from Constitutionalists who participated in the uprising in Belém on September 6. They refer to themselves as "paulistas do Pará" and the paulistas as "paraenses de São Paulo." Museu Paulista, Col. Rev. de 32, Doc. 2.769.

130. "Paulistas," *Jornal das Trincheiras* 5 (August 28, 1932): 1.

131. Milton Carneiro, "Prefácio," xxxi–xxxii, in Karam, *Um paranaense nas trincheiras da lei*. It is very likely that Carneiro was echoing language used in the widely read racist tract by Lothrop Stoddard, *Revolt against Civilization: The Menace of the Under-Man*.

132. For a hagiographical discussion of her father's oeuvre, see Ellis, *Alfredo Ellis Júnior, 1896–1974*, 18–34.

133. Penteado, "Paulistas no 'Front,'" *O Inevitável* (unpaginated).

134. Museu Paulista, Arquivo Pedro Manoel de Toledo, Pasta 1, Doc. 3698.

135. Among the more striking examples of this is the title that Paulo Duarte gave to his memoirs of combat in 1932: *Palmares pelo avesso*. Here he is invoking the role of the bandeirantes in the destruction of the seventeenth-century runaway slave community, and implying that, in the case of São Paulo, the "slaves" have seized the territory from the free (and implicitly white) inhabitants. Similarly, Mozart Firmeza referred to the federal troops as "quilombolas moraes da dictadura" ([im]moral runaway slaves of the dictatorship). *Poemas em prosa da revolução paulista*, 65. Firmeza, interestingly, was a native of Ceará.

136. Duarte, *Que é que há?*, 262; *Palmares pelo avesso* (quote on back cover).

137. Andrade, "Guerra de São Paulo."

138. The phrase "white slavery" more commonly refers to forced prostitution-related trafficking in (white) women, which carries its own implications of abomination. Here the enslavement is not sexual but involves an inversion of savage and civilized, similar to the way European Christians might have viewed the holding of "hostages" as slaves by Muslim societies in the early modern period. The point is that the outrage lies not in the immorality of slavery per se, but in the enslavement of peoples whose identities make them inappropriate for enslavement, hence the "abomination." See Weiss, *Captives and Corsairs*.

139. Carvalho, *Irradiações*, 137.

140. James Woodard, in a brilliant discussion of racism and racial ambiguities in São Paulo during the Old Republic, demonstrates that idioms of enslavement were widely used in political rhetoric before the 1932 uprising, and with the same sorts of inversions that characterized racialized discourse in the 1930s. I would argue that the Constitutionalist Revolution served to consolidate a certain white/middle-class paulista identity, and also intensified the already-existing tendency to draw a sharp contrast between paulistas and nortistas, but Woodard's point about the instability of racial categories and boundaries is well taken (if not his notion of "real people" who exist outside the cognitive realm of representation). "Of Slaves and Citizens."

141. "Paulista, Não te Desanimes," AESP, Coleção Rev. de 1932, Pasta 357, Doc. 673. The number and variety of documents that incorporate the enslavement theme are truly too numerous to mention. Ibrahim Nobre, in his widely quoted prose poem "Ainda e sempre" (Still and always), referred to runaway slaves (in this case, the paulistas) being forced back into slave quarters by the slave catchers (*capitães do mato*). (APESP, Col. 32, Pasta 342a, Doc. 327). Similarly, a flyer, "Brasileiros," which mainly targeted residents of Rio, insisted that Brazilians should not be a "slave herd" driven by a slave driver, driven in turn by other slave drivers" (APESP, Col. 32, Pasta 342a, Doc. 322). This is just a small sample.

142. See above, note 116. It should be noted that Duarte tended to be unusually overt (for a Brazilian intellectual) in his racist attitudes even well after the 1932 uprising. See, for example, his articles in *O Estadão* in 1947 in which he rebuked Gilberto Freyre for his "sociologia nigro-romântico [sic] do Nordeste." Duarte, "Os negros do Brasil."

143. Along with the motif of it being abominable or absurd to seek to "enslave" paulistas, there was the frequent claim that paulistas, by their very nature, were eager to abolish slavery, a claim that has been thoroughly rebutted by recent scholarly research. Dean, *Rio Claro*.

144. On the shift in elite sentiment toward valuing the "national" worker, see Andrews, *Blacks and Whites*, 85–88.

145. At least one manifesto issued by separatists explicitly stated that they regarded European immigrants as white and paulista. Nogueira Filho, *A guerra cívica*, vol. 1 (*Ocupação militar*), 145. Ellis claimed that the volunteer battalions were "saturated with the sons of exotics," by which he meant immigrants. *Populações paulistas*, 233.

146. Ortiz, *O que é São Paulo*, 66.

147. Dalmo Belfort de Mattos, "A influência negra na alma paulista," *Paulistânia* 4 (November 1939); Ellis, *Populações paulistas*, 96–98.

148. The official manifesto "To the Nation" cited above (note 95) does mention democracy; similarly, perrepista politician Armando Prado, at the rally on February 23, called for a movement in favor of a "democratic and liberal regime" (*A Folha da Noite*, February 24, 1932, 1). But these were isolated instances, peculiar enough to stand out.

149. APESP, Pasta 342, Doc. 298.

150. Coaracy, *O caso de São Paulo*, 18.

151. Vampre, *São Paulo terra conquistada*, 13.

152. Thus I don't entirely agree with a conclusion drawn by the renowned literary critic and sociologist Antonio Cândido de Mello e Souza. In an interview for a documentary in 1992 to mark the sixtieth anniversary of the uprising, he argued for a more appreciative view of the Constitutionalists who, despite their conservative posture on social reform, did call for legality and a democratic process. This was an understandable sentiment on his part in a Brazil that had gone nearly thirty years (1960–1989) without a direct election for president. I would argue, however, that there was little commitment to democracy in the movement, and a commitment to the law only narrowly defined as order, not justice. Thus, this exclusionary vision of democratic process could easily translate into an observance of democratic procedure on behalf of an essentially authoritarian program. For the interview with Antonio Candido, see the film *1932: A guerra civil* (directed by Eduardo Escorel, 1992).

Chapter 3: The Middle Class in Arms?

Epigraph 1. Reproduced in Donato, *A revolução de 32*, 111.

Epigraph 2. Antonio Cândido offers this Gramscian interpretation of the Constitutionalist Revolution in an interview for the film *1932: A guerra civil* (1992).

1. Burns, *A History of Brazil*, 294. For a discussion of works by Brazilian historians who frame the 1932 uprising as "tenentismo versus oligarchy," see Rodrigues, *1932*, 28.

2. Letter from Oswaldo Aranha to Vargas, May 1, 1932; calls the Constitutionalist

Movement a "campaign of a popular character." FGV, CPDOC (Rio), GV, R2, F0557, 32–01–05.

3. Carvalho, *A guerra civil de 1932 (em São Paulo)*, 17.

4. The most thorough critique is Decca, *1930: O silencio dos vencidos*, which rejects the very notion of 1930 as a "revolution."

5. For more discussion of the memory of 1932, see below, chapter 8.

6. The brief time span is not an explanation for the short shrift given this uprising by new social historians, who are fascinated by the 1904 Revolt against the Vaccine in Rio, which lasted only a few days. For a discussion of the historiography of this even briefer revolt, see Weinstein, "Postcolonial Brazil," 221.

7. The concept of "history from the bottom up" was crucial for moving historians away from an almost exclusive focus on the privileged and powerful, but it also produced a tendency to homogenize the perspectives and the interests of the popular classes and to treat the formation of those interests as preceding historical process. This is especially problematic when dealing with a movement, such as the 1932 uprising, involving many people who identified with the middling ranks of society. On the global formation of middle-class identity, see López and Weinstein, *The Making of the Middle Class*.

8. Given ample evidence of mass participation in the uprising, the problem is not a lack of research but a matter of intelligibility—it was difficult for historians after the social turn to perceive such a movement as having a mass base. By the 1990s, with social history on the wane and the global situation arguing for a rethinking of popular agency, we can see a significant shift in views of 1932 in the interviews with scholars such as Paulo Sérgio Pinheiro, Antônio Cândido, Boris Fausto, Vavy Pacheco Borges, Aspásia Camargo, and José Murilo de Carvalho that accompanied the documentary film *1932: A Guerra Civil* (1992), directed by Eduardo Escorel and funded by various paulista state and municipal agencies.

9. The two best accounts by witnesses of the events leading up to the armed conflict are Leite, *Martírio e glória*, vol. 1; and Nogueira Filho, *A guerra cívica—1932*, 4 vols. Street-fighting between paulista protesters and Miguel Costa's Revolutionary Legion on May 23 led to the deaths of four young men—Mário Martins de Almeida, Euclides Miragaia, Dráusio Marcondes de Sousa, and Antônio Camargo de Andrade—whose initials, MMDC, became a near mystical symbol for the regional revolt. (A fifth wounded student, Orlando de Oliveira Alvarenga, only died three months later so he was not included in the original pantheon of martyrs.)

10. A quick scan of Getúlio Vargas's diary entries for the first few months of 1932 indicates that he was at least as concerned about unrest in Rio Grande do Sul, and somewhat (if less) concerned about Minas Gerais. *Diário*, vol. 1. For more on the national dimensions, see Morais, *Chatô*, 272–290; and Carneiro, *XII de Agosto!*

11. On the consequences of Klinger's premature provocation, see Hilton, *A guerra civil brasileira*, 15.

12. Hilton, *A guerra civil brasileira*, 15. Hilton's account, based on research in the Ministry of War's Arquivo do Exército, is the best source on the military machinations. Isidoro Dias Lopes had been retired by the time the uprising began.

13. On the state police forces, see Love, *São Paulo in the Brazilian Federation*, 117–129.

14. Even when Vargas appointed a paulista as interventor (Laudo Ferreira de Camargo, July–November 1931), it was seen by many paulista politicians as a sham since Miguel Costa continued to control the state Força Pública. Borges, *Tenentismo e revolução brasileira*, 43–46.

15. Levy, *A coluna invicta*, 20; Coaracy, *A sala da capela*, 13.

16. Jardim, *A aventura de outubro*, 174. In the same passage in which he notes newsies and "old blacks" wearing "fascist" armbands, he also cites members of the Força Pública wearing them. On the exclusion of blacks from the Civil Guard, see Andrews, *Blacks and Whites*, 150–151.

17. Ellis, *A nossa guerra*, 149. Though less insulting in tone than Ellis, other observers noted the social distance between middle-class recruits and the lower-level officers in the Força Pública. The U.S. military attaché remarked upon the young men not used to taking orders who "found themselves under command of an abrupt and perhaps uncouth military police officer." NARA, RG59, M1472, Brazil (Revolutions): Sackville, Report no. 1035, "Tenth Week of São Paulo Revolt"—September 15, 1932. On the broader problem of the tension between military and social hierarchies, see Beattie, *The Tribute of Blood*, 36.

18. Ellis, *A nossa guerra*, 155; Mello, *Renda-se paulista*, 37–38.

19. Santos, *A epopéia de São Paulo em 1932*, 73. The distinction I am drawing here between ethnic and racial identity reflects the Black Legion's emphasis on blackness/color, rather than on African descent.

20. An anonymous letter (signed "uma patrícia") not only accused men of joining the MMDC to avoid going to the front, but urged the director, José Cassio de Macedo Soares, to allow women to enlist in the MMDC so men could be freed up to go into combat. APESP, Col. Rev. de 32, Pasta 380, Doc. 1885.

21. Nogueira Filho, *A guerra cívica*, vol. 2, 361; Picchia, *A revolução paulista*, 34–35.

22. Carvalho, *Irradiações*, 139; Martins, *Album de família 1932*, n.p.

23. Museu Paulista, Col. Rev. de 32, Pasta 5, Docs. 2775–2958. One particularly hyperbolic flyer declared: "Paulistas! Keep an eye out for the spies. The rumor-monger is a spy, LYNCH HIM!!"

24. Luiz Gonzaga Naclério Homem does mention a friend who fled to Rio out of fear of being coerced into enlisting in a volunteer battalion. *Lembranças de um belo ideal*, 2.

25. If paulistinidade was a regional cum national identity, then it follows (as Benedict Anderson argues) that many paulistas would kill and die for São Paulo. *Imagined Communities*, 7.

26. IHGSP, Col. Rev. de 1932, Recortes, Pasta 7.

27. Vavy Pacheco Borges notes that between 1932 and 1937 over 150 memoirs and chronicles about the experience of 1932 were published, a large portion of them by individuals who then or later would have regarded themselves as middle class. *Memória paulista*, 47.

28. The term "near-elite" is from Kittleson, *The Practice of Politics*, 162.

29. Leite's speech is reproduced in NARA, RG59, M1472, Roll 7, São Paulo Political Report no. 47, June 11, 1932. Cameron also declared that the paulistas were defending their "white man's culture."

30. Mello, *Renda-se, paulista!*, 3. Historically there is certainly a pattern of wealthier families seeking to spare their sons the hardships and dangers of war, but this does not seem to have been a salient aspect of the 1932 uprising, nor is it a plausible explanation for its failure.

31. The Batalhão 14 de Julho, composed almost entirely of law students and other students from institutions of higher learning, suffered about a dozen deaths. Although this is not a very large proportion of the total of 350 volunteers in the battalion, it is probably a higher *rate* of casualties than that suffered by the Força Pública. Queiroz, *Batalhão 14 de Julho*. The estimates of death rates are based on the roll of the paulista fallen in Montenegro, *Cruzes paulistas*.

32. A pioneering study of the tiers of middle-class culture in Rio and São Paulo is Owensby, *Intimate Ironies*. My thinking about middle-class identity has also been shaped by my many conversations with Ricardo López on this subject.

33. Gonçalves, *Carne para canhão*, 160. See also Mello, *Renda-se paulista*, 3. Gonçalves's remarks have to be taken with many grains of salt. At another point in his chronicle (pp. 99–100) he claims that the paulistas are deliberately putting blacks in the front lines to terrify the federal troops and compares this alleged "strategy" with France's use of colonial African soldiers in the Rhineland during the Great War, which incited a racist frenzy among the German population of the region.

34. Queiroz, *Batalhão 14 de Julho*. This more reliable source also indicates (p. 99) that the Legião Negra was widely deployed in the areas of most intense combat.

35. See my article, "Racializing Regional Difference," in Appelbaum, *Race and Nation in Modern Latin America*, especially 245–247.

36. Andrade, "A guerra de São Paulo," 4. Nogueira Filho (*A guerra cívica*, vol. 1, 141) noted the increasing involvement of the "burguesia média" in the Constitutionalist Campaign, apparently regarding this as a broadening of its base. Reporting on the rally that took place on May 23, Consul Cameron referred to it as "this mass of people, made up in part by the bluest blood of the City." NARA, RG59, M1472, Brazil (Revolutions), Political Report no. 45, May 25, 1932.

37. Levy, *Coluna invicta*, 41.

38. *A Gazeta*, September 4, 1932, 3. In her weekly column, "Cartas de Mulher," Vina Centi addressed her article "To the Paulista Intellectual Military Volunteer." In the final paragraph, she concludes: "I knew you when you were rich, in full enjoyment of all the superficial pleasures of a corrupt and arid worldliness. . . . You were elegantly useless and indifferent." But now that he has joined the battle, he is the true heir of the bandeirante spirit. *Jornal das Trincheiras*, September 22, 1932, 2.

39. Picchia, *O despertar de São Paulo*, 207–217.

40. Herbert Levy notes the salutary effects of having soldiers from relatively privileged families dig trenches. *Coluna invicta*, 41.

41. Naclério Homem, *Lembranças de um belo ideal*, 38.

42. *A Gazeta*, September 4, 1932, 3. On the low regard in which Brazilians of all classes held military service until well into the twentieth century, see Beattie, *The Tribute of Blood*, especially 207–237.

43. For descriptions of these mass protests, see Nogueira Filho, *A guerra cívica 1932*, vol. 1, 422–426.

44. FGV, CPDOC, BK 1932.05.22. Emphasis added.

45. This incompetence, however, should not be interpreted as synonymous with cowardice (a frequent charge by the getulistas against well-off paulistas). However questionable their motives, many young men (and some women) put themselves at considerable risk in fighting for São Paulo, and the record of those killed in battle includes many paulistas who likely regarded themselves as middle- or upper-class. Montenegro, *Cruzes paulistas.*

46. Pacheco, *Revivendo 32*, 21. The battalion changed its name to "14 de Julho," perhaps in an effort to be less overtly elitist. Souza Queiroz, *Batalhão 14 de Julho*, makes a point of mentioning (p. 99) the battalion fighting side by side with the Legião Negra.

47. Pacheco, *Revivendo 32*, 22. See also Queiroz, *Batalhão 14 de Julho.*

48. Pacheco, *Revivendo 32*, 22.

49. Pacheco, *Revivendo 32*, 194–199.

50. Levy, *Coluna invicta*, 111. For an excellent study of representations of black men on the battlefield and whites' insistence on the need for white officers, see Kaplan, "Black and Blue on San Juan Hill," 219–236.

51. A film produced by the State Department of Culture and the Universidade de Campinas in 1978, and which included a number of interviews with veterans of 1932, put special emphasis on this theme. *A respeito do Movimento Constitucionalista de 1932*, Cinemateca Brasileira (São Paulo).

52. AESP, Col. Rev. de 1932, Pasta 378, Doc. 1587, 9–10. Note that the "racial" identity of the nordestinos in the paulista gaze was quite unstable. The "racial type" deprecatingly referred to as cabeça chata could be vaguely described as a mixture of Portuguese, Indian, and African, whereas in other contexts, nortistas are referred to as *negro* or *mulato.*

53. For example, the film *A respeito do Movimento Constitucionalista de 1932*, which included some "dramatic re-creations," always depicts the soldiers on the opposing side as nordestinos.

54. *O Estado de São Paulo*, July 31, 1932, 5.

55. "A cooperação paulista: A dictadura lança mão dos jagunços fanáticos contra o exército consciente da liberdade," *A Gazeta* (São Paulo), August 7, 1932, 3.

56. NARA, RG59, M1472, Brazil (Revolutions): Cameron to Thurston, August 9, 1932, SPPR, no. 49.

57. *A Folha da Noite*, September 15, 1932, 2.

58. Separatist manifesto appealing to immigrants reproduced in Nogueira Filho, *A guerra cívica*, vol. 2 (Ocupação Militar), 145.

59. APESP, Col. 32, Pasta 343, Doc. 394; Pasta 385, Doc. 2034; "A cooperação da Colônia Syrio-Lebanesa," *OESP*, July 19, 1932, 3.

60. Picchia, *A revolução paulista*, 68–69; Nogueira Filho, *A guerra cívica*, vol. 3, 130.

61. APESP, Pasta 385, Doc. 2034; Pasta 386, Doc. 2041. For a chronicle by a propaulista combatant of Syrian descent, see Karam, *Um paranense nas trincheiras da lei.* Herbert Levy mentions a volunteer in his battalion, Sallah Sallib, who was a "son of Syrians": *A coluna invicta*, 51. Gastão Goulart, the (white) commander of the Legião Negra, includes a list of immigrant communities that contributed to the Constitutionalist Campaign. *Verdades da revolução paulista*, 167–168. Miguel Reale mentions

his dear friend and platoon mate, José Preiz, who died in combat. According to Reale, Preiz, a Hungarian Jew, "wasn't even a naturalized Brazilian." *Memórias*, vol. 1, 62–63. Within weeks, the presence of immigrants got translated into a claim that the paulistas were "contract[ing] Hungarians and other [foreign] elements to combat Brazilians." *O Povo* (Fortaleza), August 17, 1932, 1.

62. Museu Paulista, Col. Rev. de 32, Pasta 3, Doc. 2951.

63. A list of immigrant women's clubs (including the date they were founded) is available in Porta, *Guia dos documentos históricos na cidade de São Paulo*.

64. Montenegro, *Cruzes paulistas*. Also NARA, RG59, M1472, Brazil (Revolutions), 832.00/408, Sackville, "Memorandum on trip to São Paulo," October 12–15, 1932.

65. Ellis, *Populações paulistas*, 233.

66. Reale, *Memórias*, vol. 1, 62–63.

67. Cited in Lesser, *Immigration, Ethnicity, and National Identity*, 163. My thanks to Jeffrey Lesser for bringing these individuals to my attention.

68. Nogueira Filho, *A guerra cívica*, vol. 3 (*O povo em armas*), 175. Conde Andrea Matarazzo was arrested a few weeks after the armistice as he was attempting to flee Brazil on an Italian ship. According to a *cearense* newspaper, "The Matarazzo firm, as is well known, provided many services to the cause of the insurrectionists during the armed movement in São Paulo." *O Povo*, October 17, 1932, 1.

69. Ellis, *Populações paulistas*, 233. For an excellent discussion of Ellis's novel *Jaraguá* (1936), which exalts the role of immigrants in 1932 and disparages the conduct of a mulatto from the Nordeste, see Ferreira, *A epopéia bandeirante*, 333–346. To quote Ferreira, "the regionalism of Ellis Jr. reveals itself in *Jaraguá* with its full segregationist force" (346).

70. Andrade, "Guerra de São Paulo," 8.

71. On the worker clinics founded by industrialists during the 1932 uprising, see Weinstein, *For Social Peace in Brazil*, 63–65.

72. "Para o povo em geral," *A Plebe*, January 7, 1933, 3. In that same issue, an article "O ano terrível de 1932" (p. 2) referred to the uprising as an "abomination," and as "those cursed and horrendous three months of war, of counterrevolution, and of incredible violence."

73. Carvalho, *Guerra civil de 32*, 18. Emphasis mine.

74. NARA, RG59, M1472, 832.00, Reel 7, July 22, 1932, political report form Consul Cameron.

75. Montenegro, *Cruzes paulistas*; APESP, Col. 32, Pasta 353 contains manifestos and photos from interior towns, including Bragança, Iguape, Itapetininga, Mogy-Mirim, Monte Azul, Presidente Prudente, Ribeirão Bonito, São Simão, Taubaté, and Sertãozinho.

76. On the uneven development of working-class identification in this period, see French, *The Brazilian Workers' ABC*, 41–67.

77. The flyer for the rally on February 24 is reproduced in Donato, *A revolução de 32*, 54.

78. The formal, government-recognized union for local textile workers in Taubaté wasn't founded until 1937, but given that the Companhia Taubaté Industrial dated back to 1897 and was one of the largest textile factories in the state of São Paulo, it is very

likely that there were some precursors to the "official" labor union. Ortiz, *A trajetória da Companhia Industrial Taubaté* CTI.

79. APESP, Col. 32, Pasta 353, Doc. 567.

80. Although its coverage of events during the 1932 uprising was sometimes inaccurate, the cearense daily *O Povo* twice reported on campaigns against "Communists" in São Paulo in the weeks and months leading up to the armed phase of the movement. *O Povo*, May 31, 1932, 1; "O comunismo em S. Paulo," July 7, 1932, 1.

81. *A Cigarra*, 19, no. 427 (September 30, 1932). This issue of the monthly magazine not only ran several pages of photos of the jailed "Communists," but also included a full-page photo of Thyrso Martins, the chief of police. Despite this obvious concern among paulista leaders with the "red menace" in São Paulo, I think Vavy Pacheco Borges overstates the significance of anticommunism in the political conflicts of this period. See her *Tenentismo e revolução brasileira*, 207–211.

82. *Diário Nacional*, July 31, 1932, 2; September 14, 1932, 4.

83. APESP, Col. 32, Pasta 340, Doc. 237, no. 4 (July 29, 1932). This flyer referenced Washington Luís's notorious comment when mayor that the social question was a question for the police, not for politics.

84. APESP, Acervo DOPS, Prontuário Ibrahim Nobre, 40547.

85. On the labor policies of the early Vargas period, see Pinheiro, *Política e trabalho no Brasil*; French, *The Brazilian Workers' ABC*; and Gomes, *A invenção do trabalhismo*. Although many studies of this period focus on disputes over the specific features of labor legislation, the major point of contention, I would argue, was the question of how and how much the laws would be enforced.

86. Museu Paulista, Col. 32, Pasta 1, Doc. 2777/13.

87. Museu Paulista, Col. Rev. de 1932, Doc. 2766. The document also calls Miguel Costa a fascist.

88. The federal *Boletim de Informações* similarly referred to violence against workers in Brás and Moôca and laid the blame on the paulista insurgent government. Museu Paulista, Arquivo Pedro de Toledo, Pasta 1, Doc. 2795.

89. "Aviso aos sitiantes e trabalhadores do município de Pres. Prudente," APESP, Pasta 353, Doc. 554.

90. According to Consul Cameron (writing on July 18, 1932), "Ladies of best families volunteering for Red Cross which has been obliged to refuse further volunteers." NARA, RG59, M1472, 832.00, Revolutions/Reel 7.

91. The following articles critical of popular support/ingenuousness regarding the Causa Paulista, appeared in *A Plebe*: "A grande mistificação e os grandes mistificadores," December 17, 1932, 3; "O ano terrível de 1932," January 7, 1933, 2; "A tragédia operária na farça dos comensais," January 28, 1933, 3; "A grande ofensiva eleitoral," February 25, 1933, 1. The anarchist newspaper *O Trabalhador*, in its July 1932 issue, published two articles, "A Federação Operária," 2, and "A Federação de São Paulo em faze dos últimos acontecimentos políticos militares," 3, that referred to workers manifesting support for the Constitutionalists as "ingenuous" and "perplexed."

92. On the PD and the question of labor reforms, see Prado, *A democracia ilustrada*, 158–172. Paulo Nogueira Filho, a democrático, insisted that regional autonomy was

compatible with labor reforms, but the PD's alliance with the PRP made this contention less persuasive. *A guerra cívica*, vol. 2, 146–147.

93. *A Folha da Noite*, July 14, 1932, 4; July 20, 1932, 4.

94. On police, workers, and public space in São Paulo during the early decades of the twentieth century, see Paoli and Duarte, "São Paulo no plural," 53–99.

95. For an excellent discussion of the Gramscian formulation of a "historic bloc," see Laclau, "Toward a Theory of Populism."

96. Hence Ellis's enthusiasm for immigrants in *Populações paulistas*, 127–131. He expresses special pleasure at the high rate of intermarriage between Italians and native (white) paulistas.

97. See Butler, *Freedoms Given, Freedoms Won*, 67–178; Alberto, *Terms of Inclusion*, 23–150; Gomes, *Negros e política, 1888–1937*. Documentation in the DEOPS file of Bahian-born Joaquim Guaraná de Sant'Anna, who self-identified as "negro" in São Paulo, indicates his father self-identified as "pardo" in Bahia. APESP, Acervo DEOPS, J. G. de Sant'Anna, Prontuário 2029, November 17, 1932.

98. Butler, *Freedoms Given, Freedoms Won*, 67–87; Alberto, *Terms of Inclusion*, 138–143.

99. Alberto, *Terms of Inclusion*, 63–64.

100. After years of neglect, the scholarship on the Legião Negra has burgeoned over the last decade. See Alberto, *Terms of Inclusion*, 133–140; Butler, *Freedoms Given, Freedoms Won*, 123–127; Paula, *1932*, 164–170, and especially Domingues, "Os 'Pérolas Negras.'"

101. Museu Paulista, Arquivo Pedro de Toledo, Pasta 1, Doc. 2804; *Jornal das Trincheiras*, September 15, 1932, 1. The most credible discussion of the size of the Legião Negra can be found in Domingues, "Os 'Pérolas Negras,'" 233–234. This author estimates some ten thousand black soldiers on the paulista side, including volunteers, army troops, and members of the Força Pública.

102. Mello, *Renda-se paulista*, 67, claims that because of poor lines of communication, the Black Legion was still engaged in combat after the armistice.

103. Blackness may also have been a primary identity in the far South of Brazil; see the chapters on Rio Grande do Sul in Gomes and Domingues, *Da nitidez e invisibilidade*.

104. Domingues, "Os 'Pérolas Negras,'" 206–208; APESP, Acervo DEOPS, Sant'Anna prontuária 2029, Letter to Penteado, September 5, 1932.

105. Duarte, "Os negros do Brasil," 5. In the article Duarte claimed blacks and whites were becoming less estranged in the United States but "in Brazil the opposite is happening: it seems that the Negro wants to be separate from the white. Already in the Revolution of 1932, they made a point of having a black battalion."

106. Photographs of battalions, especially from Santos and the interior, indicate many were multiracial. Luíz Naclério Homem commented repeatedly on two men in his platoon who became good friends—one, Spencer Kuhlmann, blond and average height, and the other, Cícero Trindade, short and "black as ebony." He apparently found the sight of the two of them—at one point eating from the same dish—both amusing and touching. *Lembranças de um belo ideal*, 44–46.

107. *A Gazeta*, July 16, 1932, 3. For an account of the founding of the Legião Negra by a leading member of the FNB, see the interview with José Correia Leite in Barbosa, *Frente Negra Brasileira*, 75–78. On the schism that led to the formation of the Legião Negra, see Roger Bastide, "O negro em São Paulo," 37.

108. *Diário Nacional*, July 31, 1932, 3.

109. Montenegro, *Cruzes paulistas*, 69.

110. Hilton, *A guerra civil brasileira*, 105. Emphasis added.

111. Montenegro, *Cruzes paulistas*, 194, 188, 426. The website "Tudo por São Paulo" has pictures of the Batalhão Marcílio Franco, which seems to have been a predominantly white battalion. http://tudoporsaopau101932.blogspot.com/2010/08/amadeu -augusto-batalhao-marcilio-franco.html.

112. *Diário Nacional*, September 18, 1932, 1. One could argue that "African" would not have been considered equivalent to "black," but in racist writings of the time, the two were treated as interchangeable, and it seems likely that no amount of distance from African culture could divorce blackness from Africanity in the white/racist imagination.

113. Andrade, "Guerra de São Paulo," 8.

114. *Diário Nacional*, August 14, 1932, 5. For an excellent discussion of "social assistance in the black community during the war," see Domingues, "Os 'Pérolas Negras,'" 227–232.

115. APESP, Acervo DOPS, J. G. Sant'Anna, pron. 2029, flyer IABLN (n.d.).

116. Domingues, "Os 'pérolas negras,'" 215.

117. APESP, Acervo DOPS, J. G. Sant'Anna, pron. 2029, September 5, 1932.

118. Gomes, *Negros e política*, 73.

119. Vampré, *São Paulo terra conquistada*, 266; Picchia, *A revolução paulista*, 34–35.

120. Nogueira Filho, *A guerra cívica*, vol. 4, bk. 2 (*Resistência indômita*), 264. Emphasis added.

121. Marcha in appendix to Andrade, "A guerra de São Paulo," 145.

122. Marcha in appendix to Andrade, "A guerra de São Paulo," 225–238.

123. For biographical information on the poet Lino Guedes, see Oliveira, *Quem é quem na negritude brasileira*, vol. 1, 170.

124. Domingues, "Os 'pérolas negras,'" 214. The quote is Domingues's words.

125. Rodriguez, "Black on Both Sides," 3; Bastide, *O negro em São Paulo*, 36–37. See also the testimony of Marcello Orlando Ribeiro, a member of the FNB who joined the Guarda Civil when it was integrated in 1932. It is interesting that Ribeiro gives particular emphasis to the relatively high pay, which allowed the wives of black *guardas* to be housewives rather than work as domestics for other families. Barbosa, *Frente Negra Brasileira*, 81–93.

126. Domingues, "Os 'pérolas negras,'" 209.

127. *Jornal das Trincheiras*, September 8, 1932, 4.

128. Correia Leite (see note 98 above) implies that Guaraná de Sant'Anna worked out some deal with the dissident military officers, which involved Gastão Goulart as commanding officer. Also see Kaplan, "Black and Blue on San Juan Hill," 219–236.

129. On the dismissal of Guaraná de Sant'Anna for malfeasance and "defeatism," see APESP, Acervo DEOPS, J. G. Sant'Anna, pron. 2029. Sant'Anna claimed that the case

against him had been fabricated by his political enemies, Arlindo and Isaltino Veiga. On the installation of his successor, see *Jornal das Trincheiras*, September 22, 1932, 4.

130. Goulart, *Verdades da revolução paulista*, 230–231; 244–245.

131. NARA, RG59, M1472, Brazil (Revolutions)—Consul Cameron, São Paulo Political Report no. 50, August 23, 1932, enclosure: "Os homens de côr e a Causa do Brasil."

132. IHGSP, Arq. Rev. 32, Album de cortes de jornais, July 1932, 14. According to a newspaper item on "Indian" troops, "They are all men already familiarized with civilization, and that is why they responded to the call to arms of the Constitutionalist cause." I assume the decision about where to lodge the soldiers came from above.

133. A photo of the women's auxiliary of the Legião Negra (nurses) can be found in Museu Paulista, Col. Rev. de 32, Pasta 4, Doc. 2951. A photo of white nurses can be found in Martins, *Album de família 1932*, n.p. Roughly contemporaneous photos of the Black Cross nurses of the Universal Negro Improvement Association (Garveyites) show uniforms that are more modern and similar to the ones worn by white nurses during the 1932 uprising.

134. On insinuations of racism, see below, chapter 5. On the extent and limits of racial integration and black social mobility in São Paulo in the early decades of the twentieth century, see Woodard, "Of Slaves and Citizens." For a very thoughtful discussion of the relationship between modernity and racial democracy, see Gomes and Domingues, "Raça, pós-emancipação, cidadania e modernidade no Brasil."

135. It is interesting that Clovis Gonçalves tries to turn the tables, using the same racist premises but claiming that it was the paulistas, because of the prominent role of the Legião Negra, who were hurling savages against the civilized federal forces. *Carne para canhão*, 99–100.

136. *A Folha da Noite*, July 11, 1932, 1.

137. The Belmonte commemorative "Gold Campaign" drawing has been reproduced in many publications. See Donato, *A revolução de 32*, 113. It is worth noting that Belmonte—creator of the popular caricature of the (white) paulista recruit—was himself a man of mixed racial background.

138. Dalmo Belfort de Mattos, "A influência negra na alma paulista," *Paulistânia* 3 (October 1939) (emphasis mine).

139. Ellis, *Populações paulistas*, 98.

140. Anita Malfatti was especially visible at events involving female supporters of the uprising—for example, at a meeting on September 6 of the Department of Assistance to the Wounded (DAF). APESP, Col. 32, Pasta 384, Doc. 2026. On Guiomar Novaes's radio address, see IHGSP, Arq. Rev. 1932, Recortes de jornais, no. 21.

141. Mário's political disenchantment does not seem to have diminished his affective attachment to paulistinidade, judging from the exhaustive collection of memorabilia from 1932 that were among his personal effects when he died. The collection is housed at the Instituto de Estudos Brasileiros, USP.

142. On Oswald de Andrade, see Eleutério, *Oswald*. See his novelized treatment of post-1932 São Paulo: *Marco Zero*. The other modernist writer of some repute who declined to participate was Plínio Salgado, the antiliberal leader of the fascist-friendly Integralists.

143. Dunn, *Brutality Garden*, chapter 1. On the nationalist turn among certain modernists, see Velloso, "A brasilidade verde-amarela," 89–112.

144. Morse, *From Community to Metropolis*, 260–270; and "The Multiverse of Latin American Identity," 17–26.

145. Velloso, "A brasilidade verde-amarelo," 36, 47.

146. Velloso, "A brasilidade verde-amarelo," 41–42. In the letter Mário argued against using "paulista" in this heroicized way and warned Milliet about the rise of *bairrismo histérico* (hysterial localism) in Brazil. This polemic is also discussed in de Luca, *A Revista do Brasil*, 285–286.

147. Amaral, *Tarsila*. Not only did "Operários" (1933) portray proletarians, but also a decidedly diverse group of them, racially speaking.

148. Andrade, "Guerra de São Paulo," 8.

149. Andrade, "Guerra de São Paulo," 8. Originally Mário referenced "Indians" from "Guatemala," but that was crossed out, apparently because of indecision about the correct spelling.

150. On the expedition that Mário sponsored to recuperate folkloric music in the North and Northeast, see Sandroni, "Missão de pesquisas folclóricas," 275–277.

151. See above, note 131.

152. Dunn, *Brutality Garden*, 15–16; on the industrialists' self-fashioning as engineers and technocrats, see Weinstein, *For Social Peace in Brazil*, chapters 1–2.

153. Oswald also (in the "Manifesto Pau Brasil") mocked the excessively Europeanized Bahian statesman Ruy Barbosa as "a top hat in Senegambia." This image was later recycled by Paulo Duarte, who described the nordestinos who came to São Paulo to assume administrative posts in the aftermath of the Revolution of 1930 as "perform[ing] the same role as those Negroes in Dakar, top hat on their heads and [bare]feet on the floor, who are convinced that they hold the high position of 'French citizen.'" (Duarte, *Que é que há?*, 257–258). One has to marvel at the agility with which Duarte transformed Oswald's skewering of the belle epoque Brazilian into a means to ridicule colored "mimic men." One might argue that Duarte resignified the phrase, but I think Oswald's ridiculing of Ruy already had embedded within it the imperialist's disdain for the colonial "mimic man." On the latter concept, see Bhabha, *The Location of Culture*, 85–92.

154. For an intriguing discussion of the relationship between 1932 and the formation of paulista middle-class identity, see Mehrtens, *Urban Space and National Identity in Early Twentieth-Century São Paulo*, especially chapter 3.

155. Many of the memoirs and chronicles of the uprising were published immediately after it ended, but those that appeared in the subsequent decades are typically by middle- or upper-class paulistas. See the nearly complete list of such publications in Paula, *1932*, 293–310.

156. Speech by Cesar Salgado, Clube Piratininga, August 20, 1935, Museu Paulista, Col. Rev. de 32, Pasta 5, Doc. 5336, Recorte. See also Donato, *A revolução de 32*, 211–212; APESP, Col. 32, Pasta 354, Docs. 632–635. The quote is from Alfredo Ellis Júnior, cited by his daughter in Myriam Ellis, *Alfredo Ellis Júnior, 1896–1974*, 125.

157. Montenegro, *Cruzes paulistas*, 382–386.

158. Copies of these can be found in APESP, Col. Rev. de 32, Pasta 354, Docs. 633–635.

159. "Maria da Legião Negra," *A Gazeta*, September 5, 1932, 3; APESP, Col. Rev. de 32, Pasta 357, Doc. 692. Elias Karam recalled hearing that a nearby battalion of the Legião Negra included "five women, dressed as men, who for over a month avoided scrutiny [*burlaram a vigilância*]." Karam, *Um paranense nas trincheiras da lei*, 95–96.

160. "Homenageada d. Maria José Barroso, a Mulher-Símbolo de 32," *A Gazeta*, July 5, 1957, 24. In a film made to commemorate the 1932 uprising, Maria Soldado appears in the flag-raising scene. *São Paulo em festa* (Vera Cruz, 1954), Cinemateca Brasileira.

161. On Maria Soldado's role in the uprising, see Domingues, "Os 'Pérolas Negras,'" 222–225.

162. In at least one source, Maria Soldado is identified as Maria José Bezerra, not Barroso, but the other details are the same. Lopes, *Dicionário escolar afro-brasileiro*, 107.

163. Indeed, Stanley Hilton opens his history of the "civil war" of 1932 with an imagined scenario in which certain details are changed (such as Klinger's premature provocation) and speculates that São Paulo, under these slightly altered circumstances, might have won. *A guerra civil brasileira*, 9–15.

164. According to Warren Dean, the absence of a modern steel forge made the manufacture of rifles and cannon impossible. *The Industrialization of São Paulo*, 194.

165. Among the war dead were eighty-four members of Minas's Força Pública. In 1937 the mineiro state government made a short film, *Homenagem aos soldados mortos de 1932*, to honor them. Cinemateca Brasileira.

166. The Força Pública reached an accord with the Vargas regime on September 29, an act that the most fanatic paulistas denounced as treason. Levy, *Coluna invicta*, 182. Honório de Sylos, another combat veteran, did not accuse the Força Pública of treason, but did believe its officers' timidity cost São Paulo the war. *Gente e Fatos*, 151.

167. IEB, Coleção Guilherme de Almeida, Recorte s/d, Série 41. The newspaper clipping has no date but from other details it seems like the interview was given in the 1950s.

168. In the final section of *A sala da capela*, when the leaders of the revolt are about to depart for exile, Vivaldo Coaracy includes a "manifesto" issued by the imprisoned conspirators exalting São Paulo as the "symbol of Brazil's grandeur within the law" (149–150).

169. On southern literature of the Lost Cause, see Blight, *Race and Reunion*, especially chapter 8.

170. Nogueira Filho, *A guerra cívica*, vol. 3 (*O povo em armas*), 170, 247.

171. Reprinted in Horácio de Andrade, *Tudo por São Paulo*, 114.

172. Hilton, *A guerra civil brasileira*, 105.

173. APESP, Col. Rev. de 32, Pasta 342a, Doc. 320, "Ao povo paulista livre." Ironically, in 1937, when the paulistas feared (as it turns out, rightly so) that Vargas might cancel the presidential elections, Waldemar Ferreira paid Vargas a visit and insisted that the paulista civilian leadership, in 1932, had been coerced into supporting the revolt by General Klinger. Vargas, *Diário*, vol. 2 (1937–1943), 27.

174. According to Herbert Levy, "São Paulo was crushed unconditionally because the chiefs of the Força Pública had not even considered defending it." *Coluna invicta*, 182. Gastão Goulart, who was the (white) commanding officer of the Legião Negra, based his explanation of the FP's "treason" on Gustave Le Bon's notion of "residuals of ancestral personalities"—the largely nonwhite members of the FP "did not feel the impulses of bandeirante ancestry." Goulart, *Verdades*, 244–245. The final manifesto of the insurgent government portrayed Klinger in a relatively favorable light, claiming that he only considered surrender once it became clear that the Força Pública was negotiating with Vargas. It also stressed that he rejected the dictatorship's terms as "humiliating," but the FP raised no such objections. Andrade, *Tudo por São Paulo*, 116.

175. *Diário de São Paulo*, July 9, 1960 in APESP Col. Rev. de 32, Caixa 16, Recortes.

176. Hilton, *A guerra civil brasileira*, 61–72.

177. In an unpublished reevaluation of 1932, Alfredo Ellis, in typically hyperbolic style, blamed the defeat mainly on Klinger, whom he disparages as "neurotic . . . of evident intellectual deficiency . . . and perhaps [having been] in cahoots with the enemy." Quoted in M. Ellis, *Alfredo Ellis Júnior*, 71–72.

178. For comments regarding support in Rio Grande do Sul for the paulista uprising, see NARA, RG59, M1472, 832.00, Internal Affairs of Brazil, July 20, 1932; Report no. 1029 (Wm. Sackville), September 9, 1932.

179. According to his biographer, Assis Chateaubriand, who supported the paulistas, acted as a go-between for Lindolfo Collor, who joined the insurgency, and Olegário Maciel, governor of Minas, who stayed loyal to Vargas. Morais, *Chatô*, 277.

180. U.S. Consul Cameron seems to have been an especially unreliable source of information about Minas Gerais. Days after the uprising began, he sent a cable claiming (incorrectly) that the anti-Vargas forces had seized control of the state, a claim he soon had to retract. And a few weeks later he claimed there was a "nonaggression pact" between the two states, yet we know that eighty-four members of the mineiro Força Pública lost their lives in the fighting. NARA, RG59, M1472, Brazil (Revolutions)—Cameron to U.S. embassy, July 17, 1932; August 3, 1932.

181. Paulistas who sympathized with or participated in the 1924 tenente revolt were especially hostile to Bernardes. See Duarte, *Agora nós!*, 233.

182. However, Vivaldo Coaracy expressed skepticism over this newfound solidarity. *A sala da capela*, 39.

183. Vargas feared Waldomiro was being "overly tolerant" and that this posture would be interpreted as a sign of weakness by the paulistas. Vargas, *Diário*, vol. 1, 140, 175. His term as interventor lasted from October 6, 1932, to July 27, 1933.

184. Vianna, *Companheiros de viagem*, 23. Even though Deocélia had volunteered in support of the uprising, she still felt vulnerable as someone who was not paulista-born, and (perhaps) as someone unsure of her social and racial status. It is also significant that she uses the term "legalist" to refer to the federal forces. My enormous thanks to James Woodard for indicating this source and for his insights into Vianna's background.

185. The consular reports mention two incidents in early 1933 that resulted in deaths, including one in which a nordestino soldier, enraged by mocking comments, opened fire on a crowd and killed eight people. I could not find any confirmation

that such incidents occurred, a search complicated by the prevailing censorship, but I did find references in the press to the need for calm and to avoid provocation. NARA, RG59, M1472, Brazil (Revolutions)—Cameron, Political Report no. 55, March 28, 1933. The closest I could find to a confirmation was the commentary by General Daltro Filho, commander of the occupying forces, in which he lamented the "disagreeable" events of recent days and enlisted the press to help in the "pacification of the spirits." "A situação," OESP, March 3, 1933, 3.

186. The founding of the Escola Livre de Sociologia e Política (1933) and the Universidade de São Paulo (1934) prompted modernist critic Sérgio Milliet to declare, "From São Paulo there will no longer emerge anarchic civil wars, but rather an 'intellectual and scientific revolution' capable of changing Brazilians' social and economic conceptions." FGV, CPDOC, A Era Vargas: dos anos 20 a 1945 (2012), "Criação da Universidade de São Paulo." http://cpdoc.fgv.br/producao/dossies/AEraVargas1/anos30–37 /RevConstitucionalista32/USP.

187. NARA, RG59, M1472, 832.00, Reel 7, Thurston, August 3, 1932.

188. Coaracy, A sala da capela, 15.

189. Castro, Diário de um combatente desarmado, 191–197; Sandroni and Sandroni, Austregésilo de Athayde, 309.

190. Coaracy, A sala da capela, 46–48.

191. A number of elite paulista women in the capital and Santos stayed in contact with exiles and raised money to make sure they weren't suffering privations. The most active was Mariana Anna do Vale Neto. Several of her letters to men in exile are in the state archive. APESP, Col. Rev. de 32, Pasta 328. The leftist newspaper A Plebe sarcastically urged the "senhoritas" of Santos to consider raising money for exiled anarchists. "A solidariedade da gente 'boa,'" A Plebe, January 14, 1933, 3.

192. Duarte, who found work with a printing house in Paris, returned a check sent by José Maria Whitaker (possibly drawn from funds left over from the Gold Campaign, which Whitaker coordinated). FGV, CPDOC, JMW 32.07.11. Ellis had been wounded in the battle of Cunha and stayed in the interior until it was safe to resume public life. M. Ellis, Alfredo Ellis Júnior, 67.

193. On the Gold Campaign see Firmeza, Poemas em prosa da revolução paulista, 99–101; Mehrtens, Urban Space and National Identity, 48–51.

194. Vieira de Mello, Renda-se paulista, 3.

195. Quoted in Gomes, Negros e política, 76–77. Sant'Anna's bitterness may have been heightened by his legal troubles and his summary ejection from the leadership of the Legião Negra.

196. A dentist having difficulty establishing his credentials wrote to Armando asking for his intercession. He stressed his service in 1932 and his willingness "to give the last drop of my blood for the liberation of my State and my Brazil." APESP, Arquivo Armando de Salles Oliveira, doc. no. 101, August 15, 1937.

197. Mehrtens, Urban Space and National Identity, 95.

198. The documentary film A respeito do Movimento Constitucionalista de 1932 (1978) includes an interview with a veteran from the 1932 uprising, evidently working-class, who expresses his disappointment that he never received monetary compensation or the support for his family that he was promised when he volunteered.

199. IHGSP, Arquivo Carlota Pereira de Queiroz, Recortes: "Homenagem da Assembleia Constituinte aos Mortos da Revolução de 32," *OESP*, April 13, 1935. For similar sentiments, see Sylos, *Gente e Fatos*, 159–161, in which he re-creates a dialogue with his son and recounts his days as a soldier of the law.

200. Sampaio, *Renembranças*, 210–213.

Chapter 4: Marianne into Battle?

Epigraph 2. Rodrigues, *A Mulher Paulista no movimento pro-constituinte*, front matter.
Epigraph 3. IHGSP, Arq. Rev. 1932, Recortes, 29; also in Andrade, "Guerra de São Paulo" (Gonçalves da Costa, org.), 88–89.

1. On women's patriotic support during the Paraguayan War (1864–1870), see Ipsen, "Patrícias, Patriarchy, and Popular Demobilization." See also the longer discussion of this issue in her dissertation, "Delicate Citizenship."

2. *O Povo* (Fortaleza), October 4, 1932, 1. See also Gonçalves, *Carne para canhão!*, 163–164.

3. An example of this assumption about the Revolution of 1932 can be found in Schpun, "Carlota Pereira de Queiroz."

4. Here I am drawing on the approach to gender history that, rather than making a sharp distinction between representations and "real women," seeks to understand how gendered constructions constrain roles for women and men, but also can be shaped and, occasionally, even subverted. See, for example, the discussion of the figure of the *mujer obrera* and women factory workers in Farnsworth-Alvear, *Dulcinea in the Factory*, chapter 2.

5. Duarte, *Que é que há?*, 284–285. See also Coaracy, *O caso de São Paulo*, 139.

6. From a radio speech "Exaltação da Mulher Paulista," by João Neves de Fontoura, a politician from Rio Grande do Sul who came to São Paulo to support the revolution. Cited in Picchia, *A revolução paulista*, 129. This quote is especially interesting since it implies that elite women had been active in Brazilian politics all along; what was different this time was their ability/willingness to act publicly.

7. Pereira, *O Brasil e a raça*, 58.

8. Museu Paulista, Col. 32, Doc. 2777.

9. My thanks to James Woodard for his insight on this last point. See also Prado, *A democracia ilustrada*, 123–133. For a fierce historical critique of the getulista discourse on 1932, see Paula, *1932*.

10. In this arsenal of family metaphors, children played a role analogous to women. Thus there were many visual representations of a young boy, dressed as a volunteer, with the slogan, "If necessary, we will go, too." Martins, *Album de família 1932*.

11. For a pathbreaking study of how women's virtue is both deployed politically but treated as outside politics, see Kerber, *Women of the Republic*.

12. Carvalho, *Irradiações*, 129.

13. Duara, "Historicizing National Identity," 151–174.

14. On the prevalence of female-headed households in late colonial São Paulo, see Kuznesof, *Household Economy and Urban Development*.

15. The best scholarly treatment of the bandeiras and regional identity is Ferreira, *A epopéia bandeirante*. On women and the bandeiras see Bittencourt, *A Mulher Paulista*

na história, 37–80; Eurico de Góes, "Heroínas paulistas" (Radio address, August 18, 1932), in Museu Paulista, Col. 32, Pasta 3, Doc. 2948.

16. John Chasteen constructs a similar image of elite women in nineteenth-century rural Rio Grande do Sul. See *Heroes on Horseback*, 30–31, 117, 146.

17. A historical retrospective on paulista fashion published in 1954 sustained this image. Praising the paulista woman's fashion sense, it concluded: "The fundamental feature of her personality is discretion. She does not tend toward the exaggerations so common in tropical regions." "Quatro séculos de modas no Planalto," *Diário de São Paulo*, January 25, 1954, section 5, 4–7.

18. Góes, "Heroínas paulistas," Museu Paulista, Col. 32, Doc. 2948; Picchia, *A revolução paulistânia*, 17.

19. Picchia, *A revolução paulista*, 17; Dirce de Mello, "A Mulher Paulista na história," *Paulistania*, 2, no. 7 (May–June 1940): 31–33. For the use of this imagery in connection to Brazilian women who were fascist sympathizers, see Deutsch, "Spartan Mothers."

20. For a pre-1932 version, see Miranda, *São Paulo e o verdadeiro liberalismo*, 14–17. According to Veiga Miranda, the "matronas paulistas . . . had a touch of the Spartan" (14).

21. Luiz Naclério Homem, in a passage from his memoirs in which he considers why São Paulo went to war, cites the fervor of the paulista mothers, whom he compares to the "matrons of Sparta." He then quotes the words of the mother of his platoon mate, Alaôr Rolemberg: "My son, never beat a retreat because a Rolemberg never runs away! Never abandon your fellow soldiers! Die at your post if necessary! . . . But don't think that your mother doesn't fear for you, for whenever you are on guard duty, I will spend my nights wide awake asking God to protect you!" *Lembranças de um belo ideal*, 80.

22. Cited in Nogueira Filho, *A guerra cívica 1932*, vol. 1, 422–426.

23. Andrade, "Guerra de São Paulo," 254–255. Chasteen observes that the women of the Saraiva family—progenitor of two renowned caudillos—were often described as having masculine qualities, "as if to imply a superabundance of testosterone in the bloodline." *Heroes on Horseback*, 117.

24. My thanks to Deborah Silverman for drawing this contrast to my attention. The poster with the pointing male soldier is obviously inspired by the classic World War I British recruiting poster with the image of Lord Kitchener, which also inspired the "Uncle Sam Wants You" poster in the United States. On this famous pose and its implications, see Ginzburg, "'Your Country Needs You,'" 1–22.

25. From an article reprinted in *A Gazeta*, July 9, 1957, 7.

26. Rodrigues, *A Mulher Paulista no movimento pro-constituinte*, 58.

27. On women in the workforce, see Besse, *Restructuring Patriarchy*, 129–163.

28. *Diário de São Paulo*, Edição Comemorativa, January 25, 1954 (Modernismo), 4; Miceli, *Nacional estrangeiro*, 75–87; Sevcenko, *Orfeu extático na metrópole*, 244.

29. On the extent and limits of Guedes Penteado's feminism, see Schpun, "Regionalistas e cosmopolistas."

30. In using the phrase "the public sphere" here I do not mean to imply that there is a sharp distinction between the so-called private sphere of the home and family, and

the public sphere of politics and commerce, nor that one is "traditional" and the other "modern." For a brief critical discussion of this issue, see de Grazia, *How Fascism Ruled Women*, 14. However, it is clear to me that the women involved in this movement did draw such distinctions and did see their participation as a departure from "normal" roles for women.

31. "Eu sou a Mulher Paulista," radio address by Dulce Amara, in *A Folha da Noite*, July 14, 1932, 2.

32. Rodrigues, *A Mulher Paulista no movimento pro-constituinte*, 14.

33. IHGSP, Arq. Rev. 1932, Recortes de Jornais, 29.

34. To quote José Murilo de Carvalho on the absence of (respectable) women from the public sphere: "A mulher, se pública, era prostituta." *A formação das almas*, 92–93. On the image of the prostitute in Brazil during the early decades of the twentieth century, see Pereira, *"Que tenhas teu corpo."* On prostitution in São Paulo in a slightly earlier period, see Dias, *Power and Everyday Life*, especially 79–80, 135–137.

35. Carvalho, *A formação das almas*, chapter 4. As it turns out, Marianne's image was not universally rejected in Brazil. See Coelho, "Uma aparição tardia."

36. The classic study of the "combative" image of Marianne (and the source of the title for this chapter) is Agulhon, *Marianne into Battle*.

37. On women's growing presence in public life, and the anxiety it provoked, see Besse, *Restructuring Patriarchy*, 12–37.

38. Rodrigues, *A Mulher Paulista no movimento pro-constituinte*, front matter.

39. Among the first historical works to connect gendered interpretations with issues of racism and colonialism were Burton, *Burdens of History*; and Sinha, *Colonial Masculinity*. It is interesting to note that the cearense daily, *O Povo*, a vigorous critic of paulista chauvinism, claimed that (in response to the new electoral code) "the cearense women . . . similar to what is occurring in the most civilized nations, took the initiative and organized themselves." July 2, 1932, 1.

40. On the modernization of gender inequality in urban Brazil, see Besse, *Restructuring Patriarchy*; and Rago, *Do cabaré ao lar*. According to Deniz Kandiyoti, "On the one hand, nationalist movements invite women to participate more fully in collective life by interpellating them as 'national' actors: mothers, educators, workers and even fighters. On the other hand, they reaffirm the boundaries of their gender interests within the terms of reference set by nationalist discourse." "Identity and Its Discontents," 380.

41. Castro, *Política, és mulher!* The odd title of this book—literally, "Politics, You Are a Woman!"—is an excellent example of the way in which entities can be feminized in a manner that actually heightens the exclusion of women.

42. For the earlier period see Bederman, *Manliness and Civilization*; and McClintock, *Imperial Leather*. On the anxieties provoked by the figure of the *chica moderna* in Mexico, see Hershfield, *Imagining la Chica Moderna*.

43. On women street sellers in the nineteenth century, slave and free, see Dias, *Power and Everyday Life*, 96–109.

44. It is useful to make a distinction between public spaces as physical locations (the street, the square, etc.) and the symbolic public space of political life, the res publica. Subaltern women had long been present in the former but invisible in the latter.

The 1932 campaign allowed middle-class and elite women to enter not only physical public space, but also the space of political life. On these distinctions, see Benhabib, "Models of Public Space."

45. Nogueira Filho, *A guerra cívica*, vol. 2, 169, 199.

46. On the unaccustomed circulation of well-off women in public spaces during the Constitutionalist Campaign, see Schpun, "Carlota Pereira de Queiroz," 176.

47. On the enduring significance of this experience for elite women, see Schpun, "Carlota Pereira de Queiroz," 173–175. Referring to 1932 as a "Revolution for the Women," Schpun argues that "in a state of war, [women] have more efficient alibis for the exercise of citizenship" (174). I agree with this argument up to a point, but her perspective simultaneously gives too much (implicitly feminist) agency to women and neglects the ways in which women's "agency" involved circumscribing their own claims to citizenship.

48. *A Cigarra* (São Paulo) 424 (July 1932): 1. For a photo of women wearing caps, see Paula, *1932*, 244. A particularly striking photo of a pro-Constitutionalist rally shows men dressed in everyday clothes accompanied by two women wrapped in paulista flags.

49. Martins, *Album de família 1932*, unpaginated.

50. Such portrayals can also be found in the press. An article on "A Mulher Paulista" in a leading newspaper described the various sorts of manual labor being performed by her "delicate hands," thereby highlighting the idea that such labor was an unaccustomed activity for her. *A Gazeta*, August 7, 1932, 3.

51. APESP, Col. 32, Pasta 342a, Doc. 322.

52. Rodrigues, *A Mulher Paulista no movimento pro-constituinte*, 19.

53. This theme, that mothers might prefer a child's death to dishonor by that child, arose in a very different context a few months before the outbreak of civil war. Susan Besse cites the case of a middle-class paulista woman who went on trial in May 1932 for having shot and killed her favorite son because his behavior dishonored the family. Besse notes that this woman's response was regarded as extreme, but it nonetheless reflected the intensified emphasis on the mother's duty to ensure the honorable character of her children. Moreover, this choice of death over dishonor is an excellent example of how behavior stigmatized as deviant, or even criminal, at one moment, might be refashioned as "normative" in a very different historical context. Besse, *Restructuring Patriarchy*, 89–92.

54. The subhead for this section borrows from the title of a pathbreaking study of women, gender, and militarization: Enloe, *Does Khaki Become You?*

55. "Soldado que era mulher," *Jornal das Trincheiras*, September 8, 1932, 4; *O Diário Nacional*, September 18, 1932, 4.

56. Stanley Hilton quotes a captured soldier of the Força Pública who told his getulista interrogators that paulista morale was extremely high, and that "even young women [were] accompanying the platoons as nurses." *A guerra civil brasileira*, 105.

57. And apparently it was not only paulista women who were eager to serve in a military capacity. A cearense newspaper recounted the story of Hildovar Moreira, from Juiz de Fora, Minas Gerais, who repeatedly attempted to enlist in the federal volunteer forces and was finally sent to the front as a nurse. *O Povo*, September 1, 1932, 1.

58. Rodrigues, *A Mulher Paulista no movimento pro-constituinte*, 43.

59. Museu Paulista, Col. 32, Pasta 3, Doc. 2948. For an excellent discussion of the participation of women in the auxiliary unit of the Legião Negra, see Domingues, "Os 'pérolas negras,'" 222–225.

60. Domingues, "Os 'Pérolas Negras,'" 222–225.

61. *Diário Nacional*, September 18, 1932, 4.

62. Andrade, "Guerra de São Paulo," 254–255. This is very much in the same vein as the North American Civil War–era folksong "The Cruel War," in which a woman begs her husband/lover to let her dress as a man and accompany him to war because she "longs to be with [him], morning and night," though there is also, in this case, the intimation that she shares her partner's zeal for the Causa Paulista.

63. As Petrônio Domingues observes, it is quite remarkable that a poor, black woman would emerge as a celebrated heroine of the Constitutionalist Movement ("Os 'Pérolas Negras,'" pp. 222–225). However, it also needs to be considered whether her racial and social-class identities made it less subversive to celebrate her for doing something typically regarded as unfeminine.

64. Karam, *Um paranaense nas trincheiras da lei*, 95–96.

65. For a brief biography of Stela Rosa Sguassábia/Mário Soldado by a local (São João, São Paulo) historian, Eduardo Menezes, see Mulheres de São João, Maria Sguassábia (Biografia), 2008, http://www.mulheresdesaojoao.com.br/index_arquivos/Maria SguassabiaBiografia1.htm. An issue of *Paulistânia* commemorating the Constitutionalist Revolution included a photo of Maria Isguassabia [*sic*]. *Paulistânia* 35 (July–August 1950): 25.

66. Levy, *A coluna invicta*, pp. 111–112.

67. "Soldado que era mulher," *Jornal das Trincheiras*, September 8, 1932, 4. The photo appeared in *Paulistânia* 35 (July–Aug. 1950): 25 and is also available online at the website in note 65, above. Amilcar Salgado dos Santos describes another "paulista heroine," Anita Travassos, as "always being in the trenches and even engaging in combat." *A epopéia de São Paulo em 1932*, 83–84.

68. *A Gazeta*, September 4, 1932, 3.

69. For example, one newspaper article claimed that when Vargas's troops entered São Paulo unchallenged in 1930, some analysts "condemned us as a collectivity that had been rendered sterile by wealth and prosperity." "Povo Másculo," *A Folha da Noite*, August 1, 1932, 2.

70. *Diário de São Paulo*, Ed. Comemorativa do IV Centenário, January 25, 1954, Cad. de História, 12.

71. Nogueira Filho, *A guerra cívica*, vol. 2, 168–169.

72. *A Gazeta*, September 4, 1932, 3. In her weekly column, "Cartas de mulher," Vina Centi addressed her article to the "Voluntário intelectual paulista." In the final paragraph, she concludes: "I knew you when you were rich, in full enjoyment of all the superficial pleasures of a corrupt and arid worldliness. . . . You were elegantly useless and indifferent." But now that he has joined the battle, he has become "splendidly strong, splendidly masculine, splendidly Brazilian"; he's the true heir to the bandeirante spirit. *Jornal das Trincheiras*, September 22, 1932, 2.

73. For typical photos, see Donato, *A revolução de 32*, 79, 81, 83, 133, 151–153.

74. Leite, *Martírio e glória*, 154.

75. Andrade, "Guerra de São Paulo," 302.

76. NARA, RG 59, M1472, 832.00, Political Report no. 48, July 30, 1932. The modifier "wealthy" was hardly necessary given that such "crude" tasks would be unremarkable if he were talking about the majority of paulista women.

77. "Histórico e apreciação do movimento de 1932," APESP, Col. 32, Pasta 385, Doc. 2034.

78. APESP, Col. 32, Pasta 385, Doc. 2034.

79. "Dei Ouro Pelo Bem de S. Paulo" was the motto that appeared on the metal rings given to those who donated their wedding bands. Borges, *Memória paulista*, 65.

80. Martins, *Album de família 1932*, includes posters from the campaign, one of which depicts a manicured feminine hand depositing a gold ring on a pile of jewelry; another, painted by the eminent artist Oscar Pereira da Silva, portrays semi-naked (and very white) women as Ladies Bountiful.

81. "Ouro da Victória," *A Cigarra* 426 (August 1932): 13. This issue's cover portrayed an otherwise naked woman, draped with the flag of São Paulo, lifting arms covered with gold necklaces, and so forth, to a "sun" that is a radiant flag of Brazil.

82. Picchia, *A revolução paulista*, 139.

83. Picchia, *A revolução paulista*, 164.

84. NARA, RG 59, M1472, 832.00, Political Report no. 48, July 30, 1932.

85. Picchia, *A revolução paulista*, 165–166.

86. Castro, *Diário de um combatente desarmado*, 158–161.

87. *A Cigarra* 19, no. 427 (September 30,1932); *Diário Nacional*, July 31, 1932, 2; *A Gazeta*, September 21,1932, 1.

88. This may have been due in part to an appeal for women to show their support for the Causa Paulista by wearing the "bibi" cap, but the robust response indicates that they didn't need much prompting. "Apello à Mulher Paulista," *A Folha da Noite*, July 18, 1932, 3.

89. A photograph of the women's auxiliary of the Legião Negra can be found in a photo magazine produced to raise money for the Constitutionalist cause: *A epopéia de Piratininga*, unpaginated. Museu Paulista, Col. Rev. de 32, Doc. 2952.

90. On the participation of mulheres negras in the Legião Negra, see Domingues, "Os 'Pérolas Negras,'" 222–225.

91. Museu Paulista, Col. 32, Pasta 4, Doc. 2951.

92. Goulart, *Verdades da revolução*, 34.

93. On the Mãe Preta, see Seigel, *Uneven Encounters*, 206–234; Alberto, *Terms of Inclusion*, 69–139; Lopes, "História e memória do negro em São Paulo," 81–160. Also chapter 7, herein.

94. Although open presidential campaigning took place in 1936–1937, many historians would argue that the state of emergency declared in 1935, after the abortive revolt of the Aliança Libertadora Nacional, initiated "the definitive turn away from the liberal constitutionalism promised in 1934." Williams, *Culture Wars in Brazil*, 63.

95. "Sobre o voto feminino," *A Folha da Noite*, January 28, 1933 (clipping file, IHGSP).

96. On the response of her male colleagues to the presence of a woman in a previously all-masculine space, see Schpun, "Carlota Pereira de Queiroz," 192–194.

97. "Visitou a constituinte," *A Platéa*, April 24, 1935, 6. Toledo is clearly using the phrase in its archetypical sense; if he were simply referring to the presence of a specific paulista female, the polite locution would have been "senhora paulista" or "dama paulista."

98. The best source of information on women's roles in social services is Rodrigues, *A Mulher Paulista no movimento pro-constituinte*.

99. "Quanto deve São Paulo à Mulher Paulista," *Diário de São Paulo*, edição comemorativa do IV Centenário da Cidade de S. Paulo (January 25, 1954), 4. In retrospective accounts there is an increased tendency to refer to the women participants as *mães paulistas* (paulista mothers). "A câmara dedica sessão à comemoração do 9 de Julho," *A Folha de São Paulo*, July 10, 1962.

100. Sertório de Castro, *Política, és Mulher!* Despite the post-1932 publication date, it is clear from the book's contents that it was written before the Constitutionalist uprising. Still, the author did not feel compelled to alter his arguments in any way prior to publication.

101. See, for example, "The Sears Case," in Scott, *Gender and the Politics of History*, 167–177.

102. Picchia, *A revolução paulista*, 165–166.

103. "Eco da revolução: Voz da Mulher Paulista," *A Plebe*, December 3, 1932, 2 (emphasis in original). The depiction of "bourgeois ladies" as frivolous is a classic anarchist discursive strategy conflating class critiques with gender stereotypes. See also Capelato, *O movimento de 1932*, 43–44.

104. de Grazia, *How Fascism Ruled Women*, 14–15.

105. Similarly, the Constitutionalist leadership extolled the bravery of the Legião Negra—the battalions of black soldiers who fought for São Paulo—all the while constructing an identity for São Paulo that was white and European. See chapter 3, herein.

Chapter 5: Provincializing São Paulo

Epigraph 1. Letter reprinted in Silva, *1932*, 281.

1. Albuquerque, *A invenção do Nordeste*, 101.

2. *Diário de Pernambuco*, May 25, 1932, 3. While Barata's comments could be regarded as typical political flattery, there's no indication that his paulista hosts felt compelled to return the compliment. And the latter would certainly never have lauded any other region of Brazil as "the greatest expression of Brazil's vitality," or the "leader state."

3. APESP, Col. 32, Pasta 342, Doc 292, 294. Góes's flattering comments are especially noteworthy given that his brother Cícero had been killed by paulista forces a month earlier.

4. Blake, *The Vigorous Core of Our Nationality*, especially chapter 4. This vision informed political discourse in and about the Nordeste well into the late twentieth century. See Sarzynski, "Revolutionizing Identities." For a Marxist approach to regional inequality, see Silveira, *O regionalismo nordestino*.

5. Albuquerque, *A invenção do Nordeste*, 242–251.

6. APESP, Col. 32, Pasta 342b, Doc. 360.

7. On the 1932 drought, see Blake, *The Vigorous Core of Our Nationality*, 209–210.

8. Thus an article in *O Estadão* in 1920 praised the progress of southern Brazil, in contrast to "the North, with its deserts, its ignorance, its lack of hygiene, its poverty, its servility." "O Bloco Politico do Norte," OESP, September 3, 1920, 4, cited in Albuquerque, *A invenção do Nordeste*, 43.

9. It has been fairly well established that Freyre later retitled and rewrote his presentation at the regionalist congress to inflate his role and significance in it. But the features emphasized here were likely in the "manifesto" when it was presented in 1926 and also appeared in several journal and newspaper articles that Freyre authored in the 1920s. On the congress and these publications, see Blake, *The Vigorous Core of Our Nationality*, 191–195.

10. For a wonderful discussion of how food can be used to consolidate a national identity in the face of strong denationalizing forces, see Derby, "Gringo Chickens with Worms."

11. Freyre, *Manifesto regionalista*, 67. For an excellent discussion of Freyre's regionalist writings in the 1920s, see Blake, *The Vigorous Core of Our Nationality*, 190–196.

12. For pre-1932 manifestations of paulista disdain for the North of Brazil, see chapter 1, herein.

13. On the North's relationship with the Vargas regime in its early phase, see Pandolfi, "A trajetória do Norte," 339–425.

14. On the processes by which certain (economic) spaces get defined as separate from others, see Harvey, *Spaces of Global Capitalism*, especially "Notes toward a Theory of Uneven Geographical Development," 71–116.

15. For a discussion of the overlapping discourses of racial democracy and conservative modernization, see Mitchell, "Miguel Reale and the Impact of Conservative Modernization," 116–137.

16. Albuquerque, *A invenção do Nordeste*, 120–145.

17. Freyre, *Manifesto regionalista*, 33–34.

18. Aside from Freyre being pernambucano, he argued that the mixture of African, European, and Indian in the state of his birth made it the most emblematic of the Nordeste, and perhaps of Brazil. Blake, *The Vigorous Core of Our Nationality*, 190–200.

19. On Assis Chateaubriand's activities and alliances in this period, see Morais, *Chatô*, 273–289.

20. Chatô was arrested in Minas, where he was traveling under an assumed name for the purpose of presenting the paulistas' case to the mineiro political leadership. On his arrest and the *empastelamento* (sacking) of the *Diário de Pernambuco* see *O Povo*, September 9, 1932, 1. For the *Diário*'s own commentary, see DP, September 18, 1932, 1.

21. DP, April 23, 1932, 2. This was a long-standing theme for regional landed elites fearful of losing their access to cheap labor, but at the height of a drought, it was not merely a continuation of that lament.

22. DP, April 16, 1932, 1.

23. *O Povo* is still one of the leading daily papers in Ceará. Rocha was born in Bahia of an educated but modest family that was left impoverished when his father died. Rocha became a railroad worker, studied dentistry, then moved to Fortaleza and started the newspaper in 1923. Bonavides, *Democrito Rocha*. Early contributors to the

paper included the novelist Rachel de Queiroz, journalist Antônio Drummond, and socialist writer Jáder Moreira de Carvalho.

24. "O retorno do Brasil ao regime legal," *DP*, April 5, 1932, 1. This article was on various entities in the North that "decisively" endorsed the campaign in favor of constitutionalization, including the Instituto de Advogados in Alagoas and the Associação Comercial in Maranhão.

25. "A situação política nacional," *DP*, April 23, 1932, 2.

26. "Política paulista," *DP*, May 13, 1932, 1.

27. In "Constituinte," Austregésilo de Athayde declared the movement to be a "national" one. *DP*, May 19, 1932, 2.

28. "O movimento cívico empolga S. Paulo em defesa de sua autonomia moral," *DP*, May 25, 1932, 25.

29. Assis Chateaubriand, "O Brasil das capitanias," *DP*, May 31, 1932, 2. It is interesting to note that Chatô's main preoccupation is to deflect charges that the paulistas are motivated strictly by material interests, which perhaps reflects sentiment in the North to the effect that paulista prosperity had come at the other regions' expense.

30. Assis Chateaubriand, "O Brasil das capitanias," *DP*, May 31, 1932, 2.

31. "Pela União Nacional," *DP*, June 19, 1932, 3; "Sentimento federalista no Brasil," *DP*, June 21, 1932, 1.

32. *DP*, June 26, 1932, 1.

33. *DP*, June 21, 1932, 1.

34. "Revista das revistas," *DP*, July 1, 1932, 3.

35. "A situação política nacional," *DP*, July 7, 1932, 1.

36. According to an article published in *O Povo* on May 31, 1932 (p. 1), aside from the MMDC militia, the paulistas were also considering forming a militia that "will have as its purpose to offer the most tenacious means to combat the Communist elements that are agitating in the great state." See also "O comunismo em S. Paulo," July 7, 1932, 1.

37. *OP*, July 13, 1932, 1.

38. *OP*, July 13, 1932, 1. Here it is worth noting that Juraci Magalhães was cearense.

39. *OP*, July 19, 1932, 1.

40. *OP*, August 17, 1932, 2. "Peasant" is not an entirely satisfactory translation for "caboclo" since even though the latter term typically refers to rural people, it also has a quasi-racial and regional connotation that is lacking in "peasant."

41. "O Norte e o momento," *O Imparcial* (S. Luis, Maranhão), July 20, 1932, 8. Maranhão is an example of the instability of regional boundaries. Lying to the west of Ceará, it is sometimes grouped with the Amazonian states as part of the Norte, and at other times it is included in the Nordeste.

42. "Um telegramma sobre o levante em S. Paulo," *DP*, July 24, 1932, 1.

43. *O Povo*, August 30, 1932, 1.

44. *O Povo*, August 30, 1932, 1. While this seems to be a paraphrase of Barros's remarks, the actual comments were every bit as pejorative. Barros also authored one of the unflattering articles that ran in *O Estadão* in the 1920s in the series that clearly was meant to portray the huge contrast between modern São Paulo and the backward Nordeste. Paulo de Moraes Barros, "Impressões do Nordeste," *OESP*, August 16, 1923,

3. A 1923 speech by Moraes Barros on "racial degeneration" in the Nordeste was also cited (in this instance, favorably) in Lobo, *São Paulo na federação*, 155–156.

45. *O Povo*, August 30, 1932, 1. Comstock spent two years in the Nordeste and claimed that all of Barros's statistics were inaccurate.

46. On the strategic uses of the Brazil/U.S. comparison, see Seigel, *Uneven Encounters*, chapters 4 and 5.

47. *O Povo*, August 22, 1932, 2.

48. "Contra o Brasil, Não," *O Imparcial*, July 31, 1932, 8. The article also says that São Paulo might become the Brazilian Catalonia.

49. "Paulista, Não te Desanimes," APESP, Col. 32, Pasta 357, Doc. 673.

50. FGV, CPDOC, Arquivo Bertoldo Klinger, BK32.09.00/00. This report, written during the last weeks of the uprising, claimed that many paranenses and gaúchos were refusing to fight against the paulistas. See also "Manifesto aos Mineiros," Arquivo Virgílio de Mello Franco, VMF32.07.13.

51. "Como o Sr. Toledo qualifica os voluntários do Norte," *O Povo*, September 10, 1932, 1. According to the documentation in the Pedro de Toledo Archive in the Museu Paulista (Pasta 1, Doc. 6080), while ambassador to Argentina (1919–1926) Toledo joined (January 18, 1920) the Liga Patriótica Argentina, an ultra-right-wing/nationalist group that was openly xenophobic and anti-Semitic.

52. DP, August 18, 1932, 8. Emphasis added.

53. *O Povo*, August 17, 1932, 1. A non-naturalized Hungarian-Jewish immigrant, José Preiz, died fighting for São Paulo, and this may have been the starting point for this accusation.

54. Zebedee was the father of two disciples of Christ, and he was "left behind" when his sons were called by Jesus. The reference here seems to imply that the paulistas would also be left behind, whereas the nordestinos would be called to Jesus. APESP, Col. 32, Pasta 357, Doc. 685.

55. See entry for Barroso in Nobre, *1001 Cearenses notáveis*. I have not been able to find definitive evidence, but it seems very likely Magdaleno was related to the notorious anti-Semite and anti-paulista Gustavo Barroso, author of *A Sinagoga paulista* and a native of Ceará. For further evidence of anti-Semitic denunciations of paulista presidential candidate Armando de Salles Oliveira, see "O Leon Blum do Brasil," in APESP, Arquivo Campanha Eleitoral de Armando de Salles Oliveira, Caixa 1, Doc. 270.

56. "Contra o Brasil, Não," *O Imparcial*, July 3, 1932, 8.

57. FGV, CPDOC, Arquivo José Maria Whitaker, JMW32.07.11.

58. For example, Diniz, *São Paulo e a sua guerra de secessão*, 9; Gonçalves, *Carne para canhão*, "Aos Leitores" (n.p.)—both authors describe paulista politics as "reaccionarismo."

59. OP, October 3, 1932, 1. Also October 4, 1932, 8.

60. One article it quoted from *O Radical* claimed that "the great mass of paulista workers currently lack the means of subsistence" and were "veritable pariahs within the industrial opulence of São Paulo." OP, October 2, 1932, 1. *O Diário de Pernambuco* reported on a labor rally in Recife called to protest against the paulista uprising. "O comício de ontem," July 15, 1932, 1.

61. OP, July 23, 1932, 3.

62. *OP*, October 4, 1932, 1.

63. Diniz, *São Paulo e sua guerra de secessão*, 47.

64. Osório, *A guerra de São Paulo*, 149. On the millenarian movement in Joaseiro, see della Cava, *Miracle at Joaseiro*.

65. Osório, *A guerra de São Paulo*, 110.

66. On the ways in which the regional history of millenarian movements has been used to construct the Nordeste as a space of irrationality and backwardness, see Sarzynski, "Revolutionizing Identities."

67. Cited in Moura, *A fogueira constitucionalista*, 148–149.

68. See introduction, note 77, for another example of telluric reasoning.

69. On the permutations and persistence of race thinking, see de Luca, *A Revista do Brasil*, especially 131–235.

70. Carneiro, "Prefácio," xxiii–xxviii, in Karam, *Um paranense nas trincheiras da lei*.

71. Carneiro, "Prefácio," xxxi–ii, in Karam, *Um paranense nas trincheiras da lei*. It is very likely that Carneiro was echoing the language used in the widely read racist tract by Stoddard, *Revolt against Civilization: The Menace of the Under-Man*.

72. Carneiro, "Prefácio," xxxii, in Karam, *Um paranense nas trincheiras da lei*. For a particularly unrestrained use of racist arguments, see Amaral, "Nobreza paulista," in *Rotulas e mantilhas*, 89–109. Amaral insisted that the paulista forefathers were very zealous about racial purity and created an "Aryan nucleus" that became the foundation of the "paulista family." He goes on to describe the "Aryan" paulistas as "austere and grave," and able to control the mestiço population. In short, "it was from that Aryan unity of the nobility that the Bandeira emerged and the nationality was formed." Later in this essay he refers to Trotsky the Jew and Lenin the Mongoloid, and praises Hitler and Mussolini and the "miracle of fascism."

73. For an incisive study of Oliveira Vianna's intellectual production, see Bresciani, *O charme da ciência e a sedução da objetividade*. Bresciani's study is especially useful since she goes beyond the "stigma" of racism to explore the way Vianna used new ideas in the social sciences.

74. Azevedo Amaral, "Raça e política," *DP*, July 8, 1932, 2.

75. "Renovação naval," *DP*, August 20, 1932, 1.

76. "Problema da unidade," *DP*, August 27, 1932, 1. Although these articles did not directly address the conflict in São Paulo, the preoccupations they reflect surely were provoked by the paulista uprising.

77. For example, Lambert, *Os dois Brasis*.

78. "Détective—uma revista francesa—publicou um artigo mentiroso e ultrajante ao Brasil," *OP*, October 6, 1932, 3.

79. "Détective—uma revista francesa—publicou um artigo mentiroso e ultrajante ao Brasil," *OP*, October 6, 1932, 3. The reference to blacks remembering/recalling slavery was clearly meant as pejorative; it implies that they were tainted by their direct connection to those who had been enslaved.

80. "Détective—uma revista francesa—publicou um artigo mentiroso e ultrajante ao Brasil," *OP*, October 6, 1932, 3.

81. On northern Italians' efforts to distance themselves from pejorative repre-

sentations of Italy and to displace them onto the Mezzogiorno, see Jane Schneider, "Introduction," in Schneider, Italy's "Southern Question," 1–23.

82. On Minas under the Old Republic see Wirth, Minas Gerais in the Brazilian Federation.

83. The paulista leadership claimed the support of the renowned aviator, who died shortly after the uprising began, but his deathbed testament reads more like a call to lay down arms than a battle cry for São Paulo, even though the Dumont family had its roots in São Paulo and its most famous son died in the seaside paulista city of Guarujá. On Santos Dumont and the Constitutionalist Revolution, see Hilton, A guerra civil brasileira, 200.

84. NARA, RG59, M1472, Brazil (Revolutions)—Consul Cameron, August 3, 1932.

85. On the politics of Minas Gerais during the first phase of the Vargas regime (roughly, 1930–1934), see Bomeny, "A estratégia da conciliação."

86. Letter from Raúl Pilla to Pedro de Toledo, Museu Paulista, Arq. Pedro de Toledo, Pasta 1, Doc. 2801. Pilla, who was among the gaúchos openly supporting São Paulo, claimed Flores da Cunha's "betrayal" made it impossible for Rio Grande do Sul to fulfill its commitments to the paulistas. This same argument appeared in the manifesto "Ao Rio Grande do Sul, a S. Paulo e à Nação," signed by Pilla, Neves, Collor, and Baptista Luzardo and reprinted in several paulista accounts of the uprising. For the manifesto, see APESP, Col. Rev. de 32, Pasta 342a, Doc. 315. For reproductions of the manifesto and related documents, see Goulart, Verdades da revolução paulista, 125–145; and Alves Sobrinho, São Paulo triunfante, 1–150. Jair Pinto de Moura refers to the "Frente Unica dos pampas" as part of the Constitutionalist forces. A fogueira constitucionalista, 35.

87. As in Pedro de Toledo's speech to the consular community. OP, September 10, 1932, 1.

88. On the modernity of Minas's capital city see Eakin, Tropical Capitalism.

89. FGV, CPDOC, Arq Virgílio de Mello Franco, VMF32.07.13, "Manifesto aos Mineiros."

90. Casasanta, As razões de Minas. On Gustavo Capanema, who would become one of the leading figures in the Vargas regime, see Schwartzman et al., Tempos de Capanema; and Gomes, Capanema.

91. Capanema, "Prefácio," xi, in Casasanta, As razões de Minas.

92. Capanema, "Prefácio," xvi, in Casasanta, As razões de Minas.

93. Casasanta, As razões de Minas, 143.

94. Casasanta, "Ordem espiritual," in As razões de Minas, 219–228. For a similar reproach, see Osório, A guerra de São Paulo, 67–83. On Ariel and arielismo, see Miller, In the Shadow of the State, 96–114.

95. Albuquerque, A invenção do Nordeste, 65–93; Blake, The Vigorous Core of Our Nationality, 185–226.

96. Lima, Um sertão chamado Brasil, 91–131.

97. José Américo de Almeida, A bagaceira, cited in Albuquerque, A invenção do Nordeste, 138.

98. Blake, The Vigorous Core of Our Nationality, 212–216. Patricia Pessar, in her study of a millenarian community in the interior of the Nordeste, encountered

popular /religious notions of the superiority of the sertanejo to the African-descended populations on the coast. *From Fanatics to Folk*, 182–183.

99. On the issuing of a six-CD set by the Serviço Social do Comércio (SESC), consisting of music collected on the "folkloric research mission" of 1938, see Raquel Cozer, "CDs recuperam pesquisa de Mário de Andrade," *A Folha de São Paulo*, August 22, 2006. Of course, one of the ironies is that it was precisely the tentacles of modernity that allowed the music to be recorded and preserved. The phrase "fossil culture" is from Guerrero, "The Administration of Dominated Populations," 273.

100. Sandroni, "Folk Music and National Identity in Brazil."

101. One could identify some of the same ambivalence about this mission that occasionally emerges in the discussion of Alan Lomax and his role in recuperating Appalachian folk music and African-American blues. Most of the time Lomax is celebrated as a hero, but some scholars and musicians have raised questions about power, control, identity, and autonomy. See the essays in Radano and Bohlman, *Music and the Racial Imagination*. For a thoughtful discussion of these issues in the Brazilian context, see Hertzman, *Making Samba*.

102. Perhaps the most influential study in the last two decades of Freyre's masterwork is Araújo, *Guerra e paz*.

103. Oliven, *A parte e o todo*, 35; on the relationship between the discourse of racial democracy and the construction of a modern nation, see Gomes and Domingues, "O recinto sagrado: educação e anti-racismo no Brasil," in *Da nitidez e invisibilidade*, 287–308.

104. Oliven, *A parte e o todo*, 43. In Freyre's writings, to quote Oliven, "the national first passed through the regional."

105. Mitchell, "Miguel Reale and the Impact of Conservative Modernization," 116–137.

106. On the increasingly transregional vision of industrialization among São Paulo's manufacturers, see Weinstein, *For Social Peace in Brazil*, chapter 2.

107. FGV, CPDOC, Col. Getúlio Vargas, 1932.07.00, Rolo 2, Folha 0856; 1932.08.16/1, R2, F0894–0910/2; 1932.09.03, R2, F0949–0956/4. Vargas's correspondence during the uprising is full of notices about unrest in Rio Grande do Sul, but only one document indicates significant pro-Constitutionalist sentiment in the North, and this among the medical students of Bahia, who hardly constituted a major military threat. GVc, 1932.08.22/1, r2, f0913 (Juracy Magalhães to GV).

108. For a whirlwind tour of comments along these lines, see Woodard, *A Place in Politics*, 1.

Chapter 6: São Paulo Triumphant

Epigraph. "Histórias e memórias da cidade de São Paulo no IV Centenário," *Cidade* (Revista do Museu da Cidade de São Paulo) 1, no. 1 (1994): 17.

1. NARA, RG59, 832.00, Reel 7, Thurston, August 3, 1932.

2. Wilson Cano claims that the *questão regional* emerged with particular force in the late 1950s because that decade saw the first publication (1951 and 1952) of the national accounts (*contas nacionais*) that starkly illustrated enormous and growing regional disparities. *Raízes da concentração industrial em São Paulo*, 11–12. Although I

disagree that the national accounts could, on their own, explain this intensification of attention to regional disparities (especially since, as I noted above, the systematic display of disparity was nothing new), certainly the 1950s was a period when the discourse of national development both made São Paulo's growth a remarkable feat and a cause for concern. See also Weinstein, *For Social Peace in Brazil*, chapters 4 and 8; and Cardoso, *Ideologia do desenvolvimento Brasil*.

3. See chapter 3, herein.

4. As Vavy Pacheco Borges points out in her interview in the documentary *1932: A Guerra Civil* (1992), paulistas elected Vargas senator following his overthrow in 1945 and then gave him a wide majority of their votes in the presidential election of 1950.

5. See chapter 8, herein. In a sense, the implementation of the Constitution of 1934 was even briefer than this since the left-wing uprising in 1935 known as the Intentona enabled the regime to declare a state of emergency that effectively suspended the Constitution. On the Intentona, see Pinheiro, *Estratégias da ilusão*.

6. For historical interpretations of the Estado Novo, see Capelato, "Estado Novo"; and Pandolfi, *Repensando o Estado Novo*.

7. Though Vargas was attracted to one of the essential features of fascism—a strong, centralized state—his sentiments with regard to racism and anti-Semitism were more ambiguous. See, for example, Lesser, *Welcoming the Undesirables*.

8. See McCann, *The Brazilian-American Alliance*; Tota, *The Seduction of Brazil*; and Dinius, *Brazil's Steel City*.

9. On the problem of limited markets in the 1930s and limited inputs in the early 1940s, see the documents in Carone, *O pensamento industrial no Brasil*, especially 308–383.

10. On paulista industry during the war, see Weinstein, *For Social Peace*, 116–132; French, *The Brazilian Workers' ABC*, chapter 3; and Wolfe, *Working Women, Working Men*, chapter 4.

11. The best recent study of the nordestino migration to São Paulo is Fontes, *Um Nordeste em São Paulo*.

12. Weffort, "Nordestinos em São Paulo," 14–15. Weffort points out that European (especially Italian) immigration was "practically paralyzed" by 1930, whereas the full impact of nordestino migration would not be felt until after 1950. During that twenty-year interval, much of the migration to São Paulo came from the interior of the state or from neighboring Minas Gerais.

13. Michael Hall, "Prefácio," in Fontes, *Um Nordeste em São Paulo*, 13–15.

14. On the twentieth-century evolution of metropolitan São Paulo, see Azevedo et al., *A cidade de São Paulo*, especially vol. 2 (*A evolução urbana*) and vol. 4 (*Aspectos da metrópole paulista*).

15. On the "expulsion" of the laboring poor from the city center, and "autoconstruction" on the urban peripheries, see Holston, *Insurgent Citizenship*, chapter 5.

16. Some of the sociological studies conducted in the 1950s and 1960s make ethnographic contributions that transcend the limitations of their somewhat rigid interpretive frameworks. See, for example, Lopes, *Sociedade industrial no Brasil*; and Rodrigues, *Conflito industrial e sindicalismo no Brasil*.

17. Fontes, *Um Nordeste em São Paulo*, 66–67.

18. Fontes, *Um Nordeste em São Paulo*, 52–53.

19. Duarte, "Os negros do Brasil." My thanks to Marcos Chor Maio for bringing this series of articles to my attention. Much has been written about the many denunciations in postindependence Cuba of political organizing by blacks on the basis of race as "racist." See Helg, *Our Rightful Share*; and Bronfman, *Measures of Equality*.

20. Paulina Alberto, citing comments in various publications from the black press, notes that (in this period) "the intensity of racism in São Paulo, in contrast to Rio . . . was something contemporary black intellectuals in both cities openly discussed, often comparing patterns of racial discrimination in São Paulo to . . . the United States." *Terms of Inclusion*, 217.

21. On the use of the term "baiano" to refer to all nordestinos, see Fontes, *Um Nordeste em São Paulo*, 68–81. On the concept of "discursive darkening," see Findlay, *Imposing Decency*, 11.

22. For a list of pejorative terms for nordestinos, see Maior, *São os nordestinos uma minoria racial?*, chapter 10, "Glossário da discriminação." My thanks to Sarah Sarzynski for bringing this source to my attention.

23. Martuscelli, "Uma pesquisa sobre aceitação de grupos nacionais, grupos 'raciais' e grupos regionais, em S. Paulo," 56–73. For a similar discussion of this study, see Fontes, *Um Nordeste em São Paulo*, 69. It's worth noting that Martuscelli places "racial" in quotes—clearly, in Brazil this category was already being recognized as a social construction.

24. The vast majority of the students surveyed would be "white" and middle class. But not all such studies confined their scope to a white-identified population. See Bicudo, *Atitudes raciais de pretos e mulatos em São Paulo*. Bicudo was a woman of color who defended this study in 1945 as her master's thesis, completed under the direction of sociologist Donald Pierson.

25. Martuscelli, "Uma pesquisa sobre aceitação."

26. For a fascinating consideration of the fluidity of self-presentation in this period, see Maio, "Prefácio," in Bicudo, *Atitudes raciais de pretos e mulatos em São Paulo*, 11–60.

27. Fontes, *Um Nordeste em São Paulo*, 69.

28. On the optimistic response of some migrants to life in São Paulo, see Fontes, *Um Nordeste em São Paulo*, 77.

29. Souto Maior, *São os nordestinos uma minoria racial?*, 153. For examples of similarly racist "humor," see O'Dougherty, *Consumption Intensified*, 170–182.

30. On nationalism in the 1950s, see Cardoso, *Ideologia do desenvolvimento Brasil*; and Toledo, *ISEB: Fábrica de Ideologias*. This has also been identified as an era of "Americanization," which may seem to dispute my characterization of it as a time of rising nationalism, but I think fears about runaway growth in U.S. economic and cultural influence constituted an important element of the nationalist sensibility. For a thoughtful critique of claims about Americanization, see the chapter "American Seduction," in McCann, *Hello, Hello Brazil*, 129–159. Although the term "Populist Republic" exaggerates certain features of politics in this period and occludes others, I will use it here as a convenient shorthand.

31. Since much of the literature about regionalism focuses on formal political arrangements, such works imply that greater centralization inevitably means a decline in regional identification. See the studies of "the Brazilian Federation" by Robert M. Levine, Joseph L. Love, and John D. Wirth. See also Oliveira, *A questão nacional na Primeira República*, 196–198.

32. On the ritual cremation of the state flags during the first month of the Estado Novo, see chapter 8, herein. Almost immediately after the fall of the Estado Novo, the São Paulo state government officially "restored" the state symbols, but also felt compelled to note that this was not antinationalist, "considering that the state emblems, instead of competing, gravitate around the national symbols. São Paulo (Estado), "Restauração dos símbolos estaduais."

33. On the national scope of cultural changes, see McCann, *Hello, Hello Brazil*, 160–180; on the rise of the automobile and new forms of transport, see Wolfe, *Autos and Progress*, especially chapters 4 and 5.

34. For example, on the renewed significance of gaúcho identity, see Oliven, *A parte e o todo*, 69–98. On music and regional identity, see McCann, *Hello, Hello Brazil*, 96–128.

35. On the racialization of regional identity, see Gomes and Domingues, "O recinto sagrado: educação e anti-racismo no Brasil," in *Da nitidez e invisibilidade*, 287–308.

36. This is most evident in the tense relationship between Jânio Quadros and the organizing commission for the IV Centenário. Though one might expect the mayor of São Paulo to be the IV Centenário's biggest booster, Jânio—who clearly had his eyes on higher office—actually sought to minimize his identification with the commemorations. See chapter 8, this book.

37. Although there is no mistaking Florestan Fernandes's thoughtful, critical, and often brilliant analyses of the impact of capitalism on paulista society for Alfredo Ellis Jr.'s racist and ethnocentric "scholarship," I would argue that both were working with a notion of paulista exceptionalism. See Arruda, "Dilemas do Brasil moderno." For a thorough critique of Fernandes's approach to the marginalization of Afro-Brazilians in São Paulo, see Andrews, *Blacks and Whites*, 71–81.

38. Cited in Lofego, *IV Centenário da Cidade de São Paulo*, 17.

39. Arantes, *Paisagens paulistanas*; Arruda, *Metrópole e cultura*, 51–133.

40. The opportunities for financial gain were foregrounded in an article published in the *New York Times* about the paulista celebrations. Carr, "São Paulo's Fourth Centennial Fair," 46.

41. On the concept of cultural capital, see Bourdieu, *Distinction*, 70. For a similar argument, see Arruda, *Metrópole e cultura*, 75.

42. Lofego, *IV Centenário*, 27.

43. "4 séculos da vida paulista—4 décadas de trabalho industrial," *A Folha da Manhã*, January 24–25, 1954, Edição comemorativa, Suplemento Especial, 3.

44. Arquivo Histórico Municipal (AHM), Fundo IV Centenário, Caixa 62, Proc. No. 1740, "Proposta de um estudo de opinião em torno das atividades desta autarquia." My deepest thanks to Marcio Siwi for alerting me to the existence of this survey.

45. On public space at the time of the IV Centenário, see Arantes, *Paisagens paulistanas*, 17–39; and Arruda, *Metrópole e cultura*, 51–133. For an intriguing approach

to space and sociability in São Paulo in the years just before the IV Centenário, see Gama, *Nos bares da vida*, especially "Da Vila Buarque a Ibirapuera," 208–234.

46. AHM, FdoIVC, Comemorações Culturais, Cx. 231, Proc. 1341.

47. OESP, January 25, 1954, Edição Comemorativa, 90–91. The article was authored by Frederico Heller.

48. On the "genesis" of the IV Centenário, see Lofego, *IV Centenário*, 37–45.

49. Garcez ran for governor on the Partido Social Progressista ticket, with the support of Adhemar de Barros, whose famously inconsistent populist politics leaned to the right. Soon after his election, Garcez broke with Barros and fashioned a political career around his technical expertise as an engineer, eventually affiliating with ARENA, the pro-military party, during the dictatorship (1964–1985). On the politics of this period, see Schwartzman, *São Paulo e o estado nacional*, 136–162.

50. On Fábio da Silva Prado, see Mehrtens, *Urban Space and National Identity*, chapters 4 and 5. On the role of Francisco Matarazzo Sobrinho in the creation of a modern artistic patrimony, see Nelson, "Monumental and Ephemeral."

51. For an intriguing view of the role of the "bourgeoisie" in the IV Centenário, see Corrêa, "Depoimento," 33.

52. On the relationship between the IV Centenário and the rise of abstract art in São Paulo, see Nelson, "Monumental and Ephemeral," 127–142, especially 134. A semi-fictionalized version of Ciccillo Matarazzo played a central role in the TV miniseries *Um só coração* (A single heart) (2004), which depicted São Paulo's rise from the 1920s to the 1950s and coincided with the 450th anniversary of the city's founding. Nunes, *São Paulo através do minissérie "Um Só Coração."*

53. This was a rare genealogical feat—even "blue bloods" like the Prados were relatively recent arrivals by that standard. "Não há estrangeiros em São Paulo," *A Folha da Noite*, August 10, 1954, 3.

54. Lofego, *IV Centenário*, 83–84. According to the correspondence in the AHM, the favela "clearance" removed 186 shacks housing 204 families. Of these, 180 families moved to "their own plots" (*terrenos próprios*), while 6 were given building materials and relocated to another favela. The person hired (for 10,000 cruzeiros) to oversee the evacuation claimed it occurred, to the best of his knowledge, "without incident or violence." AHM, FdoIVC, Cx. 62, Proc. 1267 (1952).

55. On financial woes, see AHM, FdoIVC, Livro de Atas da CIVCCSP, June 10, 1953; July 1, 1953; August 19, 1953; November 4, 1953. On the size of the budget, see Cx. 62, Proc. 1740 (1953). The dollar equivalent here is based on the official rate (18.72 cruzeiros per U.S. dollar); the free market rate would yield a much less impressive total. Ludwig, *Brazil*, 432.

56. AHM, FdoIVC, Gabinete, Cx. 60, Fl. 19.

57. On the serious problems with housing and transport, and the hardships endured by workers and others living on the urban periphery during this period (which also saw various *quebra-quebras*—vandalizing riots—in protest), see Leal, *A reinvenção da classe trabalhadora*, especially 102–113, 163–181.

58. AHM, FdoIVC, Livro de Atas, August 19, 1953.

59. AHM, FdoIVC, Cx. 62, Proc. No. 1740, "Proposta de um estudo de opinião em torno das atividades desta autarquia."

60. Nelson, "Monumental and Ephemeral," 134.

61. AHM, FdoIV, SCC, Cx. 228, Proc. 2057: Relatórios II Bienal. See also Nelson, "Monumental and Ephemeral." Marcio Siwi's dissertation in progress will shed a great deal of light on the role of the II Bienal in the triumph of abstraction and the construction of a modern, cosmopolitan identity.

62. Elizabeth II's coronation in 1953 was repeatedly cited as a model for the IV Centenário, especially with regard to appealing to both "high" and "low" tastes. AHM, FdoIVC, Serviço de Relações Públicas, Proc. 2469, Fl. 80.

63. AHM, FdoIVC, Livro de Atas, June 16, 1953.

64. On the failure of Carnaval, in terms of organization and public participation, see OESP, March 2, 1954, 6; March 4, 1954, 1, and March 5, 1954, 1. This latter article is entitled "The Mayor's Recriminations Result in a Very Serious Crisis for the Quadricentennial Commission," and indicates that Matarazzo has been asked to resign. On Jânio's appeal to workers, see Leal, *A reinvenção da classe trabalhadora*, 437–442.

65. On his role in the creation of regional identity, see Ulrich, "Guilherme de Almeida e a construção da identidade paulista."

66. "Tomou posse ontem a nova Comissão do IV Centenário," OESP, March 19, 1954, 3. On the general strikes of this period, and the atmosphere of increasing labor militancy, see Leal, *A reinvenção da classe trabalhadora*, 235–286.

67. Lofego, *IV Centenário*, 46.

68. AHM, FdoIVC, Gabinete do CIVCCSP, Cx. 60, Proc. 1077, Letter (September 1, 1952).

69. AHM, FdoIVC, Gabinete CIVCCSP, Cx. 60, Proc. 1077.

70. "Assuntos Gerais," *A Folha da Manhã*, January 25, 1954, 20.

71. AHM, FdoIVC, Comemorações Populares, Cx. 226, Proc. 3367

72. "São Paulo faz 400 anos," *O Trabalhador Gráfico*, January 1954, 1–2.

73. The employer-sponsored May Day Workers' Olympics were increasingly shunned by labor unions by the mid-1950s, but that didn't necessarily deter workers, as representatives of their firms, from participating. On the "Jogos Olímpicos," see Weinstein, *For Social Peace*, 206–209, 236–237.

74. For the roster of scholars on the consulting board, see AHM, FdoIVC, ComCults, Cx. 235, proc. 1902, Letter from Jaime Cortesão, July 23, 1953.

75. "Aplausos do IDORT," *Boletim da Comissão do IV Centenário da Cidade de São Paulo* 6 (October 1953): 7.

76. IHGSP, Arquivo Aureliano Leite, Pacote 14, Pasta 2.

77. Arruda notes the irony of the "Aspiral" sculpture failing, whereas the older modernism, represented by Brecheret's Monument to the Bandeiras, finally came to fruition. *Metrópole e cultura*, 103. For a discussion of the Brecheret sculpture and other IV Centenário monuments, see Marins, "O Parque Ibirapuera e a construção da identidade paulista."

78. AHM, FdoIVC, SCC, Cx. 230, Proc. 2269, Fl. 124

79. On Faulkner as an influence on, and being influenced by, Latin America, see Cohn, "Faulkner, Latin America, and the Caribbean."

80. Morse was recommended by Sérgio Buarque de Holanda and Lourival Gomes Machado. AHM, FdoIVC, SCC, Cx. 230, Procs. 859, 1320, 2269 (Fl. 17, July 3, 1952), 3957.

81. AHM, FdoIVC, SCC, Cx. 299, Proc. 2101

82. Lofego, *IV Centenário*, 48, 60.

83. AHM, FdoIVC, ComemsPops, Cx. 99, proc. 2424 (1953).

84. Depending on the particular sector of the program, the pedagogical thrust of the festivities could be described as "illumination for the masses," or "moral and civic instruction," with the latter usually implying a middle-class audience in need of greater cultivation and refinement. AHM, FdoIVC, SRPIPTUR, Correspondência, proc. 2469, fl. 53; SCC, Cx. 235, proc. 1902.

85. AHM, FdoIVC, Cx. 62, Proc. 1740 (1953), "Proposta de um estudo de opinião em torno das atividades desta autarquia." Emphasis added. The researchers also interviewed three times as many men as women "based on the presumption that men are better informed than women." The commission paid IPOM 48,000 cruzeiros for this survey.

86. Thus when Roberto de Paiva Meira, then director of the Serviço de Comemorações Culturais, argued for programming at least a few events that would appeal to "popular tastes," commission members apparently questioned whether the kinds of programs he was proposing would be more appropriate for the Serviço de Comemorações Populares. AHM, FdoIVC, Cx. 234, Proc. 1092.

87. AHM, FdoIVC, SRPIPTUR, Correspondência, Proc. 3146.

88. Lofego, *IV Centenário*, 49, n. 26.

89. The commission did eventually present him with a certificate recognizing him as the composer "who translated into music the popular sentiment of joy at the city's anniversary." AHM, FdoIV, SRPIPTUR, proc. 3206. The public opinion survey conducted in 1953 mentioned plans for a contest for the official anthem of the IV Centenário, which reinforces the impression that Zan was seen as having stolen the organizing commission's thunder. Cx. 62, Proc. 1740 (1953).

90. AHM, FdoIVC, SRPIPTUR, Proc. 2469, Fl. 80.

91. AHM, FdoIVC, SRPIPTUR, Proc. 3720, Fl. 126.

92. AHM, FdoIVC, SCC, Cx. 234, Proc. 1092.

93. AHM, FdoIVC, SCC, Cx. 234, Proc. 2886. In the same file there is a letter from textile manufacturer Humberto Reis Costa offering performances, all expenses paid, by his factory's female band (whose members he describes as workers' daughters). Matarazzo notes, with palpable regret, that he has no choice but to accept.

94. AHM, FdoIVC, SCC, Cx. 236, Proc. 6723.

95. This failure is a sharp contrast to the great success, both at home and abroad, of the Ballet Folklórico de México, founded in 1952. The preference of the paulista organizers for "classical" (i.e., European) dance likely played a role in the São Paulo ballet's limited success. For the Mexican case, see Zolov, "Discovering a Land 'Mysterious and Obvious.'" The São Paulo Ballet, in the 1990s, enjoyed a revival of sorts through an exhibit, "Fantasia Brasileira," sponsored by SESC-São Paulo, displaying costumes and sets from the short-lived company. SESC-São Paulo, *Fantasia brasileira*.

96. AHM, FdoIVC, SCC, Cx. 94, Proc. 1785. Among the odder inquiries that the commission received was one from a "Hindu calculist." Gabinete, Cx. 70, Proc. 4885

97. AHM, FdoIVC, ComemsPops, Cx. 94, Proc. 1785, Fl. 11

98. AHM, FdoIVC, ComemsPops, Cx. 94, Proc. 1785, Fl. 13 (Letter from E. Carneiro dated June 15, 1954).

99. *A Folha da Manhã*, August 16, 1954, Cad. 2, 9.

100. On the folklore festival, see "O Folclore no IV Centenário," *Boletim da CIVCCSP* 6 (October 1953): 8; "Roteiro folclórico das festas do IV Centenário," *A Folha da Noite*, August 11, 1954, Cad. 2, 1. Another article, "Festa para o Povo" (August 23, 1954, 4) began "The Capital city applauded the splendor of the folklore that came to us from far away."

101. *A Folha da Noite*, January 24–25, 1954, Ed. Comemorativa, Sup. Especial, Cad. Atualidades, 16–19.

102. "O Folclore no IV Centenário," *Boletim da CIVCCSP* 6 (October 1953): 8.

103. It is interesting to contrast this with the Centers of Gaúcho Traditions in Rio Grande do Sul, the first of which were founded in 1948. Oliven, *A parte e o todo*, 74–93.

104. *A Folha da Noite*, August 20, 1954, 1, 3–4.

105. *Boletim Informativo da CIVCCSP* 11 (April–May 1954): 4. On the choro revival, see McCann, *Hello, Hello Brazil*, chapter 5.

106. SampaArt, GR SITES, Biografia: Alfredo Viana, 2014. http://www.sampa.art .br/biografias/alfredoviana/historia/.

107. Of the 1,439, 595 votes counted in São Paulo state, 925,493 were for Vargas (PTB), 357,413 were for Eduardo Gomes (UDN), and 153,039 were for Cristiano Machado (PSD). Eleição presidencial no Brasil em 1950, Wikipedia, a enciclopédia livre, September 9, 2013. http://pt.wikipedia.org/wiki/Elei%C3%A7%C3%A3o_presidencial _no_Brasil_em_1950.

108. D'Araújo, *O segundo governo Vargas*.

109. Arantes, *Paisagens paulistanas*, 26–31. In an issue of the *Folha* published in November 1954, Samuel Duarte, former president of the federal Chamber of Deputies, and not a paulista, published an article (reprinted in *Paulistânia*, no. 53, 1955) entitled "São Paulo, expressão de brasilidade." According to Duarte, "The power of private initiative is evident in the bandeirante progress, which remits vast resources to the treasury of the State and the Union whose badly managed application caused the financial crisis currently in full swing."

110. "Homenagem da UDN á Cidade," *OESP*, January 25, 1954, 151 (Ed. Comemorativa). Aureliano Leite, speaking at the inauguration of the Monument to the Bandeiras, referred to Vargas as "the great undesired one" (*o grande indesejado*). For the connection between *udenismo* and 1932, see chapter 8 below.

111. For the text of Vargas's speech, see *Última Hora*, January 25, 1954, 4. The Arquivo Nacional (Rio) has film footage of Vargas's visit to São Paulo from the Agencia Nacional—Cine Jornal Informativo (though, unfortunately, the soundtrack is missing). EH/FI1.0100, VHS278; EH/FI1.0104, VHS278.

112. The plot, probably orchestrated without Vargas's knowledge by his bodyguard Gregório Fortunato (whose blackness became a major theme in denunciations of the attack), injured Lacerda and caused the death of Air Force Major Rubens Florentino Vaz, then serving as Lacerda's bodyguard. On Vargas's suicide and its aftermath, see Williams and Weinstein, "*Vargas Morto*."

113. "Final dramático da crise política," *A Folha da Noite*, August 25, 1954, 1.

114. On the popular reaction to Vargas's suicide, see Williams and Weinstein, "*Vargas Morto*," 284–296; and Carvalho, "As duas mortes de Getúlio Vargas."

115. *O Mundo Ilustrado*, September 1, 1954, 42.

116. On the delay in the opening of the Historical Exposition see below, chapter 7.

117. The attention devoted to these moments, and especially the "silver shower" (*chuva de prata*), is evident on various online memory sites: A festa do IV Centenário, comunicação por Elmo Francfort Ankerkrone, *Sampa Online*, n.d. http://www.sampa online.com.br/colunas/elmo/coluna2001ju106.htm, and O IV Centenário: Léia as histórias (various authors), *São Paulo, Minha Cidade*, http://www.saopaulominhacidade .com.br/buscar/termo/IV%2BCenten%25C3%25A1rio.

Also, see interviews in the magazine *Cidade* 1, no. 1 (1994).

118. "Éxito dos festejos nos bairros," *Boletim Informativo da* CIVCCSP 9 (January 1954): 7.

119. On the programmed activities for January 24–25, 1954, see Lofego, *IV Centenário*, 64–66.

120. *A Gazeta* reported the chuva de prata in its issue of July 10, 1954. It is also filmed (badly) in a Vera Cruz studio documentary, *São Paulo em Festa*, on the July celebrations. And it is cited as occurring in July in Arruda, *Metrópole e cultura*, 75; and Xavier, *Arquitetura metropolitana*, 50. According to Xavier, "São Paulo is the world of artifice . . . of nature invented and controlled by man. . . . To make the skies rain silver is an apt spectacle for the paulista capital."

121. It is an indication of how thoroughly "9 de Julho" had been dissociated in the popular imagination from the specific motives and objectives of the uprising that federal air force planes could be used in the celebration without any sense of contradiction. On the evolving significance of 1932, see below, chapter 8.

122. See the blog *São Paulo, Minha Cidade*, http://www.saopaulominhacidade.com .br/buscar/termo/IV%2BCenten%25C3%25A1rio.

123. *OESP*, January 25, 1954, 160 (Edição Comemorativa). See a similar comment by FIESP president Antônio Devisate in *Diário de São Paulo*, January 25, 1954, 12. For further quotes, see Guimarães, "Festa de fundação," 131–139.

124. *Correio Paulistano*, January 26, 1954, 1, cited in Guimarães, "Festa de fundação," 134.

125. AHM, FdoIVC, Livros de Atas, June 16, 1953. The commission briefly considered making a small financial contribution to the celebrations on July 9 but it seems that it ultimately decided against it.

126. There are collections of these newspapers in the Arquivo Histórico Municipal, the Biblioteca Municipal Prefeito Prestes Maia (formerly Presidente Kennedy), and the Arquivo Edgard Leuenroth at the Universidade Estadual de Campinas.

127. *O Estado de São Paulo* converted the supplements from its commemorative edition into a huge volume, over nine hundred pages long, entitled *Ensaios Paulistas* (Contribuição de "O Estado de São Paulo" às Comemorações do IV Centenário da Cidade) (São Paulo: Editora Anhambi S/A, 1958). Few paulistas were likely to want to lift this immense tome, never mind read it.

128. *Diário de São Paulo*, January 25, 1954, 1–2.

129. All the newspapers referred to here were printed on January 25, 1954.

130. *OESP*, January 25, 1954, Caderno Histórico, 1–40.

131. See, for example, Heitor Ferreira Lima, "Condicionado pro diversos fatores o desenvolvimento industrial paulista," *A Folha da Manhã*, January 24–25, 1954, Caderno de Economia, 9.

132. *OESP*, January 25, 1954, Edição Comemorativa, 88–89 and 120.

133. Bourdieu, *Distinction*, 101–102.

134. *A Folha da Manhã*, January 24–25, 1954, Suplemento Especial, p. 3.

135. *OESP*, January 25, 1954, 89. "Point IV" referred to the program of technical assistance to developing nations created by the Truman administration in 1949.

136. *Diário da Noite*, July 9, 1954, 12.

137. On trends in advertising before and during this period, see Woodard, "Marketing Modernity"; and McCann, *Hello, Hello Brazil*, chapter 7.

138. The proposals submitted by various advertising and public relations firms can be found in AHM, FdoIVC, SRPIPTUR, Série Correspondência, proc. 118, 2466, 3720 fl. 52, fl. 126.

139. AHM, FdoIVC, Gabinete, proc. 1344, June 5, 1952.

140. The appliance manufacturer Arno requested permission to put the aspiral on products during 1954, which shows the value of an event-specific symbol. AHM, FdoIVC, SRPIPTUR, proc. 2159, July 3, 1953.

141. On the foiled plans to erect a giant aspiral, see Lofego, *IV Centenário*, 134; Arruda, *Metrópole e cultura*, 102–106; Nelson, "Monumental and Ephemeral," 128.

142. On Oscar Niemeyer's place in Brazilian (and global) modern architecture, see Williams, *Culture Wars in Brazil*, 208–209; Arruda, *Metrópole e cultura*, 67–104.

143. *OESP*, January 25, 1954, 46, 75. For a discussion of the many ways firms used the symbols of the IV Centenário, see Lofego, *IV Centenário*, 111–144.

144. The same is implied in a *Life* magazine article (April 5, 1948, 88) that described São Paulo as having "about as much Latin languor as a New York subway at 5 P.M."

145. *Diário de São Paulo*, January 25, 1954, 14.

146. *OESP*, Ed. Comemorativa, January 25, 1954, 96.

147. *A Folha da Manhã*, Cad. Assuntos Gerais, January 24–25, 1954, 3; an ad in the *Diário de São Paulo* for coffee also refers to São Paulo's success as "predestinada."

148. *Diário de São Paulo*, January 25, 1954, 12, Cad. 2.

149. *OESP*, January 25, 1954, 120. For a study of the use of black women's images in commercialized products, see Manring, *Slave in a Box*.

150. *Diário de São Paulo*, January 25, 1954, 4, Cad. Feminino.

151. *Diário de São Paulo*, January 25, 1954, 4, Cad. 5.

152. AHM, FdoIVC, SRPIPTUR, proc. 2049, March 20, 1953.

153. Brazil, *Anais da Câmara dos Deputados*, sessão November 30, 1921, 536.

154. Brasil, *Anais da Câmara dos Deputados*, sessão October 27, 1924, 364–65; May 30, 1927, 447.

155. Brasil, *Anais da Câmara dos Deputados*, sessão October 27, 1924, 368. In the

midst of a paulista deputy's insistence that his heart beats for Brazilians of all states, Armando Burlamaqui interjected: "If not I would demand my small portion for my Piauhy, with its babassú." The latter is a plant that produces oil for various industrial purposes.

156. Draibe, *Rumos e metamorfoses*; Negro, *Linhas de montagem*.

157. On the discourses of development in Brazil and Argentina in this era, see Sikkink, *Ideas and Institutions*.

158. Fontes, *Um Nordeste em São Paulo*, 77. To quote Fontes, "The expectations of the great majority of rural migrants was precisely to incorporate themselves into the 'progress' represented by the big city." Of course, few were able to fulfill their expectations, but that's another matter.

159. Lima, *A missão de São Paulo*. For reasons the author does not explain, he composed the book in 1954 but it wasn't published until 1962.

160. Lima, *A missão de São Paulo*, 9.

161. Lima, *A missão de São Paulo*, 26.

162. Lima, *A missão de São Paulo*, 14, 21, 15.

Chapter 7: Exhibiting Exceptionalism

Epigraph 1. For the lyrics of the music of the IV Centenário, see the website Vagalume, IV Centenário Hinos, http://www.vagalume.com.br/hinos/quarto-centenario .html. Epigraph 2. Helena Silveira, "Carta a quem faz 4 séculos," *A Folha da Manhã*, Ed. Comemorativa, January 24–25, 1954, Caderno da Mulher, 1.

1. Jaime Cortesão, the official historian of the commemorations, conceded that the designated date was arbitrary but argued that this "symbolic simplification" was "useful for commemorative purposes." Museu Paulista (MP), Coleção IV Centenário, A1, PR49, Pasta 15, 2.

2. On the Exposição do Mundo Português, see Williams, *Culture Wars in Brazil*, 227–251.

3. For the construction of paulista exceptionalism, see above, chapters 1 and 2.

4. On the challenges facing Rio as an urban center during this period, see Abreu, *Evolução urbana do Rio de Janeiro*.

5. The phrase is from the section of *The Communist Manifesto* where Marx and Engels assert the need of the bourgeoisie to constantly revolutionize the instruments of production: "All that is solid melts into air, all that is holy is profaned, and man is at last compelled to face with sober senses his real conditions of life, and his relations with his kind." It came into use among scholars of urban life with Marshall Berman's study *All That Is Solid Melts into Air* (1982).

6. Saliba, "Histórias, memórias, tramas e dramas da identidade paulistana," 270.

7. Vianna, *The Mystery of Samba*, 41–42.

8. As I hope is already apparent, this does not mean that racial democracy was an uncontested concept, or that its meaning was fixed and unitary—only that it was ubiquitous in discussions of Brazilian national character and identity. See Alberto, *Terms of Inclusion*, 178–181.

9. For an excellent discussion of the efforts to reconcile paulista exceptionalism and claims to authentic brasilidade, see de Luca, *A Revista do Brasil*, 260–291.

10. Rydell, *All the World's a Fair*; Pesavento, *Exposições Universais*; Tenorio-Trillo, *Mexico at the World's Fairs*; Hoffenberger, *An Empire on Display*.

11. On elite responses to the social unrest of the 1950s, see Weinstein, *For Social Peace*, especially chapter 8.

12. Gail Bederman's discussion of race, gender, and the Columbian Exposition of 1893 in Chicago is an excellent example of an analysis that focuses on the contested nature of the exhibits. See *Manliness and Civilization*, chapter 1.

13. On the Free World's Fair in the Dominican Republic, see Derby, *The Dictator's Seduction*, chapter 3.

14. Of course, São Paulo's claims to whiteness, though materialized in census figures, was equally an effect of representation, as well as the exclusion of dark-skinned arrivals from Minas and the Nordeste from the category of paulista. On the "official story" of the growing "white" portion of the paulista population, see table 1.1.

15. Fontes, *Um Nordeste em São Paulo*, 41–81.

16. AHM, CIVCCSP, SCC, Proc. 1092, Cx. 235, May 27, 1953.

17. AHM, CIVCCSP, SRPIPTUR, Processo 2469.

18. Although "povo" literally means "people," I think the more apt translation in this context would be "masses."

19. MP, CIVC, Pasta 15 (clippings).

20. AHM, CIVCCSP, SCC, Cx. 235, Proc. 1092, Fl. 240.

21. IHGSP, Arquivo Aureliano Leite, Pacote 14, Pasta 2.

22. IHGSP, Arquivo Aureliano Leite, Pacote 14, Pasta 2. The ambassador to Portugal at the time of the commemorations of 1954 was the eminent poet Olegário Mariano.

23. Detailed descriptions of the exposition can be found in MP, Col. IV-C, Pasta 15, and AHM, CIVCCSP, SCC, Cx. 235, Proc. 1092.

24. AHM, CIVCCSP, SRPIPTUR, Proc. 2469, April 22, 1953.

25. AHM, CIVCCSP, SRPIPTUR, Proc. 2469, Fl. 80; Proc. 3100, January 18, 1954. Note that "bandeirante" is being routinely used as a synonym for "paulista."

26. Dalmo Belfort de Mattos, "A influência negra na alma paulista," *Paulistânia* 3 (October 1939), n.p. He claimed São Paulo's white to nonwhite ratio during the colonial period was three to one, a statistic that seems little more than a racist's wishful thinking.

27. On the changing "memory" of the 1932 uprising, see chapter 8, herein.

28. AHM, CIVCCSP, SRPIPTUR, Proc. 2760, Fl. 80, January 10, 1954.

29. Quoted in Jaime Cortesão, "A Exposição Histórica de São Paulo: Balanço final," *OESP*, April 3, 1955, 7, in IHGSP, Col. Aureliano Leite, Pacote 14, Pasta 2.

30. Coverage of the exposition indicates that it didn't fully open until September 13. "Instalada ontem a Exposição de 4 Seculos da Historia Paulista," *OESP*, September 14, 1954, 12.

31. MP, CIVC, Pasta 15, p. 10. On the evolving images and interpretations of the bandeirantes, see Abud, "O sangue intimorato e as nobilíssimas tradições."

32. Without more information, I can merely speculate about this decision, but it does seem a little suspicious that the only objects the organizers decided not to transport due to excessive insurance costs were these African sculptures. AHM, CIVCCSP, SCC, Proc. 1092, Cx. 235, Fl. 185.

33. MP, CIVC, Pasta 15, 16–17.

34. MP, CIVC, Pasta, 19–20.

35. On the representation of slavery as backward and thus "foreign" to the progressive paulista temperament, see chapter 2, herein. In the commemorative edition of the *Diário de São Paulo*, Tito Lívio Ferreira wrote that "long before abolition, the paulista planter . . . considered slavery to be extinct." January 25, 1954, Cad. 3, 12, "Estrada econômica do café."

36. MP, CIVC, Pasta 15, 23.

37. MP, CIVC, Pasta 15, 25.

38. MP, CIVC, Pasta 15, 26.

39. The immense and imposing Monument to the Bandeiras, designed by modernist sculptor Victor Brecheret in the 1920s and inaugurated in 1954, is a "concrete" representation of this historical narrative. It shows two "white" bandeirantes, mounted on magnificent steeds, effortlessly leading the expedition, while Indians and Africans, on foot in the rear, struggle to keep the company moving forward. Arruda, *Metrópole e cultura*, 103–106.

40. Museu Paulista, CIVC, Pasta 16.

41. IHGSP, Col. Aureliano Leite, Pacote 14, Pasta 2, OESP, February 20, 1955.

42. For Freyre, race relations started to deteriorate, and the most valuable features of Brazilian culture started to decline, once slavery was abolished and the center of cultural gravity shifted to the urban areas—though Hermano Vianna would argue that Rio was able to "revive" the fusion and intimacy of the rural environs. Vianna, *The Mystery of Samba*, chapter 6.

43. On the work of Ernani Silva Bruno, see Lofego, *Memória de uma metrópole*. The judges recommended that the commission subsidize publication of "Café e Negro," but said it couldn't be granted the prize because it was not strictly economic history. AHM, CIVCCSP, SCC, Proc. 2101, Cx. 229.

44. My thanks to James Woodard for alerting me to Aureliano Leite's position on this issue. See Woodard, "Of Slaves and Citizens."

45. IHGSP, Col. Aureliano Leite, Pacote 4, Pasta 2.

46. Ernani Silva Bruno, "Café e Negro," *Diários Associados* (Edição especial dedicada ao café), July 15, 1954, Cad. 2, 1, 14.

47. Bastide, "O Negro em São Paulo," 23–40.

48. *A Folha da Manhã*, Cad. História Colonial, January 25, 1954, 20

49. *A Folha da Manhã*, Cad. História Colonial, January 25, 1954, 2–3.

50. Tito Lívio Ferreira, "Evolução econômica, social e cultural de São Paulo," *Diário de São Paulo*, January 25, 1954, Cad. 3, 6–13.

51. Once again, I am indebted to James Woodard for calling to my attention an essay by Freyre, "São Paulo e a unidade brasileira."

52. Cassiano Ricardo's revisionism regarding Afro-descendentes in the bandeiras is discussed in Carneiro, *Antologia do Negro Brasileiro*, 216–217.

53. On the discourse of conservative modernization and its compatibility with the Freyrean vision of racial democracy, see Mitchell, "Miguel Reale and the Impact of Conservative Modernization on Brazilian Race Relations," 116–137.

54. Gilberto Freyre, "Uma interpretação de São Paulo," *Diário de São Paulo* (Edição

Comemorativa), January 25, 1954, Cad. 3, 13–15. This and other special editions of paulista newspapers can be found in the AHM, Jornais Comemorativos do IV Centenário. For a nonscientific survey of attitudes about "miscegenation" among prominent paulistas (such as Plínio Barreto and Julio de Mesquita Filho), see Freyre, *Order and Progress*, chapter 6.

55. Given the paulistas' frequent recourse to Euclides da Cunha's account of the war on Canudos, *Os sertões*, to draw pejorative portraits of nordestinos, I think Freyre was deliberately trying to turn the tables and associate paulista fervor for progress with an "irrational" messianic tradition.

56. Queiroz, "Ufanismo paulista," 78–87.

57. "Não há estrangeiros em São Paulo!," *A Folha da Noite*, August 10, 1954, 1.

58. "Não há estrangeiros em São Paulo!," *A Folha da Noite*, August 10, 1954, 1.

59. In the case of Assis, located in a region into which coffee production expanded after abolition, this may well have been the case. But Emílio Carlos's statement was clearly a broader claim. On the role of immigrants in the coffee economy, see Holloway, *Immigrants on the Land*.

60. Sampaio Ferraz, "O homem do planalto paulista," OESP, Ed. Comemorativa, January 25, 1954, 120. Sampaio Ferraz was a native paulista and former police chief in the federal capital. Freyre mentions him as a member of the "Clube Caboclo" in *Order and Progress*, 199.

61. "Mais de 2,5 milhões de imigrantes ajudaram, desde 1820, a construir São Paulo de 1954," *A Folha da Manhã*, Edição comemorativa-Suplemento especial, January 24–25, 1954, Cad. Assuntos Especializados, 1, 4. The "start date" of 1820 for the immigrant contribution is worth noting.

62. "Os 3 milhões de imigrantes vindos a São Paulo em meio século," *Diário de São Paulo*, Edic. Comemorativa, January 25, 1954, Cad. 5, 10. *Diário Popular*, Ed. Comemorativa, January 23, 1954, 3. It is possible that "hegemony" is being used here in the sense of "preponderance," but the word choice seems significant enough to warrant a more literal translation.

63. Frederico Heller, "O caminho para a economia metropolitana: 3 séculos de preparo lento e um de impulso gigantesco," OESP, Ed. Comemorativa, January 25, 1954, 90–91.

64. Helena Silveira, "Carta a quem faz 4 séculos," *A Folha da Manhã*, Ed. Comemorativa, January 24–25, 1954, Caderno da Mulher, 1.

65. "Aspectos geográficos do crescimento de São Paulo," OESP, Ed. Comemorativa, January 25, 1954, 97.

66. *Diário de São Paulo*, Ed. Comemorativa, January 25, 1954, Cad. 3, 12.

67. *A Folha da Manhã*, Ed. Comemorativa, January 24–5, 1954, Cad. Assuntos especializados, 1, 4.

68. *O Tempo*, Sup. Comem., January 24, 1954, 11.

69. Giles Lapouge, "A vocação industrial de S.Paulo," OESP, January 25, 1954, 88–89.

70. "As lutas dos escravos e a abolição," *Notícias de Hoje*, Sup. Dominical, May 9, 1954, 1.

71. *A Folha da Manhã*, Ed. Comemorativa, January 24–5, 1954, Cad. Assuntos especializados, 4.

72. AHM, CIVCCSP, SRPIPTUR, Proc. 3100 (emphasis added).

73. AHM, CIVCCSP, SCC, Proc. 4171.

74. On the complicated ethno-racial identities of Japanese-Brazilians, see Lesser, *Negotiating National Identity*, chapter 6.

75. AHM, CIVCCSP, SRPIPTUR, Proc. 5255.

76. AHM, CIVCCSP, SCP, Cx. 226, Proc. 3428. On the national appeal of northeastern regional music, see McCann, *Hello, Hello Brazil*, chapter 3.

77. On the figure of the "Mãe-Preta," see Seigel, *Uneven Encounters*, 206–234; Alberto, *Terms of Inclusion*, 69–139; Lopes, "História e memória do negro em São Paulo," 81–160.

78. Lopes, "História e memória do negro em São Paulo," 81–160.

79. The child is presumably "white" because that is the convention—no visual elements indicate the baby's whiteness. Black militant José Correia Leite, who had long campaigned for this monument, protested that the modernist statue rendered the Black Mother "grotesque," whereas historically slaveholders selected the most attractive black women as wet nurses. Alberto, *Terms of Inclusion*, 210–211. Guerra, somewhat ironically, is best known for his gigantic (and to this critic's eyes, hideous) statue of the bandeirante Borba Gato on Avenida Santo Amaro.

80. AHM, CIVCCSP, Gabinete, Proc. 4740, Cx. 59 (emphasis added).

81. AHM, CIVCCSP, Gabinete, Proc. 4740, Cx. 59, Fl. 10.

82. AHM, CIVCCSP, Gabinete, Proc. 4740, Cx. 59, Fl. 16. A request from a black Bahian dance troupe for a subsidy was summarily dismissed by the commission on the basis of the group not being "authentically folkloric" and their performances being too "sensual." Comemorações Populares, Proc. 1785, Cx. 94.

83. On the Clube 220, see Andrews, *Blacks and Whites in São Paulo*, 215–216. Andrews identifies the club as primarily middle class but that adjective has to be regarded in relative terms. On the club's role in the campaign for the monument, see Alberto, *Terms of Inclusion*, 209–211.

84. AHM, CIVCCSP, SCC, Procs. 859, 1320, 2269, and 3957.

85. In marked contrast to the Afro-paulistas, the commission actively encouraged activities to celebrate the role of the Japanese in paulista life, many of them funded by well-heeled members of the Japanese-Brazilian community. AHM, CIVCCSP, SRPIPTUR, Procs. 5251–5255.

86. On the relationship between the discourse of racial democracy and the construction of Brazilian modernity in the age of developmentalism, see Gomes and Domingues, "Raça, pós-emancipação, cidadania e modernidade no Brasil."

87. Alberto, *Terms of Inclusion*, 149.

88. According to the recollections of José Correia Leite, the members of the Clube 220 denounced the critics of the statue as "communists." Alberto, *Terms of Inclusion*, 211.

Chapter 8: The White Album

Epigraph: Queiroz, *Batalhão 14 de Julho*, 6

1. Stanley Hilton notes that there was no *grito* (battle cry) that marked the outbreak of war, but that the ninth of July is generally agreed upon as the date the uprising began. *A guerra civil brasileira*, 84.

2. Portal Pró-TV, História das emissoras, 2010. http://www.museudatv.com.br/programação/expo400_chuvadeprata.htm.

3. Other examples of regional/national identities based on "lost causes" or dramatic defeats include the former (U.S.) Confederacy and the Boers in South Africa. See Blight, *Race and Reunion*, chapter 8; and McClintock, "'No Longer in a Future Heaven,'" 271–277.

4. It is interesting to note that the organizing commission of the IV Centenário ceded the responsibility (and the expenses) of the 9 de Julho celebrations almost entirely to the Associação de Rádios Emissoras. AHM, CCIVCCSP, Livro de Atas (1), December 30, 1953.

5. On memory and 1932, see Borges, *Memória paulista*; and Rodrigues, *1932 pela força da tradição*.

6. The industrialists of FIESP (Federação das Indústrias do Estado de São Paulo), once the Constitutionalists were defeated, quickly sought to create a modus vivendi with Vargas. Weinstein, *For Social Peace in Brazil*, 64–66. And then there was the effort by Waldemar Ferreira, supporter of Armando's candidacy for the presidency, to convince Vargas that the military conspirators had coerced the civilian paulista government into supporting the uprising. Vargas, *Diário*, vol. 2, 27.

7. The phrase quoted is from the final sentence of Vargas's suicide letter. See Levine and Crocitti, *The Brazil Reader*, 224.

8. See chapter 2, herein.

9. On memory and symptomatic misremembering, see Portelli, *The Death of Luigi Trastulli*. On the shift from contemporary accounts to concrete places of memory, see Nora, *Realms of Memory*, vol. 3.

10. "O quinto aniversário da inesquecível jornada de nove de julho foi commemorado nesta capital com numerosas solemnidades," OESP, July 10, 1937, 12.

11. The presence of the Legião Negra is worth noting in light of Guaraná de Sant'Anna's highly pessimistic comments quoted in chapter 3, herein.

12. *A Gazeta*, July 9, 1936, 1.

13. On the fragile alliance of the PD and the PRP, see Prado, *A democracia ilustrada*, 123–140; on the aftermath of the Constitutionalist uprising, see chapter 3, herein.

14. On the trajectory of the Chapa Única, see Ramos, *Os partidos paulistas e o Estado Novo*, 159–164.

15. "Paulistas contra paulistas," *A Gazeta*, July 7, 1937, 1.

16. The founding in 1934 of the Partido Constitucionalista—clearly a vehicle for Armando's political ambitions—coincided with the formal dissolution of the Partido Democrático. According to one student of paulista politics in this era, who dubbed the governor "a political contortionist," Armando "did not have a very significant participation in the events of 9 de Julho, although he sought to make others believe the opposite." Ramos, *Os partidos paulistas e o Estado Novo*, 165–167 (quote on p. 165).

17. However, Armando may have been less objectionable to the perrepistas than the circle around him. According to James Woodard, although Armando signed the original PD manifesto, that was the extent of his active participation in the party. *A Place in Politics*, 158.

18. On José Américo's role in the invention of nordestino identity, see Albuquerque, *A invenção do Nordeste*, 137–141.

19. On the maneuvers employed by Oswaldo Aranha to ensure that there was no reconciliation between the paulista factions, see Vargas, *Diário*, vol. 2, 24.

20. The editor of *A Gazeta*, Casper Líbero, was a veteran of the 1932 uprising, and his remains (he died in 1943) were later moved to the obelisk that was the main memorial to that rebellion's veterans and war dead.

21. *OESP*, July 4, 1937, 1.

22. "Paulistas contra paulistas," *A Gazeta*, July 7, 1937, 1.

23. *OESP*, July 10, 1937, 1, 11–12. There was also considerable (and as it turns out, justified) anxiety about Vargas possibly suppressing the armandista campaign. In his diary for these years Vargas reports hearing (unsubstantiated) rumors of arms shipments to São Paulo in preparation for a new regional revolt. Vargas, *Diário*, vol. 2, 11, 13, 17.

24. *A Gazeta*, July 5, 1937, 3.

25. *A Gazeta*, July 5, 1937, 3; "Despojos de uma data," July 10, 1937, 1. *A Gazeta* also attacked the Institute for Rational Organization of Work (Idort), in which Armando, an engineer, was involved: "Isto de 'Idort' é bobagem estrangeira," September 10, 1937, 3. The headline translates as "This 'Idort' is a foreign idiocy."

26. "Despojos de uma data," *A Gazeta*, July 10, 1937, 1.

27. Penteado, *O Inevitável*. For the text of his poem "Paulistas at the 'Front'" see herein chapter 2.

28. For a list of all lectures delivered at the Clube Piratininga during the first five years following its founding, see *Paulistânia* 6 (March–April 1940): 47–48.

29. "O Clube Piratininga em sua nova sede social," *Paulistânia* 16 (July–September 1943): 16. Toledo Piza's political career indicates the different routes followed by club members; he ran (successfully) for state deputy and (unsuccessfully) for governor on the pro-Vargas *trabalhista* ticket.

30. Dalmo Belfort de Mattos, "A influência negra na alma paulista," *Paulistânia* 3 (October 1939): n.p.

31. Mattos, "A influência negra," part 2, *Paulistânia* 4 (November 1939): n.p.

32. Mattos, "O verdadeiro papel do Rio São Francisco," *Paulistânia* 2, no. 7 (May–June 1940): 49.

33. Mattos, "O drama dos sampauleiros," *Paulistânia* 5 (December 1939), n.p.

34. Americo R. Netto, "Sulistas e Nortistas no Brasil: Um caso de geografia humana," *Paulistânia* 5, no. 19 (December 1944): 26–30.

35. Mattos, "A influência negra," part 2, *Paulistânia* 4 (November 1939), n.p.

36. The original Portuguese lyrics are: "Paulistinha querida / Qual é tua cor / Que tanto disfarças / Com teu pó de arroz? / Não és loura nem morena / Não tens nada de mulata / Paulistinha querida/ A tua cor é 'trinta e dois!'" On Ary Barroso's role in the genre that became known as "samba exaltação" (loosely, patriotic samba), see McCann, *Hello, Hello Brazil*, 67–78.

37. "Paulistinha querida" may also have been intended by Barroso as a foil to the hit "Your Hair Doesn't Deny (Mulata)" from the Rio Carnaval of 1932. Sprinkling powder was a traditional element of carnaval pranks, but took on more explicit racial

meanings at *futebol* (soccer) games where fans of "popular" teams, like the Corinthians, would sprinkle powder on the "São Paulo" club fans to mock their whiteness (or pretensions to whiteness). On the class and ethnic implications of futebol in São Paulo, see Bocketti, "Italian Immigrants, Brazilian Football, and the Dilemma of National Identity."

38. On the centralization of political authority, see Gomes, *Regionalismo e centralização política*. On the "flag cremation" ceremony, see Vargas, *Diário*, vol. 2, 86, n.57. As Bryan McCann notes, the Vargas regime simultaneously implemented centralization and cultivated nordestino regional identities "as ideal fodder for nationalist propaganda." *Hello, Hello Brazil*, 100, 121.

39. Soon after the declaration of the Estado Novo, Armando was forced into exile. Prominent armandistas who remained in São Paulo had their movements and correspondence monitored by the political police (DEOPS). See the remarkably detailed dossiers for Paulo Duarte, Paulo Nogueira Filho, and others in the DEOPS files, Arquivo Público do Estado de São Paulo (APESP).

40. Weinstein, *For Social Peace in Brazil*, 86–100; French, *The Brazilian Workers' ABC*, 97–98.

41. Editorial comment on the cessation of publication appears in *Paulistânia* 3, no. 10 (January–March 1942): n.p.

42. "A Morte do Zumbi," *Paulistânia* 3, no. 13 (October–December 1942): front cover.

43. For a brief history of this review, see the website urbanismobr.org, Revista Paulistânia—Documentário, http://www.urbanismobr.org/bd/periodicos.php?id=65.

44. Rego Canticaval, "O falso lirismo da escravatura," *Paulistânia* 20 (July–August 1947): 9; "Palmares 1697–Canudos, 1897," *Paulistânia* 21 (November–December 1947): 27. The author of these articles was almost certainly writing under a pseudonym (probably inverting Cavalcanti to make Canticaval).

45. *Paulistânia* 32 (January–February 1950): 46–48.

46. "Minha Terra, Minha Pobre Terra," *Paulistânia* 20 (July–August 1947): 24–25; Ceciliana, "Paulista por Mercê de Deus," *Paulistânia* 23 (May–June 1948): 8; "9 de Julho," *Paulistânia* 30 (July–September 1949): 5.

47. "Na surda revolta íntima dos gigantes acorrentados," *Paulistânia* 23 (May–June 1948): 4.

48. "9 de Julho," *Paulistânia* 20 (July–August 1947): 7.

49. Given the absurd lack of comparability between World War II and the 1932 Guerra Paulista, I would normally assume that the author of this article was writing with tongue in cheek, but given that the subject was the projected monument to the war dead and war veterans, it seems likely that the author was writing in dead earnest. "O Monumento ao Soldado de 32," *Paulistânia* 22 (March–April 1948): 1.

50. *Paulistânia* 35 (July–August 1950): 3.

51. "As eleições," *Paulistânia* 36 (September–October 1950): 3.

52. MP, CIVC, Pasta 15, 26.

53. Scholars of memory have noted that rapid changes in the present produce a tendency to be nostalgic about an idealized past. Boym, *The Future of Nostalgia*.

54. *São Paulo em festa*—Vera Cruz documentary, 1954, directed by Lima Barreto.

Studio Vera Cruz, whose slogan was "From the blessed plateau to the screens of the world," was founded in 1949 by a group of paulista investors, including Ciccillo Matarazzo. It operated for less than five years and this documentary may have been its final production.

55. On ecclesiastical support for the 1932 uprising, see Carvalho, *O clero solidário com o povo em 32*. This text was originally prepared as part of a history course on the Constitutionalist Revolution.

56. On the ambiguous role of the Força Pública in the 1932 uprising, see herein, chapter 3.

57. The lyrics are from "São Paulo, Coração do Brasil" (1951), by David Nasser and Francisco Alves.

58. On the changing landscape of São Paulo, see Arantes, *Paisagens paulistanas*.

59. Martins, *Álbum de família 1932*. The book is unpaginated.

60. Martins, *Álbum de família 1932*.

61. On the epic as a genre for paulista narratives, see Ferreira, *A epopéia bandeirante*, 23–24.

62. For a discussion of the atmosphere that produced such screeds, see chapter 3 above.

63. On how circulating representations influence "experience," see Hall, *Representation*.

64. These images were associated with the most recent major regional revolt, the Federalist Revolution (the War of the Maragatos) in Rio Grande do Sul, 1893. See Chasteen, *Heroes on Horseback*.

65. Ellis, *A nossa guerra*, 80.

66. In a similar vein, see the dedication in Aureliano Leite's *Martírio e glória de São Paulo*.

67. Such images *were* included in the facsimile collection published in 1982 and prepared by the Arquivo do Estado de São Paulo to mark the fiftieth anniversary of the uprising, but the purpose of that collection was not to cultivate sentimental identification but rather to provide materials for historical critique and interpretation.

68. See herein, chapter 3, on representations of the "enemy" troops. Chronicles published immediately after the defeat tended to be particularly lurid in their portrayal of the "nortista" troops, with Alfredo Ellis claiming the northerners wanted to "drink the paulistas' blood." *A nossa guerra*, 282.

69. On concerns about the "national" workers and their alleged inferiority to European immigrants, see Weinstein, *For Social Peace in Brazil*, 123.

70. On the major strike movements in the 1950s, see Leal, *A reinvenção da classe trabalhadora*, 235–286.

71. Bittencourt, *A Mulher Paulista na história*, 311.

72. On Vargas's capture of the democratic/populist position, see French, *The Brazilian Workers' ABC*, chapter 4.

73. *O Dia*, July 19, 1957, 2.

74. Kubitschek, who was a medical doctor by training, served as a medic in the federal troops in 1932.

75. On the efforts of the Kubitschek administration to realize its motto of "fifty

years in five," see Benevides, *O governo Kubitschek*. On the paulista industrialists and the JK government, see Trevisan, *50 anos em 5*.

76. Weinstein, *For Social Peace in Brazil*, 299–306.

77. *Correio da Manhã* (Rio), July 9, 1957, 4, 7.

78. *Correio da Manhã* (Rio), July 9, 1957, 4. On Porfírio da Paz's role in paulista politics during this period, see Leal, *A reinvenção da classe trabalhadora*, 437–442.

79. The town of his birth, Araxá, is very close to the border with São Paulo.

80. *A Gazeta*, July 5, 1957, 4, 18. It is noteworthy that Antônio d'Avila's course was entitled "São Paulo, Brazil, and National Unity."

81. The paulista dailies consulted included *O Estado de São Paulo, A Folha de São Paulo, O Dia, O Diário Popular, Correio Paulistano, A Gazeta, Ultima Hora*, and *Tribuna dos Santos*.

82. *Diário Popular*, July 10, 1957, 18.

83. *O Dia*, July 9, 1957, 2.

84. *Correio Paulistano*, July 7, 1957, 7–8; July 9, 1957, Cad. 2, 1.

85. *A Gazeta*, July 9, 1957, 6.

86. *O Estado de São Paulo*, July 9, 1957, 3.

87. *O Estado de São Paulo*, July 9, 1957, 3.

88. See herein, conclusion.

89. *Correio Paulistano*, July 9, 1957, 1; *O Dia*, July 9, 1957, 12.

90. "Exaltada a participação da mulher em 1932," *Diário Popular*, July 6, 1957, 1; "Homenageada d. Maria José Barroso, Mulher-símbolo de 32," *A Gazeta*, July 6, 1957, 24.

91. Carlota Pereira de Queiroz, "A Mulher Paulista também foi para o campo de batalha em 32," *Correio Paulistano*, July 9, 1957, Cad. 3, 4.

92. Carlota Pereira de Queiroz, "A Mulher Paulista também foi para o campo de batalha em 32," *Correio Paulistano*, July 9, 1957, Cad. 3, 4.

93. "Pedro de Toledo, a grande figura da epopéia de 32," *Correio Paulistano*, July 9, 1957, Cad. 3, 1–2, 6.

94. "Os Bombeiros de São Paulo defenderam a retaguarda," *A Gazeta* (Edição comemorativa retrospectiva da epopéia de 32), July 9, 1957, 84.

95. "Homenagem aos Chefes e os Soldados de 1932," *Tribuna de Santos*, July 9, 1957, 14.

96. "Pedro de Toledo, a grande figura da epopéia de 32," 2 (emphasis added).

97. Cel. José Moreira Cardoso, "A epopéia de 32: Glória à Mulher Paulista," *O Dia*, July 9, 1957, 4.

98. "Movimento Constitucionalista de 32," *A Gazeta*, July 9, 1957, 2. The lead article went on to claim that Vargas's imposition of an interventor "tossed us into the inferno of a genuine enslavement."

99. "O Povo nas Ruas," OESP, July 10, 1957, 9.

100. Not every media outlet embraced the Silver Jubilee commemorations: the getulista/trabalhista daily, *Última Hora*, did not run a single article in its editions on July 9 and 10 on the various festivities and ceremonies, which contrasts with its extensive coverage in 1954.

101. Rubens do Amaral, "9 de Julho, um compromisso com o Brasil," *A Gazeta*, July 9, 1957, 44; "Notas e informações: a lição de uma data," OESP, July 9, 1957, 3.

102. João de Scantimburgo, "A lição do movimento de 32," *Correio Paulistano*, July 9, 1957, 1.

103. "Manifesto do Instituto de Engenharia sobre o 9 de Julho," *Diário Popular*, July 9, 1957, 12.

104. *O Estadão*, for example, virulently opposed expanding the right to vote to illiterates. See editorials on February 5, 1964, February 15, 1964, March 17, 1964, and March 21, 1964, cited in Franco, "O papel da grande imprensa na preparação dos golpes militares."

105. This lecture, originally delivered at the IHGSP, was printed as "Prodromos da Revolução Constitucionalista," *OESP*, July 9, 1957, 23.

106. Although the scale of the memorialization indicates factors beyond the nostalgia and introspection of the aging veterans of 1932, I would agree with James Woodard that this factor contributed to the intensification of memory work. *A Place in Politics*, 233–234.

107. On the enterprise of "memory work," see the preface to Stern, *Remembering Pinochet's Chile* (2006). On memory and shifting historical interpretations, see Rappaport, *The Politics of Memory*.

108. See above, chapter 4, for the way women's participation served the cause of rendering the 1932 uprising as a moral crusade rather than a political struggle.

109. *Viagem ao passado* (1950). This short film is in the Cinemateca Brasileira (São Paulo).

Epilogue and Conclusion

Epigraph 1: Foucault, *Archaeology of Knowledge*, 12.
Epigraph 2: Dimenstein, *Folha de São Paulo* (October 19, 2003).

1. "O paulista e a Nação em perigo," *OESP*, March 21, 1964, 4. On the support for the march among key figures in FIESP, see Weinstein, *For Social Peace in Brazil*, 321.

2. "S. Paulo repete 32," *OESP*, April 1, 1964, 4. For another editorial that directly compares the Constitutionalist Movement and the military coup, see "23 de Maio," *OESP*, May 23, 1964, 4.

3. *A Folha de São Paulo*, March 20, 1964, 2; "Retorno a 32," *Última Hora*, March 20, 1964, 2.

4. There is a growing scholarly literature on the military coup of 1964 and its historical context. Two of the earliest studies, with quite different perspectives, are Skidmore, *Politics in Brazil, 1930–1964*, 284–309; and Dreifuss, *1964*. For a brief overview of this literature, see Weinstein, "Postcolonial Brazil," 243–245.

5. Here I am drawing on Roger Chartier's very useful discussion of the question of "origins" (as opposed to causes). See *The Cultural Origins of the French Revolution*, 2.

6. For a perceptive scholarly study of anticommunism in Brazil, see Motta, *Em guarda contra o "perigo vermelho."*

7. "Os paulistas não se intimidaram," *OESP*, January 24, 1964, 4.

8. The "vigorous core" is a paraphrase of a famous quote from Euclides da Cunha's *Os sertões*, used in reference to the man of the northeastern backlands, as indicated by Stanley Blake (*The Vigorous Core of Our Nationality*, 66).

9. See editorials in *OESP* opposing the vote for illiterates on February 5, 1964,

February 15, 1964, March 17, 1964, and March 21, 1964. Franco, "O papel da grande imprensa na preparação dos golpes militares."

10. On unrest in Paraíba, see "O foco da agitação," OESP, January 19, 1964; on Pernambuco see "O estado de revolução em Pernambuco," OESP, March 5, 1964.

11. O'Dougherty, *Consumption Intensified*, chapter 7.

12. O'Dougherty, *Consumption Intensified*, chapter 7. See also Dimenstein, "Capital de São Paulo é o Brasil."

13. O'Dougherty, *Consumption Intensified*, 176.

14. Garcia, *O que é Nordeste brasileiro?*, 65.

15. Souto Maior, *São os nordestinos uma minoria racial?*

16. On the formation of the Partido dos Trabalhadores, see Keck, *The Workers' Party*.

17. The film is an adaptation of the biography by Denise Paraná, *Lula—Filho do Brasil*.

18. http://tnh1.ne10.uol.com.br/noticia/brasil/2012/05/16/187873/justica-condena -universitaria-paulista-mayara-petruso-que-ofendeu-nordestinos-no-twitter. Mayara Petruso was sentenced to a year, five months, and fifteen days in prison for her remarks, but the sentence was commuted to community service and a fine.

19. http://www.cartacapital.com.br/politica/as-eleicoes-e-o-preconceito-contra -o-nordeste/. Bolsa 171 is the monthly payment that indigent families receive if their children regularly attend school.

20. See chapter 2, herein.

21. O'Dougherty, *Consumption Intensified*, 181.

22. O'Dougherty, *Consumption Intensified*, 137–139.

23. I discuss these issues at greater length in "Developing Inequality."

24. As late as 1983, paulista journalist (and 1932 veteran) Honório Sylos engaged in a polemic with Gilberto Freyre (in the columns of OESP and *Diário de Pernambuco*, respectively) over the question of whether "special favors" from the newly formed First Republic had played a crucial role in São Paulo's surge to the forefront of the Brazilian economy (Freyre's position), or whether it was a result of qualities internal to São Paulo. Sylos, *Gente e fatos*, 166–172.

25. Alberto, *Terms of Inclusion*, 127–143; Gomes, *Negros e política*, 73.

26. On the complexity of non-radical politics within São Paulo, see Prado, *A democracia ilustrada*; Woodard, *A Place in Politics*; Borges, *Tenentismo e revolução brasileira*.

27. The 1932 uprising continued to be an opportunity for immigrants to affirm their love for their new "land." The *Tribuna de Santos* noted with enthusiastic approbation that Tufic Abdalla Agia, a Syrian immigrant, had decorated his clothing store for the 9 de Julho festivities. *Tribuna de Santos*, July 10, 1957, 3.

28. Petrônio Domingues opens his study of the Black Legion by discussing the ongoing scholarly neglect of the participation of black paulistas in the uprising. "Os 'Pérolas Negras,'" 199–200.

29. On party politics in Brazil in the decade after the end of the Estado Novo, see Skidmore, *Politics in Brazil*, 48–142.

30. *Life*, April 5, 1948, 88–98.

31. John French demonstrates very persuasively that paulista workers solidly sup-

ported populist candidates following the fall of the Estado Novo. *The Brazilian Workers'* *ABC*, 132–267. See also Gomes, *A invenção do trabalhismo*, 288–321.

32. On the much more muted and historically oriented commemoration of the Golden Jubilee in 1982, see the facsimile collection "São Paulo, 1932," organized by Ana Maria de Almeida Camargo and issued by the Arquivo Público do Estado de São Paulo, to mark the occasion.

33. The use of the term *epopéia* (epic) also makes sense at a moment when nationalist feelings ran high, and paulistas probably sought to downplay the idea that the movement was a "civil war."

34. See, for example, the sneering, disparaging review of João Alberto's memoirs by Júlio de Mesquita Filho, which was issued as a small book in time for the IV Centenário. Mesquita Filho, *"Memórias de um revolucionário."*

35. *1932: A Guerra Civil*, a film about the Constitutionalist uprising marking its sixtieth anniversary, included several leading paulista scholars who, though critical of the movement, sought to recuperate the pro-democracy aspects of the Causa Paulista, an understandable impulse at a time when Brazil was still transitioning from two decades of authoritarian rule. But my point is precisely that not only was the movement, in 1932, weakly identified with democratic impulses, but that even later, talk of democracy tended to define citizenship and constitutionalism in ways that opened the door for the shift to an authoritarian register.

36. For a largely positive World Bank evaluation (August 22, 2007) of the Bolsa-Família program (171), see http://web.worldbank.org/WBSITE/EXTERNAL/COUNTRIES /LACEXT/BRAZILEXTN/0,,contentMDK:21447054~pagePK:141137~piPK:141127 ~theSitePK:322341,00.html. There are, to be sure, critics of the Bolsa-Família program who, from a left or feminist perspective, question its tying of payments to mothers and families, rather than to workers and citizens. But these critics typically want to increase redistribution, or make it more effective, not challenge it in principle or reverse it.

37. See "Italy's Northern League vows to paralyze next government," Reuters, February 13, 2013, http://www.reuters.com/article/2013/02/13/us-italy-vote-league -idUSBRE91C11720130213. Unity, as I use it here, refers to unifying commitments, not the pursuit of homogeneity.

38. For a longer historical perspective on the struggles of Santa Cruz with the Bolivian central government, see Pruden, "Santa Cruz entre la post–Guerra del Chaco y las postrimerias de la revolución nacional."

39. On recent cruceño regionalism and separatism in Bolivia, see Lowrey, "Bolivia multiétnico y pluricultural"; Gustafson, "Flashpoints of Sovereignty"; and Barragán, "Oppressed or Privileged Regions?"

40. How vigorously the cruceños construct their "racial" identity in contrast with "Andean" Bolivia is almost comically evident in the response, spoken in English at the Miss Universe Pageant in Ecuador in 2004, by Miss Bolivia, Gabriela Oviedo, to the question "What is one of the biggest misconceptions about your country?" "Um . . . unfortunately, people that don't know Bolivia very much think that we are all just Indian people from the west side of the country: it's La Paz that reflects this image that we are all poor people and very short people and Indian people. . . . I'm from the

other side of the country, the east side and it's not cold, it's very hot and we are tall and we are white people and we know English so all that misconception that Bolivia is only an "Andean" country, it's wrong, Bolivia has a lot to offer and that's my job as an ambassador of my country to let people know how much diversity we have." Quoted in Canessa, "Sex and the Citizen," 56. My thanks to Sinclair Thomson for bringing this comment to my attention.

41. For critiques of the tendency to overdraw the distinction between "biological" and "cultural" racism, see Wade, "Afterword," in Appelbaum et al., *Race and Nation in Modern Latin America*, 274–275; Larson, *Trials of Nation Making*, 63–70; Balibar, "Racism and Nationalism," 37–67.

42. See, for example, Lomnitz-Adler, *Exits from the Labyrinth*.

43. Gilroy, "One Nation under a Groove," 357.

44. Here I would reiterate the point made in the introduction; in line with the work of Prasenjit Duara (*Rescuing History from the Nation*, 177–204), I see the ongoing (and perhaps endless) struggles involved in nation building as animating, not diminishing, regional identities.

BIBLIOGRAPHY

Archival Sources
ARCHIVES

Arquivo Edgard Leuenroth, IFCH, Universidade de Campinas

Arquivo Público do Estado de São Paulo (APESP)
    Coleção Revolução de 1932
    Arquivo Campanha Eleitoral de Armando de Salles Oliveira
    Acervo DEOPS-SP (Delegacia Especializada de Ordem Político e Social)
    Prontuários of Paulo Duarte, Ibrahim Nobre, Paulo Nogueira Filho and J. Guaraná
    de Sant'Anna

Arquivo Histórico Municipal de São Paulo (AHM)
    Fundo do IV Centenário
        Livros de Atas
        Gabinete
        Serviço de Comemorações Culturais
        Serviço de Comemorações Populares
        Serviço de Relações Públicas, Imprensa, Propaganda, e Turismo

Biblioteca Nacional (Rio de Janeiro)

Cinemateca Brasileira

Fundação Getúlio Vargas, Centro de Pesquisa e Documentação (FGV, CPDOC),
Rio de Janeiro
    Acervo Bertoldo Klinger
    Acervo Getúlio Vargas (1932)
    Acervo José Maria Whitaker
    Acervo Virgílio de Mello Franco

Instituto de Estudos Brasileiros (IEB), Universidade de São Paulo
    Coleção Mário de Andrade
    Coleção Guilherme de Almeida
    Coleção Antônio de Alcântara Machado

Instituto Histórico e Geográfico de São Paulo (IHGSP) [extinct]
  Arquivo da Revolução de 32, Recortes de Jornais
  Arquivo Aureliano Leite, Pacote 13
  Arquivo Carlota Pereira de Queiroz

Museu Paulista (MP)
  Coleção Revolução 1932
  Arquivo Pedro Manoel de Toledo
  Arquivo Olga de Souza Queiroz
  Coleção IV Centenário

National Archives and Records Administration (NARA), College Park
      RG59, M1472, Brazil, Rolls 1–7

COMMEMORATIVE NEWSPAPER EDITIONS, JANUARY 24–25, 1954

Correio Paulistano
Diário de São Paulo
Diário Popular
O Estado de São Paulo
Folha da Manhã
O Tempo
Última Hora

COMMEMORATIVE NEWSPAPER EDITIONS, JULY 9, 1957

Correio Paulistano
A Folha de São Paulo
O Dia
O Diário Popular
O Estado de São Paulo
A Gazeta
Tribuna de Santos

PERIODICALS CONSULTED

NEWSPAPERS

Correio da Manhã (Rio)
Correio Paulistano
O Estado de São Paulo
Folha da Manhã
Folha da Noite
A Folha de São Paulo
Diário Nacional
A Gazeta
A Platéia
A Plebe
Notícias de Hoje
Última Hora
Jornal das Trincheiras

O Separatista
Diário de Pernambuco
O Povo (Fortaleza)
O Imparcial (São Luiz)

JOURNALS/MAGAZINES
Revista do Brasil
Cigarra
Paulistânia
Revista Nova
Anhembi
Cidade
O Mundo Ilustrado
Boletim da Comissão do IV Centenário da Cidade de São Paulo

Published and Secondary Sources

Abreu, Maurício de Almeida. *Evolução urbana do Rio de Janeiro*. Rio de Janeiro: Iplanrio, 1987.

Abud, Katia M. "O bandeirante e a Revolução de 32: Alguma relação?" 36–46. In Maria Isaura Pereira de Queiroz, ed. *O imaginário em terra conquistada*. São Paulo: CERU, 1993, 36–46.

Abud, Katia M. "O sangue intimorato e as nobilíssimas tradições: A construção de um símbolo paulista: O bandeirante." PhD diss., USP, 1986.

Adduci, Cássia Chrispiniano. *A "Pátria Paulista": O separatismo como resposta à crise final do império brasileiro*. São Paulo: Arquivo do Estado, 2000.

Adelman, Jeremy. *Worldly Philosopher: The Odyssey of Albert O. Hirschman*. Princeton, NJ: Princeton University Press, 2013.

Agulhon, Maurice. *Marianne into Battle: Republican Imagery and Symbolism in France, 1789–1880*. New York: Cambridge University Press, 1981.

"AHR Forum: Histories of the Future." *American Historical Review* 117, no. 5 (December 2012): 1402–1485.

Alberto, Paulina. *Terms of Inclusion: Black Intellectuals in Twentieth-Century Brazil*. Chapel Hill: University of North Carolina Press, 2011.

Albuquerque Jr., Durval Muniz de. *A invenção do Nordeste e outras artes*. Recife: Fundação Joaquim Nabuco/Ed. Massangana, 1999.

Almeida Jr., A. "A Faculdade de Direito e a Cidade." *Ensaios Paulistas*. São Paulo: Ed. Anhambi, 1958.

Almeida, Guilherme de. "São Paulo e o espírito moderno." In *São Paulo e sua evolução*. Rio de Janeiro: Centro Paulista, 1927, 103–113.

Alves Sobrinho, Rufino. *São Paulo triunfante*. São Paulo: n.p., 1932.

Amado, Janaína. "História e região: Reconhecendo e construindo espaços." In Silva, ed., *República em migalhas*, 7–15.

Amaral, Aracy A. *Tarsila: Sua obra e seu tempo*. São Paulo: EDUSP, 2003.

Amaral, Edmundo. *Rotulas e mantilhas*. São Paulo: Typ. Bancaria, 1931.

AmCham-São Paulo. *Paulista*, third quarter (1930).

Anderson, Benedict. *Imagined Communities: Reflections on the Origin and Spread of Nationalism*. London: Verso, 1991.

Andrade, Horácio de. *Tudo por São Paulo*. São Paulo: n.p., 1932.

Andrade, Mário de. *Cartas Mário de Andrade/Oneyda Alvarenga*. São Paulo: Duas Cidades, 1983.

Andrade, Mário de. "A guerra de São Paulo." Unpublished manuscript, Acervo Mário de Andrade, IEB/USP.

Andrade, Oswald de. *Marco Zero: A revolução melancólica*. São Paulo: J. Olympio, 1943.

Andrews, George Reid. *Blacks and Whites in São Paulo, Brazil, 1888–1988*. Madison: University of Wisconsin Press, 1991.

Appelbaum, Nancy P. *Muddied Waters: Race, Region, and Local History in Colombia, 1846–1948*. Durham, NC: Duke University Press, 2003.

Appelbaum, Nancy P. "Whitening the Region: Caucano Mediation and 'Antioqueño Colonization' in Nineteenth-Century Colombia." *Hispanic American Historical Review* 79, no. 4 (1999): 631–667.

Appelbaum, Nancy P., Anne Macpherson, and Karin A. Rosemblatt. "Introduction: Racial Nations." In *Race and Nation in Modern Latin America*. Chapel Hill: University of North Carolina Press, 2003, 1–31.

Appelbaum, Nancy P., Anne Macpherson, and Karin A. Rosemblatt. *Race and Nation in Modern Latin America*. Chapel Hill: University of North Carolina Press, 2003.

Arantes, Antonio Augusto. *Paisagens paulistanas: Transformações do espaço público*. Campinas: Ed. Unicamp, 1999.

Araújo, Ricardo Benzaquen de. *Guerra e paz: Casa Grande e Senzala e a obra de Gilberto Freyre nos anos 30*. Rio de Janeiro: Editora 34, 1994.

Arruda, Maria Arminda do Nascimento. "Dilemas do Brasil moderno: A questão racial na obra de Florestan Fernandes." In *Raça, ciência e sociedade*, edited by Marcos Chor Maio and Ricardo Ventura Santos. Rio de Janeiro: Ed. Fiocruz, 1998, 195–203.

Arruda, Maria Arminda do Nascimento. *Metrópole e cultura: São Paulo no meio século XX*. São Paulo: EDUSC, 2001.

Azevedo, Aroldo de, et al. *A cidade de São Paulo: Estudos de geografia urbana*, vols. 2 and 4. São Paulo: Cia. Ed. Nacional, 1958.

Azevedo, Célia Maria Marinho de. *Onda negra, medo branco: O negro no imaginário das elites século XIX*. São Paulo: Paz e Terra, 1987.

Balibar, Etienne. "Racism and Nationalism." In Balibar and Immanuel Wallerstein, *Race, Nation, Class*. London: Verso, 1991, 37–67.

Barbosa, Márcio, ed. *Frente Negra Brasileira: Depoimentos*. São Paulo: Quilombhoje, 1998.

Barickman, B. J. "Revisiting the Casa-Grande: Plantation and Cane-Farming Households in Early Nineteenth-Century Bahia." *Hispanic American Historical Review* 84, no. 4 (2004): 619–659.

Barragán, Rossana. "Oppressed or Privileged Regions? Some Historical Reflections on the Use of State Resources." In *Unresolved Tensions: Bolivia Past and Present*, edited by John Crabtree and Laurence Whitehead. Pittsburgh: University of Pittsburgh Press, 2008, 83–103.

Barroso, Gustavo. *A Sinagoga paulista*. Rio de Janeiro: Ed. ABC, 1937.

Bastide, Roger. "O negro em São Paulo." In *São Paulo em quatro séculos*. Vol. 2. São Paulo: IHGSP, 1954, 23–40.

Beattie, Peter M. *The Tribute of Blood: Army, Honor, Race, and Nation in Brazil, 1864–1945*. Durham, NC: Duke University Press, 2001.

Bederman, Gail. *Manliness and Civilization: A Cultural History of Gender and Race in the United States, 1880–1917*. Chicago: University of Chicago Press, 1995.

Beiguelman, Paula. *A formação do povo no complexo cafeeiro: Aspectos políticos*. São Paulo: Pioneira, 1968.

Beiguelman, Paula. "A grande imigração em São Paulo." *Revista do IEB* 3 (1968): 99–116; 4 (1968): 145–157.

Belmonte. *No tempo dos bandeirantes*. São Paulo: Departamento de Cultura, 1939.

Benevides, Maria Victória de Mesquita. *O governo Kubitschek*. Rio de Janeiro: Paz e Terra, 1976.

Benhabib, Seyla. "Models of Public Space: Hannah Arendt, the Liberal Tradition, and Jürgen Habermas." In *Habermas and the Public Sphere*, edited by Craig Calhoun. Cambridge, MA: MIT Press, 1992, 73–98.

Berman, Marshall. *All That Is Solid Melts into Air: The Experience of Modernity*. New York: Simon and Schuster, 1982.

Bernardez, Manuel. *Le Bresil: Sa vie, son travail, son avenir*. Buenos Aires: Ortega y Radaelli, 1908.

Besse, Susan K. *Restructuring Patriarchy: The Modernization of Gender Inequality in Brazil, 1914–1940*. Chapel Hill: University of North Carolina Press, 1996.

Bezerra, Holien Gonçalves. *O jogo do poder: Revolução paulista de 32*. São Paulo: Moderna, 1988.

Bhabha, Homi. *The Location of Culture*. London: Routledge, 1994.

Bicudo, Virgínia Leone. *Atitudes raciais de pretos e mulatos em São Paulo*. Edited by Marcos Chor Maio. São Paulo: Ed. Sociologia e Política, 2010.

Bieber, Judy. *Power, Patronage, and Political Violence: State Building on a Brazilian Frontier, 1822–1889*. Lincoln: University of Nebraska Press, 1999.

Bittencourt, Adalzira. *A Mulher Paulista na história*. Rio de Janeiro: Livros de Portugal, 1954.

Blaj, Ilana. "O paulista enquanto construtor da nação: A produção 'paulística.'" Paper presented at IV BRASA meetings, November 1997, Washington, DC.

Blaj, Ilana. *A trama das tensões: O processo de mercantilização de São Paulo colonial, 1681–1721*. São Paulo: Humanitas/USP, 2002.

Blake, Stanley E. *The Vigorous Core of Our Nationality: Race and Regional Identity in Northeastern Brazil*. Pittsburgh: University of Pittsburgh Press, 2011.

Blauner, Robert. "Internal Colonialism and Ghetto Revolt." *Social Problems* 16, no. 4 (1969): 393–408.

Blight, David. *Race and Reunion: The Civil War in American Memory*. Cambridge, MA: Harvard/Belknap Press, 2002.

Bocketti, Gregg P. "Italian Immigrants, Brazilian Football, and the Dilemma of National Identity." *Journal of Latin American Studies* 40, no. 2 (May 2008): 275–302.

Bomeny, Helena M. Bousquet. "A estratégia da conciliação: Minas Gerais e a abertura política dos anos 30." In Gomes, ed., *Regionalismo e centralização política*, 133–235.

Bonavides, Paulo. *Democrito Rocha: Uma vocação para a liberdade*. Fortaleza, Brazil: Fundação Democrito Rocha, 1988.

Borges, Dain. "'Puffy, Ugly, Slothful and Inert': Degeneration in Brazilian Social Thought, 1880–1940." *Journal of Latin American Studies* 25, no. 2 (May 1993): 235–256.

Borges, Vavy Pacheco. *Getúlio Vargas e a oligarquia paulista: História de uma esperança e muitos desenganos*. São Paulo: Brasiliense, 1979.

Borges, Vavy Pacheco. *Memória paulista*. São Paulo: EDUSP, 1997.

Borges, Vavy Pacheco. *Tenentismo e revolução brasileira*. São Paulo: Brasiliense, 1992.

Bourdieu, Pierre. *Distinction: A Social Critique of the Judgement of Taste*. Cambridge, MA: Harvard University Press, 1984.

Bourdieu, Pierre. "Identity and Representation: Elements for a Critical Reflection on the Idea of Region." In *Language and Symbolic Power*. Cambridge, MA: Harvard University Press, 1991, 220–228.

Boym, Svetlana. *The Future of Nostalgia*. New York: Basic Books, 2001.

Brazil. Congresso Nacional. Câmara dos Deputados. *Anais da Câmara dos Deputados*, 1920–1929.

Bresciani, Maria Stella. *O charme da ciência e a sedução da objetividade: Oliveira Vianna entre interpretes do Brasil*. São Paulo: Ed. UNESP, 2005.

Bronfman, Alejandra. *Measures of Equality: Social Science, Citizenship, and Race in Cuba, 1902–1940*. Chapel Hill: University of North Carolina Press, 2003.

Brubaker, Rogers and Frederick Cooper. "Beyond 'Identity.'" *Theory and Society* 29 (2000): 1–47.

Burchell, Graham, Colin Gordon, and Peter Miller, eds. *The Foucault Effect: Studies in Governmentality*. Chicago: University of Chicago Press, 1991.

Burke III, Edmund, and David Prochaska, eds. *Genealogies of Orientalism: History, Theory, Politics*. Lincoln: University of Nebraska Press, 2008.

Burns, E. Bradford. *A History of Brazil*. New York: Columbia University Press, 1970.

Burton, Antoinette. *Burdens of History: British Feminists, Indian Women, and Imperial Culture, 1865–1915*. Chapel Hill: University of North Carolina Press, 1994.

Bushnell, David. *The Making of Modern Colombia: A Nation In Spite of Itself*. Berkeley: University of California Press, 1993.

Butler, Kim D. *Freedoms Given, Freedoms Won: Afro-Brazilians in Post-Abolition São Paulo and Salvador*. New Brunswick, NJ: Rutgers University Press, 1998.

Camargo, Ana Maria de Almeida, org. *São Paulo, 1932—edição facsimile*. São Paulo: Arquivo do Estado, 1982.

Canessa, Andrew. "Sex and the Citizen: Barbies and Beauty Queens in the Age of Evo Morales." *Journal of Latin American Cultural Studies* 17, no. 1 (2008): 41–64.

Cano, Wilson. *Raízes da concentração industrial em São Paulo*. São Paulo: Difel, 1977.

Capelato, Maria Helena. *Os arautos do liberalismo: Imprensa paulista, 1920–1945*. São Paulo: Brasiliense, 1989.

Capelato, Maria Helena. "Estado Novo: Novas histórias." In *Historiografia brasileira em perspectiva*, edited by Marcos Cezar de Freitas. São Paulo: EDUSP/Contexto, 1998, 183–213.

Capelato, Maria Helena. *O movimento de 1932: A causa paulista*. São Paulo: Coleção Tudo é História, 1981.

Capelato, Maria Helena Rolim, and Maria Lígia Coelho Prado. *O bravo matutino: Imprensa e ideologia: O jornal O Estado de São Paulo*. São Paulo: Alfa-Omega, 1980.

Cardoso, Miriam Limoeiro. *Ideologia do desenvolvimento Brasil: JK–JQ*. Rio de Janeiro: Paz e Terra, 1978.

Carneiro, Edison. *Antologia do Negro Brasileiro*. Rio de Janeiro: Agir, 2005.

Carneiro, Milton. "Prefácio." In Elias Karam, *Um paranaense nas trincheiras da lei*. Curitiba, Brazil: Cruzada, 1933, i–xxxii.

Carneiro, Nelson de Souza Carneiro. *XII de Agosto! O Movimento constitucionalista na Bahia*. São Paulo: Cia. Editora Nacional, 1933.

Carone, Edgard, ed. *O pensamento industrial no Brasil, 1880–1945*. São Paulo: DIFEL, 1977.

Carone, Edgard. *A república velha: Evolução política*. São Paulo: DIFEL, 1974.

Carr, Francesca. "São Paulo's Fourth Centennial Fair." *New York Times*, June 13, 1954, 46.

Carvalho, Florentino de (Primitivo Soares). *A Guerra Civil de 1932 em São Paulo: Solução imediata dos grandes promblemas nacionais*. São Paulo: Ariel, 1932.

Carvalho, José Murilo de. "As duas mortes de Getúlio Vargas." In *Pontos e bordados*. Belo Horizonte: Ed. UFMG, 1998, 409–412.

Carvalho, José Murilo de. *A formação das almas: O imaginário da república no Brasil*. São Paulo: Companhia das Letras, 1990.

Carvalho, Monsenhor João Baptista de. *Irradiações: Homenagem das senhoras santistas*. São Paulo: Saraiva, 1933.

Carvalho, Monsenhor João Baptista de. *O clero solidário com o povo em 32*. São Paulo: Instituto Histórico e Geográfico de S. Paulo, 1957.

Casasanta, Mário. *As razões de Minas*. Belo Horizonte: Imprensa Oficial do Estado, 1932.

Castro, Sertório de. *Diário de um combatente desarmado*. São Paulo: J. Olympio, 1934.

Castro, Sertório de. *Política, és Mulher!* São Paulo: Paulo de Azevedo, 1933.

Caulfield, Sueann. *In Defense of Honor: Sexual Morality, Modernity, and Nation in Early Twentieth-Century Brazil*. Durham, NC: Duke University Press, 2000.

Caulfield, Sueann. "Interracial Courtship in the Rio de Janeiro Courts, 1918–1940." In *Race and Nation in Modern Latin America*, edited by Nancy P. Appelbaum, Anne Macpherson, and Karin A. Rosemblatt. Chapel Hill: University of North Carolina Press, 2003, 163–186.

Centro Paulista. *São Paulo e a sua evolução: Conferencias realisadas no Centro Paulista em 1926*. Rio de Janeiro: S.A. Gazeta da Bolsa, 1927.

Cerri, Luis Fernando. "NON DUCOR, DUCO: A ideologia da paulistinidade e a escolar." *Revista Brasileira de História* 18, no. 36 (1998): 115–136.

Chaloult, Yves. "Regional Differentials and Role of the State: Economic-Political Relationships between the Northeast and Southeast of Brazil." PhD diss., Cornell University, 1976.

Chartier, Roger. *The Cultural Origins of the French Revolution*. Durham, NC: Duke University Press, 1991.

Chasteen, John C. *Heroes on Horseback: A Life and Times of the Last Gaucho Caudillos.* Albuquerque: University of New Mexico Press, 1995.

Coaracy, Vivaldo. *O caso de São Paulo.* São Paulo: Ferraz, 1932.

Coaracy, Vivaldo. *A sala da capela.* São Paulo: J. Olympio, 1933.

Coelho, Geraldo Mártires. "Uma aparição tardia: A presença de Marianne no Pará." In *História: fronteiras.* Anais do XX Simpósio Nacional de História. São Paulo: Humanitas/FFLCH/USP: ANPUH, vol. 2 (1999): 983–993.

Cohn, Deborah. "Faulkner, Latin America, and the Caribbean: Influence, Politics, and Academic Disciplines." In *A Companion to William Faulkner*, edited by Richard Moreland. Oxford: Blackwell Publishing, 2006, 499–518.

Confino, Alon. *The Nation as a Local Metaphor: Württemberg, Imperial Germany, and National Memory, 1871–1918.* Chapel Hill: University of North Carolina Press, 1997.

Corrêa, Anna Maria Martínez. *A rebelião de 1924 em São Paulo.* São Paulo: Hucitec, 1976.

Corrêa, José Celso Martínez. "Depoimento: 1954, o ano das imagens," *Cidade*, 1, no. 1 (1994): 33.

Costa, Emilia Viotti da. *The Brazilian Empire: Myths and Histories.* Chicago: University of Chicago Press, 1985.

Costa, Emilia Viotti da. *Da senzala à colônia.* São Paulo: DIFEL, 1966.

Costa, Emilia Viotti da, "The Myth of Racial Democracy: A Legacy of the Empire." In *The Brazilian Empire: Myths and Histories.* Chicago: University of Chicago Press, 1985, 234–246.

Costa, Emília Viotti da. *1932: Imagens contraditórias.* São Paulo: Arquivo do Estado, 1982.

Cunha, Euclides da. *Rebellion in the Backlands.* Trans. Samuel Putnam. Chicago: University of Chicago Press, 1957.

Cunha, Euclides da. *Os sertões.* Rio de Janeiro: Laemmert & Cia., 1902.

Cunha, Olívia Gomes da. *Intenção e gesto: Pessoa, cor e a produção cotidiana da (in) diferença no Rio de Janeiro, 1927–1942.* Rio de Janeiro: Arquivo Nacional, 2002.

Dávila, Jerry. *Diploma of Whiteness: Race and Social Policy in Brazil, 1917–1945.* Durham, NC: Duke University Press, 2003.

Dean, Warren. *The Industrialization of São Paulo.* Austin: University of Texas Press, 1969.

Dean, Warren. *Rio Claro: A Brazilian Plantation System, 1820–1920.* Stanford, CA: Stanford University Press, 1976.

Decca, Edgar de. *1930: O silêncio dos vencidos.* São Paulo: Brasiliense, 1981.

De Grazia, Victoria. *How Fascism Ruled Women: Italy, 1922–1945.* Berkeley: University of California Press, 1993.

della Cava, Ralph. *Miracle at Joaseiro.* New York: Columbia University Press, 1970.

de Luca, Tania Regina. "O centenário da independência em São Paulo." *História* (Passo Fundo) 4, no. 2 (2003): 136–150.

de Luca, Tania Regina. *A Revista do Brasil: Diagnóstico para n(ação).* São Paulo: Ed. UNESP, 1999.

Derby, Lauren. *The Dictator's Seduction: Politics and the Popular Imagination in the Era of Trujillo.* Durham, NC: Duke University Press, 2009.

Derby, Lauren. "Gringo Chickens with Worms: Food and Nationalism in the Dominican Republic." In *Close Encounters of Empire*, edited by Gilbert Joseph, Catherine LeGrand, and Ricardo Salvatore. Durham, NC: Duke University Press, 1998, 451–493.

D'Araújo, Maria Celina Soares. *O segundo governo Vargas*. Rio de Janeiro: Zahar, 1982.

Deutsch, Sandra McGee. "Spartan Mothers: Fascist Women in Brazil in the 1930s." In *Right-Wing Women: From Conservatives to Extremists around the World*, edited by Paola Bacchetta and Margaret Power. London: Routledge, 2002, 155–168.

Dias, Arthur. *The Brazil of To-day*. Nivelles, Belgium: Lanneau et Despret, 1907.

Dias, Maria Odila Leite da Silva. *Power and Everyday Life: The Lives of Working Women in Nineteenth-Century Brazil*. New Brunswick, NJ: Rutgers University Press, 1995.

Dimenstein, Gilberto. "Capital de São Paulo é o Brasil." *Folha de S. Paulo*, October 19, 2003.

Dinius, Oliver. *Brazil's Steel City: Developmentalism, Strategic Power, and Industrial Relations in Volta Redonda, 1941–1964*. Stanford, CA: Stanford University Press, 2010.

Diniz, Almachio. *São Paulo e a sua guerra de secessão*. Rio de Janeiro: Irmãos Pongetti, 1933.

Domingues, Petrônio. *Uma história não contada: Negro, racismo e branqueamento em São Paulo no pós-abolição*. São Paulo: SENAC, 2003.

Domingues, Petrônio. *A nova abolição*. São Paulo: Selo Negro, 2008.

Domingues, Petrônio. "Os 'Pérolas Negras': A participação do negro na revolução constitucionalista de 1932." *Afro-Ásia* 29/30 (2003): 199–245.

Donato, Hernani. *A revolução de 32*. São Paulo: Livros Abril, 1982.

Draibe, Sônia. *Rumos e metamorfoses: Estado e industrialização no Brasil, 1930–1960*. Rio de Janeiro: Paz e Terra, 1985.

Dreifuss, René Armand. *1964: A conquista do estado*. Petrópolis: Vozes, 1981.

Duara, Prasenjit. "Historicizing National Identity, or Who Imagines What and When." In *Becoming National*, edited by Geoff Eley and Ronald Grigor Suny. Oxford: Oxford University Press, 1996, 151–174.

Duara, Prasenjit. *Rescuing History from the Nation: Questioning Narratives of Modern China*. Chicago: University of Chicago Press, 1997.

Duarte, Paulo. *Agora nós! Chronica da Revolução Paulista*. Preface by Boris Fausto. São Paulo: Fundap, [1927] 2007.

Duarte, Paulo. "Os negros do Brasil." *O Estado de S. Paulo*, April 15, 1947, 4; April 16, 1947, 5.

Duarte, Paulo. *Palmares pelo avesso*. São Paulo: Progresso, 1947.

Duarte, Paulo. *Que é que há? . . . Pequena história de uma grande pirataria*. São Paulo: n.p., 1931.

Dunn, Christopher. *Brutality Garden: Tropicália and the Emergence of a Brazilian Counterculture*. Chapel Hill: University of North Carolina Press, 2000.

Eakin, Marshall. *Tropical Capitalism: The Industrialization of Belo Horizonte, Brazil*. New York: Palgrave, 2001.

Eleutério, Maria de Lourdes. *Oswald: Itinerário de um homem sem profissão*. Campinas: Ed. Unicamp, 1989.

Eley, Geoff, and Ronald Grigor Suny, eds. *Becoming National*. Oxford: Oxford University Press, 1996.

Elliott, L. Elwyn. *Brazil Today and Tomorrow*. New York: Macmillan, 1917.

Ellis Jr., Alfredo. *Confederação ou separação?* São Paulo: Paulista, 1932.

Ellis Jr., Alfredo. *A evolução da economia paulista e suas causas*. São Paulo: Cia. Ed. Nacional, 1937.

Ellis Jr., Alfredo. *A nossa guerra*. São Paulo: Ed. Piratininga, 1933.

Ellis Jr., Alfredo. *Populações paulistas*. São Paulo: Cia. Editora Nacional, 1934.

Ellis Jr., Alfredo. *Os primeiros troncos paulistas e o cruzamento euro-americano*. São Paulo: Cia. Ed. Nacional, 1936.

Ellis Jr., Alfredo. *Raça de gigantes: A civilização no planalto paulista*. São Paulo: Editora Helios, 1926.

Ellis Jr., Alfredo. "São Paulo e o Brasil-Colonia—Os bandeirantes—Amador Bueno." Centro Paulista, *São Paulo e sua evolução*. Rio de Janeiro: Typ. Gazeta da Bolsa, 1927, 59–79.

Ellis, Myriam. *Alfredo Ellis Júnior, 1896–1974*. São Paulo: Bentivigna ed., 1997.

Ellis, Myriam. "The Bandeiras in the Geographical Expansion of Brazil." In Morse, ed., *The Bandeirantes*, 48–63.

Enloe, Cynthia. *Does Khaki Become You? The Militarization of Women's Lives*. London: Pluto Press, 1983.

Falcão, Joaquim, and Rosa Maria Barboza de Araújo, eds. *O imperador das idéias: Gilberto Freyre em questão*. Rio de Janeiro: Topbooks, 2001.

Fan, C. Cindy. "Uneven Development and Beyond: Regional Development Theory in Post-Mao China." *International Journal of Urban and Regional Research* 21, no. 4 (1997): 620–639.

Farnsworth-Alvear, Ann. *Dulcinea in the Factory: Myths, Morals, Men, and Women in Colombia's Industrial Experiment, 1905–1960*. Durham, NC: Duke University Press, 2000.

Fausto, Boris. *A revolução de 1930: Historiografia e história*. São Paulo: Brasiliense, 1980.

Ferreira, Antonio Celso. *A epopéia bandeirante*. São Paulo: Ed. UNESP, 2001.

Ferretti, Danilo José Zioni. "A construção da paulistinidade: Identidade, historiografia e política em São Paulo (1856–1930)." PhD diss., USP, 2004.

Ferretti, Danilo José Zioni. "O uso político do passado bandeirante: O debate entre Oliveira Vianna e Alfredo Ellis Jr., 1920–1926." *Estudos Históricos* 21 (2008): 59–78.

Fields, Barbara J. "Whiteness, Racism, and Identity." *ILWCH* 60 (fall 2001): 48–56.

Findlay, Eileen M. *Imposing Decency: The Politics of Sexuality and Race in Puerto Rico, 1870–1920*. Durham, NC: Duke University Press, 2000.

Firmeza, Mozart. *Poemas em prosa da Revolução Paulista*. Rio de Janeiro: A. Coelho Branco Filho, 1933.

Fontes, Paulo. *Um Nordeste em São Paulo: Trabalhadores migrantes em São Miguel Paulista, 1945–66*. Rio de Janeiro: FGV Editora, 2008.

Foucault, Michel. *The Archaeology of Knowledge*. New York: Pantheon Books, 1972.

Franco, Geisa Cunha. "O papel da grande imprensa na preparação dos golpes militares (Um estudo comparativo entre o Brasil, 1964, e a Argentina, 1976)." MA thesis, USP, 1997.

Frank, Zephyr. "Wealth Holding in Southeastern Brazil, 1815–60." *HAHR* 85, no. 2 (May 2005): 223–257.

French, John D. *The Brazilian Workers' ABC: Class Conflict and Alliances in Modern São Paulo*. Chapel Hill: University of North Carolina Press, 1992.

Freyre, Gilberto. *Casa-Grande e senzala: Formação da família brasileira sob o regime da economia patriarcal*. Rio de Janeiro: José Olympio, [1933] 1980.

Freyre, Gilberto. *Manifesto regionalista de 1926*. Recife: Instituto Joaquim Nabuco, 1967.

Freyre, Gilberto. *O mundo que o português criou: Aspectos das relações sociaes e de cultura do Brasil com Portugal e as colónias portuguesas*. Rio de Janeiro: J. Olympio, 1940.

Freyre, Gilberto. *New World in the Tropics: The Culture of Modern Brazil*. Westport, CT: Greenwood Press, 1959.

Freyre, Gilberto. *Order and Progress: Brazil from Monarchy to Republic*. New York: Alfred Knopf, [1959]1970.

Freyre, Gilberto. "São Paulo e a unidade brasileira." In *São Paulo: Espírito, Povo, Instituições*, edited by J. V. Freitas Marcondes et al. São Paulo: Livraria Pioneira, 1968, 1–24.

Gama, Lúcia Helena. *Nos bares da vida: Produção cultural e sociabilidade em São Paulo, 1940–1950*. São Paulo: Ed. SENAC, 1998.

Garcia, Carlos. *O que é Nordeste brasileiro?* São Paulo: Ed. Brasiliense, 1984.

Gilroy, Paul. *The Black Atlantic: Modernity and Double Consciousness*. Cambridge, MA: Harvard University Press, 1993.

Gilroy, Paul. "One Nation Under a Groove." In *Becoming National*, edited by Geoff Eley and Ronald Grigor Suny. New York: Oxford University Press, 1996, 352–370.

Ginzburg, Carlo. "'Your Country Needs You': A Case Study in Political Iconography." *History Workshop Journal* 52 (autumn 2001): 1–22.

Godoy, Joaquim Floriano de. *A província de S. Paulo: Trabalho estatístico, histórico e noticioso*, 2nd fac. ed. São Paulo: Governo de Estado, [1875] 1978.

Gomes, Angela M. de Castro, ed. *Capanema: O ministro e seu ministério*. Rio de Janeiro: FGV, 2000.

Gomes, Angela M. de Castro. *Essa gente do Rio*. Rio de Janeiro: Editora FGV, 1999.

Gomes, Angela M. de Castro. *A invenção do trabalhismo*. Rio de Janeiro: IUPERJ/Vértice, 1988.

Gomes, Angela M. de Castro, ed. *Regionalismo e centralização política: Partidos e constituinte nos anos 30*. Rio de Janeiro: Ed. Nova Fronteira, 1980.

Gomes, Flávio dos Santos. *Negros e política, 1888–1937*. Rio de Janeiro: Jorge Zahar, 2005.

Gomes, Flávio dos Santos and Petrônio Domingues. *Da nitidez e invisibilidade: Legados do pós-emancipação no Brasil*. Belo Horizonte, Brazil: Fino Traço, 2013.

Gomes, Flávio dos Santos, and Petrônio Domingues. "Raça, pós-emancipação, cidadania e modernidade no Brasil." In *Da nitidez e invisibilidade: Legados do pós-emancipação no Brasil*. Belo Horizonte, Brazil: Fino Traço, 2013, 287–307.

Gomes, Flávio dos Santos, Petrônio Domingues, and Anamaria Fagundes. "Idiossincrasias cromáticas: Projetos e propostas de 'imigração negra' no Brasil republicano." In *Da nitidez e invisibilidade*, 185–201.

Gomes, Tiago de Melo. "Problemas no paraíso: A democracia racial brasileira frente à imigração afro-americana (1921)." *Estudos Afro-Asiáticos* 25, no. 2 (2003): 307–331.

Gonçalves, Clovis. *Carne para canhão! O front em 1932*. Rio de Janeiro: Renascença Ed., 1933.

González Casanova, Pablo. "Internal Colonialism and National Development." *Studies in Comparative International Development* 1, no. 4 (1965): 27–37.

Goswami, Manu. *Producing India: From Colonial Economy to National Space.* Chicago: University of Chicago Press, 2004.

Gotkowitz, Laura. *A Revolution for Our Rights: Indigenous Struggles for Land and Justice in Bolivia, 1880–1952.* Durham, NC: Duke University Press, 2007.

Goulart, Gastão. *Verdades da revolução paulista.* São Paulo: José Olympio, 1933.

Gouveia, Saulo. *The Triumph of Brazilian Modernism: The Metanarrative of Emancipation and Counter-Narratives.* Chapel Hill: University of North Carolina Press, 2013.

Graham, Richard, ed. *The Idea of Race in Latin America.* Austin: University of Texas Press, 1990.

Gramsci, Antonio. *Selections from the Prison Notebooks.* New York: International Publishers, 1971.

Gramsci, Antonio. "The Southern Question." In *The Modern Prince and Other Writings,* edited by L. Marks. New York: International Publishers, 1983, 28–51.

Guerrero, Andrés. "The Administration of Dominated Populations under a Regime of Customary Citizenship: The Case of Postcolonial Ecuador." In *After Spanish Rule,* edited by Mark Thurner and Andrés Guerrero. Durham, NC: Duke University Press, 2003, 272–309.

Guimarães, Antonio Sérgio Alfredo. *Classes, raças e democracia.* São Paulo: Editora 34, 2002.

Guimarães, Dulce Maria Pamplona. "Festa de fundação: Memória da colonização nas comemorações do IV Centenário da cidade de São Paulo." *História* (São Paulo) 13 (1994): 131–139.

Gustafson, Bret. "Flashpoints of Sovereignty: Natural Gas and Spatial Politics in Eastern Bolivia." In *Crude Domination: An Anthropology of Oil,* edited by A. Behrends et al. London: Berghahn, 2011, 220–240.

Hall, Michael M. "Origins of Mass Immigration in Brazil." PhD diss., Columbia University, 1969.

Hall, Stuart, ed. *Representation: Cultural Representations and Signifying Practices.* Thousand Oaks, CA: Sage Publications, 1997.

Hall, Stuart. "The Whites of Their Eyes: Racist Ideologies and the Media." In *The Media Reader,* edited by Manuel Alvarado and John O. Thompson. London: British Film Institute, 1990, 271–282.

Halperin Donghi, Tulio. "Argentina: Liberalism in a Country Born Liberal." In *Guiding the Invisible Hand: Economic Liberalism and the State in Latin American History,* edited by Joseph L. Love and Nils Jacobsen. New York: Praeger, 1988, 99–116.

Hanchard, Michael, ed. *Racial Politics in Contemporary Brazil.* Durham, NC: Duke University Press, 1999.

Harvey, David. *Justice, Nature and the Geography of Difference.* Cambridge, MA: Wiley-Blackwell, 1996.

Harvey, David. *Spaces of Global Capitalism: A Theory of Uneven Geographical Development.* London: Verso, 2006.

Havens, A. Eugene, and William L. Flinn, eds. *Internal Colonialism and Structural Change in Colombia.* New York: Praeger, 1970.

Hechter, Michael. *Internal Colonialism: The Celtic Fringe in British National Development.* Berkeley: University of California Press, 1975.

Helg, Aline. *Our Rightful Share: The Afro-Cuban Struggle for Equality, 1886–1912.* Chapel Hill: University of North Carolina Press, 1995.

Hershfield, Joanne. *Imagining la chica moderna: Women, Nation, and Visual Culture in Mexico, 1917–1936.* Durham, NC: Duke University Press, 2008.

Hertzman, Marc. *Making Samba: A New History of Race and Music in Brazil.* Durham, NC: Duke University Press, 2013.

Hilton, Stanley E. *A guerra civil brasileira: A revolução constitucionalista de 1932.* Rio de Janeiro: Nova Fronteira, 1982.

Hirschman, Albert O. *The Strategy of Economic Development.* New Haven, CT: Yale University Press, 1958.

Hoffenberger, Peter H. *An Empire on Display: English, Indian, and Australian Exhibitions from the Crystal Palace to the Great War.* Berkeley: University of California Press, 2001.

Holanda, Sérgio Buarque de. *Raízes do Brasil.* Rio de Janeiro: Liv. José Olympio, [1936] 1976.

Holloway, Thomas. *Immigrants on the Land: Coffee and Society in São Paulo, 1886–1934.* Chapel Hill: University of North Carolina Press, 1980.

Holston, James. *Insurgent Citizenship: Disjunctions of Democracy and Modernity in Brazil.* Princeton, NJ: Princeton University Press, 2008.

Homem, Luiz Gonzaga Naclério. *Lembranças de um belo ideal: Diário (reescrito) de um pelotão de voluntários da Revolução de 32.* Rio de Janeiro: Biblioteca do Exército, 1992.

Ipsen, Wiebke. "Delicate Citizenship: Gender and Nation-building in Brazil, 1865–1891." PhD diss., University of California, Irvine, 2005.

Ipsen, Wiebke. "Patrícias, Patriarchy, and Popular Demobilization: Gender and Elite Hegemony in Brazil at the End of the Paraguayan War." *Hispanic American Historical Review* 92, no. 2 (May 2012): 303–330.

Jacobson, Matthew Frye. *Whiteness of a Different Color: European Immigrants and the Alchemy of Race.* Cambridge, MA: Harvard University Press, 1999.

Janotti, Maria de Lourdes Monaco. "Historiografia: uma questão nacional?" In Silva, ed. *República em migalhas,* 81–101.

Jardim, Renato. *A aventura de outubro e a invasão de São Paulo.* São Paulo: Paulista, 1932.

Jiménez de Asúa, Luis. *Un viaje al Brasil.* Madrid: Editorial Reus, 1929.

Kandiyoti, Deniz. "Identity and Its Discontents: Women and the Nation." *Millennium: Journal of International Studies* 20 (1991): 429–443.

Kaplan, Amy. "Black and Blue on San Juan Hill." In *Cultures of United States Imperialism,* edited by Kaplan and Donald E. Pease. Durham, NC: Duke University Press, 1993, 219–236.

Karam, Elias *Um paranaense nas trincheiras da lei.* Preface by Milton Carneiro. Curitiba, Brazil: Cruzada, 1933.

Keck, Margaret. *The Workers' Party and Democratization in Brazil.* New Haven, CT: Yale University Press, 1992.

Kerber, Linda K. *Women of the Republic: Intellect and Ideology in Revolutionary America.* Chapel Hill: University of North Carolina Press, 1980.

Kirkendall, Andrew. *Class Mates: Male Student Culture and the Making of a Political Class in Nineteenth-Century Brazil.* Lincoln: University of Nebraska Press, 2002.

Kittleson, Roger. *The Practice of Politics in Postcolonial Brazil: Porto Alegre, 1845–1895.* Pittsburgh: University of Pittsburgh Press, 2005.

Knight, Alan. *The Mexican Revolution.* 2 vols. Cambridge: Cambridge University Press, 1986.

Kuznesof, Elizabeth A. *Household Economy and Urban Development: São Paulo, 1765–1836.* Boulder, CO: Westview Press, 1986.

Laclau, Ernesto. "Toward a Theory of Populism." In *Politics and Ideology in Marxist Theory.* London: New Left Books, 1977, 143–200.

LaFrance, David G. *Revolution in Mexico's Heartland: Politics, War, and State Building in Puebla, 1913–1920.* Lanham, MD: Rowman and Littlefield, 2007.

Lake, Marilyn, and Henry Reynolds. *Drawing the Global Colour Line: White Men's Countries and the International Challenge of Racial Equality.* Cambridge: Cambridge University Press, 2008.

Lambert, Jacques. *Os dois Brasis.* Rio de Janeiro: INEP, 1959.

Larson, Brooke. *Trials of Nation Making: Liberalism, Race, and Ethnicity in the Andes, 1810–1910.* New York: Cambridge University Press, 2004.

Lazzari, Alexandre. "Entre a grande e a pequena pátria: Literatos, identidade gaúcha e nacionalidade, 1860–1910." PhD diss., Universidade de Campinas, 2004.

Leal, Murilo. *A reinvenção da classe trabalhadora, 1953–1964.* Campinas, Brazil: Ed. Unicamp, 2011.

Lebovics, Herman. *True France: The Wars over Cultural Identity, 1900–1945.* Ithaca, NY: Cornell University Press, 1992.

Leff, Nathaniel H. "Economic Development and Regional Inequality: Origins of the Brazilian Case," *Quarterly Journal of Economics* 86, no. 2 (May 1972): 243–262.

Leite, Aureliano. *Martírio e glória de São Paulo.* São Paulo: E. G. "Revista dos Tribunaes," 1934.

Lesser, Jeffrey. *Immigration, Ethnicity, and National Identity in Brazil, 1808 to the Present.* Cambridge: Cambridge University Press, 2013.

Lesser, Jeffrey. *Negotiating National Identity.* Durham, NC: Duke University Press, 1999.

Lesser, Jeffrey. *Welcoming the Undesirables: Brazil and the Jewish Question.* Berkeley: University of California Press, 1994.

Levi, Darrell E. *The Prados of São Paulo, Brazil: An Elite Family and Social Change, 1840–1930.* Athens: University of Georgia Press, 1987.

Levi-Moreira, Silvia. "Ideologia e atuação da Liga Nacionalista de São Paulo, 1917–1924." *Revista de História* 116 (1984): 67–74.

Levi-Moreira, Silvia. "Liberalismo e democracia na dissidência república paulista: Estudo sobre o Partido Republicano Dissidente de São Paulo, 1901–1906." PhD diss., USP, 1991.

Levine, Robert M. *Pernambuco in the Brazilian Federation, 1889–1937.* Stanford, CA: Stanford University Press, 1978.

Levine, Robert M., and John J. Crocitti, eds., *The Brazil Reader.* Durham, NC: Duke University Press, 1999.

Levy, Herbert V. *A coluna invicta.* São Paulo: Martins, 1967.

Lewin, Linda. *Politics and Parentela in Paraíba: A Case Study of Family-based Politics in Brazil*. Princeton, NJ: Princeton University Press, 1987.

Lima, Alceu Amoroso. *A missão de São Paulo*. Rio de Janeiro: Agir Editora, 1962.

Lima, Ivana Stolze. *Cores, marcas e falas: Sentidos da mestiçagem no Império do Brasil*. Rio de Janeiro: Arquivo Nacional, 2003.

Lima, Nísia Trindade. *Um sertão chamado Brasil*. Rio de Janeiro: Ed. Revan-IUPERJ, 1999.

Lobo, T. de Souza. *O Brasil confederado*. São Paulo: Lyceu Coração de Jesus, 1933.

Lobo, T. de Souza. *São Paulo na federação*. São Paulo: n.p., 1924.

Lofego, Sílvio Luiz. *IV Centenário da Cidade de São Paulo: Uma cidade entre o passado e o futuro*. São Paulo: Annablume, 2004.

Lofego, Sílvio Luiz. *Memória de uma metrópole: São Paulo na obra de Ernani Silva Bruno*. São Paulo: Annablume, 2001.

Lomnitz-Adler, Claudio. *Exits from the Labyrinth: Culture and Ideology in the Mexican National Space*. Berkeley: University of California Press, 1992.

López, A. Ricardo, and Barbara Weinstein, eds. *The Making of the Middle Class: Toward a Transnational History*. Durham, NC: Duke University Press, 2012.

Lopes, Juárez Rubens Brandão. *Sociedade industrial no Brasil*. São Paulo: DIFEL, 1964.

Lopes, Maria Aparecida de Oliveira. "História e memória do negro em São Paulo: efemérides, símbolos e identidade,1945–1978." PhD diss., UNESP-Assis, 2007.

Lopes, Nei. *Dicionário escolar afro-brasileiro*. São Paulo: Selo Negro, 2006.

Loureiro Junior. *São Paulo Vencido*. São Paulo: E. G."Revista dos Tribunaes," 1932.

Love, Joseph L. "A república brasileira: Federalismo e regionalismo (1889–1937)." In *Viagem incompleta: A experiência brasileira, 1500–2000*. Vol. 2, edited by Carlos Guilherme Mota. São Paulo: Ed. SESC, 2000, 121–160.

Love, Joseph L. *Rio Grande do Sul and Brazilian Regionalism, 1882–1930*. Stanford, CA: Stanford University Press, 1971.

Love, Joseph L. *São Paulo in the Brazilian Federation, 1889–1937*. Stanford, CA: Stanford University Press, 1980.

Lowrey, Kathleen. "Bolivia multiétnico y pluricultural: White Separatism in the Lowlands." *Latin American and Caribbean Ethnic Studies* 1, no. 1 (August 2006): 63–84.

Ludwig, Armin K. *Brazil: A Handbook of Historical Statistics*. Boston: G. K. Hall, 1985.

Machado, António de Alcântara. *Brás, Bexiga e Barra Funda: Notícias de São Paulo*. Belo Horizonte, Brazil: Editora Itatiaia, [1927] 2001.

Machado, José de Alcântara. *Vida e morte do bandeirante*. São Paulo: E. G. "Revista dos Tribunaes," 1929.

Machado, Maria Helena P.T. *O plano e o pânico: Os movimentos sociais na década da abolição*. São Paulo: EDUSP, 1994.

Maio, Marcos Chor. "Tempo controverso: Gilberto Freyre e o Projeto UNESCO." *Tempo Social* 11 (1999): 111–136.

Maio, Marcos Chor, and Ricardo Ventura Santos, eds. *Raça, ciência e sociedade*. Rio de Janeiro: Ed. Fiocruz, 1998.

Mallon, Florencia E. *Peasant and Nation: The Making of Postcolonial Mexico and Peru* Berkeley: University of California Press, 1995.

Manring, M. M. *Slave in a Box: The Strange Career of Aunt Jemima*. Charlottesville: University of Virginia Press, 1998.

Marcondes, Renato Leite. "Small and Medium Slaveholdings in the Coffee Economy of the Vale do Paraíba, Province of São Paulo." *Hispanic American Historical Review* 85, no. 2 (May 2005): 259–281.

Marinho, Maria Gabriela S. M. C. "A presença norte-americana na educação superior brasileira: Uma abordagem histórica da articulação entre a Fundação Rockefeller e estruturas acadêmicas de São Paulo." PhD diss., USP, 2005.

Marins, Paulo César Garcez. "O Parque Ibirapuera e a construção da identidade paulista." *Anais do Museu Paulista*, vols. 6/7 (1998–1999): 9–36.

Martin, John. "Inventing Sincerity, Refashioning Prudence: The Discovery of the Individual in Renaissance Europe." *American Historical Review* 102, no. 5 (December 1997): 1309–1342.

Martínez-Echazábal, Lourdes. "O culturalismo dos anos 30 no Brasil e na América Latina: Deslocamento retórico ou mudança conceitual?" In *Raça, ciência e sociedade*, edited by Marcos Chor Maio and Ricardo Ventura Santos. Rio de Janeiro: Ed. Fiocruz, 1998, 107–124.

Martins, José de Barros. *Álbum de familia 1932*. São Paulo: Livraria Martins, 1954.

Martins, Paulo Henrique. "O Nordeste e a questão regional." In Silva, ed., *República em migalhas*, 51–66.

Martuscelli, Carolina. "Uma pesquisa sobre aceitação de grupos nacionais, grupos 'raciais' e grupos regionais, em S. Paulo." *Psicologia*—USP (1950): 56–73.

McCann, Bryan. *Hello, Hello Brazil: Popular Music in the Making of Modern Brazil*. Durham, NC: Duke University Press, 2004.

McCann, Frank D. *The Brazilian-American Alliance, 1937–1945*. Princeton, NJ: Princeton University Press, 1974.

McCann, Frank D. *Soldiers of the Pátria: A History of the Brazilian Army, 1889–1937*. Stanford, CA: Stanford University Press, 2004.

McClintock, Anne. *Imperial Leather: Race, Gender and Sexuality in the Colonial Contest*. New York: Routledge, 1995.

McClintock, Anne. "'No Longer in a Future Heaven': Nationalism, Gender, and Race." In Eley and Suny, eds., *Becoming National*, 260–285.

Meade, Teresa, and Gregory Alonso Pirio. "In Search of the Afro-American El Dorado: Attempts by North American Blacks to Enter Brazil in the 1920s." *Luso-Brazilian Review* 25, no. 1 (1988): 85–110.

Mehrtens, Cristina Peixoto. *Urban Space and National Identity in Early Twentieth-Century São Paulo, Brazil: Crafting Modernity*. New York: Palgrave Macmillan, 2010.

Mello, Luiz Vieira de. *Renda-se, paulista!* Lorena, SP: n.p., 1932.

Melo, Evaldo Cabral de. *O Norte agrário e o Império*. Rio de Janeiro: Nova Fronteira, 1984.

Menezes, Emílio de. *Útimas rimas*. Rio de Janeiro: Liv. José Olympio, 1980.

Mesquita Filho, Júlio de. *"Memórias de um revolucionário": Notas por um ensaio sociologia-política*. São Paulo: Anhembi, 1954.

Metcalf, Alida C. *Family and Frontier in Colonial Brazil: Santana de Parnaíba, 1580–1822*. Berkeley: University of California Press, 1992.

Miceli, Sérgio. *Nacional Estrangeiro: História social e cultural do modernismo artístico em São Paulo*. São Paulo: Companhia das Letras, 2003.

Miller, Nicola. *In the Shadow of the State: Intellectuals and the Quest for National Identity in Twentieth-Century Latin America*. London: Verso, 1999.

Mioto, Ricardo, et al. "Apesar da aura mítica, bandeirante era assassino do sertão." Folha.com, January 25, 2011.

Miranda, J. P. da Veiga. *São Paulo e o verdadeiro liberalismo* (conferência realizada em Ouro Preto a 20 de novembro de 1929). Rio de Janeiro: Imprensa Nacional, 1930.

Mitchell, Michael. "Miguel Reale and the Impact of Conservative Modernization on Brazilian Race Relations." In *Racial Politics in Contemporary Brazil*, edited by Michael Hanchard. Durham, NC: Duke University Press, 1999, 116–137.

Monteiro, John. "Caçando com gato: Raça, mestiçagem e identidade paulista na obra de Alfredo Ellis Jr." *Novos Estudos CEBRAP* 38 (1994): 79–88.

Monteiro, John. *Negros da terra: Índios e bandeirantes nas origens de São Paulo*. São Paulo: Cia. das Letras, 1994.

Monteiro, John. "Tupis, Tapuias e História de São Paulo: Revisitando a velha questão Guaianã." *Novos Estudos CEBRAP* 32 (1992): 127.

Montenegro, Benedito. *Cruzes paulistas: Os que tombaram, em 1932, pela glória de server São Paulo*. São Paulo: E. G. "Revista dos Tribunaes," 1936.

Moraes, Marcos Antonio de, ed. *Correspondência Mário de Andrade e Manuel Bandeira*. São Paulo: EDUSP/IEB, 2000.

Morais, Fernando. *Chatô: O Rei do Brasil*. São Paulo: Companhia das Letras, 1994.

Morse, Richard M., ed. *The Bandeirantes: The Historical Role of the Brazilian Pathfinders*. New York: Alfred Knopf, 1965.

Morse, Richard M. *From Community to Metropolis: A Biography of São Paulo, Brazil*. Gainesville: University of Florida Press, 1958.

Morse, Richard M. "The Multiverse of Latin American Identity, c. 1920–c. 1970." In *Ideas and Ideologies in Twentieth-Century Latin America*, edited by Leslie Bethell. Cambridge: Cambridge University Press, 1996, 1–129.

Motta, Rodrigo Patto Sá. *Em guarda contra o "perigo vermelho": O anticomunismo no Brasil, 1917–1964*. São Paulo: Ed. Perspectiva, 2002.

Moura, Jair Pinto de. *A fogueira constitucionalista*. São Paulo: Ed. Paulista, 1933.

Múnera, Alfonso. *El fracaso de la nación: Región, clase y raza en el caribe colombiano, 1717–1821*. Bogotá: El Ancora Editora, 1998.

Nascimento, Abdias do. "Inaugurando o Congresso do Negro." *Quilombo* (June–July 1950): 1.

Needell, Jeffrey D. "Identity, Race, Gender, and Modernity in the Origins of Gilberto Freyre's Oeuvre." *American Historical Review* 100, no. 1 (1995): 51–77.

"Os negrinhos do Rio desgostam S. Paulo." *Revista Civilização Brasileira* 1 (March 1965): 53–57.

Negro, Antonio Luigi. *Linhas de montagem: O industrialismo nacional-desenvolvimentista e a sindicalização dos trabalhadores*. São Paulo: Boitempo, 2004.

Nelson, Adele. "Monumental and Ephemeral: The Early São Paulo Bienais." In *Constructive Spirit: Abstract Art in South and North America, 1920s–50s*, edited by Mary Kate O'Hare. Newark, NJ: Newark Museum, 2010, 127–142.

Nobre, F. da Silva. *1001 Cearenses notáveis*. Rio de Janeiro: Casa do Ceará, 1996.

Nogueira Filho, Paulo. *Ideais e lutas de um burguês progressista: A guerra cívica—1932*. 4 vols. Rio de Janeiro: José Olympio, 1965, 1966, 1967, 1971.

Nora, Pierre. *Realms of Memory: The Construction of the French Past*. Vol. 3, *Symbols*. New York: Columbia University Press, 1998.

Nunes, Cassiano. *O patriotismo difícil: A correspondência entre Monteiro Lobato e Artur Neiva*. São Paulo: n.p., 1981.

Nunes, Valentina. *São Paulo através do minissérie "Um Só Coração."* São Paulo: Ed. Globo, 2004.

O'Dougherty, Maureen. *Consumption Intensified: The Politics of Middle Class Daily Life in Brazil*. Durham, NC: Duke University Press, 2002.

O Estado de S. Paulo. *Ensaios Paulistas* (Contribuição de "O Estado de São Paulo" às Comemorações do IV Centenário da Cidade). São Paulo: Editora Anhambi S/A, 1958.

Oliveira, Eduardo de, ed. *Quem é quem na negritude brasileira*. Vol. 1. São Paulo: Congresso Nacional Afro-Brasileiro, 1998.

Oliveira, Francisco de. "A questão regional: A hegemonia inacabada." *Estudos Avançados* 7, no. 18 (1993): 43–63.

Oliveira, Lúcia Lippi. *A questão nacional na Primeira República*. São Paulo: Brasiliense, 1990.

Oliven, Ruben George. *A parte e o todo: A diversidade cultural no Brasil-Nação*. Petrópolis: Vozes, 1992.

Ortiz, Lacerda. *O que é São Paulo*. São Paulo: n.p., 1932.

Ortiz, Marco Antônio Moreira. *A trajetória da Companhia Industrial Taubaté* CTI. São Paulo: FAPESP/EDUC, 2006.

Osório, Manoel. *A guerra de São Paulo, 1932: Esboço crítico do maior movimento armado no Brasil*. São Paulo: Americana, 1932.

Owensby, Brian. *Intimate Ironies: Modernity and the Making of Middle-Class Lives in Brazil*. Stanford, CA: Stanford University Press, 1999.

Pacheco, José Aranha de Assis. *Revivendo 32*. São Paulo: n.p., 1954.

Pandolfi, Dulce Chaves, ed. *Repensando o Estado Novo*. Rio de Janeiro: FGV, 1999.

Pandolfi, Dulce Chaves. "A trajetória do Norte: Uma tentativa de ascenso político." In Gomes, ed., *Regionalismo e centralização política*, 339–425.

Pang, Eul-Soo. *Bahia in the First Brazilian Republic: Coronelismo and Oligarchies, 1889–1934*. Gainesville: University of Florida Press, 1979.

Paoli, Maria Célia, and Adriano Duarte. "São Paulo no plural: Espaço público e redes de sociabilidade." In *História da cidade de São Paulo*. Vol. 3. São Paulo: Paz e Terra, 2004, 53–99.

Paraná, Denise. *Lula—Filho do Brasil*. 3rd ed. São Paulo: Perseu Abramo, 2009.

Patai, Daphne. *Brazilian Women Speak: Contemporary Life Stories*. New Brunswick, NJ: Rutgers University Press, 1988.

Paula, Jeziel de. *1932: Imagens construindo a história*. Campinas, Brazil: Editora da Unicamp, 1998.

Penteado, Lauro Teixeira. *O Inevitável*. São Paulo: n.p., 1935.

Pereira, Antônio Baptista. *O Brasil e a raça*. São Paulo: E. G. Rossetti, 1928.

Pereira, Antônio Baptista. *Pelo Brasil Maior*. São Paulo: n.p., 1934.

Pereira, Cristiana Schettini. *'Que tenhas teu corpo': Uma história social da prostituição no Rio de Janeiro das primeiras décadas republicanas*. Rio de Janeiro: Arquivo Nacional, 2006.

Pesavento, Sandra Jatahy. *Exposições universais: Espetáculos da modernidade do século XIX*. São Paulo: Hucitec, 1997.

Pesavento, Sandra Jatahy. "História regional e transformação social." In Silva, ed., *República em migalhas*, 67–79.

Pessar, Patricia. *From Fanatics to Folk: Brazilian Millenarianism and Popular Culture*. Durham, NC: Duke University Press, 2004.

Picchia, Paulo Menotti del. *O despertar de São Paulo*. Rio de Janeiro: Civ. Brasileira, 1933.

Picchia, Paulo Menotti del. *A revolução paulista*. São Paulo: n.p., 1932.

Pinheiro, Paulo Sérgio. *Estratégias da ilusão: A revolução mundial e o Brasil, 1922–1935*. São Paulo: Companhia das Letras, 1991.

Pinheiro, Paulo Sérgio. *Política e trabalho no Brasil*. Rio de Janeiro: Paz e Terra, 1975.

Poovey, Mary. *A History of the Modern Fact: Problems of Knowledge in the Sciences of Wealth and Society*. Chicago: University of Chicago Press, 1998.

Poovey, Mary. *Uneven Developments: The Ideological Work of Gender in Mid-Victorian England*. Chicago: University of Chicago Press, 1988.

Porta, Paula, ed. *Guia dos documentos históricos na cidade de São Paulo*. São Paulo: Hucitec, 1998.

Portelli, Alessandro. *The Death of Luigi Trastulli and Other Stories: Form and Meaning in Oral History*. Albany: SUNY Press, 1991.

Prado Jr., Caio. *Formação do Brasil contemporâneo*. São Paulo: Livraria Martins, 1942.

Prado, Maria Lígia. *A democracia ilustrada: O Partido Democrático de São Paulo, 1926–1934*. São Paulo: Ática, 1986.

Prado, Maria Lígia. "O pensamento conservador paulista: O regionalismo de Cincinato Braga." *Anais do Museu Paulista* 31 (1982): 233–245.

Pruden, Hernan. "Santa Cruz entre la post–Guerra del Chaco y las postrimerias de la revolución nacional:Cruceños y cambas." *Historias: Revista de la Coordinadora de la Historia* 6 (2003): 1–61.

Queiroz, Augusto de Souza. *Batalhão 14 de Julho: Revolução Constitucionalista de 1932*. São Paulo: Grafica Sangirard, 1982.

Queiroz, Maria Isaura Pereira de. "Ufanismo paulista." *Revista USP* 13 (1992): 78–87.

Radano, Ronald M., and Philip V. Bohlman. *Music and the Racial Imagination*. Chicago: University of Chicago Press, 2001.

Radcliffe, Sarah, and Sallie Westwood. *Remaking the Nation: Place, Identity and Politics in Latin America*. London: Routledge, 1996.

Rago, Margareth. *Do cabaré ao lar: A utopia da cidade disciplinar—Brasil, 1890–1930*. Rio de Janeiro: Paz e Terra, 1985.

Ramos, Plínio de Abreu. *Os partidos paulistas e o Estado Novo*. Petrópolis: Vozes, 1980.

Rappaport, Joanne. *The Politics of Memory: Native Historical Interpretation in the Colombian Andes*. Cambridge: Cambridge University Press, 1990.

Reale, Miguel. *Memórias*. Vol. 1. São Paulo: Saraiva, 1986.

Rivera Cusicanqui, Silvia. "La Raíz: Colonizadores y Colonizados." In *Violencias encubiertas en Bolivia: Cultura y política*. Vol. 1, edited by Raúl Barrios and Xavier Albo. La Paz: CIPCA/Aruwiyiri, 1993, 27–139.

Rodrigues, João Batista Cascudo. *A Mulher Paulista no movimento pro-constituinte*. São Paulo: E. G. Revista dos Tribunaes, 1933.

Rodrigues, João Paulo. "O levante 'constitucionalista' de 1932 e a força da tradição: Do confronto bélico à batalha pela memória, 1932–1934." PhD diss., UNESP-Assis, 2009.

Rodrigues, João Paulo. *1932 pela força da tradição: Do confronto bélico à batalha pela memória (1932–1934)*. São Paulo: Annablume, 2012.

Rodrigues, Leôncio Martins. *Conflito industrial e sindicalismo no Brasil*. São Paulo: DIFEL, 1966.

Rodríguez, Jared. "Black on Both Sides: Racial Reimagining and Afro-Paulista Participation in the 1932 São Paulo Constitutionalist 'Revolution.'" BA thesis, CCNY, 2009.

Rydell, Robert. *All the World's a Fair: Visions of Empire at American International Expositions, 1876–1916*. Chicago: University of Chicago Press, 1987.

Sábato, Hilda. *The Many and the Few: Political Participation in Republican Buenos Aires*. Stanford, CA: Stanford University Press, 2001.

Saes, Flávio. "São Paulo republicana: Vida econômica." In *História da cidade de São Paulo*. Vol. 3, edited by Paula Porta. São Paulo: Paz e Terra, 2004, 226–234.

Safford, Frank. *Colombia: Fragmented Land, Divided Society*. New York: Oxford University Press, 2001.

Said, Edward W. *Culture and Imperialism*. New York: Vintage Books, 1994.

Said, Edward W. *Orientalism*. New York: Vintage Books, 1979.

Saint-Hilaire, Auguste. *Viagem à provincia de São Paulo*. São Paulo: EDUSP, 1972.

Saliba, Elias Thomé. "Histórias, memórias, tramas e dramas da identidade paulistana." In *História da cidade de São Paulo*. Vol. 3, edited by Paula Porta. São Paulo: Paz e Terra, 2004, 555–587.

Sampaio, Francisco Ribeiro. *Renembranças*. Campinas: Academia Campinense de Letras, 1975.

Sandroni, Carlos. "Folk Music and National Identity in Brazil: Mário de Andrade and the 1938 Mission." Paper presented at the American Historical Association meetings, January 3, 2008, Washington, DC.

Sandroni, Carlos. "Missão de pesquisas folclóricas: Música tradicional do Norte e do Nordeste, 1938" (resenha). *Revista do Instituto de Estudos Brasileiros*. 46 (2008): 275–277.

Sandroni, Cícero, and Laura C. A. A. Sandroni. *Austregésilo de Athayde: O século de um liberal*. Rio de Janeiro: Agir, 1998.

Santos, Amílcar Salgado dos. *A epopéia de São Paulo em 1932: Diário da linha de "Frente."* São Paulo: n.p., 1932.

São Paulo (State). *A epopéia de Piratininga: São Paulo em armas pela grandeza do Brasil*. São Paulo, 1932.

São Paulo (State). *O Estado de São Paulo: Seu progresso, suas riquezas*. São Paulo: Pocaí, 1917, unpaginated.

São Paulo (State). "Restauranção dos símbolos estaduais." Decree-Law No. 16.349, November 27, 1946. São Paulo: Depto. Estadual de Informações, 1947.

Sarzynski, Sarah. "Revolutionizing Identities: Popular Culture and Political Struggle in Northeastern Brazil in the Era of the Cuban Revolution." Unpublished manuscript.

Schneider, Jane, ed. *Italy's "Southern Question": Orientalism in One Country*. Oxford: Berg, 1998.

Schpun, Mônica Raisa. "Carlota Pereira de Queiroz: Uma mulher na política." *Revista Brasileira de História* 17, no. 33 (1997): 167–200.

Schpun, Mônica Raisa. "Regionalistas e cosmopolistas: As amigas Olívia Guedes Penteado e Carlota Pereira de Queiroz." In *Reprises (c) Arteologie* 2 (2011). http://cral.in2p3.fr/artelogie/spip.php?article81.

Schwarcz, Lilia M. *The Spectacle of the Races: Scientists, Institutions, and the Race Question in Brazil, 1870–1930*. New York: Hill and Wang, 1999.

Schwartzman, Simon. *São Paulo e o estado nacional*. São Paulo: DIFEL, 1975.

Schwartzman, Simon, et al. *Tempos de Capanema*. São Paulo: EDUSP, 1984.

Schwarz, Roberto. *Misplaced Ideas: Essays on Brazilian Culture*, edited with an introduction by John Gledson. London: Verso, 1992.

Scott, Joan W. *Gender and the Politics of History*. New York: Columbia University Press, 1988.

Seigel, Micol. "Beyond Compare: Historical Method after the Transnational Turn." *Radical History Review* 91 (winter 2005): 62–90.

Seigel, Micol. *Uneven Encounters: Making Race and Nation in Brazil and the United States*. Durham, NC: Duke University Press, 2009.

Serje, Margarita. *El revés de la nación: Territorios selvajes, fronteras y tierras de nadie*. Bogotá: Uniandes/CESO, 2005.

Serva, Mário Pinto. *Problemas Brasileiros*. São Paulo: Livraria Liberdade, 1929.

SESC-SP. *Fantasia brasileira: O balê do IV Centenário*. São Paulo: SESC, 1998.

Sevcenko, Nicolau. *Literatura como missão: Tensões sociais e criação cultural na Primeira República*. São Paulo: Brasiliense, 1983.

Sevcenko, Nicolau. *Orfeu extático na metrópole: São Paulo, sociedade e cultura nos frementes anos 20*. São Paulo: Companhia das Letras, 1992.

Sheriff, Robin E. *Dreaming Equality: Color, Race, and Racism in Urban Brazil*. New Brunswick, NJ: Rutgers University Press, 2001.

Sikkink, Kathryn. *Ideas and Institutions: Developmentalism in Brazil and Argentina*. Ithaca, NY: Cornell University Press, 1991.

Silva, Hélio Ribeiro da. *1932: A guerra paulista*. Rio de Janeiro: Civilização Brasileira, 1967.

Silva, Marcos A. da, ed., *República em migalhas: História regional e local*. São Paulo: Marco Zero, 1990.

Silva, Sérgio. *Expansão cafeeira e origens da indústria no Brasil*. São Paulo: Ed. Alfa Omega, 1976.

Silveira, Rosa Maria Godoy. *O regionalismo nordestino*. São Paulo: Moderna, 1984.

Sinha, Mrinalini. *Colonial Masculinity: The "Manly Englishman" and the "Effeminate Bengali" in the Late Nineteenth Century*. Manchester, UK: Manchester University Press, 1995.

Skidmore, Thomas. *Black into White: Race and Nationality in Brazilian Thought.* Durham, NC: Duke University Press, 1993.

Skidmore, Thomas. *Politics in Brazil, 1930–1964: An Experiment in Democracy.* London: Oxford University Press, 1967.

Slater, Candace. *Entangled Edens: Visions of the Amazon.* Berkeley: University of California Press, 2003.

Sommer, Doris. "*O Guaraní* and *Iracema*: Brazil's Two-Faced Indigenism." In *Foundational Fictions: The National Romances of Latin America.* Berkeley: University of California Press, 1991.

Souto Maior, Laércio. *São os nordestinos uma minoria racial?* Londrina: Livraria Arles, 1985.

Souza, Laura de Mello e. "Vícios, virtudes e sentimento regional: São Paulo, da lenda negra à lenda áurea." *Revista de História-USP* 142–143 (2000): 262–276.

Spivak, Gayatri C. "Can the Subaltern Speak?" In *Marxism and the Interpretation of Culture*, edited by Cary Nelson and Lawrence Grossberg. London: Macmillan, 1988, 271–313.

Stam, Robert, and Ella Shohat. *Race in Translation: Culture Wars around the Postcolonial Atlantic.* New York: New York University Press, 2012.

Stepan, Nancy Leys. *"The Hour of Eugenics": Race, Gender, and Nation in Latin America.* Ithaca, NY: Cornell University Press, 1991.

Stern, Steve J. "Between Tragedy and Promise: The Politics of Writing Latin American History in the Late Twentieth Century." In *Reclaiming the Political in Latin American History: Essays from the North*, edited by Gilbert Joseph. Durham, NC: Duke University Press, 2001, 32–77.

Stern, Steve J. *Remembering Pinochet's Chile: On the Eve of London 1998.* Durham, NC: Duke University Press, 2006.

Stoddard, Lothrop. *Revolt against Civilization: The Menace of the Under-Man.* New York: Charles Scribner's Sons, 1922.

Sylos, Honório de. *Gente e fatos: Relembranças jornalísticas.* São Paulo: IBRASA, 1988.

Taunay, Affonso de Escragnolle. *História geral das bandeiras paulistas.* 11 vols. São Paulo: H. L. Canton and Imp. Oficial do Estado, 1924–1936; 1946–1950.

Telles, Edward. *Race in Another America: The Significance of Skin Color in Brazil.* Princeton, NJ: Princeton University Press, 2004.

Tenorio-Trillo, Mauricio. *Mexico at the World's Fairs: Crafting a Modern Nation.* Berkeley: University of California Press, 1996.

Toledo, Caio Navarro de. *ISEB: Fábrica de Ideologias.* São Paulo: Ática, 1977.

Topik, Steven. *The Political Economy of the Brazilian State, 1889–1930.* Austin: University of Texas Press, 1987.

Toplin, Robert B. *The Abolition of Slavery in Brazil.* New York: Atheneum, 1972.

Tota, Antônio Pedro. *A locomotiva no ar: Rádio e modernidade em São Paulo, 1924–1934.* São Paulo: Secretaria de Estado da Cultura, 1990.

Tota, Antônio Pedro. *The Seduction of Brazil: The Americanization of Brazil during World War II.* Austin: University of Texas Press, 2010.

Trevisan, Maria José. *50 anos em 5: A FIESP e o desenvolvimentismo.* Petrópolis: Vozes, 1986.

Twine, Frances Winddance. *Racism in a Racial Democracy: The Maintenance of White Supremacy in Brazil.* New Brunswick, NJ: Rutgers University Press, 1998.

Ulrich, Aline. "Guilherme de Almeida e a construção da identidade paulista." MA thesis, FFLCH-USP, 2007.

Vallières, Pierre. *White Niggers of America.* New York: Monthly Review, 1971.

Vasconcelos, José. *La Raza Cosmica.* 3rd ed. Mexico DF: Espasa-Calpe Mexicana, 1966.

Vampré, Leven. *São Paulo terra conquistada.* São Paulo: Paulista, 1932.

Van Young, Eric, ed. *Mexico's Regions: Comparative History and Development.* San Diego: Center for U.S.-Mexican Studies, 1992.

Vargas, Getúlio. *Diário.* Vol. 1, 1930–1936. Rio de Janeiro: FGV/Siciliano, 1995.

Vargas, Getúlio. *Diário.* Vol. 2, 1937–1942. Rio de Janeiro: FGV/Siciliano, 1995.

Velloso, Monica Pimenta. "A brasilidade verde-amarela: nacionalismo e regionalismo paulista." *Estudos Históricos* 6, no. 11 (1993): 89–112.

Vianna, Deocélia. *Companheiros de viagem.* São Paulo: Brasiliense, 1984.

Vianna, Hermano. "A meta mitológica da democracia racial." In *O imperador das idéias,* edited by Falcão and Barboza de Araújo, 215–221.

Vianna, Hermano. *The Mystery of Samba: Popular Music and National Identity in Brazil.* Trans. John C. Chasteen. Chapel Hill: University of North Carolina Press, 1999.

Wade, Peter. "Afterword," 263–281. In Appelbaum, et al., *Race and Nation in Modern Latin America.* Chapel Hill: University of North Carolina Press, 2007.

Wade, Peter. *Blackness and Race Mixture: The Dynamics of Racial Identity in Colombia.* Baltimore: Johns Hopkins University Press, 1995.

Wade, Peter. *Race and Ethnicity in Latin America.* London: Pluto Press, 1997.

Waldstreicher, David. *In the Midst of Perpetual Fetes: The Making of American Nationalism, 1776–1820.* Chapel Hill: University of North Carolina Press, 1997.

Wasserman, Mark. *Persistent Oligarchs: Elites and Politics in Chihuahua, Mexico, 1910–1940.* Durham, NC: Duke University Press, 1993.

Weffort, Francisco C. "Nordestinos em São Paulo: Notas para um estudo sobre cultural nacional e cultura popular." In *A cultura do povo,* edited by Edênio Valle and José J. Queiróz. São Paulo: Cortez e Moraes/EDUC, 1979.

Weinstein, Barbara. *The Amazon Rubber Boom, 1850–1920.* Stanford, CA: Stanford University Press, 1983.

Weinstein, Barbara. "Brazilian Regionalism." *Latin American Research Review* 17, no. 2 (1982): 262–276.

Weinstein, Barbara. "Developing Inequality." *American Historical Review* 113, no. 1 (February 2008): 1–18.

Weinstein, Barbara. *For Social Peace in Brazil: Industrialists and the Remaking of the Working Class in São Paulo, 1920–1964.* Chapel Hill: University of North Carolina Press, 1996.

Weinstein, Barbara. "Impressões da elite sobre os movimentos da classe operária: A cobertura da greve em *O Estado de São Paulo,* 1902–1917." In Capelato and Prado, *O Bravo Matutino,* 135–176.

Weinstein, Barbara. "Postcolonial Brazil." In *The Oxford Handbook of Latin American History,* edited by Jose C. Moya. New York: Oxford University Press, 2010, 212–256.

Weinstein, Barbara. "Racializing Regional Difference: São Paulo vs. Brazil, 1932." In Appelbaum et al., eds., *Race and Nation in Modern Latin America*, 237–262.

Weinstein, Barbara. "Regional vs. National History: Rethinking Categories from a Comparative Perspective." *Territórios e Fronteiras* 4, no. 1 (2003): 23–31.

Weiss, Gillian. *Captives and Corsairs: France and Slavery in the Early Modern Mediterranean*. Stanford, CA: Stanford University Press, 2011.

Williams, Daryle. *Culture Wars in Brazil: The First Vargas Regime, 1930–45*. Durham, NC: Duke University Press, 2001.

Williams, Daryle, and Barbara Weinstein. "*Vargas Morto*: The Death and Life of a Brazilian Statesman." In *Death, Dismemberment and Memory: Body Politics in Latin America*, edited by Lyman Johnson. Albuquerque: University of New Mexico Press, 2004, 273–315.

Williams, Raymond. *Marxism and Literature*. Oxford: Oxford University Press, 1977.

Winant, Howard. "Racial Democracy and Racial Identity: Comparing the United States and Brazil." In Hanchard, ed., *Racial Politics*, 98–115.

Wirth, John D. *Minas Gerais in the Brazilian Federation, 1889–1937*. Stanford, CA: Stanford University Press, 1977.

Wolfe, Joel. *Autos and Progress: The Brazilian Search for Modernity*. New York: Oxford University Press, 2010.

Wolfe, Joel. *Working Women, Working Men: São Paulo and the Rise of Brazil's Industrial Working Class, 1900–1955*. Durham, NC: Duke University Press, 1993.

Wolff, Larry. *Inventing Eastern Europe: The Map of Civilization on the Mind of the Enlightenment*. Stanford, CA: Stanford University Press, 1994.

Woodard, James P. "'All for São Paulo, All for Brazil': Vargas, the Paulistas, and the Historiography of Twentieth-Century Brazil." In *Vargas and Brazil*, edited by Jens R. Hentschke. New York: Palgrave, 2006, 83–108.

Woodard, James P. "Marketing Modernity: The J. Walter Thompson Company and North American Advertising in Brazil, 1929–1939." *Hispanic American Historical Review* 82, no. 2 (May 2002): 257–290.

Woodard, James P. "Of Slaves and Citizens: The Places of Race in Republican São Paulo, 1880s–1930s." Unpublished paper presented to New York City Latin American History Workshop, February 2008.

Woodard, James P. *A Place in Politics: São Paulo, Brazil, from Seigneurial Republicanism to Regionalist Revolt*. Durham, NC: Duke University Press, 2009.

Woodard, James P. "Regionalismo paulista e política partidária nos anos vinte." *Revista de História* 150 (2004): 41–56.

Xavier, Denise. *Arquitetura metropolitana*. São Paulo: Annablume, 2007.

Xavier, Regina Célia Lima. *A conquista da liberdade: Libertos em Campinas na segunda metade do século XIX*. Campinas, Brazil: Centro de Memória/Unicamp, 1996.

Zeitlin, Maurice. *The Civil Wars in Chile (or the Bourgeois Revolutions That Never Were)*. Princeton, NJ: Princeton University Press, 1984.

Zolov, Eric. "Discovering a Land 'Mysterious and Obvious': The Renarrativizing of Postrevolutionary Mexico." In *Fragments of a Golden Age: The Politics of Culture in Mexico since 1940*, edited by Gilbert Joseph et al. Durham, NC: Duke University Press, 2001, 234–272.

Zureik, Elia T. *The Palestinians in Israel: A Study in Internal Colonialism*. London: Routledge and Kegan Paul, 1979.

Films (Cinemateca Brasileira, São Paulo)

Homenagem aos soldados mortos de 1932. Governo de Minas Gerais, 1937.
1932: A Guerra Civil. Eduardo Escorel, Departamento Estadual de Cultura, 1992.
A respeito do Movimento Constitucionalista de 1932. Secretaria de Cultura de S. Paulo, 1978.
São Paulo em Festa. Lima Barreto, Studio Vera Cruz, 1954.
Viagem ao passado. São Paulo, Agência de Turismo, 1950.

Websites

FGV, CPDOC, "A Era Vargas: Dos anos 20 a 1945, Criação da Universidade de São Paulo," posted 2012, accessed September 2013. http://cpdoc.fgv.br/producao/dossies/AEraVargas1/anos30–37/RevConstitucionalista32/USP.

SampaArt, GR SITES, Biografia: Alfredo Viana/Pixinguinha, accessed June 2013. http://sampa.art.br/index.php?option=com_content&view=article&id=366:-biografia pixinguinha&catid=47:biografias&itemid=61.

Eleição presidencial no Brasil em 1950, *Wikipédia, a enciclopédia livre*, accessed August 2013. http://pt.wikipedia.org/wiki/Elei%C3%A7%C3%A3o_presidencial_no_Brasil_em_1950.

A festa do IV Centenário, comunicação por Elmo Francfort Ankerkrone, *Sampa Online*, n.d., accessed December 2012. http://www.sampaonline.com.br/colunas/elmo/coluna2001ju106.htm.

O IV Centenário: Léia as histórias (Lembranças), *São Paulo, Minha Cidade*, accessed April 2011. http://www.saopaulominhacidade.com.br/list.asp?id=98.

Vagalume, IV Centenário, Hinos, accessed April 2011. http://www.vagalume.com.br/hinos/quarto-centenario.html.

Portal Pró-TV, Associação dos Pioneiros, Profissionais e Incentivadores da Televisão Brasileira, História das emissoras, posted 2010, accessed June 2011. http://www.museudatv.com.br/programação/expo400_chuvadeprata.htm.

Urbanismobr.org, Revista Paulistânia—Documentário, accessed April 2011. http://www.urbanismobr.org/bd/periodicos.php?id=65.

"Justiça condena universitária paulista Mayara Petruso, que ofendeu nordestinos no Twitter," TNH1, Pajuçara Sistemade Comunicação, posted May 16, 2012, accessed August 2012. http://tnh1.ne10.uol.com.br/noticia/brasil/2012/05/16/187873/justica-condena-universitaria-paulista-mayara-petruso-que-ofendeu-nordestinos-no-twitter.

Cynara Menezes, "As eleições e o preconceito contra o Nordeste," Carta Capital, posted November 3, 2010, accessed June 2011. http://www.cartacapital.com.br/politica/as-eleicoes-e-o-preconceito-contra-o-nordeste/.

The World Bank: "Bolsa Família: Changing the Lives of Millions in Brazil," posted 2013, accessed September 2013. http://web.worldbank.org/WBSITE/EXTERNAL/NEWS/0,,contentMDK:21447054~pagePK:64257043~piPK:437376~theSitePK:4607,00.html.

Barry Moody and Sara Rossi, "Italy's Northern League Vows to Paralyze Next Government," Reuters, posted February 13, 2013, accessed June 2013. http://www.reuters.com/article/2013/02/13/us-italy-vote-league-idUSBRE91C11720130213.

FGV, CPDOC, posted 2012, "A Era Vargas: Dos anos 20 a 1945: Miguel Costa," accessed September 2013. http://cpdoc.fgv.br/producao/dossies/AEraVargas1/biografias/miguel_costa.

Ricardo della Rosa, blogspot "Tudo por São Paulo," posted August 26, 2010, accessed August 2013. http://tudoporsaopaulo1932.blogspot.com/2010/08/amadeu-augusto-batalhao-marcilio-franco.html.

Eduardo Menezes, Mulheres de São João, Maria Sguassábia (Biografia), 2008, accessed February 2011. http://www.mulheresdesaojoao.com.br/index_arquivos/MariaSguassabiaBiografia1.htm.

INDEX